Published for
**OXFORD INTERNATIONAL
AQA EXAMINATIONS**

International A2 Level
ECONOMICS

Stuart Luker
Wendy Davis

OXFORD
UNIVERSITY PRESS

Great Clarendon Street, Oxford, OX2 6DP, United Kingdom

Oxford University Press is a department of the University of Oxford. It furthers the University's objective of excellence in research, scholarship, and education by publishing worldwide. Oxford is a registered trade mark of Oxford University Press in the UK and in certain other countries

British Library Cataloguing in Publication Data available

978-138-200679-8

10 9 8 7 6 5 4

Paper used in the production of this book is a natural, recyclable product made from wood grown in sustainable forests. The manufacturing process conforms to the environmental regulations of the country of origin.

Printed in Great Britain by CPI Group (UK) Ltd., Croydon CR0 4YY

Acknowledgements

The publisher and authors would like to thank the following for permission to use photographs and other copyright material:

Cover: Michael Melnikoff/Shutterstock.

Photos: p1(m): msmsha/Shutterstock; p3: Oxford University Press; p7: Halfpoint/Shutterstock; p9: PR Image Factory/Shutterstock; p12: Aleksandar Mijatovic/123RF; p14: JeremyRichards/Shutterstock; p15: Chatchai.wa/Shutterstock; p20: 360b/Shutterstock; p21: Naufal MQ/Shutterstock; p22: Richard Lewisohn/Alamy Stock Photo; p23: mokjc/Shutterstock; p24: TRISTAR PHOTOS/Alamy Stock Photo; p27: Photodisc/Getty Images; p29(m): vovan/Shutterstock; p31: Kletr/Shutterstock; p34: Afanasieva/Shutterstock; p38: KRITFOTO/Shutterstock; p41: Richard Griffin/Shutterstock; p50: Kuznetsov Dmitriy/Shutterstock; p53: Julie Clopper/Shutterstock; p58(tl): isak55/Shutterstock; p58(tr): Nick_Nick/Shutterstock; p58(bl): FUN FUN PHOTO/Shutterstock; p58(br): Lee Yiu Tung/Shutterstock; p63: Curioso.Photography/Shutterstock; p68: The History Collection/Alamy Stock Photo; p71: Anna Jedynak/Shutterstock; p75: Zai Di/Shutterstock; p77: danielo/Shutterstock; p87: tanuha2001/Shutterstock; p92: Tyler Olson/Shutterstock; p94: martin berry/Alamy Stock Photo; p98: AliaksaB/Shutterstock; p107: Harun Ozmen/Shutterstock; p111: ostill/Shutterstock; p113: Kris Jacobs/Shutterstock; p117: r.nagy/Shutterstock; p119(tl): Iakov Filimonov/Shutterstock; p119(tr): daniel catrihual/Shutterstock; p119(bl): anyaivanova/Shutterstock; p119(br): Monkey Business Images/Shutterstock; p122: viki2win/Shutterstock; p129: Anton Romaniuk/Shutterstock; p132: Oxford University Press; p138: Elnur/Shutterstock; p145: Azhar Hassan/Shutterstock; p150: vitmark/Shutterstock; p152(tl): Matthew Dixon/123RF; p152(tr): Ruta Saulyte-Laurinaviciene/Shutterstock; p152(bl): alekstock.com/Shutterstock; p152(br): hzrth/Shutterstock; p157: SoleilC/Shutterstock; p165: Photo Spirit/Shutterstock; p167(m): Christos Georghiou/Shutterstock; p168: Historic Collection/Alamy Stock Photo; p171: Rob Crandall/Shutterstock; p172: StockStudio Aerials/Shutterstock; p174: RoClickMag/Shutterstock; p177: Igor Kardasov/Shutterstock; p178: French Jessica Lee/Shutterstock; p180: Panwasin seemala/Shutterstock; p183: A and N photography/Shutterstock; p185: SGr/Shutterstock; p186: Teun van den Dries/Shutterstock; p189: begalphoto/Shutterstock; p190: Art Collection 2/Alamy Stock Photo; p194: panda3800/Shutterstock; p199: marog - pixcells/Shutterstock; p206: Olivier Le Moal/Shutterstock; p207: Jeff Morgan 14/Alamy Stock Photo; p211: pp1/Shutterstock; p214: Lightboxx/Shutterstock; p217: Katsiaryna Pleshakova/Shutterstock; p219: Bettmann/Contributor/Getty Images; p222: ricochet64/Shutterstock; p205(tl): Ashwin/Shutterstock; p205(tr): OkFoto/Shutterstock; p205(bl): Frank11/Shutterstock; p205(br): spatuletail/Shutterstock; p226: VectorKnight/Shutterstock; p230: Viacheslav Lopatin/Shutterstock; p243: heru sukma cahyanto/Shutterstock; p258: Stuart Miles/Shutterstock; p259: bluebay/Shutterstock; p262: pryzmat/Shutterstock; p264: ChameleonsEye/Shutterstock; p265: Yasemin Yurtman Candemir/Shutterstock; p266: JHVEPhoto/Shutterstock; p270: Douglas Olivares/Shutterstock; p274: Ilene Perlman/Shutterstock; p276: Paul Carstairs/Alamy Stock Photo; p280: Isabelle OHara/Shutterstock; p281: Howard Davies/Alamy Stock Photo; p282: REUTERS/Alamy Stock Photo; p286: klublu/Shutterstock; p289: hafakot/Shutterstock; p294(m): Chelsea Green Publishing; p296: Puwadol Jaturawutthichai/Shutterstock; p298: andrea trevisani/Shutterstock; p302: Efimova Anna/Shutterstock; p305: Milosh Kojadinovich/123RF; p306: Chelsea Green Publishing; p307: foto-kriegner/Shutterstock; p323: Beata Tabak/Shutterstock; p326: Simon Mayer/Shutterstock; p328: CAHYADI SUGI/Shutterstock; p342: Thinglass/Shutterstock; p351: Tavarius/Shutterstock; p354: Anton_Ivanov/Shutterstock.

Artwork by Aptara and Oxford University Press.

Every effort has been made to contact copyright holders of material reproduced in this book. Any omissions will be rectified in subsequent printings if notice is given to the publisher.

Contents

How to use this book

This book fully covers the syllabus for the Oxford AQA international A2 Level Economics course (9640). Experienced examiners and teachers have been involved in all aspects of the book, including detailed planning to ensure that the content adheres to the syllabus.

Using this book will ensure you are well prepared for the assessment at this level and will give you a solid foundation for further study at university level and beyond. The features below are designed to make learning interesting and effective.

Activities

These are exercises that relate to the chapter content. They can be done in class or as part of individual study.

Progress questions

These questions appear throughout the book. They are designed to check that you understand the content as you learn. Answers for all progress questions are available in the back of the book.

Key terms

These are the most important vocabulary and definitions that you need to learn. They are also compiled at the end of the book in a glossary.

Get it right

These are helpful tips and hints to give you the best chance of success.

Link

Links are provided to other parts of the book, and to the AS course/book where appropriate, for you to find related information.

Case study

These are real-life examples to illustrate the subject matter in the chapters. These examples are accompanied by questions to test your understanding.

Exam-style questions

These questions appear at the end of each chapter section. They use the same command words, structure and mark assignment as the OxfordAQA exams. Answers for all exam-style questions are available in the back of the book.

Quantitative skills

These are the skills required to calculate, illustrate, apply and interpret data and key economic concepts. The nine specific QS are listed in the syllabus.

The questions, example answers, marks awarded and/or comments that appear in this book were written by the authors. In examinations, the way marks would be awarded to answers such as these may be different.

At the end of the book, you will find a glossary of the key terms highlighted in bold in the text.

1 The objectives of individuals and firms

The economics of business behaviour and the distribution of income

Individual decision making

An important part of microeconomic theory involves analysing factors that affect the decisions made by individuals and households. Individuals and households have limited incomes and they must decide how best to use this income. In particular, they have to decide which goods and services to buy. However, they may also decide to save some of their income, to allow them to consume more goods and services in future.

Traditional economic theory assumes that individuals are motivated by self-interest, focusing on their own needs and wants. When deciding which goods and services to buy and in what quantities, people aim to maximise their own satisfaction or welfare. Their income limits what they can buy, so they have to make choices, weighing up alternatives and the opportunity cost of each decision. If they buy more of one good, they will have less income available for others.

Some households may be able to consume more than they can buy from their current income by using past savings, reducing their wealth. Also, household incomes are not necessarily fixed. Some people may be able to work longer hours to increase their income.

Traditional economic theory assumes that people prefer leisure to work. The hours they choose to work will depend on the value they place on leisure compared to the value they place on the goods and services they could buy with the extra income earned from working more.

More recent developments in Economics question this approach to individual decision making and they will be explored further when considering behavioural economics.

Utility theory

Utility theory assumes that individuals are motivated by self-interest, focusing on their own needs and wants. They are rational economic decision makers. They consider alternative choices, making decisions that will provide them with the most benefit, welfare or satisfaction. Individuals will try to maximise their utility. This is the classical or traditional view.

Link

Rational behaviour was introduced in 1.3 "Scarcity, choice and the allocation of resources" in the AS book, when discussing opportunity cost.

Total, marginal and average utility

If consumers act rationally, they weigh up the welfare or satisfaction they believe they will obtain from products in relation to their price. In Economics, this satisfaction is called **utility**. Utility in Economics is not the same as usefulness. It is based on the view of the consumer of the expected pleasure they will gain from consuming a product at a particular time. Some products which may be bad for us, such as cigarettes, provide utility to the individuals who consume them.

Utility is difficult to measure but sometimes, economists use theoretical units called utils to represent the amount of satisfaction a person believes they will obtain from consuming a particular product at a given time. This estimate of utility is subjective. It will vary from person to person and be different at different times. For example, the estimated utility from consuming a biscuit is likely to be lower if that person has just eaten a meal compared to if they are hungry.

For each decision, a person will need to consider the price of the items, the satisfaction gained from them and the opportunity cost. They may, for example, be weighing up the satisfaction gained from spending an extra $1 on biscuits or a soft drink.

The **total utility** (for a product) is the amount of satisfaction obtained from consuming different amounts of a product and **marginal utility** is the change in total satisfaction when one more unit or one unit fewer of the product is consumed. For example, if the total satisfaction from consuming three biscuits is 205 utils and the satisfaction obtained from consuming two biscuits is 150 utils, then the marginal utility of the third biscuit is 55 utils, the difference between the total utility for two and three biscuits (as shown in Table 1.1.1).

Average utility is the amount of satisfaction per item. It is calculated by dividing the total utility by the number of units consumed. If the total utility of consuming two units is estimated to be 150 utils, then the average utility of each unit is 75 utils.

The hypothesis of diminishing marginal utility

For most products, the more you have, the less satisfaction you gain from consuming another item. There is diminishing (falling) marginal utility. It is likely that consuming the first biscuit will give you the most satisfaction and that each extra biscuit you consume will give you less satisfaction than the one before. This principle is often known as the law or **hypothesis of diminishing marginal utility**.

If a person continues to consume more biscuits, there is likely to come a point where they receive no, or even negative, utility from an extra biscuit.

▲ **Figure 1.1.1**: Diminishing marginal utility?

Key terms

Utility: the satisfaction obtained from consuming a good or service.

Total utility: the satisfaction obtained from consuming a particular number of units of a product, the aggregate of the utility for all the units consumed.

Marginal utility: the addition to total utility from consuming an extra unit of a product.

Average utility: the satisfaction per item, calculated by dividing total utility by the number of items.

The hypothesis of diminishing marginal utility: the idea that the more you have of something, the less satisfaction you gain from consuming an extra unit.

Activity

Think of the last **three** items you bought. To what extent did you consider the satisfaction you would gain from consuming each of these items in relation to their price?

The hypothesis of diminishing marginal utility and the demand curve

If people receive less satisfaction from extra units when they consume more, this suggests that they will be willing to pay less for additional units. To persuade people to buy more, the price will need to be lower, which suggests that the individual and market demand curves are likely to be downward sloping. If someone receives little pleasure from consuming a fifth biscuit, the price may need to be low to persuade them to buy five biscuits.

The hypothesis of diminishing marginal utility helps to support a downward-sloping demand curve, where demand is the quantity that consumers are willing and able to buy at a given price in a given period of time. The lower the price, the greater the quantity demanded. The price of a good relative to the price of others will affect the quantities we buy of each.

The relationship between marginal utility and total utility

Table 1.1.1 shows what happens to marginal and total utility as a person's consumption of biscuits rises.

▼ **Table 1.1.1:** Diminishing marginal utility

Number of biscuits	Marginal utility (utils)	Total utility (utils)
1	80	80
2	70	150
3	55	205
4	35	240
5	10	250
6	0	250
7	−10	240

Table 1.1.1 shows a situation where marginal utility falls the more biscuits a person consumes. Diminishing marginal utility sets in after the first biscuit. The marginal utility of the second biscuit of 70 utils is less than the satisfaction of 80 utils obtained from the first biscuit.

Total utility rises as long as marginal utility is positive but as marginal utility falls, total utility rises at a decreasing rate. For example, the marginal utility of the fourth biscuit adds only 35 utils to the previous total utility, compared to the 55 utils added from consumption of the third biscuit. When the sixth biscuit provides no additional satisfaction, sometimes called the saturation point, total utility stays the same and if even more biscuits are consumed, the resulting negative marginal utility (sometimes called disutility) causes total utility to fall.

Sometimes, the satisfaction gained from an additional unit can rise before falling. For example, if the marginal utility of the first three biscuits had been 70 for the first, 80 for the second and 55 for the third, then diminishing marginal utility would have set in after the consumption of the second biscuit.

Link

The relationship between price and quantity demanded was covered in 2.1 "The demand for goods and services" in the AS book.

Quantitative skills

When drawing a diagram to show the change in a variable such as marginal utility, when there is one more or one fewer unit, it is conventional to plot the points opposite 0.5 units, 1.5 units, and so on, as can be seen in Figure 1.1.3. For example, the marginal utility of 55 utils for the third biscuit represents the difference between the total utility obtained from two biscuits (150 utils) and the total utility from three biscuits (205 utils). This is plotted halfway between these two values, at 2.5 biscuits.

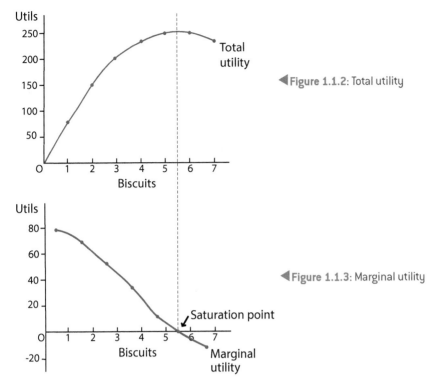

Figure 1.1.2: Total utility

Figure 1.1.3: Marginal utility

Figure 1.1.2 and Figure 1.1.3 are drawn using the data in Table 1.1.1. Figure 1.1.2 shows total utility increasing but at a decreasing rate, until no extra satisfaction is obtained from the sixth biscuit. This is because marginal utility is falling for every extra biscuit consumed until no utility is obtained from the sixth biscuit, as shown in Figure 1.1.3. Since the marginal utility of the seventh biscuit is negative, this causes total utility to fall.

Utility maximisation

Economic theory often assumes that economic agents are maximisers. The goals they set are driven by self-interest. For example, firms are assumed to be profit maximisers. A rational consumer will try to obtain the most benefit, welfare or satisfaction from the goods and services they consume. This is known as **utility maximisation**. Utility theory assumes that households try to maximise their total utility from spending their income but this does not mean that they try to maximise the total utility from each product they buy.

For a single product, total utility is maximised when marginal utility is zero. Up to this point, if marginal utility is positive, it will increase total utility. In the biscuit example in Table 1.1.1, total utility is maximised when six biscuits are consumed. This can also be seen in Figures 1.1.2 and 1.1.3. When the seventh biscuit is consumed, marginal utility is negative (−10 utils), resulting in the total utility of seven biscuits (240 utils) being lower than the total utility of six biscuits (250 utils). If the biscuits are free, utility will be maximised by consuming six biscuits. However, even if biscuits are free, a rational consumer will not consume the seventh biscuit, since it will reduce their total satisfaction.

Since they require resources to make them, it is unlikely that the biscuits will be free. Rational consumers need to consider the amounts spent on different goods and services and the satisfaction gained from

Key term

Utility maximisation: obtaining the highest possible satisfaction.

Progress questions

1 What is utility?
2 Use Table 1.1.1 to calculate the average utility of:
   i. 4 biscuits
   ii. 5 biscuits.

Link

Other maximising situations are covered later, including the fact that total revenue is maximised where marginal revenue is zero in 2.4 "Marginal, average and total revenue curves".

them to decide which combination of products would enable them to maximise their satisfaction with a given sum of money. When a consumer is choosing between alternative products, they must weigh up how much utility they will gain from extra units of the different products in comparison to their prices.

Utility maximisation is limited by people's incomes. People cannot buy everything that will give them some satisfaction. They must weigh up the opportunity cost of their decisions, in terms of what they must sacrifice when they choose to buy an extra item of a particular product. However, satisfaction is difficult to measure and a consumer cannot know exactly how much benefit they will obtain from every product they might consider.

The importance of information for decision making

One of the assumptions underlying utility theory is that everyone has perfect information. Consumers need all relevant information to make a rational decision about which products to consume and in what quantities. They will need to know the price and quality of different goods and services. They must then consider the satisfaction they will gain from alternative choices to make a decision about which combination of products will give them the most satisfaction. If they have imperfect information, such as incomplete or incorrect information, they may make the "wrong" decision.

Imperfect information may lead to the underconsumption of merit goods and overconsumption of demerit goods. If people are unaware of, or do not understand, the full effects both in the short term and the long term of consuming certain products, they may make an irrational or wrong decision about which products to buy and in which quantities, so they do not maximise their satisfaction.

Sometimes consumers have too much choice and/or it may relate to a technical issue which they know little about. For example, there may be many health insurance policies to choose from in some countries and the details may be difficult to understand and compare. Similarly, is it easier to choose the best ice cream flavour if there are five or twenty-five different flavours available?

Also, the satisfaction a person expects to obtain may not be the satisfaction they receive from the experience. For example, a football supporter may spend $200 on travel and entrance fees to an away game, believing that the expenditure is worth the likely satisfaction obtained. A poor match when her team loses may make her regret her choice. At the time, it was a rational decision but afterwards she may think that there would have been better ways of spending the money to gain more satisfaction.

The significance of asymmetric information

Asymmetric information is a form of imperfect information where one party, usually the seller, has more or better information than the other, usually the buyer. For example, in the market for second-hand cars, the seller has far more knowledge of their quality than the buyer.

Link

Imperfect information, including asymmetric information, was explained in 5.5 "Market imperfections" in the AS book, as a possible cause of market failure.

The buyer may buy a car which proves to be faulty and therefore does not provide the satisfaction expected but he could also miss out on buying a good car if he does not trust the seller. In this case, the seller also loses out on the sale. When buying health insurance, for example, it is the buyer that has more knowledge of their past and current health than the insurance company. Either way, if one party has more information, the "wrong" decision could be made.

Information failure, where individuals or firms have inaccurate or incomplete information, or have misunderstood the data, makes it difficult for economic agents to make rational decisions and is another possible cause of market failure. Consumers will be unable to weigh up all the costs and benefits to maximise their utility/satisfaction.

Summary of utility theory and its limitations

Utility theory has, for a long time, underpinned economic ideas about which products individuals buy and in what quantities. It assumes that an individual considers the satisfaction they will obtain from alternative goods and services to try to maximise their total utility from the package of goods and services they buy, given their limited income.

However, the theory has a number of limitations including:

- measurement of utility is difficult
- there may be imperfect information
- habit and impulse may cause us not to weigh up utility.

These and other influences on individual economic decision making are considered further in the next section.

Case study: The utility of water

▲ Figure 1.1.4: Parkrunners

The first parkrun was in London, England in 2004. Parkruns are usually held once a week, are free to enter and involve people covering a distance of 5km. Fifteen years later, there were typically over 250,000 runners taking part on a Saturday in about 1,500 locations in over 20 countries. After the United Kingdom and Australia, the country with the third most parkruns is South Africa.

Bandile completed his usual parkrun on a hot day in Johannesburg in a personal best time of just under 21 minutes. Cups of water were available at the finish. Table 1.1.2 lists some details of the utility he estimated he would obtain from different numbers of cups of water, measured in utils.

▼ Table 1.1.2: Bandile's utility schedule

Cups	Marginal utility (utils)	Total utility (utils)	Average utility (utils)
1		42	
2	28		
3			29
4		96	
5	4		
6			16.5

1 Copy and complete the table.

2 If water is free, how many cups will Bandile drink to maximise his utility?

3 How might Bandile's consumption of water be different if he had not just completed the parkrun?

This section will develop your knowledge and understanding of:

→ bounded rationality and bounded self-control
→ biases in decision making: computational problems, inertia, rules of thumb, anchoring and social norms
→ the importance of altruism and perceptions of fairness.

Key terms

Homo economicus: economic man – someone who always acts rationally and in their self-interest.

Behavioural economics: the study of the effects of psychological, emotional and social factors on economic decision making.

Traditional economic theory assumes that individuals are rational economic decision makers, motivated by self-interest, focusing on their own needs and wants. This theory assumes that individuals aim to maximise their utility, making decisions that provide them with the most benefit or satisfaction. Sometimes the term, **homo economicus**, or economic man, is used to describe someone who is always rational and aims to maximise their utility.

In recent years, there has been increasing interest in **behavioural economics**, which considers the effects of psychological, emotional and social factors on the decisions of individuals and institutions. For a variety of reasons, consumers may not act rationally and are not always motivated by self-interest. As a result, individuals do not necessarily make decisions that will provide them with the most utility. Through experiments, by looking at real-world examples and observing people's behaviour, new theories have emerged to explain why people may act in different ways. Firms and governments around the world are now making more use of aspects of behavioural economics when deciding on their policies.

Bounded rationality and bounded self-control

Traditional economic theory assumes that individuals are completely rational and have unlimited self-control when making decisions. In reality, there are limits to these – both the rationality and self-control of individual consumers are "bounded". If individuals act in a completely rational way, we assume that they are able to weigh up the welfare or satisfaction they believe they will obtain from alternative products in relation to their price. This is not always the case.

When individuals are making decisions, there are limitations that include:

- imperfect information about alternatives and their effects
- limited ability to process all the relevant information
- limited time to reach the "right" decision.

As a result of these limitations, behavioural economists argue that individuals have **bounded rationality**, which may lead to **utility satisficing** (combining the words satisfying and sufficing) rather than maximising. Satisficing provides adequate satisfaction but not the most that could have been obtained.

Key terms

Bounded rationality: the idea that limitations mean that individuals are not completely rational when making choices and economic decisions.

Utility satisficing: where an economic decision provides sufficient satisfaction but not the most that could have been obtained.

An individual may have a view about the level of satisfaction that would be acceptable and given the limitations they face when making decisions, they may choose the first item they believe will provide at least this amount of satisfaction. The choice is good enough but does not provide the optimal or most satisfaction. Bounded rationality and satisficing were first introduced by the American economist and psychologist Herbert Simon in the 1950s, rejecting the idea that we act like homo economicus, trying to maximise the satisfaction we obtain from every economic decision.

As well as not being completely rational when making decisions, individuals may also be limited in their ability to act in their best interests, they have **bounded self-control**. Even if they have all the information that would enable them to maximise their utility, limited self-control may stop them having the optimal consumption of a product.

Someone may sign up for an exercise class, particularly at the beginning of a year, knowing that they would benefit from being fitter. However, even though they have paid for the course of sessions at the start, they may lack the commitment to continue with the class after a few weeks. Similarly, a person may know that too many sugary drinks are bad for their teeth but they continue to consume them. In both examples, the individual knows what would be best but lacks the self-control to achieve this outcome.

Key term

Bounded self-control: the idea that individuals lack full self-control to make decisions that act in their self-interest.

Progress questions

1   What is the term sometimes used to describe someone who always acts rationally, to maximise their utility?

2   Identify **two** factors that could influence decision making, according to behavioural economists.

3   What does "bounded" mean in bounded rationality and bounded self-control?

4   What is meant by utility satisficing?

Case study: Boundless exercise?

▲ Figure 1.2.1: A popular fitness activity

With the Olympic Games due to be held in Japan, Naomi was inspired to become fitter. A new gym had just opened five miles away from her home in Tokyo and she had heard that it was better than the sports centre at the end of her street. She found information on the internet about some of the activities they offered. Any booking made in the next 24 hours would receive a 6% discount. She decided to choose a class from the 12 classes she had read about, each of which cost different amounts. She also had to decide whether she should sign up for five, ten or twenty weeks, since the price per class depended on the length of the course.

Naomi was surprised to find that it took her 45 minutes to travel to the new gym but she enjoyed the first two sessions, both of which were attended by the full class of 15. On the way home, she treated herself to a burger and a fizzy drink, as a reward. The third week it snowed and the week after that she had a cold and stayed at home. Having paid for twenty weeks, she felt she should continue. She went to the fifth session but found that only three other people were there and she did not enjoy the experience as much. She then heard that the Olympic Games had been postponed. After this announcement, she convinced herself that she had better ways of spending her time.

Use examples from the case study to explain what is meant by:

i.   bounded rationality

ii. bounded self-control.

Biases in decision making

Individuals may not behave rationally because they are influenced by a variety of **biases**, sometimes known as **cognitive biases**. Our beliefs and past experience can affect our judgement when choosing between alternatives. These biases include:

- computational problems
- inertia
- rules of thumb
- anchoring
- social norms.

Computational problems

Many decisions involve processing a large quantity of information, which may be quite technical, in order to choose the option that will provide the individual with the greatest utility. People do not necessarily have the ability or the time to spend on such a decision. Also, they may not have all the information they need. These are **computational problems**.

In 2019, New Zealand, with a population of less than five million, had over 40 different companies involved in the supply of energy. It would take a long time to examine what each company is offering, to be able to reach a decision that would maximise a person's utility, and this also assumes that they understand all the technical differences.

Insurance policies are another good example. For many people, buying their first car is a complex and time-consuming procedure. If the car is bought second hand, there is the extra complication of the seller probably knowing more about the vehicle than you do. In most countries, before they can be driven, car insurance must be bought. There are usually many insurance companies to choose from, each offering a range of policies. It may take a long time to research all the possible insurance policies, weighing up alternative prices and coverage to choose the policy that will give the greatest utility.

Therefore, when taking out insurance, computational problems may prevent individuals from being able to consider and weigh up all the possible alternatives. People may have another way of choosing their insurance company. It may have been recommended by a friend or relative. Perhaps they have seen some recent advertising or publicity for the company. It may be the first one they looked at and it seemed to offer a reasonable deal.

Inertia

Inertia is the tendency to stick with what is familiar and is sometimes called the **status-quo bias**. Many consumers are concerned about change and believe that this could leave them worse off. Inertia results in people buying the same products again, without checking if there are better alternatives now available.

Returning to the car insurance example, most policies last for a year. Particularly if a person has not had to claim, or maybe has had a good experience after claiming on the policy, they may decide to remain with the same company, without looking at alternatives, even if the policy is now much more expensive.

Also, many people stay with their electricity provider or bank for many years, possibly their whole lifetime and in the case of their bank, it may even be the one their parents used. Unlike an insurance policy, there may not be an obvious time to consider switching to another firm, which makes it even more likely that they will remain with the same company. Provided that they are receiving sufficient satisfaction from the service, inertia will result in many consumers not looking for an alternative to maximise their utility.

In both these situations, computational problems will contribute to the inertia, as some people are not confident when comparing complex financial alternatives. Having found a policy or firm with which they are reasonably happy, they do not want to risk changing to an inferior product.

In recent years, websites have been set up in several countries to compare different electricity companies or insurance policies. This has cut down the time and knowledge required to make a decision about which is best but the number of customers switching providers remains relatively low. For example, there are websites in New Zealand that compare the prices and performance of the main electricity providers but in most years less than 1 in 8 households change their electricity supplier.

Rules of thumb

Previously, it was noted that individuals have bounded rationality. When faced with alternative choices, their ability to make the "right" decision is affected by limited information, time and ability to process all the relevant information. So, how do they make their choice? Many people make decisions based on rules of thumb.

Rules of thumb are mental shortcuts, which enable the individual to make a decision more quickly and easily. Based on past experience, rather than theory, this will generally result in an acceptable outcome. It provides an adequate level of utility (utility satisficing) but not necessarily the maximum that could have been obtained. Individuals will develop general principles for making certain choices based on what has worked in the past.

When taken out for a meal in a restaurant, an individual may always choose a mid-priced meal, neither wishing to choose something too cheap which they assume they will not enjoy as much nor wanting to make the other person pay for the most expensive meal. Alternatively, they may have enjoyed the chicken dinner on previous visits, and even though the menu has now changed, they automatically choose their "usual" meal. In a café, a person may always order the same size and type of drink, regardless of changing menus and prices.

> **Key term**
>
> **Rules of thumb:** mental shortcuts, based on experience, which enable individuals to make decisions more quickly and easily.

▲ **Figure 1.2.2:** 5 a day

Key terms

Anchoring: where someone relies heavily on the first piece of information they obtain when making a decision.

Social norms: behaviour consistent with what is considered acceptable in that society at that time.

In a number of countries, people are encouraged to eat "5 a day" in the context of different fruit and vegetable portions, on the basis that this is good for you. Packets are labelled to let you know how much of that fruit or vegetable is equal to one of your five portions, so this makes it easy for people to try to eat enough fruit and vegetables each day.

One financial rule of thumb is "don't put all your eggs in one basket". This means that it is probably safer to put your savings in more than one financial institution or product, in case something goes wrong. However, it may be easier to stick to the institution or product you know. People may also have a rule of thumb about how much is required in savings in case they need it, perhaps if they lose their job. For example, they may always try to have three months' income in their savings account.

These examples illustrate how people have simple rules, based on their past experience, which enable them to make quick decisions which they expect to give them a reasonable amount of utility, rather than trying to find out and process all the relevant information about alternative choices.

Anchoring

Anchoring is another bias, where, when making a decision, someone relies heavily on the first piece of information (or anchor) they obtain. This first piece of information is given disproportionate importance and continues to be used as a reference point even when more information is obtained.

For example, when buying a house or car, the first price that is mentioned acts as the anchor. If a lower price is then agreed, the buyer may believe they have a bargain, even though this is still above the market price of the house or car. When negotiating to buy a product, the opening price may be well above its cost and/or market value but it still acts as an anchor.

People may be anchored by historic or irrelevant prices, affecting their judgement. An individual is more likely to buy a suit if its price has been reduced from $300 to $200, than if it is simply priced at $200. Having bought shares in a company at a particular price, the owner may be unwilling to sell them if the price falls, because the purchase price acts as an anchor, even though the business may now be less profitable.

Social norms

Most people are partly influenced by the behaviour of others around them, rather than making choices entirely based on their own self-interest. **Social norms** refer to behaviour consistent with what is considered acceptable in that society at that time. Local traditions and pressure from peers and family members to behave in certain ways can have an important influence on our decision making. If there is an accepted way of behaving, this can make it quicker and easier to make decisions about alternatives, since the individual may assume that if most other people do or buy something, it is also in their interest to follow these social norms.

Social norms vary from country to country and will change over time. Recycling waste has become more common in many places in recent years, helped by households being provided with a number of bins to enable them to sort out different types of waste. Cigarette smoking rates have fallen in many countries as it has become less acceptable to smoke in public places. Improved information and more regulation have also contributed to these changes. In some societies, it is viewed as a good idea to save as much as you can and this social norm affects the savings ratio. These examples illustrate how an individual's behaviour may be affected by the actions of those around them.

The importance of altruism and perceptions of fairness

An important assumption behind rational behaviour is that people (and firms) act in their own self-interest, focusing on their own needs and wants. Experience shows that this is not always the case. Altruism is when someone acts in the interests of other people, putting their welfare first. This may involve the person perhaps giving up some of their money or time for no financial gain. This could be because of their perception of fairness – that people do not like to see (too much) inequality, considering it to be unfair. Views on this vary from person to person and depend on value judgements.

In some cases, an individual may obtain satisfaction from giving money to charity or volunteering in their community but they may also believe that it is the right thing to do. Some firms give a percentage of their profits to charity. This action may attract extra customers to the business but the firm may also believe that they have a social responsibility, to benefit society as a whole. In both these cases, people and firms could be behaving altruistically.

How behavioural influences affect the actions of governments and firms

Through observing what happens in practice and by conducting experiments, behavioural economists have identified a number of influences on individual decision making, which question the assumption of traditional economic theory that individuals are rational decision makers who aim to maximise their utility. Both governments and firms have made increasing use of this information in recent years to adapt their policies.

The idea of "nudges" became popular after the publication of the 2008 book by Richard Thaler and Cass Sunstein, *Nudge: Improving Decisions about Health, Wealth and Happiness*. They defined a nudge as "any aspect of the choice architecture that alters people's behaviour in a predictable way without forbidding any options or significantly changing their economic incentives", where choice architecture refers to the different ways that choices can be presented to individuals.

Key term

Altruism: when someone acts in the interests of other people, putting their welfare first.

Link

The different motives of firms are explained in 1.3 "The objectives of firms".

Progress questions

5   Which behavioural influence do the following statements illustrate?
    i. according to a recent survey, the proportion of Europeans worried about the environmental impact of plastic has increased to 87% and 65% now separate their waste for recycling
    ii. after checking with the local council, Jorge planted flowers on some waste ground near his home to benefit others
    iii. when Aarav decided to buy a new car, he bought one from Tata because he had bought a Tata car on the two previous occasions
    iv. when Chun received a pay rise, she increased the amount of money she saved each month to keep her savings equal to at least three months of her income.

Key term

Choice architecture: a framework or way that choices can be presented to individuals.

Put simply, a **nudge** is an action that encourages a particular behaviour without removing choice. The action aims to help or persuade the individual to make a choice that is in their self-interest and should be cheap and easy to achieve. These nudges make use of knowledge about how consumers may be influenced by a range of cognitive biases and usually involve small changes.

Using behavioural policy can be a quick, cheap and effective way to persuade people to take certain actions which could benefit themselves and/or others. This may be at no financial cost to the individual.

Impact of behavioural influences on the actions of governments

Thaler and Sunstein's ideas about nudges encouraged a number of governments around the world including those in Australia, Peru, Singapore and the United Kingdom, to set up "nudge units". These are departments or organisations which look in depth at behavioural influences, to develop alternatives to traditional solutions such as taxation or regulation, which are sometimes, by contrast, called "shove" policies.

▲ Figure 1.2.3: A nudge to improve fitness

Examples of nudges include:

- sending letters saying that most people in their area have paid their tax on time
- sending text messages as reminders of doctors' or hospital appointments
- using cigarette "ballot bins" in London with two sections, giving people the chance to vote for the better of two footballers, Ronaldo and Messi, whilst reducing litter
- painting stairs like piano keys or with positive messages in public areas, such as in Stockholm, Shangdu and San Francisco, to encourage more people to use the stairs for exercise, instead of using an escalator.

Governments may present individuals with a **mandated choice**. This involves being given options but having to make a choice. For example, in Sweden, everyone is required by law to choose what happens to their organs when they die. In some countries, there is a **default choice**, an option chosen for you which is considered to be in the person's and/or society's best interest. The option can be changed but the person must take action to achieve this.

Spain has the highest organ donation rates in the world and it is believed that this is mainly because they have an opt-out system rather than opt-in. Everyone has a choice but if you do not wish to donate your organs after your death, you have to take action to opt out of the system. With both mandated and default choices, more people end up with the option thought "best", partly due to inertia.

Impact of behavioural influences on the actions of firms

Firms have been taking account of behavioural influences in their marketing strategy for many years, having studied what makes people more or less likely to buy certain products. For example, to encourage healthier eating, many supermarkets no longer put sweets near tills and place junk food nearer the back of the store. These items are then less likely to be bought on impulse.

A product may be promoted as the most popular offered by that firm to encourage more people to choose it. Restaurants and coffee shops may include a high-priced meal or drink as part of a plan to encourage more people to buy others which are less expensive but more than the average price.

Summary of behavioural influences and their limitations

Behavioural economics has provided additional insights into how individuals make decisions, particularly when the decision involves complex information and/or people have limited time to make the decision. This knowledge has been used by some governments to nudge people into making "better" decisions relatively easily and cheaply.

Behavioural policies can be seen as additional ways of correcting different market failures. They support traditional policies such as taxes and subsidies rather than replacing them. Behavioural policies may be used as the preferred method to achieve a particular aim or as part of an overall strategy, perhaps as a way of changing attitudes. What is likely to be the best solution depends on the nature of the problem.

Critics of behavioural economics argue that some behavioural theories rely too much on unrealistic experiments. Also, some people believe that the resulting policies lead to individuals being manipulated and that the government is being too paternalistic by deciding what is best for others. Firms may use the knowledge to persuade consumers to buy products that could give them less utility. Whether this is a significant problem may depend on the extent to which people know what is being done, since they still have a choice about their actions.

Behavioural economics, and its associated policies, can be seen as a complement to, rather than a substitute for, utility theory and the traditional approach to individual decision making and the correction of market failure.

Activity

Visit a local shop or supermarket. How is the business trying to nudge customers to buy certain products?

Link

Paternalism was introduced in 5.7 "Government intervention in markets" in the AS book.

Activity

To take you further, find out the meanings of the following terms, including examples. These are two other aspects of behavioural economics not covered in the specification:

i. framing

ii. loss aversion.

Case study: Workplace pensions in the United Kingdom

A workplace or occupational pension is a way of saving for your retirement. It usually involves a percentage of your weekly or monthly income being put into a pension fund, to which your employer may also be required to contribute. When you retire, you may be able to take out this money or use it to receive an income.

In the United Kingdom, in 2012, joining a workplace pension was changed from an opt-in to an opt-out scheme – workers between the ages of 21 and 65 were automatically enrolled. In 2012, 47% of workers were in a workplace pension scheme but by 2018, when the scheme had been fully implemented, this had risen to 76% overall and 90% for public sector employees, although the percentages are lower for those working part-time.

1 Does the United Kingdom workplace pension scheme have a mandated choice or a default choice? Explain your answer.

2 To what extent do you believe that the change to an opt-out scheme has been successful in encouraging people in the United Kingdom to join a workplace pension scheme? Justify your answer..

▲ Figure 1.2.4: Workplace pensions – opt-in or opt-out?

This section will develop your knowledge and understanding of:

→ how the models that comprise the traditional theory of the firm are based on the assumption that firms aim to maximise profits

→ why a profit maximising firm will produce in the short run if it can cover its variable costs but will only produce in the long run if it can make normal profit

→ the reasons for, and the consequences of, a divorce of ownership from control

→ why firms may have a variety of other possible objectives

→ the satisficing principle

→ how government ownership and/or control of a firm may affect its objectives.

Link

The objectives of firms were introduced in 4.2 "The objectives of firms" in the AS book.

Key term

Firm: an organisation that uses scarce resources to supply goods or services.

Link

The profit-maximising rule (MC = MR) will be covered in 3.2 "Perfect competition".

The traditional assumption that firms aim to maximise profits

A **firm** is an organisation that uses scarce resources to supply goods and services. It can range from a one-person business that only operates in the local area to a transnational corporation (TNC) selling all over the world. It may be one of many firms producing the same or similar products or it may be the only firm in the industry supplying that product in that country.

The models that comprise the traditional theory of the firm provide insights into how firms operate and how different market structures and objectives affect the conduct and performance of firms. They are based on the assumption that firms aim to maximise profits. Profit is total revenue minus total cost, so maximising profits involves producing an output where total revenue minus total cost is greatest.

Profit is the reward for taking risks and is used to pay the owners of the business. It provides an incentive to continue to produce that good or service and can be used to finance investment. In the same way that traditional economic theory assumes that individuals act in their self-interest to maximise their utility, firms are also assumed to be rational economic decision makers, making decisions that will provide them with the most benefit. This is generally assumed to be making the highest possible profit.

Conditions for profit maximising firms to produce in the short and long run

The short run

In the short run, when some factors of production cannot be changed, some costs, such as rent, are fixed, staying the same regardless of output. Firms also have variable costs, such as raw materials, that increase with output. In the long run, when all factors of production can be changed, all costs are variable.

In the short run, to carry on in business, a firm must be able to cover its variable costs. If it is covering its variable costs, it has enough revenue to pay its day-to-day running costs. If the firm is a profit maximiser, covering its variable costs and making a contribution towards its fixed costs, it will make less of a loss if it continues in that line of business than if it shuts down. However, if the firm's revenue is less than its variable costs, it will make a smaller loss if it stops producing.

For example, a firm's short-run total cost of $30,000 in a given time period may be made up of variable costs of $20,000 and fixed costs of $10,000. Its revenue during the same period is $24,000. The revenue is more than enough to cover the day-to-day running costs and is making a contribution of $4,000 to the fixed costs. If the firm shuts down, it would still need $10,000 to pay the fixed costs until the end of the contract, for example until the lease on the factory is due for renewal. Continuing production contributes $4,000 towards this cost. It will make a loss of $6,000 if it continues to produce, whereas the loss would be larger, at $10,000, if it stopped producing.

If the firm's revenue is not covering its variable costs, it will make a larger loss if it continues to produce in the short run. For example, if the firm's revenue is only $18,000, it will make a loss of $12,000 if it stays in business. However, if a firm is not covering its variable costs, it may still continue in business if it believes that the lack of revenue is temporary, perhaps due to a recession. It may think that it can be a profitable business in the long run and if it can obtain sufficient cash to continue, it may stay in business.

The long run

In the long run, a firm must cover all its costs, including the payment to the entrepreneur or owner. It will continue to produce in the long run if it can make at least normal profit. **Normal profit** is when revenue is just sufficient to cover costs. It is where total revenue equals total cost or average revenue equals average cost. This is the minimum amount of profit that will persuade the owner to stay in that market. Normal profit is included in the firm's total or average costs.

Anything above normal profit is known as supernormal or abnormal profit. **Supernormal or abnormal profit** is when total revenue is greater than total cost (or average revenue is greater than average cost). This will encourage the firm to continue production and attract other firms into the market. If total revenue is less than total cost in the long run, the firm will make a loss (also known as **subnormal profit**) and is likely to leave the market. However, as was the case in the short run, some firms may produce at a loss in the long run if they believe the situation is temporary and they can make profits in future.

The divorce of ownership from control

In a small business, the owner may be able to control both the day-to-day running of the firm and its overall strategy. As firms grow in size, it will become increasingly difficult for owners to control all the activities of the business. It may be necessary for business owners to hire managers, who are paid a salary but do not necessarily have a share in the firm.

Although profits can help to finance growth, to increase the size of a business may require additional money, possibly by the firm becoming an incorporated business where people or institutions buy shares in the company. Those who own shares are entitled to their part of the firm's profit.

Key terms

Normal profit: when revenue is just sufficient to cover costs, producing where total revenue equals total costs or average revenue equals average costs.

Supernormal or abnormal profit: any profit greater than normal profit, producing where total revenue is greater than total costs or average revenue is greater than average costs.

Subnormal profit: making less than normal profit, when revenue is not sufficient to cover costs.

Link

There is more on the role of profit in a market economy and the difference between normal and supernormal/abnormal profit in 2.5 "Profit".

Divorce of ownership from control: when those who own a business are different from those who control it.

Principal-agent problem: when there is a conflict of interest between one person or group, the principal, and their representative, the agent.

When those who own a business are different from those who control it, this is known as the **divorce of ownership from control**. Royal Dutch Shell, a leading oil and gas supplier, has about 8 billion shares. The largest shareholder is an investment management group with less than 4% of the shares. When there is a large number of owners, each with a very small shareholding, it is not practical for the owners to run the company. This is left to the directors or managers, who may or may not also have shares in the company.

When there is a divorce of ownership from control, there may be conflicting objectives. The shareholders are likely to want the firm to maximise profits, to increase the size of their dividends but the managers may prefer to pursue other objectives, which act more in their self-interest. This is sometimes known as the **principal-agent problem**. This is when there is a conflict of interest between one person or group, the principal, or the owners in this case, and that of their representative, the agent, or managers of the firm. It is more likely that owners and managers will both prioritise profit if the pay of the managers is linked to the firm's profits and/or part of their pay is in the form of shares in the company.

Other possible objectives of firms

Firms may have a variety of other objectives, instead of maximising profits, that could affect price, output and other aspects of their conduct and performance. This has led some to question whether the traditional model, based on the assumption that firms are profit maximisers, provides an adequate explanation of what happens in the real world. However, whether firms aim to maximise profits or not, they are still likely to need to make a profit to continue in business in the long run.

Other possible objectives include:

- survival
- growth
- increasing market share
- maximising sales revenue
- quality
- corporate social responsibility.

Survival

Survival is the most basic aim of any firm. This could apply to new firms trying to establish themselves in a market or to others facing difficulties, perhaps because of a fall in demand for their products or a recession generally. These firms may be doing everything they can to stay in business in the hope that their situation will improve in the future. However, if they cannot cover their costs, they must decide whether they should leave the market.

Growth

Although firms usually have to start on a small scale, many owners and managers will want their firm to grow. For firms to grow, they will either have to sell more of their existing product or sell a wider range of products, which may or may not be related to their original product.

This may be achieved through internal growth and/or by joining with other firms.

Particularly if the firm grows by producing more of the same or related products, it may be able to take advantage of economies of scale, such as bulk buying. This lower average cost will enable a firm to make a greater profit per unit if the price of the good or service stays the same. Being in charge of a larger firm may also bring managers more status or help their future careers. If there is a divorce of ownership from control, managers may favour the growth of the firm over maximising profit.

Increasing market share

A firm may be able to grow because the demand for its product is growing but a firm may also be trying to increase its market share. This may be done by growing faster than its rivals if the market is expanding and/or by trying to attract customers from other firms. This may involve both price and non-price competition.

For example, a firm may reduce its prices to try to increase demand for its products, or even to try to force a rival firm out of business. It may also try to attract customers by perhaps promoting the superiority of its products. Either way, this may reduce profits and/or increase costs in the short run but in the long run, it may give the firm more monopoly power and enable it to raise prices and profits later.

Maximising sales revenue

Maximising sales revenue involves gaining the highest possible income from sales. If the sale of an extra unit brings in extra revenue, total sales revenue will rise. However, the total profit will fall if the cost of the extra unit is higher than the revenue obtained from it. If managers' pay is linked to sales rather than profit, they may try to increase sales beyond the profit-maximising output by charging less than the profit-maximising price.

Quality

Many business owners gain satisfaction from providing a good-quality product. They are more concerned about doing a good job at a reasonable price than gaining the most profit they can from their business. However, high-quality products and a good reputation may increase brand loyalty, where customers continue to buy products from that firm and it may also attract new buyers. This strategy could be successful in achieving high profits and may make it easier to increase prices without losing many customers.

Corporate social responsibility

Business owners and managers may also have other objectives, which will affect the firm's behaviour and performance. **Corporate social responsibility** refers to the aim of many businesses to behave ethically in relation to their customers, workers, the local community and/or society as a whole. Examples of corporate social responsibility include trying to reduce waste or greenhouse gas emissions beyond what is required by law, providing better working conditions or giving away part of their profits to good causes.

Link

There is more on how and why firms grow in 1.4 "The growth of firms".

Link

In 1.1 "The objectives of individuals and firms", it was stated that utility maximisation occurs when marginal utility is zero. In the same way, revenue maximisation is achieved when marginal revenue, the revenue obtained from the sale of an extra unit, is zero. This will be explained further in 2.4 "Marginal, average and total revenue curves".

Get it right

It is important not to confuse profit maximisation and sales revenue maximisation. They are different objectives and involve the firm operating at a different price and output.

Key term

Corporate social responsibility: when businesses behave ethically in relation to their customers, workers, the local community and/or society as a whole.

Activity

Find out about **two** examples of firms showing corporate social responsibility in different ways.

Case study: The rise of Spotify

Spotify is a digital music service, the leader in music streaming, legally based in Luxembourg but with its headquarters in Sweden. It offers access to over 50 million songs in many parts of the world. It is free if you accept advertisements although tighter limits have now been put on what is available on its free service. You can receive a wider service without adverts if you pay a subscription.

Spotify has to pay fees to artists whose songs are played, which takes about 70% of its revenue. About half its active users pay a subscription. Spotify's main competitors are Apple, Amazon and Google but these firms also sell devices to play the music and have other sources of income.

Launched in 2008, over the next ten years, the firm grew rapidly but made continual losses. During this time, it gained funding from a range of sources, including issuing bonds, a form of debt, and from giving investors a share in the company, which they were able to sell when the company's shares started trading in 2018. On the first day of trading, Spotify was valued at about $26 billion.

▲ **Figure 1.3.1**: Music online

In early 2019, Spotify announced its first profit of about $107 million for the last quarter of 2018. If it is to survive in the future, it needs to be able to make a profit and this may require the firm to offer a greater variety of services. It will need sufficient revenue from subscriptions and other income to cover its costs.

1. When will a profit maximising firm continue to produce:
   i. in the short run
   ii. in the long run?
2. What are likely to have been the objectives of the owners of Spotify?
3. How has Spotify been able to survive without making a profit in its first ten years of operation?
4. On what does Spotify's continued survival and success depend?

Key terms

Profit satisficing: where sufficient profit is made but not the most that could have been obtained.

Stakeholders: those with an interest in the business, including owners, workers and customers.

Progress questions

1. The models that comprise the traditional theory of the firm are usually based on which assumption?
2. What is meant by sales revenue maximisation?
3. How may the divorce of ownership from control affect the behaviour and performance of firms?

The satisficing principle

The idea that economic agents may not always be maximisers was discussed previously in the context of individuals having bounded rationality, which could lead to utility satisficing. Due to imperfect information, limited time and processing ability, individuals may make a choice that gives them adequate satisfaction but not the most that they could have obtained.

In the same way that an individual may have a view about a level of satisfaction that would be acceptable, this may also apply to what different economic agents see as an acceptable level of profit or other rewards. Where there is a divorce of ownership from control, there may be **profit satisficing**, where sufficient profit is made but not the most that could have been obtained.

A firm has many **stakeholders**, those with an interest in the business, including owners, managers and other workers, customers and the wider community. Each will have their own objectives. Owners and shareholders may want a business to make a large profit to increase their income from dividends and the value of their shares in the company. Managers may be pursuing other aims which are more in their own self-interest, such as growth or sales revenue maximisation, particularly if their pay is linked to achieving this objective. However, these strategies could help the firm to become more profitable in the long run, even though it may reduce the profit made in the short run.

To keep the shareholders happy, managers must achieve a reasonable amount of profit. They may even risk losing their jobs if insufficient profit is made. The business will also want to keep its workers and customers happy, to ensure the future success of the business. Workers are likely to want high pay and better working conditions, while customers will want good-quality products at reasonable prices. This is likely to lead to **satisficing**, achieving a satisfactory minimum level of a number of variables to satisfy different stakeholders, to keep as many stakeholders as happy as possible.

It is likely that most firms will have a range of objectives, not just making a profit. It may also be difficult to know the highest profit that could be achieved by a firm. However, profit is an important objective of most firms; it is necessary for survival and depending on the competitiveness of the industry, firms may have no choice but to profit maximise. Otherwise, they may be forced out of business in competitive markets if other firms have lower costs.

Impact of government ownership or control on objectives

In most countries, some firms are owned and/or controlled by the government, often known as **state-owned enterprises** or SOEs. For example, governments may control electricity and gas supplies, rail services and airlines. These products are vital for the smooth running of the country and may be provided by monopolies, which, in the private sector, might exploit customers by charging high prices.

In theory, government services are run for the benefit of the country as a whole, so these businesses are unlikely to be aiming to maximise profits. If firms are state-owned, they will not have shareholders to whom they have to pay dividends. The government will also be able to finance losses if necessary, although this will have an opportunity cost.

If the firm is under government control, their main objectives are likely to be linked to what is in the best interest of the country as a whole. This may involve providing a reliable service at a reasonable price and there may also be the need for ongoing investment, as part of a longer-term strategy. However, those making the decisions may have their own objectives resulting in different outcomes.

> **Key term**
>
> **Satisficing**: achieving a minimum level of a number of variables to satisfy different stakeholders.

> **Link**
>
> The case for and against the public ownership of firms and industries is covered in 3.12 "Public ownership, privatisation, regulation and deregulation of markets".

> **Key term**
>
> **State-owned enterprise (SOE)**: a business with significant government ownership and control.

Case study: Railways in India

Indian Railways (IR) is run by the Ministry of Railways, a department of the Government of India, responsible for all rail transport in the country. It is the fourth longest railway network in the world. In 2018, IR carried over 8 billion passengers and over 1 billion tonnes of freight. In 2019, it was the world's ninth largest employer, with over 1.2 million workers.

All IR routes are being electrified to save on imported fuel and in 2017, India introduced the first solar-powered train. In early 2020, it was announced that IR would be issuing over $1 billion of bonds, available to international investors – borrowing to finance new engines and improvements in the railway infrastructure.

How and why are the objectives of Indian Railways likely to differ from a private sector firm? Where possible, use information from the case study to support your answer.

▲ Figure 1.3.2: One of the largest networks in the world

This section will develop your knowledge and understanding of:

→ how and why firms grow

→ the difference between internal (or organic) growth and external growth (mergers and takeovers)

→ different types of integration (vertical, horizontal and conglomerate).

▲ **Figure 1.4.1**: Steve Jobs – co-founder of Apple

How and why firms grow

How firms grow

Most firms will have to start on a small scale. Some will remain as small businesses, which could be the owner's preference or due to their inability to grow. Some new firms will stop trading after a while but others will grow over time. Apple Inc, whose products include computers and mobile phones, became the largest company in the world by 2012 (based on the value of its shares) but had only been in existence since 1976. So how and why do firms grow?

Firms can grow by making more of their existing products or by extending their range of products. This could involve making similar products, perhaps by making use of the same raw materials or technology. Alternatively, the firm may start to produce completely different goods and services. In all these cases, a firm may join together with other firms or just grow independently. In both situations, they will need money to achieve this, which may be obtained by reinvesting their profits, borrowing or issuing shares.

Firms may be able to grow because the market for their product is growing. For example, in the case of Apple, technological developments and changing tastes have increased the demand for computers and mobile phones, both from businesses and individuals. If demand rises, the firm can sell more products. With technological developments lowering the costs of production, profit per unit may rise or prices could fall, further encouraging demand. Alternatively, firms may grow by attracting customers from their rivals.

Why firms grow

Growth is one of the objectives of firms. If a firm grows, it may be able to increase its profit. Profit is usually an important objective of firms, with the owners acting in their self-interest. Entrepreneurs or shareholders will benefit if profit increases and even if the profit per unit stays the same, selling more units will increase total profit.

If a firm increases its production, it may be able to take advantage of internal economies of scale. For example, producing on a larger scale could result in technical economies, whilst buying more raw materials or components could enable it to negotiate a cheaper price per unit, especially if they are the main buyer for a particular supplier. A fall in average cost may enable the firm to increase its profit per unit, which will add to total profit. Also, if the firm now has more monopoly power, it is more able to change its price.

Activity

Draw a supply and demand diagram showing the effects of an increase in demand on the price and quantity sold of a product such as computers, then use this diagram to also show the impact of technological progress on the market.

Link

Types and effects of economies of scale were discussed in 3.4 "Economies and diseconomies of scale" in the AS book.

Managers may want their firm to grow for a number of reasons. Their pay may be linked to the sales of the firm – they may have a set target to achieve to earn a bonus. They may believe that running a larger firm will give them more prestige and may also help them to gain another job. If they own shares in the firm, they could benefit if these rise in value as the firm becomes more successful and perhaps gains an increasing share of the market.

Progress questions

1 Explain **two** ways that firms can grow.
2 Give **two** reasons why firms may grow.

Internal and external growth

Internal growth

Internal (or organic) growth is where a firm expands without joining with other firms. It grows from within rather than through taking over or merging with other firms. This may be a slow process because it takes time for a new firm to establish a reputation and it will require money to finance the purchase or rental of larger premises and to obtain other factors of production. The firm will need to be confident that there is enough demand for its products in the future to make the expansion worthwhile.

It is likely to be easier for a firm to grow internally if demand for its products and the size of the market are growing. For example, firms making smartphones have grown considerably over the last ten years. Otherwise a firm will only be able to grow by attracting customers from its rivals.

Some firms may be able to grow internally by applying the technological developments used for one product to another product they make. For example, after Dyson became known for its "bagless" vacuum cleaners, it moved onto other products such as washing machines and hand dryers.

Probably the cheapest and easiest way to finance expansion is to reinvest the profits made by the firm. Therefore, in most cases, a firm needs to be profitable to expand, both to finance the growth and as an indication that this is worthwhile. Alternatively, taking out loans and issuing shares could be options. Loans from banks or other financial institutions require the payment of interest, so would only be worthwhile if the extra revenue from the growth is likely to be greater than the extra cost. If shares are issued, this will spread the ownership of the business and shareholders will expect dividends from future profits.

External growth

External growth is where a firm expands by joining with other firms. This may be through merging with or taking over (acquiring) other firms. The process may involve firms in the same or a different industry.

Get it right

Check carefully whether questions ask "how" or "why", since these command words require a different response. "How" is looking for methods and "why" is asking for reasons.

Key term

Internal or organic growth: when a firm expands without joining with other firms.

▲ **Figure 1.4.2**: One development may lead to another

Key term

External growth: when a firm expands by joining with other firms.

A **merger** usually means that the firms are joining on a roughly equal basis and often the name of the new firm combines those of the two (or more) previous firms. For example, ExxonMobil, the American oil and gas company, was formed in 1999 from the merger of Exxon and Mobil. However, there may be a dominant partner and in the case of ExxonMobil, effectively Mobil was bought by Exxon, with Mobil's shareholders receiving a 30% stake in the new company to Exxon's 70%.

Sometimes, a firm is absorbed by another, usually larger, firm and loses its identity, although some of the more popular brand names may be continued for a while. This is known as a **takeover** or acquisition. Nestlé, a Swiss firm, is the largest food and drinks company in the world, by revenue. It bought the British confectionery firm Rowntree Mackintosh in 1988, dropping the old firm's name from some products quickly but keeping well-known brand names such as Kit Kat.

In recent years, many airlines have formed alliances. These are arrangements between two or more firms, in this case airlines, to cooperate on certain aspects of their work, while still keeping the firms separate. This may involve sharing staff at airports for checking in and baggage handling, to reduce costs. For example, Star Alliance has over 20 members including Lufthansa, Thai Airways and Air Canada. As more firms form alliances, it may increase the pressure on non-members to join, to take advantage of the cost savings and other benefits.

▲ **Figure 1.4.3:** Airlines working together

Different types of integration

Integration is another term used for the joining or combination of two or more firms, whether this is through merger or takeover. There are three main types of integration:

- horizontal
- vertical
- conglomerate.

Integration is a quicker way for a firm to expand than through internal growth.

Horizontal integration

Horizontal integration refers to the joining of two or more firms at the same stage of production of the same good or service – the merger of two car manufacturers, for example.

Benefits of horizontal integration

If two firms that were previously rivals join to become one firm, then the new combined firm will have a larger market share. For example, if the two firms previously had market shares of 26% and 25%, other things being equal, they will now have a combined share of 51% of the market. This will give the new firm more monopoly power. It will have more influence over the price for its products and may find it easier to take action to force rivals out of the market.

The new firm will be producing more units of the same or similar products and should be able to take more advantage of internal economies of scale. It may be able to use more division of labour and larger, more economic machines. The firm may also be able to obtain its raw materials or components at a lower price per unit. Internal economies of scale will reduce the long-run average cost of the new firm.

Horizontal integration may be an aggressive move by firms hoping to increase their power in the market or it may be defensive. With their competitors growing in size, whether in that country or on the international market, some firms may be forced to join together to survive.

Whatever the circumstances, horizontal integration gives the firms an opportunity to rationalise. **Rationalisation** involves reorganising the firm's operations, perhaps closing their less efficient or underused plants to concentrate production in more profitable areas.

Costs of horizontal integration

By reducing the number of firms selling a particular product, there will be less competition in the market. This will give buyers less choice of firms to buy from and may result in higher prices if the new firm has considerable market power. The firm may also decide to reduce the range of products they offer as part of the rationalisation process.

Workers could lose out if the integration results in redundancies. For example, if two banks join, they may each have a branch in a particular town. It would pay them in the long run to only have one outlet. Some employees will no longer be required and will lose their jobs.

Vertical integration

Vertical integration refers to the joining of two or more firms at different stages of production of the same good or service – a bakery buying a flour mill, for example. To gain the most benefit, it is likely that the merger or takeover will involve firms at consecutive stages of the production process. There are two types of vertical integration, backward vertical integration and forward vertical integration.

Backward vertical integration is where one firm takes over another firm at an earlier stage of production of the same good. The example of a bakery buying a flour mill would be backward vertical integration, as it involves taking over a firm further back in the supply chain.

Forward vertical integration is where one firm takes over another firm at a later stage of production of the same good. If a firm owning a tea plantation takes over a tea manufacturer, this could be classified as forward vertical integration as it involves taking over a firm further on in the supply chain.

> **Key term**
>
> Rationalisation: making a firm more efficient by reorganisation and consolidation.

> **Key terms**
>
> Vertical integration: the joining of two or more firms at different stages of production of the same good or service.
>
> Backward vertical integration: where one firm takes over another firm at an earlier stage of production of the same good.
>
> Forward vertical integration: where one firm takes over another firm at a later stage of production of the same good.

Benefits of vertical integration

The main benefits of backward vertical integration are security of supply, restricting the supplies to competitors and absorbing the intermediate profit margin. Owning their supplier, for example the flour mill, enables a firm such as the bakery to control the quantity and quality of the flour produced for them, rather than dealing with an independent firm.

The firm will also be able to control sales of the product to their competitors, perhaps increasing the price of the flour and/or no longer selling to their rivals. As separate firms, the bakery would also have to pay a price which would enable the flour mill to make a profit. As the owner of the flour mill, the bakery can now obtain their flour at cost price, absorbing the profit margin of the flour mill.

The main benefits of forward vertical integration are connected with making sure the firm has somewhere to sell its product. If it owns the next stage, there is a guaranteed market. For example, the firm owning the tea plantation may choose to buy a tea manufacturer to make it easier to sell their tea but they may be forced into it if other tea manufacturers have also been bought up by firms owning plantations and they are concerned about finding an outlet for their tea.

If a firm owns an outlet for its goods, it can also control the quality of the final product. As with backward vertical integration, the intermediate profit margin is absorbed.

With vertically integrated businesses, there may be opportunities to take advantage of economies of scale. For example, a larger firm may find it cheaper and easier to borrow money since they have more assets and are more likely to be able to pay back the loan. It is also possible that new developments may be adopted more quickly. For example, if a new type of tea is grown, the firm also has the facilities to manufacture it, rather than having to persuade another firm to develop the new product.

Costs of vertical integration

It can be difficult to find a firm to combine with that is just the right size. There may still be a need to buy supplies from elsewhere or to find other buyers for the final product. Particularly if one stage involves a primary product, the firm will not be able to take advantage of lower prices if there is a recession and demand falls. They may also be left with a worthless asset, if a substitute is later developed.

Vertical integration may restrict competition in the market and make it more difficult for new firms to enter. This could limit choice and lead to higher prices for consumers if cost savings are not passed on.

Conglomerate integration

Conglomerate integration or conglomeration is the joining of two or more firms making unrelated products – the merger of a tea plantation and an oil refinery for example.

Key term

Conglomerate integration: the combination of two or more firms making unrelated products.

Benefits of conglomerate integration

Conglomerate integration reduces risk, since the firm is no longer reliant on one market. This may be particularly relevant if there is no more scope for growth in the firm's existing market or demand for the product is declining. By joining with another firm operating in a different market, there will be other goods or services to fall back on. This spreading of risk by increasing the range of products is sometimes known as **diversification**.

Costs of conglomerate integration

Given that the firms are making different products, probably in different locations and maybe with different management styles, it could be difficult to bring them together as a single business. There may be some opportunities for rationalisation and through being a larger firm there may also be some economies of scale but these savings may be offset by the costs involved in trying to unite the separate businesses.

Benefits and costs of integration generally

Integration is a quicker way for a firm to expand than through internal growth. If successful, any type of integration should lead to higher profits which can then be used to further improve the business and strengthen its position in the market.

However, there will also be costs involved in two firms becoming one. A new brand name and/or logo may have to be promoted and perhaps different management styles brought together in a new location. There is also more likelihood of managerial diseconomies of scale, since it is more difficult to communicate and coordinate activities, and to maintain workers' morale in larger firms.

Activity

Investigate how a large firm has grown. This could be a local, national or transnational firm. Was it by internal and/or external growth? If external, was it mainly through horizontal, vertical or conglomerate integration?

Key term

Diversification: increasing a firm's or country's range of products, to spread risk.

Progress questions

3 What is the difference between internal and external growth?

4 Who may lose from integration and why?

Case study: The growth of Gepetto's Toys

▲ Figure 1.4.4: A wooden toy

Gepetto makes wooden toys for children. There is one other wooden-toy maker in the local area, Antonio. They decide to merge their firms, believing they will be better off as a combined business, which they name Gean Toys. After a while, they find it increasingly difficult to obtain the raw materials they need and buy a small firm, Pinocchio

Woods, that owns a piece of woodland. Some years later, when they are struggling to expand further, they buy a local coffee shop, Carlo's.

1 Use the information in the case study, to give an example of each of the following:
   i. conglomerate integration
   ii. horizontal integration
   iii. vertical integration.

2 Is the example of vertical integration, backward or forward vertical integration? Explain your answer.

3 What are the likely benefits of the merger between Gepetto's and Antonio's businesses?

Exam-style questions

1   Which one of the following is the best example of using a rule of thumb when choosing a meal in a restaurant?

   Choosing

   A   a different meal from the last visit   C   a mid-priced meal

   B   a meal based on the opinions of others   D   the meal that will maximise utility   (1 mark)

2   In the short run, a profit-maximising firm will continue to produce if it can at least cover its

   A   average total costs.   C   total costs.

   B   fixed costs.   D   variable costs.   (1 mark)

3   The most likely reason for a firm to choose conglomerate integration is to

   A   increase the firm's market share.   C   spread the risks of trading.

   B   obtain raw materials at cost price. D   take advantage of technical economies of scale. (1 mark)

4   The table below shows the units of utility obtained from a person's consumption of cakes.

Cakes	Total utility	Marginal utility	Average utility
1	100	100	100
2			75

   (i) Define "average utility".   (2 marks)

   You are advised to show your working for the calculations below.

   (ii) Calculate the total utility when two cakes are consumed.   (2 marks)

   (iii) Calculate the marginal utility of the second cake.   (2 marks)

5   Explain reasons why two firms may decide to integrate horizontally.   (12 marks)

6   Assess whether the maximisation of profits is the main objective of firms.   (25 marks)

   Note: To answer this as a data response question, use the data provided in the case studies on "The rise of Spotify" and "Railways in India" in 1.3 "Objectives of firms" to support your answer.

7   Evaluate whether governments should use behavioural policies rather than traditional policies to increase the consumption of merit goods.   (25 marks)

2 Costs, revenue and profits

The economics of business behaviour and the distribution of income

This section will develop your knowledge and understanding of:

→ the difference between marginal, average and total returns

→ the law of diminishing returns

→ returns to scale

→ the difference between increasing, constant and decreasing returns to scale.

Total, marginal and average returns

Total returns

In the short run, at least one factor of production is fixed in supply. For example, when growing wheat, it may only be possible to increase or decrease production by changing the amount of labour. The **total product or total returns** is the output at different levels of employment of the variable factor of production. If two workers can produce 5 tonnes of wheat, as shown in Table 2.1.1 (in the case study "The law of diminishing returns in action"), the total product is 5 tonnes.

Marginal returns

The **marginal product or marginal returns** is the change in total product/output when one more unit or one unit fewer of the variable factor of production is employed. For example, in Table 2.1.1, four workers produce 14 tonnes of wheat and three workers produce 9 tonnes of wheat. Therefore, the marginal product or returns of the fourth worker is 5 tonnes. This is the amount the fourth worker adds to the total product.

In general terms:

Marginal product of the nth worker = Total product of n workers − total product of n−1 workers

and in this example:

Marginal product of the 4th worker = Total product of 4 workers − total product of 3 workers

= 14 − 9

= 5 tonnes

Average returns

The **average product or average returns** is the amount of output per unit of the variable factor of production. It is the total product divided by the number of units of the variable factor. For example, in Table 2.1.1, the total product of six workers is 21 tonnes, so their average product is 3.5 tonnes.

In general terms:

$$\text{Average product} = \frac{\text{Total product}}{\text{Units of variable factor}}$$

and in this example:

$$\text{Average product of 6 workers} = \frac{21}{6}$$

$$= 3.5 \text{ tonnes}$$

Key terms

Total product or total returns: the output at different levels of employment of the variable factor.

Marginal product or marginal returns: the change in total product/output when an extra unit of the variable factor is employed.

Average product or average returns: the output per unit of the variable factor of production, calculated by dividing the total product by the number of units of the variable factor.

Get it right

The concepts of total product, average product and marginal product may also be referred to as total physical product, average physical product and marginal physical product. This is to emphasise that they are quantities of output, not money values. The terms total revenue product, average revenue product and marginal revenue product will be used when looking at the monetary value of the output when the number of workers is changed (see Chapter 4 "The labour market").

The law of diminishing returns

The **law of diminishing returns** (sometimes known as the law of variable proportions or the law of diminishing marginal productivity) states that as more units of a variable factor are added to a fixed factor of production, both the marginal and average returns to the variable factor will fall.

Using the wheat example, if there is a fixed amount of land and capital, if more workers are employed, then at some point, an extra worker will add less to output than the one before. Marginal product will start to fall – there will be diminishing returns. Although both the marginal and the average returns will fall, the law usually focuses on **diminishing marginal returns**.

The law of diminishing returns has three assumptions:

- There is only one variable factor.
- All units of the variable factor are equally efficient.
- There is no change in technology.

Since some factors of production are fixed in supply, it is a short-run concept.

Link

The idea of diminishing returns was introduced in a discussion of short-run costs in 3.3 "Costs of production" in the AS book. The link with short-run costs will be explained further in 2.2 "Short-run cost curves".

Key terms

Law of diminishing returns: as more units of the variable factor are added to a fixed factor of production, both the marginal and average returns to the variable factor will eventually fall.

Diminishing marginal returns: when marginal product falls after an extra unit of the variable factor is employed.

Activity

Explain what could happen to output if each of the three assumptions of the law of diminishing returns no longer applies, for example if there are two variable factors.

Case study: The law of diminishing returns in action

▲ **Figure 2.1.1**: Some factors of production are fixed in the short run

Wheat is a cereal grain, grown for its seed. It is used in a variety of products including bread, pasta and noodles. More land is used for wheat than for any other food crop. Production of wheat has tripled since 1960 with China, India and Russia producing about 40% of the world's wheat. Over time, wheat yields have increased considerably with more use of fertiliser, irrigation and different types of wheat, but can these rates of growth be maintained?

Table 2.1.1 shows the output when a different number of workers is employed to grow wheat on a fixed area of land and with a fixed amount of capital, such as equipment. Up to a point, when another worker is added, total output increases at an increasing rate but eventually an additional worker adds less to output than the previous worker. Diminishing marginal returns set in.

▼ Table 2.1.1: The law of diminishing returns

Fixed factor (land in hectares)	Variable factor (workers)	Total product (tonnes)	Average product (tonnes)	Marginal product (tonnes)
1	1	2		
	2	5		
	3	9		
	4	14		
	5	19		
	6	21		
	7	21.5		
	8	21.5		
	9	21		

Copy and complete the table, giving your answers to **one** decimal place.

Quantitative skills

In Figure 2.1.2, the gradient (or slope) of the total product curve indicates the type of return:

- when the gradient is increasing, there are increasing marginal returns
- the gradient stays the same if there are constant marginal returns
- when diminishing marginal returns set in, the gradient lessens as total product is rising more slowly
- with zero marginal returns, total product does not change
- if there are negative marginal returns, total product has a negative gradient because total product falls.

Key terms

Increasing marginal returns: when marginal product rises after an extra unit of the variable factor is employed.

Constant marginal returns: when marginal product stays the same after an extra unit of the variable factor is employed.

Zero marginal returns: when marginal product is zero after an extra unit of the variable factor is employed.

Negative marginal returns: when marginal product is negative after an extra unit of the variable factor is employed.

Figure 2.1.2 shows the total output of wheat when different numbers of workers are employed, using the information in Table 2.1.1.

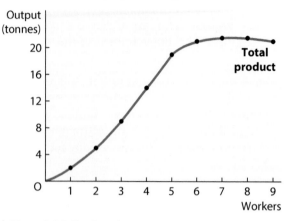

▲ **Figure 2.1.2:** Total product

For every worker up to and including the fourth worker, each worker adds more to total product/output than the one before. Marginal product is increasing, so total product is increasing at an increasing rate. There are **increasing marginal returns**. By working together, each worker can be more productive. The fifth worker adds the same to total output as the fourth worker. There are now **constant marginal returns**. Marginal product is constant and total product is increasing at a constant rate.

After the employment of the fifth worker, each extra worker adds less to output than the previous worker. Marginal product is diminishing (falling) and although total product is increasing, it is now rising at a slower rate. There are diminishing marginal returns. The fixed factors are becoming more thinly spread and the workers may even be getting in each other's way. In this example, diminishing marginal returns set in after the employment of the fifth worker.

Eventually, there could come a point where an extra worker adds nothing to output because their marginal product is zero. This happens with the 8th worker and is known as **zero marginal returns**. The employment of the ninth worker causes total output to fall because the worker's marginal product is negative. This is known as **negative marginal returns**.

Figure 2.1.3 shows the marginal and average product of wheat when different numbers of workers are employed, using the figures in Table 2.1.1.

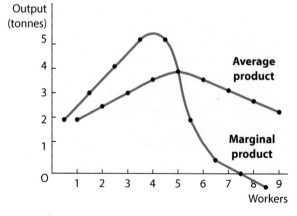

▲ **Figure 2.1.3:** Marginal and average product

Relationship between marginal product and average product

As long as a worker adds more to total output than the previous average (marginal product is greater than average product), this will cause average product to rise. This happens up to and including the fifth worker. After this number of workers is employed, marginal product is less than average product so average product falls. It therefore follows that marginal product is equal to (and intersects) average product at the highest point of the average product curve.

Application and significance of the law of diminishing returns

Although labour is likely to be the variable factor in the short run, the law of diminishing returns applies whichever factor of production can be changed. The example of wheat grown on a hectare of land could have used bags of fertiliser as the variable factor, with a fixed amount of labour. Up to a certain number of bags of fertiliser, the addition of another bag may result in increasing marginal returns, as each bag of fertiliser adds more to output than the one before. However, after this point, diminishing marginal returns will set in.

The law of diminishing returns shows the relationship between inputs and output in the short run. On its own, it does not indicate which combination of inputs is best. There may be alternative combinations of different factors of production that could produce the same output.

Returns to scale

In the long run, all factors of production are variable. It is possible to change all the factors of production in response to changes in market conditions. **Returns to scale** is the relationship between a change in inputs and the resulting change in output when all factors of production are variable. The firm may have decided that a particular combination of land, labour and capital to produce wheat is the best. As the firm expands, it may use multiples of this combination. It is not just changing one input, as occurred in the short run, it is changing all its inputs by the same percentage. The firm is able to change the *scale* of its production.

For example, the wheat grower may use one unit of land, for every 2 units of labour and 4 units of capital. Demand increases and the owners of the firm decide to expand their business. They may then use 2 units of land, 4 units of labour and 8 units of capital. In the same way, a manufacturing firm could buy a second or a third factory. As a result of the increase in the scale of production, does the firm's output increase more or less than proportionally, or even at the same rate?

Increasing returns to scale

If an increase in inputs results in a more than proportionate increase in output, there are **increasing returns to scale**. For example, if inputs increase by 100%, as in the earlier example, and output increases by 150%, there are increasing returns to scale.

Constant returns to scale

If an increase in inputs results in the same proportionate increase in output, there are **constant returns to scale**. For example, if inputs increase by 100% and output also increases by 100%, there are constant returns to scale.

Quantitative skills

In a similar way to Figure 1.1.3 of marginal utility in 1.1 "The individual as a rational economic decision maker", the values for marginal product have been plotted against 0.5 workers, 1.5 workers, and so on.

Link

The effect of factor prices and productivity on firms' costs of production and their choice of factor inputs will be explained further in 2.2 "Short-run cost curves".

Progress questions

1 What is meant by the short run?
2 If the average product of 5 workers is 12 tonnes, what is their total product?
3 Using the same figures, if the marginal product of the fifth worker was 8 tonnes, what was the total product of 4 workers?
4 What type of marginal returns are operating if output is increasing at a decreasing rate?
5 Is the law of diminishing returns an input-output or a cost relationship?

Key terms

Returns to scale: the relationship between a change in inputs and the resulting change in output when all factors of production are variable.

Increasing returns to scale: when an increase in inputs results in a more than proportionate increase in output.

Constant returns to scale: when an increase in inputs results in the same proportionate increase in output.

Key term

Decreasing returns to scale: when an increase in inputs results in a less than proportionate increase in output.

Link

The idea of returns to scale was introduced in a discussion of the shape of the long-run average cost curve in 3.4 "Economies and diseconomies of scale" in the AS book. The link with long-run costs will be explained further in 2.3 "Long-run cost curves".

Decreasing returns to scale

If an increase in inputs results in a less than proportionate increase in output, there are **decreasing returns to scale**. For example, if inputs increase by 100% but output only increases by 80%, there are decreasing returns to scale.

Summary of law of diminishing returns and returns to scale

Both the law of diminishing returns and returns to scale look at what happens to output as more factors of production are employed. However, the law of diminishing returns applies to the short run and shows the effects of changing only one factor of production. Returns to scale applies to the long run and involves changing all the factors of production.

The law of diminishing returns and returns to scale are both technical relationships, comparing the changes in the quantities of inputs and (physical) output. However, both relationships have implications for costs of production and the shape of the firm's cost curves.

Get it right

Make sure you use the correct technical language for the two time periods. In the long run, the returns are "to scale".

Case study: Returns to scale in action

▲ **Figure 2.1.4:** An end product of barley

Russia is the world's largest producer of barley, a grain crop with a number of uses, including for animal feed and bread. Alexei grows barley on a small farm in Southern Russia. For some time, he had only a small area of land and experimented with different combinations of units of land, labour and capital to see what happened to his output. He found that if he used his units of land, labour and capital in the ratio of 1:2:4, he could minimise his costs. Demand for wheat has been increasing in recent years and so Alexei decided to expand his business. He rented additional land and hired other factors of production but maintained the ratio of 1:2:4 for the units of land, labour and capital he employed.

Table 2.1.2 shows what happened to output when Alexei expanded his business, using five different combinations of factors of production, labelled A, B, C, D and E in Table 2.1.2.

▼ **Table 2.1.2:** Changing returns to scale with different combinations of factors of production

Combination of factors of production	Units of land	Units of labour	Units of capital	Total product (tonnes)
A	1	2	4	50
B	2	4	8	120
C	3	6	12	240
D	4	8	16	320
E	5	10	20	360

What types of returns to scale are there when Alexei increases his scale of production from:

i **B** to **C**

ii **C** to **D**

iii **D** to **E**?

Explain your answers.

This section will develop your knowledge and understanding of:

→ marginal, average and total costs

→ reasons for the shape of the marginal, average and total cost curves

→ how factor prices and productivity affect firms' costs of production and their choice of factor inputs.

Short-run total, marginal and average costs

Short-run total cost

The total cost of a business relates to all its costs. In the short run, at least one factor of production is fixed in supply, so there are fixed costs such as rent, as well as variable costs such as raw materials. In the short run, the total cost (TC) is made up of fixed costs (FC) and variable costs (VC) combined.

$$TC = FC + VC$$

For example, if the fixed costs of a business this month are $10,000 and its variable costs are $5,000, its total cost for the month are $15,000.

Short-run marginal costs

Marginal cost is the change in total cost when one more unit or one unit fewer is produced. For example, if the total cost of producing eight units is $400 and the total cost of producing nine units is $423, the marginal cost of the ninth unit is $23. This is the amount that producing the ninth unit adds to the total cost.

In general terms:

Marginal cost of the nth unit = Total cost of n units – total cost of n–1 units

and in this example:

Marginal cost of the 9th unit = Total cost of 9 units – total cost of 8 units

$$= 423 - 400$$

$$= \$23$$

In the short run, some costs are fixed, so the marginal cost, that is the cost of an extra unit, is the same as the change in variable cost. In the example above, the variable cost of the ninth unit was $23.

Short-run average cost

Average or unit cost is the cost per item. It is the total cost (TC) divided by the number of units produced (Q). In the example above, the average cost of eight units is $50 and the average cost of nine units is $47.

In general terms:

$$AC = \frac{TC}{Q}$$

> **Link**
>
> Fixed costs, variable costs, total costs and average costs were introduced in 3.3 "Costs of production" in the AS book.

> **Key term**
>
> **Marginal cost:** the change in total cost due to the production of an extra unit.

Progress questions

1   If the TC of 12 units is $400, and the MC of the 12th unit is $6, what is the TC of 11 units?

2   If the AFC of 8 units is $200, what is the AFC of 10 units?

3   If the AFC of 6 units is $60 and AVC is $12, what is the TC of 6 units?

4   Why is the addition to variable cost also the marginal cost when an extra unit is produced in the short run?

Link

The relationship between inputs and output in the short run, including the law of diminishing returns, was explained in 2.1 "The law of diminishing returns and returns to scale".

and in this example:

$$\text{AC of 8 units} = \frac{400}{8}$$
$$= \$50$$

The short-run average (total) cost is also the sum of the average fixed cost and the average variable cost. In this example, the total cost of producing 8 units may have been made up of fixed costs of $120 and variable costs of $280.

In general terms:

$$AC = AFC + AVC \text{ where } AFC = \frac{FC}{Q} \quad \text{and} \quad AVC = \frac{VC}{Q}$$

and in this example:

$$\$50 = \$15 + \$35 \text{ where } AFC = \frac{120}{8} \quad \text{and} \quad AVC = \frac{280}{8}$$

Shapes of different short-run cost curves

The shape of the short-run marginal cost curve

In the short run, if output changes, only the variable costs will change since the cost of the fixed factors stays the same. Therefore, the marginal cost of an extra unit will be the same as the change in the variable cost.

If only one factor can be changed, for example labour, the cost of extra units of output will depend on the wage of each worker and their productivity. Initially increasing the number of workers could lead to an increase in their marginal product. Assuming the wage rate does not change, as extra workers are more productive, the cost of producing extra units of output, that is the marginal cost, will fall. However, after a time, the law of diminishing returns will set in. Now, adding more workers will lead to a fall in their marginal product and marginal cost will rise. Therefore, the marginal cost is determined by the marginal returns.

As a result, if marginal product is increasing, marginal cost will be falling, but once diminishing returns set in and extra units of the variable factor are less productive, more and more workers will be needed to produce additional units of the good. The marginal cost will then be rising. Marginal cost falls before rising and is often drawn as a tick-shaped curve.

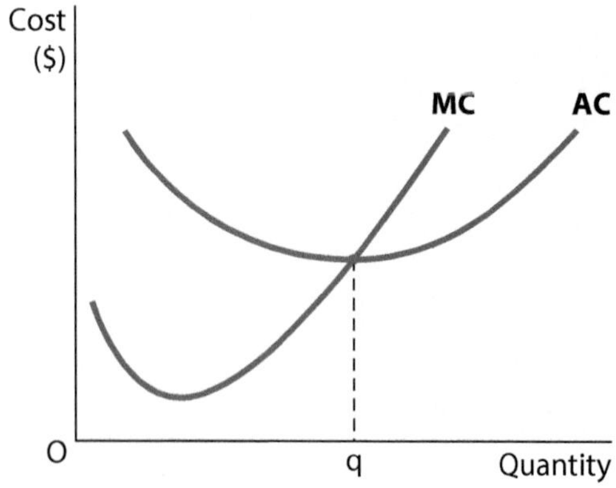

The shape of the short-run average cost curve

The shape of the short-run average variable cost curve (AVC) is determined by the average returns. When average returns are rising, AVC falls but when average returns start to fall, due to the law of diminishing returns, AVC increases.

The marginal cost curve will intersect both the AVC and average total cost (AC) curves at their lowest points. If the marginal cost of producing extra units of output is less than the existing average cost, then this will bring down the average cost. Using the figures in the previous example, if the AC of producing 8 units is $50 and the MC of the ninth unit is $23, then the AC of producing 9 units will fall to $47.

▲ **Figure 2.2.1**: The relationship between marginal cost and average cost

However, when the marginal cost of producing an extra unit of output becomes higher than the average cost, this will increase the average cost. For example, if the AC of producing 15 units is $40 and the MC of the 16th unit is $56, then the AC of 16 units will rise to $41. MC = AC at the lowest point of the AC curve.

In Figure 2.2.1, for units of output below q, MC is less than AC, causing AC to fall. Above this level of output, MC is greater than AC, causing AC to rise. MC is equal to AC at output q, the lowest point of the AC curve.

As said previously, in the short run, average cost is made up of average fixed cost and average variable cost. Although fixed costs stay the same in the short run, average fixed costs do not. The greater the output, the lower the average fixed costs because the fixed costs are spread over a greater number of units.

Total variable costs increase with output, but if there are increasing returns, although total variable costs will rise, they will do so at a decreasing rate and average variable costs will fall. This is because the marginal cost, that is the cost of producing an extra unit, will be falling. However, when diminishing marginal returns set in, marginal cost will increase and total variable costs will increase at an increasing rate.

At first, average total costs fall as output increases because average fixed costs and average variable costs are both falling. When average returns start to fall, due to the law of diminishing returns, average variable costs will rise. Average total costs will rise when the increase in average variable costs is greater than the fall in average fixed costs.

Figure 2.2.2 shows that the values for average (total) cost (AC) at each output level are found by adding the average fixed cost (AFC) and the average variable cost (AVC) for this output. Initially, both AFC and AVC fall, resulting in a fall in AC but after a certain level of output, AVC rises. Eventually, when the increase in AVC becomes greater than the fall in AFC, AC starts to rise.

The shape of the short-run total cost curve

Short-run total cost is made up of fixed costs and variable costs. Total fixed costs stay the same, but since total variable cost increases with output, total cost will also increase with output. However, variable and total costs do not increase at a constant rate. The increase in total cost as a result of the production of an extra unit is the marginal cost, which is also the increase in the total variable cost in the short run.

To start with, due to increasing marginal returns, the marginal cost will fall as output rises. This will mean that the total variable cost and the total cost will increase but at a decreasing rate. However, after diminishing marginal returns set in, the marginal cost will start to rise. This will cause the total variable cost and the total cost to rise at an increasing rate.

In Figure 2.2.3, total cost (TC) is the sum of total fixed costs (TFC) and total variable costs (TVC) at all levels of output. TFC is a horizontal line since these costs stay the same at all levels of output in the short run. TC will be the same shape as TVC because the increase in TVC is also the increase in TC. When TVC increases more steeply at high levels of output, so does TC.

Quantitative skills

If the marginal figures for a variable rise and then fall, the marginal and average figures will be equal at the highest point of the average curve. If the marginal figures for a variable fall and then rise, the marginal and average figures will be equal at the lowest point of the average curve. In both cases, this is where the curves cross.

The law of diminishing returns says that marginal product rises before falling, so the marginal product curve will cross the average product curve at the highest point of the average product curve. In the case of marginal and average cost, where marginal cost falls before rising, the marginal cost curve will cross the average cost curve at the lowest point of the average cost curve.

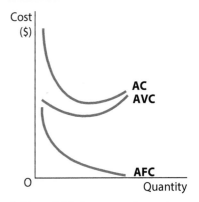

▲ Figure 2.2.2: Average total cost, the sum of average fixed cost and average variable cost

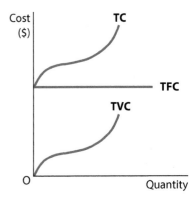

▲ Figure 2.2.3: Total fixed costs, total variable costs and total cost

Get it right

Assuming that factor prices do not change, short-run marginal cost will start to rise when diminishing marginal returns set in. AVC will start to rise when diminishing average returns set in. Average total cost will start to rise when the rise in AVC is greater than the fall in AFC.

Quantitative skills

You should be able to calculate marginal, average and total costs. You should also be able to draw and interpret short-run cost curves.

Progress questions

5   Explain the shape of the AFC curve.

6   Explain the relationship between marginal cost and average cost.

How factor prices and productivity affect firms' costs of production and inputs

Short-run marginal, average and total costs depend on the type of returns being experienced by the firm. Although the law of diminishing returns shows the relationship between inputs and output, it does not indicate which combination of inputs is best. For a given level of output of the firm, there may be alternative combinations of different factors of production.

For example, with a fixed amount of land, it may be possible to produce the same amount of wheat by using 2 units of labour and 4 units of capital or by using 3 units of labour and 3 units of capital. Which combination of inputs the firm chooses will depend on the prices of these different factors of production as well as their productivity.

If a firm is trying to maximise its profits, it will need to minimise its costs at the chosen level of output. A given quantity of output will produce a certain amount of revenue and since profit is total revenue minus total cost, choosing the cheapest set of inputs for producing any given level of output will maximise the difference between the firm's revenue and its costs. The firm will therefore have to consider both the productivity of each factor of production and its price to decide on the best combination of factor inputs to use.

Case study: Application of short-run costs

▲ **Figure 2.2.4**: Completing the test

Sofia wants to take on an extra person to work in her business. All the job applicants are expected to have studied Economics. As part of a numeracy and basic Economics test, she gives them the following short-run cost table to fill in, plus some accompanying questions.

1   Copy and complete the table, giving your answers **to the nearest whole number**.

2   What is the total cost if no units are produced?

3   After which unit will the marginal cost curve cross the average cost curve?

▼ **Table 2.2.1**: Short-run costs (all figures are in $)

Units	Fixed cost (FC)	Average fixed cost (AFC)	Variable cost (VC)	Average variable cost (AVC)	Total cost (TC)	Average cost (AC)	Marginal cost (MC)
1	500		300				
2			560				
3			780				
4			980				
5			1200				
6			1500				
7			1890				

This section will develop your knowledge and understanding of:
→ the relationship between the short-run and long-run average cost curves
→ the L-shaped long-run average cost curve
→ the minimum efficient scale of production.

The link between returns to scale and long-run cost curves

Returns to scale show the relationship between a change in inputs and the resulting change in output in the long run, when all factors of production are variable. When the scale of production increases, with more of a particular combination of land, labour and capital being employed, the firm may experience increasing, constant or decreasing returns to scale. This depends on whether output increases by a larger, the same or a smaller percentage compared to the change in inputs.

If there are increasing returns to scale, with output increasing by a larger percentage than inputs, if factor prices do not change, long-run average cost will fall. The firm may be able to take advantage of economies of scale such as technical economies, lowering the cost per unit. It will be cheaper to produce extra units so marginal cost will be less than the current average cost, helping to reduce average cost. Total cost will be rising but at a decreasing rate.

There are constant returns to scale when a given percentage increase in inputs leads to the same percentage increase in output. Average cost will stay the same as output increases and total cost will rise at a constant rate.

There are decreasing returns to scale when output increases by a smaller percentage than inputs. Average cost will rise as output increases, perhaps partly because of difficulties in management. Total cost will rise at an increasing rate.

If a business can take advantage of economies of scale up to a certain level of output as it increases its scale of production, and after this, diseconomies of scale set in, the firm's long-run average cost curve (LRAC) will be U-shaped, as shown in Figure 2.3.1.

The same relationship exists in the long run between marginal and average costs as in the short run. If the cost of producing an extra unit, the marginal cost, is less than the average cost, then this will reduce the long-run average cost. If long-run marginal cost is greater than long-run average cost, this will increase the long-run average cost. Long-run marginal cost will therefore cross (and be equal to) long-run average cost at the lowest point of the long-run average cost curve.

> **Link**
>
> Returns to scale were explained in 2.1 "The law of diminishing returns and returns to scale".

> **Link**
>
> Examples of economies and diseconomies of scale and the link between economies and diseconomies of scale and long-run average cost were introduced in 3.4 "Economies and diseconomies of scale" in the AS book.

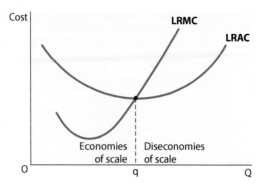

▲ **Figure 2.3.1**: A U-shaped LRAC curve

Figure 2.3.1 shows that up to output q, the firm is experiencing increasing returns to scale (increased inputs resulting in more than proportionate increases in output) and so LRAC is falling – there are economies of scale. If the scale of production increases so that output is greater than q, there are then decreasing returns to scale (increased inputs resulting in less than proportionate increases in output) and so LRAC rises – there are diseconomies of scale.

Up to output q, LRMC is less than LRAC, causing LRAC to fall. Beyond q, LRMC is greater than LRAC, causing LRAC to rise. LRMC cuts (and is equal to) LRAC at the lowest point of the LRAC curve.

The relationship between short-run and long-run average cost curves

In the short run, at least one factor of production is fixed, so there is a limit to how much a firm can increase its output. For example, a business may start with one, fully equipped factory. When demand is low, the firm may be operating below full capacity. As its products become better known, it can increase output to match the increasing demand, making better use of its fixed factors. This may be through using increased specialisation and by bringing more of its equipment into use. Fixed costs will be more thinly spread.

In the short run, the firm can only increase its variable factors. Eventually, the law of diminishing returns could set in as fixed factors are more thinly spread. Therefore, it is likely that the short-run average cost curve will be U-shaped.

In the long run, it is possible to change all the factors of production. At some point, a decision may be made about whether to change the scale of the firm's operations, by perhaps buying a second factory, so doubling the inputs of the firm. Figure 2.3.2 shows the relationship between the firm's short-run average cost curves (SRAC) and its long-run average cost curve.

In Figure 2.3.2, $SRAC_1$ shows the short-run average cost curve faced by the firm when it has only one factory. It can operate at any point on this curve. If, for example, it is producing an output of q_1, its SRAC is c_1. If it then increases its capacity to two factories, it will operate on $SRAC_2$. The same output of q_1 can now be produced at a lower SRAC of c_2. The different SRAC curves show different sizes of the firm and changes in the fixed factors of production. If the firm expands its capacity again, so it is operating on $SRAC_3$, producing output q, its SRAC is c.

Get it right

Returns to scale is a technical relationship, comparing increases in inputs and the resulting change in output. This then has an impact on the long-run costs of a firm. Similarly, the law of diminishing returns also illustrates an input-output relationship which affects short-run costs.

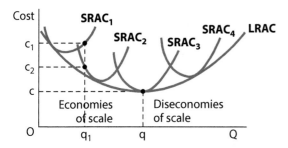

▲ Figure 2.3.2: The relationship between a firm's SRAC curves and its LRAC curve

The firm's LRAC curve is made up of a series of points on the firm's SRAC curves. The LRAC curve is sometimes known as an envelope curve since it just touches (is tangential to) points on its SRAC curves. There are numerous possible SRAC curves and the LRAC curve shows the lowest possible average cost for each output when all factors of production are variable.

In Figure 2.3.2, the lowest point on $SRAC_3$ is also the lowest point on the firm's LRAC curve. This is the **optimum size** of the firm, where the firm is producing at minimum average cost. The firm is productively efficient, having taken full advantage of economies of scale. It is operating at the scale and level of output that will minimise its cost per unit of output.

The LRAC curve in Figure 2.3.2 is drawn as U-shaped, reflecting economies of scale up to output q after which diseconomies of scale set in and LRAC starts to increase. For example, if the firm continues to expand its operations beyond $SRAC_3$ and now operates on $SRAC_4$, it will be experiencing diseconomies of scale and rising long-run average costs.

Quantitative skills

In Figure 2.3.2, each SRAC curve would have a short-run marginal cost curve going through the lowest point of that SRAC curve. For example, $SRMC_1$ would intersect $SRAC_1$ at the lowest point of $SRAC_1$. Similarly, LRMC would go through LRAC at q, which is the lowest point of the LRAC curve (as well as being the lowest point of $SRAC_3$). The marginal cost curves have not been included on Figure 2.3.2 to simplify the diagram.

Key term

Optimum size: producing at minimum long-run average cost, achieving productive efficiency.

Case study: Alexei's barley farm revisited

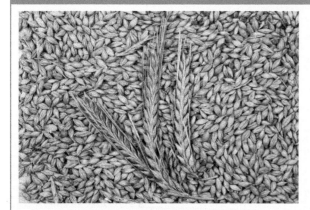

▲ Figure 2.3.3: Barley

When Alexei decided to expand his barley farm, he was concerned not only with how much his output of barley was likely to increase but also what would happen to his total costs. He has decided to review how much land he rents but intends to keep his factors of production in the ratio of 1:2:4 for land: labour: capital. The current factor prices for a given time period are $4000 per unit of land, $1500 per unit of labour and $1250 per unit of capital.

Table 2.3.1 shows different possible scales of production and their expected output of barley.

▼ Table 2.3.1: Output and costs in the long run

Land	Labour	Capital	Total product (tonnes)	Total cost ($)	Average cost (S)
1	2	4	50		
2	4	8	120		
3	6	12	240		
4	8	16	300		
5	10	20	330		

1   Copy and complete the table, calculating total cost and average cost for the different scales of production.

2   What is the shape of the LRAC for Alexei's LRAC curve and why is it this shape?

3   Which combination of land, labour and capital will result in productive efficiency? Explain your answer.

The L-shaped long-run average cost curve

The shape of the LRAC curve will depend on the good or service produced by the firm. It will not necessarily be U-shaped, with falling LRAC due to economies of scale up to a certain level of output being followed by rising LRAC, as diseconomies of scale start to offset the economies of scale.

Some activities have either considerable technical economies of scale available and/or a limited market. Even if the firm produces all the output of that product, it is possible that this level of output does not enable the firm to take full advantage of all the economies of scale available or that the LRAC curve is L-shaped.

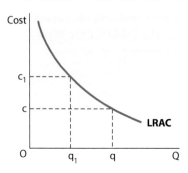

▲ **Figure 2.3.4**: A falling LRAC curve

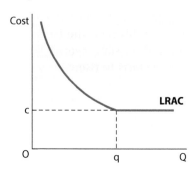

▲ **Figure 2.3.5**: An L-shaped LRAC curve

Figure 2.3.4 shows that even if output q can satisfy all the demand, there is still the potential to reduce long-run average cost below c if demand increases in future. In Figure 2.3.5, LRAC falls before becoming constant at c when the firm produces output q or more. Although there may be some diseconomies of scale setting in, perhaps due to problems of coordinating a large firm, these are balanced by further technical economies of scale.

Minimum efficient scale

The **minimum efficient scale** of an activity is the lowest level of output where long-run average cost is minimised. Whether this occurs at a low or a high level of output will depend on the good or service being produced.

Both the shape and the position of the LRAC curve will depend on what is being produced. For example, for many personal services such as hairdressing, there may be few economies of scale available as well as difficulties in coordinating a larger business. The LRAC curve is likely to be U-shaped, with diseconomies of scale setting in at low levels of output.

With other activities, for example aircraft or car manufacture, there may be considerable technical economies of scale available. With aircraft, there may be limited worldwide demand and even if there is only one firm, it may be unable to produce enough planes to achieve minimum LRAC. The firm may be operating at an output and average cost illustrated by q and c on Figure 2.3.4.

> **Key term**
>
> **Minimum efficient scale**: the lowest level of output where a firm's long-run average cost is minimised.

A firm facing a downward-sloping LRAC curve is sometimes described as a **natural monopoly** because, to be cost-effective, the activity is best carried out by one firm. In comparison, if two firms make the product, their LRAC will be higher. For example, if both firms produce output q_1 on Figure 2.3.4, their LRAC will be c_1. Even with only one producer, minimum efficient scale is not reached.

With modern cars, the same part may be used on several different models, enabling millions of identical products to be made. The firms producing these parts may be operating somewhere on the horizontal section of an L-shaped LRAC curve, where, with different economies and diseconomies of scale offsetting each other, LRAC is approximately constant. However, if output continues to increase, diseconomies of scale may eventually offset the economies of scale and LRAC may start to rise. In this case, the LRAC curve will be U-shaped but with a flat section of constant average cost in the middle, after LRAC falls and before it starts to rise.

Significance of minimum efficient scale for structure of industry and barriers to entry

If an activity has a low minimum efficient scale, it is likely to consist of many small firms. If there are few economies of scale, it will be easier to start making the product, since economies of scale will not act as a barrier to entry. This applies to hairdressing, which is an example of monopolistic competition.

However, for activities such as manufacturing aircraft and cars, the economies of scale act as a barrier to entry, making it more difficult for new firms to enter and survive in the industry. If they operate on a smaller scale than existing firms, their long-run average cost will be higher and they may not be able to produce at a profit. The industry is likely to be dominated by one or a few large firms – it is likely to be a monopoly or oligopoly.

Key term

Natural monopoly: where due to significant economies of scale, an activity is best carried out by one firm.

Link

The different types of market structure and the significance of barriers to entry were introduced in 4.1 "Market structures" in the AS book.

Activity

Apart from hairdressing and aircraft and car manufacture, list **three** examples of activities with a low minimum efficient scale and **three** examples of activities with a high minimum efficient scale. Explain why these activities have different minimum efficient scales.

Progress questions

1   If a firm is experiencing decreasing returns to scale, other things being equal, what will happen to its long-run average costs, and why?

2   Apart from the scale of production, what else could change in the long run to affect what happens to long-run average cost?

3   For a U-shaped LRAC curve, when will LRMC = LRAC?

4   If the firm faces a downward-sloping LRAC curve, where must LRMC be in relation to LRAC?

This section will develop your knowledge and understanding of:

→ marginal, average and total revenue

→ the relationship between average and marginal revenue

→ the relationship between marginal revenue, total revenue and price elasticity of demand.

Link

The difference between average and total revenue was introduced in 3.5 "Average revenue, total revenue and profit" in the AS book.

Total, marginal and average revenue

Total revenue

The total revenue (TR) of a business is its income from sales. It is all the money the firm receives in a given time period from selling its goods and/or services. If all the units are sold for the same price, total revenue can be calculated by multiplying the price of the product (P) by the number of units sold (Q).

$$TR = P \times Q$$

For example, if a farm sells 50 tonnes of barley in a month for $180 per tonne, its total revenue for that month is $180 \times 50 = $9,000$.

Marginal revenue

Key term

Marginal revenue: the change in total revenue due to the sale of an extra unit.

Marginal revenue (MR) is the change in total revenue when one more unit or one unit fewer is sold. For example, if the total revenue from the sale of 6 tonnes of barley is $1080 and the total revenue from selling 7 tonnes is $1260, the marginal revenue of the seventh tonne is $180. This is the amount that selling the seventh tonne adds to the total revenue.

In general terms:

Marginal revenue of the nth unit = Total revenue of n units – total revenue of n–1 units

and in this example:

Marginal revenue of the 7th unit = Total revenue of 7 units – total revenue of 6 units

= 1260 – 1080

= $180

Average revenue

Average revenue (AR) is the revenue per item sold. It is all the money the firm receives, the total revenue (TR), divided by the number of items sold (Q). In the previous example, the average revenue of six units is $180. AR is the same as price when all the units are sold for the same price.

In general terms:

$$AR = \frac{TR}{Q}$$

and in this example:

$$\text{AR of 6 units} = \frac{1080}{6}$$
$$= \$180$$

The relationship between average and marginal revenue

The relationship between average and marginal revenue depends on the market structure of the industry which determines the demand curve faced by an individual firm. The types of market structure range from perfect competition, where a large number of firms make the same product, to a pure monopoly, where there is only one firm in the market.

Average and marginal revenue under perfect competition

Marginal revenue affects average revenue. If the price stays the same regardless of the quantity sold, then average revenue (which is the same as price) will also be the same as marginal revenue, and both will be constant. This is the case because the demand curve for an individual firm in perfect competition is perfectly elastic. Each firm is a price taker, with the firm's price determined by supply and demand in the market. An individual firm can sell as much as it wants at this price.

In the previous numerical example (and as shown in Table 2.4.1), the average revenue of 6 tonnes of barley was $180. The 7th tonne also sold for $180. Since this increase in total revenue, that is the marginal revenue, was $180, it kept the average revenue of 7 tonnes constant at $180, the same as it was for 6 tonnes.

▼ **Table 2.4.1**: Revenue under perfect competition

Sales (tonnes)	Price ($)	TR ($)	AR ($)	MR ($)
1	180	180	180	180
2	180	360	180	180
3	180	540	180	180
4	180	720	180	180
5	180	900	180	180
6	180	1080	180	180
7	180	1260	180	180

In Table 2.4.1, the market price for a tonne of barley has been set at $180. This is both the price and the average revenue. Every extra tonne sold adds $180 to total revenue, so the marginal revenue is also $180.

Figure 2.4.1 illustrates the information in Table 2.4.1, where price, marginal revenue and average revenue are all constant at $180. This is also the firm's demand curve.

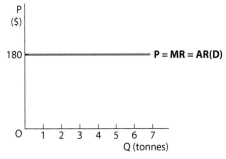

▲ **Figure 2.4.1**: Average and marginal revenue for a firm in perfect competition

Average and marginal revenue under other market structures

In market structures other than perfect competition, individual firms face a downward-sloping demand/average revenue curve. To persuade consumers to buy more products, the price needs to be lower. This means that the marginal and average revenue will both fall as sales increase. For example, in Table 2.4.2, as the price falls from $17 to $14, the firm gains an extra sale at $14 but loses $3 on each item compared with selling two products at $17 each. This results in the marginal revenue of the third item being $14 − (2 × $3) = $8. As the marginal revenue of $8 from selling the third item is less than the existing average revenue of $17, average revenue falls, to $14.

▼ **Table 2.4.2**: Revenue under monopoly

Sales	Price ($)	TR ($)	AR ($)	MR ($)
1	20	20	20	20
2	17	34	17	14
3	14	42	14	8
4	11	44	11	2
5	8	40	8	−4
6	5	30	5	−10

Quantitative skills

Marginal revenue affects average revenue in a similar way to how marginal cost and marginal utility affect average cost and average utility. If marginal revenue is less than average revenue, then average revenue will fall.

Table 2.4.2 shows the situation faced by a monopoly, for example, where the firm can choose either the price or the quantity it sells, since the demand/average revenue curve for the firm is also the market demand curve. The lower the price, the more products consumers will be willing and able to buy.

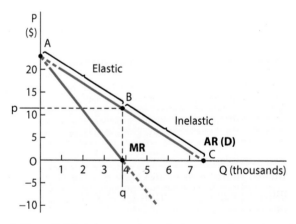

▲ **Figure 2.4.2**: Average and marginal revenue for a monopoly

Activity

Draw a graph of the relationship between MR and AR using the figures in Table 2.4.2, with the MR figures plotted against 0.5 thousand, 1.5 thousand, etc. and extend the curves so that both curves reach the two axes. Check that the two curves meet at the vertical axis and that the MR curve crosses the horizontal axis halfway between the origin and the quantity where AR = 0.

Figure 2.4.2 illustrates the information in Table 2.4.2. Both the MR and AR curves are downward sloping. Since the marginal revenue from selling additional units is lower than the average revenue, this will bring down the average revenue. The MR curve will be below the AR curve. In the diagram, the two curves have been extended to show that they start at the same point on the vertical/price axis and that the quantity where MR = 0 is halfway between the origin and where AR = 0.

The relationship between MR, TR and price elasticity of demand

As can be seen in Figure 2.4.1, a firm operating in perfect competition has a horizontal demand curve, where P = MR = AR (D). Demand is perfectly elastic. Marginal revenue is constant and so total revenue will increase at a constant rate, as shown in Table 2.4.1. Total revenue will be a straight line starting at the origin with a constant upward-sloping curve.

In other market structures, such as monopoly, marginal revenue is downward sloping, as each extra item sold adds less to total revenue than the previous one. This is because the firm has to cut its price to increase sales. Total revenue will be maximised where marginal revenue is zero. For items sold up this point, shown as quantity q on Figure 2.4.2, marginal revenue is positive. Total revenue is increasing. However, for items beyond q, marginal revenue is negative, reducing total revenue.

According to the graphical relationship between MR and AR, quantity q, where MR = 0, is halfway between the origin and where AR = 0. Quantity q is directly below point B, the mid-point of the demand/AR curve.

If a product has a downward-sloping, straight-line demand curve, its price elasticity of demand (PED) changes with price, with demand becoming less elastic as price falls. At prices above p, demand is elastic. If price falls when demand is elastic, total revenue will rise. For prices below p, demand is inelastic. If price falls when demand is inelastic, total revenue will fall. This is another way of confirming that total revenue will be maximised at q, where MR = 0. Demand is elastic between A and B (PED < –1) and inelastic between B and C (–1 < PED < 0). At B, price elasticity of demand = –1 and demand is of unit elasticity.

This section will develop your knowledge and understanding of:

→ the difference between normal and abnormal (supernormal) profit

→ the role of profit in a market economy.

> **Link**
>
> The difference between normal and abnormal or supernormal profit was introduced in 1.3 "The objectives of firms".

The difference between normal, supernormal and subnormal profit

The amount of profit made by a firm will depend on a variety of factors including the nature of the good or service being produced, the costs of the firm and the market structure.

Normal profit

Profit is total revenue minus total costs – all the income received from selling the goods or services produced minus all the payments to the factors of production involved. If total revenue equals total cost and so total revenue minus total costs equals zero, then to an accountant, there is no profit. However, in Economics, if total revenue equals total cost (or average revenue equals average cost), a firm is said to be making normal profit. Normal profit is the minimum amount of profit that will enable the firm to stay in that market in the long run a nd is included in the firm's total (and average) costs.

The costs of a business consist of the rewards to the factors of production – rent for land, wages for labour, interest for capital and normal profits for the entrepreneur. Although, normal profit suggests that the firm is making zero profit, in Economics, normal profit takes account of the owner receiving a reasonable reward, which has been included in the firm's costs. When total costs are subtracted from total revenue, this has already taken account of the owner receiving a return for their time and the risks they have taken. If the firm is not making enough money to pay this minimum requirement, the entrepreneur is likely to choose to use their money elsewhere, in the next most profitable business opportunity.

Normal profit therefore considers the opportunity cost of the inputs involved. The owner has risked money in the business – how much could it earn elsewhere, for example? If a firm is making normal profit, this is just enough to keep it in its present line of business. Normal profit will vary according to the activity and the risk involved. It is not a set sum of money. For example, a window-cleaning firm is likely to have a lower normal profit than an oil exploration business.

Supernormal or abnormal profit

Supernormal or abnormal profit is when total revenue is greater than total costs, or when average revenue is greater than average costs. It is any profit greater than normal profit. If a firm can make supernormal profit, this may attract other firms into the market.

Subnormal profit

Subnormal profit is when total revenue is less than total costs, or when average revenue is less than average costs. The firm is making a loss. If a firm is making subnormal profit in the long run, it is likely to leave the market.

The role of profit in a market economy

It is usually assumed that firms try to maximise profits but, depending on the market structure, some firms will make supernormal profit in the long run and others will make only normal profit.

In a market economy, decisions about what to produce, how to produce it and who should benefit are taken by buyers and sellers. The goods and services that are most wanted are likely to be the ones that are produced. People will be willing to pay more money for these goods and services, and sellers will want to make these products to earn more profit.

Profit has a number of roles in a market economy including:

- reward for risk taking
- incentive
- resource allocation
- source of funds
- source of income.

Reward for risk taking

Profit is the reward to the factor of production enterprise. When people start a business, they hope that it will be successful, making at least enough profit to compensate them for the risks involved. There is considerable uncertainty involved in starting and operating a business. Profit is the reward for bearing this uncertainty.

Large firms may have many thousands of owners who have bought shares (shareholders) in the company. If the business is successful, they will receive regular payments through dividends and the value of their shares may increase. If the business is unsuccessful, the owners/shareholders risk losing their money. The prospect of receiving profit may make this risk worthwhile.

Incentive

Profit provides an incentive both to set up and to continue in business. If supernormal profit is being made, it acts as a signal to the firm to produce more of their existing goods or services and for other firms to enter the industry. It also provides an incentive to develop new products. Similarly, if firms are not even making normal profit, this will cause them to leave the industry.

Resource allocation

Higher profits will attract entrepreneurs to enter a growing industry. In this way, more resources are allocated to the production of these goods and services in response to changes in demand in the economy. Similarly, fewer resources will be allocated to the production of goods and services in declining industries where profits are lower.

Source of funds

Profit is often used by firms to finance investment. The owners of the business will not necessarily receive all the profit the firm makes. Some profit may be retained (kept) to provide spare funds if needed in difficult times in the future, or to pay for the development and growth of the business. For example, the profit may be used to finance the improvement of existing products or to develop new ones. If the firm has no spare money of its own to finance these projects, it may have to issue shares, spreading the ownership of the business, or take out a loan from a bank or another financial institution, on which it will have to pay interest.

Source of income

Many people buy shares as a source of income. Shareholders, as the owners of a business, are due part of the profits, depending on the type and number of shares they own. This money is paid as a dividend, usually twice a year. If people have savings, buying shares in a business may be an alternative to putting the money in a bank to earn interest or using it to buy other assets.

Case study: Not everyone is a winner

▲ **Figure 2.5.1**: A risky business?

Mariana had a great idea for a simple new product. She had some savings and was able to obtain a loan from the bank, using her home as security for the loan. She applied for a patent to try to ensure that no one could copy her idea. She rented a workshop and started to produce the items. After a year, three local shops stocked her product and sales were increasing. However, the income from sales was only just enough to keep Mariana in business.

Mariana then decided to rent a larger workshop to expand production, encouraged by the increased demand. Her grandmother put some money into the business so

Mariana could afford to rent bigger premises. Mariana and her grandmother now each owned 50% of the firm and agreed that they would receive a payment from the profits every six months.

Unfortunately, shortly after, another well-established, local firm started making a similar product, since Mariana had not been granted a patent for her idea. The rival firm had also been attracted by the increasing demand and had the facilities to produce on a larger scale than Mariana. It could also sell the product at a lower price. Mariana cut her price to try to maintain sales, and in the short run, she was able to cover her day-to-day running costs. Eventually, however, she decided to close her business. As it now had no competition, the rival firm was able to increase its prices.

1 After a year, was Mariana's business making normal or supernormal profit?

2 Using examples from the case study, explain **three** roles of profit.

3 After Mariana's business closed, was the other firm likely to make normal or supernormal profit? Justify your answer.

The difference between invention and innovation

Invention is the creation of a new idea, product or process. For example, when Alexander Graham Bell created the telephone, this was an invention. Innovation involves making changes to existing products by introducing new ideas that better satisfy people's wants and/or have been adapted to deal with new requirements. For example, Apple's introduction of the iPhone was an innovation.

When the Apple iPhone was launched in 2007, it was able to offer a number of new features together, including a touchscreen with keyboard and connection to the internet, to access emails and social media. It was no longer just a device to make telephone calls. This and other smartphones have taken the basic product of a device that can be used to make telephone calls to a different level for both business and personal use. Since mobile phones already existed, the iPhone with its extra features was an innovation, not an invention.

Most sources agree that the idea of a vacuum cleaner dates from the 1860s but the first motorised version was not developed until the early 20th century. It has continued to evolve ever since. For example, after coming up with over 5,000 variations in 13 years, Sir James Dyson, a British inventor, developed the bagless vacuum cleaner. The product was launched in the 1990s. At first, this innovation was not popular, partly due to its high price. However, it is now the market leader in many countries.

Both the examples of the telephone and the vacuum cleaner show how initially an entirely new product was invented, but over time, innovation takes place. Various improvements can be made as new technology becomes available and people's wants change.

How technological change affects methods of production, productivity, efficiency and firms' costs of production

Technological change covers invention, innovation and the diffusion or spread of these new ideas and processes. Research and development may lead to new products or ways of working which can affect

> **Link**
>
> Invention and innovation were introduced as potential benefits from monopoly in 4.4 "Monopoly and monopoly power" in the AS book.

> **Key term**
>
> Technological change: invention, innovation and the diffusion (spread) of new ideas and processes.

production, productivity, efficiency and firms' costs of production, as it spreads through an economy.

Technological change could lead to the development of new equipment. This may replace existing equipment and/or labour. It may be more economic for the production process to become more capital intensive. It is likely that technological progress will increase labour productivity, particularly with fewer workers employed.

For example, there have been many changes to agricultural techniques due to technological change over the last 50 years. Changes to irrigation, new varieties of crops and new equipment have increased crop yields across the world. In the 1980s, the first genetically modified plants were introduced. Satellite technology enables farmers to see their land from the air and there is much more data now available. There is even the equivalent of "Fitbits" for cows to track changes in their activity and behaviour.

Technological change may lead to different ways of organising the production process, perhaps with more specialisation. The workers employed may need to be more or less skilled to work with the new equipment or processes. Some activities have become fully automated, not requiring workers as operatives, and the optimum size of the business may become larger or smaller as a result of technological change. The spread of ideas around the world has happened more quickly due to the growth of transnational corporations and the liberalisation of international trade.

Profit-maximising firms try to be as efficient as possible, to minimise their costs for a given output and to lower these costs over time. Although it may increase firms' costs in the short run to research and develop new technology, train workers in new techniques and replace outdated equipment, when successfully applied, technological change can reduce the cost of producing each unit in the long run.

A new technique may result in less waste for example. Perhaps fewer raw materials or workers are required, reducing variable costs. Perhaps the activity takes up less space, reducing the cost of buying or renting land. This will lower the total cost of producing a given output and therefore reduce the average and marginal cost.

Figure 2.6.1 shows the possible impact of technological change on a firm's long-run average cost (LRAC) curve. A shift down of the curve from $LRAC_1$ to $LRAC_2$ shows that any given quantity can now be produced at a lower LRAC than before. For example, quantity q can be produced at a long-run average cost of c_2 instead of c_1. In this diagram, the shape of the LRAC curve remains the same but technological change may also change the shape of the LRAC curve, leading to LRAC being minimised at a smaller or greater output. Lower LRAC will enable the firm to charge a lower price per unit and/or to increase its profit margin.

Link

The role of transnational corporations in a globalised world economy is explained further in 6.1 "Globalisation".

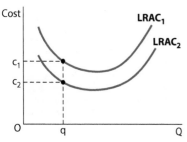

▲ **Figure 2.6.1**: Effect of technological change on LRAC

Progress questions

1   What is the difference between invention and innovation?

2   As well as invention and innovation, what else does technological change involve?

3   Explain how technological change could affect a firm's costs.

Case study: Technological change in the automotive industry

▲ Figure 2.6.2: A Model T Ford

The first car assembly line dates back to 1901, when the American automotive manufacturer, Ransom Olds, patented the concept. His stationary assembly line helped him to increase production of his Curved Dash Oldsmobile from 425 cars in 1901 to 2,500 in 1902. Henry Ford, another American car manufacturer, was also attracted by the idea of using an assembly line, with one person doing the same task repeatedly.

Between 1903 and 1908, the Ford Motor Company produced a number of different models of car, usually selling only a few hundred each year of each model. By 1913, Henry Ford was using a moving assembly line to build the Model T Ford car. The factory was divided into sections, the process was split into 45 steps and it took 93 minutes to produce one car. Fewer workers were needed and the number of person-hours per car fell from 12.5 to just over 1.5.

The lower costs were also reflected in the price. In 1908, the price of a Model T Ford was $825 but by 1912, it had fallen to $575. By 1914, an assembly-line worker could buy one of these cars with only four months' pay. Cheaper prices due to the large volumes produced and the use of mass production methods by other firms enabled the technology to spread across American society. Between 1913 and 1927, more than 15 million Model T Fords were produced.

1 Explain how assembly-line production is likely to increase labour productivity.

2 How could assembly-line production reduce average costs?

3 What led to the diffusion of this technological change in American society?

How technological change leads to new products and markets but may destroy existing markets

Technological change can lead to new products and greatly change existing ones. The smartphones of today are unrecognisable, both in their appearance and functions, compared to the telephones of the late 19th century. As a result, in many countries, the number of homes with telephone landlines is falling.

There are many examples of products that were once popular being replaced with new ideas and methods. Transport is one area that has evolved over time. Hundreds of years ago, passengers and goods were usually transported by boat or a horse-drawn vehicle. Now there are trains, cars, lorries and aeroplanes.

In many countries, for a long time, coal was an important source of fuel for both homes and industry. Energy sources later extended to oil, gas and electricity. However, if resources are non-renewable, there is a particular need for alternatives. Now, there is increasing use of "green energy", such as solar and wind power.

The American, George Eastman, developed photographic film in 1885, with the first Kodak camera introduced in 1888. Over time, there were many changes to both the appearance and operation of cameras, but they continued to use film, with Kodak being the world leader.

Link

There is another case study looking at how the Ford Motor Company operates in the 21st century in 6.1 "Globalisation".

Although Kodak developed the first digital camera in 1975, it failed to keep pace with the new developments and with digital cameras no longer requiring film, the firm experienced a massive decline, filing for bankruptcy in 2012.

The concept of **creative destruction** is often associated with the Austrian-born economist Joseph Schumpeter, although the idea came from the writings of Karl Marx. Schumpeter claimed that as technological change introduces new products and ways of working more efficiently, this will inevitably lead to the replacement of some products, firms and markets with others. What happened to Kodak is a good example of creative destruction. Even though Kodak dominated the market, it failed to adapt quickly enough to the technological change occurring. Its key product, camera film, was replaced by digital technology, destroying its traditional market.

The process of creative destruction, which results from technological change, enables resources to move to more productive processes as old less profitable firms and industries close down. New markets can develop in any economy but creative destruction is an inevitable process of free market economies/capitalism and results in constant change. The threat of being left behind and going out of business will force many firms to regularly update their practices. For example, many newspapers now have online sites as well as selling physical copies.

How technological change influences the structure of markets

As new products and processes are developed, this may change the optimum size of a firm for an activity. This can influence the structure of markets. The internet has enabled smaller firms to compete more effectively in some activities. For example, traditional travel agencies in town centres have found it harder to compete with online businesses. Without having to pay for expensive premises in the centre of cities, the costs of online businesses offering similar services can be much lower and there are now fewer barriers to entry into the market. Comparison websites also enable buyers to find cheaper services online.

If technological change reduces the barriers to entry into a market, it is likely to become less concentrated. However, some markets have become more concentrated, perhaps due to the ability to take more advantage of economies of scale. Amazon, the American e-commerce firm, now dominates the book-selling market in many countries with smaller bookshops being unable to compete with its low prices. In this case, what used to be a competitive market has become much less so.

Patents and intellectual property rights

Intellectual property rights (IPR) refer to the ownership of a creation of someone's mind, such as a design or an invention. If there are no intellectual property rights, another person or firm could copy or sell someone else's idea or product. This would lead to fewer new products and ideas being developed because there would be less financial incentive to do so. If markets are less efficient, this would cause market failure, and may also be inequitable.

A patent is a legal right to stop others from making or selling a new product or creation for a number of years. Patents allocate intellectual property rights and enable those who have created new ideas to earn money from them. This acts both as an incentive and as a means of financing more research and development. Rather than carrying the idea through to the manufacturing process, if they wish, the owner of the patent may allow another firm to exploit the idea under licence for a fee. They can then focus on more innovation.

A patent requires the owner to make public what they have developed, so that after the period of the patent ends, others can copy the idea. Otherwise, the creators may keep their idea a secret.

Critics of patents believe that they restrict competition and do not enable new ideas to be used as productively and as quickly as they could. Those producing the new product may exploit their position, charging excessive prices for the period of the patent. This is particularly controversial for life-saving drugs, which may be too expensive for those who need them. Although there are international agreements and the World Trade Organization (WTO) is trying to gain more worldwide coordination, patents are currently enforced on a country-by-country basis.

The role of governments in generating technological change

Invention, innovation and technological change can be generated in both the public and private sectors of an economy. Free-market economists view technological change as both inevitable and mainly positive because of the resulting lower costs and improved standards of living. Governments can also encourage technological change either directly or indirectly.

Profit-maximising firms in the private sector will have the incentive to innovate to keep down costs but governments can offer further assistance, through direct financing and tax relief schemes. This may involve giving firms money towards their research and development (R&D) if they meet certain conditions or reducing the tax they pay, leaving them with more money to finance R&D.

Some projects may be considered too expensive or risky for private sector firms to undertake and therefore the government may choose to take on these projects. Also, some managers may prefer short-term projects with quicker pay-offs rather than investing their profits in longer-term projects. This short-termism may reduce the long-term potential output of the economy.

Governments may have their own research facilities. If firms are state run, the government can take the lead in developing and implementing technological change, also making it available to others to help the economy. In some countries, increasing R&D is a policy objective. However, the government will not necessarily know which are the best technologies to back. Some projects will not be successful and there could be a large financial and opportunity cost.

Link

Intellectual property rights were introduced in 5.3 "Positive and negative externalities in consumption and production" and patents in 5.7 "Government intervention in markets" in the AS book.

Key term

Short-termism: when people, firms or the government focus on short-term results rather than their longer-term interests.

Activity

The European Union (EU) set a target for R&D as a percentage of GDP to be 3% by 2020.

1 What percentage of GDP is spent on R&D in your country?
2 Has this gone up or down in recent years?
3 What schemes does your government offer to encourage R&D?

Progress questions

4 What is creative destruction theory?

5 How can technological change affect the structure of markets?

Get it right

Look out for extreme words such as "always", "only", "never", etc. Is it likely that the event or effect will be true in all circumstances? This can be a useful point of evaluation in an answer. Question 6 in the "Exam-style questions" is an example showing how this may be used.

There will inevitably be winners and losers from technological change. Fifty years ago, cars were seen to be the future of land transport – more efficient than railways. So, in some countries, many less-used railway lines were closed and money was put into roads instead. However, this came at a cost of increased pollution and congestion, and the demand for rail travel has increased again.

Some people will lose their jobs and may not have the skills required to find another in an expanding market. Government support may be needed to manage the inevitable changes to an economy, including structural and regional unemployment. For example, they may support the unemployed by providing help with retraining.

There may be considerable spin-offs for the private sector or society generally of government-led research, including a number of applications using space technology. For example, in the 1960s, NASA (the National Aeronautics and Space Administration), an agency of the United States government which carries out space research, started to develop software to process pictures of the moon, which was then adapted for use on the human body to help diagnose illnesses.

Exam-style questions

1 The table below shows the output of a crop according to the number of workers employed when all other factors of production are fixed. Which one of the following applies when the number of workers employed rises from 2 to 3?

Workers	Total product (tonnes)
1	3
2	7
3	12
4	16

A Decreasing returns to scale

B Diminishing returns

C Increasing returns

D Increasing returns to scale

(1 mark)

2 If a firm faces a downward-sloping straight-line demand curve, price elasticity of demand

A becomes less elastic as price falls.

B becomes more elastic as price falls.

C is elastic at all prices.

D is of unit elasticity at all prices.

(1 mark)

3 Normal profit is

A included in a firm's total costs.

B required to continue producing in the short run.

C the difference between total cost and total revenue.

D the profit usually made in that industry.

(1 mark)

4 The table below shows the short-run costs of a small firm making chairs.

Chairs	Average fixed cost ($)	Average variable cost ($)
10	50	10
20		8

(i) Define "fixed cost". (2 marks)

You are advised to show your working for the calculations below.

(ii) Calculate the total cost when 10 chairs are produced. (2 marks)

(iii) Calculate the average fixed cost when 20 chairs are produced. (2 marks)

(iv) Explain, using a diagram, the shape of the average fixed cost curve. (4 marks)

5 The table below shows the output and long-run average cost (LRAC) for a firm over a number of years.

Year	Output	LRAC ($)
1	100	50
2	200	40
3	300	30
4	400	20
5	500	30
6	600	30
7	700	40

(i) Explain why changes in output may cause the firm's LRAC curve to be U-shaped. (4 marks)

(ii) To what extent do the data suggest that changes in output cause the firm's LRAC to be U-shaped? (4 marks)

Use the data in the table to support your answer.

6 Assess whether technological change is always beneficial to an economy. (25 marks)

Note: To answer this question as a data response question, use the data provided in the case study on "Technological change in the automotive industry" in 2.6 "Technological change" to support your answer.

3 Perfect competition, imperfectly competitive markets and monopoly

The economics of business behaviour and the distribution of income

This section will develop your knowledge and understanding of:

→ the spectrum of competition ranging from perfect competition at one end of the spectrum to pure monopoly at the other

→ how factors including the number of firms, the degree of product differentiation and ease of entry are used to distinguish between different market structures.

The spectrum of competition

The term market structure refers to the characteristics of an industry which affect the behaviour of firms producing a particular good or service. There are four main types of market structure:

- perfect competition
- monopolistic competition
- oligopoly
- monopoly.

The **spectrum of competition** refers to the range of market structures from perfect competition to pure monopoly. These two types of market structure are largely theoretical extremes. Some markets may have some of the characteristics of perfect competition and there may be rare examples of firms being the only supplier of a product, but the vast majority of the world's firms lies somewhere between these two extremes – on the spectrum of competition.

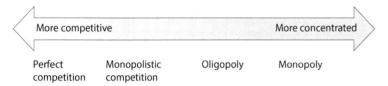

▲ **Figure 3.1.1**: The spectrum of competition

Figure 3.1.1 shows the four main types of market structure on the spectrum of competition. Perfect competition and monopolistic competition are both very competitive markets, with individual firms having little if any market power.

In perfect competition, where there is a large number of firms making identical products, the market is very competitive and individual firms are price takers. In a pure monopoly, where there is only one firm, there is no competition, enabling the firm to set either the price or quantity it sells.

As well as a pure monopoly, concentrated markets include oligopolies, and in some cases, the oligopoly may be a **duopoly**, where two firms control the supply of a good or service. As markets become more concentrated, there may be less competition, but this also depends on the other characteristics of the industry and whether the firms in an oligopoly work together or not.

> **Link**
>
> The different types of market structure were introduced in 4.1 "Market structures" in the AS book. Each of the four main types will be discussed in depth later in Chapter 3.

> **Key term**
>
> **Spectrum of competition**: the range of market structures from perfect competition to pure monopoly.

> **Key term**
>
> **Duopoly**: a market where two firms control the supply of a good or service.

Key term

Imperfect competition: market structures between perfect competition and monopoly, where there is competition between firms but there is not a perfectly competitive market.

The term **imperfect competition** may be used to describe market structures between perfect competition and monopoly, since in these market structures, there is competition between firms, but it is not perfect competition. This involves monopolistic competition and oligopoly. However, some sources include pure monopoly as an example of imperfect competition.

Factors used to distinguish between different market structures

The factors which are used to distinguish between different market structures include:

- the number of firms
- the degree of product differentiation
- ease of entry.

These factors affect the amount of competition faced by firms in that industry and how the firms behave.

Link

The full significance of these factors for firms' behaviour in different market structures will be discussed later in Chapter 3, together with the availability of information and other relevant factors.

The number of firms

The first important factor is how many firms operate in that market, which could be viewed as referring to the local area, the firms in that country or even the world as a whole. The number of firms in an industry can range from a very large number to only one.

Firms in monopolistic competition, where the products are similar, face a large number of competitors and have limited market power. Firms in perfect competition, where the products are identical, also face a large number of competitors but have no market power.

Many markets are oligopolistic, where there is a small number of firms in the market. Individual firms have more market power, since they have fewer competitors and a large share of the market. However, how oligopolistic firms behave also depends on factors such as the market shares of the other firms in the market and whether the firms work together or not.

If there is only one firm in the industry, it has much more influence on the market, but again this may depend on how narrowly the market is defined. There may be many airlines flying between large countries but only one flying to a small island. Also, a state-controlled monopoly, such as a water company, may operate in a different way from one in the private sector.

The degree of product differentiation

A second characteristic which is used to distinguish between different market structures is product differentiation. This refers to the extent to which there are differences in the goods and services offered by competing firms. Product differentiation includes differences in packaging, design or the image presented through advertising. This is particularly important in monopolistic competition and oligopoly, where firms are trying to attract customers from their rivals by emphasising the differences in their products.

If the products are the same or similar, it is likely that the price charged will also have to be similar. If firms are able to make their products different, or at least to appear to be different (perhaps through advertising), then the products will not be as close substitutes for each other. This will give the firms more market power.

Ease of entry

A third key characteristic is ease of entry. In market structures such as perfect competition and monopolistic competition there will be no or low barriers to entry into the market. In oligopolies and monopoly, there are often economies of scale. This means that new firms are unable to achieve low enough average costs to compete with existing firms, acting as a barrier to entry. It may also be difficult for a firm to be successful if the existing firms are well known due to large amounts of spending on advertising.

Whether it is easy or not for new firms to start producing the good or service will affect the behaviour of firms already in that market. The easier it is for new firms to come into the market, the less power existing firms have to set prices. If the firms set high prices and are making high profits, this will attract other firms but whether they enter the market or not depends partly on the barriers to entry.

Link

The significance of barriers to entry is discussed further in 3.7 "Contestable markets".

Progress questions

1   What is a duopoly?
2   What are the **four** main types of market structure?
3   Give **two** examples of barriers to entry into a market.

This section will develop your knowledge and understanding of:

→ the main characteristics of a perfectly competitive market

→ the formal diagrammatic analysis of the perfectly competitive model in the short and long run

→ why firms operating in perfectly competitive markets are price takers

→ the proposition that, given certain assumptions, including the absence of externalities, perfect competition will result in an efficient allocation of resources.

Link

Perfect competition was introduced in 4.3 "Competitive markets" in the AS book.

The main characteristics of a perfectly competitive market

A perfectly competitive market is a theoretical extreme in the spectrum of competition. The model of perfect competition requires the following:

- a large number of buyers and sellers
- homogeneous/identical products
- free entry and exit
- perfect information.

A large number of buyers and sellers

There may be thousands, or even millions, of buyers and sellers in a perfectly competitive market. The significance of this is that no buyer or seller has any influence on the price of the product. Even if they double or treble the amount they buy or sell, this will make no difference to the market as a whole because each buyer and seller makes up such a tiny percentage of the total purchases and sales.

Homogeneous goods

Another characteristic of a perfectly competitive market is that the products are identical, alternatively known as homogeneous goods or services. The products are not differentiated, for example, by using brand names. This means that buyers will not prefer one firm's products instead of others.

Free entry and exit

There are no barriers to entry or exit in a perfectly competitive market, so in the long run, there is nothing to stop new firms from starting to supply the good or service or to stop existing firms from leaving the market.

Perfect information

A final requirement for a perfectly competitive market is that there should be perfect information. Anything that may affect a buyer's or seller's decision making is known and understood. The information, including the price of the product and the factors of production, is known by everyone at the same time. Since there is perfect information, there is no need for advertising.

Case study: The Tsukiji fish market

▲ **Figure 3.2.1**: Fish for sale

The Tsukiji fish market in Tokyo, Japan, used to be the largest wholesale fish and seafood market in the world until part of it closed in 2018. Until 2018, the inner market at Tsukiji contained about 900 small wholesale fish sellers while the outer market had a wider variety of stalls and restaurants. The market handled about 500 different types of seafood, including seaweed, sardines, tuna and caviar. About $14 million of seafood was sold each day.

The inner market was famous for its tuna auctions, where, in January 2017, $632,000 was paid for a 466-pound (212-kilogram) bluefin tuna. Buyers (possibly agents for restaurants or food-processing firms, or other stallholders in the market) needed a licence and would bid for what they wanted at a price they thought was reasonable.

The business of the inner market now takes place at Toyosu, a short distance away. Although the fish auction part has moved to Toyosu, many tourists still visit the Tsukiji outer market, either as part of a guided tour or independently. There are plenty of similarly priced stalls and sushi bars and in total, there are currently nearly 90 eating places to choose from.

To what extent did the different parts of the Tsukiji fish market display the characteristics of perfect competition? Use the information in the case study to discuss each of the four characteristics and state what other information would be useful.

Diagrammatic analysis of perfect competition in the short and long run

How price is determined in a perfectly competitive market and for an individual firm

In a perfectly competitive market, there is a large number of buyers and sellers, none of whom has any power in the market. The price of the product is determined by the market demand and supply. Figure 3.2.2 shows the market for a product in a perfectly competitive market. The market demand and supply curves show the total demand and supply at different prices, during a given time, of all the buyers and sellers in the market. As would be expected, the lower the price, the higher the quantity demanded and the lower the quantity supplied. The equilibrium price of the product is p where q_m will be sold.

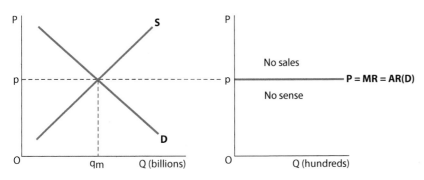

▲ **Figure 3.2.2**: Price in the market   ▲ **Figure 3.2.3**: Price for an individual firm

Activity

Copy Figures 3.2.2 and 3.2.3 and use them to show how an increase in market demand will affect the price and demand for an individual firm in perfect competition.

An individual firm can sell as much as it likes at the market equilibrium price, so faces a perfectly elastic demand curve at p. This demand curve is the firm's average revenue curve and it is also the firm's marginal revenue curve because the firm can sell additional units at the same price (shown as P = MR = AR (D) in Figure 3.2.3).

As can be seen in Figure 3.2.3, charging a price above p leads to no sales and charging a price below p makes no sense. If the firm charges more than price p, no one will buy its products because they know that they can buy identical products more cheaply elsewhere. Why would the firm sell its products for a price less than p if it can sell as much as it likes at a higher price? Note the different scales on the horizontal axes which show that the output of a single firm will be a very small percentage of the output for the market as a whole.

Why does profit maximisation occur where MC = MR?

Profit is total revenue (TR) minus total cost (TC) and profits are maximised where the difference between TR and TC is greatest. Profits will rise if the amount added to revenue from an extra unit is greater than the amount added to cost. In other words, profits rise if marginal revenue (MR) is greater than marginal cost (MC). If the firm increases its output where MR is less than MC, profits will fall.

Normal profit takes account of the owner receiving a reasonable reward and is included in the firm's costs. It is therefore just worthwhile producing the unit if MC = MR, so to maximise profits, a firm will choose the output where MC = MR.

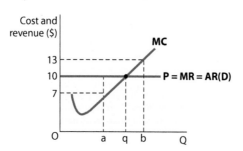

▲ **Figure 3.2.4**: Profit maximisation for a firm in perfect competition

To create Figure 3.2.4, a marginal cost curve has been added to Figure 3.2.3. This has been drawn as the usual tick shape (falling a little as output increases, then rising). At output a, MR is greater than MC, with the revenue from unit a being $10 and its cost $7. This unit will add $3 to profit. However, total profit will rise by increasing output beyond this point until q is reached. At quantities beyond q, such as b, MR is less than MC, so profit is now falling. Revenue for unit b is still $10 but its cost is $13, so producing and selling this unit would reduce the profit by $3. Profit is maximised at q, where MC = MR. There is no incentive for a profit-maximising firm to move away from this output unless costs or revenues change.

Perfect competition in the short run – supernormal profit

In the short run, at least one factor of production is fixed. Perhaps due to an increase in demand for the product, the market price rises and firms find that they can make supernormal profit. This is shown in Figure 3.2.5.

Figure 3.2.5 shows an individual firm in a perfectly competitive market making supernormal profit. An average cost (AC) curve has been added, compared with Figure 3.2.4, showing the usual relationship of MC cutting AC at the lowest point of the AC curve. A profit-maximising firm will produce where MC = MR, at quantity q.

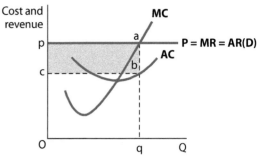

▲ **Figure 3.2.5**: Short-run supernormal profit for a firm

At q, the firm's total revenue will be Opaq, since q units are sold at a price of p (this area is p × q **or** AR × q). The average cost of producing q units is Oc (or qb), which makes the total cost Ocbq (AC × q). Since AR is greater than AC at output q and TR is greater than TC (Opaq > Ocbq), the firm makes supernormal profit of cpab, shown by the shaded area, or pc (or ab) per unit.

Adjustment from short-run supernormal profit to long-run equilibrium

So, what happens in the long run?

There is perfect information, so everyone knows that firms are making supernormal profit and this will provide an incentive for other firms to enter the market. There is free entry into the market, so there is nothing to stop new firms from starting to produce the good or service. As new firms enter the market, this will increase the total supply and lower the market price.

As can be seen in Figure 3.2.6, as more firms enter the market, the overall supply increases, and the market supply curve shifts to the right, to S_1. This will lower the equilibrium price in the market to p_1, which becomes the new price faced by an individual firm. At this new price, the individual firm is now only making normal profit, as shown in Figure 3.2.7, where TR = TC (both are Op_1eq_1), at the new profit-maximising output of q_1.

The firm's output has fallen to q_1, where MC = MR_1. However, at this quantity, AC = AR_1, so there is no longer any supernormal profit. Firms will enter the market until this long-run equilibrium position is achieved and the short-run supernormal profit has been competed away, removing the incentive to join the market.

> ### Quantitative skills
>
> Figure 3.2.7 has "Cost and revenue" on the vertical axis, since the diagram has both cost and revenue curves. Alternatively, a monetary unit sign, such as "$", can be used. Figure 3.2.6 just has "P" on the vertical axis, since it is a basic supply and demand diagram.

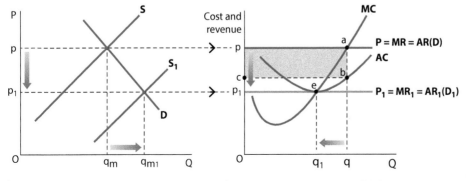

▲ **Figure 3.2.6**: Market adjustment (from short-run profit)

▲ **Figure 3.2.7**: Long-run equilibrium for a firm

Perfect competition in the short run – loss

Perhaps due to a fall in demand for the product, the market price falls, firms cannot cover all their costs and are making a loss.

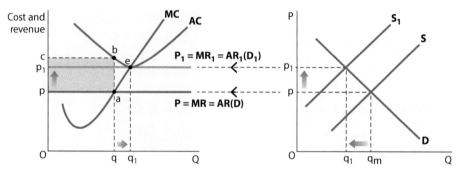

▲ **Figure 3.2.8**: Short-run loss then long-run equilibrium for a firm

▲ **Figure 3.2.9**: Market adjustment (from short-run loss)

Link

The conditions for profit-maximising firms to produce in the short run and long run were explained in 1.3 "The objectives of firms".

Figure 3.2.8 shows an individual firm in a perfectly competitive market making a loss when the price is p. A profit-maximising firm will produce at quantity q, where MC = MR. However, at q, the firm's total revenue is Opaq (AR × q) but its total cost is Ocbq (AC × q). Since AC is greater than AR at quantity q (b > a) and TC is greater than TR (Ocbq > Opaq), the firm makes a loss of cpba, shown by the shaded area, or cp (or ba) per unit.

In the short run, if the firm can cover its variable costs, it will stay in business. However, if it cannot cover its total costs, it will leave the market in the long run.

As can be seen in Figure 3.2.9, as some firms leave the market, the overall supply decreases, and the market supply curve shifts to the left, to S_1. This will raise the equilibrium price in the market to p_1, which becomes the new price faced by an individual firm. At this new price, the individual firm is now making normal profit, as shown in Figure 3.2.8, where TR = TC (both are Op_1eq_1).

The firm's output has risen to q_1, which is the new profit-maximising output, where MC = MR_1. At this quantity, AC = AR_1, so there is no longer any loss, just normal profit, which is just sufficient to keep firms in the market. Firms will continue to leave the market until this long-run equilibrium position is achieved.

Why firms in perfectly competitive markets are price takers

Firms in perfectly competitive markets are price takers. This means that they have no power to determine the price of their product and have to accept the market price. By looking again at each characteristic of the market structure, it can be seen why this must be the case.

- There are limitless sellers in the market, so each has a tiny market share, insufficient to have any influence.

Progress questions

4   Explain what will happen to market supply if firms in perfect competition make supernormal profit in the short run.

5   If some firms make losses in the short run and leave the market, what happens to the price and quantity sold of those firms that remain in the market in the long run?

- With identical products, there is no way for firms to differentiate what they sell to give them any market power.
- With no barriers to entry, new firms can easily add to the market supply if existing firms are making more than normal profit.
- Since there is perfect information, everything about the market will be known by everyone, so no firm will have an advantage.

The price for an individual firm is set by supply and demand in the market as a whole. Firms must accept this price and will only sell at this price. No one will pay a higher price since they know they can buy cheaper identical products elsewhere and there is no incentive to sell at a lower price. All firms in perfect competition are therefore price takers due to the nature and characteristics of the market structure.

Will perfect competition result in an efficient allocation of resources?

Firms in perfect competition will only survive in the long run if they can keep their costs as low as possible. If there are any developments which reduce firms' costs, due to perfect knowledge, these will be known by all firms. As a result, it is claimed that, given certain assumptions, including the absence of externalities, perfect competition will result in an efficient allocation of resources. The extent to which a market structure is efficient or inefficient enables us to judge the impact of the market structure on human welfare.

Types of efficiency

Firstly, it is important to distinguish between static and dynamic efficiency. **Static efficiency** considers whether a firm meets the criteria for a particular type of efficiency at a point in time whereas **dynamic efficiency** looks at changes in efficiency over a period of time.

A firm is productively efficient if it produces the output where average cost (AC) is minimised. This is also where MC = AC, since the marginal cost (MC) curve cuts the average cost curve at the lowest point of AC. Productive efficiency will only exist if there is **technical efficiency**. Technical efficiency exists if a given output is produced with minimum inputs, or put another way, if maximum output is obtained from a given set of inputs.

Technical efficiency refers to the quantities of inputs in relation to their output whereas productive efficiency is a cost relationship. For example, if a firm produces 100 units using 8 workers but could have produced this output with 7 workers, it would be technically inefficient. However, not all technically efficient outputs are productively efficient.

What is productively efficient also depends on the relative prices of the factors of production. For example, a firm may be able to produce the same output by using either 10 units of capital and 100 units of

> **Link**
>
> Productive and allocative efficiency were explained in the context of a production possibility diagram in 1.4 "Production possibility diagrams", and productive efficiency in the context of a firm in 3.4 "Economies and diseconomies of scale" in the AS book. Productive efficiency in the context of a firm was revisited in 2.3 "Long-run cost curves" and 2.6 "Technological change".

> **Key terms**
>
> **Static efficiency**: efficiency at a point in time.
>
> **Dynamic efficiency**: changes in efficiency over a period of time.
>
> **Technical efficiency**: when a given output is produced with minimum inputs or maximum output is obtained from given inputs.

labour or by using 20 units of capital and 30 units of labour. To be productively efficient, the firm should consider the cost of the two methods and choose the cheaper method.

The term **X-inefficiency** is sometimes used in this context when a firm fails to minimise its costs of production, perhaps due to overstaffing. Given that perfect competition is an extremely competitive structure and there is perfect knowledge, firms in perfect competition will be forced to be X-efficient to survive.

Dynamic efficiency results from improvements in technical and productive efficiency over a period of time, due to improved methods of producing existing goods and also the development of new products. Invention, innovation and research and development can lead to significant improvements in technical efficiency. However, individual firms in perfect competition are unlikely to have the money to fund significant improvements and with perfect knowledge, there is no incentive to do so.

Allocative efficiency occurs when P = MC in all industries and markets – the firms are therefore producing the types of goods and services which best meet people's preferences. If this happens in all markets, it will not be possible to make someone better off by reallocating resources between products and markets without making someone worse off – this is known as **Pareto efficiency** or **Pareto optimality** (after Vilfredo Pareto, the Italian economist and sociologist). By equating price and marginal cost, this is weighing up the opportunity cost of consumption from the buyer's point of view and the opportunity cost of production for the firm.

Perfect competition and efficiency

In the long run, if there are no externalities, a firm in perfect competition will be both productively and allocatively efficient.

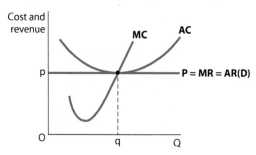

▲ **Figure 3.2.11**: Long-run equilibrium for a firm

Figure 3.2.11 shows the long-run equilibrium position of a profit-maximising firm in perfect competition. The profit-maximising output is q where MC = MR. At this output, the firm is operating at the lowest point of the AC curve, minimising AC, so the firm is productively efficient. At this output, P = MC, so it is also allocatively efficient.

However, this assumes that there are no externalities, either positive or negative, since, strictly speaking, for allocative efficiency, price

Link

There is more explanation and application of the different efficiency concepts in 3.9 "Static efficiency, dynamic efficiency and resource allocation".

▲ **Figure 3.2.10**: Vilfredo Pareto

must equal the "true" marginal cost, that is the marginal social cost. The firm in Figure 3.2.11 only takes account of the private costs of production.

If there are externalities, the profit-maximising output chosen by the firm, where its marginal private cost is equal to its marginal revenue, will result in too little or too much being produced for the benefit of society as a whole. If the externalities are positive, q will be less than the social optimum, and if the externalities are negative, perhaps due to pollution, q will be above the socially optimum output. The socially optimum output takes account of social costs (private plus external costs) not just private costs. So, if there are externalities, an individual firm will not be allocatively efficient.

In theory, if firms cannot take full advantage of economies of scale, they will not be able to reach the lowest point of the AC curve. This would make them productively inefficient. However, in such circumstances, where the minimum efficient scale is large, the market is likely to be dominated by a few large firms, not a large number of small firms.

Summary

Perfect competition is a theoretical extreme, which shows what would happen if a market were made up of a very large number of buyers and sellers, identical products, free entry and exit, and perfect information. Although there are examples of real-world markets which have many of the characteristics of perfect competition – the market for the dollar and other widely traded currencies, and many agricultural products such as fruit and vegetables – it would be extremely difficult for a market to display all the characteristics.

However, in both product and factor markets, the model of perfect competition provides a useful yardstick (benchmark) against which the behaviour and performance of real-world firms can be judged. For example, the model can be used to assess the extent to which real-world markets perform efficiently, and to what extent a misallocation of resources occurs.

Key term

Marginal social cost: the change in social cost (private plus external) due to the production of an extra unit.

Marginal private cost: the change in private cost due to the production of an extra unit.

Link

Externalities were explained in 5.3 "Positive and negative externalities in consumption and production" in the AS book.

Progress questions

6   Look again at Figures 3.2.5 and 3.2.8. Are firms that make short-run supernormal profits or losses productively efficient? Justify your answers.

7   Why may firms in perfect competition not be allocatively efficient?

Link

The model of perfect competition will be revisited when it is used as a yardstick (benchmark) for the labour market in 4.3 "The determination of relative wage rates and levels of employment in perfectly competitive labour markets".

This section will develop your knowledge and understanding of:

→ the main characteristics of monopolistically competitive markets

→ the formal diagrammatic analysis of the monopolistically competitive model in the short and long run

→ non-price competition in monopolistically competitive markets.

Link

Monopolistic competition was introduced in 4.1 "Market structures" in the AS book and as part of the spectrum of competition in 3.1 "Market structures" in this book.

Link

Price elasticity of demand and cross elasticity of demand were explained in 2.2 "Price, income and cross elasticities of demand" in the AS book.

Progress questions

1 Explain why price elasticity of demand for a product in monopolistic competition is likely to be elastic.

2 Explain why cross elasticity of demand for products in monopolistic competition will be high.

Monopolistic competition is a common market structure. It is a type of imperfect competition, which combines elements of perfect competition and monopoly. Hairdressers and cafés are good examples of monopolistic competition in many countries.

The main characteristics of monopolistically competitive markets

The main characteristics of a monopolistically competitive market are:

- a large number of buyers and sellers
- differentiated but similar products
- no or low barriers to entry and exit
- imperfect information.

A large number of buyers and sellers

Like perfect competition, there is a very large number of independent buyers and sellers, each making up a very small percentage of the market. The large number of firms will lead to considerable competition between them. Firms will have some ability to determine the price of their good or service, but demand is likely to be fairly elastic, at least in the long run, because of the number of close substitutes.

Differentiated but similar products

Unlike perfect competition, the products are similar but not identical. The products are differentiated, for example by using brand names. This means that the products are not perfect substitutes for each other and that buyers may prefer one firm's products to those of other firms. Each firm will have some monopoly power, for example there may be only one hairdresser shop called *Cutting Edge* in the local area.

Since each firm has a different product, it will face a downward-sloping demand curve and although it has the power to set price, it may have to charge a similar price to other firms to compete. To give them more power, firms try to emphasise differences in their product including, for example, in design, colours, the service offered, location and advertising, to build up brand loyalty. However, cross elasticity of demand will be high.

No or low barriers to entry and exit

Another difference from perfect competition is that there may be some barriers to entry and exit, but these are low and will not stop firms coming into or leaving the market in the long run.

Imperfect information

Unlike perfect competition, no buyers or sellers have perfect information, that is knowing everything about individual firms' products or the market as a whole. However, most information will be well known. For example, it will be easy to find out the price of a coffee in competing coffee shops but not necessarily how good the whole experience will be. Similarly, for sellers, is everything known about firms' costs, technology and methods of production?

Case study: The market for tuk-tuks

▲ **Figure 3.3.1**: A tuk-tuk

Tuk-tuks, sometimes known as trishaws, were first developed when a small engine was fitted inside a traditional rickshaw. They are commonly used as taxis in many parts of the world, particularly Asia.

In Sri Lanka, there are 1.2 million tuk-tuks for a population of just over 20 million. They are sometimes used to transport goods or for advertising, but most carry locals and tourists on short journeys. They are painted in a variety of colours and often decorated with ornaments or in other ways to make them look different. Tuk-tuks are usually bought with the help of a loan, but second-hand vehicles are plentiful, as are spare parts.

On the streets of Galle, a popular tourist destination in the south west of the country, tuk-tuks can be found on almost every street corner and there are often several travelling side by side along the main roads. Fares are agreed between the driver and passengers, although in some countries, fares are controlled by the government. There may be some negotiation, but fares are likely to be similar for a particular distance or journey, although tourists may pay more than local people.

Consider each of the four main characteristics of monopolistic competition:

    i   a large number of buyers and sellers

    ii   differentiated but similar products

    iii no or low barriers to entry and exit

    iv imperfect information.

How well does the market for tuk-tuks in Sri Lanka fit the model of monopolistic competition?

Analysis of the monopolistically competitive model in the short and long run

The short run

As explained previously, a firm in a monopolistically competitive market faces a downward-sloping demand curve for its product, since it is the only provider of that version or brand of the product. To sell more units, the firm has to lower its price. This means that its marginal revenue is less than its average revenue.

Link

The relationship between AR (D) and MR when the demand curve for the firm is downward sloping was explained in 2.4 "Marginal, average and total revenue curves". The changing value of price elasticity of demand when a product has a downward-sloping straight-line demand curve, with demand becoming less elastic as price falls, was also covered in this section.

Link

The reason why profit is maximised where MC = MR in any market structure and how to find the profit area on a diagram were explained in 3.2 "Perfect competition".

Figure 3.3.2 shows the situation for a firm in monopolistic competition, with downward-sloping AR and MR curves together with its AC and MC curves.

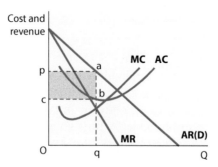

▲ **Figure 3.3.2**: A monopolistically competitive firm in the short run

If we assume that the firm is aiming to maximise profits, it will produce at q where MC = MR. For this quantity, buyers will be willing to pay price p, according to the AR (D) curve. At q, the total revenue is Opaq (AR × q) and the total cost is Ocbq (AC × q). In the short run, firms in monopolistic competition can make supernormal profit as shown by the shaded area cpab.

The long run

Other firms know that supernormal profit is being made and this will act as an incentive to enter the industry. In the long run there are no barriers to entry, so they will also be able to join the market. This will add to the market supply of similar products and reduce the market share of an individual firm. As a result, the demand for an individual firm will fall, shifting its AR (D) curve to the left, to AR_1 (D_1) in Figure 3.3.3, MR will also shift to the left, to MR_1.

Figure 3.3.3 shows the long-run equilibrium position for a monopolistically competitive firm. The supernormal profit has been competed away. At the new profit-maximising output of q_1, where MC = MR_1, AC also equals AR_1 so only normal profit is made. At output q_1, both the total revenue and the total cost are equal to Op_1eq_1. At any other output, less than normal profit is made because AC > AR at all other outputs. If some firms are not able to make normal profit in the long run, they are likely to leave the market and are free to do since there are no barriers to exit.

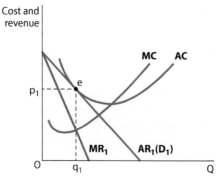

▲ **Figure 3.3.3**: A monopolistically competitive firm in the long run

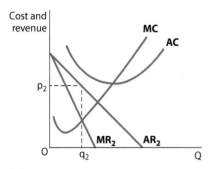

▲ **Figure 3.3.4**: A loss-making firm in monopolistic competition

Figure 3.3.4 shows a firm in monopolistic competition making a loss. The AC curve is above the AR curve at all output levels and even at the profit-maximising/loss-minimising output of q_2, the firm is unable to make normal profit, so will leave the market in the long run.

A firm in the long-run equilibrium situation is neither productively nor allocatively efficient since at q_1, AC is not minimised and P > MC. The productive inefficiency results from the firm not producing enough to reach the lowest point of the AC curve, and this may be viewed as a situation of excess capacity in the market.

Non-price competition in monopolistically competitive markets

Since there are many competing sellers in monopolistic competition offering similar but not identical products, prices are likely to be similar, at least in the long run. To survive in the market, firms will be forced to minimise their costs and will have little flexibility to try to undercut the prices of their rivals. Similarly, if their prices are much higher, many buyers will switch to alternatives, depending on the extent of brand loyalty.

Firms may have limited power over price, but non-price competition is a means by which firms can strengthen their monopoly power, to try to differentiate their products and build up brand loyalty. Advertising is an important way of promoting the differences in the product and to let more people know about it. One coffee shop may have more comfortable seats or give better customer service than another. It may be in a convenient location, try to appeal to a particular type of customer or have a loyalty scheme where, for example, customers qualify for a free cake after buying six coffees.

Non-price competition enables firms to strengthen their monopoly power but also increases the competitiveness of the market. This can benefit consumers, increasing welfare, by offering more variety and choice than perfect competition. However, it could be argued that there may be too much choice and that advertising is a waste of resources.

Quantitative skills

When drawing diagrams for a monopolistically competitive firm in the short run and the long run, try to keep the cost curves in the same position, since it is the AR/demand and MR for the firm that change, not the costs. In the long-run diagram, the profit-maximising output (q_1 in Figure 3.3.3) where MC = MR_1 is also the output where AC is tangential to the new AR/demand curve.

Activity

Choose either hairdressers or cafés in your local area, and find out what they do to differentiate their products. If there are none of these in your community, either choose a different local product which may be in monopolistic competition or try to find the answers online.

Progress questions

3 Is a firm in monopolistic competition a price taker or a price maker?

4 Why can firms in monopolistic competition only make normal profit in the long run?

5 If you were starting a business as a cleaner or a gardener, how could you try to differentiate your business to attract customers and to build up brand loyalty?

This section will develop your knowledge and understanding of:

→ the main characteristics of oligopolistic markets

→ how oligopolistic markets can be very different including in relation to the number of firms, the degree of product differentiation and ease of entry

→ factors which influence the conduct and performance of firms in oligopolistic industries

→ collusive and competitive oligopoly

→ tacit and overt collusion, and cartels

→ the kinked demand curve model

→ reasons for and types of non-price competition, including branding and advertising

→ pricing behaviour, including price leadership, price agreements, predatory pricing, limit pricing and price wars

→ the importance of spending on research and development in oligopolistic markets

→ strategic and innocent barriers to entry

→ the significance of interdependence and uncertainty in oligopoly

→ how objectives affect behaviour and the performance of firms in oligopolistic markets

→ advantages and disadvantages of oligopoly.

Link

Oligopoly was introduced in 4.1 "Market structures" in the AS book and as part of the spectrum of competition in 3.1 "Market structures" in this book.

Oligopoly is a common market structure throughout the world and the most significant by value of sales. It is a type of imperfect competition, on the spectrum of competition between monopolistic competition and monopoly, where a small number of firms controls the supply of a good or service. Examples include oil companies and airlines.

The main characteristics and differences between oligopolistic markets

Number and size of firms

By definition, an oligopolistic market is made up of a few firms. This could be where as few as two firms dominate the market, in the case of a duopoly. For example, Airbus and Boeing are the main two firms (although there are others) in the large jet airliner market, but there is no commonly agreed upper limit. Firms are likely to be large relative to the size of the market, so each has some monopoly power. Some sources claim that the market is an oligopoly if there is a five-firm concentration ratio of at least 50% or 60%. There may also be smaller firms operating in the market, but they are not large enough to have much effect on price or output.

Degree of product differentiation

Products in oligopoly may be almost identical or quite different. The market for cement could be described as an oligopoly, with the current world leader, the Swiss transnational company LafargeHolcim, operating in over 70 countries. Although cement comes in different qualities and is used for different purposes, it is difficult to differentiate the product, apart from a brand name and the reputation of the company.

If the firms produce homogeneous products, it is sometimes known as a **perfect oligopoly** or **pure oligopoly**. Some minerals can only be found in a few countries. For example, Australia, Brazil, China and Indonesia control over 70% of the market for bauxite, which is used to make aluminium.

In other oligopolies, known as **imperfect oligopolies**, the products may be quite different. The global automotive market includes a number of well-known firms, each with their own brands and features to appeal to different sections of the market. For example, Bugatti and Rolls Royce aim their cars at different income groups from the Tata Nano or the electric Changli Nemeca, which was on sale in 2020 for only $930 (or $1200 including the battery pack) from Alibaba, the Chinese e-commerce website.

▲ **Figure 3.4.1**: Cement – it is difficult to differentiate between products

Ease of entry
There are likely to be significant barriers to entry into the market, which will enable firms to make supernormal profits in the long run. These barriers may be due to the size of the firm, meaning that new smaller firms are unable to compete on costs. Alternatively, the incumbent (or existing) firms may use strategies (which will be discussed later) to keep firms out of the market.

Interdependence
The significance of there being a few large firms is that the actions of one firm will have an impact on the others. For example, if one firm changes its price, it will affect its own sales and profits but also those of its rivals. Similarly, a firm will be affected by the actions and reactions of its competitors. The firms are interdependent.

Non-price competition
A key characteristic of oligopolistic markets is the large amount of non-price competition. Advertising and other ways of differentiating a firm's products are commonly used to increase or maintain market share.

Factors which influence conduct and performance of firms in oligopolies

Conduct refers to how firms choose to behave or operate. **Performance** concerns how they can be judged and how well they are doing. Conduct concerns the policies chosen by the firm and performance refers to the outcomes of these policies. Unlike other market structures, there is no single model of how firms in an oligopoly will behave and perform.

In terms of conduct, this includes whether firms are using price or non-price competition, the extent of innovation, whether the firms are colluding (working together), and their pricing strategies. For example, are prices being set to deter new entrants and/or to drive out rivals? All of these are likely to be affected by the objectives of the firm. Is it profit satisficing, perhaps due to the divorce of ownership from control? Is it aiming to increase its market share, or just survive in the market? Or does it have multiple objectives?

> **Key terms**
>
> **Perfect or pure oligopoly:** where a small number of firms dominate the market for a homogeneous product.
>
> **Imperfect oligopoly:** where a small number of firms dominate the market for a differentiated product.

> **Key terms**
>
> **Conduct (of firms):** how firms choose to behave or operate in a market.
>
> **Performance (of firms):** outcomes on which firms may be judged, in terms of how well they are doing.

Link

For more information on X-efficiency, see 3.9 "Static efficiency, dynamic efficiency and resource allocation.

Progress questions

1   What is meant by a five-firm concentration ratio of 60%?
2   What are the key features of an oligopoly?
3   What is meant by interdependence in oligopoly?
4   Giving **two** examples of each, explain the difference between conduct and performance of firms.

Key terms

Collusion: when rival firms work together for their mutual benefit.

Collusive oligopoly: when some or all of the main firms in an oligopolistic market work together.

Quantitative skills

Collusion may allow oligopolists to act as a monopolist, trying to maximise their joint profits. In this case, you could draw the monopoly diagram as part of your analysis of the situation.

Key term

Competitive (or non-collusive) oligopoly: where the firms in an oligopolistic market act individually in their own self-interest.

In terms of performance, this includes how much profit is being made – whether it is normal or supernormal profit, is the firm meeting the needs of its customers, and whether the firm is operating efficiently, which could refer to productive, allocative or X-efficiency.

The key characteristics of an oligopolistic market – the number and size of firms, the degree of product differentiation, the ease of entry – influence the conduct and performance of firms in oligopolies.

If there are few firms in the market and/or the firm has a large market share, it will have more power to choose how to behave. It is also likely to make more profit but perhaps be less efficient if it has considerable power over the market. This is even more likely if its product is differentiated, with a low cross elasticity of demand, and if there are significant barriers to entry.

Collusive and competitive oligopoly

As said previously, there is no single model of oligopoly to explain how the market operates. Much depends on whether the firms work together or not. There are two main types of oligopoly – collusive and competitive.

Collusive oligopoly

Collusion is when rival firms work together, so a **collusive oligopoly** is where some or all of the main firms in the market work together, at least to some extent. They all hope to benefit from the arrangement. Examples of collusion include agreeing a set price or price range for the product, not competing against each other for contracts, and sharing research facilities. This reduces competition in the market and could effectively lead to the firms acting as a monopoly, since between them they would control the supply of the market. In this way, they may be able to maximise their joint profits, at the expense of consumers.

Collusion removes some of the uncertainty about what actions rival firms may take, but the arrangement relies on trust. For example, it may pay a firm to collude with others by agreeing to charge a set price, but an individual firm may benefit even more by undercutting this price. If one firm undercuts the agreed price, then others may do the same and the arrangement is likely to collapse.

Therefore, under oligopoly, there is a strong incentive for firms to collude to maximise their joint profits. However, there is also an incentive for an individual firm to cheat on the agreement, which means that such arrangements may not last for long.

Competitive oligopoly

A **competitive (or non-collusive) oligopoly** is where the firms act separately in their own self-interest. This may involve price competition and/or non-price competition. Firms will need to anticipate what their rivals may do, for example a price cut or increased advertising, and be ready to react quickly.

Tacit and overt collusion, and cartels

Collusion can be divided into two main types – tacit and overt. **Tacit collusion** is when firms have an informal arrangement or understanding about some aspect of the business. This may involve, for example, one firm setting the price, and others following. There is no formal agreement, just an accepted understanding of how the firms in the market will behave.

Overt collusion is a formal arrangement between firms. For example, a **cartel** is an example of overt collusion. This is where producers (which could be firms or perhaps countries who dominate the supply of a commodity) make a formal agreement to work together to reduce competition, controlling output and/or price. The price set will need to be high enough for all those involved, including the least efficient, to make a profit. This can cause tensions between members and may lead some to cheat on the agreement. OPEC (Organization of the Petroleum Exporting Countries) is possibly the best-known example of a cartel.

Collusion is illegal in most countries. However, it is not always easy to prove and may require one of the firms involved to act as a **whistle-blower**, informing the authorities of the illegal activity, usually in exchange for not being penalised. For example, in 2007, British Airways was fined by both the British and American authorities for entering into an arrangement with Virgin Atlantic about how much extra to charge to cover higher fuel costs. Virgin Atlantic escaped punishment for reporting this tacit collusion.

The kinked demand curve model

One commonly used model of oligopoly is the **kinked demand curve** model. Usually associated with the American economist Paul Sweezy, the kinked demand curve helps to explain why prices are often stable in non-collusive oligopolies.

Key terms

Tacit collusion: when firms have an informal arrangement or understanding about their actions, to reduce competition.

Overt collusion: when firms have a formal arrangement designed to control the market and reduce competition.

Cartel: an example of overt collusion, where producers make a formal agreement to control output and/or price.

Whistle-blower: a person who informs on another person or organisation that is involved in illegal activities.

Kinked demand curve model: a model of oligopolistic behaviour that assumes if a firm changes its price, other firms will follow decreases but not increases.

Case study: An example of a cartel – OPEC

▲ **Figure 3.4.2**: An oil well

The Organization of the Petroleum Exporting Countries (OPEC) was set up in 1960 by Iran, Iraq, Kuwait, Saudi Arabia and Venezuela. In 2020, it had 13 member countries. Ecuador, Indonesia and Qatar are former members. In 2019, OPEC controlled about 40% of world oil production and 80% of the world's viable oil reserves. However, in the early 1970s, OPEC controlled over 50% of world oil production.

The countries in OPEC work together to try to stabilise the oil market. There have been several times when the organisation has set production targets for members and when output was limited, prices rose.

1   With the help of a supply and demand diagram for the market for oil, explain why the price of oil is likely to rise if production targets for members are cut.

2   Why may countries want to join a cartel such as OPEC?

3   What does the success of a cartel depend on?

4   If collusion is illegal in most countries, how can a cartel such as OPEC continue to exist? If unsure of the answer, look up "state immunity".

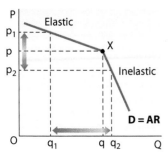

▲ **Figure 3.4.3**: A kinked demand curve

Figure 3.4.3 shows the demand curve for an oligopolistic firm, Firm A, kinked at point X, at the current price, p. If Firm A increases its price from p to p_1, it assumes, based on past experience, that its rivals will not follow but keep their prices the same. As a result, Firm A will suffer a larger percentage fall in demand from q to q_1. Demand in this price range will be elastic and its revenue from sales will fall. How much demand will fall will partly depend on product differentiation and brand loyalty.

However, if Firm A reduces its price by a similar amount, from p to p_2, it assumes that other firms will also cut their prices. As a result, although there will be an extension of demand at the cheaper price to q_2, there will be little change in market shares and the quantity sold will rise by a smaller percentage than the fall in price. Revenue from sales will fall since demand in this price range is inelastic.

According to the model, the firm will lose revenue if it changes its price, regardless of whether it increases or decreases it. This suggests that the price is likely to be stable at its current level, at p, an idea often referred to as **price stickiness** or **price rigidity**. The firm would need a good reason to risk changing its price. For example, if all firms are facing a significant increase in costs, they are more likely to follow an increase in price. Alternatively, if the firm is in a strong position, it may use a lower price to start a price war, to try to drive at least one of its rivals out of business. Otherwise, oligopolistic firms may have to rely heavily on non-price competition to maintain or increase their market share.

The kinked demand curve model illustrates the interdependence between firms and offers insights into a limited number of features in some oligopolistic markets. It is not the only model of oligopolistic behaviour, but it helps to explain why prices may be more rigid in some oligopolistic markets and the reliance on non-price competition. It also does not explain how the starting price, p, was arrived at, just why this is unlikely to change.

Reasons for and types of non-price competition

Non-price competition involves using methods other than lowering price to outdo rival firms. It is an important feature of oligopoly, whether the oligopoly is competitive or collusive. In both cases, a firm aims to promote and differentiate its product from those of its competitors. This will enable the firm to attract more buyers and build up brand loyalty. If relative prices change, when either this firm or others change their prices, it is then less likely that buyers will switch to another firm's products. If firms, for example, have decided not to compete on price, they will have to rely on non-price competition to gain an advantage.

Large amounts of money are often spent on advertising in oligopolistic markets. Advertising has two main functions, to inform and to persuade. **Informative advertising** provides people with more information, perhaps letting them know about a new product or telling them more about the features of an existing one. **Persuasive advertising**, as the name suggests, is designed to persuade more people to buy one firm's product instead of another's. It emphasises the differences between products and perhaps why one firm's product is better than that of others. Firms also sponsor sporting or other events, such as the Olympic Games and Formula 1 motor racing, to promote their brand. Advertising may be both informative and persuasive.

Through advertising, a distinctive brand image can be created, perhaps supported by a slogan or styling associated with the product. This makes the product and/or others produced by that firm, easily recognisable. The name of the firm may be written in an unusual way or it may be associated with a particular colour, as with Coca-Cola, the soft drinks firm. If firms spend large sums of money on advertising, this can also make it difficult for new firms to become established in that market.

Attractive packaging can make consumers more likely to buy the product, together with the image that has been created by the advertising. For more expensive, durable products, such as electrical goods or cars, other factors can be used to attract buyers. The length of the warranty, the after-sales service or the experience of visiting the showroom may make it more or less likely that customers will buy this and their next product from the same firm.

The use of loyalty schemes is also common in oligopolies. If there are only a few supermarket firms in a country, they may try to keep their customers returning to their stores by giving them points in relation to their spending, which they can use for their shopping or on other rewards. Kellogg's, the American food manufacturer, used to offer prizes and include gifts inside their packets of breakfast cereals to encourage people to buy more.

Pricing behaviour, including price leadership, price agreements, predatory pricing, limit pricing and price wars

The kinked demand curve model predicts that prices in competitive oligopolies are likely to be stable. This may also be true if firms collude on price. However, there are situations where changes in price may be used as part of a firm's strategy.

Price leadership is where one firm, which may be the largest, always tends to be the one that changes its price first, and then the other firms in the market follow its lead by making similar price changes. This is usually tacit collusion, where there is an understanding between the firms that this is how they will operate. Airlines have been observed to do this on certain routes.

In some industries, there may be a firm, for example, that stocks up on raw materials more regularly, and so is likely to be the first that would be affected by a significant change in costs. The firm may alternatively be good at identifying market trends. This firm may act as a price leader because it is more sensitive to market conditions, rather than due to its size. This is known as barometric pricing.

There may be other agreements on price. For example, firms may agree to fix their price at a certain level and use non-price competition instead. The price will need to be high enough to benefit all the firms involved. OPEC has at times tried to control the output of its members to keep the price of oil within a particular range, to reduce the fluctuations in price and incomes that may occur otherwise.

Sometimes a firm may cut its price to reduce competition and to maintain or increase the firm's market share. **Predatory pricing** is where one firm cuts its prices to drive one or more of its rivals out of business. This may set off a **price war**, where a price cut by one firm then leads to price cuts by others. Depending on how long the price war lasts, eventually some firms may have to leave the market. The firm that starts the price war must be prepared to make a short-run loss, but once there is less competition, it will be able to raise its prices again. Predatory pricing and price wars are more likely to occur if there is excess supply in the market.

Limit pricing is where the price of the product is set below the profit-maximising level, so the profits made by existing firms in the market look less attractive. This will deter potential new entrants if the price set by the incumbent firms is too low for a new firm to cover its costs. Although this may reduce short-run profits, it is a way of increasing the long-run profits of the firms in the industry. Predatory and limit pricing both involve setting prices below the short-run profit-maximising level, but the reasons for doing this are different. Either way, consumers are likely to lose out in the long run with less choice and higher prices than would have happened otherwise.

The importance of oligopolies spending on research and development

Another way that oligopolies can compete with their rivals is to develop new products or to make improvements to existing products. This may attract or keep customers if the new products are better or cheaper. It may also help to strengthen barriers to entry, leading to higher long-run profits. Firms in some oligopolies may therefore spend large sums of money on research and development (R&D) to maintain or increase their market share, but it may depend partly on the nature of the product and arrangements between the firms.

If barriers to entry are high and firms are working together, they may not feel the need to innovate. However, if a firm does not invest in R&D and one of its rivals (or even another firm, through the process of creative destruction) comes up with a new and better alternative, they may lose market share. Can they afford to take the risk?

R&D is also another area where firms may work together. Unlike collusion on price and output, this cooperation between firms can benefit consumers, since it may be more likely that improvements will be made and help a variety of firms' products if they pool their resources.

Strategic and innocent barriers to entry

Barriers to entry may be divided into two main types – strategic and innocent. **Strategic barriers to entry** are restrictions on new firms entering the market that have been created deliberately by existing firms – as part of their strategy. If large amounts of money are spent on advertising, this will make it difficult for new firms to enter the market, since they may not have the funds to make their products widely known and overcome brand loyalty.

If a firm has several brands, a new firm with only a single product will find it particularly hard to capture much of the market. For example, there are a few large firms in the global chocolate confectionery market. In 2020, the biggest three were Mars Wrigley, Ferrero and Mondelez. Each of these firms had a large number of different brands and products and often launched new variations.

Limit pricing is another strategic barrier to entry, designed to make it more difficult for new firms to join the market. The use of strategic barriers to entry may be more common if the industry lacks natural barriers.

Innocent barriers to entry are those that occur naturally, including economies of scale. For example, the activity may have a large minimum efficient scale and is therefore best done by one or a few large firms, for example manufacturing jet airliners. Firms competing on a smaller scale would have much higher average costs and would not be able to compete on price.

Alternatively, there may be high **start-up costs**, where, for example, expensive equipment may need to be bought by new firms. This is even more of a risk for a new firm if the equipment has no alternative use and would be difficult to sell if the business fails.

There may be statutory barriers, enforced by law. For example, if a firm has a patent, this will prevent others from copying the idea for a set period of time. Regardless of how an entry barrier arises, it has the same effect of making it more difficult for new firms to join the market and helps to preserve the market power of existing firms.

The significance of interdependence and uncertainty in oligopoly

Interdependence and the associated uncertainty are two other features of oligopolistic markets. Since there are only a few large firms, unlike perfect or monopolistic competition, the actions of one firm can have a significant impact on the others. Therefore, firms will try to anticipate what their rivals may do and must be ready to react or they may lose some of their market share.

For example, if one firm lowers its price, others may have to follow even though this may turn into a price war. If a firm is considering increasing its advertising, it has to take into account whether its rivals will do the same. Firms are affected by both the actions and reactions of their competitors – they are interdependent.

However, firms cannot be sure what their rivals will do, either in terms of actions or reactions. This leads to uncertainty. To reduce some of this uncertainty, firms may collude but even then, the uncertainty is not eliminated because it depends on how much rival firms trust each other to stick to the agreement.

Get it right

We usually talk about "cooperation" when firms are working together on something that might lead to improvements in the market, such as research and development, but "collusion" if the arrangement aims to reduce competition.

Key terms

Innocent barriers to entry: restrictions on new firms entering the market that occur naturally.

Start-up costs: the expenses involved when setting up a new business.

Activity

Game theory looks at alternative strategies where the decisions of those involved are influenced by the expected reactions of others, as in oligopoly. To take you further (since this is not in the specification), find out how game theory, including the prisoner's dilemma, is used to examine alternative strategies.

How objectives affect behaviour and performance of oligopolistic firms

Since there are only a few firms in an oligopoly, they have some choice about how they behave. This will be affected by the objectives of the firm, its relative size in the market and whether it is colluding with other firms. If the firm is a profit maximiser, it is more likely to aim to profit maximise in the long run, since in the short run, it may be limit pricing or possibly taking part in a price war.

Oligopolistic firms are usually large, so there is likely to be a divorce of ownership from control. If the owners and managers have different objectives, there may be profit satisficing, where sufficient profit is made but not the most that could have been obtained.

If an oligopolistic firm is trying to increase its market share, it may use price and/or non-price competition. If it is struggling to compete in the market, a firm may just be trying to survive. Successful innovation may help a firm increase both its market share and its profits. The firm may focus on quality and being socially responsible. This could affect the prices it charges, the wages it pays and other aspects of its business.

It is likely that firms in oligopolistic markets will have a range of objectives. However, oligopolistic firms are interdependent, uncertain of the actions and reactions of their rivals, so regardless of a firm's objectives, there is no guarantee that these will be achieved.

Advantages and disadvantages of oligopoly

Every real-world oligopoly is different, which makes it difficult to generalise about the behaviour and performance of firms, and the advantages and disadvantages of this market structure. Much will depend on the degree of concentration, product differentiation, ease of entry and whether the firms collude or not.

Firms are likely to set prices higher than in a more competitive market, but this depends partly on whether the firms are colluding or not. Prices are likely to be relatively stable, but perhaps at a high level and there may be the risk of a price war, which can lead to advantages and disadvantages to different economic agents in both the short run and the long run.

Firms are likely to make supernormal profits, which may or may not be used to pay for research and development into new and improved products. However, they may also make losses. Large firms should be able to take advantage of economies of scale, lowering their long-run average costs but these will not necessarily be passed on to consumers in lower prices. Large oligopolistic firms may also be in a strong bargaining position with their suppliers. There is more choice of firm and product than with a monopoly, but too much non-price competition can be a waste of resources and may act as a barrier to entry.

Governments often try to limit some of the potential problems of markets dominated by a few large firms. However, it is not always easy to identify when firms are abusing their power and there is little that can be done if the firms are controlled by governments.

Link

How and why governments may try to reduce the power of large firms, including oligopolies, is explained further in 3.11 "Competition policy".

Get it right

If asked to evaluate the advantages and disadvantages of a particular market structure, issues including efficiency and resource allocation, innovation, prices and quality could be considered. It is also useful to consider different perspectives – advantages and disadvantages to whom? Buyers, other firms in the market, possible new entrants, suppliers? In comparison with what? Perfect competition? Monopoly? Also, what do the effects depend on?

Progress questions

8   What is the difference between predatory and limit pricing?

9   State **two** strategic and **two** innocent barriers to entry.

10 Why is it difficult to generalise about the advantages and disadvantages of oligopoly?

Diagrammatic analysis of the monopoly model

A pure monopoly is where there is only one supplier of a product. It is the most concentrated market structure at one extreme of the spectrum of competition. More commonly, a monopoly is also said to exist where one firm controls the supply of a good or service, even though there may be other smaller firms in the market with little power. Monopolies will have considerable monopoly power and will therefore be able to determine price or output.

A monopoly faces the downward-sloping market demand curve because it is the only supplier of that product. It can choose either the price or the quantity it sells but not both at the same time, since the higher the price, the less consumers will be able and willing to buy. To sell more, the firm will need to lower its price. Therefore, a monopoly's marginal revenue is less than its average revenue.

A profit-maximising monopoly will produce at q, where MC = MR. The price that can be charged for this quantity (according to the AR/D curve) is p. At q, the total revenue is Opaq (AR × q) and the total cost is Ocbq (AC × q). The supernormal profit is the difference between them, that is the shaded area cpab.

The diagram used for a profit-maximising monopoly is the same as the one used for a firm in monopolistic competition in the short run. However, unlike monopolistic competition, where the supernormal profit will be competed away in the long run, a monopoly can earn supernormal profit in both the short run and the long run. This is because there are barriers to entry, so the diagram will apply to a profit-maximising monopoly regardless of the time period.

However, a monopoly (or firm with monopoly power) may have different objectives. Perhaps due to the divorce of ownership from control, it may be profit satisficing or aiming to maximise its sales revenue. Figure 3.5.2 illustrates both situations on the standard monopoly diagram.

Revenue maximisation occurs where MR = 0, at quantity q_r which can be sold for a price of p_r. If the firm is profit satisficing, where sufficient profit is made but not the most that could have been obtained, the firm will be producing somewhere between the profit-maximising output of q, and the normal profit output of q_n, where AC = AR. Therefore, its price will be between p and

> **Link**
>
> Monopoly and monopoly power were introduced in 4.4 "Monopoly and monopoly power" in the AS book.

> **Link**
>
> The relationship between marginal revenue and average revenue under monopoly was explained in 2.4 "Marginal, average and total revenue curves".

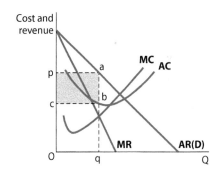

▲ **Figure 3.5.1**: A profit-maximising monopoly

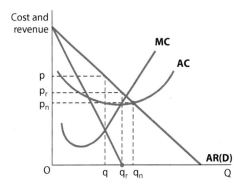

▲ **Figure 3.5.2**: Revenue maximisation and profit satisficing under monopoly

p_n. In both situations, the quantity sold is higher and the price is lower than if the firm aims to maximise profit.

Natural monopolies

Some activities may be natural monopolies. This is where, due to significant economies of scale, an activity is best carried out by one firm. This is most likely to be due to the availability of considerable technical economies (and maybe a limited market) in some activities. This results in a very high minimum efficient scale compared to the size of the market, which will only support one efficient producer.

There may also be high start-up costs in the form of the required infrastructure. For utilities, such as water and gas, it would be inefficient and a waste of scarce resources to have more than one set of pipes down a street. Average cost will be lower if there is only one supplier of such utilities unless firms can share the infrastructure. Even if one firm produces the output for the whole region, the country, or maybe even the world, it may not produce enough to achieve minimum long-run average cost. Its LRAC curve is therefore downward sloping.

Figure 3.5.3 shows the cost and average revenue curves faced by a natural monopoly. With a downward-sloping LRAC curve, LRMC will be less than LRAC. This is because LRMC cuts LRAC at the lowest point of the LRAC curve, an output which has not been reached. A single firm could make profit up to output q, where LRAC = AR. If there is more than one firm in the industry, each firm's output will be less than q and they will have higher long-run average costs.

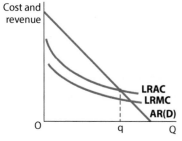

▲ **Figure 3.5.3**: A natural monopoly

What influences monopoly power?

Monopoly power is the ability of a firm to influence price and output. A firm's monopoly power is influenced by a number of factors including:

* barriers to entry
* the number of competitors
* advertising
* the degree of product differentiation.

Barriers to entry

If there are high barriers to entry, it will be difficult for new firms to join the market. These barriers could be natural, such as significant economies of scale, or strategic, for example limit pricing. If there is a monopoly (or oligopoly) operating in a market, it is likely that there will be significant economies of scale. New firms operating on a smaller scale would have higher average costs and not be able to compete on price.

Alternatively, or as well as the natural barriers, firms may use strategic barriers to increase their market power. If the existing firm(s) in the market use limit pricing to set their prices at a level where new firms cannot cover their average costs, this will remove the incentive to enter the market. This price will be below the short-run profit maximising price of p, in Figure 3.5.1.

However, even with high barriers to entry, monopoly power is not guaranteed in the long run. If another firm can develop a new product to replace the existing one, the former monopoly power will be reduced. The likelihood of this creative destruction occurring depends partly on the nature of the product and technological developments. Where large profits are being made, there will be a greater incentive to overcome the barriers to entry.

The number of competitors

In the extreme case of a pure monopoly, there are no competitors. In theory, the firm has the greatest monopoly power in this situation. However, the firm can only directly influence price or output, since it is limited by the market demand curve, which, under monopoly, is also the demand curve of the firm. As can be seen in Figure 3.5.1, showing a profit-maximising monopoly, if the firm chooses to sell output q, where MC = MR, the market will only pay price p. If it chooses a higher price, above p, then less will be sold.

If the firm is not a pure monopoly, it will have less monopoly power. The more firms there are in the market and the larger their market shares, the lower the monopoly power of an individual firm. A firm with one small competitor is likely to have more monopoly power, other things being equal, than one competing with a number of similar-sized firms. The greater the number of competitors, the more alternatives there are, giving more choice and power to consumers. Firms in monopolistically competitive and oligopolistic markets are price makers but have varying degrees of monopoly power.

Monopoly power also depends on how the market is defined. A firm may have monopoly power in its own country or the local area but face strong competition in other countries.

Advertising

Advertising may be used to increase a firm's monopoly power. It lets potential customers know more about the firm's products and how they are different from those of other firms in the market. Advertising helps to build up a strong brand image and brand loyalty. Successful advertising will give the firm more power over the price it charges since it is less likely that buyers will switch to rival firms if the firm increases its price. Advertising is particularly important in oligopolistic and monopolistically competitive markets. However, it could be questioned whether a pure monopoly needs to advertise if it provides an essential product and has no close substitutes.

Advertising may also act as a barrier to entry. Advertising can be expensive and there is no guarantee that it will be successful. In some markets, a new entrant may have to spend a large sum of money to let people know about its products and to persuade buyers to switch away from established well-known brands. This is another way that advertising can increase a firm's monopoly power.

The degree of product differentiation

The greater the differences between products, the more monopoly power firms will have. These differences could be actual or perceived (believed

Link

Natural monopolies were introduced in 2.3 "Long-run cost curves" and the natural monopoly argument will be revisited as part of the case for public ownership in 3.12 "Public ownership, privatisation, regulation and deregulation of markets".

Progress questions

1 If a monopoly chooses the amount it wishes to sell, how is the price determined?
2 What is a natural monopoly?
3 Why is LRMC below the LRAC in a natural monopoly?

Link

Barriers to entry, the number of competitors, advertising and the degree of product differentiation were discussed earlier in the chapter when explaining the characteristics of different market structures.

Get it right

A monopoly is not the only market structure with monopoly power. Firms in monopolistic competition and oligopolistic markets also have varying degrees of monopoly power.

Progress questions

4 How can advertising increase monopoly power?

5 How and why might a monopoly be run differently if it is in the public sector?

by individuals), perhaps due to the image created by advertising. They include differences in design, packaging and quality, perhaps to appeal to different income groups or other sections of the market. If products are believed to be different, they will be less easily substituted for each other. This will give firms more influence over price and output.

For example, firms in imperfect oligopolies will have more monopoly power than those in perfect oligopolies where firms struggle to differentiate their products. In perfect oligopolies, if one firm reduces its price, it is likely to be able to increase its market share unless other firms follow.

General

Barriers to entry, the number of competitors, advertising and the degree of product differentiation can all influence the monopoly power of firms, particularly if used together. If advertising and product differentiation are successful, this will give firms more influence over price and output. They will increase demand for the product and make the demand more inelastic. However, the resulting lack of competition may cause consumers and other firms to lose out and so governments may take action to limit monopoly power, particularly when the market is dominated by one or a few firms.

Advantages and disadvantages of monopoly

Advantages

Monopoly has two main potential advantages:

- economies of scale
- more invention and innovation.

Some activities will have lower costs if there is only one firm dominating the market. This is when, due to the availability of significant economies of scale, there is a large minimum efficient scale and is particularly relevant to a natural monopoly. Electricity and rail services are often quoted as examples. It would be inefficient to have more than one set of power cables or rail tracks.

A monopoly is also more likely to have more funds available for research and development (R&D), due to the amount of supernormal profit it makes. This could lead to more invention and innovation, with the development of new products and improvements to existing ones, which could benefit consumers in the form of better products and lower prices. Successful innovation will help the firm maintain its monopoly position but if barriers to entry are high, there may be less incentive for a monopoly to spend on R&D.

Disadvantages

Disadvantages of monopoly include:

- higher prices
- inefficiency and a misallocation of resources.

The monopoly model suggests that higher prices and profits result, compared to a more competitive market. To earn supernormal profit, a monopoly is likely to produce less and charge a higher price than would occur in a competitive market. This causes inefficiency and a misallocation of resources, although the extent of this depends partly on the firm's monopoly power, which in turn depends on factors such as product differentiation. The lack of competitive pressure may also result in X-inefficiency and higher costs in a monopoly, which will mean that welfare is not maximised.

In reality, the advantages of monopoly may be limited. Even if the firm has lower costs, it does not necessarily mean that these will be passed onto consumers in the form of lower prices. This will depend partly on how much costs are reduced and whether the firm is operating in the public or private sector. Invention and innovation can strengthen a firm's monopoly power but if there are high barriers to entry already, a monopoly may not invest much in R&D. This will depend partly on the likelihood of another firm developing a replacement product.

Activity

Find out why Microsoft was investigated by the European Union and the United States authorities. How was Microsoft said to be abusing its monopoly power?

Link

Efficiency and resource allocation in monopoly are explained further in 3.9 "Static efficiency, dynamic efficiency and resource allocation".

Case study: Microsoft

▲ **Figure 3.5.4**: A well-known image of Microsoft

Microsoft, the transnational American technology company, was founded in 1975. Among its best-known products are its Windows and Office software, its Internet Explorer and Edge web browsers and the Xbox video game console. By the mid-1980s, it dominated the personal computer operating system market. It has regularly developed and launched new and improved software and other products and has also diversified, acquiring Skype, an app for video chat, in 2011 and LinkedIn, a social network for business professionals, in 2016.

Microsoft has been fined over $1 billion in total by the European Union for anti-competitive practices and at one time, the United States government threatened to split up the firm. Microsoft's gross profit for the year to March 2020 was over $94 billion. Windows is still the main operating system on desktops but as more people are using smartphones, the importance of desktops and laptops has declined.

The first Android device was launched in 2008. Since their development, there has been a rapid increase in the use of smartphones. By 2017, Android had become the leading operating system for global internet usage at 37.93% against Microsoft's 37.91%, despite Microsoft having had 80% of the market in 2012. Smartphones are increasingly being used to access information and the growing Asian market mainly uses devices with Android systems.

1 How does the story of Microsoft support the view that firms with monopoly power may still undertake considerable research and development?

2 What evidence is there in the case study to suggest that Microsoft may have abused its monopoly power?

3 How does the case study illustrate the concept of creative destruction?

3.6 Price discrimination

This section will develop your knowledge and understanding of:

→ third-degree price discrimination

→ conditions necessary for price discrimination

→ advantages and disadvantages of price discrimination.

Third-degree price discrimination

Price discrimination is when a firm charges different prices to different consumers for the same product for reasons other than differences in cost. By splitting the market into groups willing and able to pay different amounts, the firm can charge a higher price to those willing and able to pay more. This enables the firm to increase its total revenue and profit.

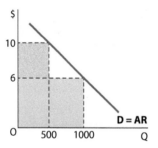

▲ **Figure 3.6.1**: Increased revenue from price discrimination

If the monopolist charges a single price of $6, its revenue is $6,000 ($6 × 1,000). However, if it can separate its customers into two groups, charging one group $10 without affecting the price it charges the other group, the firm can gain extra revenue of $2,000 ([$10 – $6] × 500). This increases the monopolist's total revenue from $6,000 without price discrimination to $8,000 when it charges two different prices to the two separate groups based on their ability and willingness to pay.

The reason for the different prices is not that one group costs more to supply than another. For example, a child may pay less for public transport than an adult but still requires a seat. Similarly, someone over the pension age may pay less for a haircut, even though it takes the same time.

Conditions necessary for price discrimination

Certain conditions are necessary for price discrimination to work:

* control of supply
* separation of markets
* differences in demand.

Control of supply

The firm must be able to control the supply of the product, to give it the ability to set prices. If there are other similar products available, the firm could be undercut if it charges a higher price in some markets. The firm will need to have monopoly power, with a substantial share of the market and/or an agreement with its competitors not to undercut its prices.

Separation of markets

The markets must be capable of being kept apart, to prevent resale. If products can be bought in the cheaper market and resold at a higher price in a more expensive market, known as arbitrage, this will undermine the firm's strategy. Markets may be separated by:

- time
- geography/distance
- characteristics of consumers.

> ### Key term
>
> Arbitrage: when products can be bought in a cheaper market and resold at a higher price in a more expensive market.

Separation by time

It may be more expensive to use public transport, such as railways, at peak times. The overall market for rail travel can be split into off-peak and peak travel, with different prices charged and no possibility of arbitrage. It may be more expensive to travel by ferry, particularly in holiday locations, on a summer weekend, compared to a winter weekday. Tickets to watch a film or play may be cheaper during the week or for an afternoon performance.

Time can also be used to separate markets in terms of when the product is bought. Fares for some methods of transport such as flights and rail travel will vary depending on how far ahead the ticket is bought. For example, when first released, tickets may be relatively cheap. The firm may be unsure of how popular that date will be and will also receive the payment earlier. Nearer the time of the journey, if there are few tickets left, the price is likely to rise, but if there are still plenty of tickets available, the price is more likely to fall, to try to sell as many more tickets as possible, given that the journey will go ahead regardless. As long as the revenue from an extra passenger covers their cost (MR > MC), total profit will rise.

Geographical separation

Separation of markets geographically involves charging different prices in different locations, perhaps in different countries or different regions within the same country. This may be due to one area having higher incomes and people in the area being able and willing to pay a higher price. However, the difference in price should not be high enough to make it worthwhile for someone to buy the products in the cheaper area and then transport them to the more expensive area to resell.

However, transport costs and tariffs are other reasons why a product may be sold at a higher price in different countries. In this case, the price difference is not due to price discrimination but because of differences in cost.

Ways of categorising consumers

Different prices can be charged if consumers can be identified according to some characteristic and the product cannot be transferred between buyers. The most common example is probably age. For example, children under a certain age may pay a reduced rate or may not pay at all to enter a tourist attraction. An adult would not be able to pass themselves off as a three-year-old to pay a lower price. Similarly, people beyond the pension age may be charged reduced rates for some activities, such as bus travel. Proof of age, perhaps with an accompanying photo, can ensure that only those who are eligible pay the lower price.

Businesses may pay less than households for electricity in some countries, although this may be partly because they buy a greater quantity.

Differences in demand

As well as being able to separate buyers into different markets, these sub-sections of the overall market must have a different demand to make charging a different price worthwhile. One group must be willing and able to pay more than another. For example, those of working age are generally likely to have more income than pensioners. Those who travel at peak times may be doing so to reach their workplace, while those travelling off-peak may not have jobs or may not need to make the journey. These factors will affect both the quantity demanded and its elasticity.

The price elasticity of demand is very likely to be different for different groups. The demand of some buyers will be less sensitive to changes in price, so their demand will be less elastic. People who have to arrive at work by a particular time and choose to travel by train are likely to be willing and able to pay a higher price. They are also less likely to stop using the service if the price rises than those who are not required to travel by a certain time and/or who may have less money. Therefore, peak travellers will be charged a higher price than off-peak travellers if a firm is price discriminating.

Figures 3.6.2 and 3.6.3 show what happens if the market for rail travel is separated into two markets, peak and off-peak, by the supplier of the service. Since price discrimination is for reasons other than differences in costs, the cost curves are the same in both diagrams. For this example, to simplify the situation, it has been assumed that the marginal cost is constant, which will also make MC = AC. Assuming the

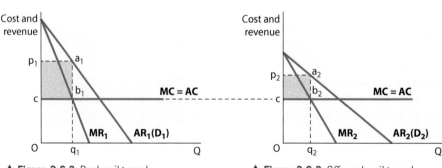

▲ **Figure 3.6.2**: Peak rail travel   ▲ **Figure 3.6.3**: Off-peak rail travel

firm is profit maximising, it will choose the output where MC = MR, q_1 in Figure 3.6.2 and q_2 in Figure 3.6.3.

Figure 3.6.2 shows that buyers are willing and able to pay a higher price for peak rail travel, as shown by the fact that AR_1 (D_1) starts higher up the vertical axis than AR_2 (D_2). Also, at any given price, the demand for rail travel at peak times is more inelastic than at off-peak times. The profit-maximising price is higher at p_1 than it is for non-peak rail travel at p_2. The profit areas, showing the difference between total revenue and total cost in each market, are the shaded areas, $cp_1a_1b_1$ and $cp_2a_2b_2$, for peak travel and non-peak travel respectively.

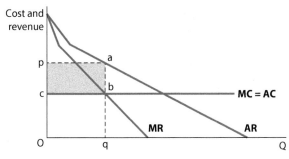

▲ **Figure 3.6.4**: Combined rail travel

Figure 3.6.4 combines the two diagrams for peak and off-peak travel to show what the total demand would be at each price. To profit maximise in the market as a whole, the firm will choose output q (where MC = MR) which can be sold for price p. The overall market price will be between p_1 and p_2 (on Figures 3.6.2 and 3.6.3). The supernormal profit of cpab will be less than the profits of $cp_1a_1b_1 + cp_2a_2b_2$ when the market is divided into peak and off-peak travel and two different prices are charged.

Advantages and disadvantages of price discrimination

For producers
Firms price discriminate to increase their sales and profits. The increase in sales may enable them to take more advantage of economies of scale, which would lower their long-run average cost. This may strengthen their position in the market. Higher profits would provide more funds to invest in research and development, although they will not necessarily be used for this. Profits could be used to lower prices where the firm faces more competition, making it more difficult for new firms to enter the market. With a stronger market position, this may also help the firm in its negotiations with suppliers. Price discrimination can therefore be advantageous to those firms using it but may cause problems for other firms.

Price discrimination also enables firms to make better use of their capacity and to spread their fixed costs. If a flight will take place regardless of whether there are five or 50 people on board, charging different prices to increase demand will make better use of its resources. On trains and buses, for example, the marginal cost of an extra passenger is close to zero, so any extra revenue will add to their profit. Also, by charging lower

Quantitative skills

When analysing price discrimination, you would be expected to include diagrams. Note how the diagrams of the two separate markets have the same cost curves but different revenue curves. The combined AR and MR curves for the market as a whole are plotted by adding the two separate AR (AR_1 and AR_2) and MR (MR_1 and MR_2) curves horizontally at each price. There is a kink in both curves because at the highest prices, demand only exists in one of the markets.

Activity

Find out about **three** examples of price discrimination in your country. In each case, how are the markets separated and what are the different prices charged?

Progress questions

1 What is price discrimination?
2 Why may an airline charge a lower price if you book six months before a flight is scheduled to leave than if you book a week before?

prices to persuade some passengers to travel at off-peak times, fewer buses and trains are needed in total, further reducing fixed costs.

For consumers

By price discriminating, the firm is charging closer to the maximum price that individuals are willing to pay (reducing their consumer surplus). This increases producer welfare, often at the expense of consumer welfare. Those in the more expensive market (peak rail travel in the previous example) will pay more than they would have done if there was a single price charged for the product, so they lose out. This could be considered to be unfair and exploitation of the firm's monopoly power.

Those in the cheaper market (for example, off-peak travel) pay less than if there was a single price, so these buyers gain. Some may not have been able to consume as much of the product otherwise or even buy it at all. It is likely that many (but not all) of those paying a lower price are in lower-income groups, so this could be viewed to be fairer, even though this is unlikely to be the main motive of the firm.

If price discrimination leads to economies of scale and so to lower average costs, these could be passed on in the form of lower prices. Then, at least in theory, all consumers could gain from the arrangement. For example, selling more cheaply in the export market would add to total sales and output. Similarly, if the extra profits are used to develop improved and/or cheaper products, all consumers could benefit in the long run. Much, however, depends on the objectives and conduct of the firm.

Link

The welfare effects of price discrimination will be explained further in 3.10 "Consumer and producer surplus".

Progress questions

3   Give **two** examples of economic agents who may gain and **two** who may lose from price discrimination. Explain your reasons.

Case study: Price discrimination in the pharmaceutical industry

▲ **Figure 3.6.5**: Cheaper for some than others

Price discrimination on an international basis is common in the pharmaceutical industry. Prices for many prescription medicines in the United States are the highest in the world. According to one study, prices for the same products in Europe, where salaries are generally lower, are on average 44% of those in the US. Furthermore, a study a few years ago found that for patented medicines, developing countries paid on average 27% of the prices paid in industrialised countries.

Even though products are sold more cheaply in poorer countries, where average incomes are lower, the ability of the leading pharmaceutical companies to control prices remains a concern. In such countries, those who cannot afford imported branded medicines may turn to cheap copies, which may be ineffective or even poisonous.

The use of patents encourages the leading firms to develop improved medicines, but they then charge high prices to recover the development costs and to pay for new research. The average cost of developing a new medicine can be over $1 billion, including research and testing over several years. Meanwhile, there are many who desperately need medicines but cannot afford them.

1   Why are pharmaceutical companies able to use price discrimination?

2   Explain how differences in price between countries could be due to factors other than price discrimination.

3   Should pharmaceutical firms be stopped from using price discrimination? Justify your answer.

This section will develop your knowledge and understanding of:

→ the significance of market contestability for the performance of an industry

→ sunk costs and hit-and-run competition.

The significance of market contestability for the performance of an industry

Contestable market theory was introduced by the American economist William Baumol in 1982. The theory explained why firms in concentrated markets, such as oligopolies and monopolies, may behave competitively if there is the threat of competition from new entrants into the market. The equilibrium output and price will then be closer to the outcomes predicted in more competitive market structures.

This could lead to consumers having the benefits of firms operating on a large scale without the exploitation of high prices. Many governments now consider the contestability of a particular market as part of their competition policy and do not necessarily assume that an oligopoly or monopoly must be bad for consumers.

A **contestable market** exists if there are low barriers to entry and exit, and a **perfectly contestable market** has no barriers to entry or exit. It will be easy for firms to join or to leave these markets. The extent of market contestability affects the behaviour and performance of firms. Baumol argued that if markets are contestable, then whatever the market structure, competitive outcomes would be achieved with firms producing at or near their minimum average cost.

According to contestable market theory, price and output depend on the threat of competition rather than the market structure and actual competition. If existing firms earn supernormal profit, this acts as an incentive for new firms to enter the market and if the market is contestable, they will be able to do so. Supernormal profits are then competed away.

A perfectly competitive market is perfectly contestable because one of the assumptions of this model is that there are no barriers to entry and exit. If existing firms make supernormal profits in the short run, others will enter the market, increasing the market supply and reducing the price and profits. If firms are making losses, there is nothing to stop them leaving the market, reducing the market supply and raising the price. In the long run, only normal profits will be made. Assuming there are no externalities, firms will be productively and allocatively efficient in the long run.

In monopolistic competition, it is assumed that there are no or low barriers to entry and exit. Therefore, this is also a contestable market. For example, in popular tourist locations, there have been increasing numbers of people offering walking tours in recent years.

Link

The significance of the contestability of markets for competition policy is explained in 3.11 "Competition policy".

Key terms

Contestable market: when there are low barriers to entry and exit.

Perfectly contestable market: when there are no barriers to entry or exit.

▲ **Figure 3.7.1**: A contestable market

Link

Figure 3.3.3 in 3.3 "Monopolistic competition" shows the long-run equilibrium for a firm in monopolistic competition.

Get it right

The contestability of a market is determined by the extent of barriers to entry or exit, not the number of firms in the market. Although markets with fewer firms are often less contestable, this is not always the case.

Key terms

Sunk costs: costs that have been incurred but cannot be recovered if a firm leaves the market.

Barriers to exit: factors that make it difficult for firms to leave a market.

Again, short-run profits will attract other firms. They will be able to enter the market and loss-making firms will be able to leave, resulting in normal profits being made in the long run.

In concentrated markets (oligopolies or monopolies), there are likely to be considerable barriers to entry or exit. For example, there may be high start-up costs and a large minimum efficient scale, making it difficult for new smaller firms to compete on cost and price. A patent will also prevent another firm from producing the good. Alternatively, incumbent firms may use limit pricing to make joining the market less attractive, to increase their long-run profits.

Existing firms in these non-contestable markets are able to make supernormal profits knowing that this will probably not lead to new firms entering the market to compete them away. They may lack the competitive pressure to operate efficiently. However, in industries where there is rapid technological progress, existing firms may be concerned about the possibility of creative destruction. This may lead to more dynamic efficiency in the market if the firms invest in the development of new and improved products. The internet has also increased the contestability of some markets.

So, even if a few firms dominate the market, consumers are not necessarily exploited. It is not just the number of firms in the market that is significant but also the threat of entry into the market that can make firms perform differently. A market with only a few firms is likely to be non-contestable, but this cannot be assumed. Overall, the lower the entry and exit barriers, the more contestable the market. Firms are then more likely to be efficient and not make excessive profits.

Link

The significance of barriers to entry and exit was explained earlier in this chapter when discussing each of the different market structures. The types of efficiency were explained in 3.2 "Perfect competition".

Sunk costs and hit-and-run competition

Sunk costs are costs that must be paid for a firm to enter a market but which cannot be recovered if the firm then leaves the market. Sunk costs include spending on advertising, R&D, or specialist equipment with no resale value. If the firm has to leave the industry later, it risks making a large loss since there will be a considerable amount of money that it has spent but cannot recover. If an activity has sunk costs, this makes the market less attractive to enter, and so less contestable.

Although sunk costs could be viewed as a **barrier to exit** (a factor that makes it difficult for firms to leave a market), since they may encourage a firm to stay in a market for longer, they are often quoted as a barrier to entry because entering the market is more of a risk. Another barrier to exit could be the large costs involved with closing some businesses such as having to carry out an environmental clean-up.

If there are few or no sunk costs, it will be easy to enter and leave the industry, making the market more contestable. This can lead to **hit-and-run competition**, where firms may be able to enter a market with low or no barriers to entry and exit if the price is significantly above average cost, to take advantage of the supernormal profit. They then leave the market when the increased competition has eliminated the supernormal profit.

The increase in supply reduces the price and when the market is no longer profitable, these firms leave. This will also happen if the original firms deliberately lower their prices to persuade firms to leave. The lack of entry and exit barriers makes this possible and so hit-and-run competition is a feature of contestable markets.

If a market has no or low sunk costs, and there is the threat of hit-and-run competition, the firms already in the market are likely to offer lower prices, closer to their minimum average cost. They will make less profit than if the market was less contestable.

Activity

Think about businesses in your local area or country. Identify **two** which are in contestable markets and **two** which are not. Justify your choices.

Progress questions

1 What is a perfectly contestable market?
2 Is a monopoly a non-contestable market?
3 How can hit-and-run competition affect the performance of firms in a contestable market?
4 How has the internet enabled some markets to become more contestable?

This section will develop your knowledge and understanding of:

→ short-run and long-run benefits which may result from competition

→ how firms do not just compete on the basis of price; that competition will, for example, lead firms to strive to improve products, reduce costs and improve the quality of the service provided

→ the process of creative destruction.

Link

How firms compete was introduced in 4.5 "The competitive market process" in the AS book.

Key term

Competition: when rival firms use strategies to try to increase their sales, market share and/or profits.

Short-run and long-run benefits which may result from competition

Competition occurs when rival firms use strategies to try to increase their sales, market share and/or profits. If there is excess supply in the market, firms may be competing just to survive. Competition is a key feature of market economies. It is an ongoing dynamic process which can bring a number of benefits to consumers and society as a whole.

Firms' strategies include changing price and also non-price methods such as lower costs, improved products and improved quality of service. As discussed earlier in the chapter, the methods used by firms to compete may depend on the market structure, whether the market is contestable and if the firms are working together or not.

Competition can benefit consumers in both the short run and the long run. If there is a price war, when price cuts by one firm lead to price cuts by others, consumers will gain from cheaper prices in the short run. However, the price war may lead to one or more firms leaving the market. This could lead to less choice and higher prices in the long run, particularly if there are only a few firms or perhaps only one left in the market after the price war is over.

Competition may encourage or force firms to look for ways to reduce their costs. This will increase efficiency and make better use of scarce resources. It can also benefit consumers if these lower costs are passed on in the form of lower prices. In perfect competition, firms are forced to keep their costs as low as possible, achieving both allocative and productive efficiency in the long run.

As well as cheaper products, competition may lead to innovation and a better-quality service, or higher-quality products with new features, responding to the wants and preferences of consumers and overall, providing better value for money. Competition will alert buyers to new opportunities. Firms will try to improve their products to attract customers from their rivals and to persuade existing customers to buy the next version. This will be an ongoing process over time which contributes to higher living standards.

How firms compete

Firms compete in a number of ways including:

- price
- improvements to products

- reductions in costs
- improvements in the quality of the service provided.

Price

Other things being equal, a lower price should lead to an increase in the firm's quantity demanded because people are now able and willing to buy more. This could apply to the firm's existing buyers, but this is also done to attract buyers from rival firms, the success of which will depend on both the price and cross elasticity of demand for the product.

Whether price competition is effective partly depends on product differentiation and brand loyalty. If products are similar and there is little brand loyalty, lowering price is more likely to increase sales and market share. Customers switch between sellers as they can now buy a similar product more cheaply elsewhere. If, however, other firms also lower their prices, there is the risk of a price war, which may force one or more of the firms to leave the market. A firm starting a price war needs to be sure that it can cope with making a loss in the short run if necessary.

With the interdependence and uncertainty associated with oligopoly, firms may have an agreement not to compete on price. However, regardless of whether they have an agreement on price, they may rely mainly on non-price competition.

Improvements to products

Another way to persuade buyers to switch to a firm's products is to make them better. Putting money into R&D may result in products performing better, lasting for longer or having more features. This gives the firm a competitive edge over its rivals and helps to differentiate its products. Buyers may be willing to pay more for what they believe to be superior products, particularly if they are advertised well. This may also encourage existing users to buy the new model.

Reductions in costs

If a firm is able to reduce its costs of production, it has the ability either to reduce its prices or to make more profit, possibly to fund more improvements. In both cases, this can strengthen its position in the market, by making its products more competitive.

Lower costs may be because of technological developments which could result in more efficient equipment or methods of production. Alternatively, if the firm is growing, it may be able to take more advantage of economies of scale, for example by making better use of larger pieces of equipment or transport.

Improvements in the quality of the service provided

For some products, the quality of the product or the accompanying service may be more important than its price, giving firms another way to compete with their rivals. For example, for consumer durables such as cars or electrical products, the quality of the service provided may encourage buyers to choose one firm over another. This may be the service provided when the consumer is considering buying the product or the after-sales service to maintain the equipment or repair it if necessary.

Link

The process of creative destruction was explained in 2.6 "Technological change".

Progress questions

1. State **three** benefits to consumers from competition between firms.
2. How may a firm be able to maintain monopoly power in the long run?

Activity

Find out:

1. what improvements have been made to mobile phones over the last 10 years
2. how the market shares of the leading manufacturers of mobile phones have changed.

The process of creative destruction

The process of creative destruction is where existing products, markets and firms are replaced with new ones as an inevitable outcome of technological change. There are many recent examples including phones, transport, energy and numerous applications of computer technology. The process of creative destruction is therefore a fundamental feature of the way in which competition operates in a market economy.

One way to enter a market to take advantage of supernormal profits is to develop a new product which replaces the existing product or better satisfies the preferences of buyers. If firms with monopoly power are making large profits, there will be an incentive for new firms to enter the market by innovating to overcome the barriers to entry. The threat posed by the process of creative destruction could encourage existing firms to innovate and/or to set their prices lower to make the market less attractive.

The possibility of creative destruction will generally make markets more competitive. The threat of being left behind and going out of business will force many firms to try to continually improve their products and practices. Otherwise, when a firm develops an alternative, this could give it a competitive edge and monopoly power in the short run, particularly if it has a patent. However, this new product could soon be replaced by another development, by another firm. Therefore, there is a constant threat and a need to do whatever it takes to remain competitive in that market. As older less profitable firms and industries decline, resources will be reallocated to more productive processes, benefiting society as a whole.

Case study: Uber

▲ **Figure 3.8.1**: The dynamics of competition

Travelling by taxi in many countries traditionally involved contacting a firm and paying a fixed charge plus extra for the distance travelled. Taxis were subject to local rules and regulations. For example, in London, black cab drivers typically spent two to four years, learning 'the knowledge', information about streets, landmarks, museums, and so on. They then had to pass tests before a licence was granted.

Uber Technologies Inc, often known as Uber, believed they could offer a similar service more cheaply. Rides are booked using a mobile app, which quotes a price based on supply and demand for that route at that time. This is usually cheaper than a metered journey. Increased competition has led to lower fares but complaints from existing drivers whose earnings have fallen. Uber currently operates in a large number of countries, often in combination with local businesses.

Drivers were self-employed but could rent a car from Uber. They were registered and had background and vehicle checks but effectively, anyone could offer a seat in their car, raising concerns about safety. There have been other complaints, including predatory pricing and illegal taxi services being offered, resulting in new rules being introduced and Uber no longer operating in some areas. For example, in 2016, Hungary banned the app.

Uber has also launched a car-sharing service and a food delivery service, Uber Eats. Meanwhile, the company has been trialling driverless cars.

1. What have been the benefits of Uber offering taxi services?
2. How does the case study illustrate the process of creative destruction?

The difference between static and dynamic efficiency

Static efficiency is concerned with how well scarce resources are allocated at a point in time. Is a firm operating efficiently now, for example? This may relate to productive, technical or allocative efficiency. Dynamic efficiency looks at efficiency over a period of time. Has a firm become more technically or productively efficient over the last 10 years, for example?

Conditions required for productive and allocative efficiency

Productive efficiency

Productive efficiency for a firm occurs when it produces where average cost (AC) is at its minimum. Since marginal cost (MC) cuts AC at the lowest point of the AC curve, this is also the output where MC = AC. So productive efficiency can also be said to take place at the output where MC = AC.

Allocative efficiency

Allocative efficiency for a firm occurs when it produces where price = marginal cost (P = MC). At this output, firms are producing the goods and services which best meet people's preferences. This is because buyers are considering the opportunity cost of consumption in relation to the price of the product and firms consider the opportunity cost of production in relation to its marginal cost.

For the buyer, the price, for example $1, is the value they place on the last unit they consume. If they spend $1 on a particular good, that money is not available to spend on other goods. For the firm, the marginal cost of the last item is the cost of the resources used to produce that good, which cannot then be used to produce other goods. If resources costing $1 are used to produce one good, they are not available to produce others. If P > MC, the value placed on the product is greater than the value placed on the resources used to produce it, hence more of the good should be produced. If P < MC, the value of the resources is greater than the value placed on the product and so fewer units should be produced.

> **Link**
>
> The different types of efficiency were introduced in 3.2 "Perfect competition".

For the economy as a whole, allocative efficiency is achieved when P = MC in all markets. It is then not possible to make one person better off without making someone else worse off, by switching resources from one good to another (assuming a particular distribution of income and wealth). Overall, the welfare of the population cannot be increased by reallocating resources between markets and industries.

Application of efficiency concepts to different market structures

Perfect competition

Figure 3.9.1 shows the long-run equilibrium position of a profit-maximising firm in perfect competition. The profit-maximising output is q, where MC = MR. The firm is productively efficient because it is operating at the lowest point of the AC curve, where MC = AC. The firm is also allocatively efficient because P = MC at this output.

However, Figure 3.9.1 only takes account of the private costs and benefits. If there are externalities, either in production or consumption, this output will not be allocatively efficient. This is because buyers and sellers only consider the marginal private cost and benefit not the marginal social cost and benefit when choosing the quantity they wish to produce or consume.

▲ **Figure 3.9.1**: Perfect competition and efficiency in the long run

If a firm in perfect competition is making a profit or loss in the short run, it will not be operating at the lowest point of its AC curve and so will not be productively efficient. However, in perfect competition, marginal revenue is the same as average revenue and price (P = MR = AR), so by choosing the output where MC = MR, to maximise profits, this will also be the output where P = MC. Therefore, assuming no externalities, a firm in perfect competition will be allocatively efficient in both the short run and the long run.

Monopolistic competition

Figure 3.9.2 shows the short-run position of a profit-maximising firm in monopolistic competition. The profit-maximising output is again at q, where MC = MR. According to the AR/D curve, it can charge p for this quantity. At output q, the firm is neither productively nor allocatively efficient. It is not operating at the lowest point of its AC curve, nor is it producing where P = MC.

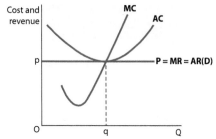

Activity

Draw a diagram for each of the following situations to check whether a firm in perfect competition will be productively or allocatively efficient:

1 a firm making short-run supernormal profit

2 a firm making a short-run loss.

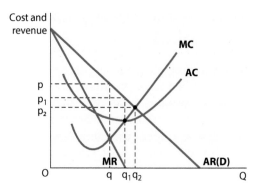

▲ **Figure 3.9.2**: Monopolistic competition and efficiency in the short run

Productive efficiency occurs at q_1 which would sell for price p_1, since this is where AC is lowest and MC = AC. Allocative efficiency occurs at q_2, where MC = P (AR). This quantity would sell for p_2. This shows that a profit-maximising firm in monopolistic competition will choose to sell too low a quantity and charge too high a price to achieve either productive or allocative efficiency.

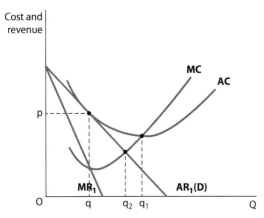

▲ **Figure 3.9.3**: Monopolistic competition and efficiency in the long run

In the long run, new firms will enter the market, attracted by the supernormal profit and low barriers to entry. The demand for an individual firm in monopolistic competition will fall, shifting AR/D to the left. The profit-maximising output q, where MC = MR_1, will now be where AC = AR_1, so only normal profit is made. Here, the firm is neither productively nor allocatively efficient. For productive efficiency, the firm should produce quantity q_1, where AC is lowest. For allocative efficiency, they should produce q_2 where MC = P (AR_1).

Therefore, a profit-maximising firm in monopolistic competition will choose to sell too low a quantity and charge too high a price to achieve either productive or allocative efficiency.

Oligopoly

Oligopolies may be competitive or collusive so there is no single theory to explain the behaviour of firms in this market structure. In a competitive oligopoly, firms may be forced to be more efficient, both in a static and dynamic sense. This will help them to gain an advantage over their rivals or sometimes, just enable them to survive in the market. If the firms are working together, there may be less pressure to increase efficiency. However, if working together involves joint research and development, this may lead to more improvements in dynamic efficiency.

It is highly unlikely that profit-maximising oligopolists will be either productively or allocatively efficient, although how efficient they are also depends on the contestability of the market. If there are low barriers to entry and exit, the market will be contestable. The more contestable the market, the more efficient the firms are likely to be. However, there are often high barriers to entry and/or exit in oligopolistic markets.

Quantitative skills

You should be able to illustrate whether firms are operating efficiently or not, when applying efficiency concepts to different market structures.

Link

Figure 3.5.3 in 3.5 "Monopoly and monopoly power" illustrates a natural monopoly in the long run.

Get it right

Efficiency concepts can be used to compare the performance of firms in different market structures and both conduct and performance indicators can be used when making comparisons and judgements between markets. For example, whether a firm is likely to be productively or allocatively efficient can be used to help evaluate the advantages and disadvantages of competitive as opposed to concentrated markets.

Progress questions

1   What is the difference between static and dynamic efficiency?
2   State **two** facts about marginal and/or average costs which apply when a firm is productively efficient.

Key term

X-efficiency: when a firm uses the ideal combination of factors of production at their lowest cost.

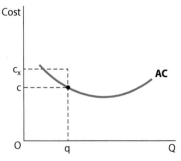

▲ **Figure 3.9.4**: X-inefficiency

Monopoly

A profit-maximising monopolist will also be productively and allocatively inefficient. This can be seen in Figure 3.9.2, which was used earlier for a firm in monopolistic competition in the short run. The same diagram applies to a monopoly in both the short run and the long run. A monopoly is likely to lack the competitive pressure to be efficient. However, this depends on whether the market is contestable and whether creative destruction is likely. If the market is contestable and/or creative destruction is possible, this is likely to encourage the monopoly to be more efficient, both in the short run and long run. A monopoly or oligopoly is also more likely to have money from supernormal profit to finance R&D and so be more dynamically efficient than more competitive market structures.

However, if the firm is in the public sector, run by the government for the benefit of the country as a whole, it may have different objectives. It is possible that the firm could be instructed to produce where MC = P, to aim for allocative efficiency.

X-inefficiency

X-inefficiency is when a firm fails to minimise its costs of producing any given level of output. Productive efficiency can only exist if there is technical efficiency. Technical efficiency is when a given output is produced with minimum inputs, or put another way, when maximum output is obtained from a given set of inputs. To achieve **X-efficiency**, a firm must use the ideal combination of factors of production, taking account of the prices of the different factors of production.

A firm may not be producing the most it can from its resources and is therefore likely to be employing more people than it needs. It may be paying too much for its resources, for example, paying large management salaries, or perhaps it could buy its raw materials more cheaply elsewhere. Both situations cause X-inefficiency because the firm is paying more than necessary for a given output.

In Figure 3.9.4, AC shows the lowest possible average cost for each output. If the firm is producing at a higher average cost, then it is X-inefficient. The firm is paying more than it needs for its chosen output. In Figure 3.9.4, the firm will be X-efficient if it produces output q for an average cost of c, but it will be X-inefficient if it produces this output for c_x.

X-efficiency was first identified by the American economist Harvey Leibenstein in the 1960s. He noted that when businesses are not competitive, there is often 'organisational slack', particularly when there is a divorce of ownership from control. In competitive markets such as perfect competition and monopolistic competition, firms may be forced to be X-efficient to survive. In concentrated markets (oligopoly and monopoly), firms are more likely to be X-inefficient since there is less competitive pressure. However, much depends on the contestability of the market, how the firm is managed, and in the case of an oligopoly, whether the firm is colluding or not.

Influences on dynamic efficiency

Dynamic efficiency results from improvements in technical and productive efficiency over time. Invention, innovation and R&D can lead to significant improvements in technical efficiency. The firm may invest in human or non-human capital to increase its productivity. Training is an example of investment in human capital and the development of a faster machine would be investment in non-human capital. There could be improved methods of producing existing goods and the development of new products. More output can then be gained from the same resources, lowering the firm's marginal and average costs.

To finance research and development, firms need funds, which could be from profits, their shareholders or loans. Small firms, and those in competitive markets generally, are less likely to be able to access this finance. Firms in perfect competition are unlikely to have the money to fund significant improvements and with perfect knowledge, there is no incentive to do so. Firms in monopolistic competition may be able to make some supernormal profit in the short run to finance improvements that could give them an advantage over their rivals. Remember that the large transnational companies of today were once small firms. As they grew, they were perhaps able to take advantage of economies of scale to lower their average costs.

Oligopolists and monopolists are the firms most able to finance new developments that could lead to dynamic efficiency. This is because of the supernormal profits they make in both the short run and the long run. Usually, significant amounts of R&D occur in oligopolistic markets as firms try to gain sales and market share from their rivals. This is most likely if it is a competitive oligopoly, where firms are concerned about other firms' reactions to a change in price.

Whether a firm tries to increase its efficiency over time depends on the competitive pressure it faces. This could be actual pressure, in a competitive oligopoly, for example, or perceived pressure from the possibility of creative destruction and/or new entrants in a contestable market.

A monopoly may have no need to improve its efficiency if there is a lack of competitive pressure. However, if it does nothing, there may be more risk of a new product being developed by another firm which could destroy its market. Some industries have been more affected by technological change than others and firms operating in these industries may be forced to improve their efficiency or be left behind by their competitors.

Progress questions

3   Why must a firm be technically efficient to be productively efficient?

4   Explain **two** factors which can influence a firm's dynamic efficiency.

This section will develop your knowledge and understanding of:

→ consumer and producer surplus and the concept of a deadweight loss

→ applications including the welfare effects of price discrimination, monopoly and tariffs.

Activity

Draw a diagram and use it to explain what happens to consumer and producer surplus in each of the following situations:

1   the cost of raw materials increases

2   consumer incomes rise assuming the product is a normal good.

Consumer and producer surplus and the concept of a deadweight loss

Consumer and producer surplus

Consumers may be willing to pay more for an item than the market price. Similarly, firms may be willing to sell their goods and services for a lower price than they receive. These situations result in consumer and producer surplus.

Consumer surplus is the difference between the price consumers would be willing to pay and what they actually pay. It is the extra welfare, or benefit, they gain by paying less than they would have been willing to pay. For example, if someone was willing to pay $2 for a cookie but they only have to pay a price of $1.20, then their consumer surplus is $0.80.

Producer surplus is the difference between the lowest price sellers are willing to charge for a product and the price they receive. It is the extra welfare or benefit firms gain from receiving more money for a product than they would have been willing to accept. For example, if a firm was willing to sell the cookie for $1.50 but it receives $2, then its producer surplus is $0.50.

The demand curve shows the different prices that consumers are willing to pay for each item of a good or service. The consumer surplus for an individual or the market as a whole is the area between the demand curve and the market price. This is the difference between what the individual or market was willing to pay for each item, as indicated by the demand curve, and what they actually paid, as shown by the market price.

The supply curve shows the different prices that producers are willing to supply any given quantity for and the producer surplus is the area between the supply curve and the market price. This is the difference between what the firm or market was willing to produce each item for, as indicated by the supply curve, and what they actually charge, as shown by the price.

Figure 3.10.1 shows the market supply and demand for a product, where at the equilibrium, quantity q is sold at price p. The area of consumer surplus in this market is pab, the area between the demand curve D, and the equilibrium price, p. Similarly, the area of producer surplus in this market is cpb, the area between the supply curve S and the equilibrium price, p.

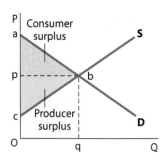

▲ **Figure 3.10.1:** Consumer and producer surplus

Deadweight welfare loss

The **deadweight welfare loss** (DWL) is the consumer or producer surplus lost when production and consumption are not at the social optimum. Situations when this might happen include where there is monopoly pricing, externalities, a tax or subsidy, or price controls. It is a loss of welfare to society because the optimal quantity is not being produced and sold. Total welfare is less than it could be because either too much or too little is being produced and consumed.

Welfare effects of price discrimination, monopoly and tariffs

Price discrimination

When it uses price discrimination, a firm charges different prices to different consumers for the same product for reasons other than differences in cost. For example, different prices may be charged for peak and off-peak travel or for entrance to a sports event for children and adults. The firm must be able to control the supply of the product and be able to separate the consumers into different markets, to prevent resale.

Figure 3.10.2 shows the market for rail travel, with and without price discrimination. To simplify the diagram, cost curves have not been included. If there is no price discrimination and a single price of p_1 is charged, the quantity sold will be q_1 and consumer surplus at this output and price will be p_1ab_1, the area between the price p_1 and the demand curve D. This is the difference between the price consumers are willing to pay and the price they actually pay.

If price discrimination is used, the market is divided into groups of consumers. Those who are willing and able to pay the higher price, for example those travelling at peak times, may be charged price p_2. At this price, their demand is q_2 and their consumer surplus is p_2ab_2. The remaining consumers buy quantity $q_1 - q_2$, at price p_1. Their consumer surplus is eb_2b_1. The total consumer surplus has fallen from p_1ab_1 to $p_2ab_2 + eb_2b_1$. The rectangle $p_1p_2b_2e$ has been transferred to the seller in the form of increased producer surplus. Splitting the market into peak and off-peak travel leads to the firm charging peak travellers a higher price, closer to the maximum they were willing to pay. By charging closer to what consumers are willing to pay, some of the consumer surplus has been transferred to producers, increasing producer welfare at the expense of consumer welfare.

Those in the off-peak market may have lower incomes on average. Some would argue that if they pay a lower price than other better-off consumers, the welfare they may gain from price discrimination is more important than the welfare loss of those who can afford to pay a higher price.

Price discrimination enables firms to increase their supernormal profit. Although the overall loss of consumer surplus is an argument against price discrimination, if it enables firms to develop better products or take more advantage of economies of scale, lowering their costs and prices, consumer welfare may increase in the long run. Also, if price discrimination involves setting a lower price to one group, compared

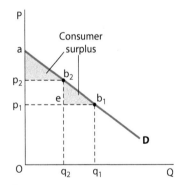

▲ **Figure 3.10.2**: The market for rail travel, with and without price discrimination

with charging a single price, then consumer surplus could increase as a result of price discrimination.

Monopoly

Even if a monopoly does not use price discrimination, if it is profit maximising, a monopoly can lead to a net welfare loss compared to a perfectly competitive market.

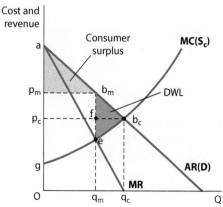

▲ **Figure 3.10.3**: The impact of a profit-maximising monopoly on welfare

Figure 3.10.3 compares the outcomes of a perfectly competitive market and a monopoly. The MC curve for the monopoly is assumed to be the same as the MC curve under perfect competition. In these circumstances, the monopolist's MC curve will also be the supply curve for the industry if it is perfectly competitive. In a perfectly competitive market, the equilibrium price is where the market supply and market demand are equal. This is at a price of p_c where q_c is sold. The consumer surplus is p_cab_c and producer surplus of gp_cb_c.

If the market then becomes a profit-maximising monopoly, output will be q_m where MC = MR and the price for this output will be p_m. Consumer surplus falls to p_mab_m. Part of the lost consumer surplus, $p_cp_mb_mf$, has been transferred to the firm (as supernormal profit) and overall, the producer surplus becomes gp_mb_me. However, this leaves a deadweight welfare loss triangle (DWL) of eb_mb_c. This is the combined loss of consumer surplus fb_mb_c and producer surplus efb_c.

Welfare loss is often quoted as a disadvantage of monopoly. However, it is possible that one large firm may be able to take advantage of economies of scale or be more dynamically efficient than many competing small firms. This could result in lower average and marginal costs than would occur in a perfectly competitive market. If this then leads to a lower price being charged by a monopoly, it may result in an increase in total welfare compared to a more competitive market. This is because the deadweight welfare loss will be more than offset by the gains in consumer and producer surplus.

Tariffs

A tariff is a tax on imports. It causes the price to rise above the market equilibrium, resulting in less being sold. In a similar way to a monopoly setting a higher price, there will be a loss of consumer surplus and a deadweight welfare loss. Part of the former producer and consumer surplus will go to the government in the form of tariff revenue but overall, there will be a net loss of benefits.

Link

Full analysis of the effects of a tariff, including a diagram, will be explained in 6.2 "Trade".

Progress questions

1   What is consumer surplus?
2   Why does price discrimination lead to a loss of consumer surplus?
3   A market is transformed from perfect competition to a monopoly. Is this likely to result in a loss of consumer surplus, producer surplus or both?
4   Why might having a monopoly in a market, rather than perfect competition, lead to an increase in welfare?

3.11 Competition policy

The prevention of dominant firms abusing their monopoly power

The biggest companies in the world have a larger annual revenue than many governments or even countries. Walmart, the American retailer, was the firm with the largest revenue in 2019, at over $500 billion. In 2016, Walmart's annual revenue was greater than the government revenue of all except nine of the world's economies. Walmart and the next three largest companies, all Chinese, had more revenue than the South Korean government, for example, while the largest eight firms, including Royal Dutch Shell and Volkswagen, had more revenue than the government of India.

▲ **Figure 3.11.1**: Walmart has more income than some economies

Although a government's revenue is smaller than the country's national income, there are still many large transnational corporations with an annual revenue greater than the GDP of many countries. This can lead to concerns about whether such large companies may abuse their power. However, it is not just the overall size of a firm that may be of concern. It is also important to consider the size of the firm compared to the market in which it operates and the size of the other firms in that market.

Dominant firms are firms that have a significant market share. What is considered "significant" varies from country to country. This may be as low as 25% or more commonly, 40% or more. Dominant firms are also likely to have a significantly larger market share than their next largest rival. This can lead to concerns about the amount of competition there is in the market. Dominant firms have considerable monopoly power, which may be abused. As a result of this, most countries have rules about what firms can and cannot do but how well these rules are enforced varies between countries.

Competition policy and monopoly power

Competition policy involves the ways that governments regulate markets, to protect consumers from firms abusing their monopoly power and to encourage a more efficient allocation of resources. Theory suggests that a profit-maximising monopoly will charge a higher price and sell a lower quantity than if the market is competitive. Other things being equal, this leads to a fall in consumer surplus, an inefficient allocation of resources and a deadweight welfare loss. This may also be inequitable, particularly if people on

Key terms

Dominant firm: a business with a significant market share and a significantly larger market share than its next largest rival.

Competition policy: state regulation of markets to protect consumers and other firms from dominant firms abusing their monopoly power.

Key terms

Per se rule or dogmatic approach: a general rule which does not require the individual circumstances to be investigated further.

Rule of reason or pragmatic approach: where individual circumstances are considered and actions, such as having a monopoly, are not illegal unless there is an unreasonable restraint of trade.

Monopoly busting: breaking up a dominant firm into smaller separate firms.

Activity

Find out what is done in your country about dominant firms. Is the policy dogmatic or pragmatic?

low incomes are unable to afford necessities and have no choice of supplier. Competition policy may cover dominant firms, mergers/takeovers and restrictive practices.

There are two basic types of anti-monopoly (anti-trust) policy. Many countries, for example the United States, view monopoly to be illegal if the company has achieved its monopoly position through behaving in an anti-competitive way. This is a **dogmatic approach** or *per se* **rule**. This is a general rule that does not require the individual circumstances to be investigated further. If a monopoly is behaving anti-competitively, this is viewed to be wrong, even if no one is harmed. However, if the firm has taken sales from its competitors by being more efficient, this is not against anti-trust (anti-monopoly) law.

Other countries, for example the United Kingdom, take a **pragmatic approach** using the **rule of reason**. According to the rule of reason, being in a monopoly position is not unlawful. Individual cases can be examined to see if there is an unreasonable restraint of trade, with each case that is investigated judged on its merits. On balance, is it in the public interest or not? The principles of the *per se* rule and the rule of reason are also the basis of China's anti-monopoly law, where monopolies may be allowed to exist if there is "reasonable cause".

If countries have laws about anti-competitive behaviour, they must also have penalties for breaking these laws. Firms found guilty of abusing their position may be fined and stopped from continuing their anti-competitive behaviour. For example, Google, the technology company, was fined €2.42 billion by the European Union (EU) in 2017 for "promoting its own shopping comparison service at the top of search results". It was also told to stop using its dominance to promote itself for online price comparisons.

In some countries, individual managers may be held responsible or the firm could be broken up into smaller units, known as **monopoly busting**. The United States considered breaking up Microsoft but then chose not to.

Remember that monopolies, especially natural monopolies, can be beneficial both to individuals and the economy as a whole. For example, if they can take advantage of economies of scale and offer lower prices, this may be better than having a number of smaller firms in the market.

Regulation of mergers and takeovers

One way that dominant firms can develop is through mergers and takeovers. Therefore, competition policy is also likely to cover planned mergers and takeovers. The concern may be that there will be a substantial lessening in competition and/or the creation of a monopoly. Rules may require potential mergers fulfilling these criteria to be notified to the authorities before they happen. A planned merger might be investigated if the new firm will have a significant share of a market. The criterion may be the value of assets involved. Alternatively, the authorities may simply choose which mergers/takeovers to investigate.

The merger/takeover may be permitted if it is believed that it will not be anti-competitive or if the resulting increase in efficiency is sufficient to offset any likely harm. If there are concerns that the merger/takeover will lead to a substantial lessening in competition, it may not be allowed to go ahead. Alternatively, it may be permitted, subject to certain conditions. For example, this may involve selling off part of the new business.

There is likely to be a limited number of cases that the competition authorities can deal with relatively quickly, so it may not be possible to consider all large mergers/takeovers and on balance, many mergers could be beneficial. There is also the complication that the firms involved may be based in (or operate in) different countries which have different approaches to competition policy.

Policies to control restrictive practices and protect consumers

Restrictive practices (sometimes known as anti-competitive practices) are actions taken by a dominant firm or combination of firms to limit competition. These include colluding with other firms about where products are sold, fixing prices, or any other measure which prevents fair competition. This makes it difficult for new firms to enter the market. The firms are abusing their monopoly power and may cause harm both to consumers and other firms which are not part of the agreement.

Many countries have laws preventing restrictive practices, with penalties for firms who break these laws. For example, the EU can fine a firm up to 10% of its turnover from the previous year if it breaks the rules on cartels and other restrictive agreements. The restrictive practice will also be stopped. However, if a firm acts as a whistle-blower and tells the authorities about an agreement in which it is involved, it may receive a lower fine or possibly no fine.

Laws preventing restrictive practices are in place to enable firms to compete openly and fairly and to protect consumers from exploitation. However, some restrictive practices may be allowed if their benefits outweigh their anti-competitive disadvantages. For example, this may apply if the practice enables the firms to achieve more technical progress than would occur without this agreement.

Measures to promote competition and reduce entry barriers

Having an effective competition policy is one way a government can help to promote competition. As part of this, as mentioned earlier, it may be possible to break up an existing monopoly, if it has been behaving anti-competitively. However, this is not easy to do and although it results in more firms in the market, some of the advantages of a larger firm, such as economies of scale, may be lost.

One way of creating competition where there is a natural monopoly is to set up a system where firms share the infrastructure, for example pipes or cables. In many countries, where industries such as gas,

Link

How firms grow, including the difference between mergers and takeovers, was covered in 1.4 "The growth of firms".

Activity

1 Find out how your country deals with potential mergers and takeovers.
2 Find out what happened in a recent case, in your country or elsewhere, involving the investigation by the competition authorities of a dominant firm or a planned merger/takeover.

Key term

Restrictive practices: actions by a dominant firm or combination of firms to limit competition.

Link

Types and examples of collusion were covered in 3.4 "Oligopoly".

Progress questions

1 What is a dominant firm?
2 What problems could arise from a firm dominating a market?
3 What could a competition authority do to reduce the potential problems of a monopoly?
4 Why might a country have a competition policy to deal with mergers and takeovers?
5 Give **two** examples of restrictive practices.

Link

The case for and against privatisation and deregulation of markets is explained in 3.12 "Public ownership, privatisation, regulation and deregulation of markets".

electricity and water have been privatised (transferred from the public to the private sector), competing firms share the infrastructure, creating a competitive market. This reduces the barriers to entry and avoids the waste of resources which would occur if different firms had to have their own set of pipes or cables, adding to the cost of providing the service. The market becomes more contestable, reducing the potential for abuse of monopoly power.

In a similar way, markets can be deregulated, which involves the removal of rules, particularly those that restrict competition. For example, in some countries, local bus services may be run by the local or regional government. No other firms are allowed to offer alternative services. If the rules are relaxed, this removes the statutory barrier to entry and enables competing firms to set up in this market. The increased competition will increase choice and hopefully, lower costs and prices.

Price and profit controls

Other ways of influencing the behaviour of dominant firms are through price and profit controls. There may be limits on how much prices can be increased, perhaps linked to the country's annual inflation rate. This will stop dominant firms from exploiting their position by charging consumers high prices. This may be appropriate for state-run or privatised firms with monopoly power, especially if they are providing vital services. If firms wish to increase their profits, they will have to improve their efficiency.

An alternative approach is to limit the profits that firms can make. This may stop them from charging high prices, if they cannot make more than a certain level of profits without being fined. It is difficult to know what would be a fair level of profit and to maintain this for a long period, particularly if the firm is in the private sector. Also, controls on profits may lead to inefficiency and limit technical progress in that market because the profits to finance it and the incentive to carry it out have been limited. There is less incentive to control costs, so higher prices could still result.

Summary of competition policy and its limitations

Competition policy is generally believed to be necessary to stop dominant firms abusing their monopoly power. For example, they may charge high prices to consumers or behave in ways that increase barriers to entry for other firms. Consumers may also need protection in terms of the quality and safety of products, particularly from firms with little or no competition. However, such policies have costs and limitations. Resources are required to monitor the activities of firms and conduct investigations, which also take time.

There are limits to how many cases a competition authority can deal with and inevitably, some abuse by dominant firms will continue. However, if a country has laws and penalties in place, this may be enough to stop some potential abuse from happening.

The advantages of large firms need to be considered against any negative behaviour when reaching a final judgement about the activities of a firm or group of firms. When deciding on a proposed merger or takeover, it is difficult to know exactly what will happen after the firms join together and some mergers that may have been beneficial might be prevented.

Dominant firms are not necessarily undesirable and whether they have the ability to abuse their position partly depends on the contestability of the market.

Link

The significance of market contestability for the behaviour of firms was discussed in 3.7 "Contestable markets".

Case study: Competition policy in Brazil

▲ **Figure 3.11.2**: A well-known Brazilian landmark, Rio de Janeiro

In 2011, a new Competition Law introduced reforms to Brazilian competition policy. It led to the setting up of a single independent competition agency, CADE (Administrative Council for Economic Defence), to replace the three different agencies that operated before. It also introduced a pre-merger notification system. These reforms followed recommendations from the 2005 and 2010 reviews by the OECD (the Organisation for Economic Cooperation and Development), an international organisation which aims to encourage economic progress and world trade.

The new agency is still understaffed and struggling to hire enough experts, yet the pre-merger notification system has led to a high number of notifications and decisions are required by set deadlines. Its cartel enforcement programme has been modernised and in 2014, it imposed a record fine. Reduced fines are available if firms cooperate. There have been relatively few investigations into dominant firms.

CADE works with other international competition policy agencies, both in its region and in other parts of the world. This can be particularly useful in merger cases.

Source: http://www.oecd.org/daf/competition/oecd-peer-reviews-of-competition-law-and-policy-brazil-ENG-web.pdf; accessed 20 September 2019

1   How may the reforms made in Brazil reduce the potential problems of dominant firms and restrictive practices?
2   What else could the Brazilian government do to encourage more competition in markets?

This section will develop your knowledge and understanding of:

→ the case for and against the public ownership of firms and industries

→ the case for and against the privatisation of state-owned enterprises

→ arguments for and against the regulation and deregulation of markets

→ regulatory capture.

Key terms

Public ownership: when the government owns a firm, industry or asset.

Nationalisation: when private sector firms or industries are transferred from the private sector to state ownership or control.

The case for and against the public ownership of firms and industries

Public ownership (also known as state ownership or government ownership) is when the government owns a firm, industry or asset. This may apply to national or local governments. State-owned enterprises (SOEs) are also called nationalised industries and when a private sector firm or industry is taken over by the public sector, this process is called **nationalisation**. The firms then supply goods and services to consumers and/or other businesses. Some of the products are public goods, for example street lighting, and others are private goods, for example education or water.

Decisions about what should be nationalised and how the business should be run may be made for political rather than economic reasons and the amount of public ownership varies considerably between countries. Interventionist supply-side economists believe that private companies may not invest enough in long-term projects but focus more on short-term profits for their shareholders.

Without government intervention, spending on research and development in key areas important to the economy may be too low. However, a nationalised industry may lack the incentive to be efficient, compared to a firm in the private sector, but this depends on how it is managed. Also, there may be more or less innovation, depending on the funds made available by the government. An argument for privatisation is that private firms can raise money on capital markets and investment is not restricted by limited government expenditure.

Public goods and merit goods

Some goods would be undersupplied or not supplied at all if the government did not provide them. Public goods are non-excludable and non-rival in consumption. It is usually not possible to prevent non-payers from using street lighting and the amount they use cannot be determined, so why would people pay for it and how can an appropriate price be set? This could be a missing market unless the government intervened.

If a product is undersupplied or not supplied at all by the private sector and it is considered important enough, then there is a case for a government to either supply it themselves or to enable a firm to collect money to pay for it if this is possible. For example, government spending on infrastructure, such as roads, improves efficiency and reduces transport costs. In most cases, this is paid for directly by governments out of tax revenue, although there may be some roads that people pay to use.

The government can also take account of externalities and inequality. Private sector firms only consider the private costs and benefits. Merit goods are products that society or government judges are desirable and too little is provided by the market for the benefit of the country as a whole. For example, many countries provide at least some education and health care free to consumers. This is because these services are considered to be important for the quality of people's lives and some people would be unwilling or unable to buy enough education or health care for their own well-being and that of others. A healthy, well-educated population is important for economic growth.

The state may also provide some housing at low rents for families on low incomes. However, what is considered a merit good depends on the government's value judgements and priorities. In some countries, people have to pay for health care or take out insurance.

Other key industries

Nationalisation of key industries may be justified as part of a belief that state planning is more effective than leaving the industries to market forces. Some industries may be considered too important to be left to the private sector. Industries such as rail services, electricity, water and other utilities are crucial to the smooth operation of the economy.

These industries may be natural monopolies, where an activity is best carried out by one firm due to significant economies of scale. There are high start-up costs acting as a barrier to entry and it would be a waste of resources to have more than one set of pipes or cables, for example. A private sector profit-maximising monopoly may choose to charge high prices and limit output, exploiting consumers.

If the industry is state-owned, or taken over by the state, the government can run the industry for the benefit of consumers and the economy. This will probably involve charging lower prices and maintaining some services that are uneconomic but considered important. Externalities, both positive and negative, can be considered. For example, a loss-making rail service to a remote town may not be provided by a firm in the private sector, unless subsidised. State ownership also removes the problem of having to regulate private sector monopolies providing vital services.

There may be issues of national security or safety involved in the operation of some industries. For example, in France, nuclear power is the largest source of electricity, generating about 70% of the total, the highest proportion in the world. Électricité de France (EDF) manages the country's 58 nuclear power reactors, but the French government has 85% of the shares in the company.

Accidents at nuclear power plants, including major incidents at Three Mile Island (US), Chernobyl (Ukraine) and Fukushima (Japan), have added to the safety concerns associated with this method of producing energy and there is also the problem of what to do with the nuclear

> ### Link
> Public goods were explained in 5.2 "Private goods, public goods and quasi-public goods" in the AS book, and merit goods were covered in 5.4 "Merit and demerit goods" in the AS book.

▲ **Figure 3.12.1:** Water – a key industry, often under state control

waste. Although nuclear power reactors have a good safety record, many people remain concerned about radiation and other issues. The government may believe that it should be involved with such activities.

Occasionally, exceptional circumstances may lead to a temporary nationalisation of firms. For example, in the global financial crisis of 2007–2008, some governments put money into some banks and took over others that may have stopped trading otherwise. This was done to increase confidence and stability in the economy. The government's shares may be sold back to the private sector when the situation improves.

▼ **Table 3.12.1**: Advantages and disadvantages of public ownership

Advantages	Disadvantages
• Provision of public goods • Increased provision of merit goods • Can take account of externalities and inequality • Control of key industries to help the economy • Control of industries where they are security or safety concerns • Benefits of natural monopolies without exploitation • Less regulation needed	• Decisions may be made for political rather than economic reasons • May be difficult to carry through long-term plans if government priorities change • Difficult to know which products to supply and in which quantities • Lack of incentive to be efficient if no competitive pressure • Prices not necessarily lower or investment higher than if in private ownership

The case for and against the privatisation of state-owned enterprises

Over the last 40 years, many countries have privatised (or denationalised) some of their industries, where government-owned businesses are sold and become private sector businesses. Privatisation started to spread worldwide after a number of successful sales of state-owned enterprises (SOE) under the government of Margaret Thatcher in the United Kingdom in the 1980s. Inevitably, some of the arguments for privatisation are similar to those against state ownership. Free market supply-side economists are in favour of the privatisation of government-owned firms because they believe that these firms are inefficient.

As some economies have moved from being largely state-planned towards becoming market economies, it has been necessary to transfer the ownership of many resources from the public to the private sector. This has worked more effectively in some countries than others.

Increased efficiency

Private sector firms have owners and shareholders who want their firm to be profitable, so that they receive a reasonable income and/or the value of their shares increases. This gives the firms more incentive to be efficient, to cut costs and to look for ways of improving their products and prices. Where there is competition, market forces provide an additional incentive for firms to be efficient.

In some countries, one of the motives for privatisation is to have wider share ownership so more people have a direct interest in the business doing well. This is particularly relevant if workers in the firm are given or encouraged to buy the shares. However, if the firm is a monopoly, the firm may be inefficient and have the potential to exploit its customers.

If the market is, or can be made, contestable, for example by firms being able to share pipes, cables or rail track, then there can be competition without unnecessary duplication of resources. This has been done successfully in the privatisation of electricity, gas and rail services in many countries. However, privatisation may need to be accompanied by regulation, controlling how the firms operate. Also, if there are too many competing firms, some of the benefits of economies of scale may be lost.

Lack of political interference

State-owned enterprises may be subject to regular interference from politicians, which could affect their long-term strategy. This is a particular concern when an election leads to a different political party in charge. They may have different priorities and views, including whether the industry should be in the public sector or not. Money for the industry may be cut and projects may be changed or stopped.

Firms in the private sector will not be subject to the same interruptions to the running of their business and can make longer-term plans, knowing that they should be able to see them completed. Investment decisions can be made for commercial rather than political reasons.

Raise revenue for the government

The transfer of a state-owned enterprise to the private sector usually involves the sale of shares in the company. This will provide money for the government to use for other priorities. However, since a private sector business will not consider the externalities, the government may still have to subsidise some activities or impose rules on how the firm operates. In 2009, the year with the highest world privatisation revenue, the amount raised was over $250 billion. This is a one-off source of revenue but if the privatised firm makes profits in future, this can increase tax revenue.

▼ **Table 3.12.2**: Advantages and disadvantages of privatisation

Advantages	Disadvantages
• More incentive to improve efficiency • Freedom from direct government interference in decision making • Able to make longer-term investment plans • Raises money for government • Wider share ownership • Market can determine the appropriate price and quantity	• May be less efficient and able to exploit monopoly power if lacking competition • Loss of economies of scale if more firms in the market • Private sector firms only consider private costs and benefits • Need for effective regulation and risk of regulatory capture • Some goods and services may still need to be paid for by government

Activity

Choose an industry or activity in your country that has been privatised. How well has it performed since it was privatised?

Arguments for and against the regulation and deregulation of markets

Regulation

Regulation involves laws or rules that control the behaviour and activities of individuals and firms. In the context of privatisation, the transfer of ownership of a state-owned enterprise (SOE) to the private sector may be done alongside imposing regulations about what it must or cannot do. This is particularly important if a public sector monopoly is replaced by a private sector monopoly. Regulation can ensure that monopoly power is not exploited and that externalities are considered, to reduce the market failures that could occur.

For example, if the water industry is privatised, the government may set up a regulatory body (sometimes known as a "watchdog" or regulator) at the same time. This body may put limits on how much prices can rise. There may be other requirements of the privatisation, for example to provide water supplies to remote properties, even though it is uneconomic to do so. Regulation helps to achieve the potential benefits of privatisation while protecting customers.

However, regulation adds to costs and may restrict competition, acting as a barrier to entry. Operating the regulatory body costs money and complying with the regulations adds to the costs of firms. If the industry becomes more competitive, there may less need for regulation and the market may eventually be able to regulate itself.

Deregulation

Deregulation involves the removal of rules, particularly those that restrict competition. When an industry is state run, other firms may not be allowed to supply the product. Deregulation aims to increase the contestability of markets and with fewer rules, firms' costs can fall. If restrictions are removed, competition can increase, leading to more choice for consumers, increased efficiency and lower prices. As countries have privatised some of their industries, there has also been more deregulation, as part of a move towards freer markets.

Regulation versus deregulation

On balance, there needs to be the right amount of regulation – to protect consumers and other firms, and deregulation – where restrictions are not necessary. For example, regulations may be imposed to reduce pollution and tackle climate change or to protect consumers from products that could be unsafe. There may also be particular circumstances where the need for more regulation is identified. For example, after the global financial crisis of 2007–2008, many countries looked again at their regulation of banks and other financial institutions and introduced new rules.

Regulatory capture

Regulatory capture is where regulatory agencies operate in the firms' interests rather than the interests of the consumers or other economic agents they are trying to protect. It is an example of government failure.

Get it right

The term denationalisation is sometimes used as an alternative term for privatisation, where a state-owned enterprise is transferred to the private sector. Deregulation is the removal of rules, usually those that restrict competition. They are separate actions but may occur together.

Link

Regulation was explained in 5.7 "Government intervention in markets" in the AS book. Deregulation and regulatory capture were introduced in 5.8 "Government failure" in the AS book.

For example, the firm or industry may be able to persuade the regulator to let it increase prices by more than necessary. This may happen because the regulatory body works closely with the industry and is sympathetic to its problems. Alternatively, the firms may provide the regulator with inaccurate information or officials may be corrupt, acting in their self-interest rather than those they are trying to protect. Consumers on low incomes may then find it more difficult to afford these vital services.

Progress questions

3 What is regulation and why may the government regulate a privatised industry?

4 Explain **two** advantages and **two** disadvantages of privatising state-owned enterprises.

Case study: Privatisation in the Philippines

▲ **Figure 3.12.2**: Manila, capital of the Philippines

The Philippines is an emerging market, moving towards services and manufacturing away from its traditional agricultural base. It has a population of over 100 million. According to the Philippine government, it is committed to being a free market economy, but the government is still involved in economic planning, as well as owning companies involved in banking, oil, transport and power. The government is focusing on areas where it is not practical for the private sector to be involved or where some people could be disadvantaged.

Privatisation was introduced for political as well as economic reasons, to meet requirements for loans

from international institutions such as the International Monetary Fund (IMF) and World Bank. Most privatisations occurred between 1991 and 1998.

When the energy sector was privatised, it was divided into four sectors; two were subject to regulation and the other two were open to competition. Competition in the industry has increased, but the price of electricity rose considerably and there have been claims of regulatory capture. Critics also argue that vital services such as water and electricity should be run by the government.

Although some jobs have been lost to reduce costs, privatisation has increased investment and government revenue. By 2001, 490 government-owned assets and companies had been privatised for 200.76 billion Philippine pesos and some of the money was used to pay off the government's debts.

1 If the exchange rate of the Philippine peso to the US dollar is 1 peso = USD 0.02, calculate how much money was received from privatisation by 2001 in US dollars, to the **nearest billion**.

2 Use the information in the case study to identify some advantages and disadvantages of privatisation.

Exam-style questions

1 The table below shows the total revenue and total cost of a firm selling different quantities in the short run.

Sales	Total revenue ($)	Total cost ($)
10	300	400
20	600	700
30	900	900
40	1,200	1,050
50	1,500	1,400

The firm is most likely to be operating in which market structure?

A Monopolistic competition

B Monopoly

C Oligopoly

D Perfect competition   (1 mark)

2 A perfectly contestable market must have

A a large number of firms. **C** no barriers to entry.

B high sunk costs. **D** perfectly elastic demand. (1 mark)

3 A firm is productively efficient when it operates where marginal cost is equal to

A average cost. **C** marginal revenue.

B average revenue. **D** price. (1 mark)

4 (i) Define "consumer surplus". (2 marks)

(ii) Explain, using a diagram, how an increase in labour costs, other things being equal, will affect the consumer surplus in a competitive market. (4 marks)

5 The table below shows the number of firms in the industry and the total price change for electricity over a 10-year period in five countries.

Country	Number of firms	Change in price (%)
A	1	60
B	2	40
C	6	30
D	20	50
E	50	70

(i) Explain why the number of firms in the electricity market may affect the percentage change in price over the 10-year period. (4 marks)

(ii) To what extent do the data suggest that the number of firms affects the percentage change in price over the period? (4 marks)

Use the data in the table to support your answer.

6 Explain the short-run and long-run costs and benefits which may result from competition in the market for taxi services. (12 marks)

Note: To answer this question as part of a data response question, use the data provided in the case study on "Uber" in 3.8 "The dynamics of competition and competitive market processes" to support your answer.

7 Discuss whether oligopolistic industries benefit consumers. (25 marks)

Note: To answer this question as a data response question, use the data provided in the case study "An example of a cartel – OPEC" in 3.4 "Oligopoly" to support your answer.

8 Assess whether perfect competition will result in an efficient allocation of resources. (25 marks)

Get it right

The data response context in the A-level papers includes a 12-mark question, as well as short-answer data interpretation questions and an extended 25-mark response question. In this set of exam-style questions, to provide practice applying the material, the 12-mark question has been linked to one of the case studies in the chapter. As with the 25-mark questions, you should apply your answer to the context in the question and support your points with some of the information provided. The Level 3 band (9–12 marks) in the levels mark scheme for these questions makes reference to "good application of relevant economic principles and/or good use of data to support the response".

4 The labour market

The economics of business behaviour and the distribution of income

This section will develop your knowledge and understanding of:

→ how the demand for a factor is derived from the demand for the product

→ the marginal productivity theory of the demand for labour

→ how the demand curve for labour shows the relationship between the wage rate and number of workers firms wish to employ

→ causes of shifts in the demand curve for labour

→ determinants of the elasticity of demand for labour.

How the demand for labour is derived from the demand for the product

Labour is not wanted for its own sake but for its contribution to the production of goods and services. A firm is unlikely to employ more workers unless it believes that the extra items it produces can be sold and that this will increase the firm's total profit. In the long run, the firm must be able to sell its output for at least normal profit, to make it worthwhile producing in that market.

The demand for labour and the other factors of production is a derived demand. This is where the demand for the factor of production results from the demand for the product it makes. If the demand for a product falls, there will be less demand for the factors of production involved.

For example, with the growing use of the internet and people reading news online, the demand for newspapers has decreased. This has led to fewer people being needed to manufacture and deliver newspapers. Similarly, if demand for a good or service increases, other things being equal, this will increase the demand for factors of production, including labour.

The marginal productivity theory of labour

When an extra worker is employed, the resulting increase in total output or total physical product (TPP) is known as the **marginal physical product (MPP)**. The value of this increase in output is the **marginal revenue product (MRP)**. This is the amount that the total revenue product (TRP) increases due to the employment of an extra worker. For example, if a firm making wooden toys produces 57 wooden toys a week with 2 workers, and 81 wooden toys with 3 workers, then the MPP of the third worker is 24 wooden toys. If the wooden toys sell for $10 each, then the worker's MRP is $240. This is the amount they add to the firm's total revenue product.

The MRP is found by multiplying the MPP by the marginal revenue (MR) for each additional unit of output. In a perfectly competitive goods market, P = MR = AR for a firm, so the MRP can be found by multiplying the MPP by the price of the product. In this case:

$$MRP = 24 \times \$10 = \$240$$

The **marginal (revenue) productivity theory** states that a firm will employ additional workers up to the point where their marginal revenue product is equal to their marginal cost. The firm should employ extra workers as long as MRP > MC for labour. This applies the same principle that a profit-maximising firm uses to determine its output, with the firm producing where MC = MR. The extra cost of producing one more item is equal to the extra revenue from its sale. Similarly, according to the marginal productivity theory, a profit-maximising firm should employ workers up to the point where the extra revenue the worker generates is equal to the extra cost of employing them.

In the numerical example above, where the worker's MRP is $240, it is not worth employing them if their cost is more than $240. They would be employed (assuming a constant wage rate) at an extra cost of $220 a week but not if the extra cost of employing them is $260, because then they would add more to the firm's costs than its revenue.

MRP theory, the demand curve for labour and the relationship between wage rates and employment

MRP theory and the demand curve for labour

If we assume that there is a perfectly competitive goods market, then the price of the product will be determined by the supply and demand in the market as a whole. An individual firm will face a perfectly elastic demand curve for its product and can sell as much as it likes at the market price. We will also assume that the firm is operating in the short run, with labour as the only variable factor of production. As the firm employs more workers, other things being equal, their marginal product will fall according to the law of diminishing returns.

A profit-maximising firm will not employ someone if their cost is greater than their MRP. Therefore, the higher the wage, the fewer the number of workers the firm will employ and the lower the wage, the greater the number of workers employed, other things being equal. If the market for labour is also perfectly competitive, an individual firm is one of many buyers of labour and the number of workers employed by an individual firm does not affect the market wage rate. Each worker is paid the same wage, so MC = AC for labour and this also equals the wage rate. The MRP curve is effectively the demand curve for labour, as shown in Figure 4.1.1.

The **wage rate** is the pay for a given time period, for example an hour or week. At a wage rate of $100 a week, if fewer than 45 workers are employed, MRP > wage (MC) and employing more workers will increase profit. If more than 45 workers are employed, MRP < MC of labour, so profits would rise if the firm reduced employment. If we assume that the wage rate is the marginal cost of the worker, then if the wage rate is $100 a week, the firm will employ 45 workers. However, if the wage rate is $200 a week, according to the MRP curve, it is only profitable to employ 30 workers.

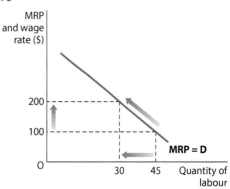

▲ Figure 4.1.1: MRP as the demand curve

Case study: Marginal revenue product

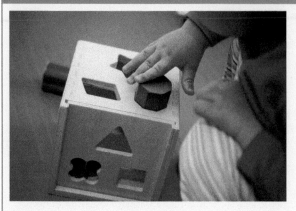

▲ Figure 4.1.2: How many to produce?

Gepetto has a small business making wooden toys for children. He sells each toy for $10. Gepetto is considering how many workers to employ. Table 4.1.1 shows his estimates of the total physical product per week for different numbers of workers.

▼ Table 4.1.1: Impact of changing employment

Number of workers employed	Total physical product, TPP	Marginal physical product, MPP	Total revenue product, TRP ($)	Marginal revenue product, MRP ($)
1	30			
2	57			
3	81			
4	102			
5	120			
6	135			

1 Copy and complete the table.
2 Explain how many workers Gepetto should employ if the weekly wage per worker is:
   i. $155   ii. $260   iii. $320.

Key terms

Wage rate: the pay for a given time period.

Average revenue product: the revenue per worker, calculated by dividing the total revenue product by the number of workers.

At each wage rate/cost, the demand for labour will be the point where the wage rate = MRP. Therefore, the MRP curve shows the demand curve for labour, which is the quantity demanded of labour at each wage rate. If the wage rate changes, this causes a movement along the demand curve, in the same way as happens with the demand for any product when its price changes.

If the goods market is not perfectly competitive, the firm will face a downward-sloping demand curve for its product. This means that if the firm wishes to sell more, it will have to charge a lower price. This causes the MRP to fall more steeply as more workers are employed, since the MRP is now falling for two reasons – the law of diminishing returns and falling product prices. The market demand curve for labour can be found by adding the demand of every firm at each wage rate.

Is the demand curve for labour based on the whole of the MRP curve?

The **average revenue product (ARP)** is the revenue per worker and can be calculated by dividing the total revenue product (TPP × Price of the product) by the number of workers who have produced this output. For example, in Table 4.1.1, the ARP of 5 workers was $240 because the TPP was 120 and each product sold for $10, resulting in a TRP of $1,200 (and $1,200 ÷ 5 = $240).

It could be that MPP (and therefore MRP) increases for the first few workers before the law of diminishing returns sets in. This will cause both the MRP and the ARP to rise before falling, as shown in Figure 4.1.3. If the MRP of an extra worker is higher than the current ARP, this will cause the ARP to rise and if the MRP is less than the current ARP, this will cause ARP to fall. It follows that the MRP curve will cut the ARP curve at the highest point of the ARP curve.

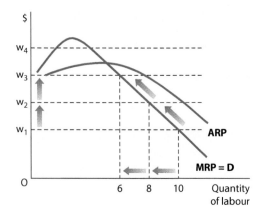

▲ Figure 4.1.3: ARP, MRP and the demand curve for labour

If the wage rate is w_1, the firm will employ 10 workers and if the wage rate rises to w_2, only 8 workers will be employed, because for those extra 2 workers, their MRP is now less than their cost. If the wage rate rises to w_3, only 6 will be employed. If the wage rate is greater than the ARP, for example at w_4, then ARP < AC of labour and so the total revenue generated by employing this type of labour is less than their total cost. None of these workers will be employed but the firm may employ other factors of production or other types of labour. Only the part of the MRP curve below the ARP curve forms the demand curve for labour, which is downward sloping.

Causes of shifts in the demand curve for labour

The demand curve for labour, which is derived from the MRP curve, will shift if there is a change in workers' MRP. Since MRP = MPP × MR, then if either the MRP or the MR changes (or both change), this will change the MRP and the demand for labour.

Changes in MPP

If workers can now produce more or less than they could before, this will increase or reduce their MPP. For example, training may enable them to produce more, increasing their productivity. This will increase their MPP. Assuming that MR stays the same, MRP will also rise, increasing the demand for labour, shifting the curve to the right. If something happens to reduce worker productivity, the demand for labour will fall, shifting the demand curve to the left.

Changes in MR

Assuming a perfectly competitive goods market, P = MR = AR, so if the price of the product changes, this also changes the MR and the MRP. For example, if demand for the product increases because of a rise in incomes, this will result in a rise in price, other things being equal. It will then be worthwhile employing extra workers. Similarly, if there is a change in tastes and demand for the product falls, this could lead to a fall in its price. Workers' MRP will also fall reducing the demand for labour.

In Figure 4.1.4, $MRP_1 = D_1$ shows the original demand curve for labour. If MRP increases because of an increase in MPP, MR, or both, this shifts the MRP = D curve to the right, to $MRP_2 = D_2$. At any given wage rate, the demand for labour is now higher than before. For example, at wage rate w, the demand for labour, determined by the workers' MRP, is now q_2 instead of q_1.

Determinants of the elasticity of demand for labour

The **price elasticity of demand (PED) for labour** (also known as **wage elasticity of demand**) measures the responsiveness of the demand for labour to a change in the wage rate, which is effectively the price of labour.

$$\text{PED for labour} = \frac{\text{Percentage change in quantity demanded}}{\text{Percentage change in wage rate}}$$

If the percentage change in the wage rate causes a larger percentage change in the quantity demanded of labour, then demand for labour is elastic. If the percentage change in the wage rate causes

Progress questions

1 Explain why the demand for labour is a derived demand.

2 If the MRP of the 14th worker in a week is €374 and the goods they produce are sold for €11, what is their MPP that week?

3 If the TRP of 18 workers in a day is £2,700, what is their ARP?

Link

The relationship between MRP and ARP is the same as that between MP and AP in Figure 2.1.3 in 2.1 "The law of diminishing returns and returns to scale". This is because MP and AP are multiplied by a constant price to give MRP and ARP in a perfectly competitive goods market.

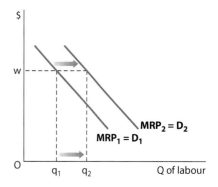

▲ Figure 4.1.4: A shift of the demand curve for labour

Key term

Price elasticity of demand for labour or wage elasticity of demand: a measure of the percentage change in the quantity demanded of labour as a result of a given percentage change in the wage rate, or simply, the responsiveness of the quantity demanded of labour to a change in the wage rate.

a smaller percentage change in quantity demanded, then demand is inelastic.

Factors affecting the PED for labour include:

- PED for the final product
- wages as a proportion of total cost
- ability to substitute other factors of production
- time.

PED for the final product

If the demand for the good or service produced is inelastic, then the demand for labour will also be inelastic. An increase in the wage rate will increase the firm's costs and is likely to result in it charging a higher price for the final product. If demand for the product is inelastic, there will be a relatively small change in the quantity demanded as a result of the increased price. This will then cause a relatively small change in the quantity demanded of labour as well. Similarly, if the demand for the product is elastic, there will be a larger fall in the demand for the product and hence the demand for labour. The more elastic the demand for the product, the more elastic the demand for the labour.

Wages as a proportion of total cost

If the wage bill is a large proportion of the total costs of a firm, demand will tend to be elastic. This is because an increase in labour costs will have a large effect on the firm's total costs and is likely to have a significant effect on the price and hence the demand for the product. The firm may choose, or be forced, to reduce the quantity of labour employed rather than increase its prices. Also, there may be more potential to reduce the amount of labour employed if the activity is labour intensive.

Ability to substitute other factors of production

If wages increase and it is easy to replace workers with other factors of production, such as a new machine, then the demand for labour is likely to be elastic. This is more likely to apply to unskilled workers. However, if workers are highly specialised or the work cannot easily be automated, an increase in wages may not have much effect on the number of workers employed and so the demand for labour will be more inelastic. As assembly lines have become more automated, the demand for many factory workers has fallen and become more elastic, whereas those providing personal services, such as nurses, tend to have less elastic demand.

Time

The demand for a particular type of labour is likely to become more elastic the longer the time period under consideration. Therefore, in the short run, the demand for labour is likely to be less elastic than in the long run. It takes time to make changes to the methods of production. Depending on the legislation in that country, it may also be difficult and costly to reduce employment quickly.

Link

PED in the context of the goods market was explained in 2.2 "Price, income and cross elasticities of demand" in the AS book.

Progress questions

4   Explain how each of the following should be illustrated on a diagram showing the demand for labour in a factory:

   i. increased training

   ii. an increase in the wage rate.

5   Explain why the demand for labour is likely to be elastic if the demand for the product it makes is also elastic.

6   If a 15% increase in the wage rate leads to a 12% fall in the demand for labour, what is the value of PED? Is demand elastic or inelastic?

7   Explain whether the demand for workers who deal with payments into a bank is likely to be more or less elastic than the demand for hairdressers.

How the supply of labour is influenced by monetary and non-monetary considerations

The supply of labour

The **supply of labour** is concerned with how many people are willing and able to work at different wage rates and how many hours they are willing to offer. It is the total number of hours that potential workers are willing and able to offer at different wage rates. For the economy as a whole, the supply of labour is affected by, for example, the working age and the total population but for a particular occupation, there will be both monetary and non-monetary considerations.

There are two requirements affecting the supply of labour: people being willing to work and being able to work. Someone may be willing to work as a doctor at a given wage rate but lack the qualifications to do so. Similarly, someone may be able to work as a doctor but chooses not to at a particular wage rate.

Monetary considerations

The wage rate and any other monetary considerations will have a large effect on how many people offer their services for a particular occupation. As well as the usual wage rate per hour or per week, there may be regular overtime payments at a higher rate of pay. If the job involves selling a product, the worker may be paid commission according to how many products they sell. There may be bonuses available based on productivity or the successful completion of contracts. Some workers, particularly managers, may receive shares in the firm as part of their total pay.

Non-monetary considerations

Non-monetary considerations that may influence the supply of labour to a particular occupation involve any factor not related to the financial rewards of the job. These include:

- the education, skills and experience
- job satisfaction, working conditions, hours and promotion prospects
- pension schemes and other benefits.

Education, skills and experience

Some jobs, for example doctors or architects, require many years' training and certain qualifications which are not easy to obtain.

> **Key term**
>
> **Supply of labour:** the number of hours that people are willing and able to work at different wage rates.

Before this, potential workers may have to study for a degree related to the subject, adding to their total years in education. There will be fewer people able and willing to offer their services for these jobs than for serving in a restaurant, for example. Other jobs require rare skills. For example, few people have the talent to become professional athletes. Generally, the supply of labour will be lower for skilled than unskilled jobs.

Job satisfaction, working conditions, hours and promotion prospects

Job satisfaction often plays an important part in people's choice of work. If they obtain considerable pleasure from their job, for example by helping others in a nursing home, people may be more willing to do this job than one which requires a similar amount of skill and is less satisfying but pays a higher wage.

The working conditions for jobs vary considerably. The worker may be doing a dangerous or dirty job, perhaps down a mine or collecting waste, or they may be working in an air-conditioned office. Other things being equal, it is likely that fewer people will choose to supply their services for jobs with unpleasant working conditions.

Some jobs require people to work unsocial hours, such as nights or weekends and/or do shift work, where the hours worked vary from week to week. Many people, perhaps because of their family commitments, are unable or unwilling to work at these times. This reduces the supply of labour to these occupations compared with those requiring similar skills but which only require people to work the hours normally expected in a working week.

Some jobs have better promotion prospects than others and for some people, this will make a difference as to how attractive a particular job is. They may start on low pay doing basic tasks but if they believe that they could be promoted to a more rewarding job, both in terms of pay and job satisfaction, this may increase the supply of labour to these jobs relative to those that do not offer this possibility.

Pension schemes and other benefits

The firm may contribute towards a pension for the worker, enabling them to have an income after they retire. They may provide a company car, private medical insurance or other allowances, depending on the nature of the job. The firm may also provide a subsidised canteen or leisure facilities. These additional benefits all help to make a job more attractive and increase the supply of labour to that firm or occupation.

Net advantage

Workers are likely to consider all aspects of a job, both monetary and non-monetary considerations. There may be good and bad aspects of the work. For example, a boring job may be better paid than one that offers more variety for a similar level of skill. Taking all factors into consideration is considering the net advantage of the job.

> **Key term**
>
> Net advantage: combining the monetary and non-monetary benefits of a job when deciding how much labour to supply.

The supply curve for labour showing the relationship between the wage rate and number of workers willing to work

Generally, the higher the wage rate, the more people will be willing to work in a particular occupation. Other things being equal, if the wage rate increases, this occupation will now appear to be relatively more attractive than alternatives. However, as well as being willing to work at a particular wage rate, people must also have the ability to carry out this work.

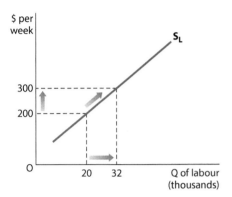

▲ Figure 4.2.1: The supply curve of labour in a particular occupation

In Figure 4.2.1, at a wage rate of $200 per week, the supply of labour for a particular occupation is 20,000 workers. If the wage rate increases to $300 per week, the supply of labour rises to 32,000 workers. More workers are willing to offer their services at a higher rate of pay. If the wage rate changes, this causes a movement along the supply curve, in the same way as happens with the supply for any product when its price changes.

The elasticity of supply of labour

The **price elasticity of supply (PES) for labour** (also known as **wage elasticity of supply**) measures the responsiveness of the supply of labour to a change in the wage rate/price of labour.

$$\text{PES for labour} = \frac{\text{Percentage change in quantity supplied}}{\text{Percentage change in wage rate}}$$

If the percentage change in the wage rate leads to a larger percentage change in the quantity supplied of labour, then the supply of labour is elastic. If the percentage change in the wage rate causes a smaller percentage change in quantity supplied, then supply is inelastic.

Factors affecting the PES for labour include:

* the skills and qualifications required
* time.

Skills and qualifications

Generally, if a particular occupation requires considerable training, skill and/or qualifications, then the supply of labour is likely to be more inelastic than for unskilled work. A given percentage increase in the wage rate is likely to lead to a smaller percentage increase in the supply of labour because there will be relatively few extra people who would be able to offer their services. Ease of access to training

Quantitative skills

In Figure 4.2.1, the supply curve for labour has been labelled S_L. In a similar way, the demand curve for labour may be labelled D_L. This is to distinguish the supply and demand for labour from the supply and demand for the product it makes. However, S and D are also acceptable when labelling labour market curves.

Key term

Price elasticity of supply for labour or wage elasticity of supply: a measure of the percentage change in the quantity supplied of labour as a result of a given percentage change in the wage rate, or simply, the responsiveness of the quantity supplied of labour to a change in the wage rate.

Get it right

When considering the supply and demand for a product, it is the consumers that determine demand and the firms that control supply. In the labour market, the supply is determined by workers, in terms of how many hours they are willing to offer and the demand is determined by firms, in terms of how many workers they are willing to employ at different wage rates.

Link

PES in the context of the goods market was explained in 2.4 "Price elasticity of supply" in the AS book. Immobility of factors of production, including labour, was discussed in 5.5 "Market imperfections" in the AS book, as a possible cause of market failure.

Progress questions

1 What is meant by the supply of labour?

2 Is the supply of labour directly or inversely related to the wage rate?

3 Explain **three** factors that could influence the supply of labour to a particular occupation.

4 If a 10% increase in the wage rate leads to a 15% rise in the supply of labour, what is the value of PES and is supply elastic or inelastic?

5 Explain whether the supply of doctors is likely to be more or less elastic than the supply of cleaners.

Activity

Think of **four** jobs in your country that you think are well paid and **four** that are low paid, then research how much workers in these occupations are actually paid.

to obtain the necessary skills also affects the elasticity of supply of labour. Many workers are likely to be occupationally or geographically immobile, at least in the short run.

Time

It follows that the longer the time period, the more elastic the supply of labour is likely to be because people will have had longer to respond to changes in the relative wage rates of different jobs. Potential workers will have had time to undertake the necessary training or to obtain the qualifications. Workers will be more occupationally and geographically mobile in the long run than the short run.

Quantitative skills

Direct and inverse relationships were explained in the context of supply and demand in the goods market in Chapter 2 of the AS book. A direct relationship is where both variables, such as quantity supplied and price move in the same direction, and an inverse relationship is where the two variables move in opposite directions, for example price and quantity demanded.

Causes of shifts in the market supply curve for labour

The supply curve for a product will shift if there is a change in any of the factors affecting supply apart from the price of that product. Similarly, the market supply curve for labour, which is the supply curve for a particular occupation, will shift if there is a change in any factor affecting the supply of labour apart from the wage rate. If supply increases, the curve shifts to the right and a decrease in the supply of labour will shift the supply curve to the left.

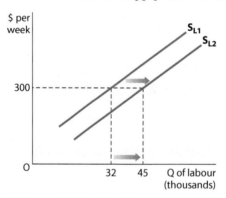

▲ Figure 4.2.2: A shift of the supply curve for labour

Figure 4.2.2 shows an increase in supply from S_{L1} to S_{L2} so that at any given wage rate, the supply of labour is now higher than before. For example, at a weekly wage rate of $300, the supply of labour has increased from 32,000 to 45,000.

This increase in the market supply of labour could have been caused by a change in one or more of the following:

• non-monetary factors

• demographic factors

• social attitudes.

Non-monetary factors

The supply of labour to a particular occupation could increase if there is a change in any of the non-monetary factors associated with that job. For example, if there are more people with the education, skills or experience required for a particular job, then the supply of labour will increase. If working conditions, promotion prospects or job satisfaction improve, the job will become more attractive. Perhaps, the amount of paid annual holiday has increased relative to similar jobs. Alternatively, there may now be more benefits offered with the job, for example help with child care.

Demographic factors

An increase in the population of working age will make more people available for work generally, including for a particular occupation. This could be affected by a number of factors such as a reduction in the school leaving age, an increase in the retirement age and net immigration. Also, as people are living longer, they may retire later, either because they wish to work longer or because the pension age has increased.

Social attitudes

Over time, there may be a change in social attitudes in a country. For example, it may become more or less acceptable for women to work in certain occupations, or even at all. People may choose to retire earlier or later depending on how much they value the extra income compared with the extra leisure time. This may partly depend on how much they would receive in pensions if they stop working.

Activity

Find out the following labour market information for your country:

1. What are the minimum and maximum ages that people are allowed to work, or are there no limits?
2. Have these limits changed in the last 20 years?
3. What proportion of women work, both now and 20 years ago?

Case study: Bruce's Boards

▲ Figure 4.2.3: Surfboards

Bruce has a made-to-order surfboard business based in a small town by the coast in New South Wales, Australia. Six months after starting his business, he had so many orders that he decided to employ four workers to help him make the boards. Bruce advertised the jobs at a wage rate of AUD $810 per week, just above the minimum that must be paid for employees aged 21 or older. He also required applicants to have some basic educational qualifications and training.

Bruce received only two applications for the jobs. He had hoped to employ all four workers at the same time and thought he may be able to attract other people to apply, so decided to readvertise the jobs. He invited the two original applicants to apply again.

1. Identify **three** changes, either to his requirements or what he is offering, that Bruce could make to attract more applicants.

2. Bruce later readvertised the jobs at a wage rate of $972 per week and this time attracted five applicants, including the two who applied originally. Calculate the price elasticity of supply for labour between the original and new wage rate offered and state whether it is elastic or inelastic.

This section will develop your knowledge and understanding of:

→ wage determination in a perfectly competitive labour market

→ the role of market forces in determining relative wage rates.

Link

The characteristics of perfect competition in the goods market and the determination of price were explained in 3.2 "Perfect competition".

Wage determination in a perfectly competitive labour market

The main characteristics of a perfectly competitive labour market

The main characteristics of a perfect labour market are similar to those of a perfectly competitive goods market. Similarly, it is a theoretical extreme which can be used as a benchmark (standard) against which real-world labour markets can be judged. The main characteristics of a perfectly competitive labour market are:

- a large number of buyers and sellers of labour
- homogeneous/identical workers
- free entry and exit
- perfect information.

A large number of buyers and sellers of labour

It is assumed that there are many small firms willing and able to buy labour and many individual workers offering their services for a particular occupation. No buyer or seller of labour has any influence over the wage rate. This is set by the market supply and demand for labour. All are price/wage takers.

Homogeneous workers

Workers are identical, offering the same skills and experience. There is no reason to prefer one worker to another. Likewise, there is no reason for a worker to prefer one firm instead of another.

Free entry and exit

There are no barriers to entry or exit in the labour market. In the long run, there is nothing to stop workers starting to offer their services to a particular labour market or leaving that market. Workers are perfectly mobile, so can transfer easily between jobs. In the same way, firms are free to start to employ people or to leave the market.

Perfect information

Everyone has perfect information. Everything that may affect a buyer's or seller's decision is known and understood. All information, including the wage rate, is known by everyone at the same time.

As said previously, these characteristics will not apply in their extreme forms but there may be some labour markets which have some of these characteristics. For example, in a large agricultural area, particularly during the harvesting or picking season, there may be large numbers of willing workers with similar skills and many small farms willing to employ these workers. As a result, there is likely to be a standard wage rate set by the market supply and demand for labour in that area at that time. But how is this wage rate determined?

Wage determination

Figures 4.3.1 and 4.3.2 show the situation for a perfectly competitive labour market and one firm within it. In Figure 4.3.1, the equilibrium wage rate is w where q_m is the quantity of labour/number of workers employed. If the wage rate is less than w, there will be excess demand for labour and wages will be bid upwards. Similarly, if the wage rate is above w, there will be excess supply of labour causing the wage rate to fall.

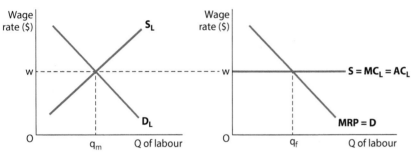

▲ Figure 4.3.1: Wage determination in a perfectly competitive labour market

▲ Figure 4.3.2: A firm in a perfectly competitive labour market

At the equilibrium wage rate, set by the supply (S_L) and demand (D_L) for labour in that market, an individual firm can employ as many workers as it likes. As Figure 4.3.2 shows, a firm in a perfectly competitive labour market faces a perfectly elastic supply curve of labour (S). The firm would not need to pay any more than this wage rate to attract as many workers as it wants and no one would work for a lower wage, knowing that they can earn more elsewhere.

The wage rate the firm has to pay does not change, regardless of the number of workers it employs, since it is one of many firms in the market and has an insignificant impact on the demand for labour. Therefore, w is also the firm's marginal cost (MC_L) and average cost (AC_L) of labour. The **marginal cost of labour** is the addition to total cost from employing an extra worker. The **average cost of labour** is the cost of employing each worker, calculated by dividing the total labour cost by the number of workers employed.

According to the marginal revenue productivity theory, a profit-maximising firm will employ additional workers up to the point where their marginal revenue product (MRP) is equal to their marginal cost (MC). This compares the revenue obtained from employing an extra worker to their cost. The firm will employ q_f workers at wage rate w, because this is where the firm's MRP = D curve crosses the $S = MC_L = AC_L$ curve of labour. At q_1 workers, the MRP equals the marginal cost of labour.

Key terms

Marginal cost of labour: the change in a firm's total cost due to the employment of an extra worker.

Average cost of labour: the cost of employing each worker, calculated by dividing the total labour cost by the number of workers employed.

Get it right

Figures 3.2.2 and 3.2.3 in 3.2 "Perfect competition" showed similar diagrams for a perfectly competitive product market. The market price was determined by the supply and demand for the good and an individual firm faced a perfectly elastic demand curve, which was also its MR and AR curves. A firm could sell as much as it liked at this price, but it made no sense to charge less, and due to perfect knowledge, it would make no sales if it charged more. In a perfectly competitive product market, a firm faces a perfectly elastic demand curve for the good but in a perfectly competitive labour market, the perfectly elastic curve faced by a firm is the supply curve of labour.

Case study: Fruit picking in New Zealand

▲ Figure 4.3.3: Kiwifruit – grown in large quantities in New Zealand

New Zealand is well known for growing a wide variety of fruit and has a large demand for fruit pickers when the fruit is ready for harvest. The three main fruit crops in New Zealand are kiwifruit, grapes and apples, but harvest times vary. For example, grapes and apples require extra workers from February to May, while the peak season for kiwifruit can last from March to July. There may also be work available on fruit farms at other times, for example to prune the plants or to work in the packing houses.

Fruit pickers need to be physically fit but other qualifications are not usually required. Fruit-picking work is often attractive to backpackers who want to earn money to pay for their travels, with New Zealand being a popular country to visit. In 2020, the minimum wage for those 18 or over in New Zealand was NZ$15.25 an hour.

There are many different websites advertising farming jobs at many different farms in various parts of New Zealand. One refers to: 'thousands of jobs available in some of New Zealand's most stunning regions'. Three examples of jobs available in different regions of New Zealand on a particular date are listed below:

- Fruit pickers, Bay of Plenty NZ$18.90
- Vineyard workers, Blenheim NZ$18.90 + holiday pay
- Potato harvest worker, Pukekohe NZ$18.90 + 8% holiday pay.

None of these jobs required any experience.

To what extent, does the New Zealand fruit-picking market have the characteristics of a perfectly competitive labour market? Use the information in the case study to compare with the requirements of this type of labour market.

Link

The marginal revenue productivity theory was explained in 4.1 "The demand for labour, marginal productivity theory".

Key terms

Relative wage rate: the pay of one job compared to that of others.

Wage differentials: differences in wages between workers with similar or different skills.

If the firm employs another worker beyond this level, then their extra cost will be greater than the extra revenue from their output, reducing the firm's total profit. In a similar way, if it employs fewer than q_f workers, the firm will lose out on profits by not employing workers whose MRP is greater than their cost.

The role of market forces in determining relative wage rates

The previous section showed how the wage rate was determined in a particular perfectly competitive labour market, for example the market for fruit pickers, assuming that this market demonstrates all the characteristics of a perfect labour market. However, the wage rate for this job may be higher or lower than for others requiring different skills or in different locations. The term, **relative wage rate** is used to refer to the pay of one job compared to that of other jobs. **Wage differentials** simply refers to differences in pay.

For example, if one worker earns $8 an hour and another earns $10 an hour, the wage differential is $2 an hour, the difference between the two rates of pay. However, the relative wage rate is 1:1.25, expressed as a ratio, to show one wage rate as a proportion of the other.

Each job has its own labour market with its own supply and demand for labour, which determine the equilibrium wage rate. Generally, a job requiring considerable skill or qualifications is likely to have a higher wage rate than one with fewer requirements. For example, the pay of a doctor is higher than the pay of a cleaner. This is partly because there are fewer people able and willing to offer their services as a doctor. This limits the supply of doctors and it is also less elastic than the supply of cleaners. If workers could move freely between these labour markets, the differences in wage rates would fall, as workers are attracted to jobs with higher pay.

In Figure 4.3.4, the equilibrium wage rate for doctors is w_d where the supply and demand for doctors (S_d and D_d) are equal. This is higher than the equilibrium wage rate of w_c for cleaners in Figure 4.3.5, partly because of differences in the supply of workers to the two markets. If the supply of doctors increases in future, perhaps because working conditions improve, this could help to reduce the relative gap in wages between doctors and cleaners, other things being equal. Similarly, if cleaners are now required to have a certain qualification, this will reduce their supply and raise their wage rate, which is also likely to narrow the gap in relative wage rates.

The wage rate of one job relative to another is also affected by differences in demand, for example doctors have a much higher MRP than cleaners. If the demand for labour in a particular market rises, so will the wage rate in comparison with other jobs, other things being equal. This may be due, for example, to an increase in demand for the product, its price, or workers' productivity, because these factors increase MRP and hence the demand for labour in this market. For example, an ageing population could increase the demand for health care, increasing the demand for doctors.

Summary

In a perfectly competitive labour market, the wage rate is determined by the supply and demand for labour in that market. If the demand for the product increases, for example due to an increase in incomes, there will be an increase in demand for labour to produce it, raising the equilibrium wage rate. If there is an increase in the supply of labour in the market, perhaps because working conditions improve, this will lead to a fall in the wage rate.

It is unrealistic to expect any labour market to have all the characteristics of a perfectly competitive labour market. For example, workers are not perfectly mobile and some large firms may be able to influence wage rates. All real-world labour markets are imperfectly competitive to a greater or lesser extent, but the model of a perfectly competitive labour market helps us to understand how wage rates and levels of employment are determined in competitive labour markets which may have some of these characteristics.

Link

Factors affecting the demand for labour were explained in 4.1 "The demand for labour, marginal productivity theory" and factors affecting the supply of labour were explained in 4.2 "The supply of labour to different labour markets".

Activity

Find out how much two particular jobs are paid in your country, both now and at an earlier date. Has the relative wage rate changed and if so, why?

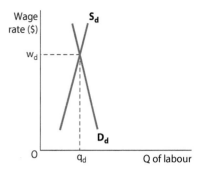

▲ Figure 4.3.4: The market for doctors

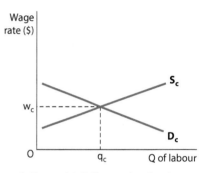

▲ Figure 4.3.5: The market for cleaners

Progress questions

1 State **two** characteristics of a perfectly competitive labour market.

2 In a perfectly competitive labour market, does an individual firm face a perfectly elastic demand curve for labour, a perfectly inelastic demand curve for labour, a perfectly elastic supply curve of labour or a perfectly inelastic supply curve of labour?

3 If the wage rate for workers in a perfectly competitive labour market is $20 an hour, what is the average cost of labour, and what is the marginal cost of labour?

4 Draw a diagram to show what is likely to happen to the wage rate for lawyers if more qualifications are required to do this work and demand increases for their services.

The determination of relative wage rates and levels of employment in imperfectly competitive labour markets

This section will develop your knowledge and understanding of:

→ how various factors including monopsony power, trade unions and imperfect information contribute to imperfections in a labour market

→ the determination of wages and employment where there is a monopsonist

→ factors that affect the ability of trade unions to influence wages and levels of employment

→ how wages and employment are likely to be affected by the introduction of a trade union into a previously perfectly competitive labour market and into a monopsony labour market.

Factors that contribute to imperfections in a labour market

All labour markets are imperfect to a greater or lesser extent. Factors contributing to imperfections in a labour market include:

- monopsony power
- trade unions
- imperfect information
- immobility of labour.

Monopsony power

A **monopsony** is the only or main buyer in a market. In the context of the labour market, a monopsonist is the only buyer of a particular type of labour, or in a certain location. For example, in many countries, including China, education is mainly provided by the state and as the major employer, the state can set the wage rate and teachers have few, if any, alternatives. The state is a wage maker and teachers are wage takers.

In a perfectly competitive labour market, no firm/buyer of labour has any influence over the wage rate. As the only buyer of a particular type of labour, the government or firm has considerable **monopsony power**, in the same way that a single seller has monopoly power. This situation also occurs if a firm is the main employer in a small town. For example, a coal mine may employ most of the workers in the local area.

Trade unions

A **trade union** is an organisation of workers that aims to protect and promote the rights and interests of its members. This may include trying to obtain higher pay or better working conditions for workers doing a particular job or perhaps providing support for individual members. This is normally achieved through **collective bargaining**, which is where a trade union negotiates with employers, or their representatives, on behalf of its members. A trade union will have much more bargaining power than an individual worker. If an agreement cannot be reached, this may result in industrial action, such as a strike. There may also be professional organisations setting standards and representing the interests of doctors, for example.

> ### Key terms
>
> **Monopsony:** the only or main buyer of a product or factor of production.
>
> **Monopsony power:** the ability of a single buyer to influence the price or wage rate.
>
> **Trade union:** an organisation of workers that aims to protect and promote the rights and interests of its members.
>
> **Collective bargaining:** where trade unions negotiate and agree pay and working conditions with employers.

Trade unions may represent those working in a particular industry, for example copper mining, or perhaps those doing a particular job, for example electricians, who work in a variety of industries. There may also be general unions that anyone can join, perhaps if there is no union representing their trade or industry. For example, in Malawi, trade unions include a Sugar Plantation and Allied Workers Union and a Transport and General Workers Union.

In a perfectly competitive labour market, there are large numbers of individual workers operating independently, who have no influence over the wage rate. A trade union can represent all, or a significant number, of those willing to work in a particular labour market. This may make the trade union a monopoly seller of this type of labour, giving them monopoly power. The trade union is likely to have more influence if it is dealing with a large number of small firms and may be able to negotiate a higher wage rate than would occur otherwise. Alternatively, there may be both a trade union and a monopsonist employer in that labour market, known as a **bilateral monopoly**, and their influence on the wage rate and employment will depend partly on their relative strengths.

Imperfect information

In a perfectly competitive labour market, everyone has perfect information. Everything that affects a buyer's or seller's decision is known and understood, and all information, including the wage rate, is known by everyone at the same time. This is not realistic. There is imperfect information in all labour markets. Both workers and employers may not be aware of the wage rates offered by other firms. Firms may not be profit maximisers or may be unable to calculate workers' MRP, not employing the number of workers suggested by MRP theory.

Immobility of labour

Many workers are geographically or occupationally immobile – unable or unwilling to move from one area or type of job to another. This may be partly because they do not know about job opportunities elsewhere. If workers are immobile, either occupationally and/or geographically, this can lead to difference in wage rates.

The determination of wages and employment where there is a monopsonist

Where there is a monopsonist, the wage rate and employment level will be different from those in a perfectly competitive market, but they also depend on whether there is a trade union operating in the market as well.

Determination of wages and employment with a monopsonist and no trade union

A monopsonist, as the only or main buyer of a particular type of labour, is able to pay a lower wage rate than would be offered in a competitive market and at this lower wage rate, fewer workers will be employed.

> ### Key term
>
> **Bilateral monopoly**: where there is a single buyer (monopsonist) and a single seller (monopolist) in the market for a product or factor of production.

> ### Get it right
>
> If a trade union is the sole seller of a particular type of labour, it acts as a monopoly in that labour market. If a firm or the government is the sole buyer of labour, it is a monopsony.

In a perfectly competitive labour market, the wage rate is determined by the supply and demand in that labour market and an individual firm can employ as many workers as it chooses at this wage rate. For an individual firm, the marginal and average cost of labour are the same. However, as the only buyer of the labour, the monopsonist faces the market supply curve for labour. This also shows the average cost of labour, which is the wage rate.

Since the market supply curve for labour curve is upward sloping, the firm has to offer a higher wage rate to persuade an extra worker to offer their services. The higher wage rate must be paid to all its existing workers as well as to the extra worker employed. Therefore, the marginal cost of an extra worker will be higher than the average cost or wage, which can be seen in Table 4.4.1.

▼ Table 4.4.1: The cost of labour for a monopsonist

Wage rate ($)	Supply of workers (S_L)	Average cost of labour ($)	Total cost of labour ($)	Marginal cost of labour ($)
10	1	10	10	10
20	2	20	40	30
30	3	30	90	50
40	4	40	160	70
50	5	50	250	90

Table 4.4.1 shows that one worker would be willing to work for a wage rate of $10, but to attract a second worker, a wage rate of $20 must be paid, not just to the second worker but also to the first. This increases the average cost of labour from $10 to $20. The total cost of labour rises from $10 for one worker to $40 for two workers, giving a marginal cost of $30 for the second worker, higher than the average cost of $20. This pattern continues as the firm employs more workers. This is shown in Figure 4.4.1.

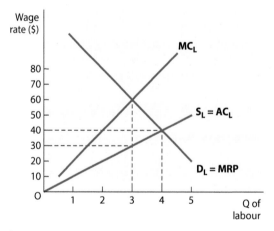

▲ Figure 4.4.1: Wage determination in a monopsonistic market

Figure 4.4.1 is drawn using the information in Table 4.4.1 and a D_L = MRP curve has been added. In a perfectly competitive labour market, the equilibrium wage rate will be $40 and 4 workers will be

Quantitative skills

As usual with marginal figures, the marginal cost of labour figures are plotted above 0.5 workers, 1.5 workers, etc.

employed. This is where the supply and demand for labour are equal ($S_L = D_L$).

A profit-maximising monopsonist will employ workers up to the point where their marginal cost (MC_L) is equal to their marginal revenue product (MRP). If the firm employs any more workers, profits will fall because MC > MRP (the extra cost is greater than the extra revenue earned). Therefore, the firm will only employ 3 workers and according to the supply curve for labour ($S_L = AC_L$), the monopsonist will only need to offer a wage rate of $30 to obtain these 3 workers.

Compared to the competitive market outcome of 4 workers employed at a wage rate of $40, a monopsonist will only employ 3 workers at $30. Both the wage rate and the employment level are lower if there is a monopsonist than if there are many small firms buying labour in that market.

Factors that affect the ability of trade unions to influence wages and employment

The ability of trade unions to influence wages and employment may be affected by a number of factors including:

- legislation
- the proportion of workers in the union
- the good or service supplied
- the profitability of the firm
- the state of the economy
- whether there is a monopsonistic employer.

Legislation
Some countries may not allow trade unions to exist or may have laws that limit their powers. For example, a trade union may have to allow its members to vote in secret about whether they want to strike before a strike can begin. This will give unions less ability to influence wages and employment. **Closed shops** may or may not be allowed. This is where all workers doing a certain job or working in a particular place must be members of a particular union. Firms will not be able to employ anyone who is not a member of this union. If a closed shop is allowed, this gives the trade union considerable monopoly power over the supply of workers in that labour market.

The proportion of workers in the union
A union is more likely to be successful in improving the pay and working conditions of its members if most of the workers in that labour market belong to the same trade union. A high **trade union density** will give the union more monopoly power, especially if it is dealing with a number of small firms that may be unable to find alternative workers. If there are several trade unions in that labour market or few workers are members, unions will have less power.

The good or service supplied

Trade unions may have more power if the product supplied is vital to the running of the country and would cause inconvenience if, for example, workers stop working overtime or go on strike. For example, a trade union trying to gain higher wages or employment for electricity workers may be more successful, at least up to a point, than a trade union representing workers making tennis balls.

The profitability of the firm

If a firm is doing well, it will be more able to afford to pay higher wages and/or increase employment. If workers obtain higher wages, the firm may be able to increase prices to help pay for this. A trade union will have less power if the firm or firms it is dealing with are making losses or only normal profits, since any increase in wages may result in firms having to cut costs, perhaps by making some of their workers unemployed. It may even cause some firms to go out of business.

The state of the economy

In a similar way, if the economy is doing well, then demand for most products is likely to be high. Firms will be more willing and able to increase wages and/or employment to take advantage of the high demand. If the economy is near full employment, it will be easier for the trade union to negotiate a higher wage with the firm.

Whether there is a monopsonist employer

Trade unions will have more power to influence wages and levels of employment when they are dealing with many firms than if they are in a bilateral monopoly situation, dealing with a monopsonist buyer of labour. For example, unions will have more bargaining power when dealing with a small firm than the government.

Activity

Find out about a trade union in your, or another, country. How many workers are members of this union and what has it achieved in the last 10 years?

Case study: The impact of a trade union

▲ Figure 4.4.2: Should workers be paid more?

The government of a small country has recently passed new laws affecting the labour market. Closed shops are now illegal, but workers are allowed to strike if 51% of those who vote are in favour of striking compared to the previous figure of 67%.

In one of the towns, shoe making has been the main industry for many years, and there are several small firms making a variety of shoes. There is no minimum wage rate for the job, but workers are usually paid around $10 an hour. A new union has just been formed to try to improve the pay and working conditions in the industry. It costs $120 a year to be a member and 55% of local shoe workers are now members of the new union. Shoe-making firms have done well in recent years, but the country's unemployment rate is now rising.

Use the information in the case study to discuss how effective the new trade union is likely to be in improving pay and working conditions for those employed in the local shoe industry.

How wages and employment are likely to be affected by trade unions in different labour markets

The effect of a trade union on wages and employment depends upon whether it is operating in:

- a perfectly competitive labour market
- a monopsony labour market.

A trade union in a perfectly competitive labour market

If there is a trade union operating in an otherwise competitive labour market, the union will control the supply of labour and there will be many firms buying/demanding labour, none of which can influence the wage rate or level of employment.

There are two main ways that a trade union can try to increase the wage rate in a particular perfectly competitive labour market. It can limit the supply of labour available to firms or negotiate that all the workers are paid a wage higher than the equilibrium wage rate.

Limiting the supply of labour

As can be seen in Figure 4.4.3, if the trade union can reduce the supply of labour in a particular market, then the supply of labour will shift to the left, from S_{L1} to S_{L2}. The excess demand at the old equilibrium wage rate of w_1 is likely to cause the wage rate to rise to w_2. At this higher wage rate there will be a contraction in demand for labour and employment will fall from q_1 to q_2.

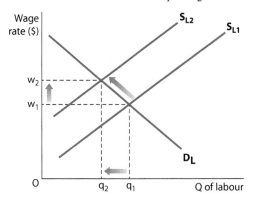

▲ Figure 4.4.3: A trade union reducing the supply of labour

The lower supply may be caused by the trade union introducing a closed shop that limits the number of people who can join the union and be able to work in that labour market. This may also make the supply of labour less elastic. Alternatively, the union may insist on workers having more qualifications or longer training which will reduce their supply. Either way, reducing the supply of workers in that labour market may be successful in increasing the wage rate but this could be at the expense of the number of workers employed.

Setting a higher minimum wage rate

A trade union may also negotiate that workers in a particular labour market are paid more than the current equilibrium wage rate.

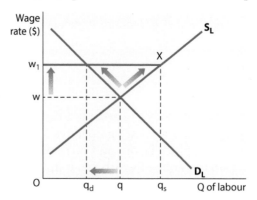

▲ Figure 4.4.4: A trade union setting a minimum wage rate

In Figure 4.4.4, the equilibrium wage rate is w where q workers are employed. If the trade union is able to achieve a minimum wage rate of w_1 in that labour market, no one will be able or willing to work for less than this. The supply curve for labour will become w_1XS_L. At w_1, the demand for labour will contract to q_d but the supply of labour will extend to q_s, resulting in employment falling to q_d and an excess supply of labour at w_1 of $q_s - q_d$. The trade union has been successful in increasing the wage rate but again at the expense of the number of workers employed.

However, in both situations where a trade union can increase the wage rate in an otherwise perfectly competitive labour market, employment may not fall if the demand for labour increases at the same time, perhaps due to higher demand for the product.

A trade union in a monopsony labour market (bilateral monopoly)

If there is a trade union operating in a labour market where there is also a monopsony, then a single seller of labour will be dealing with a single buyer of labour.

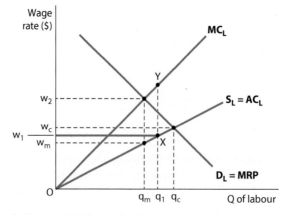

▲ Figure 4.4.5: Determination of wages and employment in a bilateral monopoly

A profit-maximising monopsonist in a perfectly competitive labour market would choose to employ q_m workers where $MC_L = MRP$ but would only need to pay w_m to obtain this number of workers. A trade union operating in this market could try to negotiate that no one is paid less than a certain wage, above that chosen by the monopsonist.

If, for example, the trade union negotiates a wage rate of w_1, the supply curve for labour will become $w_1 XS_L$. For workers up to and including q_1, $MC_L = AC_L$. However, beyond this level of employment, the supply curve of labour becomes upward sloping and the marginal cost becomes greater than the average cost of labour. To persuade more than q_1 workers to offer their services, a higher wage rate will be necessary. There is now a discontinuity in the marginal cost curve for labour of XY, so the curve becomes $w_1 XYMC_L$. This means that $MRP = MC_L$ now occurs between X and Y and the profit-maximising monopsonist will employ q_1 workers if the minimum wage rate is set at w_1.

In a bilateral monopoly, a trade union can increase both the wage rate and the level of employment. The extent to which the union is successful in raising the wage rate and employment depends on its bargaining power relative to the monopsony. However, if it negotiates a wage rate above w_c, employment will fall below the competitive level and if the wage is above w_2, employment will fall below q_m.

Summary

All labour markets are imperfect. The assumptions of a perfect labour market are not realistic and in the real world, there is always imperfect information and some labour immobility. Also, trade unions or monopsonist employers may be able to influence wage rates and employment through controlling the supply or demand for labour in particular labour markets.

In an otherwise perfectly competitive labour market, a monopsony is likely to reduce both the wage rate and employment. A trade union may negotiate a higher wage rate, but this may lead to a fall in employment. However, if MRP rises at the same time, perhaps due to higher demand for the product, employment may stay the same or possibly even rise.

In a bilateral monopoly, trade unions may be able to negotiate both a higher wage rate and employment level, even if there is no increase in MRP. In all situations, the power of the trade union or monopsonist employer will depend on a number of factors, including for example, trade union density and whether there are any other employers, perhaps in a different industry.

Progress questions

4   What are the **two** main ways that a trade union can obtain a higher wage rate?

5   In what circumstances could a trade union negotiate a higher wage rate for its members without employment falling?

6   Copy Figure 4.4.4 and then add another demand curve for labour that would result in the quantity of labour employed staying at q.

This section will develop your knowledge and understanding of:

→ conditions necessary for wage discrimination

→ the impact of gender, ethnicity and other forms of discrimination on wages, levels and types of employment.

Conditions necessary for wage discrimination

Discrimination involves treating people differently, by classifying them into different groups according to particular personal characteristics. For example, price discrimination in the product market is when a firm charges different prices to different consumers for the same product for reasons other than differences in cost. This is because some consumers are able and willing to pay a higher price than others.

Wage discrimination involves offering different pay to different groups of workers for the same or similar work for reasons other than differences in their MRP. In its extreme form, perfect wage discrimination involves paying every worker the minimum amount they are willing to accept. This relies on firms having this knowledge and on workers not being able to transfer easily to other firms. Wage discrimination may be considered unfair because employers gain at the expense of workers and some workers will be worse off through no fault of their own.

For wage discrimination to occur, the following conditions are necessary:

- The employer must have some monopsony power.
- The employer must be able to identify personal characteristics of workers and separate the workers according to these characteristics.

Monopsony power

Wage discrimination can occur if the labour market is imperfectly competitive. If the employer is the sole buyer of labour, they will have considerable power in deciding who they employ and how much pay they offer to different individuals. Workers may have no or few other sources of employment and will have to accept the wage rate offered if they wish to be employed, even if this is less than the pay offered to other workers with different personal characteristics.

Identification of different characteristics and groups

Employers must be able to identify different groups of workers according to their personal characteristics. This involves separating workers according to gender, age, social class, ethnicity or other factors. On this basis, some workers are valued more highly than others. The employer believes that the possession of a particular characteristic makes a person a better worker than one who does not have this characteristic.

Link

Discrimination in the product market was discussed in 3.6 "Price discrimination".

Key terms

Discrimination: treating people differently by classifying them into different groups according to particular characteristics.

Wage discrimination: when different groups of workers are offered different pay for the same or similar work, for reasons other than differences in their MRP.

Impact of gender, ethnicity and other discrimination on wages, levels and types of employment

When discrimination occurs, this is because the employer believes that workers with certain characteristics are better workers simply because they possess this characteristic, even though their MRP is the same as the group being discriminated against. For example, some employers may think that men are better workers than women and offer men a higher wage rate. This is negative discrimination against women. A contributing factor may be that one group of workers believes the other to be less productive and/or would prefer not to work with them. Wage discrimination is based on imperfect information and is an example of labour market failure.

The employer may also be more likely to offer promotion to certain groups of workers, adding to wage differentials between groups. The MRP for one group is undervalued, reducing demand, wages and employment for this group, whereas for the other group their MRP is overvalued, resulting in higher demand, wage rates and employment.

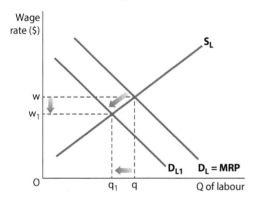

▲ Figure 4.5.1: Wage discrimination by gender

In Figure 4.5.1, D_L = MRP shows the actual MRP for both men and women, assuming all workers are equally productive. Employers who do not discriminate will employ q workers at a wage rate of w. Employers who discriminate against women will undervalue their MRP and their demand for female workers will be lower, at D_{L1}. With a lower demand for female workers, their wage rate will be lower, at w_1, and at this lower wage rate, there will be a contraction in the supply of female workers, resulting in a lower level of employment of q_1 women.

If some employers discriminate and this leads to fewer of the group discriminated against being employed in that firm or industry, this is likely to increase the supply of this group of workers to other firms and industries where such discrimination does not happen.

Figure 4.5.2 shows the knock-on effects on other labour markets of some firms discriminating between groups of workers. Without discrimination, the supply of labour will be S_L. This is made up of both/all groups of workers. If one group, for example women, is discriminated against in another labour

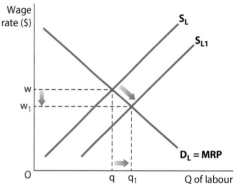

▲ Figure 4.5.2: The effects of wage discrimination on other labour markets

market and fewer women are employed there, this will increase the supply of women in other labour markets, raising the overall supply of labour there to S_{L1}. As a result, the equilibrium wage rate in this labour market will fall from w to w_1 and at this lower wage rate, there will be a higher level of employment at q_1 instead of q.

In both labour markets, there will be a lower wage rate than without any discrimination but for different reasons. In the market where discrimination takes place, demand is less than it should be for the group experiencing discrimination and as wage rates are lowered as a result, this increases the supply of these workers in other markets, which lowers the wage rate for these jobs as well.

This analysis could apply equally to any group that is discriminated against, for example those of a particular ethnicity. Workers who are undervalued may also choose not to apply for certain jobs, for example those in management, further reducing the supply of (this type of) labour. They may believe that they have less chance of obtaining these jobs. Therefore, groups that experience negative discrimination may be disproportionately represented in lower-paid jobs or even choose not to work at all. This will widen inequality and could increase the amount of welfare benefits paid by governments.

Summary of effects of wage discrimination for workers, employers and the economy

Workers who experience negative wage discrimination are likely to have lower wage rates and are less likely to be employed in firms or industries that discriminate. They are also likely to have lower wage rates but higher employment levels elsewhere. However, employment overall for this group could be lower if some individuals are then not employed at all as a result of discrimination. Workers who receive positive wage discrimination will experience the opposite effects, with higher wage rates and employment, particularly in firms and industries that discriminate.

It is irrational for employers to discriminate because they may have to pay a higher wage rate, raising the firm's costs, if the workers discriminated against go elsewhere for work, reducing the supply of labour to the firm or industry. Firms may also be paying more if they overvalue the MRP of the group they believe to be better workers.

If discrimination leads to higher costs, this could reduce profits and efficiency, harming the firm's competitiveness, both at home and abroad. Lower international competitiveness and higher welfare payments to those who are unable to find work or who are put off looking for work, could harm the economy.

However, just because one group of workers earns less on average than another does not necessarily mean that there is discrimination. For example, if a particular gender or ethnic group chooses to work more in certain lower-paid jobs, bringing down their average pay, this may not be because of discrimination in other types of work.

Case study: Management quotas for women

▲ **Figure 4.5.3**: More women in management roles

Since 2008, at least 40% of board members in public sector and large private sector companies in Norway must be women. This is in response to the low proportion of women in senior roles in large companies. For example, in 2002, only about 6% of private sector board members were women. Other countries have since set quotas of 30%.

In Norway, the current Prime Minister is female and although many women have obtained senior jobs in the public sector, only 15 of 213 public limited companies in 2017 (7%) were run by women. According to the World Economic Forum Global Gender Gap report for 2020, which looks at gender parity in four ways, including 'economic participation and opportunity', Norway was second out of 153 countries, behind Iceland. Only three countries, France, Iceland and Norway, had more than 40% female directors on companies' boards and many countries had less than 10%.

India has also made considerable progress in recent years in relation to the proportion of women on company boards. The law requires at least one woman to be on company boards although around 25% of female company board members in India are related to the owner. With women on boards, some believe there can be a wider variety of experiences and views, leading to better decision making. Malaysia has also been encouraging women at the top of industry. At the end of 2019, women made up 29.6% of board members in the top 100 companies, nearly double the 2015 figure.

Explain possible advantages and disadvantages of setting minimum quotas for management roles for women or other particular groups of workers.

This section will develop your knowledge and understanding of:
→ the effects of minimum wage controls on labour markets
→ advantages and disadvantages of a national minimum wage.

The effects of minimum wage controls on labour markets

What are minimum wage controls?

A minimum wage control or **minimum wage rate** is the lowest amount that can be paid by law for a given period of work. It sets a wage floor, and employers cannot legally pay less than this. It usually takes the form of a minimum sum of money that must be paid per hour. This may increase with age to reflect greater experience and productivity. It works in a similar way to a minimum price for a good but in this case, the product being bought and sold is labour, with the wage rate being the price of labour.

Many countries have a minimum wage rate (a **national minimum wage rate**) and some cities or regions may have a higher rate if these areas have a higher cost of living. In November 2020, Geneva, in Switzerland, introduced the highest minimum wage rate in the world of 23 Swiss francs an hour, equivalent to $25.

Minimum wage rates are usually set at a level that will enable workers to be able to afford to live in that city or country. This will take account of the cost of living, the level of inequality and views about fairness. In some countries, where there may be no, or a very low, minimum wage, groups such as Fairtrade encourage employers to pay a "living wage" to agricultural workers to enable them to have a reasonable standard of living.

Effects in a competitive labour market

If the labour market is competitive, or even perfectly competitive, with large numbers of buyers and sellers of a particular type of labour, the effects will be the same as if a trade union negotiates a minimum wage in this market.

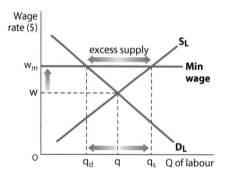

▲ Figure 4.6.1: A minimum wage in a competitive labour market

As with any minimum price, it only directly affects the wage rate if the equilibrium wage rate for this type of work is less than the minimum wage rate. In Figure 4.6.1, the equilibrium wage rate is w where q workers are employed. A higher (minimum) wage rate, w_m, encourages more workers to offer their services in this market causing an extension in supply to q_s. However, at a higher wage rate, there will be a contraction in the demand for labour to q_d. Other things being equal, employment will fall from q to q_d and there will be unemployment in this market of $q_d q_s$ because this is the excess supply of labour at w_m.

In a competitive labour market, a higher minimum wage will cause an increase in pay of those who continue to be employed but some workers may lose their jobs. The fall in unemployment depends on the price elasticity of demand for labour in this market. The more elastic the demand for labour, the greater the fall in employment. Similarly, the extent of the unemployment will also depend on the price elasticity of supply for labour. The more elastic the supply and demand for labour, the greater the excess supply of labour, and hence unemployment, at the new higher wage rate.

However, a higher wage rate may act as an incentive for workers to increase their productivity and reduce absenteeism. They may be more motivated to work hard and they may also be worried about losing their jobs. This could increase their MRP and the demand for labour. If demand for labour increases, it could reduce the number made unemployed. It could maintain or even increase employment, depending on the extent of the increase in demand for labour.

Introducing a minimum wage rate may encourage some employers to invest in more training for their workers, given that they will have to pay them a higher wage rate. This could also increase the demand for labour.

Although labour markets are not perfectly competitive, many real-world labour markets are very competitive and a higher wage rate could cause some unemployment. However, this also depends on the level of the minimum wage rate. The higher it is above the current equilibrium, the greater the effects are likely to be.

Effects in a monopsonistic labour market

If there is a monopsony employer in the labour market, with one large buyer but many sellers of a particular type of labour, the effects are again likely to be the same as if a trade union forces up the minimum wage in this type of labour market.

Activity

Draw two diagrams, one with elastic supply and demand for labour and another where supply and demand for labour are inelastic, to compare what happens to employment and the excess supply of labour if a minimum wage rate is set above the equilibrium.

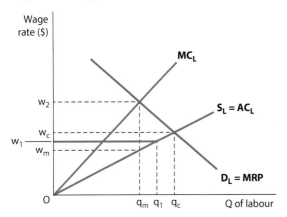

▲ Figure 4.6.2: A minimum wage in a monopsonistic labour market

In Figure 4.6.2, a monopsonist would choose to employ q_m workers but will only need to offer a wage rate of w_m to attract this number of workers. If the national minimum wage rate is higher than w_m, for example at w_1, then the wage rate paid in this labour market must rise to at least this new higher level. Unlike in a perfectly competitive labour market, a higher wage rate can increase employment, in this case to q_1, so a national minimum wage can increase both the wage rate and the employment in an imperfectly competitive market. However, if the minimum wage is set above w_2, then employment may fall. Again, this assumes that other things stay the same, for example that there is no change in productivity.

Advantages and disadvantages of a national minimum wage

Advantages

A national minimum wage will raise the pay per hour of those who receive the lowest wage rates. This should increase the income of these low-paid workers, assuming their hours worked stay the same. A minimum wage will increase the standard of living of those who benefit and help to reduce inequality. By setting a legal minimum, it can help to stop exploitation and may be considered fairer, especially in monopsonistic labour markets, where workers can be paid less than their MRP.

According to the **efficiency wage theory**, higher wages can lead to higher labour productivity because workers feel more motivated and this increases the efficiency of the economy. Workers feel more valued and/or they may be more concerned that they could lose their job and need to raise their MRP.

Similarly, if firms have to pay higher wages, it may be more worthwhile investing in training to raise workers' MRP. The higher wage rate will also encourage more workers into the labour market, particularly if there is now a greater gap between the income they would receive in and out of work.

If those who were earning below the minimum wage receive an increase in pay, this could also lead to an increase in pay for those who previously received the minimum wage rate or just above this wage rate, to maintain the wage differentials. When those on low incomes receive more pay, they are likely to spend most of the increase (because they have a high marginal propensity to consume), which will help to increase aggregate demand and also the demand for labour. This may help to offset any fall in demand for labour due to the introduction of a minimum wage rate.

Disadvantages

A national minimum wage rate will add to the costs of firms if they have to pay more to their employees. Some firms may find it difficult to pay the higher wages. They may reduce their demand for labour, which will cause some workers to lose their jobs, especially in competitive labour markets. Some firms may even employ people illegally at less than the minimum wage rate.

> **Key term**
>
> **Efficiency wage theory**: the idea that higher wages can lead to higher labour productivity because workers feel more motivated, increasing the efficiency of the economy.

> **Link**
>
> The marginal propensity to consume (MPC) was explained in 7.3 "Determinants of aggregate demand" in the AS book.

It is likely that some groups will be worse affected than others, such as the young and unskilled who are more likely to be low paid. Also, if there is a single national wage rate, it may not improve the living standards of those on low incomes living in more expensive areas because they are already paid above the minimum wage.

Firms may pass on the higher wage costs in the form of higher prices. This will be inflationary and reduce the real incomes of workers. This will be worse for those people on low incomes, for example the unemployed or pensioners, who do not benefit from higher pay but now have to pay higher prices. Higher prices will also affect firms' international competitiveness if rates of pay are lower in other countries, enabling firms there to charge lower prices.

Summary of effects of minimum wage controls for workers, employers and the economy

Free-market economists are in favour of leaving price and wage determination to market forces and believe that the disadvantages of the government intervening to set a (national) minimum wage are greater than the advantages. Evidence about whether a minimum wage rate causes unemployment varies from country to country, but experience suggests that the effects on unemployment are limited.

Many people support a minimum wage to prevent 'poverty pay' and exploitation and to ensure that workers can afford a reasonable standard of living. Most countries have minimum wage rates, but they may vary between different states and cities.

The effects of setting a minimum wage rate depend on the rate at which it is set and how well it is enforced. Clearly, the higher the minimum wage rate, the greater its effects are likely to be. However, the effects on the demand and supply of labour depend on the price elasticities of demand and supply and the state of the economy at that time. When an economy is growing, introducing a national minimum wage may be accompanied by falling unemployment because the demand for labour is rising. The effects also depend on whether most workers are employed by firms in competitive labour markets or by monopsonist employers.

Some firms will find it easier than others to pay more to their workers and if unemployment and/or higher prices result, this could damage the economy. Larger firms may be able to absorb the increase in costs, accept lower profits or increase prices. However, if a minimum wage rate leads to an increase in productivity, labour costs may change little and the advantages could outweigh the disadvantages.

Progress questions

1 Is a minimum wage rate a price floor or a price ceiling?

2 Give **two** reasons why MRP may increase after a minimum wage has been introduced.

3 Why might the introduction of a minimum wage rate worsen the international competitiveness of firms?

Case study: Minimum wage rates in Thailand

▲ **Figure 4.6.3**: Phuket – the highest minimum wage rate in Thailand

Thailand introduced a minimum wage in 1972. This was changed to become a national minimum wage rate of 300 baht a day in 2013. In 2017, its basis was changed again, so it could reflect certain economic indicators in the different regions of Thailand, such as the cost of living. Rates in different parts of Thailand in 2020 varied from 308 baht to 330 baht a day.

For most types of work, the daily rate is based on 8 hours work, with a 48-hour working week. The Thai government has also designated some jobs which could affect a worker's health or safety as only requiring a 7-hour working day (and a 42-hour working week).

The government has also classified some other more skilled jobs as worth a higher minimum wage rate, for example HVAC (heating, ventilation and air-conditioning) technicians. The minimum wage rate per day for these workers ranges from 370 to 600 baht per day.

1   How many days a week are people in Thailand generally assumed to work?

2   In 2020, what was the lowest minimum wage rate per hour in Thailand?

3   Why might the Thai government have increased the minimum wage rate between 2013 and 2020?

4   What are the advantages and disadvantages of having different minimum wage rates in different regions of a country?

5   Why may the Thai government have set a higher minimum wage rate for certain skilled jobs?

Exam-style questions

1   Which one of the following influences the demand for labour?

   A   Job satisfaction

   B   Marginal revenue product

   C   Promotion prospects

   D   Working conditions   (1 mark)

2   A perfectly competitive labour market must have

   A   a single buyer of labour.

   B   differentiated workers.

   C   immobility of labour.

   D   perfect information.   (1 mark)

3   The diagram below shows a profit-maximising monopsony employer operating in an otherwise competitive labour market.

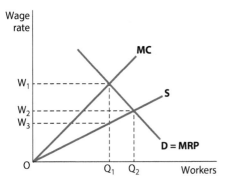

How many workers will the firm employ and at what wage rate?

	Quantity of workers	Wage rate
A	Q_1	W_1
B	Q_1	W_2
C	Q_1	W_3
D	Q_2	W_2

(1 mark)

4   The table below shows the national minimum wage for six countries in 2020.

Country	Minimum wage ($ per hour)
A	20.00
B	18.50
C	8.00
D	13.10
E	10.00
F	12.00

You are advised to show your working for the calculations below.

(i) Calculate the median national minimum wage for the six countries in 2020.   (3 marks)

(ii) Calculate the mean national minimum wage for the six countries in 2020.   (3 marks)

(iii) Explain, using a diagram, how the number of workers employed in a perfectly competitive firm is determined.   (4 marks)

5   Explain the advantages and disadvantages to firms of a government introducing a national minimum wage.   (12 marks)

6   Should governments make all types of wage discrimination illegal? Justify your answer.   (25 marks)

Note: To answer this question as a data response question, use the data provided in the case study "Management quotas for women" in 4.5 "Discrimination in the labour market" to support your answer.

5 Poverty and inequality

The economics of business behaviour and the distribution of income

Factors that affect the distribution of income

Income is a flow of money received by an economic agent over a period of time, and the distribution of income relates to how it is divided between people or regions. Income can be earned from work or it may be unearned income such as interest on savings or welfare benefits. The distribution of income within an economy will be unequal because there will be differences between individuals in terms of how much they receive from the different sources of income.

Factors affecting the distribution of income include:

- income from work
- access to health and education
- entitlement to pensions
- the distribution of wealth
- age
- government policy.

Income from work

The most important determinant of differences in income is usually differences in income from work. Much depends on the demand and supply for each type of labour, which can lead to large differences in pay, as discussed in Chapter 4. Some people work and others do not, perhaps because they are ill or too old. People who claim unemployment-related benefits are likely to receive a lower income than those in work. People may be in full-time or part-time work. They could earn the minimum wage, if there is one, or earn millions of dollars a year. Wage discrimination can also affect the distribution of income.

Access to health and education

Those who are able to access more and/or better education and health care are likely to have higher incomes than those who cannot. Good education and health can increase an individual's marginal revenue product, and hence their ability to earn higher incomes.

Entitlement to pensions

There are two main types of pension: occupational pensions result from someone's job; and the state may pay a pension after someone reaches a certain age. Occupational pension schemes usually involve

> **Link**
>
> The difference between income and wealth and how an inequitable distribution of income and wealth leads to market failure, were explained in 5.6 "An inequitable distribution of income and wealth" in the AS book.

both the employer and employee contributing a percentage of the person's pay, which the individual can use as an income after they reach a particular age. Those on higher pay will inevitably have a higher occupational pension, other things being equal.

State pensions in different countries vary greatly. Retired workers in Croatia receive 129% of the working wage but many middle-income and developing countries can only afford a minimal amount. Also, some people, including those who work in the informal sector, may not be entitled to a pension.

The distribution of wealth

The distribution of wealth affects the distribution of income because many assets generate an income. The wealth distribution is often very unequal, contributing to the unequal income distribution. For example, someone who owns a number of properties will earn rent. A person with shares in a business will receive dividends. This unearned income will add to the income of some people but not others.

Age

A country's income distribution is partly affected by its age distribution. Young people usually have few sources of income, and when they start work, their income is relatively low. Near the end of their working lives, they may be in more senior positions, with a higher income. After retiring, individuals may have a low income again, depending on the amount of their pensions and savings.

Government policy

The extent to which a government offers welfare benefits will affect the distribution of income. It also depends on the tax structure of the country – what is taxed and the rates of tax.

Factors that affect the distribution of wealth

Wealth is a stock of assets owned by an economic agent at a point in time, and the distribution of wealth relates to how it is divided between people or regions. Wealth may or may not generate income. It includes physical wealth such as works of art and property (including the house you live in), financial wealth such as savings and shares and private pension wealth. The distribution of wealth within an economy is likely to be unequal, and probably more unequal than the distribution of income, because there will be differences in the amount of assets individuals own.

Factors affecting the distribution of wealth include:

- inheritance
- success in business
- pension wealth
- housing
- the distribution of income
- age
- government policy.

Link

Policies that influence the distribution of income and wealth are explained in 5.2 "Government policies to alleviate poverty and to influence the distribution of income and wealth".

Inheritance

The most important determinant of differences in wealth is usually inheritance. Some people are left large quantities of wealth while many receive nothing from their family and friends.

Success in business

Some people have become wealthy if they have set up a business that has become successful. If they still own a significant part of the business, this can be a valuable asset and contributes to the inequality of wealth.

Pension wealth

In many countries, some people will be able to accumulate a sum of money in a pension scheme. This counts as part of their wealth and enables them to receive an income from this when they retire. This is a significant part of many people's total wealth, but others have no pension wealth.

Housing

For many people, the value of their home is their main asset, or at least the difference between its value and the amount of any mortgage they still have on the house. If house prices rise significantly, this will widen the wealth gap between those who own a house and those who do not. This gap will be even greater if some people own more than one property.

The distribution of income

The distribution of income affects the distribution of wealth because those with more income can afford to save or to buy more assets, adding to their wealth. Since the distribution of income is unequal, this contributes to the unequal distribution of wealth.

Age

As with income, young people usually have few sources of wealth and many will achieve their greatest wealth near the end of their working lives, particularly if they are saving for their old age. After retiring, their income is likely to be lower and they may start to reduce their wealth, especially if they have to pay for health care or residential care.

Government policy

In a similar way to income, what the government does or does not do to reduce inequalities in wealth will affect its distribution. For example, some countries such as Argentina and Switzerland have taxes on wealth, but most do not. Rates of income tax also vary between countries which will affect people's ability to save.

The Lorenz curve and Gini coefficient

The Lorenz curve and the Gini coefficient are two related measures used to show the inequality of income and wealth.

Progress questions

1   Identify **one** factor that influences both the distribution of income and the distribution of wealth.

2   Explain **one** other factor that influences the distribution of income.

3   How does the distribution of income affect the distribution of wealth?

Lorenz curves

The **Lorenz curve** is a graph showing the cumulative distribution of national income or wealth for a given percentage of the population.

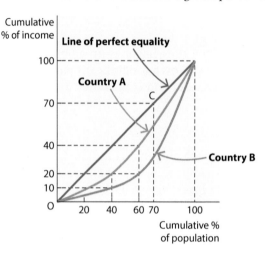

▲ Figure 5.1.1: Lorenz curves

Figure 5.1.1 shows the distribution of income for two countries, Country X and Country Y. The line of (perfect) equality shows what happens if the income is distributed equally. For example, at point C, 70% of the population have 70% of the income. This is very unlikely and so the Lorenz curve shows the extent of the inequality.

The graph shows the cumulative amount received or owned by the poorest x% of the population. For example, looking at the curve for Country A, the poorest 40% of the population have 20% of the income and the poorest 60% have 40% of the income. In Country B, the poorest 40% only have 10% of the income and the poorest 60% have 20% of the income. The further the Lorenz curve is away from the line of perfect equality, the greater the inequality of income or wealth. For all curves, 0% of the population have 0% of the income or wealth and 100% of the population have 100% of the income or wealth.

The Gini coefficient

The **Gini coefficient** (sometimes known as the Gini index or Gini ratio) is a numerical measure of the extent of a country's inequality of income or wealth. Its value ranges from 0 to 1, although it may also be quoted as a percentage.

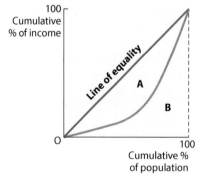

▲ Figure 5.1.2: A Lorenz curve and the Gini coefficient

The Gini coefficient $= \dfrac{\text{Area A}}{\text{Area A + Area B}}$

where Area A is the area between the Lorenz curve and the line of equality and Area B is the area under/beyond the Lorenz curve. The Gini coefficient therefore measures the area between the Lorenz curve and the line of perfect equality as a proportion or percentage of the total area under this line.

The further the Lorenz curve is from the line of equality, the greater the inequality and the higher the value of the Gini coefficient. If the income or wealth is equally distributed, there is no Area A, giving a Gini coefficient of 0 (or 0%) and if one person has all the income and wealth, the Gini coefficient is 1 (or 100%).

Relative and absolute poverty

Poverty is the state of being very poor. This involves having little or no money or means of support. The individual or community is not able to achieve a minimum standard of living. There are two types of poverty, absolute poverty and relative poverty.

Absolute poverty refers to a person not having enough money to satisfy their basic needs. According to the United Nations, an international organisation that aims to maintain peace and security, absolute poverty is: "a condition characterised by severe deprivation of basic human needs, including food, safe drinking water, sanitation

Case study: The Gini coefficient

▲ Figure 5.1.3: Inequality in the Americas

▼ Table 5.1.1: Gini indices and income per head for selected countries in the Americas

Country	Gini index	GNI per capita (US$)
Argentina	41.4	11,200
Brazil	53.9	9,130
Canada	33.3	46,370
El Salvador	38.6	4,000
Honduras	52.1	2,390
Mexico	45.4	9,430
United States	41.1	65,760

Source: The World Bank, Gini index (World Bank estimate), GNI per capita, Atlas method (current US$). Under CC-BY 4.0.

Table 5.1.1 shows the most recent estimates of the Gini index/coefficient for income and income per head for selected countries in the Americas, according to the World Bank. All Gini index figures are for 2018, except Canada (2017) and the United States (2016). All Gross National Income (GNI) per capita figures are for 2019.

1 According to its Gini index, if drawn on a diagram, which country's Lorenz curve would be closest to the line of equality?

2 Which country has the most unequal distribution of income?

3 Does there appear to be any relationship between the inequality of income, as measured by the Gini index, and the income per head of a country?

Activity

Find out the most recent figure for the Gini coefficient in your country. How has it changed over the last 20 years?

Key terms

Poverty line: the minimum level required to not be living in absolute or relative poverty.

Relative poverty: where an individual or household has less than a certain percentage of the average income in their country.

Key term

Unemployment trap: where people may be worse off, or little better off, in work than unemployed.

facilities, health, shelter, education and information. It depends not only on income but also on access to services".

The amount of money required to avoid being in absolute poverty can be calculated in terms of the cost of these "basic human needs" in a given country at a point in time. In 2015, the World Bank set this at $1.90, using PPP (purchasing power parity) exchange rates, which take account of how much money can buy in different countries. This gives a rough idea of the **poverty line**, which is the term given to the minimum level required to not be living in poverty. According to this definition, 8% of the world's population were estimated to be living in absolute poverty in 2020, but this is a third of the number who were in absolute poverty in 1990.

Relative poverty compares the standard of living of an individual or household to a measure of the average for that society at that time. For example, a person or household may be considered to be living in relative poverty if they have less than 50% (or maybe 60%) of the median income. As incomes rise in an economy, so will the relative poverty line.

Causes and effects of poverty

Poverty, whether absolute or relative, can be caused by a number of factors:

- age
- health and education
- unemployment
- low pay.

Age

Many children or old people may be living in poverty because they have no or very little income or wealth. This will make them relatively poor, and in some situations, they may be living in absolute poverty. This partly depends on the extent of any benefits paid by the government. Where there is war or conflict in a country, more people will be affected. If they become homeless, they may be in absolute poverty.

Health and education

In many countries, there is little state education or health care and those with no or low incomes may suffer ill health. The jobs they are able to do, if any, are likely to pay very low wages.

Unemployment

Those without jobs may also have very limited money or means of support. They may or may not be entitled to some unemployment-related benefits, causing many to be below the poverty line. In some countries, some people may be caught in the **unemployment trap**. This is where someone is worse off, or little better off, in work than unemployed due to the benefits they would receive if out of work. The incentive to find work is therefore low. This may apply particularly to unskilled workers who would receive low pay.

Low pay

People in work can also be in relative poverty. The country may not have a minimum wage and/or even if a person works full time, their pay may be less than the required percentage of the average income, leaving them below the country's relative poverty line. In some countries, people may be caught in the **poverty trap**, where it is difficult to escape poverty in that economic system. They may lack the skills, education, health or capital to obtain better-paid jobs.

They may be caught in a cycle of poverty, having grown up in a poor family and with their children also likely to be poor. The poverty trap may also be defined as a situation where if someone earns a higher income, they could be little better off, or even worse off, than before. This is because they are no longer entitled to certain income-related benefits and/or are paying more tax.

Effects of a more equal or more unequal distribution of income and wealth

People will disagree on whether a particular distribution of income and wealth should be made more equal or more unequal. This may depend partly on how much income and wealth they have but also on what they think is equitable (fair). There needs to be a balance between equity and efficiency. It may be argued that higher economic growth can be achieved with either a more or a less equal distribution of income and wealth.

If the distribution of a set amount of income or wealth becomes more or less equal, it could lead to a number of benefits and costs for individuals and the economy. The extent of the effects will depend on the degree of inequality, how much the distributions change and a number of other factors, including the state of the economy at that time.

Two important influences on individuals and the economy, affected by the distribution of income and wealth, are:

* aggregate demand
* incentives.

Aggregate demand

People with lower incomes have a higher marginal and average propensity to consume than those with higher incomes. Therefore, a redistribution of income and wealth so that the poor have more, is likely to increase aggregate demand, as the poor spend most of the extra income they receive. This should increase output and the demand for labour, resulting in upward multiplier effects. Supporters of a more equal distribution of income and wealth argue that it leads to higher economic growth.

However, this depends on factors such as consumer confidence and the state of the economy. If there is already full employment, a more equal distribution of income and wealth may cause higher inflation. Similarly, a less equal distribution of income and wealth could reduce aggregate demand, as the rich are more likely to save additional income.

> **Key term**
>
> **Poverty trap**: where it is difficult to escape poverty.

> **Link**
>
> The propensity to consume was introduced in 7.3 "Determinants of aggregate demand" in the AS book.

Incentives

Many people argue that some inequality in income and wealth is necessary to provide incentives, for example to work, save and invest. If everyone receives the same income, why would anyone choose to work? The prospect of receiving a higher income or having more wealth may encourage people to spend more time in education and to acquire the skills and qualifications that might enable them to obtain a more highly paid job. Supporters of a less equal distribution of income and wealth argue that the increased incentives this provides lead to higher economic growth.

Similarly, the prospect of higher income or wealth may encourage people to save and to put their money into businesses, hoping that they will be successful. This could lead to a **trickle-down effect**, where increasing incomes and wealth for the rich can lead to higher economic growth and the creation of jobs and higher incomes for many more people in society, as the effects work through the economy. For example, the successful business owner may now be able to afford to employ a gardener and a cleaner.

A less equal distribution of income could also generate more revenue from taxing income and capital that can then be used to help deal with some of the problems of inequality. However, taxes should not be set too high so that they create disincentive effects.

Too much inequality or increasing inequalities of income and wealth may be seen as unfair by many. It may lead to the creation of an underclass who feel left behind by the rest of society. Inequality of income and wealth can also lead to inequality of opportunity. The poor may not have access to decent education or health care and may have less chance of becoming better off. Those living in poverty may feel there is no incentive to make the most of their abilities, resulting in inefficiency. This can affect whole communities, for example if the major industry in the area shuts down, causing social and health problems, including lower life expectancy.

Summary

The distribution of income and wealth in a market economy is inevitably unequal, and the distribution of wealth is usually more unequal than the distribution of income. There are many reasons for these inequalities, including different incomes from employment and inheritance. Too much inequality is both a cause and a consequence of market failure, affecting both equity and efficiency in an economy. Those with little income or wealth will live in relative poverty, or possibly even in absolute poverty, if they are unable to satisfy their basic needs.

However, value judgements influence people's views of what is an equitable distribution of income and wealth. This also influences their views on what, if anything, should be done to make the distribution of income or wealth more or less equal.

Key term

Trickle-down effect: where increasing incomes and wealth for the rich leads to the creation of jobs and higher incomes for others.

Progress questions

4   Explain the difference between absolute and relative poverty, including how they can be measured.

5   Identify **two** groups of people who may be poor and explain why.

6   Explain why people may disagree about whether the current distribution of a country's income or wealth should be more or less equal.

This section will develop your knowledge and understanding of:

→ policies that can be used to influence the distribution of income and wealth and to alleviate poverty

→ consequences of such policies.

Policies to reduce poverty and influence income and wealth distributions

Policies that can be used to reduce poverty and to influence the distribution of income and wealth include the use of:

- welfare benefits
- state provision
- taxation
- wage and price controls.

Welfare benefits

Welfare benefits can be universal or means-tested and may be given in cash or in kind. A **universal benefit** is given to everyone who fits into a particular category. For example, child benefit is paid to all families in Finland with children up to the age of 17. One advantage of a universal benefit is that it does not have to be claimed, so no one loses out. If benefits have to be claimed, some people may not know they exist or may not understand what they need to do to obtain the benefit. Universal benefits are also paid to those on high incomes, who may not need the extra money. However, the money paid represents a larger percentage increase for those on low incomes, narrowing the relative gap between rich and poor.

Means-tested benefits are those where entitlement to a payment depends on a person's income and/or wealth, and on their needs. In Italy, child benefit is means-tested, with those on the lowest incomes receiving the most money, but if families with children have more than a certain income, they are not entitled to any child benefit. Another means-tested benefit available in many countries is housing benefit, which helps people on low incomes pay their rent. Benefits may or may not be included in taxable income.

Means-tested benefits can be given to those who need them most, but they have to be claimed and only those who claim them receive the benefit. Also, as they change according to income, people may be caught in the poverty trap, where when their income rises, they may be worse off if they no longer qualify for a particular benefit.

Benefits paid in cash are generally more effective than taxation in reducing inequality. Whether universal or means-tested, if benefits are paid in cash, they can be used by the individual for whatever their priority is at that time, for example to buy food. However, cash benefits may also be spent on other less important items.

Link

Factors affecting poverty and the distributions of income and wealth, and the effects of a more or less unequal distribution were explained in 5.1 "The distribution of income and wealth within an economy".

Key term

Universal benefit: provided for everyone who fits into a particular category.

Link

Welfare benefits were introduced in 5.7 "Government intervention in markets" in the AS book.

Activity

Find out about some of the welfare benefits available in your country. Which benefits are universal and which are means-tested?

Alternatively, a government may provide some **benefits in kind**, which do not take the form of money, for example free school meals for those on low incomes. These benefits are used for a set purpose, for example to obtain a school meal, and are likely to be more effective in targeting the problem, in this case adequate food for children. However, again they will need to be claimed and some who need this benefit will miss out for a variety of reasons.

State provision

As well as paying for benefits, the government may also pay for other goods and services to try to reduce the impact of poverty and the inequalities of income and wealth. In many countries, the state provides at least a basic level of education and health care, often considered to be merit goods. This is partly because of the positive externalities, since we all benefit from a healthy, well-educated population. However, this is also to provide a more equal opportunity for everyone, regardless of income and wealth, to be able to enjoy good health and to obtain employment.

Free or subsidised health care or education makes a greater relative difference to someone on a low income, helping to narrow the gap between rich and poor. If an individual has an income of $10,000 but receives health benefits of $5,000, their total income, including this benefit, rises to $15,000. A similar benefit for someone with an income of $100,000 increases their income to $105,000. Before adding the benefit, the person on the higher income had ten times the income of the poorer person but including the benefit, their income is now only seven times the amount. State provision of services such as health care may also be classed as a benefit in kind.

Without state funding, many poorer children would not be able to access education and be unable to obtain the qualifications and skills they need to earn a reasonable wage. Poor health will also affect their ability to work productively. However, if free or subsidised education and health care are provided for everyone, rich and poor, this can be very expensive.

Taxation

So far, the main focus of reducing poverty and influencing the distributions of income and wealth has been on narrowing the gap by giving more money and other support to those with less income and wealth. Another approach is to reduce the gap by taking more money away from those with higher incomes and wealth through taxing them more.

Most countries have a progressive income tax, with the tax rate increasing with income. However, the number of tax bands and the rates of tax vary considerably. For example, in 2020, Austria had a top rate of 55% for income over €1 million and five other rates, starting at 25% for income between €11,000 and €18,000. Individuals with annual incomes below €11,000 pay no income tax. In China, income tax rates range from 3% to 45%. As incomes increase, a progressive tax system takes both a larger sum of money and a greater percentage of income in tax, reducing the gap between rich and poor in both absolute (as a sum of money) and relative terms.

Some countries also have an annual wealth tax, but these rates tend to be lower and less progressive. For example, the highest rate of wealth tax in Switzerland is 0.94%. It is more difficult to tax wealth on a regular basis, since it requires a frequent valuation of assets and some people may have large amounts of wealth, such as an expensive house, but limited income to pay the tax. It may also discourage entrepreneurs from setting up businesses in that country. However, there are usually much higher rates of tax on assets left at death in most countries. This helps to reduce inequality by cutting the amount passed on through inheritance, an important cause of inequalities in the distribution of wealth.

Reduced taxation may be used instead of benefits in some countries to reduce poverty and to influence the distribution of income and wealth. For example, in Poland, **tax credits** are given according to the number of children in the family. This reduces the amount of income tax paid and increases families' disposable income.

Wage and price controls
As previously discussed, a minimum wage rate could be introduced, either for a specific region or for the country as a whole to make sure that everyone in work is paid at least a certain amount per hour or day that they work. This increases the income of those on the lowest pay and may help to reduce both poverty and the relative gap in incomes between rich and poor, as long as unemployment does not rise too much.

Some countries have considered setting a maximum wage, which could involve workers receiving no more than a set sum of money. For example, Cuba put a limit on pay of US$20 a month. There has also been discussion in other countries about whether in a particular business, the highest-paid worker should receive no more than, say, 20 times the pay of the lowest-paid worker in that firm, but this has not been made law anywhere yet.

Some countries may also use price controls such as a maximum price on a few essential products. For example, there may be a maximum price on essential foods or a maximum rent on housing, as a further support for those on low incomes. Price controls, however, distort the workings of the free market, may lead to shortages and, like any control, need to be enforced.

Consequences of policies
Different policies aimed at influencing the distributions of income and wealth may have varying success and could result in other less desirable or unintended consequences. The following effects must be considered:

- incentives
- equity.

Incentives
The impact on incentives, for example to work, save or invest, must be considered for all those affected. High income tax rates may lead to people reducing their hours worked, including whether they are

---

Key term
Tax credit: an amount that can be taken off income to reduce the amount of tax owed.

Link
The effects of minimum wage rates were discussed in 4.6 "Minimum wage laws". Price controls were explained in 5.7 "Government intervention in markets" in the AS book.

Progress questions
1 What is the difference between universal and means-tested benefits?
2 How does a progressive income tax help to reduce income inequality?

willing to work overtime, or even seek promotion to a more highly paid job. Narrower wage differentials can affect both the geographical and occupational mobility of labour, which affect resource allocation.

If benefits are too high, some people may be caught in the unemployment trap, when they may be better off out of work than in work. If there is no or little incentive for those on low incomes to work, output is less than it could be and government expenditure is higher. Also, if people are out of work for a long time, this could lead to other problems, including reducing their chances of finding work in future as they become dependent on welfare benefits.

Similarly, if income tax rates are too progressive, this may reduce incentives for those with high incomes. If there are high taxes on unearned income such as from savings, or on assets when someone dies, this may reduce the incentive to save.

High tax rates, whether on income or capital, may reduce the incentive to develop a business. Some successful business people may even leave the country, resulting in a "**brain drain**". Alternatively, they may find other ways of reducing the amount of tax they pay. **Tax avoidance** is when people try to minimise the tax they pay by using loopholes in the law, whereas **tax evasion** is when people do not declare all their income or assets. Tax avoidance is legal, but tax evasion is illegal. In all these cases, as well as possibly losing out on output and income for the economy, less tax is paid than could be expected.

Equity

With no government intervention, inequality in a market economy is likely to be substantial. Policies need to be as equitable/fair as possible, although people will disagree in terms of what they think is "fair". Views will vary about how much more a person who works hard should receive, compared with someone who contributes less to the economy. Most people think that there should be some redistribution of income and/or wealth but may believe, for example, that either too much or too little is being done or that the wrong mix of policies is being used. This could affect how they respond in terms of their attitude to work, saving and enterprise, which in turn could affect economic growth and international competitiveness.

Summary

Inequality is usually measured in relative terms and there are various policies that can be used to influence the distribution of income and wealth and to alleviate poverty. They may involve increasing the income or assets of those with little or reducing them for those who have more, narrowing the gap between the two groups. The gap may be reduced both in absolute terms, as a sum of money, and in relative terms.

It may be possible to aim to reduce or alleviate absolute poverty, where people cannot afford the basic needs, but because relative poverty is linked to the average income for that society at that time, there will probably always be people living in relative poverty. However, some people living in relative poverty in one country may

Key terms

Brain drain: when highly educated and skilled people leave the country.

Tax avoidance: using legal methods to minimise the amount of tax paid by an individual or business.

Tax evasion: illegally not paying the full amount of tax.

Activity

The American supply-side economist, Arthur Laffer, developed a theory about the relationship between tax rates and government revenue. Find out about the Laffer Curve.

have a higher standard of living than some who are not living in relative poverty in another country.

Free-market economists would argue for minimal intervention, to increase incentives and enable everyone to become better off through economic growth. However, there will always be some groups of people who need extra support, for example people with disabilities or older people. Each policy has advantages and disadvantages but to be most effective, it is probably best to use a combination of policies to address the different causes of inequality. Also, revenue gained from tax can be used to pay for the different benefits or state provision of goods and services. It should be recognised that there are moral and political perspectives involved when considering what and how much should be done to redistribute income and wealth and to alleviate poverty.

Progress questions

3   Can both absolute and relative poverty be eliminated?

4   Explain the disadvantages of **two** different policies which may be used to reduce inequalities of income and wealth.

Case study: Negative income tax

▲ **Figure 5.2.1**: New Jersey – the first negative income tax experiment

A negative income tax system involves people paying tax if their income is above a certain level or receiving a payment from the government if it is below this amount. This guarantees that everyone receives at least a minimum amount of income.

The key issues to decide are the cut-off point and the rate of negative income tax. For example, if $20,000 is the cut-off level of income used (the income at which income tax would start to be paid), and the negative income tax rate is 50%, then a person with an income of $12,000 would receive $4,000 from the government (50% of the $8,000 difference). This would give them a total income of $16,000. Above the cut-off point of $20,000, the rate of income tax paid may be the same or different from the rate of negative income tax but would probably be a fixed rate rather than being progressive.

The idea of a negative income tax, instead of people receiving a range of different benefits, is often associated with the American economist Milton Friedman. He promoted the idea in the 1960s as a way of reducing poverty. Between 1968 and 1982, there were five small-scale experiments using a negative income tax in the United States and Canada. Similar schemes have been suggested since but there are some disadvantages of a negative income tax system.

1   Using the numerical example in the case study, how much would someone who has no other income receive from the government?

2   What are the possible disadvantages of using a negative income tax system?

Exam-style questions

1 Which one of the following is a true statement about relative poverty?

Relative poverty

   A   applies to people who have incomes of less than $1.90 a day.

   B   includes everyone without a job.

   C   involves a set percentage of the population.

   D   is judged against the average income of the population.   (1 mark)

2 Which one of the following is shown by a Lorenz curve?

   A   The average percentage of income paid in tax

   B   The distribution of income

   C   The income per head of the population

   D   The total income of an economy   (1 mark)

3 Which one of the following combinations of characteristics applies to means-tested and universal benefits?

	Means-tested benefits	Universal benefits
A	Focuses on those most in need	Paid to all in a particular category
B	Paid in cash, not paid in kind	Should reduce relative poverty
C	Paid to both rich and poor	Does not need to be claimed
D	Some people may miss out	Paid to everyone in the population

(1 mark)

4 [i] Define "income".   (2 marks)

   [ii] Explain, using a diagram, how the Gini coefficient is calculated.   (4 marks)

5 The table below shows the minimum wage per hour and annual GDP per capita for five countries in 2020.

Country	Minimum wage ($ per hour)	Annual GDP per capita ($)
A	20.00	55,000
B	18.50	60,000
C	8.00	10,000
D	13.10	40,000
E	10.00	15,000

   (i) Explain why differences in annual GDP per capita may cause differences in the minimum wage per hour.   (4 marks)

   (ii) To what extent do the data suggest that differences in annual GDP per capita cause differences in the minimum wage per hour?   (4 marks)

6 Explain the factors that affect the distribution of wealth.   (12 marks)

7 Evaluate alternative policies that may be used to reduce poverty.   (25 marks)

6 Globalisation and trade

Economic development and the global economy

Key terms

Globalisation: the process through which the economies of the different countries of the world become increasingly integrated and interdependent.

Transnational corporation (TNC): an enterprise that owns assets, produces and sells goods and/or services in more than one country. Also known as a multinational corporation (MNC).

▲ **Figure 6.1.1**: Marshall McLuhan

Globalisation is a process through which the economies of the different countries of the world become increasingly integrated and interdependent. In the 1960s, the Canadian philosopher Marshall McLuhan used the phrase "global village" as a way of describing how the different parts of the world were being brought closer together through trade, **transnational corporations (TNCs)**, migration and modern methods of communication.

The first wave of globalisation occurred during the second half of the 19th century when technological advances led to a significant growth in the volume of world trade. This came to an end with the start of the First World War in 1914. The second wave of globalisation began after the end of the Second World War in 1945 and was helped by improvements in transport and communication and the reduction in the restrictions on international trade.

However, it remains to be seen how the devastating human and economic cost of the coronavirus pandemic will affect the process of globalisation. It is difficult to predict whether the effects will be temporary or more long-lasting. It is possible that some countries may decide that the risks of relying on others for supplies of some essential products are too great and globalisation might go into reverse. It may take a long while before the full effects are known.

The main characteristics of globalisation

The main characteristics of the increasingly globalised world economy are:

- trade liberalisation and the growth of world trade
- the growth and development of transnational corporations
- the integration of the world's financial markets and the reduction in the restrictions on moving financial capital between countries
- increased international migration and improved international mobility of labour
- the development of trading blocs such as the European Union (EU) and the Common Market for Eastern and Southern Africa (COMESA).

Trade liberalisation and the growth of world trade

Trade liberalisation is where countries remove or reduce restrictions on international trade, for example reducing tariffs and non-tariff barriers. The process of trade liberalisation and the resulting growth of world trade are important characteristics of globalisation.

Since the end of the Second World War in 1945, world trade has grown much more quickly than world GDP. In 1945, merchandise trade was less than 5% of world GDP whereas in 2019 it was almost 25% of world GDP. However, since the global financial crisis of 2007–2008, world GDP and merchandise exports have both grown by approximately 26% which means that merchandise trade remained at approximately 25% of world GDP over this period. In real terms, world exports are more than 40 times larger than in 1913.

In 1960, international trade in services accounted for about 6% of world GDP. Although between 2008 and 2018 **merchandise trade** grew at approximately the same rate as world GDP, international trade in services continued to grow faster than world GDP, increasing from 12.4% to 13.3% of world GDP.

In the 1930s, countries around the world used **protectionism** to try to help their economies avoid the worst effects of the **Great Depression**. However, imposing tariffs on imports led to retaliation and made most countries worse off.

After the Second World War, many countries wanted to see a reduction in the restrictions on international trade. The **General Agreement on Tariffs and Trade (GATT)** was signed by 23 countries and came into force on 1 January 1948. Its main purpose was to reduce protectionism and to promote free trade between countries. By 1994, there were 128 members of GATT and a significant reduction in the restrictions on international trade had been achieved.

In 1995, the **World Trade Organization (WTO)** was established and included the provisions of GATT. In 2020, the WTO had 164 members who accounted for 98% of world trade. GATT and the WTO have been very successful in promoting the liberalisation of international trade and this has led to a rapid growth in world exports. This change to more open economies is a fundamental characteristic of a globalised world economy.

However, not all governments are in favour of free trade and many countries have continued to protect their economies. The election of President Donald Trump in the USA in 2016 led to tariffs being imposed on a range of imports into the USA and to retaliation from countries whose goods were subject to these tariffs. If there is a return to protectionism around the world, this would almost certainly slow and may lead to a reversal in the process of globalisation. As mentioned earlier, the long-term effects of the coronavirus pandemic on the growth of world trade are difficult to predict but it may encourage some countries to make more products at home, reducing their reliance on imports.

Key terms

Trade liberalisation: the removal or reduction of restrictions on international trade, for example reducing tariffs and non-tariff barriers.

Merchandise trade: trade in goods.

Protectionism: imposing tariffs and other restrictions on imports from other countries.

Great Depression: the severe global economic depression that began in the USA in 1929 and lasted in many countries until the late 1930s.

General Agreement on Tariffs and Trade (GATT): an international treaty to promote international trade by reducing tariffs and other restrictions on imports.

Link

GATT and the WTO are covered in more detail in 6.2 "Trade".

The growth and development of transnational corporations

Another important characteristic of globalisation is the growth of transnational corporations (TNCs), also known as multinational corporations (MNCs). In the second half of the 19th century, the search for natural resources, including oil and other minerals, and the desire to expand into overseas markets, led to the growth of TNCs. Technological developments that reduced the costs of transport and communication have also contributed to the growth of TNCs. In 2014, it was estimated that TNCs accounted for approximately a third of global output and over half of world exports.

Most TNCs are still based in the more economically developed countries (MEDCs) such as the USA, the UK, Germany and Japan, but they invest heavily in less economically developed countries (LEDCs). TNCs operate in a wide variety of markets including extractive industries, manufacturing, retailing and the provision of other services. Long-established TNCs include Adidas, ExxonMobil, Microsoft, Rio Tinto Zinc, Samsung, Tata and Toyota, but there are many others. Amazon and Google are examples of large TNCs that were formed in the 1990s and are based in the USA.

In recent years, there has been a substantial growth in the number of TNCs based in China and it is estimated that in 2018, China was the home of the second largest number of TNCs after the USA. Chinese TNCs include enterprises such as Geely, Haier, Huawei and Sinopec.

The integration of the world's financial markets

During the past 50 years, financial markets throughout the world have become much more closely linked to each other. This integration of the world's financial markets is another important characteristic of globalisation.

During the 1950s and 1960s, many financial institutions focused on their domestic markets. Most countries, including the USA, imposed restrictions on international capital movements to help governments maintain the system of fixed exchange rates that was established under the Bretton Woods System.

This started to change in the 1970s and the pace of change increased during the 1980s. For example, in the UK, the government of Prime Minister Margaret Thatcher abolished exchange controls in 1979 and France abolished exchange controls in 1989. However, some large countries such as Argentina, China and India still have a system of exchange controls in place. Margaret Thatcher's government deregulated UK financial markets in the 1980s and similar changes followed in other countries including the USA and Japan. Developments in information and communications technologies have also contributed to the increasing integration of financial markets. Electronic and automated trading of securities have allowed dealers to operate 24 hours a day in different markets around the world.

As a result, governments and companies have access to a much wider range of sources of finance and there is increased competition among

Activity

Investigate three foreign TNCs that produce goods and/or services in your country's economy.

1   In which country is the Head Office of each of these TNCs based?
2   In which other countries do they supply goods and/or services?
3   How do they contribute to your country's economy?

Key terms

Financial markets: where people borrow and lend money, and where they buy and sell financial assets such as shares, bonds, foreign exchange and commodities.

Bretton Woods System: a global monetary system, agreed in 1944, that set up the International Monetary Fund (IMF) and the system of fixed exchange rates that operated between 1946 and 1973.

Exchange controls: limits imposed by a government on the buying and selling of foreign currencies.

Integration of financial markets: when the financial markets of different countries are interconnected and closely linked with each other.

the various providers of finance. These changes have contributed to the overall growth in both foreign direct investment (FDI) and **portfolio investment**.

In 2018, the flow of new FDI for the world was approximately $1.3 trillion and the stock of FDI throughout the world was over $32 trillion. However, FDI is volatile (changes unexpectedly) and the flow of new FDI peaked at over 5% of world GDP in 2007 but was under 1.4% of world GDP in 2018. This is still significantly higher than the average of under 0.5% between 1970 and 1985. Cross-border flows of short-term portfolio investment are much larger than FDI and are even more volatile.

Many of the world's TNCs are banks and other financial institutions. Examples include the Hong Kong and Shanghai Banking Corporation (HSBC) and the Prudential, a life assurance and financial services company.

The global financial crisis of 2007–2008 affected people's confidence in financial institutions and, in response to the crisis, governments around the world introduced new regulations on their activities. This has slowed the pace of change, but the integration of financial markets and international capital flows remain important features of the globalised world economy.

International migration and mobility of labour

While most people continue to live in the country in which they were born, the United Nations World Migration Report in 2020 shows that the number of international migrants has increased during the past five decades. In 1970, there were over 84 million migrants and this represented 2.3% of the world's population. In 2019, there were over 271 million migrants, representing 3.5% of the world's population. Around 74% of the international migrants in 2019 were of working age. While some people migrate to avoid conflict and persecution, the overwhelming majority migrate for reasons related to work, family and study.

Although, labour remains much more mobile within countries than between them, increasingly, firms recruit people from around the world and labour is more internationally mobile than it used to be. Some people working abroad are in temporary employment and help businesses deal with labour shortages. Construction, agriculture and tourism are examples of industries that, in some countries, employ significant numbers of migrant workers.

Some migrant workers are highly skilled and well paid, for example those working in finance, in universities and as health care professionals. TNCs often search the world when trying to recruit skilled workers to fill job vacancies.

Nevertheless, migration of labour between countries remains restricted. Highly paid, skilled professional workers have a high degree of mobility, but unskilled workers usually find it more difficult to move between countries when looking for work.

Key term

Portfolio investment: the purchase of shares, bonds and other financial assets without any involvement in the management of businesses.

Link

The role of the IMF and different exchange rate systems are covered in 7.2 "Exchange rates".

Activity

Find out all you can about the Bretton Woods System. Where is Bretton Woods? Who were the two important economists, one British and one American, who were responsible for designing the system?

Link

The nature and role of financial markets are explained in 7.3 "Financial markets".

▲ **Figure 6.1.2**: Migrant workers from different parts of the world

Key term

Trading bloc: a group of countries that agree to remove, or reduce, restrictions on trade between themselves whilst keeping restrictions on trade with countries that are not members of the trading bloc.

Link

Trading blocs are covered in more detail in 6.2 "Trade".

Progress questions

1 What is meant by globalisation?
2 What is meant by trade liberalisation?
3 What is a TNC?
4 Why does the growth of FDI contribute to the process of globalisation?
5 What is a trading bloc?

Link

The costs and benefits of international trade are covered in 6.2 in the section "Trade".

Key term

Principle of increased dimensions: where an increase in the size of a vehicle or building leads to a more than proportionate increase in capacity and a fall in average costs.

▲ **Figure 6.1.3**: Bulk carriers reduce transport costs

The development of trading blocs

Since the Second World War, in many parts of the world, there has been a move towards developing regional **trading blocs**. There are different types of trading bloc, but a common characteristic is that they reduce and sometimes eliminate restrictions on trade between member countries. In this respect, they are part of the process of globalisation. However, they may also increase the restrictions on trade with non-member countries.

Some people believe that the creation of trading blocs has made it easier to negotiate reductions in restrictions on trade. For example, it might be easier for a country to negotiate a trade deal with the European Union (EU) than to negotiate a separate deal with each of the 27 countries who are currently members of the EU.

Causes of globalisation

There are many factors that have contributed to the globalisation of the world economy since the end of the Second World War, some of which have already been mentioned. They include:

- improvements in transport
- improvements in communication
- reductions in barriers to trade
- reductions in barriers to capital flows
- the desire of large corporations to expand their operations
- the benefits countries have gained by opening their economies to trade and capital flows.

Improvements in transport

High transport costs reduce the benefits from international trade. Previously, high transport costs meant that some low-cost producers abroad, when transport costs were included, were unable to compete with higher-cost producers in their home market. Technological developments and investment in infrastructure have led to significant reductions in the cost of transporting goods by land, sea and air. As a result, countries have been able to gain the benefits obtained from international specialisation and trade.

Falling transport costs have helped to increase the volume of international trade and have contributed to the globalisation of the world economy. For example, containerisation has significantly reduced the cost of transporting goods. Containers, invented in 1956, can be transferred between different forms of transport, for example from a container ship to a train or a lorry.

The increase in the capacity of oil tankers and bulk carriers, used for products such as grain, coal, steel and cement, has also reduced the average cost (unit cost) of transporting goods between countries. The **principle of increased dimensions** is an example of an important internal economy of scale in the transport industry. For example, doubling the dimensions of a container increases its volume eight times, reducing the average cost of transporting products. Also, there is not much difference in the cost of operating a large or small vehicle.

Transporting goods by air is more expensive than by sea, road and rail, but the costs have fallen significantly during the past 50 years. Air freight is fast and reliable and may be the best way of transporting low-volume, high-value products. It also provides an efficient way to get perishable products to market.

Improvements in transport infrastructure within and between countries have helped to reduce costs and stimulate trade. For example, improvements in roads, rail networks, airports and seaports have all helped to reduce transport costs.

Improvements in communication

Technological developments leading to improvements in communications have played an important role in globalisation. Not only has our ability to communicate effectively across the world improved but the cost has also fallen dramatically. Computerisation, satellite technology, mobile phones, the internet, email and video-conferencing are just a few examples of technologies that have helped to improve our ability to communicate with each other.

These developments make it easier for TNCs to manage and control operations in different locations around the world. They help firms search for suppliers from different countries, allowing them to obtain raw materials and components from the best source. Effective communication systems make it easier for firms to sell abroad, expanding the markets for their products, helping them to benefit from economies of scale. It also makes it easier for firms to recruit workers and fill vacancies when there are labour shortages in their domestic economy.

Modern information and communication technologies make it easier for firms to raise finance from overseas. Improvements in technology have increased competition between financial institutions, including banks. This has helped to reduce the cost of borrowing and made it more likely that firms can get the money they need.

Reductions in barriers to trade

As already explained, the growth in the volume of world trade is a fundamental characteristic of globalisation. The WTO, GATT and the formation of trading blocs have contributed to the growth in world trade by encouraging reductions in the barriers to international trade. Barriers to trade make it impossible or uneconomic to import products from other countries. Reductions in tariff and non-tariff barriers mean that countries can specialise in supplying those goods and services that they are relatively most efficient at producing and can import those products that they cannot produce or can only produce at a high cost.

Reductions in barriers to capital flows

Many, but not all, countries have reduced or eliminated restrictions on capital flows into and out of their economies. This has helped TNCs to expand their operations abroad. It has also allowed banks and other financial institutions to play a bigger part in the economies of a variety of countries, for example lending to firms and governments overseas and providing a variety of other financial services.

Get it right

Make sure that you can describe the characteristics of globalisation **and** explain the causes of globalisation.

Progress questions

6   How have technological developments in transport contributed to globalisation?

7   Explain what is meant by a "barrier to international trade".

Link

The role of banks and other financial institutions is covered in 7.3 "Financial markets".

The desire of large corporations to expand their operations

Firms are in business to make a profit and expanding abroad can provide them with the opportunity to increase profits. This might be achieved by exporting or by setting up a factory in a foreign country. As firms grow, they can benefit from economies of scale and lower average costs. Lower costs can lead to lower prices, more sales and more profits. When a firm sets up a factory or an office in another country, it can make it easier to sell its products in that country.

Lower labour and other costs sometimes provide the incentive for TNCs to invest in less economically developed countries (LEDCs). Lower production costs allow the TNCs to reduce prices and compete more effectively. The goods and services produced in the LEDC can then be exported around the world.

Even if firms that are located in more economically developed countries (MEDCs) do not set up in LEDCs, they may **outsource** some of their production to firms in LEDCs so they can benefit from lower labour and other production costs. The reduction in the cost of transporting goods has helped to make this worthwhile.

Different parts of a TNC often trade with each other. Intra-firm trade represents a significant share of world trade but differs widely between countries and industries. Car manufacturing is an example of a vertically integrated industry where firms engage in intra-firm trade. The various components are often transported from several different countries to the place where the car is finally assembled.

Benefits gained by opening up economies to trade and capital flows

Many countries have benefited from reducing restrictions on international trade and capital flows. This has encouraged other

> **Key term**
>
> **Outsource**: when a firm buys some of the goods, services or components it needs from another supplier, sometimes in a different country.

Case study: Ford, a global car manufacturer

▲ **Figure 6.1.4**: Ford is a TNC that buys components from abroad

The Ford Motor Company (FMC) is the second largest car manufacturing company in the USA. Its headquarters are in Dearborn, Michigan. In 2018, Ford was the sixth largest seller of cars in Europe and is aiming to increase its sales in a number of emerging economies, including China and Russia. It makes components and assembles vehicles throughout the world. For example, FMC assembles cars in Argentina, Brazil, Canada, Germany, India, Russia, South Africa, Thailand, Turkey and Vietnam. It manufactures engines in England, Germany, Mexico, Spain, Turkey, USA and Wales.

As well as manufacturing vehicle parts, FMC has outsourced the production of some components to other firms around the world. FMC buys sliding sunroofs from Germany, instrument panel parts from China, airbags from Spain and exhaust systems from Venezuela. It has also invested around $200 million in a new Global Technology and Business Centre in Chennai, India.

1 Using the information in the case study, explain why the Ford Motor Company is a TNC.

2 Why does FMC assemble cars in different locations around the world?

3 Why does FMC outsource the production of some of the parts that it uses to build its cars?

countries to follow suit and start to open up their economies to international trade, foreign competition and capital flows. The belief that globalisation is beneficial has contributed to the process of globalising the world economy.

However, opening up an economy to overseas investment and international trade has costs as well as benefits; there are losers as well as winners. Some economists believe that protectionism is needed to support economic development.

The consequences of globalisation

Globalisation has had a profound effect on both LEDCs and MEDCs. Some of these effects are very similar for LEDCs and MEDCs, but they are not always the same. There are benefits and costs to all countries and to different groups within a country. Many people disagree about the extent to which globalisation has been beneficial and some believe that the disadvantages outweigh the benefits.

The benefits of globalisation

Those in favour of globalisation emphasise the benefits of free trade, competition and international investment flows. They point to the gains that countries such as China, India, South Korea and Thailand have derived from opening up their economies. They also believe that globalisation has made a significant contribution to the reduction in world poverty that has occurred during the past 30 years. A number of developing countries have experienced sustained growth rates of between 7% and 10%; 13 countries, including China, have grown by more than 7% per year for 25 years or more. Advocates of globalisation also stress that people in countries that have continued to protect and isolate their economies from the effects of globalisation, such as North Korea and Venezuela, have not seen much improvement in their standard of living.

The benefits of globalisation include:

- countries specialise in making products in which they have a comparative advantage
- increased ability to exploit economies of scale as countries specialise and sell in the global market
- increased competition leading to improvements in efficiency and the quality of products
- firms are able to locate where production costs are minimised
- greater choice of products and lower prices for consumers
- increased FDI in LEDCs increases economic growth and living standards
- investment by TNCs creates employment and can lead to an improvement in the skills of the working population
- investment by TNCs can lead to a transfer of technology
- improved mobility of labour allows people to move abroad to improve their job prospects.

Link

The principle of comparative advantage is explained in detail in 6.2 in the section "Trade".

Increased specialisation

Trade liberalisation leads to countries specialising in producing the goods and services in which they have a comparative advantage. They export goods and services in which they have a comparative advantage and import those that they are relatively less efficient at producing. Specialisation and trade should result in the total world output of goods and services increasing. An increase in total output makes it possible to increase consumption and improve living standards. The principle of comparative advantage illustrates why specialisation and trade can benefit all those involved.

Economies of scale

As countries specialise and the markets for products become global rather than national, firms will produce and sell more. An increase in output allows firms to benefit from economies of scale, leading to falling average costs. Lower costs can lead to lower prices for consumers.

Increased competition

Opening up markets to international trade and inward investment leads to more competition. Benefits that can result from competition include improvements in efficiency, lower prices, more choice and invention and innovation leading to better products. Reducing barriers to trade can reduce the power of local monopolies and help to prevent the exploitation of domestic consumers.

Link

The benefits of competition are explained in 3.8 "The dynamics of competition and competitive market processes".

Firms can locate where production costs are minimised

Globalisation has led many TNCs to locate factories in countries where labour and other costs are low, for example the German company Mercedes-Benz manufactures its C-Class saloon car in South Africa and exports it around the world. Locating factories in low-cost locations and outsourcing the production of goods and services to low-cost suppliers has benefited consumers through lower prices. For example, in the fashion industry, clothes may be designed in one country but manufactured in a different country with lower manufacturing costs.

At the time of writing, Nike products were made in 41 countries, in 533 factories employing over 1.16 million workers. Nearly all Nike products are obtained from independent companies that also supply products to other TNCs. Many companies have call centres that are located overseas, for example, in India or the Philippines.

More choice and lower prices

Globalisation has meant that consumers around the world are able to obtain products that are not easily available in their own country. For example, people in Europe are able to get bananas and pineapples from South America and the Caribbean. Globalisation has provided consumers with more choice and a greater variety of the same product, for example consumers can choose between different brands of mobile phone, watch or cooker.

Specialisation, economies of scale and increased competition are just some of the reasons why globalisation has led to lower costs and lower prices for many products, benefiting consumers.

Foreign direct investment (FDI) can increase economic growth

Investment is an important determinant of the rate of growth of an economy. LEDCs often have limited funds available to invest and FDI can increase investment while leaving domestic savings available to finance other investment projects. FDI usually has a multiplier effect, leading to further increases in national income. The increase in national income can help to improve living standards. It can also stimulate further investment by local firms and the government.

Investment by TNCs creates employment and improves people's skills

When transnational corporations (TNCs) invest abroad, they create employment and often, but not always, the jobs are relatively well paid. TNCs invest in human capital, increasing the skills and productivity of the labour force. Some of these skills are transferable and may benefit other parts of the economy.

Investment by TNCs can lead to a transfer of technology

TNCs are often an important means of spreading new technologies from MEDCs to LEDCs but also between MEDCs. These transfers of technology and improvements in productivity often result from the relationships developed between the TNC and local firms who are suppliers or customers of the TNC. They can lead to better methods of production and management within these organisations. Improvements in technology and productivity may also result from local firms adopting some of production methods used by the TNCs.

Figure 6.1.6 illustrates how FDI by a TNC can affect the economies of the countries in which the investment is made. In the short run, the increase in investment increases aggregate demand (AD) and in the long run, it increases capacity and should help to improve the supply-side performance of the economy, shifting the LRAS curve to the right. Since the TNC employs workers and increases output and incomes, the increase in AD should be sustained.

In Figure 6.1.6, FDI increases real national income from Y_{N1} to Y_{N2} but does not affect the price level. However, the impact on the price level is uncertain and depends on the extent to which productive capacity of the economy increases, as shown by the shift in the LRAS curve, compared to the increase in AD.

Improved mobility of labour between countries

Significant barriers to the mobility of labour between countries still exist but labour is more internationally mobile than it used to be. Increased international mobility of labour makes it easier for firms with labour shortages to recruit the staff they need. This makes it easier for firms to expand and should increase economic growth.

People who are unemployed or underemployed or earning low wages are more likely to be able to relocate, helping to reduce unemployment and

▲ **Figure 6.1.5:** Consumers have a choice of mobile phone

Link

The importance of savings as a determinant of an economy's growth rate is covered in 8.2 "Factors that affect economic development".

Link

The advantages and disadvantages of FDI are covered in 8.3 "Policies to promote development".

Get it right

A large proportion of global FDI is between the world's richest countries and MEDCs benefit from FDI as well as LEDCs.

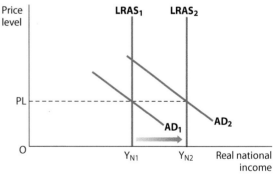

▲ **Figure 6.1.6:** The effect of FDI on the macroeconomy

Key term

International mobility of labour: the movement of workers between countries.

Case study: Vietnam has prospered during the past 35 years

▲ **Figure 6.1.7**: Hanoi, the capital of Vietnam

Since the mid-1980s, Vietnam has changed from a closed centrally planned economy to an open mixed economy in which the state plays a leading role. The integration of Vietnam into the globalised world economy started with the reforms under Doi Moi that began in 1986. Since 1986, Vietnam has been transformed from one of the world's poorest nations into a lower middle-income economy. According to the World Bank, "Between 2002 and 2018, GDP per capita increased 2.7 times, reaching over $2,700 in 2019, and more than 45 million people were lifted out of poverty".

Vietnam became a member of the World Trade Organization (WTO) in 2007 and since then, it has liberalised trade with a number of other countries. It is a member of the ASEAN Free Trade Area (AFTA) and has recently signed an agreement with the EU that will eliminate 99% of tariffs on the goods that are traded between the two regions. During the past 30 years, the average annual rate of growth of Vietnam's exports has been around 12%. Export-led growth has created millions of jobs for the people of Vietnam. The country has also benefited from large inflows of FDI. In 2019, the inflow of FDI was $16.1 billion and the total stock of FDI was $161 billion.

1 What is meant by the phrase "an open mixed economy"?
2 What evidence is there in the case study to show that Vietnam has become part of the globalised world economy?
3 Explain ways in which Vietnam may have benefited from being part of the globalised world economy.

improve their standard of living. Young people are able to study abroad acquiring valuable skills and increasing the stock of human capital. This should also help to increase economic growth and living standards.

The costs of globalisation

Some people believe that the costs of globalisation outweigh the benefits. Even those who believe that globalisation has been beneficial, improving living standards for many, recognise that there are costs that should be dealt with. Others who recognise the benefits of globalisation consider that it has gone too far and believe it ought to be controlled. Some consider that developments in technology mean that the process of globalising the world economy is irreversible but that action is needed to ensure the costs are reduced.

The costs of globalisation include:

- globalisation may lead to instability
- firms and workers are vulnerable to changes in comparative advantage
- TNCs may be too powerful and benefit MEDCs more than LEDCs
- it may lead to exploitation of workers
- it may increase inequality
- skilled workers move from LEDCs to MEDCs
- globalisation contributes to global warming and other environmental problems
- globalisation has resulted in standardisation and a reduction in cultural diversity.

Globalisation can lead to instability

Globalisation has led to increased interdependence of countries around the world. A negative economic shock in a large economy, or a part of the world, can adversely affect the rest of the world. The growth of world trade means that exports are a large injection into the circular flow of income for many economies.

If a large economy such as China, the EU or the USA goes into recession, their demand for imports will fall. This means there is a reduction in other countries' exports and a downward multiplier effect. As national incomes fall, there is also likely to be a negative accelerator effect, leading to lower investment and further reductions in aggregate demand. A recession which starts in one country can easily spread to others. Similarly, positive economic shocks in one country can help to boost the economies of other countries.

The 1997 Asian financial crisis started in Thailand but quickly spread to much of East and South East Asia. There were concerns that there would be a global economic crisis, but this did not happen. Thailand had accumulated large amounts of foreign debt and was running out of foreign currency. As a result, it was forced to let its currency, the Thai baht, float and its exchange rate fell. There was a **capital flight** from other countries in East and South East Asia, including South Korea, Indonesia, Malaysia and the Philippines. Economists disagree about the initial cause of the crisis, but it is clear that the ease with which funds can be invested and withdrawn from countries around the world added to the problem.

The global financial crisis of 2007–2008 led to a serious recession in many countries around the world and is known as the Great Recession. The crisis was linked to problems in the US housing market and risky lending by many of the world's **financial institutions**. Some important financial institutions collapsed, for example the US investment bank Lehman Brothers. Other large financial institutions were bailed out by their governments. People lost confidence in the banks, and firms and households found it difficult to borrow. Problems in global financial markets inevitably affected the real economies of many countries, leading to the worst world economic downturn since the Great Depression of the 1930s.

In 2020, the coronavirus pandemic caused the governments of many countries to impose restrictions which seriously depressed economic activity. While there have been global pandemics in the past, international tourism and the movement of people around the world have meant that the virus spread more quickly. The pandemic has had both supply-side and demand-side consequences for the world economy. In the short-run, supply chains may be disrupted, and this may affect production in a number of countries. It is likely that at least some of the effects of the pandemic will be long-lasting and will affect some sectors of the economy more than others.

Firms and workers are vulnerable to changes in comparative advantage

Over time, for a variety of reasons, the structure of economies change; some industries grow and others decline. Changes in comparative

Key terms

Capital flight: when foreign investors rapidly withdraw their money from a country, usually resulting in a large fall in the value of the country's currency.

Financial institutions: companies that provide financial services such as banks, insurance companies and investment funds.

Link

The role of financial institutions and financial markets is explained in 7.3 "Financial markets".

Activity

Find out all you can about the causes of the 2007–2008 global financial crisis and the effects it had on your country's economy.

Activity

Investigate how the coronavirus pandemic affected your country's economy. For example, how it affected economic growth, unemployment, inflation, the balance of payments, the national debt and inequality.

▲ **Figure 6.1.8**: Shipbuilding in South Korea

advantage and in restrictions on trade are important reasons why an industry may grow in one country while, at the same time, decline in another country. When an industry declines, workers are likely to become unemployed and some may be out of work for a long time. Globalisation and competition from newly industrialised economies have led to structural unemployment in a number of MEDCs.

For much of the 19th century, the UK was the largest producer and exporter of textiles but production in the UK peaked in 1926. China is currently the world's largest producer of textiles; it produces over 50% of the total world output of textiles. The next largest producer is India with a global share of nearly 7% in 2019. As comparative advantage switched from the UK to other countries, many firms closed down and jobs were lost, leading to structural unemployment in the textile-producing areas of the UK.

In the 1890s, the UK built 80% of the world's ships but now it only has a small share of the global market. By the 1960s, Japan was the largest shipbuilding nation but since then, China and South Korea have dominated this industry. In 2019, both China and South Korea had market shares of around 33% and Japan, the third largest shipbuilding nation, had a market share of 17%.

Between 2009 and 2018, China's share of global manufacturing increased from around 8.7% to 28.4% while the US share of global manufacturing fell from 22.3% to 16.6%. However, other countries, such as Vietnam and India, are also experiencing strong growth in manufacturing. As wages and therefore labour costs rise in China, labour intensive manufacturing is likely to move to countries with lower wages. However, not all manufacturing is labour intensive and capital-intensive manufacturing is important in many MEDCs, particularly when competitiveness depends on advanced technologies.

Although many MEDCs have experienced a relative decline in manufacturing, the service sectors of their economies have grown. Many services have a high income elasticity of demand and as national income increases, there is a more than proportionate increase in output and employment in the service sector. However, changes in comparative advantage and globalisation can also affect output and employment in the service sector.

Transnational corporations may be too powerful and benefit MEDCs more than LEDCs

The revenue of some TNCs is greater than the national income of some of the countries in which they invest. For example, in 2019, it has been estimated that the revenue earned by Shell was $397 billion, Volkswagen earned $278 billion and Samsung earned $222 billion.

TNCs are often **footloose** and will search the globe to find the most profitable locations for their operations. Profitability is often affected by labour costs and government incentives. TNCs provide income, employment and other benefits for the economy but they may demand concessions from the government before they invest. To attract investment from TNCs, governments often provide subsidies, tax relief and/or exempt them from regulations that are imposed on local businesses. If circumstances change, the TNC may decide to move its operations to a different country. To avoid this happening, the government may provide additional financial incentives and adjust their policies to suit the requirements of the TNCs.

Although the TNCs create income for people in the country in which they have invested, some of the profits are likely to be returned to the parent country and to shareholders. This **repatriation of profits** reduces the overall benefit to the host country.

Can lead to exploitation of workers

Some people argue that globalisation has led to the exploitation of workers in LEDCs. TNCs often locate in LEDCs because wages are low and employment regulations are weak, allowing them to increase profits. Workers employed to manufacture products for large corporations may be required to work for very long hours, in poor conditions and for wages that are far below what they would have received in a more developed economy. Sometimes, workers earn a tiny percentage of the selling price of the product. However, labour costs are not the only cost and the wages paid are often more than would have been earned in other similar occupations in that country. Many TNCs pay more than local firms, providing good working conditions and secure employment.

May increase inequality

The impact of globalisation on inequality is controversial. Some believe that globalisation has reduced the degree of inequality between countries but may have increased it within countries. However, there are many factors that influence inequality, for example technological change and government policies, and it is difficult to be certain how significant each of these factors has been.

Between 1800 and 1975, inequality between countries was increasing and there was a clear divide between the so-called developed economies and the rest of the world. Since 1975, rapid growth in much of Asia in particular means that global inequality between countries has fallen. The incomes of the poorer half of the world have risen faster than the incomes of the richer half of the world. Some believe that globalisation and the liberalisation of trade are important factors in the increasing prosperity of countries in Asia.

Estimates by the World Bank indicate that 44% of the world's population lived in extreme poverty in 1981, but since then the proportion of extremely poor people in the world has fallen faster than ever before. In 2015, fewer than 10% of the world's population was living in extreme poverty. In 1990, there were 1.9 billion people living in extreme poverty but despite the rise in the world population, this had fallen to 735 million by 2015. This is still a lot of people, but the numbers have fallen much more rapidly than in previous generations. However, it is hard to be sure how much of this is due to globalisation.

If globalisation promotes economic growth, it is not likely to benefit everyone equally. In most cases, in the early stages of growth, some people will experience a significant increase in their income while

Key term

Repatriation of profits: returning profits earned in the host country to the country where the business is owned.

Link

The role of TNCs in a globalised world economy is covered later in this section.

Link

The Kuznets curve is explained in detail in 8.2 "Factors that affect economic development".

▼ **Table 6.1.1**: Selected Gini coefficients for a selection of LEDCs

Brazil		China		Ethiopia		India		Vietnam	
Year	Gini coefficient	Year	Gini coefficient	Year	Gini coefficient	Year	Gini coefficient	Year	Gini coefficient
1990	60.5	1990	32.2	1995	44.6	1993	32.7	1992	35.7
2002	58.1	2002	42.0	2004	29.8	2004	36.8	2002	37.0
2016	53.3	2016	38.5	2014	35.0	2011	37.8	2018	35.7

Source: The World Bank; accessed June 2020

Get it right

Remember that absolute poverty can be falling while relative poverty and inequality are increasing. For example, this will happen if the income of the poor is increasing but more slowly than the income of the rich is increasing.

others will see little change. As a result, inequality within a country is likely to increase. However, if growth continues, the benefits are likely to become more widespread. The Kuznets curve suggests that if growth persists, the degree of inequality will eventually fall. However, the validity of the Kuznets curve has been questioned in recent years.

Data measuring inequality is not as readily available as many other economic statistics and the data are not always accurate or up to date. Table 6.1.1 shows the Gini coefficient for a selection of countries that have been affected by globalisation during the past 30 years.

The data in Table 6.1.1 does not clearly show that globalisation has increased inequality within these countries. For example, between 1993 and 2011, the degree of inequality in India, as measured by the Gini coefficient, has increased but in Vietnam, the Gini coefficient is the same in 2018 as it was in 1992.

In some MEDCs, particularly since 1980, economic growth has been accompanied by increasing inequality. Some economists believe that globalisation is one of the main reasons why inequality in some MEDCs has increased. Globalisation leads to increased competition and this has led to a loss of employment, particularly in manufacturing. Lower labour costs in LEDCs have meant that there has been a shift in comparative advantage away from MEDCs to LEDCs. Low-skilled workers are particularly vulnerable. Foreign competition and immigration have meant that the wages of many low-skilled workers have not increased as much as the wages of skilled workers. However, it is not just globalisation that has brought about this change, investment in new technologies has also reduced the demand for low-skilled workers, contributing to the reduction in employment and wages. On the other hand, many skilled workers are in short supply and their wages have increased significantly.

Get it right

Globalisation is not the only reason for changes in the degree of inequality within a country. Government policy and changes in technology are examples of other influences on the distribution of income and wealth.

Link

The factors that affect the distribution of income and wealth were explained in detail in 5.1 "The distribution of income and wealth within an economy".

▼ **Table 6.1.2**: Selected Gini coefficients for a selection of MEDCs since 1990

France		Germany		United Kingdom	
Year	Gini coefficient	Year	Gini coefficient	Year	Gini coefficient
1984	36.9	1994	29.2	1979	28.4
2016	31.9	2016	31.9	2016	34.8

Source: The World Bank; accessed June 2020

The top 1% of households in the USA earned less than 10% of the total national income in 1980 but now earn over 20%. According to the World Bank, in the USA, the Gini coefficient was 34.6 in 1979 but had increased to 41.4 in 2016. In 2018, the Gini coefficient in the USA was reported to be 48.6. As can be seen from Table 6.1.2, according to the Gini coefficient, the UK and Germany have also experienced an increase in inequality but inequality in France has fallen.

Skilled workers move from LEDCs to MEDCs

Some people who move from poorer countries to richer countries are **economic migrants**. They may be looking for work and/or higher wages; they want to improve their standard of living. Some economic migrants are unskilled, but others are highly skilled workers. When there are skill shortages, MEDCs are usually keen to accept foreign migrants who are able to fill important vacancies. Doctors, nurses, teachers, engineers, scientists, technicians and accountants are just some examples of workers who are often in short supply.

While this usually benefits the MEDC and the individual worker, it can be very damaging for the LEDC where such workers are also in short supply. Many LEDCs cannot compete with the wages and opportunities offered by MEDCs. The education and training of these workers is often financed by the governments of the LEDC. If skilled workers move abroad, this spending on investment in human capital provides little benefit to the LEDC.

Global warming and other environmental problems

The growth in the volume of international trade and travel has increased the amount of fossil fuels used. As a result, CO_2 (carbon dioxide) emissions have risen, contributing to global warming. The increase in economic growth that has resulted from globalisation has led to an increase in the use of natural resources. The increased use of natural resources has contributed to deforestation, overfishing and scars on the landscape from mining.

The increase in the consumption of goods and services has generated more waste. The disposal of waste can create serious environmental problems. For example, plastic material takes centuries to degrade and if dumped carelessly on land or in rivers, it may end up in the sea, threatening marine life.

Governments in some countries, wishing to attract inward investment from TNCs, have adopted weaker environment standards than in other countries. Complying with strict environmental regulations can be expensive, lead to lower profits and deter investors. Regulations and taxes on polluting activities help to internalise negative externalities, forcing businesses to take into account the full social cost of their activities. However, they may encourage firms to locate where they can avoid paying the external cost of their activities.

However, globalisation has helped to make people more aware of environmental problems and has triggered investment into developing environmentally friendly innovations. Large scale production, made possible by a global marketplace, has lowered the cost of products that can help to reduce environmental problems, for example solar panels. It has also led to some transfer of green technologies, although firms in competition with each other are often reluctant to share the results of thcir investment in research and development.

Key term

Economic migrants: people who move from one country to another to try to improve their standard of living.

▲ **Figure 6.1.9**: There are lots of opportunities for scientists to work abroad

Link

Externalities were explained in 5.3 "Positive and negative externalities in consumption and production" in the AS book.

Progress questions

8   Why is "specialisation and trade" a benefit that results from globalisation?

9   Explain **two** benefits of increased international mobility of labour.

10   Why might globalisation increase unemployment in MEDCs?

11   What is meant by a "footloose industry"?

12   Give **two** reasons why globalisation may have reduced the degree of inequality between countries.

Key terms

Per se: a Latin term that means 'by itself' or 'on its own'.

Deglobalisation: the reversal of the effects of globalisation, reducing the integration and interdependence between the economies of different countries. It occurs when the volume of international trade and investment decline.

Link

The tragedy of the commons was explained in 5.2 "Private goods, public goods and quasi-public goods" in the AS book.

Resulted in standardisation and a reduction in cultural diversity

Critics of globalisation are concerned that markets in most countries are dominated by global brands, such as Coca-Cola, Starbucks and McDonald's, and by products supplied by TNCs. They argue that the power of large international companies restricts competition, leads to a limited variety of standardised products and encourages consumerism. However, international trade and migration can help to broaden the variety of products available to people and expose them to different cultures and experiences.

Globalisation and the natural environment

As explained earlier, some people believe that globalisation has caused serious damage to the natural environment. However, many of the environmental problems the world has experienced result from the pursuit of economic growth rather than globalisation *per se*. Nevertheless, globalisation is an important reason why some countries have experienced increased rates of economic growth. While globalisation and economic growth can harm the environment, rapid rates of economic growth in some developing economies have lifted millions of people out of poverty, improving their quality of life.

While some environmentalists argue for **deglobalisation**, others adopt a different approach to reducing the adverse environmental consequences of globalisation. Many believe that it is unlikely that globalisation will be reversed and argue that more government intervention is needed to regulate the negative environmental consequences of economic activity. Where there are negative externalities, the costs of these externalities are, without government intervention, often ignored by firms and consumers. International agreement is also needed to limit the damage to the environment from globalisation. International action may be required because it is not always easy to assign property rights to some environmental resources. Without international action, shared resources, such as the atmosphere, the oceans and rivers may be overexploited. This problem is known as "the tragedy of the commons".

Globalisation and growing economic activity have been accompanied by increasing emissions of greenhouse gases, such as carbon dioxide (CO_2) and methane, into the atmosphere, contributing to global warming. More goods are transported to markets abroad, people travel more within and between countries, and more energy is consumed as production and consumption rise. Global warming can have a variety of consequences including extreme weather conditions, heatwaves, expansion of deserts, droughts, wildfires, rising sea levels and flooding.

Globalisation has also been associated with excessive use and exploitation of both non-renewable and renewable natural resources. As economic activity grows, the demand for natural resources increases and the world's stock of non-renewable resources, such as metals and fossil fuels, is depleted. There is a risk that some may run out, although new discoveries, recycling and the development of substitutes may help to prevent this happening. The stock of renewable resources, such as trees and fish, can be replenished but if overused, some potentially renewable resources will also be depleted. If natural resources are not carefully managed, the environmental damage can be significant.

Globalisation and increasing economic activity have also contributed to the problem of waste and its disposal. The amount of waste we create is closely linked to production and consumption. In production, a lot of waste is generated from mining, quarrying, manufacturing and construction. Waste from consumption includes old electrical goods, cars, batteries, plastic, paper and furniture. Rivers and the oceans can be badly affected if waste is not disposed of properly. Fish and other marine life can be threatened by waste that finds its way into the sea. Some waste is toxic and can affect crops that are grown on contaminated soil. Litter is unsightly and waste that is not disposed of safely can damage people's health.

▲ **Figure 6.1.10**: Recycling waste uses resources

Waste management uses economic resources to collect, sort and dispose of waste safely. However, the **recycling** of waste products means that fewer new materials need to be extracted. Materials that are not recycled represent an economic loss to society since labour and other factor inputs were used to produce them.

The world economy is unlikely to continue to reap the benefits of globalisation and economic growth unless problems such as global warming, the depletion of natural resources and waste are dealt with effectively. **Sustainable economic growth** requires that the natural environment is protected. Market forces have a role to play but government action and the values people hold are also very important.

Some environmentalists argue for **localisation of economic activity** rather than globalisation. Making products close to the market reduces transport costs and damage to the environment. For example, transporting fruit, vegetables and other food products that could be produced locally would help to reduce the environmental costs associated with transporting such products long distances. These externalities are not always adequately taken into account, although some fossil fuels used to transport products may be subject to a **carbon tax**. However, protecting local farmers at the expense of relatively more efficient farmers overseas may mean that the benefits from specialisation, trade and economies of scale are lost.

Some economists have argued that in the long run globalisation can be good for the environment. Specialisation and trade can lead to a more efficient allocation of resources, meaning that fewer resources are needed to produce a given level of output. It may lead to a more rapid transfer of green technologies between countries, helping to reduce environmental damage. It is also argued that a clean environment is a normal good, meaning that as incomes rise, people are more willing to devote resources to ensuring that the natural environment is protected. This idea is linked to the environmental Kuznets curve.

Key terms

Recycling: the process of converting waste into reusable material.

Sustainable economic growth: economic growth that can be maintained over time.

Localisation of economic activity: when products are made close to where they are sold, using local materials, and designed to suit local tastes and preferences.

Carbon tax: an indirect tax levied on the carbon content of fuels. Carbon taxes are used to internalise the external costs of using fossil fuels that release greenhouse gases into the atmosphere.

Link

Sustainable economic growth and development are considered in detail in 8.1 in "Measuring economic growth, development and living standards".

Link

The environmental Kuznets curve is considered in detail in 8.2 "Factors that affect economic development".

Activity

Find out all you can about the "doughnut model of the economy".

Some environmentalists recognise the benefits that globalisation has brought to many people living in LEDCs. They believe that MEDCs should aim for zero growth and introduce policies that focus on reducing emissions of greenhouse gases while supporting aspects of globalisation that help to support growth and poverty reduction in LEDCs.

In her book *Doughnut Economics*, published in 2018, the Oxford economist Kate Raworth argued for an economic system that meets the fundamental needs of people without causing severe damage to the earth's life-supporting structures, such as the ozone layer. Kate Raworth disputes the view that economic growth should be the main aim of government macroeconomic policy.

Case study: Global electricity generation is changing but is it changing fast enough?

▲ **Figure 6.1.11**: Offshore wind farms are producing more electricity

In 2015, in Paris, 197 countries signed an agreement to limit the increase in global average temperature to well below 2°C above pre-industrial levels. The general aim is to try to limit the increase to 1.5°C, but some countries believe this will be hard to achieve.

In 2019, the growth of the world economy was slower than expected and electricity consumption only grew by 1.4%, the lowest increase for a decade. According to a report by EMBER, a climate think tank, coal-fired electricity generation fell by 3% in 2019 and electricity generated

from wind and solar grew by 15%, leading to a 2% fall in CO_2 emissions from generating electricity. However, fossil fuels still supply around 62% of the world's electricity whereas only 9% comes from wind and solar. The rest comes from other sources including hydro and nuclear. The switch away from fossil fuels to green sources of energy is essential if the increase in global average temperatures is to be kept below 2°C.

Between 2009 and 2017, the price of solar panels fell by an average of 76% and wind turbines by 34%, and they have fallen further since. Improvements in technology, standardisation and economies of scale in manufacturing have contributed to these cost reductions. The rapidly falling costs of producing wind and solar energy should provide an incentive for countries to switch to low-carbon sources of energy, but will it be enough?

1 Explain why the rate of growth in the world economy affects global consumption of electricity.

2 Explain why the prices of solar panels and wind turbines have fallen since 2009.

3 Why might the fall in prices of solar panels and wind turbines help to reduce global warming?

4 How might governments encourage producers to reduce the use of fossil fuels to generate electricity?

The role of transnational corporations in a globalised world economy

Key term

Global supply chain: a worldwide network of suppliers, assembly plants, distribution centres and retailers.

TNCs are businesses that operate in more than one country. TNCs that are involved in manufacturing may have factories in several countries that assemble finished products from components that are produced in other countries. These finished products are then transported and sold throughout the world. They operate with a **global supply chain** that obtains raw materials and components, and transforms them into finished products that are distributed to consumers. Not all TNCs are manufacturing companies, some focus on extracting raw materials while others provide services. BHP Billiton and the Rio Tinto Zinc Corporation (RTZ) are TNCs that specialise in the extraction of minerals such as iron ore and copper. Google, Amazon and Vodafone are examples of TNCs that specialise in providing services for people and businesses. In recent years, TNCs with their head offices in countries in Asia have become increasingly influential, for example, Alibaba and Sinotec (China), Infosys and Tata (India) and Samsung and Daewoo (South Korea). The growth of TNCs is a key feature of globalisation.

TNCs can provide a variety of economic benefits but they can also have a negative impact on the economies of some countries. TNCs are in business to make a profit for their owners who are usually the shareholders. The pursuit of profit can be beneficial; it encourages firms to supply good-quality products that people want to buy, and to produce them efficiently. However, the desire to make large profits can also lead to decisions that have harmful effects on society.

The benefits of transnational corporations

1   TNCs are large organisations that benefit from economies of scale. They are usually very productive, efficient organisations that are able to supply goods and services at competitive prices.
2   By locating production in low-cost LEDCs, TNCs provide products to MEDCs at much lower prices than if they were produced in a more developed economy.
3   TNCs invest in both MEDCs and LEDCs helping to boost both short-run and long-run economic growth.
4   Inward investment by TNCs has a multiplier effect on the economy and may also lead to further investment to provide the infrastructure the business needs. This may benefit other local firms and the population as a whole.
5   They provide employment for people both directly and indirectly. Not only does the TNC provide jobs for people, jobs are also likely to be created in other businesses.
6   They invest in human capital, to increase the skills and abilities of their employees. Many of the skills are transferable and can be employed to benefit other parts of the economy when workers change jobs.
7   The investment, growth and jobs provided by the TNCs help to improve living standards.
8   Many TNCs export their products around the world, helping to improve the balance of payments of the host countries. Exports help to provide foreign exchange that is needed to pay for imports. Also, the products supplied by some TNCs enable **import substitution** reducing the amount of foreign currency the host country needs.
9   When TNCs become established in a country there may be a transfer of technology and management skills that benefit other firms in the host country. However, some TNCs will be reluctant to allow other firms to benefit from their knowledge and expertise.

> **Key term**
>
> **Import substitution:** where domestic production replaces foreign imports.

10 The activities of TNCs will usually lead to an increase in the amount of tax revenue received by the government of the host country. Direct taxes will be levied on the income earned by employees and company profits. Indirect taxes may be levied on products sold. The increase in tax revenue can finance more government spending, for example, improving the provision of health care and education.

11 Some TNCs provide the technology and resources that allow countries to exploit their natural resources.

Some costs of transnational corporations

1 Many governments around the world want to attract and retain investment by TNCs in their country. This desire to attract investment and the size of many TNCs gives the TNCs a lot of power and influence over the government, particularly governments of small LEDCs. TNCs may receive subsidies, tax relief and exemption from regulations, for example those designed to protect the environment and the health and safety of workers. In some cases, employees of TNCs have been found guilty of bribing corrupt government officials.

2 Many TNCs are footloose and may move to another country with very little notice. Changes in production costs and taxation may mean that a different location, in another country, is now more profitable. This can be very damaging for the original host economy, leading to a sizeable reduction in income and employment.

3 Some TNCs invest in countries that are rich in natural resources such as oil, copper and tin. While the host country may benefit from the extraction of these resources, the TNC is also likely to make large profits from its operations and their activities may damage the local environment. Once it is no longer economically viable to extract the natural resource, the TNC will move elsewhere.

4 Low labour costs are another reason why TNCs invest in some LEDCs. Many TNCs provide stable employment and pay wages that are higher than local firms. However, this is not always the case. A common criticism of some TNCs is that they exploit workers by paying low wages and providing poor working conditions.

5 While TNCs provide employment in LEDCs by investing and outsourcing production, this can lead to job losses and structural unemployment in MEDCs.

6 When TNCs locate in an economy, some local firms may go out of business because they cannot compete. Also, the existence of a large TNC can make it difficult for new domestic firms to start up in business.

7 Although TNCs increase the output and national income of the host country, the profits earned may be returned to the home country. This repatriation of profits reduces the benefits that the

TNC provide to the host country. However, some of the profits earned may be reinvested in the host country and profit is only part of the total income produced by the TNC.

8 Some TNCs attempt to minimise the amount of tax they pay to governments by using transfer pricing to affect where their profits are declared. When one part of a business supplies a good or service to another part of the same business, it has to decide how much it is going to charge. This is known as the **transfer price**. The price charged will affect how much profit is generated by the different parts of the business. If the transfer price is reduced, it will reduce the profit earned by the part of the business supplying the good or service and increase the profit earned by the part of the business that is using that good or service. A TNC can reduce the amount of tax it pays by increasing the transfer price charged by parts of the organisation located in a country where taxes on company profits are low. The part of the business that buys the component, located where taxes on company profits are high, will then declare a lower profit and pay less tax. Although the total profit made by the business remains the same, the total tax burden can be reduced by manipulating transfer prices.

9 The supply chain of many TNCs is vertically integrated with production at different stages taking place in different countries. Transporting raw materials and semi-finished products between different parts of the organisation contributes to global warming. Also, supplying the global market with final products from a few large factories can also increase emissions of greenhouse gases.

> ### Key term
>
> **Transfer price**: the price that one part of a business charges another part of the business for goods and services provided.

> ### Progress questions
>
> 13 Explain **two** ways in which globalisation may have damaged the natural environment.
>
> 14 Explain why the depletion of non-renewable resources may make recycling more profitable.
>
> 15 If a TNC, manufacturing cars, invests in a LEDC, how might it affect the LEDC's balance of trade in goods and services?
>
> 16 Explain why investment by a TNC in an LEDC may cause structural unemployment in an MEDC.

Case study: Electric bicycles – a growing global business

▲ **Figure 6.1.12**: The market for e-bikes is growing fast

A company producing e-bikes (electric bicycles) makes the electric motors for its e-bikes in Country A. In Country A, taxes on company profits are 10%. It manufactures its e-bikes in Country B where profits are taxed at 30%. The cost of producing electric motors in Country A is $80 and the cost of making the e-bikes

in Country B, excluding the electric motor, is $190. The e-bikes are sold at a price $450 to the final consumer. The company sells 20,000 e-bikes each year.

1 If the transfer price for the electric motor is set at $100, calculate:
   i the profit that the company will make in each country
   ii the amount of tax it will have to pay in each country
   iii the total amount of tax it will have to pay.

2 If the transfer price for the electric motor is increased to $200, calculate:
   i the profit that the company will make in each country
   ii the amount of tax it will have to pay in each country
   iii the total amount of tax it will have to pay.

3 If the company wants to minimise the amount of tax it pays, what transfer price should it charge for the electric motor? Losses cannot be used to reduce the company's tax liability.

This section will develop your knowledge and understanding of:

→ the model of comparative advantage

→ the difference between absolute and comparative advantage

→ causes of comparative advantage and why comparative advantage changes over time

→ why the model shows that specialisation and trade can increase total output

→ other economic benefits of trade, including economies of scale and increased competition

→ the costs of international trade

→ protectionist policies, including tariffs, quotas and export subsidies

→ reasons for and consequences of countries adopting protectionist policies

→ the changing pattern of world trade

→ the terms of trade

→ causes and effects of changes in a country's terms of trade

→ trading blocs: free trade area, customs union, common market and monetary union

→ the role of the World Trade Organization (WTO).

Link

Specialisation was explained in 3.2 "Specialisation, division of labour and exchange" in the AS book.

Get it right

The model of comparative advantage shows that specialisation and trade can make everyone better off.

▲ **Figure 6.2.1:** David Ricardo

The model of comparative advantage

The model (or theory) of comparative advantage was developed by David Ricardo and explained in his book *On principles of political economy and taxation*, published in 1817. Ricardo was an influential 19th century English classical economist.

The model explains the benefits of specialisation and trade and is often used to support the case for international free trade. If countries, or other economic agents, specialise in producing a limited range of products, they have to trade to obtain the other products they want. It shows that if people, firms or countries specialise in producing those products in which they have a comparative advantage, free trade can make everyone better off.

Economic models invariably include a number of simplifying assumptions that help us to focus on the key issues. The main assumptions of the model of comparative advantage are:

1 two countries
2 two goods (or services)
3 no transport costs
4 constant returns to scale – there are no economies or diseconomies of scale
5 perfect mobility of factors of production *within* a country
6 factors of production are immobile *between* countries.

Relaxing one or more of these assumptions can affect the predictions of the model. The effects of relaxing some of these assumptions will be considered after the model has been developed and the predictions explained.

The difference between absolute and comparative advantage

A country (or other economic agent) has an absolute advantage in the production of a good (or service) if it can produce a given amount of the good with fewer resources (factors of production) than another country. This is the same as being able to produce more of a good than another country with the same amount of resources.

A country (or other economic agent) has a comparative advantage in the production of a good (or service) if the opportunity cost of producing the good is lower than in another country.

A country can have a comparative advantage in producing a good even if, in absolute terms, it is less efficient at producing all goods. A country has a comparative advantage if it is relatively more efficient at producing a good than another country. Comparative advantage is sometimes known as relative advantage.

The following examples illustrate the difference between absolute and comparative advantage.

▼ **Table 6.2.1**: Each country has an absolute and comparative advantage in one good

	Cars		Tractors
Country A	16	**or**	4
Country B	12	**or**	6

Opportunity cost ratios for Country A: 1 car = 0.25 tractors **or**
1 tractor = 4 cars

Opportunity cost ratios for Country B: 1 car = 0.5 tractors **or**
1 tractor = 2 cars

Table 6.2.1 shows the number of cars or tractors Country A and Country B can produce with a given amount of resources. Country A has an absolute advantage in the production of cars because it can produce more cars with the same amount of resources than Country B: 16 cars compared to 12 cars. Country B has an absolute advantage in the production of tractors because it can produce more tractors with the same amount of resources than Country A: 6 tractors compared to 4 tractors.

Country A also has a comparative advantage in the production of cars because it only has to give up a quarter of a tractor to produce one car. In Country A, the opportunity cost of producing 1 car = 0.25 tractors. Country B has to give up half a tractor for each car it produces. In Country B, the opportunity cost of producing 1 car = 0.5 tractors. The opportunity cost of producing a car in Country A is lower than in Country B.

Country B has a comparative advantage in the production of tractors because it only has to give up two cars to produce one tractor. In Country A, the opportunity cost of producing 1 tractor = 2 cars. Country B has to give up 4 cars for each tractor it produces. In Country B, the opportunity cost of producing 1 tractor = 4 cars. The opportunity cost of producing a tractor in Country B is lower than in Country A.

Key terms

Absolute advantage: when a country (or other economic agent) can produce a given amount of a good (or service) with fewer resources than another country **or** when a country can produce more of a good than another country with the same amount of resources.

Comparative advantage: when the opportunity cost of producing a good (or service) is lower than in another country.

If one country has an absolute advantage in one good and the other country has an absolute advantage in the other good, each country will also have a comparative advantage in the good in which they have an absolute advantage.

In his book *An inquiry into the nature and causes of the wealth of nations*, published in 1776, Adam Smith showed that countries would benefit from trade if they specialised in producing those goods in which they have an absolute advantage.

▼ **Table 6.2.2**: One country has an absolute advantage in both goods but each country has a comparative advantage in one of the goods

	Cars		Tractors
Country A	10	**or**	5
Country B	8	**or**	2

Opportunity cost ratios for Country A: 1 car = 0.5 tractors **or**
1 tractor = 2 cars

Opportunity cost ratios for Country B: 1 car = 0.25 tractors **or**
1 tractor = 4 cars

In the situation shown in Table 6.2.2, Country A has an absolute advantage in the production of both cars and tractors. With the same amount of resources, it can produce more cars and more tractors than Country B.

However, Country B has a comparative advantage in the production of cars since the opportunity cost of producing cars in Country B (1 car = 0.25 tractors) is lower than in Country A (1 car = 0.5 tractors).

Country A has a comparative advantage in the production of tractors since the opportunity cost of producing tractors in Country A (1 tractor = 2 cars) is lower than in Country B (1 car = 4 tractors).

While it is better to compare the opportunity cost ratios when determining which country has a comparative advantage in each good, comparative advantage can also be seen by comparing the relative efficiencies. For example, in Table 6.2.2, Country A is 25% more efficient at producing cars than Country B but it is 150% more efficient at producing tractors. Therefore, Country A has a comparative (or relative) advantage in producing tractors whereas Country B has a comparative (or relative) advantage in producing cars.

In this example, in absolute terms, Country A is more efficient at producing both goods than Country B. However, as will be explained, specialisation and trade can still benefit both countries, provided each country has a comparative advantage in one of the goods.

A production possibility diagram illustrating the difference between absolute and comparative advantage

The production possibility diagrams show the various combinations of two goods that each country can produce with a given amount of resources. Figure 6.2.2 is based on the data in Table 6.2.1 and assumes each economy has four bundles of resources.

Get it right

Make sure that you understand the difference between absolute advantage and comparative advantage.

Quantitative skills

Make sure you understand what is meant by "opportunity cost ratio" and can compare opportunity cost ratios to determine which country has a comparative advantage in which product.

If Country A devotes all the resources to producing cars, it can produce 64 cars (4 × 16). If it devotes all the resources to producing tractors, it can produce 16 tractors (4 × 4). If Country B devotes all the resources to producing cars, it can produce 48 cars (4 × 12). If it devotes all the resources to producing tractors, it can produce 24 tractors (4 × 6).

In Figure 6.2.2, the slope of the production possibility boundary (PPB) shows the opportunity cost of producing each good. In Country A, the opportunity cost of producing 1 tractor is 4 cars and in Country B the opportunity cost of producing 1 tractor is 2 cars. Country A has an absolute advantage in cars because if it devotes the 4 bundles of resources to cars, it can produce more cars than Country B. Country B has an absolute advantage in tractors because if it devotes the 4 bundles of resources to tractors, it can produce more tractors than Country A. If each country has an absolute advantage in one of the products, the PPBs will cross.

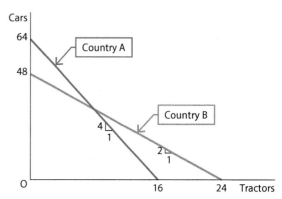

▲ **Figure 6.2.2**: Each country has an absolute and comparative advantage in one good

Progress questions

1 Which economist first developed the theory (or model) of comparative advantage?

2 What is meant by comparative advantage?

3 What does it mean if a country has an absolute advantage in the production of a good?

4 If the slopes/gradients of two countries' production possibility boundaries are different, does this show that each country has an absolute or comparative advantage in the production of a good?

Figure 6.2.3 is based on the data in Table 6.2.2 and assumes each economy has four bundles of resources.

If Country A devotes all the resources to producing cars, it can produce 40 cars (4 × 10). If it devotes all the resources to producing tractors, it can produce 20 tractors (4 × 5). If Country B devotes all the resources to producing cars, it can produce 32 cars (4 × 8). If it devotes all the resources to producing tractors, it can produce 8 tractors (4 × 2).

In Figure 6.2.3, Country A's PPB lies outside Country B's PPB. This shows that Country A has an absolute advantage in producing both cars and tractors. The slopes of the two PPBs are different, showing that the opportunity costs of production in each country are different. This means each country has a comparative advantage in one of the goods.

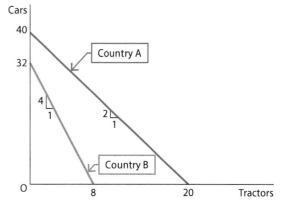

▲ **Figure 6.2.3**: One country has an absolute advantage in both goods but each country has a comparative advantage in one of the goods

Causes of comparative advantage and why it can change

A country's absolute and comparative advantage depend mainly on its **factor endowment**, infrastructure, technology and institutions.

Case study: Absolute and comparative advantage in the production of rice and wheat

▲ **Figure 6.2.4**: Working in a rice field

▼ **Table 6.2.3**: Production of rice and wheat in Countries X and Y

	Rice		Wheat
Country X	16 tonnes	or	4 tonnes
Country Y	18 tonnes	or	9 tonnes

1 Which country has an absolute advantage in the production of rice?

2 What is the opportunity cost of producing a tonne of wheat in Country Y?

3 State which country has a comparative advantage in the production of rice and explain why.

Table 6.2.3 shows the amount of rice and wheat that can be produced in Countries X and Y with a given amount of resources.

Link

Factors of production were explained in 1.2 "Economic resources" in the AS book.

Activity

Choose two products, goods or services, that your country exports. How might your country's factor endowment help to explain why these two products are important exports for your country?

A country's factor endowment is the amount of land, labour, capital and entrepreneurship that the country possesses. The factor of production land includes all the "free gifts of nature", for example natural resources, the sea and the climate of the country, as well as the land itself. Labour is not a homogeneous factor of production. People have different skills, the stock of human capital and the age structure of the population will affect productive efficiency. The stock of capital is affected by the amount of investment that has taken place over many years and its rate of depreciation. Entrepreneurship is, for example, affected by people's creativity, their willingness to take risks and their ability to organise production.

The infrastructure of a country is part of its capital stock. It includes road and rail networks and power supply and communication systems. The amount and quality of the infrastructure affect productivity and production costs and so both comparative and absolute advantage.

The state of technology in the country will also affect productive efficiency and the quality of the goods and services produced. Both productive efficiency and the quality of goods can affect both absolute and comparative advantage.

The efficiency of the country's institutions can affect how easy it is to start and grow a business and the performance of firms. For example, a well-developed financial system makes it easier for firms to raise the finance they need to set up in business and should reduce the cost of borrowing.

Whether a country has an absolute advantage in the production of one or more goods is affected by the overall level of efficiency within the country. However, a country may have a comparative advantage in some goods even if it is not the most efficient producer of those goods. For example, a low-income country with an abundant supply of cheap labour may have a comparative advantage in producing a labour-intensive manufactured good even if the same good could have been produced with fewer workers in a high-income country. The high-income country may have a comparative advantage in technologically advanced, capital-intensive products.

Comparative advantage changes over time

Over time, a country's factor endowment will change. For example, investment will increase the capital stock, education and training will improve the skills of the labour force, natural resources may be discovered and technology will improve. These changes can lead to a country developing a comparative advantage in different products.

As firms within a country develop new products and more efficient methods of production, the pattern of comparative advantage can change. Government policies may provide support for specific industries attempting to create a comparative advantage in that sector. For example, the Chinese government supported its solar panel manufacturing industry and it is now the world's largest supplier of solar panels.

As comparative advantage starts to change, it can become self-reinforcing. As output increases, firms are likely to benefit from increasing returns to scale, resulting in improvements in efficiency and lower average costs. As the industry grows and the demand for labour increases, the skills of the labour force will improve. Profits can be reinvested, helping to improve the quality of products and methods of production.

Changes in comparative advantage will lead to changes in the pattern of trade. If a country develops a comparative advantage in a good, it is likely to change from importing the product to becoming an exporter of the product.

Why the model shows that specialisation and trade can increase total output

The model of comparative advantage shows that specialisation and trade can be beneficial to those involved. If countries specialise in producing those goods in which they have a comparative advantage and then exchange them for those that they relatively less efficient at producing, it is possible to make everyone better off.

Each country has an absolute and comparative advantage in one good

Table 6.2.4 shows the number of bicycles and motorcycles that can be produced in Country A and Country B with one bundle of resources (factors of production). Country A has an absolute advantage in bicycles and Country B has an absolute advantage in motorcycles.

▼ **Table 6.2.4**: The quantity of bicycles and motorcycles that can be produced in Countries A and B with one bundle of resources

	Bicycles		Motorcycles
Country A	12	or	3
Country B	8	or	4

The opportunity cost of each good in each country is as follows:

Country A: 1 bicycle = 0.25 motorcycles **or** 1 motorcycle = 4 bicycles

Country B: 1 bicycle = 0.5 motorcycles **or** 1 motorcycle = 2 bicycles

Progress questions

5 What is meant by a country's factor endowment?

6 Why might investment into an industry and training the labour force in the skills needed by that industry lead to a change in comparative advantage?

Country A has a comparative advantage in bicycles because it only has to give up 0.25 motorcycles for each bicycle it produces whereas Country B has to give up 0.5 motorcycles for each bicycle it produces. Similarly, Country B has a comparative advantage in motorcycles because it only has to give up 2 bicycles for each motorcycle it produces whereas Country A has to give up 4 bicycles for each motorcycle produced.

For both countries to benefit from trade, the **terms of trade** must be between the **domestic opportunity cost ratios**. This could be anywhere between 1 motorcycle = 4 bicycles and 1 motorcycle = 2 bicycles, for example, 1 motorcycle = 3 bicycles.

Country A will specialise in producing bicycles and will export them to Country B in exchange for motorcycles. If the terms of trade are set at 1 motorcycle = 3 bicycles, Country A will benefit because without trade, it would have to give up producing 4 bicycles to enable it to produce 1 motorcycle whereas through trade it only has to sacrifice 3 bicycles for each motorcycle it imports from Country B. It makes a net gain of 1 bicycle for each motorcycle it imports.

Similarly, Country B benefits because it gains 3 bicycles for each motorcycle it exports whereas if it produces bicycles itself, it will only gain 2 bicycles for each motorcycle it gives up producing. Country B makes a net gain of 1 bicycle for each motorcycle it exports. It is better off producing motorcycles and trading them for bicycles rather than producing bicycles itself.

How much each country benefits from trade will be determined by the terms of trade but both countries will gain some benefit from specialisation and trade, provided the terms of trade are between the domestic opportunity cost ratios.

The benefits of specialisation and trade can also be measured by looking at the effect on the total output of the two goods. If we assume that each country has two bundles of resources, Table 6.2.5 shows total output without specialisation and Table 6.2.6 shows total output if each country devotes all its resources to producing the good in which it has a comparative advantage.

▼ **Table 6.2.5**: The quantity of bicycles and motorcycles that can be produced in Countries A and B if one bundle of resources is used to produce each good in each country

	Bicycles	Motorcycles
Country A	12	3
Country B	8	4
Total output	20	7

▼ **Table 6.2.6**: The quantity of bicycles and motorcycles that can be produced in Countries A and B if each country devotes two bundles of resources to producing the good in which it has a comparative advantage

	Bicycles	Motorcycles
Country A	24	0
Country B	0	8
Total output	24	8

Comparing Table 6.2.5 with Table 6.2.6 shows that, as a result of the countries specialising in producing the goods in which they have a comparative advantage, the total output of bicycles has increased by 4 and the total output of motorcycles has increased by 1. Specialisation has led to a more efficient allocation of resources and an increase in the output of both goods.

In this example, each country has an absolute advantage in producing one of the goods. It is not surprising that there are benefits from countries specialising in producing and exporting goods in which they have an absolute advantage and importing those in which they have an absolute disadvantage. However, the next example shows that specialisation and trade can benefit both countries even if one country has an absolute advantage in producing both goods.

One country has an absolute advantage in both goods but each country has a comparative advantage in one good

In Table 6.2.7, Country A has an absolute advantage in producing both bicycles and motorcycles. Country A also has a comparative advantage in producing motorcycles, but Country B has a comparative advantage in producing bicycles.

▼ **Table 6.2.7**: The quantity of bicycles and motorcycles that can be produced in Countries A and B with one bundle of resources

	Bicycles		Motorcycles
Country A	20	or	10
Country B	15	or	3

The opportunity cost of each good in each country is as follows:

Country A: 1 bicycle = 0.5 motorcycles **or** 1 motorcycle = 2 bicycles

Country B: 1 bicycle = 0.2 motorcycles **or** 1 motorcycle = 5 bicycles

Ricardo demonstrated that even though one country, in this case Country A, is more efficient at producing both goods, trade can be mutually beneficial (benefit both countries) provided each country has a comparative advantage in one of the goods.

The opportunity cost of producing motorcycles in Country A is less than in Country B and therefore Country A will benefit from specialising in the production of motorcycles and trading with Country B to get the bicycles it wants. Country B has a comparative advantage in bicycles and so it will specialise in producing bicycles and export them to Country A to get the motorcycles it wants.

Trade will be mutually beneficial provided the terms of trade are between the domestic opportunity cost ratios, that is between 1 motorcycle = 2 bicycles and 1 motorcycle = 5 motorcycles.

If the terms of trade are set at 1 motorcycle = 3 bicycles, Country A will benefit from specialising in producing motorcycles because it will gain 3 bicycles for each motorcycle it sells to Country B but would only be able to produce 2 bicycles itself for each motorcycle it gave up producing. It makes a net gain of 1 bicycle for each motorcycle it exports.

Progress questions

7   What is meant by the terms of trade?

8   Countries A and B can produce both oranges and apples. With a bundle of resources, Country A can produce either 100 kg of oranges or 250 kg of apples. With a bundle of resources, Country B can produce either 150 kg of oranges or 225 kg of apples. If the terms of trade are set at 1 kg of oranges = 2 kg of apples, explain why Country B will benefit from specialising in producing oranges and importing apples from Country A.

Country B will benefit because through trade it will only have to give 3 bicycles for each motorcycle it imports whereas if it decided to produce motorcycles itself, it would have to give up producing 5 bicycles for each motorcycle. Country B makes a net gain of 2 bicycles for each motorcycle it imports.

Once again, the benefits of specialisation and trade can be seen by looking at the effects on the total output of the two goods. The example that follows assumes that each country has 2 bundles of resources.

▼ **Table 6.2.8**: The quantity of bicycles and motorcycles that can be produced in Countries A and B if each country devotes one bundle of resources to producing each good

	Bicycles	Motorcycles
Country A	20	10
Country B	15	3
Total output	35	13

Table 6.2.8 shows that if each country devotes one bundle of resources to producing bicycles and one bundle of resources to producing motorcycles, the total output of bicycles will be 35 and the total output of motorcycles will be 13.

▼ **Table 6.2.9**: The quantity of bicycles and motorcycles that can be produced if Countries A and B devote two bundles of resources to producing the good in which they have a comparative advantage

	Bicycles	Motorcycles
Country A	0	20
Country B	30	0
Total output	30	20

By comparing Table 6.2.8 with Table 6.2.9, we can see that complete specialisation has resulted in the production of motorcycles increasing from 13 to 20 but the production of bicycles has fallen from 35 to 30. Given that the terms of trade are 1 motorcycle = 3 bicycles, it is reasonable to conclude that the gain of 7 more motorcycles is worth more than the loss of 5 bicycles.

However, if Country A does not specialise completely and uses some of its resources to produce bicycles, it is possible to increase the total output of both bicycles and motorcycles. For example, if Country A gives up producing 3 motorcycles, it can produce 6 more bicycles and, as can be seen in Table 6.2.10, the output of both goods can be increased through specialisation and trade.

▼ **Table 6.2.10**: The quantity of bicycles and motorcycles that can be produced if Country B specialises in producing bicycles and Country A uses most of its resources to produce motorcycles

	Bicycles	Motorcycles
Country A	6	17
Country B	30	0
Total output	36	17

Case study: Northland and Southland

▲ Figure 6.2.5: Doors and windows

Northland and Southland can produce doors and windows. Table 6.2.11 shows the number of doors and windows that Northland and Southland can produce with a given amount of resources.

▼ Table 6.2.11: Production of doors and windows in Northland and Southland

	Doors		Windows
Northland	3	**or**	6
Southland	4	**or**	16

1 Which country has an absolute advantage in the production of doors and windows?
2 What is the opportunity cost of producing one door in Northland?
3 What is the opportunity cost of producing one door in Southland?
4 Explain why Northland has a comparative advantage in producing doors.
5 Explain why Southland has a comparative advantage in producing windows.
6 If the terms of trade is 1 door = 3 windows, explain why Northland would benefit from specialisation and trade.
7 If the terms of trade is 1 door = 3 windows, explain why Southland would benefit from specialisation and trade.

By comparing Table 6.2.8 with 6.2.10, we can see that specialisation and trade have resulted in the production of bicycles increasing by 1 and the production of motorcycles increasing by 4.

Other economic benefits of specialisation and trade

While the principle of comparative advantage explains how specialisation and trade can benefit people, there are other benefits that can result from international trade.

Economies of scale and improvements in productivity

Constant returns to scale is an assumption of the model of comparative advantage. This means that the model assumes that the domestic opportunity cost ratios do not change as countries start to specialise in producing those goods in which they have a comparative advantage.

However, when countries specialise and export those products in which they have a comparative advantage, total output of these products and the scale of production increase. This may lead to increasing returns to scale and economies of scale. If productivity increases and average costs fall, this allows prices to be cut. These benefits are in addition to those illustrated by the principle of comparative advantage.

As firms within a country specialise in producing certain goods, it may lead to better methods of production which could also increase productivity. This can result from improvements in workers' skills and abilities, from spending on research and development and from "learning by doing".

Link

Economies of scale were explained in 3.4 "Economies and diseconomies of scale" in the AS book and increasing returns to scale was explained in 2.1 "The law of diminishing returns and returns to scale".

More competition

International trade means that there is more competition between firms. Increased competition encourages firms to become more efficient, reduce costs and lower prices. Where there is competition, firms need to produce high-quality products that satisfy people's needs and wants. Competition can also lead to new products being developed that benefit consumers.

In a closed economy, in some industries, there may be monopolies or firms with substantial monopoly power. Opening up an economy to trade may prevent large, dominant firms abusing their monopoly power.

A greater variety of products

Without trade, there are products that some countries are unable to produce and consume. For example, a country that has no oil must import it from countries that can produce oil. It may be too expensive for a country with a cold climate to produce certain types of food that can be produced cheaply in countries with a warmer climate.

Also, foreign firms often provide substitutes for products that are produced in the domestic economy. For example, many countries produce and export cars, but they also import cars. Car manufacturers differentiate their products, and trade allows consumers to choose a car that best meets their needs. If different countries produce similar but not identical products, it can increase consumers' welfare.

Temporary shortages can be eliminated or reduced

There are times when a country may not be able to supply the goods and services that people usually consume. If, for example, there is a natural disaster, trade makes it possible for people to satisfy some of their needs by importing essential products.

Many agricultural products are seasonal and without imports from around the world, they may not be available at certain times of the year. International trade means that many people are able to buy such products whenever they want them.

Improvements in technology can be transferred between countries

International trade allows firms to buy advanced machinery from other countries, improving their productivity and efficiency. Global supply chains allow technological improvements and other changes that increase productivity to be transferred around the world.

Faster economic growth and more employment

International trade and the ability to export increase the size of the market and allow firms to increase sales. Without international trade, firms' sales are limited by the size of their home market. The growth in exports increases aggregate demand. Exports are an injection into the circular flow of income and will have a positive multiplier effect, leading to an increase in real GDP and employment. The increase in AD and the supply-side improvements that result from specialisation and trade lead to an increase in both short-run and long-run economic growth. Although it is not the only reason, many countries such as South Korea, China and Vietnam, that have opened up their economies to international trade, have experienced rapid economic growth.

Overall, specialisation and trade should improve the allocation of resources. Free trade should lead to improvements in productive, allocative and dynamic efficiency, and reduce X-inefficiency. It should result in lower prices, an increase in consumer surplus and higher living standards.

The costs of international trade

Although international trade has improved the standard of living for many people, not everybody benefits. It should be possible to make everyone better off, but this does not always happen. Some of the costs of specialisation and trade are explained below.

Structural unemployment

For simplicity, the model of comparative advantage assumes that factors of production are perfectly mobile within a country, but this is an unrealistic assumption. When barriers to trade are reduced or the pattern of comparative advantage changes, some industries will grow and others will go into decline. If factors of production are perfectly mobile, resources will move from the declining industries to those that are growing. However, factors of production, including labour, are not perfectly mobile and those who were employed in the declining industries are likely to experience unemployment, which may last a long while. This has harmful social and personal consequences for those who are unemployed and their families.

If factors of production are unemployed, it also means that the output of the economy is lower than it could have been. This loss in output, due to unemployment, offsets the gain in output that results from countries specialising in producing those products in which they have a comparative advantage.

Transport costs

The model assumes that there are no transport costs. Resources employed in transporting products between countries could have been used to produce other goods and services. Again, this loss of output offsets some of the gains from specialisation and trade. However, as transport and communication have become more efficient, these costs have fallen.

Environmental costs

Transporting goods creates negative externalities, where the social cost is higher than the private cost. Unless government policies internalise the external costs, for example, by imposing high taxes on fossil fuels, it means that the true cost of products imported from abroad do not reflect their cost to society. Therefore, the volume of international trade is likely to be greater than the volume of trade that would maximise social welfare.

Link

Productive, allocative and dynamic efficiency, and X-inefficiency were explained in 3.9 "Static efficiency, dynamic efficiency and resource allocation". Consumer surplus was explained in 3.10 "Consumer and producer surplus".

Get it right

Remember that the principle of comparative advantage does not explain all the benefits that result from specialisation and trade.

Link

Barriers to entry were explained in 3.4 "Oligopoly".

Link

The effects of primary product dependency are explained in 8.2 "Factors that affect economic development".

Get it right

Remember that there are some disadvantages that result from specialisation and trade. These disadvantages help to explain why some countries use measures to protect their economies from foreign competition.

Activity

Find out which products or types of product your country imports. Why does your country import these products? What are the main benefits and costs of importing these products?

Also, if the production of some goods damages the environment and this is not reflected in the costs of production and the price of the product, relative prices do not reflect the true pattern of comparative advantage. As a result, the volume and pattern of trade is likely to be **suboptimal**.

LEDCs may find it difficult to compete with MEDCs

Absolute and comparative advantage are affected by economies of scale, technology and "learning by doing". Established firms usually have an advantage over new entrants. This means that firms in LEDCs that have the potential to become efficient producers are likely to find it very difficult to break into a market where there are well-established overseas producers. If existing firms have created barriers to entry, it becomes even more difficult for new firms from LEDCs to set up in markets dominated by firms from MEDCs.

Countries are more vulnerable to change

Specialisation means that countries produce a limited range of goods and services and import products that they do not produce themselves. If the pattern of comparative advantage changes and other countries develop a comparative advantage in goods and services that a country is specialising in producing, the demand for its products will fall and this may lead to low growth and rising unemployment. Changes in technology and in the pattern of demand can have similar consequences. For example, the development of substitutes for natural rubber can have a serious impact on countries that specialise in producing and exporting rubber, particularly if their economy is very dependent on the rubber industry. If a country has a diversified industrial structure, it will not be as badly affected if one sector of its economy declines.

Prices of commodities fluctuate more than most manufactured goods. Some LEDCs have a comparative advantage in a few primary products and when world market prices of primary products fall, it can be very damaging for economies that depend on these products.

Unfair competition

Some firms in MEDCs argue that they face unfair competition from low-cost producers in some LEDCs. They believe that low wages, poor working conditions and the lack of regulations to control pollution mean that they are unable to compete. In many MEDCs, minimum wage laws, regulations relating to the health and safety of workers and policies to limit pollution increase the costs of firms. If firms in LEDCs do not have to pay for negative externalities in production, they are not paying the full cost of production and can charge lower prices. However, it is the abundant supply of labour in many LEDCs, relative to other factors of production, that leads to low wages and is often their source of comparative advantage. It is comparative advantage that provides the gains from international trade.

Progress questions

9   Explain why increasing returns to scale can increase the benefits that result from specialisation and trade.

10 Explain why a country may suffer from structural unemployment when there is a change in the pattern of comparative advantage.

Protectionist policies

Despite the benefits of specialisation and trade, governments in many countries use tariffs, quotas, subsidies and other measures to protect their economies from foreign competition. Such policies are normally used to protect particular sectors of the economy, such as the car industry or agriculture.

Link

The reasons why countries use protectionist policies are explained in detail later in this section.

Tariff

A tariff is an indirect tax on imports, it might be a specific tax or an ad valorem tax. A tariff increases the price of imports and makes them less competitive. Domestic producers are protected; they can charge higher prices, will make more profit and should experience an increase in sales. A tariff is also likely to protect jobs. If domestic firms experience an increase in the demand for their products, they are likely to employ more workers. However, the increase in the prices of products with a tariff makes consumers worse off.

Link

Indirect taxes were explained in 5.7 "Government intervention in markets" in the AS book.

The effectiveness of a tariff depends on the amount of the tax and the price elasticities of demand for and supply of the product. If the demand for the product is price elastic, there will be a more than proportionate fall in the demand for imports and it should result in an increase in the demand for domestic substitutes. If the supply of domestic substitute products is price elastic, the increase in price will lead to a more than proportionate increase in domestic output.

In Figure 6.2.6, S_d and D_d are the domestic supply and demand curves for the product. If imports of the product are banned, sometimes known as **autarky**, the domestic price of the product would be P_d and quantity bought and sold would be Q_3.

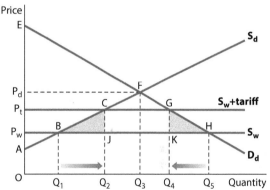

▲ **Figure 6.2.6**: The effects of a tariff

The world market supply of the product is S_w and it is shown as being perfectly elastic at a price of P_w. This means that the country can import as much of the product as it wants from the rest of the world at this price. This assumes that the price is fixed on the world market and the country is one of many buyers of the product. If this is not the case, the world market supply curve would be upward sloping.

If the economy is opened up to trade and there are no restrictions on imports of the product, the price in the domestic market would fall from P_d to P_w. As shown by the demand curve (D_d), domestic consumers would buy Q_5 units of the product at a price of P_w. The supply curve (S_d) shows that domestic firms would only be willing to supply Q_1 and ($Q_5 - Q_1$) would be imported from the rest of the world.

Key term

Autarky: where imports are banned and the economy is self-sufficient in a product.

If the government imposes a tariff of ($P_t - P_w$), the world market supply curve shifts vertically upwards, by the amount of the tariff, to S_w + tariff. As a result, the domestic demand for the product falls to Q_4. The domestic supply curve (S_d) shows that the increase in the price of imports encourages domestic firms to increase production from Q_1 to Q_2. The amount imported falls to ($Q_4 - Q_2$). The tariff revenue collected by the government is the tariff charged on each product multiplied by the number of products imported, it is [$(P_t - P_w) \times (Q_4 - Q_2)$] or the area JCGK.

The tariff means that the production of the product is diverted away from low-cost producers in the rest of the world to higher-cost producers in the domestic economy. It makes consumers worse off but protects domestic firms and raises revenue for the government. The effect on economic welfare can be analysed by considering the sum of these effects.

Before the tariff was imposed, the consumer surplus was the area P_wEH but after the tariff, consumer surplus falls to P_tEG. Therefore, the loss in consumer surplus is P_wP_tGH. However, there is an increase in producer surplus equal to P_wP_tCB and tariff revenue of JCGK. Since the reduction in consumer surplus is more than the increase in producer surplus and tariff revenue, there is an overall reduction in economic welfare. The overall loss of welfare is areas (BCJ + GHK). The sum of these two triangles is sometimes known as the deadweight loss that results from imposing a tariff.

> Loss of welfare = Fall in consumer surplus − (increase in producer surplus + tariff revenue)
>
> = $P_wP_tGH − (P_wP_tCB + JCGK)$
>
> = BCJ + GHK

Link

Consumer surplus, producer surplus and deadweight loss were explained in 3.10 "Consumer and producer surplus".

Quota

A quota is a limit on the quantity of a good that can be imported. It is usually enforced by a system of licensing. Firms that wish to import the product from abroad must apply for a licence from the government and the government will limit the quantity of products that are given a licence. Since the quota restricts the supply of a good, it is likely to lead to an increase in the price of the good in the domestic market and will help protect domestic firms and their workers but will make consumers worse off.

In Figure 6.2.7, S_d and D_d are the domestic supply and demand curves. In a situation of autarky, the price in the home market would be P_d and the quantity Q_3. The world market supply of the product is S_w and if the economy was open to free trade in this product, the price would be P_w and the quantity sold Q_5.

If the government imposes a quota on imports equal to $(Q_4 − Q_2)$, the supply of the product to the domestic market is S_d + quota. The horizonal distance between the original domestic supply curve and the new supply curve is the amount of the quota. The new equilibrium price and quantity would settle at P_q and Q_4. Compared to the situation where there is free trade, the price has increased, the quantity sold has fallen and there is a fall in economic welfare. The change in economic welfare is shown in Table 6.2.11.

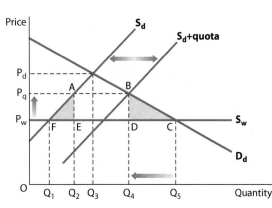

▲ **Figure 6.2.7**: The effects of a quota

Table 6.2.11: Change in economic welfare when a quota is imposed on imports

Fall in consumer surplus	P_wP_qBC
Increase in the producer surplus for domestic firms	P_wP_qAF
Increase in producer surplus on imports from abroad	ABDE
Net reduction in economic welfare (deadweight loss)	AFE + BDC

Subsidy

If the government gives a subsidy to the domestic producers of a good, it distorts the pattern of comparative advantage and protects domestic firms, but the subsidy is a cost to the taxpayer.

In Figure 6.2.8, when there is free trade in the good, the market price is P_w and the quantity bought and sold is Q_3. The domestic supply curve S_d shows that domestic producers will supply Q_1 and the amount imported will equal $(Q_3 - Q_1)$.

If the government gives a subsidy to domestic producers, the domestic supply curve shifts from S_d to S_d + subsidy. The vertical distance between the two supply curves is the amount of the subsidy per unit. In Figure 6.2.8, the subsidy per unit is $(P_x - P_w)$ or CD. The subsidy does not affect the market price of the product or the amount bought but domestic production increases to Q_2 and the quantity of imports falls to $(Q_3 - Q_2)$.

Since the subsidy has not affected the equilibrium price or quantity sold, consumer surplus is unchanged. However, domestic producer surplus has increased by $P_w P_x CB$ and taxpayers have to pay the total amount of the subsidy, which is $P_w P_x CD$. Consequently, the overall loss in economic welfare is $(P_w P_x CD - P_w P_x CB)$ shown by the area BCD.

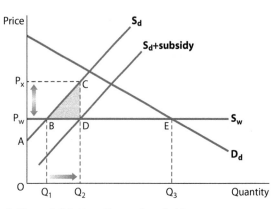

▲ **Figure 6.2.8**: The effects of a subsidy

Quantitative skills

Make sure you can draw and interpret diagrams that illustrate the effects of a country imposing tariffs and quotas or giving subsidies to protect domestic firms.

Other restrictions on trade

Some countries impose an **import ban** on some products and/or some countries. An import ban is also known as an embargo on imports. This may be to protect domestic producers, to prevent demerit goods being imported into the country or perhaps to damage a foreign country when there is a dispute between the two countries.

Governments also pass laws and regulate the sale of certain products in their domestic market. Regulations may relate to, for example, health and safety or the protection of the environment. Most regulations of this type are imposed to protect people's health or the natural environment, but they can also make it difficult for other countries to export their products to countries that have imposed such regulations. Complying with the regulations can increase the cost of the product, particularly if the regulations are different from those imposed by other countries.

Common standards for certain products may be required to ensure that they fit or work together, for example plugs for electrical sockets. If the standard is different from other countries, it can provide domestic firms with an advantage over foreign suppliers. Regulations can also relate to the labelling and packaging of products.

Some regulations and other informal controls imposed by governments can restrict international trade and are sometimes introduced for this purpose. It is often much more difficult to identify and reduce these less obvious restrictions on international trade.

Key term

Import ban (embargo on imports): when no imports of a certain type of product, or products from a particular country, are allowed.

Case study: Trade restrictions increase in 2019

▲ **Figure 6.2.9**: Tariffs restrict trade

In 2019, a report from the World Trade Organization (WTO) stated that 102 measures to restrict international trade were put in place by its members. These restrictions included tariff increases, quotas, bans and stricter customs procedures. It was estimated that in 2018, almost $1.5 trillion of world merchandise imports were affected by import restrictions, representing almost 7.5% of world imports. Import restrictions increase the price of imports and the volume of world merchandise trade was expected to grow more slowly at 1.2% in 2019, less than the previous estimate of 2.6%.

1 Explain how stricter customs procedures might affect the volume of imports.
2 Explain why an increase in restrictions on international trade is likely to increase the price of imports.
3 How might an increase in restrictions on international trade affect firms and consumers?

Progress questions

11 Distinguish between a tariff and a quota.
12 Explain why the effectiveness of a tariff depends on the price elasticity of demand for the good.
13 Explain why the introduction of a quota will reduce the consumer surplus of domestic consumers.

Why countries impose protectionist policies

The principle of comparative advantage shows that provided there are differences in the opportunity costs of production, free trade can be mutually beneficial for countries, yet many countries continue to protect their economies from foreign competition. There are many reasons why countries protect their economies, some are economic but others are social and political. Some of the so-called economic arguments are hard to justify on economic grounds but other economic arguments can be justified.

Some of the main arguments for imposing restrictions on trade are:

- the infant industry (or sunrise industry) argument
- to prevent structural unemployment
- to protect against dumping
- to allow a country to diversify
- to protect the environment
- to prevent balance of payments problems
- to improve the terms of trade
- to raise revenue for the government
- to protect against low wages and unfair competition
- to prevent imports of unsafe products
- to protect strategic industries.

Infant industry argument

When a new firm enters an established market, it will often find it hard to compete with incumbent firms. At the start, production is usually on a small scale and methods of production may be inefficient. However, if the firm is able to survive and has the chance to grow, methods of production should improve and, as the firm expands, it should be able to benefit from economies of scale. If firms in an **infant industry** are protected from foreign competition, it may give them the chance to become more efficient and to develop a comparative

Key term

Infant industry: an industry that is in its early stages of development.

advantage in producing the good or service. An infant industry is sometimes known as a **sunrise industry**. A sunrise industry is usually in a new sector of the economy that is expected to grow rapidly.

The infant industry argument for protection is often applied to new industries in LEDCs that find it hard to compete with established firms from MEDCs. If an infant industry in an LEDC is protected by a tariff, or other restrictions on imports, it will have the chance to expand in its domestic market and become competitive. If the government does not support and protect infant industries, some LEDCs may remain dependent on a few primary industries.

This argument for protectionism is also used to support the introduction of trade restrictions to help the growth of sunrise industries in MEDCs. Not only does it take time for a new industry to expand and benefit from internal economies of scale, there may also be external economies of concentration that emerge when an industry locates in a region. These include the development of a skilled labour force and component suppliers. Once these advantages have been gained, firms that were once protected may become large companies able to compete in, and sometimes dominate, the global marketplace.

Economists, such as Ha-Joon Chang, have argued that many MEDCs, including the USA and Japan, were able to develop their economies by protecting some of their key industries from foreign competition. For example, the Japanese car industry was protected in the 1950s and 1960s and was required to produce at least 90% of the components needed to build a car in Japan. In the short run, Japanese consumers paid higher prices for lower-quality cars but since the 1970s, Japanese car manufacturers, such as Toyota, have been very successful both in their domestic market and abroad.

However, protectionism does not guarantee that the industry will become efficient. The lack of competition may mean that protected firms do not have the incentive to improve and they remain inefficient. It is difficult to know which industries to support. Markets change and some governments have protected industries that have not become competitive. Domestic consumers may suffer from higher prices and poor-quality products without any long-run benefits.

Prevent structural unemployment

The theory of comparative advantage assumes that factors of production are perfectly mobile within a country. This means that when an economy is opened up to free trade, or the pattern of comparative advantage changes, no one will be unemployed. Workers made unemployed, from those declining industries in which the country has a comparative disadvantage, will immediately find employment in the expanding industries in which the country has a comparative advantage. However, in the real world, labour and other factors of production are not perfectly mobile. Some workers will be structurally unemployed and may be out of work for several years. Buildings may be left empty and machinery that cannot be used elsewhere destroyed.

Unemployment means that more could have been produced to improve living standards. This loss of output has to be weighed against

▲ **Figure 6.2.10**: The economist and author Ha-Joon Chang

Key term

Sunrise industry: an industry that is in its early stages of development, often in a new sector of the economy that is expected to grow very rapidly.

the gains from a more efficient allocation of resources. Not only that, but there are social and personal costs for the unemployed and their families. Taxes are likely to increase to help pay for the financial support given to the unemployed. While some people are better off as a result of free trade, at least in the short run, others are worse off.

However, in the long run, most workers who were made unemployed are likely to find employment in other sectors of the economy and the benefits of a more efficient allocation of resources are likely to persist. Nevertheless, there is an economically justifiable argument for providing, at least, short-term protection to allow the industry to decline more slowly. This provides time for people to be retrained, to relocate and to be absorbed into the growing sectors of the economy.

Industries that are in decline in an economy are sometimes known as **sunset industries**. Governments often use protectionist measures to slow, or try to reverse, the decline of a sunset industry. Usually, the main aim is to reduce structural unemployment. However, some believe that protectionism, combined with industrial policies that are designed to help the industry become more efficient, can stop the decline and allow growth to resume.

In some MEDCs, industries such as steel and shipbuilding are sunset industries because it is now more efficient to produce these goods in other countries. As concerns over CO_2 emissions and global warming grow, the oil and gas industry may become a sunset industry.

Protect against dumping

Dumping is where a firm exports goods to another country and sells them at a price which is significantly below the price it sells the same good in its home market. The price charged is sometimes below the cost of production. There are several reasons why firms dump their products on foreign markets.

If an exporter has monopoly power in its home market, dumping is a form of price discrimination. It can charge a high price in its home market but, in order to compete with other foreign firms, it may have to charge a lower price in export markets. Charging a high price in its home market allows the firm to convert consumer surplus into producer surplus, increasing its revenue and profits.

Dumping can also be a type of predatory pricing. The exporter may charge a low price to undercut domestic firms to gain market share or with the aim of driving them out of business. If the exporter succeeds in destroying the competition, it may then increase prices.

Another reason for dumping is to get rid of surplus production which firms are unable to sell at the normal price. In the past, the European Union (EU) supported its agricultural industry by buying up surplus agricultural products when prices fell below the price floor set by the EU. These agricultural surpluses were often exported at subsidised prices which were below world market prices.

Dumping can also allow firms to benefit from economies of scale. If a firm is able to increase its sales by dumping, output will increase and it may be able to benefit from economies of scale that reduce its average cost. Provided the price the firm charges in the export market covers its average variable cost, it will make a contribution to its fixed costs and increase its profits.

Dumping can damage firms in the importing country's domestic market but, at least in the short term, it benefits consumers by reducing prices. Dumping usually means that prices do not reflect the opportunity costs of production and distort the pattern of comparative advantage, providing an economically justifiable reason for protecting the domestic industry.

Dumping is not illegal under World Trade Organization (WTO) rules unless it causes or threatens to cause significant damage to a domestic industry in the importing country or prevents an industry starting up in the domestic market. However, if there is evidence of dumping, the WTO may allow the country to impose a tariff on the product.

Allow a country to diversify
The theory of comparative advantage explains why specialisation and trade can be beneficial but specialisation can leave countries vulnerable to economic shocks. Some LEDCs specialise in producing and exporting a few primary products. Fluctuations in primary product prices and the development of substitutes can harm their economies.

Tariffs, quotas and similar measures can be used to protect sectors of the economy from foreign competition and allow the economy to develop a more diversified economic structure. For example, LEDCs that are dependent on a few primary products may wish to develop industries in the manufacturing sector.

Protect the environment
Where there are externalities, firms' costs of production do not always reflect the social cost of supplying the product. Consequently, relative prices do not reflect the true opportunity cost of producing different products. In some countries, the government has introduced policies, such as carbon taxes and pollution permits, that increase firms' costs of production so that they take into account the external, environmental costs. In other countries, there is little attempt to adopt policies that force firms to internalise production externalities.

Firms in countries that have strict environmental policies are at a competitive disadvantage compared to firms operating in countries where such policies are weak. There is an economic argument for imposing a tariff on products where the producer does not bear the full social cost of production.

International trade also requires that products are transported between countries. Particularly where this involves fossil fuels, there may be external environmental costs that are not taken into account. Some economists argue that trade restrictions are justified to encourage local production, reducing the damage to the environment.

Prevent balance of payments problems
Trade restrictions reduce spending on imports and can help to reduce a balance of payments deficit. However, unless the same restrictions

Link

Externalities were explained in 5.3 "Positive and negative externalities in production and consumption" in the AS book.

apply to all imports, they distort relative prices and the pattern of comparative advantage. They protect high-cost, inefficient domestic firms at the expense of more efficient overseas producers, and harm domestic consumers.

A large balance of payments deficit can be damaging for an economy but there are other measures, apart from protectionism, that can be used to reduce the deficit.

Link

Policies to reduce a balance were explained in 7.1 "The balance of payments".

Link

The terms of trade are explained later in this section.

Improve the terms of trade

The terms of trade improve when the average price of a country's exports rise relative to the average price of its imports. An improvement in the terms of trade means that a country is able to import more products for a given quantity of exports.

If, for example, a country imposes a tariff on imports, the exporter may have to reduce the price to try to maintain competitiveness. Other things being equal, this fall in the price of imports will mean that fewer exports are needed to buy a given quantity of imports and so the country's terms of trade have improved. The extent to which the price of imports is reduced will be affected by the price elasticity of demand for the product. If the demand is very elastic, the exporter may need to reduce the price significantly to prevent a large fall in demand.

Raise revenue for the government

If the government imposes a tariff on imports, it raises revenue that can be used to pay for public expenditure, for example, on health care and education. However, as always, the disadvantages of a tariff have to be considered. For example, the increase in price reduces consumers' real incomes and therefore the demand for other products.

Protect against low wages and unfair competition

Firms in MEDCs sometimes claim that trade restrictions are needed to protect them from unfair competition from LEDCs. They argue that the wages they have to pay are much higher than wages paid to workers in LEDCs. Regulations to protect workers, for example, in relation to health and safety, add to the cost of labour in most MEDCs. Minimum wage laws and pension contributions also make it more expensive to employ people. It is alleged that without protection from competition from firms in LEDCs, unemployment in MEDCs will increase and it will be impossible to maintain high wages and good working conditions.

However, it is the abundance of labour that leads to lower wages in LEDCs and the large supply of labour is the LEDCs' source of comparative advantage in labour-intensive products. By specialising and trading those products in which they have a comparative advantage, MEDCs should benefit from importing labour-intensive products at a price that is lower than they could produce them for themselves.

Prevent imports of unsafe products

Some regulations that are applied to imports are designed to protect consumers from products that are judged to be unsafe or have a health risk, for example, children's toys are often subject to strict health and safety rules. The EU has banned imports of chlorine-washed chicken from the US because it argues that to disinfect chicken in this way can deter farmers from adopting good hygiene standards. However, some regulations may be excessive and used to restrict imports rather than protect people.

Protect strategic industries

A strategic industry is one that the government judges to be important for the nation's security. Agriculture is often regarded as a strategic industry since it is important that there is enough food available in times of crisis. The steel and energy industries are other examples of industries that a government might wish to protect to ensure that the country is not completely reliant on importing these products. This argument is a non-economic argument for protecting certain key sectors of the economy.

Protectionism, membership of the WTO and retaliation

Since the end of the Second World War, there has been a general trend towards trade liberalisation. The General Agreement on Tariffs and Trade (GATT) and the World Trade Organization (WTO) have encouraged countries to reduce restrictions on international trade. The 164 countries that are members of the WTO (2020) are not completely free to impose tariffs, quotas and other restrictions on trade.

Also, although there are circumstances where protectionism may be in a country's interest, there is always the possibility of retaliation and a trade war. If one country imposes restrictions on imports and other countries retaliate, it is likely that everyone will be worse off. The exports of all the countries will fall and the benefits of specialisation and trade will be reduced.

Activity

Find two industries in your country that are protected by either a tariff or a quota. Explain why the government has chosen to protect each of these industries.

Key term

Trade war: when countries impose tariffs, quotas or other trade restrictions on each other's exports.

Progress questions

14 Briefly explain the infant industry argument for protectionism.

15 What is meant by "dumping"?

16 What is meant by "retaliation"?

Case study: Banana wars

▲ **Figure 6.2.11**: Bananas are big business

The banana wars were a series of trade disputes between the European Union (EU), the USA and several countries in Latin America. The dispute began in 1993. The EU banana market is the largest in the world and is important for many developing countries. The EU does not impose a tariff on bananas imported from former European colonies in Africa, the Caribbean and the Pacific (known as the ACP countries). However, a tariff is charged on bananas imported from other countries, including those in Latin America.

The USA, Ecuador, Guatemala, Honduras and Mexico complained to the World Trade Organization (WTO) about the tariff. The USA was involved because some large transnational US companies produce bananas in Latin America. The ACP countries were against a reduction in the tariff. In 2009, the Geneva Agreement on Trade in Bananas agreed to cut the EU tariff from €176 per tonne to €114 per tonne by 2017.

1 Why did the ACP countries oppose the reduction in the tariff on bananas imported into the EU?

2 How will banana producers in Latin America, such as Ecuador, be affected by the reduction in the tariff?

3 How will households in the EU be affected by the reduction in the tariff?

The changing pattern of world trade

There are two main aspects to consider when describing the **pattern of world trade**. The first is concerned with the types of goods and services that are traded between countries, or the commodity structure of trade. The second is the geographical distribution of international trade.

When describing changes in the commodity structure of trade, economists usually distinguish between merchandise trade and trade in services, although these categories can be sub-divided. For example, merchandise trade is often divided into primary products and manufactures. Changes in the percentage of total world exports accounted for by each group of products is often used when measuring changes in the pattern of trade,

The geographical distribution considers how various countries', or regions', share of world trade is changing. The main indicator of changes in the geographical pattern of trade is the change in the percentage of total world exports accounted for by different countries or regions.

When investigating the pattern of trade for an individual country, it is usual to consider:

- the commodity structure of the country's exports
- the commodity structure of the country's imports
- the geographical distribution of its exports
- the geographical distribution of its imports.

The commodity structure of world trade

In 2018, just over 23% of total world exports were services and nearly 77% were exports of merchandise. Over 70% of merchandise exports were manufactured goods and the remaining 30% were primary products including food, raw materials and fuels. The value of merchandise exports in 2018 was almost $19.5 trillion.

In Africa, primary products accounted for around three-quarters of merchandise exports. The economies of North and Central America, Europe, and South, East and South-East Asia export mainly manufactured goods.

Exports of services have been growing faster than merchandise exports. Between 2008 and 2018, exports of services grew by 46% whereas merchandise exports grew by 20%. This has resulted in the share of world exports accounted for by services increasing. The value of services exported in 2018 was approximately $5.8 trillion.

The geographical distribution of world trade

In 2018, MEDCs accounted for just over 55% of total world exports. MEDCs' share of merchandise exports was 52% but their share of services exported was nearly 68%. China was the largest exporter of merchandise exports with nearly 13% of the world total. The USA was the largest exporter of services with 14% of the world total.

In 2018, 36% of merchandise trade was between developed economies, 28% was between developing economies and 36% was between developed and developing economies. The USA imported goods worth \$563 billion from China and exported goods worth \$168 billion to China. Around 69% of European merchandise exports were to other European countries and approximately 60% of the exports from Asian countries went to other Asian countries.

Table 6.2.12 shows how the regional pattern of world merchandise trade changed between 1980 and 2019. Exports are measured at current prices and so the figures do not show what happened to the volume of world merchandise exports, but changes in the geographical distribution (or pattern) of world merchandise exports can be seen from the table.

▼ **Table 6.2.12**: Source of merchandise exports in 1980 and 2019, \$ million at current prices

Region	Exports ($ million) 1980	Percentage of world trade 1980	Exports ($ million) 2019	Percentage of world trade 2019
Africa	121 378	5.92%	462 257	2.45%
America	405 031	19.76%	3 148 771	16.67%
Asia	509 170	24.84%	7 705 165	40.79%
Europe	984 934	48.04%	7 246 800	38.37%
Oceania	29 616	1.44%	325 807	1.72%
World	2 050 129	100%	18 888 799	100%

Source: UNCTADstat, unctadstat.unctad.org; accessed August 2020

Factors that affect the pattern of world trade

The commodity structure of world trade is affected by comparative advantage which, as explained earlier, is determined by a number of influences including the factor endowment of different countries, technology and economies of scale. The growth and diversification of newly emerging economies have affected the pattern of trade.

The commodity structure and geographical distribution of trade are influenced by tariffs, quotas, subsidies and other protectionist measures. Changes in exchange rates affect competitiveness and also cause changes in the pattern of trade.

Despite improvements in technology that have reduced transport costs, countries often trade more goods and services with countries that are located in the same region. In some cases, this has been reinforced by the creation of regional trade blocs such as the EU and AFTA (ASEAN Free Trade Area).

The terms of trade

The terms of trade measures the quantity of imports that a country can obtain for a given quantity of its exports. The formula for calculating a country's terms of trade is:

$$\text{Terms of trade} = \frac{\text{Index of export prices}}{\text{Index of import prices}} \times 100$$

The index of export prices is a weighted index that attempts to measure changes in the average price of a country's exports. The index of import prices is a weighted index that attempts to measure changes

Progress questions

17 What is meant by the commodity structure (or pattern) of world trade?

18 What is meant by the geographical distribution (or pattern) of world trade?

19 Use Table 6.2.12 to identify the main changes in the geographical distribution (or pattern) of world merchandise trade between 1980 and 2019.

Link

The nature of trade blocs is explained later in this section.

Key term

Terms of trade (for a country): the quantity of imports that a country can obtain for a given quantity of its exports, determined by the average price of exports relative to the average price of imports.

Case study: Destination of merchandise exports from African countries

▲ **Figure 6.2.12**: Africa

Table 6.2.13 shows the value of merchandise exports from African countries to developing and developed economies and the total value of world merchandise exports in 2008, 2013 and 2018.

1 Calculate, to **two** decimal places, the sum of African merchandise exports to developing and developed economies as percentage of total world exports for each of the three years 2008, 2013 and 2018.

2 Calculate the ratio of African merchandise exports to developing economies compared to African merchandise exports to developed economies in 2008, 2013 and 2018. The ratio should show the value of developing economies' exports for each dollar of developed economies' exports. Each ratio should be shown to **one** decimal place.

3 Use your answers to questions 1 and 2 to help you describe the main changes in African merchandise exports between 2008 and 2018.

▼ **Table 6.2.13**: Destination of African merchandise exports 2008 and 2018

Year	Developing economies ($ billion)	Developed economies ($ billion)	Total world exports ($ billion)
2008	186	357	16 135
2013	274	300	18 997
2018	250	227	19 414

Source: UNCTAD Handbook of statistics 2019

Key term

Improvement in the terms of trade: when the average price of a country's exports rises relative to the average price of its imports.

Link

Index numbers were explained in 6.2 "Macroeconomic indicators" in the AS book.

Quantitative skills

Remember that the terms of trade is an index and that index numbers do not have any units.

in the average price of a country's imports. The index of export prices is also known as the export unit value index because it attempts to measure changes in the average price of one unit of exports. Similarly, the index of import prices is also known as the import unit value index. Therefore, the formula for calculating the terms of trade is sometimes written as:

$$\text{Terms of trade} = \frac{\text{Export unit value index}}{\text{Import unit value index}} \times 100$$

An **improvement in the terms of trade** occurs when the average price of a country's exports rises relative to the average price of its imports. This might be caused by, for example, a rise in export prices, a fall in import prices or export prices rising faster than import prices. An improvement in the terms of trade means that a country is able to obtain more imports for a given quantity of exports. This can lead to an improvement in living standards because, potentially, there is an increase in the amount of goods and services available for people in the country to consume. For example, for an oil exporting country, such as Nigeria, an increase in the world market price of oil will mean that it can obtain more imports for a given quantity of oil exported.

A **deterioration in the terms of trade** occurs when the average price of a country's exports falls relative to the average price of its imports. For example, import prices might be rising faster than export prices or import prices might be falling more slowly than export prices are falling. Other things being equal, this can lead to a fall in average living standards because the country obtains fewer imports for a given quantity of exports.

An increase in the numerical value of the terms of trade indicates an improvement whereas a fall in the numerical value of the terms of trade shows that the terms of trade has deteriorated.

▼ **Table 6.2.14**: The indices of export and import prices for an economy, 2018–2021, (2019 = 100)

Year	Index of export prices	Index of import prices
2018	90	80
2019	100	100
2020	120	90
2021	110	105

In Table 6.2.14, the base year is 2019. In the base year, the index of export prices, the index of import prices and the terms of trade are all equal to 100.

In 2018, the terms of trade was:

Terms of trade (2018) $= \frac{90}{80} \times 100 = \textbf{112.5}$

Between 2018 and 2019, import prices rose faster than export prices and so the terms of trade deteriorated, as shown by the terms of trade index falling from 112.5 to 100.

Between 2019 and 2020, export prices rose and import prices fell, leading to an improvement in the terms of trade.

Terms of trade (2020) $= \frac{120}{90} \times 100 = \textbf{133.3}$

Between 2020 and 2021, export prices fell and import prices rose, leading to a deterioration in the terms of trade.

Terms of trade (2021) $= \frac{110}{105} \times 100 = \textbf{104.8}$

Causes of changes in a country's terms of trade

Anything that leads to a change in the average price of a country's exports or imports will lead to a change in its terms of trade. For example, other things being equal, if a country has a higher rate of inflation than other countries, the average price of its exports is likely to be increasing faster than the average price of its imports and its terms of trade will improve.

A rise in world commodity prices will lead to an improvement in the terms of trade for countries exporting primary products and a deterioration in the terms of trade for countries that import primary products.

A depreciation/fall in a country's exchange rate causes a deterioration in its terms of trade. A depreciation in the exchange rate reduces the foreign currency price of a country's exports and increases the price

Get it right

Do not confuse unit value of exports (or imports) with the value of exports. The unit value of exports is the average price of exports whereas the value of exports is the total amount spent on a country's exports. The value of exports depends on the price and the quantity sold.

Key term

Deterioration in the terms of trade: when the average price of a country's exports falls relative to the average price of its imports.

Link

The causes and effects of changes in a country's exchange rate are explained in 7.2 "Exchange rates".

Activity

Find out what has happened to the index of export prices, the index of import prices and the terms of trade for your country over the past five years. Has the terms of trade improved or deteriorated?

Get it right

Do not confuse the "terms of trade" with the "balance of trade". The terms of trade is concerned with the average price of exports compared to the average price of imports whereas the balance of trade is the difference between the value of exports and the value of imports. Changes in the terms of trade affect the balance of trade.

Get it right

The price elasticities of demand for exports and imports will affect how a change in the terms of trade affect a country's economy. An improvement in the terms of trade is most likely to harm the economy when the demand for exports and imports are price elastic.

Progress questions

20 What is the formula used to calculate a country's terms of trade?

21 What is the value of the terms of trade in the base year?

22 If the terms of trade increases from 95 to 97, has the terms of trade improved or deteriorated? Explain your answer.

23 Explain why an improvement in a country's terms of trade might lead to a deterioration in its balance of trade.

of imports in the domestic currency. This means it has to export more goods and services to obtain a given quantity of imports. Similarly, an appreciation/rise in a country's exchange rate will improve its terms of trade because it leads to a rise in the foreign currency price of exports and a fall in the domestic currency price of imports.

The effects of a change in a country's terms of trade on its economy

The effects of a change in a country's terms of trade on its economy will depend upon the causes of the change and the nature of the economy. An improvement in the terms of trade is not always good for an economy and a deterioration in a country's terms of trade is not always harmful.

An improvement in a country's terms of trade means that it can obtain more imports for a given quantity of exports. However, it might also mean that the country is becoming less competitive in world markets. For example, if high inflation is the reason why a country's export prices are increasing, it is likely to experience a fall in the quantity/volume of exports it sells. This may lead to a deterioration in its balance of trade in goods and services and a fall in aggregate demand. The fall in the volume of exports will have a downward multiplier effect on national income and is likely to increase unemployment. The magnitude of these effects will depend on the price elasticity of demand for its exports. The more elastic the demand for the products the country exports, the greater the fall in the demand for exports and the greater the damage to the economy.

If the improvement in the terms of trade is due to a fall in the price of imports, there are likely to be similar consequences. Domestic residents will start to buy cheaper imports rather than home-produced goods and services and the impact on the economy will depend on the price elasticity of demand for imports. If the demand for imports is price elastic, there will be a more than proportionate increase in the demand for imports. The balance of trade will deteriorate and the withdrawals from the circular flow of income will increase.

However, if the improvement in the terms of trade is due to a fall in the world market price of primary products, countries that import these products will benefit. The demand for commodities is usually price inelastic and therefore the amount spent on importing these essential products will fall. The balance of trade will improve and withdrawals from the circular flow of income will fall. Domestic residents will have more money to spend, leading to a rise in national income and employment. The fall in commodity prices will reduce cost-push inflationary pressures and as fewer exports are needed to buy these products, living standards should improve.

A rise in primary product prices leading to an improvement in the terms of trade of countries that export these products will benefit their economies. The inelastic demand for such products will mean that export revenues rise, improving the balance of trade. Injections into the circular flow of income will increase, leading to a rise in national income and employment.

Case study: Australia – a major exporter of primary products

▲ **Figure 6.2.13**: Symbols of Australia

▼ **Table 6.2.15**: Changes in the terms of trade for Australia, 2013–2019

Year	Unit value index of exports	Unit value index of imports	Terms of Trade
2013	147.0	123.2	119.3
2015	100.0	100.0	100.0
2017	?	99.0	116.4
2019	127.8	98.2	?

Source: UNCTADstat; accessed 6 August 2020

1 AUD = 0.702 USD. This fall in the exchange rate made Australia's exports cheaper but increased the price Australian residents had to pay for imports.

1 Distinguish between the terms of trade and the balance of trade.

2 Use Table 6.2.15 to calculate Australia's terms of trade in 2019.

3 Calculate the index of export prices (Export unit value index) in 2017.

4 Explain what happened Australia's terms of trade between 2015 and 2019.

5 Explain how, other things being equal, a fall in the exchange rate affects a country's terms of trade.

In 2019, the value of goods exported by Australia was worth US$272.4 billion. Over 70% of these exports were primary products. Changes in the world market price of these products has a significant effect on the country's terms of trade and its balance of trade.

Between 1 January 2013 and 31 December 2019, the value of the Australian dollar (AUD) depreciated against the US dollar (USD) from 1 AUD = 1.04 USD to

Trading blocs

A trading bloc, or trade bloc, is a formal agreement between two or more countries to reduce or eliminate restrictions on trade between each other while keeping restrictions on trade with countries that are not members of the trading bloc. Most trading blocs are between countries in the same region, for example the EU and Mercosur, a South American trade bloc. There are different types of trading bloc representing different degrees of integration. They include:

- free trade areas
- customs unions
- common markets
- monetary unions.

Free trade area

A **free trade area (FTA)** is when member countries remove restrictions on trade between each other but keep their own restrictions on trade with non-member countries. Since each country has its own restrictions on trade with non-member countries, border controls between countries in the FTA must be retained. Without these controls, goods from non-member countries could be imported into a country with a low tariff and then re-exported to a country in the FTA that has a high tariff on those goods.

Customs union

A **customs union (CU)** is when there is free trade between member countries and each country in the customs union has the same restrictions on trade with non-member countries. With a CU, there is a **common external tariff (CET)**. This means that every country in the CU has the same tariff on goods and services imported from non-member countries. For example, every country in the EU charges a 10% tariff on cars built in the USA. The size of the tariff varies from one product to another and may also be different for the same product imported from different countries.

The CET means that it is not necessary to have border controls between members of a CU. It is also possible for the CU to negotiate a trade deal with non-member countries for all member countries.

Common market

A **common market** is a customs union that also allows the free movement of capital and labour between member countries. This usually means that member countries must have some common rules and regulations. Common markets often go further than this by adopting a variety of policies that apply to all member countries. For example, there may be common policies for agriculture, fishing, monopolies and mergers, energy and the environment.

A common market may raise funds from member states to pay for these policies. In the EU, some of the money comes from tariffs on imports plus a small percentage of the money governments raise from taxing the sale of goods and services within their economies. Some of the money may be spent helping the less prosperous regions within the common market.

Monetary union

A **monetary union** is an agreement between two or more countries to create a single currency area. Countries in a monetary union have the same currency. They also have a single central bank which implements monetary policy for the currency area. Monetary policy in a monetary union involves the central bank controlling the supply of money, influencing interest rates and the exchange rate for the common currency.

In 2020, 19 of the 27 members of the EU were also part of a monetary union. These 19 countries have adopted the euro as their currency and are members of the Economic and Monetary Union (EMU) which is part of the EU. Some other EU countries are in the process of joining the EMU. The EMU is a common market and monetary union.

The economic consequences of joining a trading bloc will depend on the type of trading bloc. The effects of joining a FTA are different from being a member of an economic and monetary union.

Trade creation gains and trade diversion losses

Trading blocs usually result in more trade between member countries but less trade with non-member countries. Some economists believe that completely free trade is unlikely to be achieved and so the formation of trading blocs can be a second-best option. Free trade between members allows for greater specialisation and the benefits shown by the model of comparative advantage. However, restrictions on imports from non-member countries mean that countries within a trading bloc may stop buying goods and services from the lowest-cost producers who are not members of the bloc.

The Canadian economist Jacob Viner distinguished between **trade creation gains** and **trade diversion losses**.

After joining a trading bloc, free trade between members means that countries start to specialise and buy some goods and services from lower-cost producers within the bloc rather than produce these products themselves at a higher cost. This is a trade creation gain as production moves from higher-cost domestic firms to lower-cost firms within the bloc.

However, trade may also be diverted from the lowest-cost producer outside the bloc to a higher-cost producer within the trade bloc. For example, if country has a 20% tariff on all cars it imports, removing the tariff on cars produced by member countries but keeping the tariff on cars produced by non-member countries may mean that the country starts to import cars from a member country rather than the lowest-cost producer outside the trade bloc. Trade is diverted away from the lowest-cost rest of the world producer to a higher-cost producer within the trade bloc. This is a trade diversion loss.

If the trade creation gains are larger than the trade diversion losses, other things being equal, the trade bloc increases economic welfare.

Other advantages and disadvantages of trading blocs

Trade creation gains and trade diversion losses are the static resource allocation effects of forming a trade bloc. However, there are other effects which may be more significant. The advantages include:

- An increase in specialisation and trade, resulting from removing tariffs between member countries, can lead to economies of scale and lower average costs.
- Competition between the firms in a trade bloc can lead to lower prices, more choice and more innovation.
- An increase in foreign direct investment (FDI) from countries outside the trade bloc who wish to avoid trade restrictions and take advantage of the large internal market.
- The trade bloc may have more influence when negotiating trade agreements with non-member countries. The benefits to non-member countries of gaining access to a group of countries in a trade bloc is greater than gaining access to the market of one country.

▲ **Figure 6.2.14**: Jacob Viner

The disadvantages of trade blocs, other than trade diversion, include the following:

- Individual members of a customs union are unable to negotiate trade agreements with non-member countries. However, members of a free trade area can negotiate their own trade agreements with non-members.
- Free trade between member countries can lead to structural unemployment, affecting some of the less prosperous regions of the trade bloc, increasing inequality.
- Inefficient industries within the trade bloc may be protected from competition from firms outside the trade bloc, harming consumers who have to pay higher prices and have less choice.
- In a monetary union, individual countries lose control over monetary policy and some other import tools of economic policy. If the countries in the monetary union experience different economic problems, they may need different economic policies. For example, a country with low growth and high unemployment may benefit from low interest rates and a low exchange rate whereas a country with rapid growth and high inflation may need high interest rates and a strong currency.

The World Trade Organization (WTO)

The WTO is an international organisation that was set up in 1995 to deal with the rules governing international trade. Countries who are members of the WTO have accepted a set of agreements that help to promote free trade. The WTO also helps to settle disputes that might otherwise lead to a trade war.

The history of the WTO

The Great Depression started in the USA in 1929 and lasted for most of the 1930s. It was a worldwide depression that affected most countries. During this time, many countries used measures such as tariffs and quotas to restrict imports in an attempt to protect their economies from rising unemployment. Restrictions imposed by one country led to retaliation by other countries and many believe that these protectionist measures made the depression worse.

In 1944, at a conference in Bretton Woods in the USA, arrangements for a new international world monetary and trading system were proposed. The Bretton Woods agreement led to the creation of the International Monetary Fund (IMF) and the World Bank. It was also recognised that a similar organisation was needed to regulate international trade to prevent a return to the "beggar-thy-neighbour policies" of the 1930s. A number of countries agreed to the creation of the International Trade Organization (ITO), but the agreement was not approved by the United States Congress and the ITO was not set up. However, in 1947, 23 countries, including the USA, signed the General Agreement on Tariffs and Trade (GATT) which came into force on 1 January 1948. GATT helped to regulate international trade between countries until the formation of the WTO in 1995. In 1994, 128 countries had signed GATT and 123 of these countries joined

Progress questions

24 What is the main difference between a free trade area and a customs union?

25 What is a monetary union?

26 Distinguish between trade creation gains and trade diversion losses.

Key term

Beggar-thy-neighbour policies: measures adopted by a country to improve its economy but which harm the economies of other countries, for example imposing tariffs and quotas on imports or devaluing its currency.

the WTO when it was set up in 1995. In 2020, 164 countries were members of the WTO, accounting for 98% of world trade.

The GATT

The purpose of GATT was to promote international trade by reducing or eliminating restrictions on international trade. Between 1947 and 1986, it held eight rounds of trade negotiations, each of which achieved some success in reducing restrictions on international trade. The average level of tariffs for members of GATT was over 20% in 1947 but after the Uruguay Round of negotiations concluded in 1994, this had been reduced to around 5%.

An important principle of the GATT was that trade should take place without discriminating between countries. This principle was included in the most-favoured-nation (MFN) clause. This clause states that if a country agrees to reduce a tariff, or other restriction on trade, with a country that has signed GATT, the same reduction is automatically applied to all other countries who have signed GATT. This principle still applies to members of the WTO. There are, however, some exceptions, for example to allow the creation of trading blocs and to give LDCs favourable access to the markets of MDCs.

GATT also included a system for settling trade disputes between countries and this helped to prevent a disagreement between countries escalating into a trade war.

> ### Key term
>
> **Most-favoured-nation (MFN) clause**: when a country agrees to reduce a restriction on trade with one country, the same reduction automatically applies to all other countries.

The role of the WTO

The 1986 to 1994, the Uruguay Round led to changes to GATT and to the creation of the WTO. Whereas GATT dealt mainly with trade in goods, the WTO also covers trade in services and intellectual property. In recent years, international trade in services has grown faster than trade in goods and the protection of intellectual property is important for many individuals, firms and countries.

The main purpose of the WTO is to ensure that international trade takes place as freely and smoothly as possible. It does this by:

- helping member countries to negotiate trade agreements that reduce or eliminate restrictions on trade
- establishing a set of rules that govern international trade and making sure that the rules are being followed
- helping settle disputes between countries and judging whether a country has broken the rules.

Unlike GATT, the WTO can authorise sanctions on a country that breaks trade agreements and rules. If the WTO has judged that a country is breaking a trade agreement, it can give permission for other countries to retaliate. For example, in 2019, the WTO authorised the USA to retaliate against illegal EU subsidies to Airbus, a European aircraft manufacturer. As a result of this ruling by the WTO, the USA placed tariffs on a wide variety of EU imports including aircraft, clothing, machinery and agricultural products.

Case study: The European Union and Canada negotiate a trade agreement

▲ **Figure 6.2.15**: CETA encourages trade

The Comprehensive Economic and Trade Agreement (CETA) is a trade deal between the EU and Canada. The agreement was signed in 2016 but still has to be approved by the national parliaments of some EU countries. Even so, most parts of the agreement already apply to trade between the two regions. The agreement abolishes 98% of customs duties between the EU and Canada. For example, the tariff on chocolate confectionery has been removed.

It is estimated that the deal will save EU businesses €590m in customs duties each year. Import quotas have also been relaxed, for example the quota Canada imposes on cheese imported from the EU has been more than doubled from 13,500 tons to 32,000 tons. The deal gives Canadian companies improved access to the markets of the 27 countries, and half a billion consumers, in the EU. In 2018, Canada's merchandise exports to the EU were nearly $44.5 billion and in a few years' time, 99% of all Canadian goods sold in the EU will be duty free.

The agreement is not only about trade in goods, it also reduces some of the restrictions on trade in services, encourages more investment and improves the protection given to intellectual property rights. CETA will increase competition between Canadian and EU companies and it should lower prices and increase choice for consumers.

1 Explain what is meant by a 'trade deal'.
2 What is the difference between a tariff and a quota?
3 Why might some Canadian businesses be harmed by CETA?
4 Give **two** examples of the types of people who are likely to benefit from the improved protection for intellectual property.
5 Explain the benefits consumers in the EU and Canada are likely to obtain from CETA.

Exam-style questions

1 Which one of the following is an important characteristic of globalisation?

A A rise in foreign direct investment

B An increase in labour mobility within countries

C The growth of protectionism

D The introduction of exchange controls (1 mark)

2 The data in the table below show the number of bundles of resources that are needed to produce a television and a radio in Country X and Country Y.

	Television	Radio
Country X	5	1
Country Y	4	2

It can be concluded from the data in the table that

A Country X has an absolute advantage in radios and a comparative advantage in televisions.

B Country X has an absolute advantage in radios and Country Y has an absolute advantage in televisions.

C Country X has an absolute advantage in televisions and Country Y has an absolute advantage in radios.

D Country Y has an absolute advantage in televisions and a comparative advantage in radios. (1 mark)

3 The introduction of a quota on a good will benefit the country introducing the quota because it is likely to lead to an increase in

A consumer surplus.

B employment.

C the amount of competition.

D the value of exports. (1 mark)

4 The data in the table below show the index of export prices and the index of import prices for a country in January 2020 and January 2021.

	Index of export prices	Index of import prices
January 2020	100	120
January 2021	125	90

(i) Define a 'deterioration in the terms of trade'. (2 marks)

You are advised to show your workings for the calculations below.

(ii) Calculate the country's terms of trade in January 2020. (2 marks)

(iii) If the price elasticity of demand for the country's imports is -1.3, calculate the effect of the change in import prices between January 2020 and January 2021 on the volume of imports. Show your answer as a percentage, to **one** decimal place. (4 marks)

5 Explain why the creation of a trading bloc can result in trade creation gains and trade diversion losses. (12 marks)

6 Assess the view that overseas investment by a transnational corporation based in the USA benefits the economy of the USA. (25 marks)

Note: To answer this question as a data response question, use the data provided in the case study "Ford, a global car manufacturer" in 6.1 "Globalisation" to support your answer.

7 Discuss the benefits and costs of international trade. (25 marks)

7 The balance of payments, exchange rates and financial markets

Economic development and the global economy

This section will develop your knowledge and understanding of:

→ the current, capital and financial accounts on the balance of payments
→ balance of payments deficits and surpluses and their significance
→ foreign direct investment (FDI) and portfolio investment
→ consequences of investment flows between countries
→ policies that might be used to deal with balance of payments problems
→ expenditure-switching and expenditure-reducing policies
→ the effects of policies used to correct a deficit or surplus may have on other policy objectives.

The balance of payments is a record of a country's financial transactions with the rest of the world. It includes transactions carried out by individuals, firms, financial institutions and governments. The account is divided into four main sections:

- the current account
- the capital account
- the financial account
- net errors and omissions.

The balance of payments account is constructed using the double-entry bookkeeping method. This means that every transaction is entered twice, once as a debit entry (–) and once as a credit entry (+). Therefore, total debits must equal total debits and the account as a whole must balance. However, there can be deficits and surpluses on individual parts of the account, but surpluses on one or more parts of the account must be matched by equivalent deficits on other parts of the account. It is where the deficits and surpluses occur and what caused them that determines their significance for a country's macroeconomic performance.

The main sections of the balance of payments account

The different sections of the balance of payments account record different types of transaction.

The current account
The current account records trade in goods and services and other income flows between countries. The current account is divided into four sections:

- **trade in goods** such as cars, computers, machinery, wheat and other commodities, also known as merchandise trade
- **trade in services** such as financial services, legal services, the arts and entertainment services
- **primary income flows** including interest, profits and dividends earned on overseas assets and payments to individuals who are working abroad

Key terms

Capital account (of the balance of payments): a record of transactions that involve the purchase and sale of intangible assets and capital transfers between countries.

Financial account (of the balance of payments): a record of transactions that lead to changes in a country's stock of overseas assets and liabilities.

Net errors and omissions: the net value of the mistakes made when recording the transactions included on the balance of payments account.

Link

A detailed explanation of the structure of the current account of the balance of payments was included in 8.4 "The balance of payments on current account" in the AS book.

▲ Figure 7.1.1: The balance of payments

- **secondary income flows** which are transfers between countries and include gifts to people abroad, payments to overseas charities, overseas aid and payments to international institutions.

When a transaction leads to money coming into the country, it is a credit item, for example the export of goods and services or interest earned on money saved in an overseas bank account. When the transaction leads to money going out of the country, it is a debit item, for example imports of goods and services or dividends paid to overseas residents who own shares in a domestic company.

The current account balance is an important indicator of a country's economic performance. If the current account is in deficit in a given year, it means that the country did not earn enough money from its exports of goods and services and other inflows of income to pay for its imports and the income earned by overseas residents. It is sometimes said that a current account deficit means that a country is "living beyond its means" (spending more than it can afford).

When a country has a current account deficit, it has to be financed. The foreign exchange needed to pay for the deficit can come from net inflows of investment from overseas, borrowing or using up foreign exchange reserves. The deficit on the current account has to be financed by an equivalent surplus on the capital and financial accounts of the balance of payments.

When a country has a current account surplus, it can use the surplus to invest abroad, lend to other countries or increase its foreign exchange reserves. A surplus on the current account will be matched by a deficit on the capital and financial accounts. A deficit on the financial account indicates that the country is adding to its stock of overseas assets.

The capital account

In most years, the capital account is a very small part of any country's balance of payments account. The capital account includes two types of transaction.

The first is the purchase and sale of intangible assets such as patents, copyrights and trademarks. For example, if a Japanese company bought the copyright to a video game produced by a UK company, this would appear as a debit item on the capital account of the Japan's balance of payments and as a credit item on the capital account of the UK's balance of payments.

The second type of transaction is capital transfers. Two examples of capital transfer are:

- when the government of one country gives an asset that it owns to another country
- when a government writes off a debt that it is owed by another country.

Some less economically developed countries (LEDCs) that accumulated large foreign debts have benefited from **debt forgiveness** programmes designed to reduce the annual interest they pay to lenders, usually more economically developed countries

(MEDCs). The value of the debt written off is shown on the capital accounts of the borrower and the lender.

The financial account

The financial account records transactions that lead to changes in the stock of foreign financial assets owned by a country and changes in a country's overseas liabilities. Globalisation and the integration of the world's financial markets have resulted in a substantial increase in financial flows between countries and a corresponding increase in the importance of the financial account of the balance of payments.

The items recorded in the financial account include the following:

- **Direct investment** is when the investor sets up a business abroad or acquires a controlling interest in a foreign firm. Direct investment includes earnings that are reinvested in the overseas firm.
- **Portfolio investment** involves buying shares, corporate bonds, government bonds and other financial assets where the buyer does not play any part in the management of the enterprise that issues these assets.
- **Other investments** include trade credit, and deposits and withdrawals from foreign bank accounts.

Reserve assets include transactions in assets that the monetary authorities (central bank) have available to use to help deal with balance of payments problems. They are the country's foreign exchange reserves. They include the government's (official) holdings of gold, foreign currency and special drawing rights (SDRs). Foreign exchange reserves can be used by the central bank to intervene in the foreign exchange market to influence the external value of the country's currency.

Many of the items included on the financial account of the balance of payments can be moved easily and quickly between countries. For example, if it is expected that a country's exchange rate is going to fall and/or if interest rates are reduced, investors may move their money into an asset in a different currency that earns a higher rate of interest. Investors move funds between financial centres to try to achieve the highest possible rate of return. These short-term movements of money between financial centres are known as hot money flows.

Net errors and omissions

With such a large volume of transactions included on a country's balance of payments account, it is inevitable that mistakes will be made and some transactions will not be recorded. The figure for net errors and omissions shows the sum of these measurement errors. While the size of this figure gives an indication of the accuracy of the other items recorded on the balance of payments account, some errors offset each other.

If all the items on the balance of payments account were recorded accurately, the sum of the debit and credit items would be the same and, taken together, sum to zero. Therefore, if the sum of these items is a net credit, the figure for net errors and omissions will be shown as a debit of equal value, and vice versa.

Key term

Liabilities: the amount of money that is owed to individuals, firms, financial institutions, governments and other economic agents.

Link

Special drawing rights are explained in 7.2 "Exchange rates".

Key terms

Trade credit: where the seller provides a good or service to a buyer but is not paid until later. It is a type of short-term finance, provided by the seller, to help increase sales.

Reserve assets: the assets a country's central bank has available to deal with balance of payments problems. They include official holdings of gold, foreign currency and special drawing rights (SDRs).

Special drawing rights (SDRs): an international reserve asset created by the International Monetary Fund that can be used by central banks to deal with balance of payments problems and can be exchanged for a limited number of foreign currencies (Chinese yuan, euros, Japanese yen, UK pounds and US dollars).

Hot money flows: short-term movements of money between the world's financial centres to achieve the highest possible return for investors.

▼ Table 7.1.1: An example of the balance of payments account

	$ billion	$ billion
Balance of trade in goods and services	+ 200	
Primary income balance	− 50	
Secondary income balance	− 30	
Current account balance		+ 120
Capital transfers	− 3	
Net acquisition (−)/disposal of intangible assets (+)	− 12	
Capital account balance		− 15
Net direct investment	− 63	
Net portfolio investment	− 19	
Other investment	+ 11	
Reserve assets [(+) decrease (−) increase]	− 24	
Financial account balance		− 95
		+ 10
Net errors and omissions		− 10

In Table 7.1.1, there is a surplus on the current account because the surplus on the balance of trade in goods and services is larger than the sum of the primary and secondary income deficits.

The minus $15 billion shown on the capital account means that domestic firms have bought more intangible assets from abroad than have been sold overseas.

The negative figures for direct and portfolio investment mean that the country is investing more abroad than is being invested in the domestic economy by overseas residents. The positive figure for other investments shows a net inflow of funds invested in these assets. The negative figure for reserve assets means that the country's stock of reserve assets has increased.

The surplus of $120 billion on the current account means that the sum of the capital and financial accounts should show a deficit (net outflow) of $120 billion but the deficit shown is only −$(15 + 95) = −$110 billion. This means that there are net errors and omissions of −$10 billion.

Progress questions

1 Why must the balance of payments account as a whole always balance?

2 Distinguish between direct investment and portfolio investment.

3 Why does the balance of payments account include a figure for net errors and omissions?

4 A country has a current account surplus of $35 billion, a surplus of $18 billion on its primary income balance and a deficit of $6 billion on its secondary income balance. What is the value of the balance of trade in goods and services?

A different way of structuring the balance of payments account

Some countries present their balance of payments account in a different way from that shown in Table 7.1.1. Table 7.1.2 uses the same key data as Table 7.1.1 but shows inflows of money on the financial account with a minus sign and outflows with a plus sign. In Table 7.1.2, the positive figure on the financial account shows that there is an outflow of money leading to a net increase in the ownership of overseas assets.

▼ Table 7.1.2: An alternative way of presenting the balance of payments account

	$ billion
Current account balance	+ 120
Capital account balance	− 15
	+ 105
Financial account balance	+ 95
Net errors and omissions	− 10

With this method, if every transaction is recorded accurately, a surplus (+) on the combined current and capital accounts would lead to the same positive figure on the financial account. The positive figure on the financial account shows that the net surplus on the current and capital accounts was invested abroad, leading to a net increase in the country's stock of overseas assets. However, in Table 7.1.2, the financial account balance is $10 billion less than the combined current and capital account balance. This means that there are net errors and omissions of minus $10 billion.

The financial account balance must equal the current account balance + the capital account balance + net errors and omissions.

The financial account shows where the money comes from to pay for a current account deficit or what happens to a current account surplus.

When checking to see which method has been used, remember that if there are no errors or omissions, a combined surplus on the current and capital accounts must lead to the same net outflow on the financial account. This means that the country has increased its net ownership of overseas assets. A deficit on the combined current and capital accounts will have to be financed by a net inflow on the financial account and results in a reduction in the country's net ownership of overseas assets. When a country's ownership of overseas assets is less than their overseas liabilities, the value of their net overseas assets is negative.

Balance of payments deficits and surpluses and their significance

When assessing the effects of a country's balance of payments position on its economic performance, it is important to consider where the deficits and surpluses occur and what caused them.

Get it right

When analysing a country's balance of payments account, look carefully to see which method of presenting the data has been used.

Case study: France's balance of payments account

▲ Figure 7.1.2: The Eiffel Tower

1 Calculate France's balance of trade in goods and services in 2019.
2 Explain why France's current account balance deteriorated by €3.0 billion between 2018 and 2019.
3 Describe the change in portfolio investment between 2018 and 2019.
4 What happened to France's holdings of reserve assets in 2018?
5 Explain why the account shows errors and omissions of −€14.6 billion in 2019.

Table 7.1.3 shows France's balance of payments account using the second method of presenting the country's balance of payments account.

▼ Table 7.1.3: France's balance of payments account, 2018 and 2019

	2018 € billions		2019 € billions	
Balance of trade in goods	−48.1		−46.8	
Balance of trade in services	24.8		21.6	
Primary and secondary income balance	10.1		9.0	
Current account balance		−13.2		−16.2
Capital account balance		2.1		1.9
Direct investment	57.1		4.2	
Portfolio investment	9.4		−93.0	
Other investments	−100.2		57.1	
Reserve assets	10.4		2.8	
Financial account balance		−23.3		−28.9
Net errors and omissions		−12.2		−14.6

Source: Banque de France (banque-france.fr); accessed December 2020

Link

The causes of changes in exchange rates are explained in 7.2 "Exchange rates".

The current account balance is often taken as an indicator of the performance of an economy, and a large current account deficit may show that the economy is not performing well. Similarly, a current account surplus is often believed to indicate a strong economy. However, this is not necessarily true. For example, a country may have a surplus on its current account because it is in recession, resulting in a low level of demand for foreign imports.

A country can run a large deficit on its current account provided it is able to finance the deficit by inflows of funds from abroad. The inflows may result from direct investment and/or short-term investment in financial assets. However, if a large deficit causes overseas investors to lose confidence in the economy, inward investment may collapse and funds may be withdrawn from the economy leading to an unwanted fall in the country's exchange rate.

Problems with a current account deficit

For most countries, trade in goods and services is the largest component of the current account, but the primary and secondary income balances also affect the overall current account balance. For example, if a country holds a large stock of overseas assets, changes in the amount it earns on these assets will have a significant effect on the current account balance. If the world economy is in recession, leading to a fall in interest rates and company profits, the primary income balance will fall and the current account balance will deteriorate.

May indicate that the country is uncompetitive

If the current account deficit results from a deficit on the balance of trade in goods and services, it may mean that the country's firms are uncompetitive in export markets and their home market. A low value of exports suggests that foreign firms are more competitive in export markets. A high value of imports suggests that foreign firms are more competitive than domestic firms in their home market. The lack of competitiveness may, for example, have been caused by high inflation, low productivity or a failure to innovate. This may lead to low growth and rising unemployment.

Causes a net withdrawal from the circular flow of income

Exports are an injection into the circular flow of income and imports are a withdrawal. If imports are greater than exports, there is a net withdrawal from the circular flow which reduces aggregate demand (AD = C + I + G + (X − M). Other things being equal, as can be seen in Figure 7.1.3, an increase in the current account deficit will reduce national income. There will be a downward multiplier effect and unemployment is likely to increase.

Increases overseas indebtedness

As already explained, a deficit on the current account has to be financed. Exactly how this is done is shown on the financial account of the balance of payments. The inflows on the financial account represent a reduction in the country's holdings of foreign assets and/or an increase in its liabilities. A sustained current account deficit is likely to mean that the country becomes a net debtor. This will lead to a net outflow of interest, dividends and profits, causing a deterioration in the primary income balance and a further deterioration in the current account balance.

Leads to foreign ownership of domestic assets

Financing the deficit with inward investment from abroad may lead to foreign transnational corporations (TNCs) taking over domestic enterprises. Profits are likely to be returned to the parent company and the government may have less influence on their activities. However, foreign direct investment (FDI) can have significant benefits for the domestic economy, for example, it may lead to improvements in efficiency, competitiveness and long-run economic growth. This may lead to an improvement in the balance of trade in goods and services.

Activity

Find out what has happened to the current account of your country's balance of payments during the past 10 years. Draw a bar chart to illustrate the current account balance in each of these years.

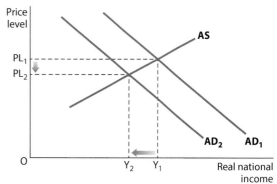

▲ Figure 7.1.3: The effect of a growing deficit on the macroeconomy

Link

The effects of transnational corporations (TNCS) are explained in 6.1 "Globalisation".

There is a risk of capital flight

When a deficit is financed by borrowing from abroad, interest has to be paid to the lender and the money borrowed has to be repaid when the debt matures. If overseas investors lose confidence in the ability of country to pay the interest or repay loans when they mature, the country will find it difficult to borrow and may have to offer high rates of interest to attract lenders. There is also the risk that existing investors will sell their assets and withdraw their money from the economy. Large, persistent current account deficits can lead to capital flight, a fall in the exchange rate, cost-push inflationary pressures and a fall in living standards.

Measures taken to reduce the deficit may harm the domestic economy

Most countries are unlikely to be able to run large, persistent deficits on the current account of their balance of payments indefinitely. There is a variety of policies that can be used to reduce a deficit, but there are likely to be conflicts with other policy objectives. For example, allowing the exchange rate to fall to restore competitiveness will add to inflationary pressures, cause a deterioration in the terms of trade and reduce living standards. Deflationary measures, to reduce imports, will increase unemployment, reduce economic growth and will also reduce living standards.

A current account deficit is not always a problem

Although a persistent, large current account deficit can cause serious economic problems for a country's economy, a current account deficit is not always damaging. When a country is importing more than it is exporting, it usually means that domestic residents are able to consume more than the country is producing. This increases their standard of living, at least in the short run.

If the deficit results from the country importing capital goods, the increase in the capital stock should help to increase the country's underlying rate of economic growth, boosting capacity and improving competitiveness. Provided the deficit can be financed, the excess of imports over exports can benefit the economy.

A deficit on the current account must be matched by inflows of funds from abroad and if the deficit is financed by foreign direct investment (FDI), this may help to improve the long-run performance of the economy. However, if the deficit leads to capital flight, high interest rates and a fall in the exchange rate, then it becomes a problem.

When assessing the significance of the deficit, it is important to consider the size of the deficit as a percentage of GDP rather than the absolute monetary value of the deficit. A large economy is generally able run a large deficit more easily than a small economy. Also, if the deficit is short term, it is much less likely to be a problem than if it persists for a long while. However, if overseas investors have confidence in the ability of the economy to finance the deficit, a country may be able to run a large current account deficit for a long time. For example, the United States has run a large current account deficit for many years. This

Link

Policies to deal with balance of payments deficits and their effects are explained later in this section.

has been possible because overseas investors are willing to hold assets valued in dollars, for example US government bonds.

The exchange rate system also affects the significance of the deficit. When a country has a floating exchange rate, if the current account is in deficit, it can allow the exchange rate to depreciate. When a country has a fixed exchange rate, it must have enough foreign exchange reserves to intervene in the market to prevent the exchange rate falling.

Should a country aim for a current account surplus?

If a country runs a current account surplus, it is able to invest abroad and increase its net holdings of overseas assets. However, a surplus means that domestic residents are consuming less than the country is producing and, at least in the short run, living standards are lower than they might have been.

A surplus increases aggregate demand and will add to any existing inflationary pressures. However, if the country has a floating exchange rate, it may also lead to an appreciation in the country's exchange rate which will help to reduce inflation. With a fixed exchange rate, the country will have to supply its currency on the foreign exchange market, and add to its foreign exchange reserves, to prevent the exchange rate appreciating.

Most countries would prefer a current account surplus to a large persistent deficit, but a large surplus is not without its problems. If some countries are running current account surpluses, others must be running deficits.

Some countries have run a current account surplus because they have substantial oil reserves. When the price of oil on the world market is high, it often leads to very large surpluses and a high exchange rate. When the exchange rate is high, it can make other sectors of the economy uncompetitive because imports are cheaper and exports more expensive. This may, for example, lead to a decline in the manufacturing sector of the economy. This is known as the **Dutch disease** after what happened to the economy of the Netherlands following the discovery of substantial reserves of oil and gas in the North Sea in the 1960s, off the coast of the Netherlands. Exports of oil and gas led to large current account surpluses and an appreciating exchange rate, damaging other parts of the Dutch economy.

The Dutch disease can be caused by the discovery of any natural resource that is in high demand in the world economy. Often, when there is a new discovery of a natural resource, it is accompanied by an inflow of FDI to provide the capital needed to extract the resource. This inflow of overseas investment adds to the demand for the country's currency and increases the pressure for the exchange rate to appreciate.

The current account balances of countries that rely on selling natural resources for their export revenues can be very unstable. When the world market price of the resource is high, they run large surpluses but if the price falls, the current account balance is likely to move into deficit.

Link

The factors that affect exchange rates and types of exchange rate system are explained in 7.2 "Exchange rates"

Key term

Dutch disease: when the discovery of a natural resource leads to an appreciation of a country's currency making other sectors of the economy uncompetitive, particularly the manufacturing sector.

Get it right

When assessing the significance of a balance of payments deficit, it is important to consider the cause of the deficit, the size of the deficit and how long it lasts.

Progress questions

5 Why does a current account deficit indicate that a country is uncompetitive?

6 Explain how, other things being equal, a current account surplus affects aggregate demand.

Foreign direct investment and portfolio investment

Both foreign direct investment (FDI) and portfolio investment are shown on the financial account of the balance of payments. Inflows of FDI and portfolio investment can help a country finance a current account deficit. If a country is running a current account surplus, it can invest abroad to accumulate foreign assets through both direct investment and portfolio investment.

FDI is when the investor acquires a controlling interest in the overseas assets in which they are investing. It includes a TNC building a new factory or office block abroad. It also includes buying shares that give the investor the right to control or take part in the management of the business, for example by purchasing over 50% of a company's issued share capital. Sometimes the ownership of a much smaller proportion of a company's share capital allows the investor to have some control over the business and would be classified as FDI. To be classified as FDI, the investor must acquire a minimum of 10% of the share capital of a foreign enterprise. Profits earned by an overseas enterprise that are reinvested in that enterprise are also classified as FDI.

Portfolio investment is when individuals, businesses, financial institutions and sometimes governments, buy shares, bonds and other financial assets to earn a return, such as interest or dividends, without acquiring a controlling or management role in the assets in which they are investing. Portfolio investment is often very liquid and the investor may only hold the assets for a short time before selling them, although some assets are held for a long while.

The consequences of investment flows between countries

Globalisation of the world economy has meant that flows of both FDI and portfolio investment have increased substantially since the Second World War.

The growing importance of TNCs has meant that there are substantial flows of FDI. Inflows of FDI can increase a country's capital stock and its underlying rate of economic growth. This is particularly important for those LEDCs that have a shortage of domestic savings to fund investment. FDI creates employment and often leads to improvements in productivity. However, profits may be sent back to the TNC's home country and if the company decides to relocate to a different country, it can be very damaging. When a TNC decides to invest overseas, it is sometimes argued that it could have invested in its home country, leading to lower growth and fewer jobs in its domestic economy.

Although, TNCs can relocate to a different country, FDI is generally more stable than portfolio investment. Financial institutions invest large sums of money in financial centres located in different countries around the world. The aim is to make a profit for themselves or their clients by investing in financial assets such as shares and bonds. The profits earned depend on the income received from the financial asset,

> **Link**
>
> The effects of FDI and TNCs were explained in detail in 6.1 "Globalisation".

what happens to the value of the asset and changes in the exchange rate. If investors believe that investment in a particular economy is less profitable than elsewhere, they may choose to sell their investments and move their money to a different country.

A large withdrawal of funds at short notice can be very damaging for the real economy of a country. Withdrawing funds and investing those funds in another country will mean that the investor will sell the country's currency and buy foreign currency. The increase in the supply of the country's currency on the foreign exchange market will lead to a fall in the exchange rate. Although a fall in the exchange rate may improve the competitiveness of domestic producers, it will add to inflationary pressures and reduce living standards. Flows of hot money between countries can cause exchange rates to be volatile. Unstable movements in a country's exchange rate can make it very difficult for firms to plan for the future and affect confidence in the economy, reducing investment and economic growth.

Despite the problems caused when there is capital flight and outflows of hot money from an economy, portfolio investment overseas can benefit the investor and the economy of the country in which the investment is made. Investors have the opportunity to earn a higher rate of return than if they were only able to invest in their own economy. This can mean, for example, that a pension fund that invests abroad is able to pay higher pensions to people. Inward investment into a country's capital market can make it easier for firms and the country's government to raise finance. This can help to increase investment in the capital stock and help the government to pay for beneficial public expenditure.

Free market economists argue that the free movement of funds between countries allows organisations and countries with surplus funds to invest in countries that have a shortage. They believe that it should result in funds being invested in projects that have the highest rate of return, providing the most benefit to people.

Policies to deal with balance of payments problems

Governments are usually more concerned about persistent current account deficits than persistent surpluses. As explained above, a deficit indicates that domestic firms are less competitive than their overseas rivals and the deficit has to be financed, leading to an increase in overseas liabilities. Most countries can easily finance a short-run deficit by overseas borrowing or by attracting inflows of funds from abroad. However, if a country has a persistent current account deficit, it may have to take measures to reduce or eliminate the deficit.

Introducing policies to correct a current account deficit is more urgent when a country is trying to maintain a fixed exchange rate than when a country has a floating exchange rate. When a country has a deficit on the current account of the balance of payments, market forces create pressure for the exchange rate to fall. With a fixed exchange rate, to prevent this occurring, the government will have to introduce policies to reduce the deficit.

> ### Key term
>
> **Real economy:** the part of the economy that uses economic resources to produce goods and services to satisfy people's needs and wants. It includes markets for factors of production and markets for goods and services but not financial and money markets.

> ### Progress questions
>
> 7 Explain why, other things being equal, an increase in interest rates in a country is likely to result in an increase in portfolio investment from abroad.
>
> 8 A country experiences a substantial outflow of hot money that leads to a fall in the exchange rate. Explain how this is likely to affect inflation.

The policies available to a government wishing to reduce a balance of payments deficit are:

- direct controls
- deflationary policies
- devaluation or allowing the exchange rate to depreciate
- supply-side policies.

Direct controls

Direct controls include restrictions on imports and subsidising exports.

A tariff is a tax on imports. A tariff is likely to increase the price of the products upon which it is imposed, although foreign firms may cut their prices to try to remain competitive. The effectiveness of the tariff in reducing imports, and the current account deficit, will depend on whether there are home-produced substitutes and the price elasticities of demand for the products on which the tariff is imposed. This is because the more price elastic the demand for imports, the more effective the tariff. The more elastic the demand for imports, the more the quantity demanded falls when the price rises.

A quota is a restriction on the volume of imports. The introduction of quotas may help to reduce a current account deficit if they are imposed on a number of products. However, as explained earlier, they usually lead to higher prices for consumers and result in a net loss of welfare.

Export subsidies make it more profitable for firms to sell their products abroad and allow exporters to reduce prices, increasing their ability to compete in overseas markets. However, subsidies can be expensive and may lead to higher taxes or reductions in other types of government expenditure.

If a country is a member of the World Trade Organization (WTO), it may not be able to use direct controls to reduce a current account deficit without breaking WTO rules. Also, countries that are members of a customs union cannot impose their own restrictions on trade to reduce a deficit. In addition, if a country imposes restrictions on imports from abroad, it is likely to face retaliation from the countries affected. These countries are likely to impose similar restrictions on its exports. Therefore, the effectiveness of direct controls to reduce a balance of payments deficit is likely to be limited.

Deflationary policies

Deflationary policies are contractionary fiscal and monetary policies that reduce aggregate demand (AD). Contractionary fiscal policy involves increasing taxes and cutting government spending. Contractionary monetary policy involves increasing the central bank's base rate of interest and adopting measures to reduce the rate of growth of the supply of money and credit.

Reducing AD will lead to a reduction in national income. As people's incomes fall, they are likely to buy fewer imports as well as fewer home-produced goods and services. The reduction in spending on imports will reduce the current account deficit. As AD falls, domestic firms will cut production and they will buy fewer imports and components from

Link

Fiscal policy and monetary policy are explained in Chapter 9 "Macroeconomic policy" in the AS book.

abroad, adding to the reduction in imports. The extent of the impact on the balance of payments depends on the marginal propensity to import (MPM) and/or the income elasticity of demand (YED) for imports. The higher the MPM (or YED for imports), the greater the reduction in the deficit resulting from a given reduction in AD and national income.

A fall in AD is also likely to reduce inflation. Over time, a lower rate of inflation will help to improve the price competitiveness of the country's products abroad and in its home market. This should increase exports and reduce imports. However, what happens to price competitiveness depends on the country's inflation rate compared to the rate of inflation in other countries.

A reduction in AD will mean that firms have spare capacity. This will encourage some firms to try to sell more abroad and will make it easier for them to supply overseas customers. If AD is high and domestic firms have sufficient sales in their home market, there is less incentive to look for customers abroad and if they are working close to capacity, they may find it hard to supply overseas customers.

Devaluation or allowing the exchange rate to depreciate

A fall in the exchange rate, known as a devaluation in a fixed exchange rate system and a depreciation in a floating exchange rate system, can help t o restore a country's price competitiveness. A devaluation is announced by the country's government and is usually a significant change in the value of the currency that takes place immediately. A depreciation usually occurs gradually over a longer period of time and generally results from the operation of market forces.

A fall in the exchange rate reduces the foreign currency price of the country's exports and increases the price of imports in terms of the domestic currency. It improves the competitiveness of the country's goods and services abroad and in its home market.

The fall in the foreign currency price of exports should lead to an increase in the demand for exports, but the extent to which the demand for exports rises depends on the price elasticity of demand (PED) for exports. The larger the PED, the greater the increase in the quantity demanded. For example, if the PED for exports is elastic (greater than 1), export revenue will increase in terms of foreign currency since the percentage increase in the quantity demanded is greater than the percentage fall in the foreign currency price of exports.

In Figure 7.1.4, the fall in the exchange rate reduces the foreign currency price of exports from P_1 to P_2. If the demand for exports is elastic (D_E), the quantity sold increases from Q_1 to Q_{2E} and export revenue also increases from ($P_1 \times Q_1$) to ($P_2 \times Q_{2E}$). However, if the demand for exports is inelastic (D_I), the quantity sold only increases to Q_{2I} and export revenue falls from ($P_1 \times Q_1$) to ($P_2 \times Q_{2I}$).

However, even if the PED for exports is inelastic ($0 < PED < 1$), export revenue will rise in terms of domestic currency since more exports will be sold, due to the fall in the foreign currency price, but the domestic currency price is not directly affected by the fall in the exchange rate.

> **Key term**
>
> Devaluation: a reduction in the value of a country's currency in terms of other currencies. It is when, in a fixed exchange rate system, the government announces a reduction in the official value of the currency.

> **Get it right**
>
> A fall in the exchange rate reduces the foreign currency price of a country's exports and increases the price of imports in terms of domestic currency. It makes domestic products more price competitive both at home and abroad. An increase in the exchange rate increases the foreign currency price of exports and makes imports cheaper in terms of domestic currency.

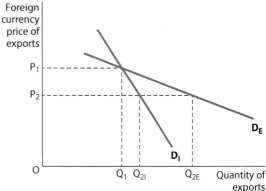

▲ **Figure 7.1.4:** The effect of a fall in the foreign currency price of exports on export revenue

237

The rise in the domestic currency price of imports should lead to a fall in the demand for imports but the extent to which the demand for imports falls depends on the PED for imports. The more elastic the PED, the greater the decrease in the quantity demanded. If the PED for imports is elastic (greater than 1), spending on imports will fall in terms of domestic currency since the percentage fall in the quantity demanded is greater than the percentage increase in the domestic currency price of imports. However, even if the PED for imports is inelastic (0 < PED < 1), spending on imports will fall in terms of foreign currency since fewer imports will be sold and the foreign currency price is not directly affected by the fall in the exchange rate.

In summary, the more price elastic the demand for both exports and imports, the greater the benefit to the current account of the balance of payments from a fall in the country's exchange rate. If the demand for exports is elastic, the fall in price will lead to a proportionately greater increase in the quantity of exports demanded and if the demand for imports is elastic, the rise in price will lead to a proportionately greater fall in the quantity of imports demanded.

However, other things being equal, it can be shown that provided the sum of the PEDs for exports and imports is greater than 1, a fall in the exchange rate will lead to an improvement in the balance of payments. This means the PED for exports and the PED for imports can both be inelastic (less than 1) but provided, when they are added together, they sum to more than 1, a fall in the exchange rate should lead to an improvement in the current account of the balance of payments. This is known as the Marshall-Lerner condition.

The J-curve effect

The effect of a fall in the exchange rate on the current account balance may be different in the short run from the long run. The **J-curve effect** explains why a fall in the exchange rate usually leads to a larger current account deficit in the short run but helps to reduce, or eliminate, the deficit in the long run.

In the short run, the elasticities of demand for exports and imports are likely to be very inelastic. This means that a fall in the foreign currency price of exports will have little effect on the volume of exports and so the value of exports will fall. Also, the rise in the domestic currency price of imports will not have much effect on the volume of imports and so the value of imports will rise. As a result, the deficit on balance of trade in goods and services, and the current account balance, will worsen in the short run. Demand is inelastic in the short run because it takes time for people to recognise the price changes and to change suppliers. Also, importers may have agreed long-term contracts with suppliers and it takes time before they can change suppliers.

Over a period of time, people respond to the change in relative prices and demand becomes more elastic. In the long run, the fall in the price of exports is likely to lead to an increase in the volume and value of exports and the rise in the price of imports is likely to lead to a fall in the volume and value of imports. As a result, in the long run, the fall in the exchange rate leads to an improvement in the current account of the balance of payments.

Figure 7.1.5 shows that immediately after the fall in the exchange rate, the deficit in the balance of trade in goods and services increases but later the deficit is reduced and moves into a surplus. The shape of the curve is like the letter J.

Recognising that in the short run a fall in the exchange rate is likely to lead to a deterioration in the balance of trade in goods and services is important. If policy makers are not aware of this effect, they may introduce other policies to try to correct the deficit when they are unnecessary.

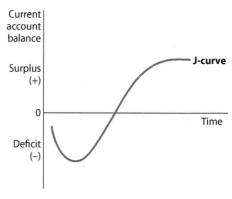

▲ **Figure 7.1.5**: The J-curve effect

Other factors to consider

While the price elasticities of demand for exports and imports are important, there are other factors that affect whether a fall in the exchange rate will improve a current account deficit.

- There must be spare capacity. The fall in the foreign currency price of exports should increase the demand for exports but domestic producers must have enough spare capacity to supply the goods and services demanded. Similarly, there must be enough spare capacity in import-competing industries to supply the increased demand for home-produced goods and services that results from the increase in the price of imports. This means that the supply of exports and the supply of goods and services produced by import-competing industries must be sufficiently elastic to respond to the increase in demand without leading to a significant rise in price. The more elastic the supply, the greater the benefit to the balance of payments.

- A fall in the exchange rate increases the domestic currency price of imports and can increase inflationary pressures. If inflation increases, over a period of time, this will reduce the improvements in price competitiveness that resulted from the fall in the exchange rate. If the economy is operating at, or close to, full capacity, it might be necessary to deflate the economy to prevent inflation reducing the benefits that result from a fall in the exchange rate. Deflationary measures will also create some spare capacity allowing the increase in demand, caused by the fall in the exchange rate, to be met.

- If the demand for a firm's products is price inelastic, the firm will get little benefit from a fall in the foreign currency price of its products since demand will not increase much. However, the firm can keep the foreign currency price unchanged and will still benefit from a fall in the exchange rate. When it converts the foreign currency that it receives from exports into domestic currency, the firm will receive more domestic currency. For example, if a Chinese firm sells solar panels in the USA at a $10,000 and the exchange rate is 6.8 CNY = 1 USD, the Chinese firm would receive CNY 68,000 for each solar panel sold, but if the yuan exchange rate fell so that 7.1 CNY = 1 USD, the Chinese firm would receive CNY 71,000 for each solar panel. As a result, exporting becomes more profitable and export revenue will increase in terms of domestic currency.

Activity

Find out what has happened to your country's exchange rate and the current account of the balance of payments during the past 5 years. How might the changes in the exchange rate have contributed to the changes in the current account balance?

Link

Supply-side policies are explained in Chapter 9 "Macroeconomic policy" in the AS book.

Progress questions 9–12

9   Other things being equal, explain why a tariff can help to reduce a current account deficit.

10 Distinguish between deflationary policies and devaluation.

11 Give **two** reasons why deflationary measures are likely to reduce a deficit on a country's balance of trade in goods and services.

12 Explain why a fall in the exchange rate is most likely to lead to a significant improvement in the balance of trade in goods and services when the demand for exports and imports are both elastic.

Key terms

Revaluation: an increase in the value of a country's currency in terms of other currencies. It is when, in a fixed exchange rate system, the government announces an increase in the official value of the currency.

Expenditure-switching policies: measures that change the relative prices of imports and exports, to persuade people to buy fewer imports and to make exports more attractive to people abroad.

Expenditure-reducing policies: measures to reduce aggregate demand to reduce spending on imports, and so reduce a deficit on the current account of the balance of payments.

Supply-side policies

In the long run, supply-side improvements in an economy make firms more competitive. It is improvements in the supply-side performance of an economy that are most likely to lead to a permanent improvement in the balance of trade in goods and services and therefore the current account of the balance of payments. Supply-side improvements enable firms to produce better goods and services at lower cost. They result, for example, from increases in productivity, new technologies, improved methods of production, quality control and better customer service.

Supply-side policies should support firms in achieving supply-side improvements. However, it can take a long time before the improvements are achieved and they are not always as effective as intended. If the economy is suffering from a large deficit that needs to be reduced quickly, the government may have to use other methods. For example, it may decide to allow the exchange rate to fall to deal with the immediate problem while using supply-side policies to try to improve the long-run competitiveness of the economy.

Policies to reduce a surplus on the current account of the balance of payments

Governments are not usually too concerned about a current account surplus but if some countries have large surpluses, others must have large deficits. Particularly under a system of fixed exchange rates, deficit countries may try to persuade surplus countries to reduce their surpluses by, for example, reflating their economies.

A current account surplus leads to pressure for the exchange rate to appreciate but if the country is willing to invest abroad, increasing its net holdings of overseas assets, this can be avoided. Alternatively, if it increases the supply of its domestic currency on the foreign exchange market (FOREX), thereby increasing its foreign exchange reserves, pressure for the exchange rate to rise is reduced.

If a country with a current account surplus wishes to reduce the surplus, policies include reducing restrictions on imports, reflationary policies to increase aggregate demand and a **revaluation** of the currency/allowing the exchange rate to appreciate. They are the opposite of the policies used to reduce or eliminate a current account deficit.

Expenditure-switching and expenditure-reducing policies

A distinction is often made between **expenditure-switching policies** and **expenditure-reducing policies**.

Expenditure-switching policies change the relative prices of imports and exports to persuade people to buy fewer imports and to make exports more attractive to people abroad. The aim is to switch demand away from foreign goods and services to home-produced goods and services. Tariffs, export subsidies and a reduction in the exchange rate are examples of expenditure-switching policies. Tariffs increase the price of imports compared to home-produced goods, export subsidies reduce the price of exports and a lower exchange rate increases the domestic currency price of imports and reduces the foreign currency price of exports.

Expenditure-switching policies are most appropriate when an economy is experiencing low growth and unemployment as well as a balance of payments deficit. Switching demand towards home-produced goods will reduce the deficit and will also help to increase economic growth and employment. However, if the economy is suffering from inflation, expenditure-switching policies are likely to add to inflationary pressures because they increase AD and may increase the price of imports.

Expenditure-reducing policies are contractionary monetary and fiscal measures to reduce aggregate demand. They are also known as expenditure-damping policies. As already explained, a fall in AD will reduce people's income and so the value of imports purchased. It will also help to reduce inflationary pressures and help to restore price competitiveness.

Expenditure-reducing policies are most appropriate when an economy is experiencing inflation and has a positive output gap. Reducing AD should reduce the current account deficit and inflation. If there is a positive output gap, a reduction in AD should not have much effect on economic growth. However, if the economy has a negative output gap, reducing AD is likely to increase unemployment and move the economy further away from its normal capacity level of output.

How policies to correct a deficit or surplus may affect other policy objectives

Countries have a variety of macroeconomic policy objectives including low unemployment, low and stable inflation and achieving a steady rate of economic growth. The impact of policies to correct a current account deficit or surplus on these policy objectives will depend on the type of policy used and the current state of the country's economy.

Changes in the exchange rate

Allowing the exchange rate to fall to correct the deficit is likely to add to inflationary pressures. It increases the price of imports which directly increases the Consumer Price Index (CPI) and it also increases the costs of firms that import raw materials and components from abroad. If the fall in the exchange rate increases inflation, the reduction in the current account deficit may not last. However, if the economy is in recession, a fall in the exchange rate may not have much effect on inflation since firms may choose to absorb the increase in costs and may not raise prices. The increase in demand that results from the improvement in competitiveness will help the economy to recover from recession, closing the negative output gap and increasing employment. The fall in the deficit will reduce the net withdrawal from the circular flow of income and will have a positive multiplier effect, supporting the recovery.

If the economy has a positive output gap and economic growth is above the long-run trend rate, allowing the exchange rate to fall to correct a current account deficit could be damaging for the economy. It will increase the inflationary pressures that are already present in the economy and may not be very effective in reducing the deficit. In such circumstances, there will be limited spare capacity to supply the increased demand for exports and import substitutes. Also, if inflation accelerates, the improvement in price competitiveness will not last.

Allowing the exchange rate to appreciate to correct a surplus, will help to reduce inflationary pressures but will reduce AD and may also reduce employment and growth. Whether this is an appropriate policy depends on the current state of the country's economy.

Direct controls

The use of tariffs, quotas and other direct controls to correct a current account deficit will also add to inflationary pressures but may help to protect employment, at least in the short run. However, such measures are likely to lead to retaliation and their effectiveness may be limited.

Changing aggregate demand

Using deflationary policies to correct a balance of payments deficit can benefit an economy that has high inflation and is working above its normal capacity level of output. Some countries experience increasing current account deficits in the boom phase of the economic cycle. Rising incomes and confidence lead to increased spending, and imports are likely to rise. Reducing AD will help to reduce inflation and prevent the economy from growing too fast and may not have much impact on employment.

If an economy has a negative output gap, high unemployment and low growth, deflationary policies are likely to be damaging for the economy. Reducing AD may help to reduce the current account deficit but is also likely to increase unemployment and may push the economy into recession.

The use of reflationary policies to eliminate a current account surplus, will add to inflationary pressures but will help to increase employment and short-run economic growth. Increasing AD may be good for an economy that has a negative output gap but could be damaging if the economy is already producing above its normal capacity level of output. If the government uses fiscal measures to increase AD, it might also result in a growing budget deficit, which some governments might not want.

Supply-side policies

If successful, using supply-side policies to correct a current account deficit should not conflict with the main macroeconomic policy objectives. Improvements in the supply side of the economy should help to keep inflation under control, increase the long-run trend rate of economic growth and create employment.

Some supply-side measures may increase the budget deficit but if the economy starts to grow more rapidly, tax revenues should rise and spending on welfare should fall. Some supply-side measures may lead to an increase in inequality, but others may support a government's aim to make the distribution of income more equitable.

Progress questions

13 Explain how the use of export subsidies to reduce a deficit on the current account of the balance of payments is likely to affect the other objectives of macroeconomic policy.

14 A country is in recession and has a deficit on the current account of its balance of payments. Would you recommend that it uses expenditure-switching or expenditure-damping polices to reduce the deficit? Explain your answer.

Get it right

Do not confuse a balance of payments deficit, or surplus, with a budget deficit, or surplus. A balance of payments deficit is when imports are greater than exports (M > X). A budget deficit is when government spending is greater than taxation (G > T).

Case study: Does Indonesia's persistent deficit on the current account of its balance of payments matter?

▲ Figure 7.1.6: Tourism in Indonesia

Since 2012, Indonesia has had a deficit on the current account of its balance of payments after having had a substantial surplus for most of the previous decade. One reason for the change from a surplus to a deficit is that Indonesia was a net exporter of oil but now imports much more oil than it exports. Between 2012 and 2019, the current account deficit ranged between 3.2% and 1.6% of GDP. In 2019, the deficit was 2.7% of GDP but by the 1st quarter of 2020, it had fallen to 1.4% of GDP and stood at US$3.9 billion. The slower growth in the domestic economy led to a fall in imports. The surplus on trade in goods increased and the deficits on trade in services and the primary income balance fell. The Covid-19 pandemic means that domestic demand is likely to remain weak and imports will continue to fall. However, the weakness in the global economy will reduce merchandise exports and the collapse in earnings from tourism will damage the balance of trade in services.

A current account deficit means that the country is a net borrower from the rest of the world and it needs inflows of FDI or other investment to finance the deficit. The deficit is not necessarily harmful since it may lead to productive investment in industry or infrastructure. However, if the deficit is used to finance consumption, it does not help to support the growth of the economy or help to generate income in the future. Countries that run persistent current account deficits can be vulnerable to capital flight. At the end of the 1st quarter of 2020, Indonesia had net overseas liabilities of US$253.8 billion (22.5% of GDP). However, its foreign exchange reserves were enough to pay for 9 months' worth of imports.

The value of the Indonesian Rupiah has fallen substantially since 2012. At the beginning of 2012, it cost nearly 9,000 rupiah to buy one US dollar, but by the middle of 2020 it cost around 14,800 rupiah to buy one US dollar. The current account deficit is one reason why the value of the rupiah has depreciated but the depreciation has also helped to improve the competitiveness of Indonesia's economy. If the government wanted to reduce the current account deficit, it could introduce contractionary monetary and fiscal measures but this would be damaging at a time when economic growth is negative and unemployment is rising. Increasing import restrictions is another option that the Indonesian government might consider.

1. What is meant by the "primary income balance"?
2. Explain how a fall in the deficit on the primary income balance would affect Indonesia's balance of payments on current account.
3. Explain why a persistent deficit on the current account of the balance of payments is likely to lead to an increase in Indonesia's net overseas liabilities.
4. State **two** expenditure-reducing policies and **two** expenditure-switching policies mentioned in the case study.

Exam-style questions

1. The financial account of a country's balance of payments shows   (1 mark)

   A   exports and imports of goods and services.

   B   how a current account deficit is financed.

   C   income earned on assets abroad.

   D   net foreign assets owned by residents of the country.

2 A country has a surplus of $540 billion on the current account of its balance of payments and a surplus of $625 billion on its balance of trade in goods and services. The country's primary and secondary income balance is a (1 mark)

A deficit of $85 billion.

B deficit of $1,165 billion.

C surplus of $85 billion.

D surplus of $1,165 billion.

3 A tariff is most likely to be successful in reducing a deficit on the balance trade in goods and services when the tariff is imposed on products that have an (1 mark)

A elastic income elasticity of demand.

B elastic price elasticity of demand.

C inelastic income elasticity of demand.

D inelastic price elasticity of demand.

4 The following table shows an extract from a country's balance of payments account in 2020. In 2020, the country's GDP was $745 billion.

	2020	
	$ billion	
Balance of trade in goods and services	?	
Primary and secondary income balance	19.0	
Current account balance		9.6
Capital account balance		?
Direct investment	93.2	
Portfolio investment	−84.1	
Other investments	−18.3	
Reserve assets	23.3	
Financial account balance		14.1
Net errors and omissions		−1.7

[i] Define 'reserve assets'.

You are advised to show your workings for the calculations below. (2 marks)

[ii] Calculate the country's balance of trade in goods and services as a percentage of GDP in 2020. Give your answer to **two** decimal places. (4 marks)

[iii] In the table, a positive figure for items in the financial account means that there is a net investment abroad. Calculate the country's capital account balance in 2020. (4 marks)

5 A country's economy goes into recession. Explain how the recession is likely to affect its balance of trade in goods and services. (12 marks)

6 Assess the different policies that Indonesia might use to try to reduce the deficit on the current account of its balance of payments. (25 marks)

Note: To answer this question as a data response question, use the data provided in the case study "Does Indonesia's persistent deficit on the current account of its balance of payments matter?" in 7.1 "The balance of payments" to support your answer.

This section will develop your knowledge and understanding of:

→ determination of exchange rates in a freely floating exchange rate system

→ causes of changes in the exchange rate, including speculation and herding behaviour

→ government intervention to influence the exchange rate

→ advantages and disadvantages of free floating, managed and fixed exchange rate systems

→ how changes in the exchange rate affect individuals, firms and economic performance

→ role of the International Monetary Fund (IMF).

An exchange rate is the price at which one currency can be converted into another currency. For example, if an exchange rate is £1 = €1.07, it means that someone who has euros (€) and wants to buy pounds (£) would have to pay €1.07 for each pound they buy. A currency does not only have one price but will also have an exchange rate in relation to most, if not all, other currencies. A currency may appreciate in relation to some currencies but depreciate in relation to other currencies.

Effective exchange rate indices

An **effective exchange rate index** measures whether, on average, a currency is appreciating or depreciating against a basket of other currencies.

To construct an effective exchange rate index, statisticians have to decide which currencies to include in the index and how changes in the value of each currency are to be weighted. The weight given to each country's currency in the index is usually determined by the proportion of total trade the country does with that country. The more trade a country does with a country, the greater the weight attached to changes in that country's exchange rate. For example, if the proportion of a country's trade with the USA was 15% and the proportion of its trade with countries that use the euro was 30%, a change in the value of its currency in terms of the euro would have more effect on the country's exchange rate index than the same change in the value of its currency in terms of the US dollar.

In the base year, the effective exchange rate index starts with a value of 100. If the numerical value of the index increases, the value of the currency has appreciated against the basket of other currencies. A fall in the index indicates a depreciation in the value of the currency.

A country's real exchange rate is calculated by adjusting for differences in the rates of inflation between countries. For example, if the country's nominal exchange rate has depreciated by 10% against another country's currency but its inflation rate is 10% higher, then its real exchange rate has not changed.

In the following example, in Table 7.2.1, a country experiences 10% inflation between 2018 and 2019 but there was no inflation in the USA. It is assumed that the domestic currency price of the good increases by 10%, the same as the rate of inflation.

Link

An explanation of index numbers is included in Chapter 6 "The measurement of macroeconomic performance" in the AS book.

Key term

Effective exchange rate index (nominal): a measure of the weighted value of a currency against a basket of other currencies.

Activity

Find out as much as you can about the way in which the effective exchange rate index for your country's currency is calculated. For example, what are the weights and how are they determined?

▼ **Table 7.2.1**: Inflation and exchange rate

Year	Price of the good in the domestic currency (peso)	Exchange rate	Price of the good in US dollars
2018	1200 peso	$1 = 300 peso	$4
2019	1320 peso	$1 = 330 peso	$4

The country's exchange rate depreciated by 10%, the same as the difference between the countries' inflation rates. The fall in the exchange rate compensates for the higher rate of inflation and the US dollar price of the product is unchanged.

The **real effective exchange rate index** takes into account the different rates of inflation experienced by countries included in the index as well as changes in their nominal exchange rates.

Determination of exchange rates in a freely floating exchange rate system

In a **freely floating exchange rate system**, the exchange rate (the price of a currency) is determined by the demand for and supply of the currency on the foreign exchange market. In a freely floating exchange rate system there is no intervention by governments or central banks to affect the value of the currency. The exchange rate is determined by market forces.

The foreign exchange market (FOREX)

Currencies are bought and sold on the **foreign exchange market (FOREX)**. The foreign exchange market is a global market and does not have a particular physical location. Any individual or organisation that buys or sells foreign currency is trading on the foreign exchange market. Firms exporting and importing goods and services, individuals buying foreign currency to go on holiday abroad and financial institutions buying shares abroad, all trade currencies on the FOREX. Central banks may also buy and sell currencies to influence the value of their country's currency. However, in a freely floating exchange rate system, governments and central banks do not intervene to influence the value of the currency.

The demand for a currency on the FOREX

The demand for a currency on the FOREX is determined mainly by:

- the value of its exports of goods and services
- investment in the economy from abroad
- speculation that the exchange rate will change.

When a country exports goods and services abroad, the overseas buyer will need to convert their currency into the currency of the exporter, leading to a demand for the currency on the foreign exchange market. Similarly, if an overseas resident wants to invest in a country's economy, including direct and portfolio investment, they will need to exchange their currency for the currency of the country in which they wish to invest. This will increase the demand for that currency on the FOREX. If people think that a currency is going to appreciate

Key terms

Real effective exchange rate index: a measure of the weighted value of a currency against a basket of other currencies, adjusted to take into account the different rates of inflation in countries.

Freely floating exchange rate system: where the price of a currency is determined by the demand for and supply of the currency on the foreign exchange market, without any government intervention.

Foreign exchange market (FOREX): where currencies are bought and sold and their prices are determined.

compared to other currencies, they may buy the currency hoping that they will profit from doing so.

The demand curve for a currency is usually shown as downward sloping, meaning that a fall in the value of the currency, its price or exchange rate, leads to an increase in the quantity demanded of the currency. An increase in the exchange rate leads to a fall in the quantity of the currency demanded. A change in the exchange rate causes a movement along the demand curve.

In Figure 7.2.1, when the euro exchange rate depreciates from €1 = \$1.21 to €1 = \$1.09, the quantity of euros demanded increases from Q_1 to Q_2. A fall in the exchange rate is likely to lead to an increase in the quantity demanded because the foreign currency price of exports will fall, resulting in an increase in the demand for exports. Provided the demand for exports is price elastic, the foreign currency value of exports, and so the demand for the currency, will increase. Also, the fall in the exchange rate makes it cheaper for overseas residents to invest in the economy which should also increase the quantity of the currency demanded.

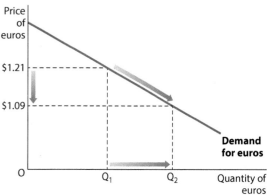

▲ **Figure 7.2.1**: The demand for a currency on the foreign exchange market

The supply of a currency on the FOREX

The supply of a currency on the FOREX is determined mainly by:

- the value of goods and services imported
- investment overseas
- speculation that the exchange rate will change.

When a country imports goods and services, the buyer will need to convert their currency into foreign currency to pay for the imports, adding to the supply of the currency on the foreign exchange market. Similarly, if a domestic resident wants to invest abroad, they will need to exchange their currency for the currency of the country in which they wish to invest. Again, this will increase the supply of the currency on the FOREX. If people think that the currency is going to depreciate compared to other currencies, they may sell the currency before the price falls.

The supply curve for a currency is usually shown as upward sloping, meaning that a rise in the value of the currency, its price or exchange rate, leads to an increase in the quantity supplied of the currency. Similarly, a decrease in the exchange rate leads to a decrease in the quantity supplied of the currency. A change in the exchange rate causes a movement along the supply curve.

In Figure 7.2.2, when the euro exchange rate appreciates from €1 = \$1.07 to €1 = \$1.16, the quantity of euros supplied increases from Q_1 to Q_2. A rise in the exchange rate will lead to an increase in the quantity supplied because the fall in the domestic currency price of imports will lead to an increase in the demand for imports. The increase in the quantity of imports will mean that foreign currency is needed to pay for them and so the supply of the domestic currency on the FOREX will increase. The rise in the exchange rate also makes it cheaper, and therefore more

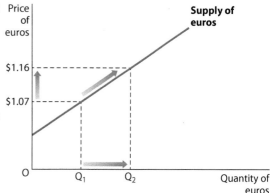

▲ **Figure 7.2.2**: The supply of a currency on the foreign exchange market

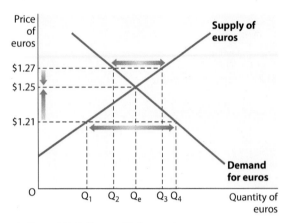

▲ **Figure 7.2.3**: The equilibrium exchange rate

attractive, for domestic residents to invest abroad. An increase in investment abroad should lead to an increase in the quantity of the domestic currency supplied on the FOREX.

The equilibrium exchange rate

In a freely floating exchange rate system, the equilibrium exchange rate is where the demand for a currency equals the supply of the currency on the FOREX. This is shown in Figure 7.2.3.

In Figure 7.2.3, the equilibrium exchange rate is $1.25 since at this exchange rate the demand for the currency equals the supply of the currency. If the current exchange rate was $1.21, there would be excess demand for euros equal to $OQ_4 - OQ_1$ and there would be pressure for the exchange rate to appreciate. The quantity of euros being placed on the market would not be sufficient to satisfy the quantity of euros people wish to buy and so the price would rise. However, if the current exchange rate was $1.27, there would be excess supply of euros equal to $OQ_3 - OQ_2$ and there would be pressure for the exchange rate to depreciate. There would be more sellers of euros than buyers and so the price of euros would fall.

Causes of changes in the exchange rate

Anything that causes a shift in the demand for and/or supply of a currency on the FOREX will lead to a change in the equilibrium exchange rate. An increase in the demand for the currency, that is a rightward shift in the demand curve, or a fall in the supply of the currency, that is a leftward shift in the supply curve, will lead to an appreciation in the exchange rate. The exchange rate will depreciate when demand for the currency decreases or the supply increases.

In Figure 7.2.4, the original exchange rate is $1 = £0.86 and a quantity of OQ_1 is traded in a particular time period. If the demand for the dollar increases, represented by a shift in the demand curve to the right from D_1 to D_2, there will be an excess demand for dollars at the original exchange rate equal to $OQ_x - OQ_1$. The excess demand for the currency causes the exchange rate to be bid up to $1 = £0.89, where the demand for dollars again equals the supply of dollars. The increase in the demand for dollars might, for example, have been caused by an increase in exports from the USA or an increase in overseas investment in the USA.

In Figure 7.2.5, the original exchange rate is $1 = £0.83 and a quantity of OQ_1 is traded in each time period. If the supply of dollars increases, represented by a shift of the supply curve to the right from S_1 to S_2, there will be an excess supply of dollars at the original exchange rate equal to $OQ_x - OQ_1$. The excess supply of the currency causes the exchange rate to depreciate to $1 = £0.81, where the supply of dollars again equals the demand for dollars. The increase in the supply of dollars might, for example, have been caused by an increase in the value of goods

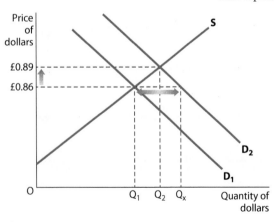

▲ **Figure 7.2.4**: An increase in the demand for a currency causes the exchange rate to appreciate

and services imported by the USA or by financial institutions located in the USA buying stocks and shares from overseas.

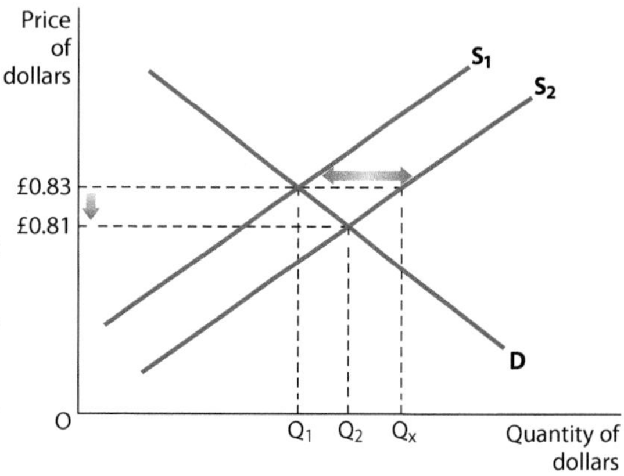

How speculation affects the exchange rate

Speculation is when economic agents buy or sell an asset, such as foreign currency, expecting that its price will change and allow them to make a profit in the future. In a floating exchange rate system, the value of a currency can change very quickly and the FOREX is a market where speculation sometimes causes significant fluctuations in exchange rates. Speculators may include financial institutions, firms involved in foreign trade and private individuals. A currency speculator will buy a currency to make a financial gain rather than, for example, buying the currency to pay for imports. Although speculators hope to make a profit, there is usually a significant risk that they will make a loss.

▲ **Figure 7.2.5**: An increase in the supply of a currency causes the exchange rate to depreciate

Destabilising speculation

If speculators believe that a currency is going to appreciate in value, they will buy the currency expecting that when its value has risen, they will be able to convert it back into the original currency for a larger amount of money. For example, if an individual buys $5,000 when €1 = $1.10, it will cost them €4,545. If the value of the dollar increases so that €1 = $1.05, they will be able to sell the $5,000 for €4,762, making a profit of €217, less dealing costs. Speculation that a currency is going to rise in value will lead to an increase in the demand for the currency and will cause the currency to appreciate. A rise in the value of the currency may lead others to speculate that the value of the currency will continue to rise, leading to a further appreciation. This type of **herding behaviour** can cause significant fluctuations in the value of a currency.

In Figure 7.2.6, the demand for dollars initially increases from D_1 to D_2 and the dollar exchange rate appreciates from $1 = €0.91 to $1 = €0.93. This increase in the value of the dollar leads to speculation that there will be a further appreciation in the dollar exchange rate and so speculators buy dollars, increasing the demand for dollars to D_3. As a result, the dollar exchange rate appreciates even more to $1 = €0.98.

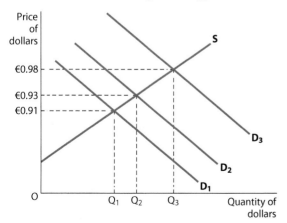

▲ **Figure 7.2.6**: The effect of speculation that the exchange rate is going to appreciate

Get it right

The exchange rate is determined by the demand for and supply of the currency on the foreign exchange market. It is not directly affected by the domestic demand for the currency or the domestic money supply.

Progress questions

1. Explain why an increase in the value of exports leads to an increase in demand for the country's currency on the foreign exchange market.

2. Explain why an outflow of FDI leads to an increase in the supply of the country's currency on the foreign exchange market.

Key term

Herding behaviour: when an individual's behaviour is influenced by the behaviour of the group.

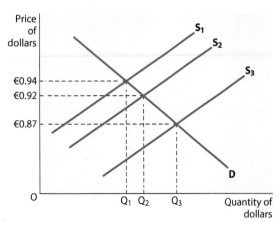

▲ **Figure 7.2.7**: The effect of speculation that the exchange rate is going to depreciate

After a while, some economic agents are likely to consider that the price of the currency is too high and will sell the currency. This will increase the supply of the currency on the FOREX and if supply exceeds demand, the exchange rate will start to depreciate. As the price starts to fall, others may sell the currency speculating that the price will continue to fall, so contributing to the fall in its value. This type of **destabilising speculation** can be very damaging for an economy.

Speculators can make a profit when a currency is falling in value by selling the currency before it has depreciated and buying it back after its value has fallen. For example, if an individual sells €12,000 when the exchange rate is €1 = \$1.10, they will receive \$13,200. If the value of the euro falls so that €1 = \$1.00, they will be able to sell the \$13,200 for €13,200, making a profit of €1,200, less dealing costs.

In Figure 7.2.7, the supply of dollars initially increases from S_1 to S_2 and the dollar exchange rate depreciates from \$1 = €0.94 to \$1 = €0.92. This fall in the value of the dollar leads to speculation that there will be further depreciation in the dollar exchange rate and so speculators sell dollars, increasing the supply of dollars to S_3. As a result, the dollar exchange rate depreciates even further to \$1 = €0.87.

As can be seen from Figures 7.2.6 and 7.2.7, speculation can lead to larger fluctuations in exchange rates than would have occurred if speculation had not taken place.

Stabilising speculation

Speculation does not always lead to large changes in exchange rates. It can also help to reduce fluctuations in exchange rates. Economic agents who speculate on the FOREX are often experts and may recognise when a change in the value of a currency is not caused by the underlying economic conditions but by temporary, random factors. For example, on a particular day, firms might choose to buy large amounts of a currency to allow them to pay for imports and this large increase in the demand for the currency may cause a significant, but temporary, increase in the value of the currency. If speculators recognise that the increase in the value of the currency is temporary, they will sell the currency at a high price and buy it back later when the price has fallen. In this case, the actions of speculators have increased the supply of the currency on the FOREX and prevented the exchange rate appreciating as much as it otherwise would have done.

In Figure 7.2.8, a temporary increase in the demand for the Japanese yen, from D_1 to D_2, would have increased the exchange rate from ¥1 = \$0.0091 to ¥1 = \$0.0095. Speculators realise that the increase in the exchange rate is only temporary and supply yen on the FOREX to take advantage of the high price. The increase in the supply of yen means that the exchange rate only increases to ¥1 = \$0.0093.

Similarly, if there is a temporary increase in the supply of a currency which leads to a fall in the value of the currency, expert speculators may recognise that the fall in the exchange rate is temporary and buy the currency in the expectation that its price will soon rise. The actions of speculators increase the demand for the currency and prevent the exchange rate falling by as much as it otherwise would have done. This is known as **stabilising speculation**.

Although speculation is most common in a floating exchange rate system, it can also occur when a country has a fixed exchange rate. It occurs when it is expected that the government is likely to revalue or devalue the currency.

Government intervention to influence the exchange rate

There are many different types of exchange rate system, but they are often categorised as follows:

* a freely floating exchange rate system
* a managed floating exchange rate system
* a fixed exchange rate system.

Freely floating exchange rate system
In a completely free floating exchange rate system, there is no deliberate intervention by governments or central banks to influence the exchange rate. As explained earlier, the exchange rate is determined by market forces, that is by the interaction of the demand for and supply of the currency on the FOREX.

Managed floating exchange rate system
In a **managed floating exchange rate system**, also known as a dirty floating exchange rate system, there is intervention by the country's monetary authorities, usually its central bank, to affect the exchange rate. The amount of intervention can vary. Sometimes the central bank only intervenes to reduce temporary, day-to-day fluctuations in the exchange rate and does not attempt to influence the underlying value of the currency. For example, if there is persistent excess supply of the currency on the FOREX, the central bank would allow the exchange rate to depreciate until the underlying equilibrium exchange rate is established. Similarly, if there is persistent excess demand for the currency, the central bank would allow the exchange rate to appreciate.

However, some central banks take a more active, interventionist role and attempt to keep the exchange rate above or below the level that would result from allowing market forces to determine the value of the currency. They may wish to keep the exchange rate low to try to make domestic firms more price competitive in their home and overseas markets. A low exchange rate should help to increase employment and economic growth. If the central bank wants to reduce inflationary pressures, it may intervene to try to strengthen the exchange rate and keep the rate above the free-market equilibrium rate.

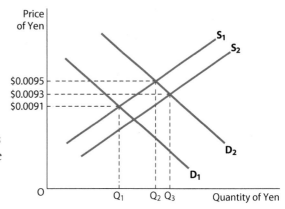

▲ Figure 7.2.8: Stabilising speculation can help reduce a temporary rise in the exchange rate

Progress questions

3 Draw a diagram to illustrate how, other things being equal, a substantial inflow of FDI is likely to affect a country's exchange rate.

4 Explain how a significant fall in the world market price of copper is likely to affect the exchange rate of a country that is a major exporter of copper.

5 It is generally believed that a country's exchange rate is going to depreciate. Explain why speculation may help to cause the exchange rate to depreciate.

Activity

Find out what type of exchange rate system your country is using.

Key terms

Stabilising speculation: when the actions of speculators lead to smaller fluctuations in the price of an asset than if speculation had not taken place.

Managed floating exchange rate system: an exchange rate system where central banks intervene in the foreign exchange market to influence the value of their country's currency.

Central banks can intervene to affect the exchange rate in two main ways:

* buying and selling their currency on the FOREX
* changing interest rates to affect the demand for and supply of the currency.

Buying and selling the currency to influence the exchange rate

Central banks have reserves of foreign currency that they can use to intervene in the FOREX. The main **reserve currencies** are US dollars, euros, Japanese yen, Chinese yuan and UK pounds sterling. If the central bank wants to increase the exchange rate, or prevent it from falling, it can use its reserves of foreign currency to buy its own currency. This increases the demand for its currency and helps to increase its price. However, a central bank's ability to intervene in this way is limited by the value of its foreign exchange reserves, although these can be increased by borrowing from abroad.

If the central bank wishes to reduce the exchange rate, or prevent it from appreciating, it can sell its own currency and buy foreign currency. This increases the supply of its currency on the FOREX and helps to prevent the price of its currency rising. Since a central bank can create its own currency, it can supply as much currency as is needed to prevent the exchange rate appreciating.

Changing interest rates to affect the demand for and supply of the currency

A central bank can also affect the demand for and supply of its currency by changing its discount rate, also known as its base rate of interest. If the central bank increases its discount rate, other interest rates in the domestic economy are also likely to increase. An increase in domestic interest rates compared to other countries, other things being equal, is likely to attract inflows of hot money as investors are attracted by the higher rate of return. This increases the demand for the currency on the FOREX. If speculators believe that the increase in interest rates will cause the currency to appreciate, this will add to the increase in the demand for the currency. Also, domestic economic agents, including financial institutions, are more likely to invest in financial assets in the domestic economy rather than overseas. This will reduce the supply of the currency on the FOREX.

In Figure 7.2.9, an increase in interest rates has increased the demand for the currency from D_1 to D_2 and reduced the supply of the currency for S_1 to S_2. The increase in demand and fall in the supply of the currency on the FOREX has caused the exchange rate to appreciate. The currency will now buy $0.46 rather than $0.41.

If the central bank wishes to reduce the exchange rate, it could reduce its discount rate. The resulting fall in domestic interest rates compared to other countries should reduce the demand for and increase the supply of the currency on the FOREX. Foreign investors are likely to move their money abroad and domestic economic

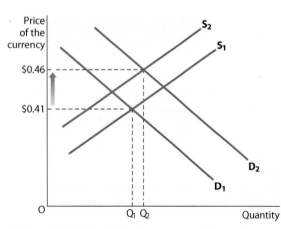

▲ **Figure 7.2.9:** The effect of an increase in interest rates on the exchange rate

agents are also more likely to invest in interest-earning assets in countries that offer a higher rate of return.

However, although changes in interest rates can affect the exchange rate by influencing portfolio investment and hot money flows, they may not always be effective. For example, if speculators believe that the currency is going to fall in value, an increase in domestic interest rates may not be sufficient to compensate for the expected fall in the value of the currency.

Changing a central bank's discount rate is a very important instrument of monetary policy. If used to influence the exchange rate, it might conflict with other macroeconomic policy objectives but does not necessarily do so. For example, if the central bank increases its discount rate to try to prevent the exchange rate falling, it may lead to higher unemployment but will help to reduce inflationary pressures.

Fixed exchange rate system

In a fixed exchange rate system, governments announce the value of their currency, usually in terms of one or more other currencies, and central banks intervene in the market to maintain the exchange rate. During much of the 19th century and the early part of the 20th century, many countries fixed the value of their currencies in terms of gold. This exchange rate system is known as the gold standard system. Since the value of each currency was fixed in terms of gold, the value of each currency was fixed in terms of every other currency. However, even in a fixed exchange rate system, governments may change the exchange rate. If the central bank is unable to maintain the value of the currency, it can be devalued or revalued.

In most fixed exchange rate systems, the exchange rate is allowed to fluctuate to a limited extent. For example, under the Bretton Woods system of fixed exchange rates, which operated from the end of the Second World War until 1971, each country announced a **par value** for its currency and agreed to keep the exchange rate within a **band** of plus or minus 1% of the par value. The par value is sometimes known as the parity or central rate. The upper limit is also known as the ceiling and the lower limit is known as the floor. This system is known as an **adjustable peg exchange rate system** since the par value can be changed when necessary.

The width of the band can vary. In a fixed exchange rate system with a wide band, the system has some of the features of a floating exchange rate system. The central bank can allow the exchange rate to be determined by the demand for and supply of the currency, provided market forces do not cause the exchange rate to move outside the band.

In a fixed exchange rate system, the central bank intervenes in the FOREX to make sure that the exchange rate stays within the band. As explained earlier, it can do this by buying and selling the currency on the FOREX and/or by changing its discount rate to influence hot money flows.

Link

Monetary policy was explained in 9.1 "Monetary policy" in the AS book.

Get it right

An increase in interest rates will tend to increase the exchange rate because it leads to an increase in the demand for and a reduction in the supply of the currency on the FOREX. An increase in interest rates makes it more rewarding for overseas and domestic investors to buy interest-earning assets in the economy. A fall in interest rates will tend to reduce the exchange rate.

Key terms

Par value: the official value of a currency in a fixed exchange rate system, also known as the parity or central rate.

Band: the limits between which an exchange rate is allowed to fluctuate in a fixed exchange rate system.

Adjustable peg exchange rate system: a system of fixed exchange rates where the exchange rate is allowed to fluctuate within an agreed band and where the par value can be changed if necessary.

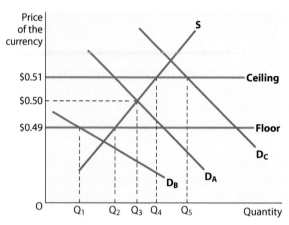

▲ **Figure 7.2.10**: Central bank intervention to maintain a fixed exchange rate

In Figure 7.2.10, the par value for the currency is $0.50 and there is a band of 2% either side of the par value. If market forces would cause the exchange rate to go above $0.51 or fall below $0.49, the central bank would intervene in the market to prevent this happening.

If the demand curve is D_A and the supply curve is S, the free-market equilibrium exchange rate is $0.50 and the central bank does not need to intervene in the market. However, if the demand for the currency decreased to D_B, market forces would cause the exchange rate to go below the floor. To prevent this happening, the central bank would have to use its foreign exchange reserves to buy at least $OQ_2 - OQ_1$ of its currency to eliminate the excess supply of the currency at the floor price of $0.49. If the demand for the currency increased to D_C, market forces would cause the exchange rate to go above the ceiling. To prevent this happening, the central bank would have to sell at least $OQ_5 - OQ_4$ of its currency to eliminate the excess demand for the currency at the ceiling price of $0.51.

If market forces continue to cause pressure for the exchange rate to rise above the ceiling or fall below the floor, the central bank could also change its discount rate to affect the demand for and supply of the currency. In the long run, the government could adopt other measures that affect the demand for and supply of its currency on the FOREX or it could revalue or devalue the exchange rate to a value that can be sustained.

When a country has a fixed exchange rate, it will often use exchange controls to affect the supply of and demand for its currency on the FOREX. Exchange controls are government-imposed limits on the purchase and sale of its currency. For example, the government may limit the amount of money domestic residents are allowed to invest abroad or on how much foreign currency they can take on holiday abroad. Limits may also be imposed on the amount of overseas investment in the domestic economy. Although exchange controls are more likely to be used in a fixed exchange rate system, they can also be used when a country has a managed floating exchange rate.

Get it right

In a fixed exchange rate system, the central bank can prevent the exchange rate falling below the lower band by using its foreign exchange reserves to buy the currency. If the exchange rate is likely to go above the upper band, it will sell the currency, adding to its foreign exchange reserves.

Advantages and disadvantages of different exchange rate systems

The advantages of a freely floating exchange rate system usually match the disadvantages of a fixed exchange rate system and the disadvantages of a freely floating exchange rate system usually match the advantages of a fixed exchange rate system. The advantages and disadvantages of a managed floating exchange rate system will depend on how much the central bank and government intervene in the market and the extent to which the exchange rate is allowed to change with market forces.

Advantages of a freely floating exchange rate system

The main advantages of a freely floating exchange rate system are:

- automatic correction of balance of payments deficits and surpluses
- allows the government to pursue independent monetary and fiscal policies
- helps to protect the domestic economy from external shocks
- demand-side monetary and fiscal policies are more effective
- allows the economy to adjust gradually to change
- less need for foreign exchange reserves.

Automatic correction of balance of payments deficits and surpluses

If a country has a balance of payments deficit, it means that the amount of currency supplied on the foreign exchange market to buy imports is greater than the demand for the currency to buy exports. The excess supply of the currency will cause the exchange rate to fall, making exports more competitive abroad and imports less competitive in the domestic economy. Provided the Marshall-Lerner condition is satisfied, this should reduce the deficit.

Similarly, if a country has a balance of payments surplus, it means that the amount of currency supplied on the foreign exchange market to buy imports is less than the demand for the currency to buy exports. The excess demand for the currency will cause the exchange rate to appreciate, making exports less competitive abroad and imports more competitive in the domestic economy. Provided the demand for imports and exports is sufficiently price elastic, this should reduce the surplus.

However, it must be remembered that for some countries, in the globalised world economy, trade in goods and services is a small part of their balance of payments account. As a result, excess supply or demand for the currency, and so changes in the exchange rate, depend more on capital flows than current account transactions. As a result, even in a freely floating exchange rate system, current account deficits and surpluses will not be corrected automatically by changes in the exchange rate. However, under a floating exchange rate system, even in a globalised world economy where capital flows are increasingly important, exchange rate changes should help a country to deal with balance of payments problems.

Activity

Find out whether your country uses exchange controls to influence the supply and/or demand for its currency. If your government has imposed exchange controls, describe two types of control that are being used.

Get it right

In a fixed exchange rate system, a fall in the value of a currency is known as a devaluation but in a floating exchange system, it is known as a depreciation. In a fixed exchange rate system, a rise in the value of a currency is known as a revaluation but in a floating exchange system, it is known as an appreciation.

Progress questions

6 Distinguish between a managed and freely floating exchange rate system.

7 Explain how a central bank can use its foreign exchange reserves to try to prevent the exchange rate depreciating.

8 Explain why, other things being equal, a fall in domestic interest rates is likely to lead to a fall in the country's exchange rate.

Link

The Marshall-Lerner condition was explained in 7.1 "The balance of payments".

Link

How changes in the exchange rate help to correct balance of payments deficits and surpluses was explained in 7.1 "The balance of payments".

Allows the government to pursue independent monetary and fiscal policies

In a freely floating exchange rate system, the government can allow the exchange rate to change to take care of balance of payments problems and it does not have to intervene in the FOREX to influence the exchange rate. As a result, it is able to use monetary and fiscal measures to achieve its internal macroeconomic policy objectives. For example, if the economy is in recession and is suffering from high unemployment, it can reduce interest rates to increase aggregate demand (AD). In a fixed exchange rate system this may not be possible because reducing interest rates could result in the exchange rate falling below the lower band.

Similarly, an expansionary fiscal policy may lead to an increase in imports, increasing the supply of the currency on the FOREX and causing the exchange rate to depreciate. In a freely floating exchange rate system, government policy is not constrained by changes in the exchange rate and the fall in the exchange rate should help the balance of payments to adjust.

If the economy is suffering from high inflation, the central bank can increase its discount rate to reduce demand-pull inflationary pressures without being constrained by an appreciating exchange rate. In fact, the appreciation in the exchange rate will help to reduce import prices and inflationary pressures.

Helps to protect the domestic economy from external shocks

If a country's main trading partners go into recession, exports are likely to fall and the domestic economy will experience a negative demand-side shock, reducing real GDP and employment. However, the fall in exports will reduce the demand for the currency and cause the exchange rate to depreciate. The fall in the exchange rate will reduce the foreign currency price of exports and increase the domestic currency price of imports. The improvement in price competitiveness will help to increase AD and reduce the impact of the negative demand-side shock. Similarly, a positive external demand-side shock, which increases exports, will cause the exchange rate to appreciate and reduce the inflationary effects of the increase in AD.

An increase in world commodity prices is a negative external supply-side shock for a country that is a large importer of commodities. Since the demand for imported commodities is likely to be price inelastic, the increase in commodity prices will lead to an increase in spending on imports and the supply of the currency on the FOREX. As a result, the country's exchange rate will depreciate. This will increase AD and help to offset the initial fall in real GDP and maintain employment, but it will add to the inflationary pressures.

A positive external supply-side shock will reduce inflation, increase real GDP and lead to an appreciation of the currency. As a result, there is a further reduction in inflationary pressure and the increase in real GDP is reduced.

Demand-side monetary and fiscal policies are more effective

In a fixed exchange rate system, expansionary fiscal and monetary policy will increase AD but some of the increase in spending will go on imports. Since imports are a withdrawal from the circular flow of income, the increase in AD and hence the impact on the domestic economy is reduced. In a freely floating exchange rate system, the increased spending on imports leads to an increase in the supply of the currency on the FOREX and a fall in the exchange rate. As a result, imports fall and exports rise so that the full impact of the expansionary policy feeds into the domestic economy.

Similarly, in a fixed exchange rate system, contractionary monetary and fiscal policies are less effective than in a floating exchange rate system. In a fixed exchange rate system, the contractionary policy reduces spending on imports and therefore the amount that is withdrawn from the circular flow of income. In a freely floating exchange rate system, the initial reduction in spending on imports causes the exchange rate to appreciate, as the supply of the currency on the FOREX falls, and AD is reduced so that the full impact of the contractionary policy feeds into the domestic economy.

Allows the economy to adjust gradually to change

Exchange rates affect the allocation of resources because they affect the prices of exports and imports. An efficient allocation of resources requires that relative prices change in response to changes in the pattern of demand, comparative advantage and competitiveness. Such changes occur all the time, for example, as a result of changes in efficiency and technological progress. In a freely floating exchange rate system, the relative prices of products in different countries should adjust to reflect these changes.

Over time, different countries experience different rates of inflation and in a fixed exchange rate system, currencies can become overvalued or undervalued. When exchange rates do not reflect the true value of the different currencies, resources are misallocated within and between countries. Eventually, this will lead to currencies being devalued or revalued, requiring a significant reallocation of resources. This can be damaging for an economy. For example, when a currency is devalued, the change in the relative price of home-produced and foreign goods leads to an increase in the demand for exports and a fall in demand for imports. This means that resources should be transferred into export industries and import-competing industries. Under a freely floating exchange rate system, the exchange rates should change gradually and by smaller amounts, allowing for a smoother, less damaging reallocation of resources.

Less need for foreign exchange reserves

In a fixed exchange rate system, central banks have to intervene in the FOREX to maintain the fixed exchange rate. There are times when this may require large amounts of the currency to be purchased. For example, when a currency is overvalued, it will take time before other policies are introduced and able to correct the overvaluation. Also,

▲ **Figure 7.2.11:** A floating exchange rate

if there is speculation that the currency is going to be devalued, the central bank will have to use its foreign exchange reserves to buy the currency and prevent its value falling. In a freely floating exchange rate system, there is less need for foreign exchange reserves.

Disadvantages of a freely floating exchange rate system
The main disadvantages of a freely floating exchange rate system are:

- may restrict international trade and foreign direct investment
- destabilising speculation
- removes the discipline from a government's use of monetary and fiscal policy
- may be inflationary.

May restrict international trade and foreign direct investment
Changes in exchange rates that occur under a freely floating exchange rate system may mean that firms are less likely to export and import goods and services. If a firm agrees to buy products from abroad but later the exchange rate depreciates, it will have to pay more for the imports than it expected. This uncertainty may mean that the firm may choose to buy the products from a domestic supplier even though, at current exchange rates, they are more expensive.

Similarly, if the currency appreciates, an exporter may receive less money than they anticipated when the sale was agreed. For example, if a Chinese manufacturer exports a pair of shoes that sells in the USA at a price of $40, when the exchange rate for the Chinese yuan is ¥1 = $0.14, the exporter will receive ¥286. However, if the exchange rate for the yuan appreciates to ¥1 = $0.16, the exporter will only receive ¥250. This uncertainty, which affects the profits made when exporting, may discourage the company from selling its products abroad.

The principle of comparative advantage shows that international trade can lead to a better allocation of resources and an improvement in living standards. If freely floating exchange rates restrict international trade, some of these benefits will be lost.

Link
The principle of comparative advantage was explained in 6.2 "Trade".

However, traders can use forward markets to buy currency for delivery in the future at an agreed price. This helps to reduce the uncertainty and helps to encourage international trade.

Exchange rate fluctuations may also discourage companies from investing abroad because changes in the exchange rate can lead to changes in the cost of investment abroad and in the profits earned. This may also mean that resources are not allocated efficiently between countries, leading to a reduction in economic welfare.

Destabilising speculation

In a freely floating exchange rate system, speculation is more likely to happen because the exchange rate is always changing. If speculators predict correctly whether the exchange rate is going to appreciate or depreciate, they can make large profits. Globalisation has been accompanied by a substantial increase in short-term capital flows between countries and these movements of hot money can lead to large fluctuations in exchange rates which restrict international trade and can be damaging for a country's economy. However, not all speculation is destabilising.

Speculation also occurs in a fixed exchange rate system and is arguably more damaging. For example, if it becomes obvious that a currency is overvalued, speculators will sell the currency and this may force the government to devalue the currency.

Link

Forward markets are explained in 7.3 "Financial markets".

▲ Figure 7.2.12: Speculation can be destabilising

Removes the discipline from a government's use of monetary and fiscal policy

A freely floating exchange rate system gives a government the freedom to use monetary and fiscal policies to achieve its internal macroeconomic policy objectives because they do not have to consider the balance of payments or the exchange rate. In addition, it makes demand-management policies more effective. However, it also means that the government can pursue a very expansionary economic policy that leads to high inflation and an unstable economy. For example, the central bank does not have to use interest rates to manage the exchange rate and could cut its discount rate to increase AD. The government could cut taxes and increase government expenditure without having to worry too much about the effect on the balance of payments. If the balance of payments goes into deficit, it can allow the exchange rate to fall. The risk is that a government wishing to increase economic growth and maintain full employment may increase AD too much. Too much demand will cause the economy to overheat, leading to high inflation and eventually a recession. The fall in the exchange rate, caused by a growing balance of payments deficit, will add to inflationary pressures, as the price of imports rises.

In a fixed exchange rate system, expansionary monetary and fiscal policies will lead to an increase in spending on imports, a deterioration in the current account of the balance of payments and pressure for the exchange rate to depreciate. To prevent the exchange rate falling below the lower band, it is likely that the central bank will have to increase its discount rate and the government will have to adopt a less expansionary fiscal policy. The fixed exchange rate imposes a discipline on the government but prevents it from adopting independent monetary and fiscal policies.

May be inflationary

If a country has a higher rate of inflation than other countries, the balance of payments will move into deficit and the exchange rate is likely to depreciate. The fall in the exchange rate will increase the cost of imports and will increase AD, adding to both cost-push and demand-pull inflationary pressures. Higher inflation will lead to higher wage demands and result in more inflation. As inflation increases, the exchange rate depreciates further so that the floating exchange rate contributes to an inflationary spiral that could get out of control.

However, governments can prevent this from happening if they adopt monetary and fiscal measures to control inflation. In some countries that have floating exchange rates, governments have set an inflation target and have an independent central bank that is required to use monetary policy to make sure that the target is met.

Advantages of a fixed exchange rate system

The main advantages of a fixed exchange rate system are:

- encourages international trade and investment
- limited speculation
- limits a government's ability to pursue inflationary economic policies.

Encourages international trade and investment

In a fixed exchange rate system, firms know how much they will receive for exports, and firms considering importing goods and services know how much they will have to pay. Unless the currency is revalued or devalued, the risk that a change in the exchange rate will make exporting or importing unprofitable is removed. Similarly, the risks of investing abroad are reduced when exchange rates are fixed.

Limited speculation

When exchange rates are completely fixed, there is no point in speculation unless it is expected that the currency is going to be devalued or revalued. An adjustable peg exchange rate system does provide speculators with the chance to make a profit but the opportunity for speculation depends on the width of the band. Even with a wide band, speculation is likely to be less than under a freely floating exchange rate system.

However, over time, the economic performance of countries will differ and it is likely that exchange rates will have to be adjusted. It will become obvious that some exchange rates are overvalued and others undervalued. In this situation, there is a problem known as the one-way option and speculators can make very large profits. If it is obvious that a currency is overvalued, speculators will sell the currency. If the overvalued currency is devalued, speculators will make large profits when they convert their money back into the devalued currency. If the currency is not devalued, speculators can still buy back the currency at the original exchange rate, although there are dealing costs to consider. In these circumstances, speculation can make it impossible to maintain the exchange rate and it can force the government to devalue its currency.

Limits a government's ability to pursue inflationary economic policies

Under a fixed exchange rate system, if a government expands the economy too much, leading to high inflation, the country's products will become uncompetitive and the balance of payments will deteriorate. As a result, there will be an excess supply of the currency on the FOREX. In the short run, the central bank may be able to buy up the surplus currency, using its foreign exchange reserves, and prevent the exchange rate falling. However, in the long run, if it wishes to maintain the fixed exchange rate, it will have to use contractionary fiscal and monetary policies to control inflation. In a fixed exchange rate system, a country cannot continue with policies that lead to significantly higher rates of inflation than other countries.

Disadvantages of a fixed exchange rate system
The main disadvantages of a fixed exchange rate system are:

- balance of payments crises
- reduced ability to respond to economic shocks
- the exchange rate may be fixed at an inappropriate rate
- the need for substantial foreign exchange reserves
- resources may be misallocated
- deflationary bias.

Balance of payments crises

In a fixed exchange rate system, differences in economic performance result in some currencies being overvalued and others undervalued. As a result, some countries will have growing deficits on the current account of the balance of payments and others will have large current account surpluses. Speculators will sell the currencies of the deficit countries and

Key term

One-way option: in a fixed exchange rate system, when a currency becomes overvalued or undervalued, it is obvious whether the exchange rate will be devalued or revalued, allowing speculators to make very large profits.

buy the currencies of surplus countries. To maintain the exchange rate, unless the country is willing and able to impose direct controls, deficit countries will have to use expenditure-reducing policies to correct the deficit. This can lead to rising unemployment and low growth.

Reduced ability to respond to economic shocks

Changes in the exchange rate affect competitiveness and aggregate demand. If a country experiences a negative demand-side shock, in a floating exchange rate system, the country could allow its exchange rate to depreciate to increase AD, helping to support growth and employment. This is not possible when the exchange rate is fixed. Also, the ability of the central bank to reduce its discount rate to increase AD is limited because interest rates are used to make sure the exchange rate stays within the agreed band.

The exchange rate may be fixed at an inappropriate rate

In a freely floating exchange rate system, the exchange rate is determined by market forces but in a fixed exchange rate system the government has to choose the exchange rate. If it is fixed at too high a value, the country's products will be uncompetitive and it may lead to low growth and high unemployment. If the exchange rate is too low, the economy may suffer from high inflation.

The need for substantial foreign exchange reserves

In a fixed exchange rate system, central banks have to intervene in the FOREX to maintain the exchange rate. There will be times when there is pressure for the exchange rate to fall. To prevent this happening, the central bank will have to use its foreign exchange reserves to buy the currency. If the country has a large balance of payments deficit and/or there is speculation that the currency is going to be devalued, the central bank will need a large stock of foreign currency to prevent the exchange rate falling. In a fixed exchange rate system, governments often borrow from other countries or international financial institutions, such as the International Monetary Fund (IMF), to add to their foreign currency reserves.

Resources may be misallocated

The exchange rate is a price and relative prices affect the allocation of resources. When a fixed exchange rate is overvalued or undervalued, factors of production will be misallocated between and within countries. For example, an undervalued exchange rate will result in too many resources allocated to export industries because the low exchange rate means that the prices of exports are artificially low. If resources are misallocated, economic welfare is reduced.

Deflationary bias

In a fixed exchange rate system, countries with balance of payments deficits are likely to have to deflate their economies to reduce the deficit and prevent their exchange rate depreciating. If they do not correct the deficit, they are likely to run out of foreign exchange reserves or will have to devalue their currency. Surplus countries do not have to reduce the surplus by reflating their economies because they can supply their currency on the FOREX and add to their foreign exchange reserves.

▲ **Figure 7.2.13**: The dollar is a reserve currency

The problem of correcting balance of payments deficits and surpluses falls on the countries with balance of payments deficits. Under a fixed exchange rate system, expenditure-reducing policies are generally used to correct balance of payments deficits, so the system has a deflationary bias. Expenditure-switching policies, such as devaluing the currency, are used as a last resort. Direct controls are also avoided by countries that are members of the WTO.

The advantages and disadvantages of a managed floating exchange rate system

A managed floating (dirty floating) exchange rate system is often viewed as a compromise between a fixed and freely floating exchange rate system. However, the extent to which a managed floating exchange rate system has the advantages and disadvantages of fixed or freely floating exchange rate systems depends on the extent to which the central bank intervenes in the market. It also depends on whether it attempts to achieve a target exchange rate or just intervenes to smooth out temporary, day-to-day fluctuations in the exchange rate.

Some countries with managed floating exchange rates attempt to keep their exchange rate below the free-market level to make domestic firms more competitive and increase economic growth and employment. They can do this by supplying their currency on the FOREX and by keeping interest rates low. Low interest rates make it less attractive for overseas residents to invest in interest-earning assets, reducing the demand for the currency. However, low interest rates may add to domestic inflationary pressures. Some countries also set up **sovereign wealth funds (SWFs)** to invest abroad, increasing the supply of their currency on the FOREX. As a result, surpluses on the current account of the balance of payments are matched by capital outflows on the financial account.

How the exchange rate affects individuals, firms and economic performance

A fall in the exchange rate makes exports cheaper in foreign currency and imports more expensive in domestic currency, making domestic products more competitive. An appreciation in the exchange rate makes domestic products less competitive at home and abroad. This change in the relative prices of home-produced and foreign goods and services affects individuals, firm and economic performance.

How a change in the exchange rate affects individuals

A fall in the exchange rate increases the prices of imports and, other things being equal, will lead to a fall in real household income and living standards. For example, if some food products are imported, the amount households pay for their shopping will increase. If people go on holiday abroad, the cost of the holiday will rise and may mean that people choose to go on holiday in their own country instead. However, if the improvement in competitiveness leads to more jobs being created, some people will be better off.

Get it right

A managed floating exchange rate system has some of the advantages of free floating and some of the advantages of a fixed exchange rate system. Similarly, it has some of the disadvantages of each. However, the amount of central bank intervention and the way in which countries manage their exchange rates vary. This will affect advantages and disadvantages of any particular real-world managed floating exchange rate system.

Progress questions

9 A country has a freely floating exchange rate and a balance of payments surplus. Explain why it is likely that the exchange rate will adjust automatically to reduce the surplus.

10 Explain why a country with a fixed exchange rate cannot pursue policies that will result in it having a permanently higher rate of inflation than other countries.

11 Explain how a country with a managed floating exchange rate may be able to maintain an undervalued exchange rate and a balance of payments surplus.

Case study: Mexico's exchange rate system

▲ **Figure 7.2.14**: Mexico City

▼ **Table 7.2.2**: Mexico's exchange rate and the Mexican central bank's official interest rate, January 2013 to January 2017

Date	US$ to Mexican peso exchange rate (pesos)	Mexican central bank's official interest rate (%)
2013 January	12.70	4.50
2013 July	12.76	4.00
2014 January	13.22	3.50
2014 July	12.99	3.50
2015 January	14.70	3.00
2015 July	15.94	3.00
2016 January	18.05	3.25
2016 July	18.56	4.25
2017 January	21.35	5.75

Source: Bank for International Settlements; accessed 21 November 2020

In 1988, the Mexican peso was pegged against the US dollar. However, between 1988 and 1994, inflation in Mexico was higher than in the USA causing the peso to become overvalued which led to a large deficit on the current account of the balance of payments. On 20 December 1994, the Mexican government devalued the peso by almost 15%, but two days later it had to abandon the fixed exchange rate and adopt a floating rate.

From 2010 until the start of 2015, Mexico's exchange rate against the US dollar was fairly stable. However, the Mexican peso depreciated rapidly in 2015 due to the fall in the price of oil (Mexico is a major exporter of oil) and speculation that interest rates in the USA were likely to increase. The central bank of Mexico intervened in the foreign exchange market to prevent the exchange rate falling too fast and also increased its interest rate. The rise in interest rates was also intended to reduce the inflationary effects of the exchange rate depreciation.

1 What is meant by the phrase "the Mexican peso was pegged against the US dollar"?
2 Explain why higher inflation in Mexico than in the USA may have contributed to Mexico having to devalue its currency and then adopt a floating exchange rate in December 1994.
3 Describe the main changes in the US dollar to Mexican peso exchange rate between January 2013 and January 2017 shown in Table 7.2.2.
4 Explain why the fall in the price of oil and speculation that interest rates in the USA were likely to increase led to the Mexican peso depreciating against US dollar.
5 How might the changes in the exchange rate shown in Table 7.2.2 help to explain why Mexico's central bank increased its official rate of interest from 3.00% to 5.75% between July 2015 and January 2017?

A rise in the exchange rate will mean that households will pay less for foreign goods and services and, other things being equal, real incomes and living standards will improve. However, it may lead to some job losses, particularly for people who work for firms that export goods and services.

How a change in the exchange rate affects firms

A change in the exchange rate mainly affects firms that are directly involved in exporting and/or importing goods and services, but it will have some indirect effects on other firms. For example, if a fall in the exchange rate leads to an increase in sales and employment for exporters, there will be a multiplier effect that will benefit other firms.

A fall in the exchange rate will benefit firms that export goods and services. The fall in the exchange rate will reduce the foreign currency price of exports and should lead to an increase in the quantity sold. It also makes exporting more profitable. If the exporter keeps the foreign currency price unchanged, the revenue received in domestic currency from the same volume of sales will increase. The extent to which exporters choose to reduce the foreign currency price of exports will be affected by factors such as the competitiveness of the market, the price elasticity of demand for their products and the amount of spare capacity. If firms export more goods and services, they are also likely to employ more workers and may be able to afford to increase wages.

However, if the exchange rate falls, a firm that imports goods and services will experience an increase in costs and a fall in profits. The higher the proportion of the firm's total costs that are imports, the larger the reduction in profits. If the firm passes on the increase in costs by raising the price of their products, the volume of sales is also likely to fall. The extent to which an individual firm benefits or is harmed by a fall in the exchange rate will depend on the extent to which the firm relies on imports of raw materials and components and how many of its products are exported.

An appreciation in the exchange rate will benefit firms that import raw materials, components and other goods and services from abroad but will harm firms that export a large proportion of their output.

A change in the exchange rate will also affect a firm's willingness to invest abroad. A rise in the exchange rate will make it cheaper for firms to invest overseas. Since a rise in the exchange rate also makes exports dearer, a manufacturing firm that exports its goods, for example, may find it more profitable to build a new factory abroad rather than build the factory in its home country.

▲ Figure 7.2.15: A factory producing washing machines

How a change in the exchange rate affects economic performance

Changes in the exchange rate affect many aspects of economic performance, including economic growth, living standards, unemployment, inflation and the balance of payments. In the short run, a fall in the exchange rate is likely to increase economic growth, reduce unemployment and improve the balance of payments but will

Link

How the exchange rate affects the main macroeconomic policy objectives was explained in Chapter 8 "Economic performance" in the AS book.

Progress questions

12 Explain why a fall in the exchange rate may lead to a fall in a household's real income.

13 Why might a rise in the exchange rate increase the profits of some firms?

Key terms

International Monetary Fund (IMF): an international organisation whose role is to maintain the stability of the international monetary system and to provide financial support to countries experiencing balance of payments problems.

IMF quota: an allocation that determines how much a country has to pay to the IMF, its voting rights and its allocation of SDRs.

increase inflation. Whether a fall in the exchange rate benefits the economy in the long run depends mainly on whether the inflationary effects of the lower exchange rate are controlled. If the fall in the exchange rate is the start of an inflationary spiral, the improvement in competitiveness will soon disappear.

A rise in the exchange rate will help to reduce inflationary pressures and will lead to a short-run improvement in living standards. However, the fall in competitiveness may lead to lower growth and higher unemployment which may cause living standards to fall in the long run.

When assessing the impact of a change in the exchange rate on the performance of an economy, it is important to consider why the exchange rate changed. For example, if the exchange rate appreciated because supply-side improvements increased competitiveness and led to a current account surplus, the rise in the value of the currency may not have much, if any, effect on growth and employment.

The role of the International Monetary Fund

The **International Monetary Fund (IMF)** was created in December 1945 when 29 countries signed its articles of agreement. The IMF had an important role in supporting of the Bretton Woods system of fixed exchange rates which ended in 1971. After the collapse of the Bretton Woods system, members of the IMF were free to choose any type of exchange rate system, other than pegging their currency to gold. In 2020, there were 190 member countries. The IMF's main role is to maintain the stability of the international monetary system.

The IMF aims to:

- encourage monetary cooperation between countries
- support the balanced growth of international trade
- help countries maintain stable exchange rates
- support countries with balance of payments problems
- monitor the global economy, the economic performance of member countries and to provide advice regarding suitable economic policies.

To achieve its aims, the IMF raises funds from its members through the quota system, it provides short-term loans to countries experiencing balance of payments problems and reports on the economic performance of its members.

IMF quotas

Each country that is a member of the IMF has a quota. The **IMF quota** determines the amount a member country has to pay to the IMF and provides the IMF with much of the finance it needs to lend to member countries that are experiencing serious balance of payments problems. The size of a country's quota determines its voting power in IMF decision making and how much it is able to borrow from the IMF, should it need to do so. The quota also determines a country's allocation of SDRs. The size of each country's quota is decided by a formula that reflects its position in the world economy. Quotas are reviewed at regular intervals. At present, the sum of the quota resources available to the IMF equal SDR 477 billion which is over US$650 billion.

▲ Figure 7.2.16: The IMF

Special Drawing Rights (SDRs)

SDRs were first created in 1969 and add to the foreign exchange reserves of countries that are members of the IMF. They increase international liquidity and the ability of countries to support their currencies. The value of an SDR is determined by a weighted basket of five major world currencies. These currencies are: the US dollar, the euro, the Japanese yen, the Chinese yuan and the UK pound sterling. The SDR is not a currency but can be exchanged for any of the five major world currencies. These currencies can then be used to pay for imports, deal with balance of payments problems and support the country's exchange rate.

IMF lending

The IMF provides short-term loans to member countries that are experiencing balance of payments problems but, unlike the World Bank, it does not lend to help finance specific projects, such as building a dam. Most of the money the IMF has available to lend comes from the members' quotas, but some members have also agreed to provide additional funds to the IMF when needed.

The IMF helps countries that are affected by economic crises that may have resulted from internal or external causes. These include expansionary fiscal and monetary policies leading to inflation, a large balance of payments deficit and the loss of official reserves. An external shock could be caused by a fall in the world market price of a primary commodity, leading to a large fall in the value of exports for a country that is dependent on that commodity. As a result of the shock, the country may be unable to pay for essential imports or pay the interest on its overseas debts.

If a member country experiences an economic crisis, it can apply to the IMF for a loan to help stabilise its economy while measures are taken to deal with the problems. Countries usually ask the IMF for a loan when they are unable to borrow from financial markets. The IMF provides loans at a lower rate of interest than banks and other lenders, but there are conditions attached. Some loans are provided to poorer countries with no interest payable. The IMF will only provide a loan if the country's government agrees a set of economic policies to correct the problems the country is experiencing.

Stand-By Arrangements (SBA) provide most of the financial help to members experiencing balance of payments problems. With an SBA, a country can borrow up to 145% of its quota in any 12-month period and up to 435% of its quota over the life of the loan. However, the IMF also has a variety of other lending arrangements, some of which are more flexible and may be better suited to the needs of low-income countries.

Monitoring the global economy, the performance of member countries and to provide advice

IMF monitoring attempts to identify risks to the stability of individual countries and the global economy. IMF monitoring is known as surveillance.

The IMF produces reports that analyse global economic trends, identify possible threats to the stability of financial markets and the world economy. The IMF also monitors the performance of individual member countries and offers advice to member countries to help them improve their economic performance and prevent financial crises.

Key term

Stand-By Arrangement (SBA): a facility through which the IMF provides financial help to member countries experiencing balance of payments problems.

Link

The role of the World Bank is explained in 8.3 "Policies to promote development".

Activity

Visit the IMF website and find out all you can about the different types of financial assistance the IMF provides to member countries.

Progress questions

14 What is the main way in which the IMF raises funds to provide loans to member countries that experience severe balance of payments problems?

15 What are SDRs and what is their purpose?

This section will develop your knowledge and understanding of:

→ the functions and characteristics of money

→ money, capital and foreign exchange markets

→ spot and forward markets in currencies and commodities

→ the role of financial markets in facilitating saving, lending, the exchange of goods and services, and insurance

→ the difference between debt and equity

→ the difference between commercial and investment banks

→ why a bank might fail, including the risks involved in lending long term and borrowing short term

→ the functions of a central bank, including lender of last resort

→ moral hazard, asymmetric information and market bubbles

→ the regulation of financial markets

→ the shadow banking market

→ systemic risk and the impact of problems in domestic and global financial markets on the real economy.

Key terms

Money: an asset that fulfils the functions of money.

Store of value: something that retains its purchasing power over time.

Measure of value: a function of money that allows the relative cost of different products to be compared.

Standard of deferred payment: a function of money that allows future payments for products bought on credit to be stated clearly.

Monetary economy: an economy that uses money as a medium of exchange when trading goods and services.

The functions and characteristics of money

Money has been used for thousands of years and replaced barter as a way of trading goods. Different societies have used many different items as money including cowrie shells, beads, salt and various metals. Today we use both physical and electronic money when we buy goods and services.

Money is an asset that fulfils the functions of money. An asset is something of value. There are many financial and non-financial assets, but most are not classified as money because they cannot be used as an efficient medium of exchange.

Functions of money

The functions of money are:

- medium of exchange
- store of value
- measure of value
- standard of deferred payment.

The last two functions of money are often known together as the unit of account function.

Medium of exchange

In a **monetary economy**, people sell their goods and services, including labour services, for money and use money to buy what they want from others. When deciding whether an asset should be classified as money, the most important consideration is whether it is a medium of exchange.

Using money as a medium of exchange to trade goods and services is more efficient than barter. The use of money avoids the need for a double coincidence of wants. In a barter economy, a trade will only take place when the buyer of a good or service is able to offer the seller something they also want. This can be very inefficient because it can take a long while to find two people who each want what the other has to offer. As people start to specialise, they have to trade to satisfy their needs and wants. Without an efficient way of exchanging goods and services, the benefits of specialisation would be reduced.

Link
The role of money in the development of specialisation was explained in 3.2 "Specialisation, division of labour and exchange" in the AS book.

Store of value

A store of value is something that retains its purchasing power over time. For people to accept an asset as a medium of exchange, it must retain its purchasing power. If an asset became worthless shortly after it was exchanged for a good, the seller would not be willing to accept it. People can exchange goods and services for money and keep the money until they are ready to use it to buy other goods and services. Money allows people to delay their consumption. One reason why precious metals, such as gold and silver, have been used as money is because precious metals are a good store of value.

Measure of value

In a monetary economy, every product has a price expressed in terms of money. This makes it easy to compare the relative cost of different goods and services. In a barter economy, the price of each product has to be expressed in terms of every other product. In a monetary economy, each product has a single price but in a barter economy each product has lots of different prices. If there are n products, there are n prices in a monetary economy, but in a barter economy there are $[n \times (n - 1)] \div 2$ different prices. For example, if there are 10 products, in a barter economy, there will be $(10 \times 9) \div 2 = 45$ different prices, expressed in terms of the other products.

Standard of deferred payment

Money is widely used to value debts and makes borrowing and lending much easier. It allows goods and services to be bought now but paid for in the future. When goods are bought on credit, interest is normally paid to the lender and repayments are often made in instalments. Money is a convenient way of showing the amount borrowed, the interest on the loan and the repayments that have to be made in the future. To act as a standard for deferred payments, money must maintain its value over time. That means it must be a store of value.

Characteristics of money

For an asset to be able to fulfil the functions of money it must have a number of characteristics, these include being:

- **acceptable**: people must have trust that money will retain its value otherwise they will not accept it in exchange for goods and services. Unless money is accepted by the majority of the population it will not fulfil the medium of exchange function. This is the most important characteristic of money

- **durable**: money must last otherwise it cannot act as a store of value. Perishable items such as eggs are not an effective store of value

Get it right
When there is inflation, the value of money falls and it is less effective as a store of value. If the rate of inflation is very high, people lose confidence in their currency and may refuse to accept it in exchange for products. They may use other currencies or barter to obtain the goods they need.

- **divisible**: it must be possible to divide it into small amounts so that items of different value can be purchased
- **portable**: it must be easy to carry around and/or use in different places. It must also be easy to transfer from one person to another
- **limited in supply**: if there was an unlimited supply of money, it would not have any value and people would not accept it in exchange for goods and services. For money to keep its value it must be scarce. Governments need to limit the supply of money and to prevent forgery.

These characteristics of money enable money to fulfil its functions and they are also, to some extent, linked to each other.

Case study: Hyperinflation in Venezuela

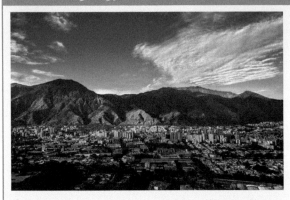

▲ Figure 7.3.1: Caracas, the capital city of Venezuela

Venezuela has had double-digit inflation every year since 1983. In 2018, the rate of inflation was estimated to be over 65,000% although it has fallen since then.

Venezuelan hyperinflation and the rapidly falling value of the exchange rate have had a number of effects, including reducing the ability of the bolivar, Venezuela's currency, to perform the basic functions of money. With prices rising so fast, restaurants stopped including them on their menus and shops no longer displayed the prices of their products. At one point, a chicken cost 14.6 million bolivars, which would have required the use of 14,600 one thousand

bolivar notes, weighing 14.6 kg. Some people had to use a suitcase to collect their wages and some companies started paying bonuses in eggs or foreign currencies which were more stable.

The bolivar, has been devalued five times since 2003. An illegal black market for the currency developed with the currency trading at an exchange rate lower than the official rate against the US dollar. Eventually, a new currency was issued in 2018. However, according to one survey, about 54% of transactions in September 2019 were in dollars. Almost all electrical goods purchased were paid for in dollars.

1 What is meant by "hyperinflation"?
2 Using the information in the case study, explain how high inflation in Venezuela affected the ability of the bolivar to fulfil each of the following functions of money:
   i medium of exchange
   ii store of value
   iii measure of value.
3 Explain why many people in Venezuela use dollars to buy goods and services.

The money supply

The money supply is sometimes a target of monetary policy. Even when the money supply is not a specific target of monetary policy, the central bank will monitor what is happening to the money supply and take it into consideration when deciding whether, for example, to change interest rates. Some economists, known as monetarists, believe that changes in the money supply determine the future rate of inflation and so that the rate of growth of the money supply must be controlled. Most economists believe that the rate of growth of the money supply will have some effect on the rate of growth of aggregate demand and so will affect economic activity and inflation. However, there is more than one definition of the money supply and central banks often monitor more than one **monetary aggregate**.

Key term

Monetary aggregate: a measure of the money supply.

There are narrow and broad definitions of the money supply. Narrow definitions of the money supply include notes and coins, **banks' balances at the central bank** and **demand deposits** in people's bank accounts. Banks hold deposits with the central bank that can be exchanged for cash or used to make payments to other banks. Demand deposits in people's bank accounts are those that that can be spent without giving any notice of withdrawal. They can, for example, be transferred to pay for goods and services by writing a cheque, using a debit card or with a direct debit. Demand deposits are a type of electronic money and are the largest part of the money supply. Narrow definitions of the money supply only include very liquid assets that are commonly used as a medium of exchange.

Broad definitions of the money supply also include some more illiquid assets that can be converted easily into money. Savings accounts, that have a **notice of withdrawal**, are usually included in broad definitions of the money supply. Government securities with a short time to maturity may also be part of a broad definition of the money supply. However, shares and other long-dated securities are not included in any definition of the money supply since they are not sufficiently liquid.

Progress questions

1   Why is using money a more efficient way of trading goods and services than barter?

2   If there are 30 products traded in an economy, how many different prices would there be in a monetary economy and how many different prices in a barter economy?

3   Why are shares not included in any definition of the money supply?

Money, capital and foreign exchange markets

Financial markets are where economic agents buy and sell financial assets. They include markets for shares, bonds, insurance, foreign currencies and commodities. Many markets do not have a specific physical location, for example, trading securities often takes place online and markets may be global.

Financial markets play an important role in allocating resources and increasing the liquidity of financial assets. They help to channel funds from those who have surplus funds, that is savers and investors, to those who need additional money, perhaps to buy a house or expand their business. Funds can be channelled from savers to borrowers through a financial intermediary, such as a bank, or directly through financial markets, for example when a government issues bonds to finance public expenditure.

Key terms

Banks' balances at the central bank: deposits banks hold with the central bank that can be exchanged for cash or used to pay other banks.

Demand deposits: money in people's bank accounts that can be spent without giving any notice of withdrawal.

Link

The nature and functions of a central bank are explained later in this section on financial markets.

Key term

Notice of withdrawal: the depositor must tell the bank in advance when they want to take money out of the account. The period of notice can vary but is typically between 7 days and 3 months.

Activity

Visit the website of the central bank of your country and find out what is included in the money supply (monetary aggregate) of your economy. There may be more than one monetary aggregate and they might, for example, be named M0 or M1.

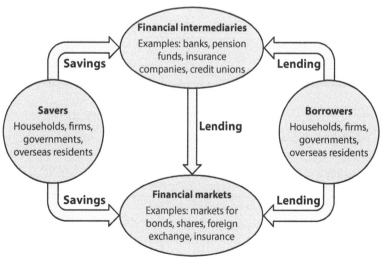

▲ Figure 7.3.2: The role of financial markets

Key terms

Money market: the market that provides funds to those who want short-term finance.

Maturity: the time that a loan lasts for and when it has to be repaid.

Interbank market: short-term lending between banks, usually for a week or less.

Treasury bills: short-term securities issued by the government.

Commercial bills: short-term securities issued by firms.

Redeemed: paying back the money borrowed to the holder of a security, usually on maturity.

Capital market: the market that provides medium-term and long-term finance for individuals, firms and governments.

New issue market: part of the capital market where securities are offered for sale for the first time.

Securities: financial assets that can be bought and sold on financial markets, including shares and bonds.

Bonds: securities that represent a loan to the government or organisation that issued the bonds. Bonds pay interest to the holder and are usually redeemed at a specified date in the future.

Shares: securities that represent ownership of part of a company. Shares pay dividends to the holder depending on the amount of profit made by the company. Shares are not usually redeemed by the company.

Figure 7.3.2 shows that funds are channelled from savers to borrowers through financial institutions and financial markets. Households, firms, governments and overseas residents can be borrowers and lenders. The chart indicates that there are flows of funds between countries. Examples include a bank in Germany providing a loan to a company in Brazil, and the Kuwait Investment Authority (KIA), a sovereign wealth fund (SWF), investing in a variety of assets in different parts of the world.

Money market

The **money market** provides short-term finance. Funds borrowed on the money market have a **maturity** of between 24 hours and 12 months. Economic agents that use the money market include individuals, firms, financial institutions and governments. Lending between banks, the **interbank market**, is a central part of the money market. Banks must have sufficient liquidity to be able to pay depositors who want to withdraw their money and, in some countries, they have to meet the reserve ratios set by the government or central bank. If a bank is not sufficiently liquid, it can borrow on the money market. If it has surplus liquidity, it can lend to other banks.

Securities that are traded on the money market include **treasury bills** and **commercial bills** of exchange. Treasury bills are issued by some governments, including the governments of India, the USA and the UK, to raise short-term finance. Commercial bills are issued by firms that wish to borrow short term, often to finance the purchase of goods from other firms. Bills are issued at less than their face value so that the holder makes a small profit when they are **redeemed** on maturity. Bills can be bought and sold before they mature, allowing the buyer to get their money back before the maturity date.

Calculating the rate of return on a bill

A bill is issued to raise $4,000,000 for the firm issuing the bill. The bill has 3 months (one quarter of a year) until it matures and pays the holder $4,012,000 on maturity. The rate of return over 3 months is:

$$(12,000 \div 4,000,000) \times 100 = 0.3\%$$

Therefore, the annual rate of return on the bill is $0.3\% \times 4 = 1.2\%$.

Capital market

The **capital market** provides medium-term and long-term finance to individuals, firms and governments. Individuals may borrow to buy a house or a car, a firm may borrow to finance investment and governments borrow when they are running a budget deficit. There are two parts to the capital market: the **new issue market** and the secondary market.

The new issue market

The new issue market is sometimes known as the primary capital market. This market is where companies and governments raise finance by offering new issues of **securities** for sale. A new issue is when the securities are offered for sale for the first time and the money raised goes to the company or government issuing the securities. The securities issued by firms can be either corporate **bonds** or **shares**. Buyers of corporate bonds provide a long-term loan to the company whereas people who buy shares own part of the company. Governments raise finance by offering medium-term and long-term bonds for sale.

The secondary market

Secondary markets trade securities that were issued in the past; they are markets in second-hand securities. In the new issue market, investors buy securities from the company or government issuing the securities whereas in the secondary capital market, investors buy securities from each other. The world's stock exchanges are important institutions in secondary markets. The main function of a secondary market is to increase the liquidity of securities. Secondary markets allow people who own securities to sell them very easily. If selling securities was difficult, people would be reluctant to buy new issues of securities, making it hard for companies and governments to raise finance.

Foreign exchange market

The foreign exchange market (FOREX) allows economic agents to obtain the currencies they need to buy goods and services from abroad and to invest abroad. As the values of world trade and international investment flows have increased, the foreign exchange market has grown. It is the largest financial market in the world. Anyone who buys or sells foreign currency is participating in the FOREX, including people who want foreign currency when they go on holiday. However, the main participants in the FOREX are the large international banks who may trade on their own behalf but also for clients who need foreign currency. Central banks also participate in the market to influence the value of their currency.

Spot and forward markets in currencies and commodities

A spot market is where currencies, securities and commodities are traded and delivered immediately. Spot markets are also known as cash markets because items are paid for as soon as the sale has been agreed and the items exchanged. The current price of an item is known as the spot price.

A forward market is also known as a futures market. A forward contract is where traders agree the price and quantity of an item, but the item is delivered and paid for at a specified date in the future.

Forward contracts and forward markets, in commodities and foreign exchange, help businesses reduce the uncertainty and risks of trading in volatile markets. The prices of commodities, such as metals and agricultural products, are likely to fluctuate significantly and sometimes unpredictably.

A business that imports a commodity from abroad to use in the manufacture of its products may find that an unexpected rise in the world market price of the commodity could lead to a large fall in its profits. By using forward markets to fix the price it pays for the commodity, the firm's production costs, and so its profits, are more predictable. If the prices of the commodity remain high, the firm has

Link

The foreign exchange market was explained in section 7.2 "Exchange rates".

▲ **Figure 7.3.3**: Picking coffee beans

Progress questions

4   What is the difference between the money market and the capital market?

5   State the **two** main differences between bonds and shares.

6   What is the difference between a spot market and a forward market?

time to increase the selling price of its products. The use of forward markets can also help the sellers of a commodity protect themselves against an unexpected fall in the price of the commodity.

Firms involved in exporting goods and services can find that changes in exchange rates might turn a profitable export order into an unprofitable one. For example, if a firm based in Austria agreed to export goods to the USA for US$40,000, it would receive €50,000 if $1.00 = €1.25. If the euro appreciated against the US dollar so that $1.00 = €1.00, the exporter would only receive €40,000 and this might make the deal unprofitable. However, if the exporter had entered into a forward contract to sell the US dollars at an agreed price in the future, the risk of changes in the exchange rate turning a profitable sale into a loss-making sale would be removed.

Role of financial markets

Financial markets fulfil a number of important functions that help economies develop and operate efficiently. These functions include facilitating:

- saving
- lending
- the exchange of goods and services
- insurance.

Saving

Saving involves postponing current consumption. When people save, they do not spend all of their current income. This allows them to consume more in the future. Savings also provide funds that can be used to finance investment and increase a country's capital stock.

In a closed economy with no government, since output = income = expenditure, if there is no saving and all the income is spent on consumer goods, there will be no investment. Households can either consume or save their income, therefore $Y = C + S$. Firms can either produce consumer goods or capital goods, therefore $Y = C + I$. So, if households consume all of their income, in a closed economy with no government, there will be no investment.

However, in the real world, the government can levy taxes, reducing households' disposable income, and use at least some of the tax revenue to pay for capital projects such as building roads, schools and hospitals. Also, borrowing from abroad and foreign direct investment can add to domestic savings, helping to increase the capital stock and economic growth.

A well-developed financial system makes it easier and more attractive for people to save. For example, households are more likely to save if there is a trusted bank near to their home. In a well-developed financial system, savings are generally more liquid and can be withdrawn when households want to spend their money. Banks offer interest on money saved to attract people to postpone current consumption and to compensate for inflation and risk. Competition between financial institutions should help to ensure that the rate of return offered is sufficient to attract enough people to save to meet the needs of borrowers. Regulation by the government and central bank should ensure that people's savings are protected.

Some financial institutions specialise in providing pensions for people when they retire. People make contributions into a pension fund and the money is invested in a variety of financial assets and property. The contributions into the fund are a form of long-term saving. People will only put money into such schemes if they are confident that the financial institution is secure and will be able to pay their pension when they retire.

Lending

In well-developed financial markets, there are many ways in which households, firms and the government can raise funds. Banks provide households and firms with medium-term and long-term loans, and **overdrafts** to finance short-term needs. Mortgages, paid back over many years, are available to finance the purchase of property. Most people would be unable to pay the full price of a house without the help of a mortgage. Credit cards can provide a convenient way for households to buy goods that they want now but cannot afford out of their current income. Companies can raise long-term funds by issuing shares or corporate bonds. The government can also borrow by selling treasury bills and bonds on capital markets. Global financial markets also make it possible for economic agents to borrow from abroad.

Borrowing from banks and other financial institutions enables some households to consume more than their current income. This can be important when people are young and may want to start, and provide for, their family. Firms may wish to raise funds to invest and expand their business. Governments may borrow so that they can spend more than they raise in taxes. The money borrowed may be spent on infrastructure projects to improve the productive capacity of the economy. However, it is sometimes used to pay for current expenditure, for example the salaries of public sector workers or welfare benefits.

Financial markets provide the channel through which savings are made available to people who wish to borrow and finance investment. Interest rates have a role to play in this process. If more people want to borrow than save, interest rates are likely to increase to make it more rewarding to save and less attractive to borrow. When there is a surplus of funds available, interest rates are likely to fall, encouraging people to borrow and invest and making it less attractive to save.

The exchange of goods and services

Financial institutions, particularly banks, provide a variety of ways in which people can pay for goods and services. This reduces transaction costs and provides a more flexible, convenient way for people to buy goods and services. The fall in the costs of trading helps firms and supports the development of a specialised, efficient economy.

The most obvious way in which banks help people exchange goods and services is by supplying cash. People can withdraw money from their

> ### Key term
>
> **Overdrafts:** when a bank agrees that a household or firm can withdraw more money from their account than they have paid in. The bank sets a limit on the amount that can be borrowed and charges interest daily on the amount overdrawn.

> ### Activity
>
> To take you further, find out about the loanable funds theory of interest rates which argues that the rate of interest is determined by the demand for and supply of loanable funds. It explains the role of saving and investment in affecting interest rates. This theory is not included in the specification.

Activity

Find out how each of the following helps people pay for goods and services:

1   a standing order
2   a direct debit
3   a debit card.

Key term

Premium: an amount of money paid for insurance.

▲ **Figure 7.3.4**: Lloyd's in the city of London

Key terms

Equity: funds provided by the owners of the business.

Debt: funds raised by borrowing.

Dividends: money paid by a company to its shareholders out of its profits. Dividends are usually paid twice a year but sometimes more often.

bank account by going into the bank or using a cash machine. However, increasingly, cash has been replaced by other means of payment. These include cheques and the use of standing orders and direct debits to pay regular bills. Debit and credit cards are used to make purchases in shops and through the internet without withdrawing cash. Electronic bank transfers may also be used to pay for goods and services.

Banks and other financial institutions also help firms pay for imports. For example, they supply foreign currency and arrange for funds to be transferred electronically between the bank accounts of importers and exporters.

Insurance

Another important function of some financial institutions is to provide insurance for households and firms. Insurance helps people share the risk of an unforeseen event that may result in a loss. An insurance company agrees to provide financial compensation for a specified loss in return for the payment of a **premium**. The loss insured against may relate to events such as fire, flood, theft and accidental damage. The risk to any individual is generally small and hence a small premium paid by many people is usually sufficient to fully compensate anyone who suffers a loss.

Unforeseen events, such as a large fire, can be very costly for the individual or business that is affected. A large fire or flood, for example, could result in a profitable business going bankrupt and having to stop trading. Insurance protects businesses from this happening and helps to support an economy. However, it is not possible to insure against all risks, for example a business cannot insure against a fall in sales.

Debt and equity

All businesses need to raise funds to finance their growth and development. Firms can either obtain funds from the owners of the business or by borrowing. Money raised from the owners of the business is known as **equity** and money raised by borrowing is **debt**.

In a small firm, equity includes the money that the owner used to start and expand the business and, in a company, it includes the money raised by selling shares. Shareholders are the owners of a company. Equity also includes any profits that have been retained within the business to help it grow. **Dividends** are usually paid to shareholders when the company makes a profit and they represent the return the owners receive on the equity they have invested in the business. Similarly, the owner of a small business may withdraw some of the profit made from the business for their personal use. If the business does not make a profit, the owners may not receive any return on their investment. If a business goes bankrupt, the owners will only receive any money if there is anything left after everyone else has been paid what they are owed.

Firms do not rely solely on the money raised from their owners to help them grow. They also borrow to raise both short-term and long-term finance. Firms may need short-term finance to bridge the gap between paying for raw materials and wages and receiving the money from sales. They need long-term funding to invest in capital assets and to finance spending on research and development (R & D). There is a variety of ways in which firms can borrow and they are all types of debt finance. Firms pay interest on debt and this has to be paid whether the firm makes a profit or not. The rate of interest on some debt is fixed, but on other types of debt it is variable. Interest on debt finance is usually regarded as a fixed cost of the business because it has to be paid whatever the output produced. If a business goes bankrupt, providers of debt finance will be paid before the owners receive any money from selling the assets of the business.

Commercial and investment banks

Although the activities and functions of **commercial banks** and **investment banks** differ, many banks are involved in both commercial and investment banking. However, some economists believe that the development of financial institutions that are both commercial and investment banks added to the severity of the global financial crisis of 2007–2008. Some investment banking activities are riskier than those carried out by commercial banks. The losses made by the investment banking divisions of some large banks meant that the business had to be bailed out by the government because otherwise the activities of the commercial banking division, which are essential for an economy, would also have been lost.

Since the crisis, some governments have introduced regulations requiring that the commercial and investment banking divisions of such banks are kept separate. The purpose of these regulations is to try to ensure that even if the investment banking division fails, the commercial banking division can continue operating.

The Hong Kong and Shanghai Banking Corporation (HSBC), the Bank of America, the Agricultural Bank of China (ABC), Barclays Bank and BNP Paribas are examples of banks that provide both commercial and investment banking services.

Commercial banks

Commercial banks are also known as retail banks and high street banks. They provide banking services to the general public. Like other financial intermediaries, commercial banks play a vital role in channelling funds from economic agents who have surplus funds (savers) to those who can make use of those funds (borrowers). The three main functions of a commercial bank are to:

* accept deposits
* provide loans and overdrafts
* provide an efficient means of payment.

Accept deposits

Commercial banks offer two main types of bank account: current/cheque accounts and savings/deposit accounts. **Current accounts** are used by individuals and firms for making payments, for example by cheque, debit card or bank transfer. Individuals usually have their salary paid into their current account. **Deposit accounts** are for people

Progress questions

7 Why are savings important for the growth and development of an economy?

8 How do governments usually borrow on financial markets?

Activity

Lloyd's of London is one of the world's largest insurance and reinsurance markets. Find out how Lloyd's differs from an insurance company such as the Prudential, AXA or AIA Group.

Progress question

9 State **three** differences between equity and debt.

Key terms

Commercial banks: financial institutions that provide financial services to the general public and business. The services provided include accepting deposits, giving loans and providing means of payment.

Investment banks: financial institutions that help businesses, and sometimes governments, carry out complex financial transactions such as issuing new shares or helping with mergers.

Current account: an active account from which payments are made without any notice of withdrawal and into which there are frequent deposits.

Deposit account: a savings account that pays interest but may require a notice of withdrawal.

who want to save. They pay interest but may require a notice of withdrawal. However, some current accounts pay interest and savings accounts do not always insist on a notice of withdrawal.

There is a range of reasons why individuals and firms open bank accounts, including to keep money safe, to receive interest and to make it easier to pay bills.

Provide loans and overdrafts

Commercial banks provide different types of loan to suit the various needs of personal and business customers. For example, they offer mortgages to people who want to buy a house and personal loans to customers who want to buy expensive consumer durables, such as a car. They also offer credit cards to provide a more flexible form of borrowing. The length of the loan and the interest payable will depend on the purpose of the loan and the creditworthiness of the borrower.

Overdrafts are particularly important for business customers since there are times when they have to pay for raw materials and wages but have to wait until they receive money from sales. An overdraft allows the customer to withdraw more money from a current account than has been paid in and interest is only charged when the account is overdrawn. Overdrafts are also available to personal customers.

Provide an efficient means of payment

By providing their customers with a convenient way of paying for goods and services, commercial banks reduce transactions costs. Increasingly, people pay for goods and services without using cash. This has been made possible by developments in information technologies and innovation by the banks. As mentioned earlier, means of payment provided by commercial banks include supplying cash, cheques, standing orders, direct debits, debit cards, credit cards, and other means of transferring funds electronically.

Other services provided by commercial banks

Commercial banks offer a number of other services to their customers including providing foreign currencies, insurance, financial advice, buying and selling securities and a place for storing valuables.

How do commercial banks make a profit?

Commercial banks raise funds by accepting deposits which they lend to individuals, firms and the government. Many commercial banks also raise funds by borrowing on financial markets, for example by issuing bonds. They make a profit by charging a higher rate of interest on the money they lend than they pay to depositors. They may also charge for some of the other services they provide.

Credit creation

Whenever a commercial bank gives a loan to a customer, it increases the value of the deposits in the customer's account by the amount of the loan. When a bank provides a loan, because it also creates a deposit, it increases the supply of money. Bank deposits are money because they can be used to pay for goods and services and are generally accepted by people. They are a medium of exchange and store of value. This process through which commercials banks create deposits/money is known as **credit creation**.

However, the bank must be careful when creating deposits because it must have sufficient cash to pay anyone who wants to take cash out of their account. Also, when customers in one bank make payments to customers in a different bank, the first bank must have sufficient funds in its account at the central bank to transfer the money owed to the other bank. In practice, payments are made in both directions and the banks transfer the net amount owed at the end of each day. Nevertheless, the amount of deposits a bank can create is limited by its holdings of cash and other liquid assets that can be converted easily into cash.

Investment banks

Goldman Sachs, Morgan Stanley, Nomura and UBS are examples of investment banks that operate in many countries around the globe. The clients of investment banks include companies, other financial institutions, governments and wealthy individuals. The main role of an investment bank is to help their clients access financial markets.

They help companies raise finance by arranging new issues of shares and corporate bonds. Firms involved in a merger or takeover will consult with investment banks who advise them regarding the price they should pay and how to manage the operation. Governments that wish to privatise state-owned enterprises (SOEs) may also use an investment bank for advice and to arrange the sale of shares in the newly formed company. Investment banks charge a fee for providing these services.

Investment banks are also involved in secondary capital markets where they buy and sell securities for their clients, for example pension funds, but also on their own behalf. Buying and selling securities on their own behalf is known as **proprietary trading** and is a risky activity. Investment banks provide financial advice to their clients and manage the wealth of many of the world's rich people. In 2017, UBS was believed to manage the wealth of almost half of the world's billionaires.

Some investment banks are involved in commodity trading and the foreign exchange market, and some are **market makers**. Market makers are always ready to buy and sell certain financial assets, for example particular shares or currencies. They aim to make a profit by means of the differential between the buying and selling price. At any given time, the price they charge someone who wants to buy the financial asset is higher than they price they would pay to the seller. However, price fluctuations mean that market making can be a risky activity.

Why do some banks fail?

As with any other business, a bank that is not well managed may go bankrupt. At times of economic crisis, bank failures are not uncommon. There are two main reasons why a bank may go out of business: they might run out of cash or they might become insolvent.

An important feature of banks is that they borrow short term and lend long term. If a bank is not well managed, it could have liquidity problems. Also, some of the assets held by a bank are risky, particularly when the economy goes into recession.

Commercial banks are owned by their shareholders and are in business to make a profit, but they must be sufficiently liquid to pay depositors

> ### Key terms
>
> **Credit creation**: the process of creating bank deposits/money by giving loans to customers.
>
> **Proprietary trading**: when a trader, for example a financial institution, buys and sells securities, currencies and commodities using their own money, rather than on behalf of a client.
>
> **Market makers**: financial institutions or dealers who are always ready to buy and sell certain financial assets, for example particular shares or currencies.

▲ **Figure 7.3.5:** Morgan Chase, an investment bank

Progress questions

10 State the **three** main functions of a commercial bank.

11 Explain how a bank creates credit.

12 State **three** activities of an investment bank.

Key terms

Run on the bank: when a large number of a bank's customers withdraw their money from the bank at the same time because they are concerned that the bank might fail.

Insolvent: when the value of the liabilities (excluding the equity/shareholders' funds) of a business are greater than the value of its assets.

Get it right

The liabilities side of the balance sheet includes both liabilities and equity. In the basic accounting equation, liabilities show the money that the business owes to people other than the owners. Liabilities are debt rather than equity. It may seem confusing but it is important to remember that the total liabilities on a balance sheet include both equity and liabilities.

when they want to withdraw money from their accounts. However, there is a trade-off between liquidity and profitability. Usually, liquid assets earn a lower rate of return than illiquid assets. If the management of the bank places too much emphasis on achieving high profits, it may find it has too few liquid assets when the economy is contracting.

Liquidity problems

The main source of funds for commercial banks is customer deposits, many of which can be withdrawn without any notice or with very little notice. However, the main asset for the commercial banks is the loans that they provide for their customers. Some loans, such as mortgages, are repaid over many years, usually between 20 and 40 years. Loans to business customers are typically for a period of 5 to 10 years and personal loans to households are usually for a period of 1 to 5 years. Because much of a bank's borrowing is short term and their lending is long term, there is always the risk that a bank may not be able to pay everyone who wants to withdraw money from their account.

However, every day banks receive some loan repayments and some customers pay money into their accounts. Banks need to hold sufficient cash to meet the demands of their depositors, but they do not want to hold too much cash because they do not make any money from holding cash. Therefore, they also invest in liquid assets that pay some interest but which can be converted quickly into cash when required. They can also borrow on the money markets, often from other banks that have surplus cash.

The survival of a bank depends on confidence. If customers believe that there is a risk that the bank may not be able to pay them their money when they ask for it, there is likely to be a **run on the bank** (bank run). If too many customers attempt to withdraw their money at the same time, the bank may run out of cash even though it is profitable. In these circumstances, the bank is likely to fail.

Solvency problems

A run on the bank is not the only reason why a bank might fail. If a bank is poorly managed and/or there is an economic crisis, the value of the bank's assets may fall. If the fall in the value of its assets leads to a situation where its liabilities (excluding the owners' stake in the business) are greater than its assets, the bank is **insolvent**.

▼ **Table 7.3.1:** A simplified balance sheet of a commercial bank

Assets:	$ billion	Liabilities:	$ billion
Cash and other liquid assets	90	Shareholders' funds	40
Investments	70	Borrowing	50
Loans to customers	190	Customers' deposits	260
Total assets	350	**Total liabilities**	350

With any balance sheet, total assets must equal total liabilities, including the shareholders' funds, as shown in the example of a commercial bank's balance sheet in Table 7.3.1. The shareholders' funds represent the amount of money the bank owes its owners and is equity. It is a source of funds for the bank. The basic accounting equation is:

$$\text{Assets} = \text{Shareholders' funds (Equity)} + \text{Liabilities}$$

Shareholders' funds include the value of the issued share capital and profits that have been retained in the business. Shareholders' funds are also known as the equity in the business. The liabilities side of the balance sheet shows where the bank obtained its funds. The assets side of the balance sheet shows how the funds are being used.

The bank represented in Table 7.3.1 is solvent because the value of its assets ($350 billion) is greater than the value of its liabilities, excluding shareholders' funds ($310 billion). However, if the management of the bank has not invested the funds wisely or the economy goes into a serious recession, the value of the bank's assets could fall. For example, the bank may have to write off some customers' loans because customers are unable to repay the money they owe, perhaps because a business that borrowed money has gone bankrupt. Similarly, in a financial crisis, some of the banks' investments may become worthless. When the value of the assets fall, the shareholders' funds fall by the same amount. In Table 7.3.1, if the total value of the bank's assets fall by more than $40 billion, the bank would be insolvent. The shareholders' funds would have disappeared and the liabilities would be greater than the bank's assets. In these circumstances, the bank would have to close.

Although a run on a bank and insolvency are different reasons why a bank may go out of business, they are often linked. If people think that there is a risk that a bank may become insolvent, depositors will start to take their money out of the bank causing a liquidity crisis.

Key term

Shareholders' funds: the shareholders' stake in the business. It is the value of the total assets minus the value of the other liabilities. The shareholders' stake in the business comes from the money raised by issuing shares plus any profits that have been retained in the business.

Progress questions

13 State **two** sources of funds for a commercial bank.

14 Give **two** reasons why a bank might become insolvent.

Case study: Northern Rock

▲ Figure 7.3.6: Queues outside a branch of the Northern Rock bank in 2007

In the summer of 2007, Northern Rock was the fourth largest bank in the United Kingdom, in terms of its share of lending. It was included in the FTSE100, an index that is made up of the 100 largest companies on the London Stock Exchange. A few months later, the bank had collapsed.

Where did it all go wrong? Instead of using deposits of customers to finance its mortgage lending, it had borrowed heavily on international money markets. Only 25% of its loans were financed by deposits, with 25% coming from interbank loans and the other 50% from issuing mortgage-backed securities. Some of the money Northern Rock raised from financial markets was short term and the business

needed to keep refinancing itself. In the global financial crisis of 2007–2008, banks lost confidence in the ability of other banks to pay back their loans and stopped lending to each other. As a result, Northern Rock was in trouble.

Northern Rock's request for an emergency loan from the Bank of England was soon in the news. Customers were worried that they might lose their savings and queued in the street to try to take their money out of the bank. This was the first run on a British bank for 140 years. The bank struggled on for a while but was eventually nationalised in February 2008.

Its assets were divided into "good" and "bad", with the good assets taken over by Virgin Money. Over the next few years, almost 4,000 employees lost their jobs and many small shareholders also lost their money. Since then, the Bank of England and many other central banks have increased the regulations on financial institutions, to try to reduce the chance of such a collapse happening again.

1 What are interbank loans?

2 Explain why borrowing heavily on international money markets helped to cause the collapse of Northern Rock.

3 What is meant by a "run on a bank"?

4 Explain why a run on a bank can cause the bank to fail even if it is profitable.

▲ **Figure 7.3.7**: Bank Indonesia, a central bank

Functions of a central bank

Most countries in the world have a central bank, some of which are agencies of the government. However, many of the so-called independent central banks are influenced by their governments to a greater or lesser extent. Only a few countries do not have a central bank, including the tiny countries of Monaco and Andorra. This has not always been the case. For much of the 19th century, the USA did not have a central bank and countries such as Brazil, China, Canada, India and New Zealand did not have a central bank until the 20th century. In most countries, the central bank is wholly owned by the state, but a few central banks have some private shareholders, for example the central banks of Japan, Switzerland and Turkey. The Bank of England (UK), the People's Bank of China, the European Central Bank (ECB), the Bank of Uganda and the Federal Reserve (USA) are just a few examples of the world's central banks.

The fundamental aims of a central bank are to maintain financial stability and to help the government in maintaining macroeconomic stability. Central banks use monetary policy to support the government in maintaining macroeconomic stability, but this will not be achieved unless there is also financial stability. Crises in financial markets are likely to disrupt the real economy and send it into recession.

While the functions of a central bank may vary between countries, the main functions of a typical central bank include:

- issuing notes
- government's bank
- bankers' bank
- supporting the payments system
- lender of last resort
- monetary policy
- maintaining the stability of financial markets
- managing foreign exchange reserves.

Issuing notes

In most countries, the central bank has complete control over the issue of notes. For example, the European Central Bank (ECB) issues €5, €10, €20, €50, €100 and €200 notes. These notes are **legal tender** in the 19 euro area countries. Central banks ensure that there are sufficient notes in circulation to allow trade to take place smoothly.

Central banks have not always been in control of the note issue. In the past, many commercial banks issued their own banknotes and in some countries they still do. For example, three commercial banks in Scotland, which is part of the United Kingdom, still issue their own banknotes.

Government's bank

Central banks act as bankers to the government. They provide financial advice and will usually arrange short-term loans for the government.

Most central banks provide bank accounts for the government and government departments, but many governments will also have

> **Key term**
>
> **Legal tender:** money that the law states must be accepted in payment of a debt.

accounts with commercial banks. In some countries, tax revenues and other government receipts are paid into the government's accounts at the central bank and payments for public expenditure are made from these accounts.

Some central banks are responsible for managing the national debt for the government, but sometimes this function is carried out by a different government agency. The central bank of Kenya sells treasury bills and bonds on behalf of the government and manages the country's national debt. Even where the central bank is not wholly responsible for managing the national debt, it will often buy and sell government securities. In countries such as the UK and Japan, the use of quantitative easing has meant that the central bank owns large amounts of the national debt.

Bankers' bank

The central bank is also banker to the other banks. Commercial banks are usually required to have a bank account with the central bank. The balance in this account is part of the bank's cash reserves. The central bank will usually specify the minimum ratio of cash to deposits that banks have to keep in their account with the central bank. Some central banks change the required cash reserve ratio as part of monetary policy, for example if they want to tighten monetary policy, they will increase the ratio.

When a commercial bank needs banknotes for its customers, the central bank supplies the notes and debits the commercial bank's account. These accounts are also used to settle debts between the banks. For example, if the customers of Bank A use the deposits in their bank accounts to pay $150 million to customers of Bank B but customers of Bank B only pay customers of Bank A $120 million, Bank A will owe Bank B $30 million. The central bank will transfer funds from Bank A's account to Bank B's account.

Supporting the payments system

Payment systems support the transfer of funds between individuals, businesses and financial institutions. Making sure that payments can be made without risk is important for the economy and for financial stability. Central banks regulate and monitor the payments system to make sure that it is working effectively. Their role in supplying bank notes and in the settlement of debts between banks is part of this function.

Lender of last resort

Since commercial banks borrow short term and lend longer term, there is always a risk that they could run out of cash. The central bank, in its role as **lender of last resort**, will provide liquidity to banks that are unable to obtain liquid funds from the interbank market and/or other sources. In normal circumstances, the loan is short term and the bank is charged a higher rate of interest than they would pay if they could borrow from elsewhere. Hence, they will only borrow from the central bank if there is no alternative and will repay the loan as quickly as possible.

> **Key term**
>
> Lender of last resort: when a central bank lends to a commercial bank that is short of liquidity and unable to borrow from other sources.

In principle, the central bank should only lend to a financial institution that is solvent but has a temporary shortage of liquidity. Insolvent banks should be allowed to go out of business. However, in times of financial crisis, the central bank may decide to support a bank that is in financial difficulties for much longer.

When the central bank acts as lender of last resort, its aim is to prevent unnecessary disruption to financial markets and to prevent bank runs. Having the central bank as lender of last resort provides confidence that commercial banks will be able to provide depositors with cash whenever they want to withdraw money or pay others.

Monetary policy

Central banks conduct monetary policy on behalf of the government. Monetary policy involves influencing the supply of money and credit and the cost of borrowing. In general, the aim of monetary policy is to control inflation, maintain employment and to achieve stable economic growth. Controlling inflation is usually the main aim of monetary policy since it is generally believed that high inflation is damaging for an economy.

When a country has an independent central bank, the government usually sets the objective of monetary policy, and it is the responsibility of the central bank to use the tools of monetary policy to achieve that objective. In many countries, the government sets an inflation target, usually with a band that states an acceptable margin either side of the band, for example, in 2020, the inflation target set by the government of Egypt was 9% plus or minus 3%. However, the objective of monetary policy might be to maintain a fixed exchange rate or a specified rate of growth of the money supply. When the government sets a target for the rate of growth of the money supply, it does so because it believes that this will control inflation.

Maintaining the stability of financial markets

The central bank, acting as the lender of last resort, helps to maintain the stability of financial markets but there are other actions that a central bank can use to help it achieve this objective. Since the global financial crisis of 2007–2008, central banks around the world have increased their supervision of individual financial institutions and imposed regulations to try to reduce the risk of financial institutions going bankrupt. The regulations also aim to minimise the impact on the real economy if a financial institution does fail.

Managing foreign exchange reserves

Central banks are responsible for managing the country's foreign exchange reserves. Foreign exchange reserves are foreign currency assets that are held by central banks. They can include special drawing rights (SDRs), gold, treasury bills and government bonds, as well as foreign currencies. Countries hold foreign exchange reserves for a number of reasons including:

- to manage the exchange rate
- to pay interest on foreign debt and to repay the debt when it is due
- to pay for government expenditure overseas
- to deal with the effects of emergencies or natural disasters.

Link

Monetary policy was explained in 9.1 "Monetary policy" in the AS book.

Link

The regulation of financial markets is explained later in this section.

Changes in a country's foreign exchange reserves are affected by the current account of the balance of payments and international capital flows. A country can acquire foreign exchange reserves by borrowing or by selling its own currency. However, the effects on the exchange rate and hence the domestic economy will be different.

Moral hazard, asymmetric information and market bubbles

Well-functioning financial markets are essential for the efficient operation of an economy, but they do not always work well and may provide opportunities for dishonest traders to make large financial gains. There are times when financial markets are unstable and may cause serious harm. The global financial crisis of 2007–2008 is just the most recent example of problems in financial markets having a damaging effect on the real economy. Two other well-known examples are the Wall Street Crash of 1929 and the Asian financial crisis of 1997.

There are various sources of market failure in financial markets, as described below. These market failures can have both microeconomic and macroeconomic consequences.

Moral hazard

Moral hazard is when an economic agent has the incentive to take extra risk because they do not bear the full cost of the risk. There are various ways in which moral hazard can lead to failures in financial markets.

An individual trader working for a large financial institution may receive a bonus that is dependent upon the profit they make for their employer. If the risk pays off, the trader will receive a large bonus but if it does not, the financial institution will bear the loss. The management of the financial institutions should be monitoring the activities of its employees and limiting their ability to take too much risk, but sometimes this does not happen. The rewards of management are also often dependent on the profits made by traders, and management may have little incentive to restrict traders' activities, particularly when markets are performing well.

When someone takes out insurance, this may result in people being careless because they know that they will be compensated by the insurance company if they suffer loss.

When central banks act as lender of last resort, there is the risk of moral hazard. Commercial banks know that they can borrow from the central bank if they run out of liquidity. This may mean that banks do not manage their business properly. Some economists argue that if a bank was allowed to fail when it runs out of liquidity, other banks would be more careful and manage their business better.

Similarly, a **government bailout** of a financial institution that has failed because it has taken too much risk or is badly managed can also result in moral hazard. If financial institutions believe that they will be bailed out by the government, others may also take unnecessary risks.

Link

How a central bank can influence the exchange rate was explained in 7.2 "Exchange rates".

Progress questions

15 What is a central bank?

16 What are the **two** main ways that commercial banks use their accounts at the central bank?

17 What is the lender of last resort function of a central bank?

Activity

Research the causes of the Asian financial crisis of 1997 and its effects on the economies in the region.

Key terms

Moral hazard: when an economic agent has the incentive to take extra risk because they do not bear the full cost of the risk.

Government bailout: when the government provides financial support to a business that would otherwise have gone bankrupt.

Activity

Find out about mortgage-backed securities and how asymmetric information in the market for these securities contributed to the global financial crisis of 2007–2008.

Link

Asymmetric information was explained in 5.5 "Market imperfections" in the AS book.

Key term

Market bubble: when the price of an asset rises rapidly so that it does not reflect its true value. The price then falls rapidly when the bubble bursts.

Link

Asset bubbles, another name for market bubbles, were introduced in 2.5 "The determination of market prices" in the AS book.

▲ **Figure 7.3.8:** When the bubble busts, prices fall

Progress questions

18 Why might bailing out a financial institution by the government lead to moral hazard?

19 How does 'herding' help to cause market bubbles?

Asymmetric information

When one party to a contract knows more than the other party, economic agents may make irrational decisions leading to a misallocation of resources and market failure.

An insurance company has to assess the risk of loss when deciding on the premium to charge a customer. However, it is unlikely to know all the relevant information about economic agents who wish to take out insurance. For example, a small business may want to insure its premises but the insurance company will not know whether the owner always locks up the property when it is not occupied.

When a company wishes to raise finance, potential investors will have limited information about the business and its future prospects. This uncertainty may mean that a good company is unable to raise the money it needs. It might also mean that a company that is less well run may be able to borrow at a lower rate of interest than is justified by the risk that they might not be able to pay back the loan.

Market bubbles

Prices of many assets in financial markets are subject to frequent and sometimes large fluctuations. These fluctuations are often due to speculation. A **market bubble** occurs when the price of an asset rises rapidly and does not reflect the true value of the of the asset. Market bubbles often result from the herding behaviour of speculators who, like animals that are part of a herd, follow the behaviour of others in the market. An initial increase in the price of an asset may lead people to believe that the price will continue to rise and so they buy it, resulting in a further price rise. As more investors continue to buy the asset, the increase in demand causes the price of the asset to rise well above its real value. However, at some point, people will realise that the asset is overvalued and sell it. As a result, the price will start to fall and others will also sell. Once again, herding behaviour may lead to the price falling rapidly, causing the bubble to burst.

Large fluctuations in the prices of financial assets can be harmful for individuals, businesses and the economy as a whole. Individuals who have saved by buying securities may find that when they need the money, the value of the securities is much less than they paid for them. Firms can be affected by fluctuations in commodity prices and exchange rates. A fall in the price of financial assets reduces people's wealth and damages confidence which may reduce aggregate demand, output and employment. Uncertainty can also affect investment and hence the growth of an economy.

Regulation of financial markets

The damage caused by the global financial crisis of 2007–2008 has led to more intervention by governments and central banks to regulate financial markets. In the previous 25 years, many governments had reduced the amount they intervened in financial markets because they believed that market forces would improve efficiency and lead to a better allocation of financial resources. It was widely believed that the managers of financial institutions would act rationally to ensure that their business was secure and that intervention would prevent markets working efficiently.

However, in the financial crisis a number of large, well-known financial institutions did fail while others would have failed if governments had not bailed them out. At first, some governments were reluctant to bail out large financial institutions that had made bad decisions and taken too many risks. They were concerned that moral hazard would lead to more reckless behaviour and even more failures in the long run. However, it soon became clear that some financial institutions were **"too big to fail"** because if they failed, they would cause other financial institutions to fail and severely damage the world economy.

Financial institutions have always been regulated but since the global financial crisis, governments and central banks have introduced a variety of additional measures to control financial markets and financial institutions.

Measures to regulate financial institutions and financial markets

1 In most countries, a company must have a licence before it is allowed to provide financial services. For example, in Singapore, companies must apply for a licence to the Monetary Authority of Singapore (MAS) which regulates the country's financial institutions.

2 **Ring-fencing** requires that large banks separate the essential services they provide to the wider economy from their riskier, investment banking activities. More controls are imposed on the ring-fenced part of the bank, making it less likely that it will fail. This means that if there is a shock to the financial sector, the essential services that the bank provides to the wider community will be protected.

3 Minimum **capital ratios** have been imposed to make it less likely that a bank will become insolvent if a shock to the economy or financial system reduces the value of its assets. The capital ratio is a measure of a bank's capital (equity) to its loans. The minimum ratio is risk-weighted which means that the amount of capital the bank has to hold depends on the risk associated with the different types of loan. The riskier the loans, the more capital the bank has to have. The higher the capital ratio, the lower the risk of a bank becoming insolvent if the value of its assets fall.

4 Minimum **liquidity ratios** have been imposed to make it less likely that a bank will run out of cash in times of crisis. When financial markets are experiencing problems, more customers are likely to withdraw money from their accounts. A minimum liquidity ratio should help to ensure that the banks can always meet customers' demands for cash. When necessary, a solvent bank can borrow from the central bank in its role as lender of last resort but imposing a high liquidity ratio should reduce the need for a bank to do so.

5 Many countries offer a **deposit protection scheme** for individuals who have deposits in a licensed bank or savings institution. The banks pay into an insurance fund and if one of

the banks goes bankrupt, the fund compensates depositors, up to a certain limit. For example, in the United Kingdom the limit is £85,000, in countries that are members of the European Union the limit is €100,000 and in China the limit is ¥500,000. These schemes help to preserve trust in the banking system and make it less likely that there will be a run on the banks when there are problems in financial markets.

6   Separate organisations have been set up to monitor the activities and performance of financial institutions. In some countries, there is more than one regulatory organisation, each with a different role. They will regularly consult with the various financial institutions and recommend, or may insist on, changes that help to make the financial institutions more secure. Some of these organisations may recommend changes in the law. If the behaviour of a financial institution is inappropriate, they may prosecute or impose fines. In the USA, the Securities and Exchange Commission, which was formed in 1934, aims to protect investors and maintain orderly and efficient financial markets. In China, the Financial Stability and Development Committee (FSDC) and the China Banking Insurance Regulatory Commission (CBIRC) are two organisation that have been set up to monitor financial institutions and markets.

7   Some central banks carry out **stress tests** at regular intervals to see whether financial institutions have sufficient capital and liquidity to survive possible future shocks to financial markets and the wider economy. Stress tests are carried out using computer models (simulations). Many large financial institutions will also carry out their own stress tests. The results of the stress test warn the central bank of potential problems and lead to action being taken to deal with the problems.

Disadvantages of regulating financial markets

Some economists believe that government intervention and regulation of financial markets have more costs than benefits and can cause financial instability. Central banks may keep interest rates too low for too long, leading to rising asset prices and market bubbles. Central banks providing liquidity to financial markets and governments bailing out financial institutions can lead to moral hazard.

The costs of regulation are significant and there is always the danger of regulatory capture. The regulators may take decisions that benefit the financial institutions they are regulating rather than the general public. Regulation leads to lower profits for the banks and can reduce innovation in financial markets. It restricts competition, leading to higher costs and inefficiency.

Regulation may mean that the supply of credit is reduced. Economic agents who could make good use of additional funds may not be able to invest and develop their business, reducing economic growth. Those who are unable to borrow from regulated financial institutions may borrow from unregulated institutions, leading to a rapid growth in the shadow banking market.

Shadow banking market

Financial institutions in the shadow banking market do not accept deposits from customers and are not licensed or regulated by governments and central banks. However, like a regulated bank, they borrow short term and lend long term. The liquidity requirements and capital ratios imposed on commercial banks do not apply to institutions that operate in the shadow banking market. Therefore, they are at greater risk than regulated banks. Some financial institutions that are licensed and regulated also participate in the unregulated shadow banking market. The regulated activities of these institutions are often ring-fenced to protect them from the risks of operating in the shadow banking market.

Shadow banks provide credit to individuals and companies that might find it difficult to raise the finance they need from the traditional, regulated banks. Lending to new businesses and to some less well-known companies may be considered too risky for traditional banks. Shadow banks are often willing to take more risk and to support new ventures that turn out to be very profitable. They can also be an important source of finance in countries that do not have a well-developed banking system. Since shadow banks are not subject to the same controls as other banks, they are often more flexible and can provide credit and other financial services at lower cost than the traditional banks. The services provided through the shadow banking market can help to support the growth of the global economy but as shown by the global financial crisis of 2007–2008, shadow banking increases the risk of problems emerging in financial markets that damage the real economy.

According to the Financial Stability Board (FSB), an organisation that monitors and makes recommendations about the global financial system, the total financial assets of shadow banks grew from US$30 trillion in 2010 to US$52 trillion in 2017. Over this period, the rate of growth in the shadow banking market was highest in China (58%) and Argentina (48%).

How problems in financial markets affect the real economy

Problems in financial markets have both microeconomic and macroeconomic effects on the real economy. Firms may find it difficult to borrow to expand their business and individuals may find, for example, that they are unable to borrow to buy a new car or get a mortgage to buy a house. If a bank fails, some people may lose their savings and falling asset prices will also reduce people's wealth. If the payments system is affected, there may be delays in some firms receiving the money they are owed and workers may not be paid on time.

Problems in financial market may cause cyclical instability

Although problems in financial markets are not the only cause of cyclical instability, there is plenty of evidence to suggest that it takes more time to recover from a recession caused by a financial crisis than from a recession caused by other factors. Financial crises often happen after a long period of prosperity. Low interest rates, easy credit and

▲ **Figure 7.3.9:** The shadow banking market is growing

Activity

To take you further, find out about organisations that operate in the shadow banking market including how they raise finance and the services they provide.

Progress questions

20 Why do high capital and liquidity ratios imposed by central banks on commercial banks help to prevent bank failures?

21 According to the Financial Stability Board, the financial assets of shadow banks increased from $30 trillion in 2010 to $52 trillion in 2017. Calculate, to the nearest whole number, the percentage increase in the size of the shadow banking market between 2010 and 2017.

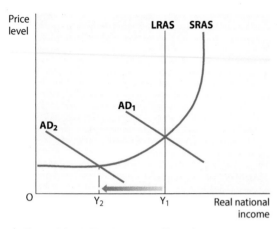

▲ **Figure 7.3.10:** The short-run effect of a financial crisis on the macroeconomy

Key terms

Credit crunch: a sudden reduction in lending by financial institutions and an increase in the rate of interest charged on loans.

Fire sale: when an organisation is in financial difficulty and has to sell some of its assets at a price that is below their true value.

Systemic risk: the possibility that the failure of a large financial institution could have a very damaging effect on other financial institutions and the real economy.

Link

Causes of cyclical instability were explained in 8.1 "Economic growth and the economic cycle" in the AS book.

Progress questions

22 Give **two** reasons why problems in financial markets may reduce aggregate demand.

23 Why may problems in financial markets reduce the long-run rate of economic growth?

rising asset prices are accompanied by high levels of debt and overconfidence. Asset price bubbles are followed by a collapse in asset prices which may result in some financial institutions becoming insolvent. Even if this does not happen, banks are likely to reduce their lending and household wealth falls. As a result, consumption and investment fall, leading to a reduction in aggregate demand (AD) and economic activity.

Figure 7.3.10 shows that the financial crisis causes aggregate demand to fall from AD_1 to AD_2, reducing national income from Y_1 to Y_2. Multiplier and accelerator effects will contribute to the fall in AD and the resulting fall in national income will be accompanied by a rise in unemployment.

A **credit crunch**, which is one part of a financial crisis, means that bank lending is restricted and interest rates will rise, causing a further fall in AD. Before the crisis, when households and firms were confident about the future, they may have borrowed heavily. When confidence falls, households and firms try to save more to reduce their debts. The credit crunch and the fall in confidence mean that it is likely to take a long time before AD and economic activity recover.

A financial crisis is also likely to reduce an economy's long-run rate of economic growth. The credit crunch will reduce investment and may force firms to cut their spending on training and on R & D. As a result, the rate of increase in the economy's productive capacity may fall.

Regulation should reduce the effects of financial instability on the real economy

Financial instability usually leads to economic instability. This is the main reason why governments around the world have increased the regulations imposed on financial institutions and markets.

A problem in one part of the global financial market can spread very easily and quickly. Financial institutions lend to each other and if one financial institution fails, the value of the assets and capital of other financial institutions falls. In a serious financial crisis, as occurred in 2007–2008, they may stop lending to each other because they do not know whether the loans would be repaid.

Financial institutions that are short of liquidity will try to sell some of their assets. The increase in the supply of these assets causes the price to fall. Such a **fire sale** of financial assets usually leads to a large fall in asset prices and reduces the capital of other financial institutions.

Systemic risk is when there is a risk that the failure of a large financial institution will spread to other financial institutions and seriously damage the real economy. Many of the regulations, including ring-fencing, aim to reduce systemic risk and try to make sure that no financial institution is too big to fail.

Exam-style questions

1 Which one of the following is recorded on the financial account of the balance of payments?

   A Errors and omissions

   B Government spending

   C Net investment income

   D Portfolio investment overseas   (1 mark)

2 The diagram below shows the foreign exchange market for a currency. The original price of the currency is P_1 and the original quantity traded is Q_1. Which one of the following combination of events is likely to cause the exchange rate to rise to P_2 and the quantity traded to increase to Q_2?

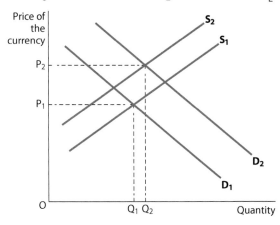

	Exports of goods	Imports of services
A	Decrease	Decrease
B	Decrease	Increase
C	Increase	Decrease
D	Increase	Increase

        (1 mark)

3 Which one of the following statements about debt and equity is correct?

   A Both equity and debt are sources of funds for a bank.

   B Debt is a loan and the return on equity is interest.

   C Equity is a long-term loan and debt is a short-term loan.

   D Equity is retained profit and debt is money raised by selling shares.   (1 mark)

4 An objective of government macroeconomic policy is to achieve a stable balance of payments position.

   [i] Define "balance of payments".   (2 marks)

   [ii] Draw a diagram to illustrate the likely effects of a growing surplus on the balance of trade in goods and services on the macroeconomy of a country.   (4 marks)

[iii] A French firm imports computer chips from the USA to use in the manufacture of its products. It bought $45,000 on the forward market at an exchange rate of €1 = $1.15. If the firm had waited and bought the dollars on the spot market, the exchange rate would have been €1 = $1.20.

Calculate, to the **nearest whole euro** (€), the effect on the firm's profit of buying dollars on the forward market rather than buying them later on the spot market.

You are advised to show your working. (4 marks)

5 The table below shows the Chilean central bank's official interest rate, known as its Monetary Policy Rate, and the US dollar exchange rate for the Chilean peso between June 2010 and December 2010.

Date (2010)	US dollar to Chilean peso exchange rate (pesos)	Chilean central bank's Monetary Policy Rate (%)
June	537	1.00
July	532	1.50
August	509	2.00
September	494	2.50
October	484	2.75
November	482	3.00
December	475	3.25

Source: Bank for International Settlements; accessed December 2020

[i] Explain why the Monetary Policy Rate set by the Chilean central bank affects the exchange rate of the Chilean peso. (4 marks)

[ii] To what extent do the data suggest that the Chilean peso exchange rate was affected by the Monetary Policy Rate set by Chile's central bank? Use the data in the table to support your answer. (4 marks)

6 Explain why imposing minimum liquidity and capital ratios on commercial banks reduces the risk of bank failures. (12 marks)

7 Discuss the view that central banks and governments should not support a failing bank. (25 marks)

Note: To answer this question as a data response question, use the data provided in the case study "Northern Rock" in 7.3 "Financial markets" to support your answer.

Economic development and the global economy

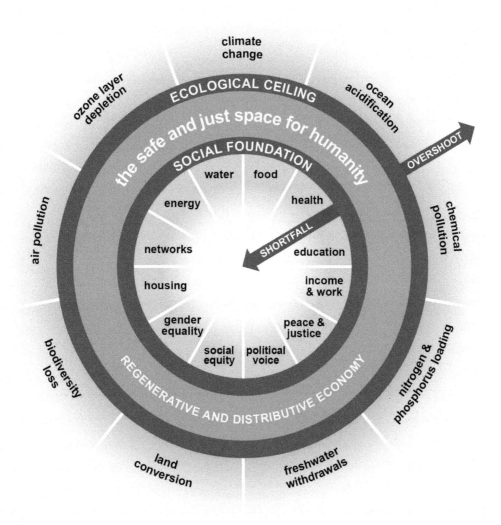

This section will develop your knowledge and understanding of:

→ the difference between economic growth and development

→ general characteristics of MEDCs, emerging economies and LEDCs

→ changes in real national income as the main measure of economic growth

→ the Human Development Index (HDI), Inequality-adjusted HDI (IHDI) and the Multidimensional Poverty Index (MPI) as indicators of economic development

→ other indicators of development, including infant mortality rates, literacy rates and measures of inequality

→ how economic development is sustainable, improving the well-being of current and future generations

→ measuring changes in living standards over time and comparing living standards between countries at a point in time

→ the use of Purchasing Power Parity (PPP) exchange rates when making international comparisons of living standards

→ strengths and weaknesses of real GDP per head as an indicator of living standards within and between countries

→ environmental and social limits to economic growth and development.

Economic growth and development

Economic growth should not be confused with economic development. Sometimes a country may experience a rapid rate of economic growth but this benefits very few people and long-run, sustainable economic development does not take place.

Economic growth

Economic growth measures the rate at which the total output of an economy is increasing and is measured by the annual percentage change in real national income. When calculating the rate of economic growth, gross domestic product (GDP) is the most commonly used measure of national income. However, economic growth is sometimes calculated using a different measure of national income, for example, gross national product (GNP) or net national income (NNI).

Economists distinguish between short-run and long-run economic growth. Short-run economic growth is the percentage change in real GDP in a particular year and it is affected by both demand-side and supply-side factors. Long-run economic growth is the average annual percentage change in the productive capacity of an economy over a number of years. Long-run economic growth is determined mainly by supply-side factors and can be illustrated by a rightward shift in the production possibility boundary (PPB) or a rightward shift in the long-run aggregate supply curve (LRAS).

Economic development

Economic development is a process that leads to a sustained improvement in the economic well-being and quality of life of people. Economic growth can contribute to economic development but it is

Link

Economic growth was explained in 8.1 "Economic growth and the economic cycle" in the AS book.

Key term

Economic development: a process that leads to a sustained improvement in the economic well-being and quality of life of people.

only one aspect of the process. Economic growth leads to an increase in output and has the potential to increase living standards. However, it cannot be concluded that economic growth improves economic welfare without considering which goods and services are produced and how the output is distributed among the population. For example, the discovery and exploitation of a valuable natural resource, that is owned by a few rich and powerful people, may increase economic growth but damage the environment and provide little, if any, benefit to the majority of the population.

Economic development occurs when the population of a country benefits from a general improvement in living standards that is accompanied by a reduction in poverty and inequality. It enables everyone to satisfy the basic human need for food, clothing and shelter. Economic development also means that people have access to good-quality education and health care. It involves satisfying people's needs and wants while taking care of the environment in which they live and work. Economic development is sustainable which means that satisfying the needs and wants of people living today does not affect the ability of future generations to meet their needs and wants.

The characteristics of MEDCs, emerging economies and LEDCs

Economists often distinguish between more economically developed economies (MEDCs) and less economically developed economies (LEDCs). The MEDCs are the richer countries of the world that have a high GDP per head, at least US$10,000. Life expectancy is high and population growth is low, usually below 1% per annum. Literacy rates are high and people have access to good-quality health care.

The proportion of the population employed in the primary sector of the economy, including agriculture, is usually low. Most MEDCs have a manufacturing sector that is technologically advanced, where labour productivity is high, but the majority of the population is usually employed in the service sector. The infrastructure, including road and rail networks, housing, schools and hospitals, is well developed. Most MEDCs are located in the Northern hemisphere but there are some exceptions, including Australia and New Zealand.

The LEDCs are mainly located in the Southern hemisphere, for example in Africa. They have a low GDP per head and often have high rates of population growth, low life expectancy and high infant mortality rates. They produce many of the world's primary products which are sold to the MEDCs who use them to make high-value manufactures. Food is often produced on small subsistence farms. The housing stock is generally poor and many people do not have access to clean running water and/or electricity. Literacy rates are low and the infrastructure is not well developed.

Emerging economies are countries whose economy is not yet fully developed but which are growing rapidly and have some features of

Activity

Find out all you can about the United Nations Millennium Development Goals (MDGs) and the Sustainable Development Goals (SDGs). What progress did the world make towards achieving the MDGs by the target date of 2015?

Key terms

Life expectancy: the average number of years a person can expect to live.

Infant mortality rate: the number of infant deaths, in the first year of life, out of every thousand live births in that year.

▲ **Figure 8.1.1**: The BRICS

an MEDC. They are in the process of changing from a low-income, less developed, often pre-industrial economy into a developed, modern industrial economy. Emerging economies include the BRIC economies of Brazil, Russia, India and China. The term BRIC economies was first used by the British economist Jim O'Neill when he was working for the investment bank Goldman Sachs. In 2010, South Africa was added to the list of BRICS. Other emerging economies include Indonesia, Mexico, Hungary and Turkey. Some emerging economies are more developed than others.

Changes in real national income as the main measure of economic growth

Real national income measures the monetary value of all the goods and services produced by an economy during a given period of time, often a year. When measuring economic growth, it is essential that national income is in measured in real terms, that is after the effects of inflation are removed. An increase in real national income means that the quantity of goods and services produced by the economy has increased.

However, the impact of an increase in real national income on living standards will be affected by which goods and services have led to the increase in national income and whether national income has increased by more or less than the country's population. Living standards will also be affected by what has happened to the distribution of income and so who has benefited from the increase in output.

Key indicators of economic development

An increase in a country's real national income per head indicates that, on average, more has been produced per person and so more can be consumed. Real national income per head is an important indicator of economic development but it also has some significant weaknesses. As a result, other indicators of economic development are also used.

The Human Development Index (HDI)

The **Human Development Index (HDI)** takes into account three aspects of human development: health, education and material living standards. Health is measured by life expectancy at birth. Education is measured by the mean of years of schooling for adults aged over 24 years and the expected years of schooling for children about to start school. The standard of living is measured by gross national income (GNI) per head. The scores for each of these measures are put together to create the HDI.

The numerical value of the HDI can range from 0 to 1. A country with a high HDI is judged to have a higher level of human and economic development than a country with a low HDI. HDI is often broken down into four tiers of human development as shown in Table 8.1.1.

▼ **Table 8.1.1**: Tiers of human development according to the HDI

Tier	HDI values	Examples of countries	HDI Value in 2020
1 – Very high human development	0.80 to 1.00	Norway	0.954
		Japan	0.915
		Chile	0.847
2 – High human development	0.70 to 0.79	Mexico	0.767
		China	0.758
		Philippines	0.712
3 – Medium human development	0.55 to 0.69	Morocco	0.676
		Ghana	0.596
		Pakistan	0.560
4 – Low human development	Below 0.55	Nigeria	0.534
		Afghanistan	0.496
		Chad	0.401

Source: Human Development Index (HDI) by Country 2021

Although many economists believe that the HDI is a better indicator of human and economic development than real national income per head, some important elements of economic development are not included in the index. For example, the HDI does not take into account inequality, poverty or the environment in which people live.

Inequality-adjusted Human Development Index (IHDI)

Two countries with different distributions of income can have the same HDI value but if one country has a much more unequal distribution of income, it is difficult to argue that the level of development is the same. The **Inequality-adjusted Human Development Index (IHDI)** is a measure of economic development that is based on life expectancy, education and income but which also takes into account how these three indicators of development are distributed among a country's population. If the distribution of income is perfectly equal, the IHDI is the same as the HDI, but IHDI is below HDI when there is some inequality. The more inequality, the greater the difference between the two measures.

Multidimensional Poverty Index (MPI)

The global MPI uses 10 indicators to measure three dimensions of household poverty. The three dimensions of household poverty are health, education and the standard of living. Table 8.1.2 shows the weight attached to each of the indicators of poverty included in the MPI.

The value of the index can range from 0 to 1. The higher the value of the index, the greater the amount of poverty in the country. The index takes into account the proportion of the population who are poor and the extent, or intensity, of their poverty. In 2020, the MPI was used to assess the extent of global poverty in 107 developing countries with a combined population of 5.9 billion people. According to the global MPI, 1.3 billion of these people (22%) were identified as living

Quantitative skills

Although the HDI is usually shown as a value between 0 and 1, it is sometimes shown as a percentage with a value ranging from 0% to 100%. A value of 0.793 using the first method is the same as 79.3% when the second method is used.

Key term

Inequality-adjusted Human Development Index (IHDI): a measure of economic development that is based on life expectancy, education and income but which also takes into account how these three indicators of development are distributed among a country's population.

▲ **Figure 8.1.2**: Poor housing, an aspect of poverty

▼ **Table 8.1.2**: Dimensions and indicators in the global MPI

Dimension	Indicator
Health (1/3)	Nutrition (1/6)
	Child mortality (1/6)
Education (1/3)	Years of schooling (1/6)
	School attendance (1/6)
Living standards (1/3)	Cooking fuel (1/18)
	Sanitation (1/18)
	Drinking water (1/18)
	Electricity (1/18)
	Housing (1/18)
	Assets (1/18)

in poverty. About 84% of the multidimensionally poor lived in Sub-Saharan Africa (558 million) and South Asia (530 million). Two-thirds of the multidimensionally poor lived in middle-income countries.

Other indicators of economic development

It is unlikely that a single indicator will provide an adequate measure of the economic development of a country. This is why measures of development, such as the HDI, that include several elements were introduced. Even so, when assessing the economic development of a country, economists would usually consider a wide range of indicators, each of which reflects a different aspect of a country's development.

People's health is an important of aspect of economic well-being and quality of life. Indicators of health include life expectancy, infant mortality rates and the number of doctors per head of population. Life expectancy is the number of years a new-born infant would be expected to live and the infant mortality rate is the number of children per 1,000 that are expected to die before they reach the age of 5 years old.

Education can affect people's chance of finding a well-paid job, their sense of achievement and their ability to enjoy life. Indicators of people's access to education include literacy rates, numeracy rates, years of schooling and the proportion of the population that have a degree.

Reducing inequality is another important aspect of economic development. People may disagree about how much inequality is acceptable but high levels of inequality are likely to mean that large numbers of people are living in poverty and unable to satisfy their basic human needs. Indicators of income inequality and poverty include the Gini coefficient, the percentage of total income earned by the poorest 20% of the population, the MPI, and the proportion of the population living on less than $1.90 a day. In 2020, it was estimated that around 8.6% of the world's population lived below the international poverty line of $1.90 a day. Economic development also depends on reducing other forms of inequality, for example gender inequality.

The most frequently used measure of living standards is real national income per head, but other indicators are also used, for example the percentage of the population with access to clean water or to electricity, and the percentage of the population owning assets such as beds, TVs, telephones, computers and cars.

The quality of the environment is an important aspect of economic development. Increased levels of noise and air pollution reduce people's quality of life. Data showing changes in the environment can help provide a broader view of a country's economic development.

How economic development is sustainable

Economic development must be sustainable. A temporary improvement in living standards, perhaps caused by the discovery of a natural resource that increases the income of some people for a while, is not economic development. That does not mean that the discovery and exploitation of natural resources cannot lead to economic development. It depends on how the benefits are used and distributed among the population.

Improvements in the education, skills and health of the population are likely to lead to long-lasting benefits for the economy and for people's well-being. Investment in infrastructure can also lead to long-term benefits for society. Sustainable development means protecting the natural environment for future generations and, for example, making sure that renewable resources, such as forests and fish stocks, are not overused. The ecosystem provides the resources to produce goods and services. If not managed carefully, resources will be used up and the environment may be permanently damaged by waste generated through production and consumption.

Measuring changes in living standards

The standard of living is the ability of people to satisfy their needs and wants and includes their access to education and health care. The most commonly used indicator of the standard of living is real national income per head. Gross domestic product (GDP) and gross national income (GNI) are the most frequently used measures of national income.

Measuring changes in the standard of living of a country over time

National income is a measure of the monetary value of the goods and services produced by an economy over a period of time, for example one year. In general, what is produced by a country's economy determines what can be consumed by people living in that country and consumption affects people's material standard of living.

If a country imports more goods and services than it exports, people may be able to consume more than is produced, but for most countries, this is unlikely to be very significant. It must also be remembered that some of the output produced will be capital goods. In general, the production of capital goods does not affect current living standards but should increase economic growth and future living standards.

Progress questions

1 What is the difference between economic growth and economic development?

2 What are the **three** main aspects of human development included in the HDI?

3 What is the difference between the HDI and the IHDI?

4 What is meant by 'sustainable development'?

Link

How to convert money national income to real national income was explained in 6.2 "Macroeconomic indicators" in the AS book.

Get it right

Whenever you are presented with data showing changes in a country's national income, it is important to consider whether the data are in money or real terms. If the data are in money terms, it is not possible to draw any conclusions about what has happened to living standards without also knowing what has happened to inflation/the price level.

National income includes all the goods and services produced by an economy, for example food, clothing, new houses, medicines, health care, education, furniture, holidays, cars and haircuts. If a country's national income is rising over time, it means that people are able to consume more goods and services than in the past and so, should be better off. However, this is only true if national income is measured in real terms and changes in the size of the country's population are taken into account.

Inflation

Over time, the price level changes and so the change in money national income will not accurately reflect the change in the output of the economy. If a country has experienced inflation, the change in money national income will exaggerate the change in living standards. For example, if money national income has risen by 20% over a period of five years but the price level has risen by 15%, the increase in output, and therefore living standards, is much less than 20%. The effects of inflation have to be removed to calculate the change in real national income.

Changes in the size of the population

The change in a country's population must also be taken into account when measuring living standards. If the population is growing by 0.6% per annum, to prevent average living standards falling, real national income must increase by at least 0.6%.

To take into account the changes in both the price level and population, the change in real national income per head is used to measure the change in a country's living standards.

Limitations of using real national income per head as a measure of living standards

However, when trying to measure changes in a country's living standards over time, the change in real national income per head has some limitations, including:

- inequality
- types of goods and services
- changes in quality
- non-marketed output
- leisure time
- externalities
- statistical inaccuracies.

Inequality

An increase in real national income per head indicates that, on average, people are able to consume more goods and services but that does not mean that everyone is better off. An increase in inequality could mean that not only are some people relatively worse off but may also be poorer in absolute terms. When comparing living standards over time, it is worth considering how inequality has changed, using an indicator such as the Gini coefficient, alongside the change in real national income per head.

Types of goods and services

Changes in living standards depend on the types of goods and services produced as well as total output. An increase in the production of demerit goods, such as cigarettes, will increase national income but may, arguably, reduce people's well-being. An increase in spending on national defence may be considered necessary but it does not increase living standards. The production of capital goods may lead to an increase in future consumption but does not usually increase the current standard of living.

Changes in quality

Changes in national income do not always reflect changes in the quality of goods and services produced. For example, a modern car is likely to be more reliable and have more features than a car produced 25 years ago. Unless the change in quality is reflected in the change in the real price of the car, the benefit will not be included in the change in real national income. Over time, the quality of some goods and services increases but the quality of other products may fall.

Non-marketed output

National income measures the monetary value of goods and services that enter into exchange. It does not usually take into account services that are provided at home by members of the family. As societies get richer, some services that were provided by members of the family may be bought. For example, as a family's income increases, they may decide to pay someone to clean their house and look after the garden. These payments will add to national income but will not affect the real output of the economy.

Some transactions may not be recorded. In most countries, there is a hidden economy. The hidden economy is also sometimes known as the shadow economy or underground economy. Some transactions may not be recorded because individuals want to avoid paying tax or they may be illegal activities. Over time, the size of the hidden economy may change, and this is not reflected in the change in national income.

> **Key term**
>
> Hidden economy: where goods and services are supplied and exchanged but not recorded.

Leisure time

Living standards are affected by the amount of leisure time people have. As societies get richer, productivity usually increases and people are able to work fewer hours without it reducing the output of goods and services. For most people, a reduction in the number of hours worked per week and an increase in the number of days holiday each year increases their standard of living. If both real national income per head and leisure time increase, the increase in real national income per head understates the rise in living standards.

Externalities

The production and consumption of goods and services can create both positive and negative externalities. These indirect benefits and costs are not included in national income and so national income does not provide an accurate indication of living standards. If, for example, production and consumption lead to high levels of pollution, real national income per head will overstate average living standards.

Key term

Subsistence sector: part of the economy where individuals or families provide for their own basic needs, for example they grow their own food.

However, the costs of dealing with negative externalities, such as cleaning up litter and removing other forms of pollution, are often included in national income. If, for example, government expenditure pays for cleaning up waste, an increase in the amount of waste will lead to an increase in government spending and so national income, wrongly suggesting that average living standards are rising.

Statistical inaccuracies

Measuring national income is difficult, not all transactions are recorded and, in some countries, particularly the poorer LEDCs, the data is often inaccurate and not collected frequently enough. In a country where there is a large **subsistence sector**, a significant part of the country's output does not enter into exchange and may not be included in the national income data.

Case study: Botswana: selected indicators, 2000–2018

▲ **Figure 8.1.3**: The Okavango Delta – a popular tourist destination

Botswana is a landlocked country in southern Africa and its currency is the pula. Two of Botswana's major industries are mining and tourism. It was one of the poorest countries in the world but after rapid economic growth, Botswana's GDP per head is now one of the highest in Africa. Its HDI has also risen, from 0.581 in 2000 to 0.730 in 2018. Botswana is classified as an upper middle income country.

1 Calculate the GDP per head, at 2006 prices, for Botswana in 2000 and 2018. Give your answer to the nearest pula.

2 What is the percentage increase in GDP per head, at 2006 prices, between 2000 and 2018? Give your answer to **one** decimal place.

3 Describe what has happened to the degree of inequality in Botswana between 2000 and 2018. Use the figures in Table 8.1.3 to support your answer.

4 Explain why the data suggest that the average standard of living for people in Botswana improved between 2000 and 2018.

▼ **Table 8.1.3**: Selected economic indicators for Botswana, 2000–2018

	2000	2006	2012	2018
GDP (pula millions, 2006 prices)	45,655	59,107	75,515	89,798
Population (millions)	1.643	1.836	2.040	2.254
Share of income (top 1%)	29.6%	28.6%	25.9%	22.6%
Share of income (bottom 50%)	5.5%	5.9%	7.6%	8.7%
Life expectancy (years)	50.6	53.4	63.5	69.3
CO_2 emissions per capita (metric tonnes)	2.30	2.25	2.49	2.94*
Mobile cellular phone subscriptions (per 100 people)	13.5	44.8	151.1	150.0

* = 2016 figure

Source: World Bank, Botswana | Data (worldbank.org); except GDP Gross Domestic Product, Base Year = 2006 - OpenData for Statistics Botswana (opendataforafrica.org) and the shares of income, Botswana - WID - World Inequality Database, https://wid.world/country/botswana/, accessed 12 January 2021

Comparing the standard of living of different countries at a point in time

Real national income per head is also used to compare the living standards of different countries at a point in time. However, countries usually have different currencies and comparisons cannot be made unless each country's national income is converted into the same currency. Such comparisons are usually made by converting each country's national income into US dollars.

When converting different countries' national income per head into the same currency, the exchange rate used should reflect the purchasing power of the different currencies. For example, if $100 in the USA will buy the same basket of goods as €117 euros in Belgium, then when converting Belgian national income per head into US dollars, the exchange rate used should be $1 = €1.17. If the chosen exchange rate does not reflect the purchasing power of the different currencies, the comparison will not be accurate.

Many of the limitations of using national income to compare the changes in a country's living standards over time are also relevant when making international comparisons. However, inflation is not an issue because inflation occurs over a period of time and international comparisons are made at a point in time. If countries experience different rates of inflation, this means that the exchange rate which reflects the purchasing power of the currencies will change from one year to another.

Differences in the distribution of income

If a country has a relatively equal distribution of income, its national income per head is likely to provide a reasonable measure of the typical standard of living of people in that country. If a different country has the same real national income per head but its distribution of income is much more unequal, the typical standard of living for the average person in the two countries will not be the same.

Types of goods and services

If the types of goods and services produced by two countries are significantly different, the people in the two countries may have very different living standards even if the national income per head is the same. For example, if expenditure on defence is much higher in one country than the other, the average person in the country where defence expenditure is high will have a lower standard of living.

Non-marketed output

If a comparison is made between two countries where the size of the hidden economy, or the subsistence sector, is very different, this has to be taken into consideration. For example, the national income per head of an LEDC with a large subsistence sector is likely to understate the living standards of its people, unless an accurate estimate has been made of the value of subsistence production and it has been included in the calculation of the country's national income.

Leisure time

The leisure time for the people in two countries with a similar national income per head may be different. If people in one country have to work more hours to produce the same amount of goods and services, average living standards are likely to be lower in that country.

Externalities

The environment in which people live and other externalities should be taken into account when comparing the living standards of people in different countries. For example, if a country has high levels of pollution, it can lead to health problems and reduce living standards.

Statistical inaccuracies

Some countries collect more accurate data than others to calculate their national income. If the data is not accurate, it means that using national income per head is not a reliable indicator of differences in living standards.

Purchasing Power Parity (PPP) exchange rates and international comparisons of living standards

A **Purchasing Power Parity (PPP) exchange rate** is an exchange rate that accurately reflects the relative purchasing power of two currencies in their domestic economies. Market exchange rates are affected by international trade in goods and services. If one country has a higher rate of inflation than another country, its products are likely to become uncompetitive and its balance of payments will deteriorate. There will be an excess supply of the country's currency on the FOREX and its exchange rate will deteriorate. These changes should mean that market exchange rates move towards PPP exchange rates. However, this will not necessarily happen. Firstly, not all goods and services are traded internationally and changes in the exchange rate will depend on changes in the prices of exports and imports. Exchange rates are also affected by international capital flows and speculation. As a result, it is very unlikely that the market exchange rate will accurately reflect the purchasing power of the two currencies in their domestic economies.

As explained in the previous section, differences in national income per head will only provide a reasonable indicator of differences in living standards between countries if each country's national income is converted into the same currency using PPP exchange rates. If the market exchange rate is lower than the PPP exchange rate, the country's national income is undervalued and hence national income per head will understate the living standards of the country's people compared to people in other countries.

Strengths and weaknesses of real GDP per head as an indicator of living standards

Real GDP is a measure of national income that does not take into account net property income from abroad or capital consumption. Some of the income paid to domestic residents is generated from the ownership of overseas assets and part of the income generated in the

Key term

Purchasing Power Parity (PPP) exchange rate: an exchange rate that reflects what the two currencies are able to buy in their domestic economies.

Get it right

International organisations, such as the World Bank, publish data showing national income per head at current market exchange rates and at PPP exchange rates. When comparing living standards between countries, it is important to use national income per head at PPP exchange rates. Always check whether PPP exchange rates have been used. If not, the differences in national income per head will not provide an accurate indicator of differences in living standards.

Link

The measurement of national income and the difference between GNP and NNI was explained in 7.1 "The circular flow of income" in the AS book.

domestic economy is paid to people abroad who own assets in the domestic economy. The difference between these two income flows is net property income from abroad. If more income is flowing into the economy than is being paid out, that increases the ability of domestic residents to consume goods and services. If outflows exceed inflows of property income, GDP will overstate living standards.

Part of the output produced during a year is needed to replace the part of the capital stock that has depreciated due to use or obsolescence. Since GDP does not account for capital consumption, it overstates living standards. However, using net national income (NNI) per head as the measure of living standards removes these two problems.

However, as explained above, using national income as a measure of living standards has many weaknesses. These weaknesses relate to using both GDP and NNI per head as an indicator of living standards. When attempting to assess how living standards have changed over

Case study: Comparison of living standards in four countries in 2019

▲ **Figure 8.1.4**: B for Bangladesh, Belgium, Bolivia and Burundi

Table 8.1.4 shows selected indicators for four countries that begin with the letter "B" in four different continents but with quite different key indicators of living standards.

1   Explain why it is important to use PPP (Purchasing Power Parity) exchange rates when converting each country's GNI per capita into US dollars.

2   Why is the percentage of employment in agriculture likely to be an indicator of differences in living standards?

3   Which country appears to have the most unequal distribution of income? Use the data to support your answer.

4   Do the data suggest that average living standards are higher in Bolivia than Bangladesh? Justify your answer.

▼ **Table 8.1.4**: Selected indicators for four countries, 2019 (unless stated below the table)

	Bangladesh	Belgium	Bolivia	Burundi
Gross National Income per capita (2017 PPP $)	4.976	52,085	8,554	754
HDI	0.632	0.931	0.718	0.433
IHDI	0.478	0.859	0.546	0.303
MPI	0.104	n/a	0.096 [1]	0.403 [2]
Gini coefficient [3]	32.4	27.4	42.2	38.6
Life expectancy	72.6	81.6	71.5	61.6
Health expenditure (as % of GDP) [4]	2.3	10.3	6.4	7.5
Mean years of schooling	6.2	12.1	9.0	3.3
Employment in agriculture (% of employment)	38.6	1.0	30.7	92.0

[1]2008   [2]2016/2017   [3]2018   [4]2017

Source: Human Development Data Center | Human Development Reports (undp.org), accessed 14 January 2021

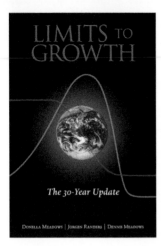

▲ **Figure 8.1.5**: *Limits to growth*, first published in 1972

time or to compare living standards in different countries, a variety of indicators should be used, including national income per head.

Environmental and social limits to economic growth and development

Environmental limits to growth and development

In 1972, a report produced for the Club of Rome called *The limits to growth*, highlighted how scarce natural resources and environmental problems would limit the extent to which the world economy and population could continue to grow. At the time, many economists disagreed with the conclusions of the report, but it has forced people to pay more attention to the sustainability of economic growth and development.

Economic growth means that more natural resources are likely to be needed to produce the higher output. Natural resources are either non-renewable or renewable. There is a finite quantity of non-renewable resources such as iron, copper, titanium, coal and oil. However, the supply available can be increased by new discoveries and some, such as metals, can be preserved by recycling. In principle, renewable resources, such as wood and fish, can always be replaced but too much use can mean that supplies are depleted (used up) and may not recover. The absence of well-defined property rights can result in the "tragedy of the commons" and lead to the supply of renewable resources being used up. As the supply of natural resources decreases, it will be difficult to maintain current levels of economic growth, and output may fall.

However, market forces and technological change may help to prevent or reduce the extent to which the limited supply of natural resources restricts economic growth. When a natural resource becomes scarcer, the excess demand will lead to an increase in its price. The higher price, and so profits, will create the incentive to search for new sources of supply. It will also encourage firms to economise on the use of the resource. The increase in price will incentivise changes in technology that lead to the development of substitutes. Recycling the natural resource will also become more profitable.

Damage to the environment that can result from economic growth may limit the extent to which economies can continue to grow and develop. Increased production and consumption may lead to more pollution, affecting people's health and well-being. More vehicles and roads affect the quality of the air we breathe and create more noise pollution. Economic growth means that more energy is consumed and the use of fossil fuels has led to more CO_2 emissions. The increase in CO_2 emissions is likely to cause global warming and may, for example, lead to drought, lost crops and shortages of drinking water in some regions and flooding in others.

However, government action and changes in technology can help to reduce the damage to the environment. The use of pollution permits, carbon taxes, subsidies and regulations can persuade people to switch to cleaner sources of energy. Changes in technology have made it possible to produce more energy cheaply from renewable sources, such as wind and solar power.

As societies become richer and basic needs are met, people may become more concerned about the environment in which they live and be willing and able to devote more resources to controlling pollution, recycling and disposing of waste in an environmentally friendly manner. However, this is not necessarily the case and depends on people's attitudes and political will.

Social limits to growth and development

As people become richer and their material needs are satisfied, some goods are not wanted for their basic worth but because they are believed to give people status. These products are known as **positional goods**. The satisfaction gained from positional goods depends on the fact that not everyone can have them. Positional goods could include a painting by a famous artist, a front seat at the theatre or a house in an attractive location. The supply of these products is very limited and they have a high income elasticity of demand. Therefore, as incomes rise, their relative price increases so that only the wealthy can afford them.

It has been argued that as societies become richer, some goods that were positional goods, such as fast cars, become less scarce and are not valued as much. The attempt to supply more positional goods can be harmful. For example, more cars and building houses in areas of natural beauty can damage the environment. As more people have a university degree, obtaining a degree does not guarantee a high-paid job and people may have to spend more time and money trying to get a higher degree to maintain their status.

People may work more hours as they try to earn the money needed to buy positional goods. Less time may be spent with family and friends, and people may have to move away to get a well-paid job. Even those who are able to buy positional goods are not really any better off and those who are unable to afford them feel worse off, even though they may be able to satisfy more of their basic needs and wants. For this reason, some people argue that continued economic growth does not increase human happiness and well-being.

Key term

Positional goods: goods and services that people value because of their limited supply and because they are believed to give people status.

▲ **Figure 8.1.6:** A luxury yacht, an example of a positional good

Progress questions

5 What does national income measure?

6 Why is it important to use real national income per head rather than nominal national income per head when assessing changes in living standards over time?

7 What is meant by a Purchasing Power Parity (PPP) exchange rate?

8 If GDP per capita at PPP exchange rates is used to compare the living standards of people in two countries, why might differences in the size of the subsistence sector in each country matter?

9 State **two** possible environmental limits to economic growth.

→ the stock of physical capital, including infrastructure

→ the flow of saving and investment

→ the Harrod-Domar model

→ access to financial services

→ the natural environment including climate and access to raw materials

→ demographic factors

→ education, skills and investment in human capital

→ health care and access to services to meet basic needs, for example clean water and housing

→ inequalities in income, wealth and opportunity

→ the inequality and environmental Kuznets curves and associated critiques

→ primary product dependency and fluctuations in commodity prices

→ the Prebisch-Singer hypothesis and associated critiques

→ the importance of foreign trade

→ public and private sector debt

→ industrialisation and urbanisation

→ the rule of law, property rights, good governance, corruption, political instability, war and conflict.

Economic development is a process that leads to a sustained improvement in the economic well-being and quality of life of people. This section will consider a variety of factors that influence the economic development of a country.

The stock of physical capital

Physical capital is the human-made factor of production and it includes, for example, tools, machines, vehicles, offices and factories. It also includes the country's infrastructure of roads, railways, power supplies, water and sewerage systems, communication networks, hospitals and schools. The stock of physical capital is the amount of this human-made factor of production that exists at a point in time.

Over time, the stock of capital depreciates due to wear and tear and obsolescence but can be increased by investment in new capital. A country's stock of physical capital increases when the value of new investment is greater than the depreciation of the capital stock.

MEDCs have a large stock of physical capital that helps their economies produce goods and services. An increase in the capital stock is likely to increase labour productivity enabling an improvement in material living standards. However, it is not just the volume of capital that matters, it is also the quality that affects what can be produced. Rapid technological change should increase the productivity of capital but may also mean that existing capital becomes obsolete more quickly.

Reliable road and rail networks allow goods to be transported more quickly and at a lower cost. They also allow people to move around more easily, increasing labour mobility and reducing unemployment.

Hospitals and schools help to improve the quality of people's lives as well as contributing to increases in productivity. Clean water and sewerage systems, improve people's health and well-being.

An increase in a country's capital stock increases economic growth and can support sustainable development. Economic growth does not necessarily lead to economic development but poor LEDCs are unlikely to develop without economic growth. The impact on economic growth can be illustrated by a rightward shift in the LRAS curve or a rightward shift in the country's production possibility boundary (PPB), as shown in Figure 8.2.1, where the PPB shifts from XX to YY.

However, some increases in the capital stock may damage the environment, for example coal-fired power stations pollute the atmosphere and contribute to global warming. Developments in technology have meant that more electricity is being produced from clean, renewable energy sources. In recent years, the cost of generating electricity from these sources has fallen significantly and is likely to continue to do so. Building roads supports an increase in the number of cars and the emission of greenhouse gases but in the future, electric vehicles are likely to replace those that use petrol and diesel.

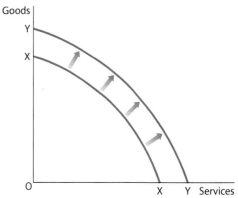

▲ **Figure 8.2.1**: An increase in the capital stock shifts the PPB to the right

The flow of saving and investment

A low level of domestic savings by households and firms can mean that there is a lack of funds to finance investment. In many poor LEDCs the savings ratio and the level of saving are low. When people are poor, they need to consume most, if not all, of their income and hence the savings ratio is low. Low incomes and a low savings ratio mean that the total amount saved is also low. Financial markets in LEDCs are not well developed, making it more difficult for people to save. This is another reason why there is a **savings gap** in many LEDCs. Low savings, and therefore investment, can result in low rates of economic growth and development, but low rates of economic growth also lead to low levels of domestic saving, as illustrated in Figure 8.2.2. Since incomes, savings, investment and economic growth depend on each other, it can make it difficult for poor LEDCs to grow and develop.

In a closed economy without a government sector, savings (S) must equal investment (I). Household income, which comes from production (output = income), can be either consumed or saved, therefore Y = C + S. An economy can produce either consumer or capital goods (investment), therefore Y = C + I. Therefore S must equal I. In poor economies, where people need to consume most of what is produced to survive, the production of capital goods is inevitably low. Freeing resources to produce capital goods means that people must save part of their income.

Firms can also invest some of their retained profits. Retained profits are a form of saving. However, in many LEDCs profits are not high and foreign firms located in LEDCs may send their

> **Key term**
>
> **Savings gap**: when domestic savings are unable to provide the funds required to finance the investment an economy needs.

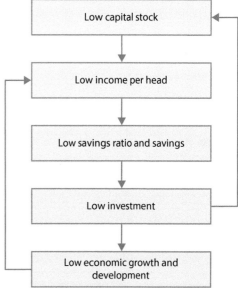

▲ **Figure 8.2.2**: How incomes, savings, investment and growth depend on each other

profits abroad. Low levels of household savings can be added to by the government raising taxes to pay for public sector investment. However, the ability of governments to raise taxes in LEDCs is also limited.

The Harrod-Domar model

The **Harrod-Domar model** of economic growth was developed independently by Sir Roy Harrod in 1939 and Evsey Domar in 1946. The model explains economic growth in terms of savings, investment and the productivity of capital.

The model suggests that economic growth depends on the value of savings and the marginal capital-output ratio (MCOR). An increase in savings allows more investment and the effect of investment on the growth of the economy depends on the MCOR. The more output that is produced from a given increase in the capital stock (net investment), the greater the effect on output and so, economic growth. In the basic Harrod-Domar model, the equilibrium rate of economic growth (g), also known as the warranted rate of economic growth, is given by the following equation:

$$g = \frac{s}{k} \quad \text{where} \quad \begin{array}{l} s = \text{the savings ratio } (S \div Y) \\ k = \text{the marginal capital-output ratio}(\Delta K \div \Delta Y) \end{array}$$

The equation indicates that an increase in the savings ratio and/or a fall in the MCOR will increase a country's equilibrium rate of economic growth. The increase in the savings ratio should lead to more investment and a fall in the MCOR means that more output is produced from a given increase in net investment.

This simple model assumes that savings leads to an increase in net investment, but some of the investment is required to replace that part of the existing capital stock that has depreciated. Therefore, the equation above overestimates the equilibrium growth rate. Even so, the overall conclusion of the model is that an increase in savings or an increase in the productivity of capital will increase a country's equilibrium growth rate.

In some versions of the model it is also assumed that the capital-output ratio is constant and so, the MCOR = the capital-output ratio = k.

The Harrod-Domar model suggests that LEDCs with low rates of economic growth should try to increase the savings ratio. This should create a positive cycle where more saving leads to more investment, an increase in national income and more saving.

If the savings ratio equals 0.2 and the MCOR is 4, then the equilibrium growth rate is $s \div k = 0.2 \div 4 = 0.05$ or 5% per annum.

If a country wishes to achieve a growth rate of 6% per annum and its MCOR = 3, then the savings ratio it needs can be calculated as follows:

$$0.06 = s \div 3$$
$$s = 0.06 \times 3 = \underline{0.18}$$

Key term

Harrod-Domar model: an economic model that suggests that the rate of economic growth depends on the savings ratio and the marginal capital-output ratio.

Link

The savings ratio and the marginal capital-output ratio were explained in 7.3 "Determinants of aggregate demand" in the AS book.

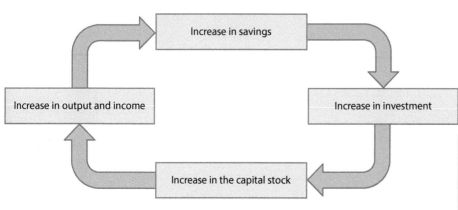

▲ **Figure 8.2.3**: How an increase in the savings ratio can create a positive cycle

As shown in Figure 8.2.3, an increase in savings can lead to more investment and a rise in national income, resulting in more savings. This positive cycle increases the rate of economic growth. However, some LEDCs find it very hard to increase savings when many people are struggling to satisfy their basic needs and undeveloped financial markets make it difficult for people to save.

The Harrod-Domar model provides an explanation of some factors that influence a country's growth rate, but it has some limitations, including:

- it does not take into account that some investment is needed to replace worn-out and obsolete capital

- it assumes that all savings are used to finance investment, but, particularly in an LEDC with undeveloped financial markets, this may not happen

- many LEDCs have limited ability to produce capital goods and may have to rely on imports. Some LEDCs may not have the foreign currency needed to pay for imports of capital goods as well as the other foreign goods and services they need

- it ignores the importance of human capital, the skills and abilities of the labour force, in the development process

- it does not take into account that domestic savings are not the only source of finance for investment. For example, countries may borrow from abroad, some investment is paid for by foreign aid, transnational corporations (TNCs) may invest in the economy (FDI) and public sector investment may be paid for by taxation

- it does not explain the role of technological progress in helping to generate economic growth.

It is also important to remember that the model focuses on what determines economic growth and not economic development.

Access to financial services

Financial institutions provide a variety of services that help support the growth and development of an economy. Financial markets in many LEDCs are undeveloped and this can restrict their growth. Financial institutions such as commercial banks accept deposits and lend these funds to households and firms who can make use of those funds. They encourage people to save and channel savings to firms and others who wish to invest, supporting the growth of the economy. Capital markets can help firms raise finance by issuing shares and corporate bonds. Governments can also borrow more easily by selling bonds to finance spending on infrastructure.

Commercial banks provide a variety of secure and efficient means of payment which reduce the cost of exchanging goods and services, making specialisation worthwhile. Specialisation usually leads to increases in productivity and hence the growth of the economy. Without an efficient means of payment, the cost of exchanging goods and services is likely to limit the degree of specialisation in the economy.

Financial institutions that provide insurance enable firms to protect themselves against risks such as theft, fire and flood damage, allowing them to focus on their main business.

In recent years, the increased use of mobile phones in many LEDCs has allowed individuals and small businesses to access a range of financial services without having a bank account. For example, M-Pesa is a mobile phone-based service that operates in a number of African countries and elsewhere. It provides banking services for people who do not have a bank account, these services include depositing and withdrawing money, paying bills and transferring money to other users of the service.

> **Link**
>
> The role of financial markets was explained in 7.3 "Financial markets".

The natural environment including climate and access to raw materials

Location, access to raw materials and climate can affect the ease with which a country is able to grow and develop. Geographical factors can affect economic development through their impact on the productivity of agriculture, transport costs, the chances of natural disasters and disease. Many of the world's poorest countries are in the tropics where it is hot, the land is less fertile and infectious diseases affect people's health. Most of the world's MEDCs are in temperate zones.

Climate

The climate in some countries means that it is more difficult to get enough food to eat and people have to work much harder to provide for their basic needs. In Europe and North America there are large areas of fertile land and sufficient rain to grow crops. In parts of Africa, land and temperature are less suitable for agriculture, and rainfall is less reliable. Agricultural productivity affects income levels and also the density of the population. Where local markets are small, the opportunities for businesses to grow and expand are limited.

Natural disasters

Some countries are more likely to be affected by natural disasters such as floods, droughts and earthquakes. For example, in Bangladesh, in the monsoon season, flooding may damage the country's infrastructure and destroy crops. Livestock and houses are washed away. Bangladesh also suffers from cyclones and earthquakes which mean that scarce resources have to be used to replace those parts of the capital stock that have been damaged. Roads, railways, bridges and houses have to be repaired or rebuilt and meanwhile, economic activity is interrupted.

Raw materials

The available stock of raw materials can also affect a country's growth and development. For example, countries such as Saudi Arabia and Kuwait have benefited from large supplies of oil. In the 18th century, the Industrial Revolution in Britain was helped by the country having supplies of coal and iron ore. Renewable resources such as wood, fish and fresh water can also be important. While some LEDCs have plenty of natural resources, others do not. Natural resources do not determine a country's rate of growth but can affect it.

Location

A country's location and its ability to transport goods at low cost can affect economic growth and development. The 18th-century British economist, Adam Smith, believed that economic growth depends on specialisation and that specialisation depends on the size of the market and the ability to trade. Transporting goods by sea is relatively cheap. Countries that do not have access to the sea are at a disadvantage. Many of the most developed regions and cities in the world are located near the coast, for example, Hong Kong, London, New York, Shanghai and Singapore. The ease with which goods can be transported within a country is also important.

Demographic factors

The size of a country's population, the rate at which it is growing, and the age structure of the population can affect the ability of a country to grow and develop.

Thomas Malthus

Malthus was an English economist who developed one of the earliest and best-known theories of the impact of population growth on living standards. Malthus believed that a country's population grows more rapidly than its ability to increase the production of food. He believed that population grows exponentially but the growth in food supplies and other basic needs is linear. An increase in the supply of food and other basic needs would lead families to have more children but this would cause living standards to fall because the supply of food and other basic needs could not grow fast enough. He believed that, as a result, population growth would be limited by hunger and disease. This is known as the Malthusian trap.

Figure 8.2.4 shows that when the population grows to a point where there is not enough food to keep people sufficiently well fed, hunger and disease cause the population to decline. This is known as the Malthusian catastrophe.

The rapid improvement in living standards in the MEDCs proved Malthus wrong, but his theories may be relevant to the problems faced by some poor LEDCs. Some people also believe that the continuing rapid growth in the size of the world's population is not sustainable and that a Malthusian catastrophe is possible.

Key terms

Age structure of the population: the distribution of the population among different age groups.

Malthusian trap: a theory that population growth is faster than the growth in the supply of food, leading to a situation where there is not enough food to feed the population.

Malthusian catastrophe: when food supplies are not sufficient to feed the population, causing hunger, disease and a fall in the size of the population.

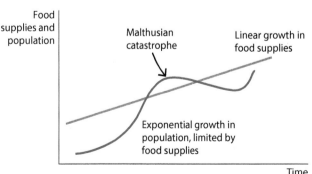

▲ **Figure 8.2.4**: The Malthusian trap

Malthus underestimated the ability of the MEDCs to accumulate capital and the improvements in technology that have sustained economic growth. For example, agricultural production has increased more rapidly than the size of the world's population. Also, in most MEDCs population growth has slowed as living standards have improved.

Demographic transition

The demographic transition model shows how the population of a country changes over time as it develops. The original model, developed in the 1920s, identifies four stages of transition but more recently a fifth stage has been added.

The first stage relates to pre-industrial societies that have high **birth rates** and high **death rates**. In this stage, population growth is slow and fluctuates.

In the second stage, improvements in health care, sanitation and living standards cause the death rate to fall and the population to grow rapidly.

In the third stage, birth rates start to fall but the **natural increase** in the population is still high. The birth rate may fall due to an increase in the availability of contraception and because, as infant mortality rates fall, families decide to limit the number of children they have. It becomes normal for people to have smaller families.

In the fourth stage, birth rates fall and are similar to death rates, and population growth is slow. There are many explanations for the falling birth rates, including more widespread use of contraception and the growing independence and status of women. More women choose to follow a career before having children.

Most LEDCs, but not all, are in second and third stages and most MEDCs are in the fourth stage. However, some MEDCs are expected to enter a fifth stage where their population declines due to people having children later in life and having smaller families. As the birth rate falls below the death rate, the population falls and the average age increases.

The model suggests that as living standards improve, the rate of increase in the world's population should eventually fall but it is not certain that this will happen. For example, in some countries, the position of women in society has not changed very much and birth rates have not fallen as much as elsewhere.

▼ **Table 8.2.1**: Estimated birth rates and death rates for a selection of countries

Country	Birth rate (2020)	Death rate (2021)
Afghanistan	36.7	12.6
Lesotho	23.2	15.1
Finland	10.5	10.3
Switzerland	10.5	9.9
Japan	7.3	10.2

Source: Death rate – The CIA World Factbook (cia.gov); Birth rate – The CIA World Factbook (cia.gov), accessed 21 January 2021

In Table 8.2.1, it can be seen that the birth rates for the two LEDCs, Afghanistan and Lesotho, are significantly higher than the death rates and so the natural increase in the population is high. The birth rates in Finland and Switzerland, two MEDCs, are slightly higher than the death rates and so the natural increase in the population is low. In Japan, another MEDC, the death rate is higher than the birth rate, the population is falling and ageing.

Population size and its rate of growth

As the population grows, there are more workers available to produce goods and services but there are also more people to feed and consume the goods and services produced.

The growth in the size of a country's population depends on birth rates, death rates and net migration. For example, if the birth rate is 27 per thousand per annum and the death rate is 15 per thousand per annum, the natural increase in the population is 12 per thousand per annum. This is a natural growth rate of 1.2% per annum. However, net migration also has to be taken into account when calculating the rate at which a country's population is changing.

The effect of an increase in the size of a country's population on economic development depends on the rate at which it is growing and the supply of other factors of production, including fertile land, the stock of capital and changes in technology. Unless investment increases significantly, rapid population growth will reduce the capital per worker, reducing labour productivity. If the growth in the population is greater than the growth in real national income, real national income per head will fall and living standards will also fall. Rapid population growth may also harm the natural environment as the increase in production and consumption cause negative externalities.

However, provided people are able to find employment, a growing population will increase the demand for goods and services. A growing market is good for business, it should encourage investment and allow firms to benefit from economies of scale. Increases in the capital stock lead to improvements in productivity and living standards. Increasing populations supported the growth of many MEDCs and some are concerned that a low birth rate may lead to a fall in the population size.

The age structure of the population

Population growth and its age structure are not independent of each other. Rapid population growth in many LEDCs is caused by high birth rates and falling death rates. As a result, the young-age dependent group and the old-age dependent groups grow more rapidly than the working age group. There is an increase in the **dependency ratio** meaning that, on average, each worker has to provide for more people. In this situation, a significant increase in labour productivity is needed to prevent average living standards falling. An increase in the size of the young age group means that more resources are devoted to educating and supporting young people, leaving fewer funds available to invest in developing the country's infrastructure. The government may also have to provide more support for the older age groups too.

When the population is growing rapidly and a high percentage of the population are in the young-age dependent group, it may be hard for

Key term

Demographic dividend: when the number of people in the workforce is growing relative to the number of people in the dependent age groups.

Progress questions

6 Identify **two** ways in which a financial markets can help any economy to grow.

7 Identify **two** ways in which a country's climate may affect its economic development.

8 Define "birth rate".

9 Assuming there is no net migration, calculate the rate of increase in a country's population if its birth rate is 22 and its death rate is 7.

10 State **two** reasons why a growing population may be good for an economy.

the economy to create enough jobs for the large number of young people who are entering the labour force. This could lead to rising unemployment and underemployment. In rural areas, there may not be enough work on farms to keep people employed throughout the year. Some workers may only be able to find part-time work. However, in the long run, there may be a demographic dividend. As young people reach working age, the working population may increase relative to the dependent population. This is most likely to happen when the country's birth rate starts to fall and more young people are entering the labour force than are being born. Also, young people may be more willing to adapt to change and are often more occupationally and geographically mobile than older people.

In many MEDCs, the population is growing slowly and the population is ageing. The old-age dependent sector is increasing, meaning that fewer workers have to provide for more older people. Governments have to spend more on pensions and health care and this leads to less government spending on other goods and services or to higher taxes. More people in MEDCs are choosing to work beyond the normal retirement age, often part time.

Education, skills and investment in human capital

Human capital is the knowledge, skills, abilities and experience of the population. Human capital is affected by the health of people. Poor health may mean that people are unable to work and is likely to reduce their efficiency when at work.

An increase in the stock of human capital should increase labour productivity and hence, economic growth. The stock of human capital is increased by education and training. It is also affected by the learning that takes place when people are working. Education should lead to improvements in productivity but that is not the only reason why it is important for economic development. Education can help people lead more interesting and satisfying lives. It also helps to ensure that growth and development are sustainable.

Skilled workers are needed to operate some machines and use modern technologies. Human capital is also needed to enable people to carry out specialist jobs such as nursing, surveying, engineering and driving a lorry. Investment in human capital can lead to more businesses being set up and provide people with the ability to manage firms. Skilled people involved in research and development contribute to the development of new technologies. Investment in human capital usually enables the individual to earn a higher wage as well as contributing to the growth and development of the economy.

Similar to investment in physical capital, investment in human capital involves giving up current consumption to increase the amount that can be produced and consumed in the future. People and other resources are needed to educate and train people. These resources could have been used to produce consumer goods and, in the short run, there is an opportunity cost.

Health care and access to services to meet basic needs

As explained earlier, people's health affects the stock of human capital and labour productivity. Labour productivity is also affected by people's ability to satisfy other basic needs such as having a suitable place to live. Providing good health care and satisfying people's basic needs is not only about increasing productivity and growth. An increase in people's ability to access to clean water, food, health care, education, a suitable place to live and other basic needs is an essential part of economic development. It affects people's quality of life and their well-being.

Inequalities in income, wealth and opportunity

If economic growth only benefits the rich and increases the degree of inequality, it is not economic development and is not likely to be sustainable. Sustainable development requires that the benefits of economic growth are shared by the majority of the population and reduce the number of people living in poverty. When the distribution of income is very unequal, the general population will have limited access to education and health care, and investment in human capital will be low. This is likely to restrict the rate of economic growth and development. In some countries, some groups may not have the same opportunities as others. For example, gender inequality in some societies means that many women do not have the chance to contribute to, and benefit from, the growth and development of the economy.

However, some degree of inequality is required to create the incentive for people to invest in their education and to develop their skills. It is also important that there is sufficient incentive for people to take risks and set up in business. Higher incomes for some people should lead to more saving and therefore investment. Rising incomes for a minority of the population may also result in a trickle-down effect, helping to create employment and incomes for others.

> **Link**
>
> The effects of inequality were explained in 5.1 "The distribution of income and wealth within an economy".

> **Key term**
>
> **Inequality Kuznets curve:** a diagram that illustrates an hypothesis of the relationship between economic growth and the degree of inequality in the distribution of income.

The inequality and environmental Kuznets curves

In the 1950s, the American economist Simon Kuznets suggested that there was a relationship between inequality and economic growth. This is the original Kuznets curve. The environmental Kuznets curve was proposed later, in the 1990s, and shows a relationship between the environment and economic growth. Both Kuznets' curves are controversial.

The inequality Kuznets curve

The original **inequality Kuznets curve** illustrates the hypothesis that as economies start to grow, the distribution of income becomes more unequal, but eventually, as growth continues and economies develop, the distribution of income will become more equal, as shown in Figure 8.2.5.

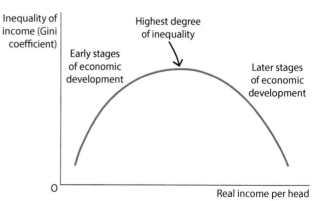

▲ **Figure 8.2.5**: The inequality Kuznets curve

In pre-industrial societies, or very poor LEDCs, almost everyone is poor and so the distribution of income is fairly equal. However, as economies start to grow, some people benefit and others do not. As a result, the degree of inequality increases significantly. In the early stages of growth, new opportunities for investment allow those with funds and entrepreneurial skills to make large amounts of money. Economic growth is often accompanied by people moving from rural areas to the towns in search of work and higher wages, but the increase in the supply of labour keeps wages for the majority low. However, as the economy develops, a middle class emerges and inequality falls. Higher incomes and higher taxes allow governments to spend more on merit goods, such as health and education, on social welfare and on public goods. Government spending and the use of progressive taxes helps to reduce inequality. Also, improved employment opportunities and investment in human capital increase the ability of most people to earn a reasonable income.

The hypothesis was originally developed after looking at data for a number of Western European countries and a few LEDCs. However, the East Asian economic miracle that began in the 1960s casts doubt on the universal application of the Kuznets hypothesis. Rapid economic growth in a number of countries, including Indonesia, Japan, Malaysia, Singapore, South Korea and Thailand, seems to have been accompanied by reductions in inequality. The experience of these countries suggests that growing inequality is not necessary for economic growth and that economic growth does not necessarily lead to increased inequality.

In 2013, the French economist Thomas Piketty in his book *Capital in the 21st Century*, pointed out that, as a result of the economic policies introduced in the last two decades of the 20th century, inequality in some developed economies increased as their economies continued to grow. He also noted that inequality in the distribution of capital/wealth is far greater, and likely to be more permanent, than the inequality in the distribution of income. Some believe that the inequality in the distribution of wealth and power is likely to preserve, and perhaps increase, the inequality in income in some countries.

The environmental Kuznets curve

The **environmental Kuznets curve (EKC)** illustrates the hypothesis that as economies develop, and real income per head increases, the damage to the environment will initially increase but, after a certain point, further increases in real income per head will lead to improvements to the environment. However, some people say that there is little, if any, evidence to support the view that economic growth will eventually lead to an improvement to the environment.

According to the environmental Kuznets curve shown in Figure 8.2.6, at low levels of real income per head, as real income per head increases, so does the damage to the environment. As an economy grows and develops, more natural resources and energy are used to produce goods and services. More waste is created from

> **Key term**
>
> **Environmental Kuznets curve (EKC):** a diagram that illustrates an hypothesis of the relationship between economic growth, or real income per head, and damage to the environment.

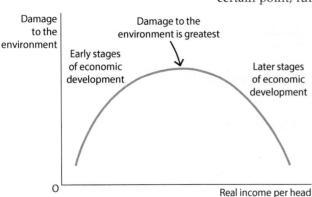

▲ **Figure 8.2.6**: The environmental Kuznets curve

the increase in both production and consumption. There are more greenhouse gas emissions and other dangerous substances enter the environment.

However, the EKC suggests that, at some point, further increases in real income per head may be associated with a reduction in environmental damage. As people become better off, they may be willing to pay more for products that are less damaging to the environment and may be willing to devote more scarce resources to improving the environment in which they live. More waste may be collected and recycled. Firms are also likely to respond to the demands of consumers for environment-friendly products. The change in people's preferences is also likely to be reflected in the willingness of their governments to pass laws and adopt other policies that require, or encourage, economic agents to reduce the damage they cause to the environment.

New technologies developed in high-income countries may also lead to more environment-friendly products and methods of production. For example, more energy may be generated from renewables rather than fossil fuels, goods may be made with less raw materials and they may be recycled more easily.

Some MEDCs have gone through a process of **deindustrialisation**. As economies develop, the output of services usually increases relative to the output of manufactured goods. Generally, supplying services uses fewer resources than supplying goods and is less damaging to the environment. This can help to reduce the environmental impact of growth in MEDCs. However, lower costs and strict environmental regulations in MEDCs have led to industrial production moving to rapidly growing LEDCs. MEDCs may be producing less waste and pollution but this is more than outweighed by the effects of **industrialisation** on the environment in some LEDCs. Also, some of the waste produced in MEDCs is shipped to other parts of the world. As a result, although rising real incomes per head in MEDCs may be associated with less damage to the environment in the local economy, the damage to the global environment may not have been reduced but shifted to a different part of the world.

The EKC suggests the economic growth will eventually cause a reduction in environmental damage, but some of the developments that have helped to reduce the impact of economic activity on the environment are not directly caused by economic growth. For example, many countries around the world are concerned about global warming and other sources of damage to the environment. The governments of these countries have adopted policies and taken action to try to protect the environment. New technologies that result in less polluting methods of production may be taken up by countries with relatively low incomes per head. Rising incomes may then lead to the reduction in some forms of environmental damage, particularly where its impact is noticeable in the local economy. However, economic growth usually means that more resources are used, there are more emissions and more waste.

Many people do not believe that rising global incomes will eventually automatically lead to a reduction the damage to environment. They argue that other measures are needed to deal with this global problem, for example government regulations and the use of new technologies

Key terms

Deindustrialisation: the absolute or relative decline in a country's, or a region's, manufacturing industry.

Industrialisation: when the manufacturing sector of an economy grows quickly and the relative size of the agricultural sector declines.

Progress questions

11 What is meant by "investment in human capital"?

12 Why should investment in human capital help to support economic development?

13 Describe the hypothesis illustrated by the original, inequality Kuznets curve.

14 State **two** reasons why economic growth may damage the environment.

that are less damaging for the environment. Some believe that countries should stop pursuing economic growth and focus on policies that are more closely linked to people's well-being, taking into account the environmental impact of economic activity.

Primary product dependency and fluctuations in commodity prices

Primary products are also known as commodities or raw materials. Coffee, iron, oil, rice, tea, tin and timber are just a few examples of primary products. Primary product industries include agriculture, forestry, fishing and mining. The economies and people of many LEDCs are very dependent on primary commodities. They account for a high proportion of the gross domestic product and exports of such countries.

According to the United Nations Conference on Trade and Development (UNCTAD), a country is considered to be dependent on exporting commodities (export-commodity-dependent) when more than 60% of the value of its total merchandise exports are commodities. The UNCTAD report *State of commodity dependence 2019* found that in the period 2013 to 2017, 102 out of 189 countries were export-commodity-dependent. Only 13% of developed countries were export-commodity-dependent, compared with 85% of the least developed countries.

Many LEDCs have a comparative advantage in primary products. They are an important source of employment, income, export earnings and tax revenue. Primary product industries may attract FDI and provide funds, which can be used to develop other parts of the economy if invested wisely. Foreign investment may help to provide the infrastructure that is needed to get the products to overseas markets. This might include new roads, railways and port facilities.

Link

The causes of fluctuations in commodity prices were explained in 2.5 "The determination of market prices" in the AS book.

However, overspecialisation in a few products can make an economy vulnerable to economic shocks. Since commodity prices are subject to large and often unpredictable price fluctuations, dependence on a few primary products can be very damaging for an economy.

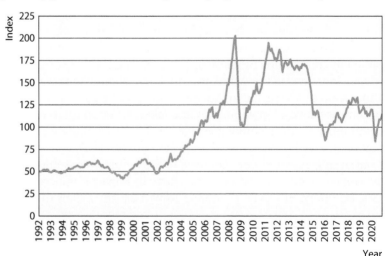

▲ **Figure 8.2.7**: All Commodity Price Index, 2016 = 100, January 1992 to November 2020

Source: The International Monetary Fund, January 2021; IMF Primary Commodity Prices

Figure 8.2.7 illustrates the fluctuations in the price of primary products between 1992 and 2020. As can be seen from the chart, prices were relatively stable between 1992 and 2002, but between 2002 and 2008, they rose rapidly. Since 2008, prices have been subject to large fluctuations. Over the whole period, primary commodity prices ranged from an index of 42.0 to an index of 202.8.

The demand for most primary products is inelastic and if the world market price falls, there is a less than proportionate increase in the quantity sold and export earnings fall. When a country is dependent on the sale of a few primary products, or perhaps only one, for the majority of its export revenue, this can affect its ability to obtain the foreign exchange it needs to import essential products from abroad and to **service debts** from overseas. The fall in export revenue reduces the demand for the currency and therefore the exchange rate, affecting living standards. Since producers have little, if any, control over the price of most primary products, it can be very difficult for governments to manage their economies and fulfil their development plans.

If the world market price of a primary commodity rises, there is likely to be an increase in export revenue. This can be beneficial in the short run, but the increase in the demand for the country's currency may also lead to an appreciating exchange rate. An appreciating exchange rate might damage other domestic firms and make it difficult for the LEDC to diversify its economy. However, the fluctuations in price and the uncertainty caused are usually the main problems for countries that depend on primary products for their export earnings.

The governments of countries that depend on a few primary commodities often obtain a high proportion of their tax revenues from the producers of these products. When the revenues and profits of the producers fall, so does the government's tax revenue. The government may have to cut its spending on infrastructure projects and other development programmes. Government borrowing and debt are also likely to increase.

In some countries, non-renewable resources such as gold, diamonds and oil, are owned by a few rich, powerful people and the general population may not obtain much benefit from the mining and sale of these resources. Sometimes, foreign direct investment (FDI) from transnational corporations is needed to enable these non-renewable resources to be mined. Often, the profits made are sent abroad and paid to overseas investors. Eventually, non-renewable resources will run out and unless the money made has been invested wisely, economic development may be limited.

The resource curse

It has been claimed that some LEDCs have suffered from a natural **resource curse**. Some countries that have an abundance of natural resources, such as Angola, the Democratic Republic of the Congo, Nigeria and Venezuela, have achieved relatively low rates of economic growth and development. Other countries with far fewer natural resources have benefited from high rates of growth and development, such as Japan and Singapore.

> **Key term**
>
> **Service debts:** the cash needed to repay the interest and principal due on money that has been borrowed.

> **Key term**
>
> **Resource curse:** when a country with plenty of natural resources finds it hard to achieve sustainable economic development.

Link

The Dutch disease was explained in 7.1 "The balance of payments".

Key term

Prebisch-Singer hypothesis: over time, the prices of primary commodities fall relative to the prices of manufactured goods.

Link

The terms of trade and the effects of changes in the terms of trade were explained in 6.2 "Trade".

Link

Income elasticity of demand was explained in 2.2 "Price, income and cross elasticities of demand" in the AS book.

Economists have identified a number of reasons why some countries may have suffered from a resource curse. Having plenty of natural resources can result in other sectors of the economy being ignored, sometimes corruption and political problems mean that the revenues earned are not used to benefit the majority of the population and fluctuating commodity prices harm development programmes. The discovery, mining and export of a valuable natural resource can lead to a significant appreciation in the country's exchange rate and damage other parts of the economy. This can be a serious problem for an LEDC when other industries are not very efficient or competitive. It also becomes difficult to set up new industries. This particular aspect of the resource curse is known as the Dutch disease. The term was first used in connection with the discovery of natural gas and oil in the North Sea in 1959, which led to an appreciation in the value of the Dutch currency, damaging the competitiveness of Dutch manufacturing firms.

The Prebisch-Singer hypothesis

The **Prebisch-Singer hypothesis** was proposed in the late 1940s by Raul Prebisch and Hans Singer. The hypothesis suggests that, over time, the prices of primary commodities fall relative to the prices of manufactured goods. Since many LEDCs export mainly primary commodities and import manufactured goods, in the long run, commodity-dependent LEDCs are likely to suffer from a deterioration in their terms of trade. This means that if the Prebisch-Singer hypothesis is correct, commodity-dependent LEDCs will have to export more commodities to obtain the same volume of imports.

One explanation for this change in the relative prices of commodities and manufactures is that the two types of product have different income elasticities of demand (YED). Most commodities, for example food products, are expected to have a YED of less than 1 and most manufactures are expected to have a YED of more than 1. Therefore, as incomes increase, the demand for manufactures will grow more quickly than the demand for commodities, causing the price of manufactures to rise more quickly than the price of commodities.

It has also been argued that, in the long run, technological change in MEDCs will mean that fewer raw materials will be needed to produce manufactured products, leading to a fall in demand for primary products. Also, if the price of a commodity rises rapidly, there is an incentive to develop a substitute, causing the price to fall again. The discovery of a new source of supply or new producers of agricultural products joining the market can also lead to the price of the commodities falling.

The Prebisch-Singer hypothesis was used to support the view that LEDCs should focus on developing the manufacturing sector of their economies. This would reduce their dependence on primary products. They would be able to substitute home-produced manufactures for foreign imports and increase their exports of manufactured goods. However, the growth of the manufacturing sectors in emerging economies and the increase in supply has helped to keep the price of some manufactured goods low.

Case study: Thailand and Togo

▲ **Figure 8.2.8**: Cotton is a commodity exported by Togo

expectancy was 60.7 years. Industry accounted for just over 20% of GDP and agriculture for around 28% of GDP. In Togo, much of the population depends on subsistence agriculture.

▼ **Table 8.2.2**: Selected economic indicators for Thailand and Togo in 2017

	Thailand	Togo
Value of merchandise exports (US$ millions)	235,000	982
Commodity exports (as a share of mechanise exports)	27%	72%
GDP per capita (constant 2010 US$)	6,180	655
HDI (value and world rank)	0.755 (81)	0.503 (162)
Gini index (in 2015)	36.0	43.1

Source: UNCTAD, *State of Commodity Dependence*, 2019

Thailand is a newly industrialised country (NIC) in Southeast Asia. According to the World Bank, in 2019, its population was nearly 70 million and the average life expectancy was 76.9 years. Industrial production accounted for almost 40% of GDP and agriculture, just over 8%. Exports were about 60% of the country's GDP.

Togo is in West Africa and is one of the poorest countries in the world. According to the World Bank, in 2019, its population was just over 8 million and the average life

1 What is meant by the phrase "much of the population depends on subsistence agriculture"?
2 Why is it likely that a significant fall in the world market price of commodities would affect Togo's terms of trade more than Thailand's terms of trade?
3 Explain why the data suggest that Thailand is a more developed country than Togo.

The evidence for the Prebisch-Singer hypothesis is mixed. Since the Second World War, there have been periods when the prices of manufactured goods have grown faster than the prices of commodities, but sometimes the opposite has been true. For example, in the first decade of the 21st century, commodity prices rose rapidly as a result of the growing demand from China and other emerging economies.

The importance of foreign trade

Some economists believe that LEDCs should adopt measures to protect themselves from foreign competition while they introduce policies to develop their economies. It is argued that without protectionism, it will be very difficult for domestic firms to survive in the face of competition from well-established overseas firms. Others believe that opening up markets to foreign trade is essential if an economy is to grow and develop. The extent to which an LEDC is able to benefit from foreign trade will depend on other aspects of its economy, for example the country's infrastructure and the skills and abilities of the labour force. It may also depend on whether it is able to attract FDI and its access to foreign markets.

The principle of comparative advantage shows that trade can benefit those who take part. If countries specialise in producing those goods and services in which they have a comparative advantage, total world output should increase which means it should be possible to make everyone better off. However, that depends on the terms of trade.

International trade also provides countries with a larger market for their products and provides the opportunity to exploit economies of scale. Exports increase aggregate demand and have a multiplier effect which can benefit other sectors of the economy. However, imports are a withdrawal from the circular flow of income and if domestic firms are not competitive, imports will increase and reduce economic activity.

Foreign trade allows countries to import goods and services that they cannot produce, or produce enough of, themselves. For example, an LEDC may benefit from importing capital goods from more developed economies. Many LEDCs also import fuel and other commodities that they cannot produce at home. Even if domestic firms can produce the product, they may only be able to do so at a high cost.

If an economy is open to foreign competition, it provides the incentive for domestic firms to be efficient. Firms will need to control their costs, keep prices competitive and produce the goods and services people want to buy. If domestic firms are protected from foreign competition, they are likely to become inefficient and may use their monopoly power to exploit consumers. Higher costs and higher prices reduce living standards.

Some LEDCs have much a much greater supply of a primary products than they can use themselves. For example, it is estimated that Chile produces over 30% of the world's copper and Peru produces much more tin than it can use. The money earned from exporting the surplus can be used to develop other sectors of the economy. However, sometimes the profits earned from **extractive industries** in LEDCs go to foreign transnational corporations and/or a few rich and powerful individuals within the country. Also, unless extractive industries are properly regulated, they may cause significant damage to the environment.

Exports provide foreign exchange that is needed to pay for essential imports and to fund development programmes. However, opening up an economy to foreign trade can lead to balance of payments problems and foreign exchange crises. If, for example, a country depends on the export of a few primary commodities and the prices of these commodities fall, it may experience a large balance of payments deficit and a significant depreciation in the value of its currency. As a result, foreign debts may increase and it may have to restrict imports.

Public and private sector debt

Types of borrowing

Public sector debt is money that has been borrowed by the government and is also known as **sovereign debt**. Private sector debt is money borrowed by households and firms. Economic agents often borrow to fund the purchase of capital assets that they cannot easily afford out of current income. For example, governments might borrow to pay for infrastructure projects, firms may borrow to build a new factory or buy machinery, and households might borrow to buy a house or a car. However, money borrowed is sometimes used by

---

Key term

Extractive industries: industries that obtain non-renewable raw materials, such as metals, oil and other minerals, by mining and quarrying. They are part of the primary sector of the economy.

Link

The principle of comparative advantage and the costs and benefits of international trade were explained in 6.2 "Trade".

Progress questions

15 If a country discovers and exports a primary commodity such as oil, explain why it may damage other sectors of the country's economy.

16 What is the Prebisch-Singer hypothesis?

17 What is meant by exports can have a multiplier effect?

Key term

Sovereign debt: the amount of money borrowed by a country's government.

governments, firms and households to finance day-to-day expenditure and not to acquire capital assets.

Debts can be internal debt or external. **Internal debt** is money borrowed from a domestic lender whereas **external debt** is money borrowed from a foreign lender. Debts can be short term or long term and can be raised in a variety of ways, for example by taking out a bank loan or by issuing bonds.

Countries borrow from international financial institutions such as the World Bank and the International Monetary Fund (IMF). When the World Bank or IMF lends to a country, the government has to agree to certain conditions that affect its economic policy. Many LEDCs borrow from MEDCs on favourable terms. A **bilateral loan** at a low rate of interest is a type of foreign aid. Countries also borrow from private sector financial institutions at market interest rates.

The type of borrowing can affect the cost of the loan and may be important when assessing the risks involved. For example, the borrower will need foreign currency to service external debt and may be at more risk of **default** if it has a large amount of debt which is due for repayment within a few months.

Benefits of borrowing
- Borrowing can help LEDCs fill the savings gap, allowing firms and the government to finance investment.
- Provided the return on the investment is greater than the interest on the loan, there will be a net benefit from the investment. The interest and the money borrowed, also known as the principal, can be paid back easily out of the money made on the investment. When interest rates are low, as they have been in recent years, there are usually plenty of investment projects that are worthwhile.
- Governments may need to borrow to finance expensive infrastructure projects, such as building hospitals and roads.
- Borrowing can help LEDCs to diversify their economy, for example to develop a new industry that reduces the country's dependence on primary products.
- It can help a country deal with emergencies, for example to pay for the resources needed to deal with a natural disaster or a pandemic.

Risks of borrowing
- If the money borrowed is in a foreign currency, for example US dollars, a fall in the country's exchange rate will make it more expensive to service the debt. It would probably need to export more to earn enough foreign currency to pay the interest and to repay the amount borrowed.
- An increase in interest rates could also mean that a country finds it difficult to service its debt. In the short run, if money was borrowed at a fixed rate of interest, this might not be a problem. However, when older loans mature, the country is likely to have to take out a new loan with higher repayments.
- Interest on government debt is part of government expenditure. If the cost of servicing the government's debt increases, unless taxes

Key terms

Internal debt: money borrowed from a domestic lender.

External debt: money borrowed from a foreign lender.

Bilateral loan: when a single lender provides a loan to a single borrower, for example one country lending to another country.

Default: when a borrower fails to make a loan repayment or to repay the debt, including interest, when it is due.

are increased, there will be less money available for the government to spend on other projects to support economic development.

- If a country is unable to service its debt, in the short run, it will have to reduce imports. In the long run, it will find it much more difficult to borrow money and, even if it is able to borrow, it will probably have to pay a much higher rate of interest.

- There is also the risk that the government will 'print money' so that it is able to continue to pay for public expenditure and to repay its internal debts. This is likely to cause high inflation and damage the economy in the long run. It may lead to a recession and high unemployment.

Assessing the risk of a country defaulting on its debt

When assessing the risk faced by an individual country, indicators that are often used include the following:

- total debt as a percentage of Gross National Income (GNI)
- external debt as a percentage of GNI
- debt servicing costs as a percentage of exports
- short-term debt as a percentage of total debt
- foreign exchange reserves as a percentage of external debt.

Case study: Argentina's debt crisis

▲ **Figure 8.2.9**: A cattle ranch in Argentina

Argentina is a country in South America with a population of almost 46 million. In 2020, Argentina defaulted on its debts for the ninth time in its history. Argentina owed over US$300 billion and failed to pay around US$500 million in interest that it owed to various holders of government bonds. The economy has been in recession since 2018 and the country's problems have been made worse by the Covid-19 pandemic. The government has agreed a deal with a group of private bondholders to change the terms of its debt and is also trying to change the terms of its US$44 billion loan with the IMF. The exchange rate fell from around

60 peso = 1 US dollar in January 2020 to 86 peso = 1 US dollar in January 2021.

▼ **Table 8.2.3**: Selected economic indicators for Argentina, 2015 and 2019

	2015	2019
GNI (US$ million)	582,648	432,302
Total external debt (US$ million)	177,185	279,306
Stock of external debt as % of annual exports	245	326
Debt servicing as a % of annual exports	25	47
Short-term debt as a % of external debt	34	24
Foreign currency reserves as a % of external debt	13	15

Source: World Bank, *International Debt Statistics 2021*; World Bank, *Debt Report 2021 Edition I*

1 What is meant by external debt?

2 What evidence is there in the extract to suggest that Argentina may have defaulted on its debts?

3 Why might the change in the value of the Argentine peso between January 2020 and January 2021 make it more difficult for Argentina to service its external debts?

4 To what extent do the data in Table 8.2.3 suggest that the ability of Argentina to pay its external debts got worse between 2015 and 2019?

A country's ability to service its external debt is affected by the total amount of external debt, the foreign exchange the country earns from exporting goods and services and its stock of foreign exchange reserves. The risk of default increases if a high proportion of its debt only has a short time until it has to be repaid.

Industrialisation and urbanisation

Industrialisation and urbanisation are often linked. Industrialisation encourages workers to move from rural areas in search of work and higher wages. The growth of the industrial sector benefits from urbanisation, but industrialisation is not the only cause of urbanisation in developing countries.

Industrialisation

In the 18th and 19th centuries, the Industrial Revolution changed Great Britain from an agricultural economy to an economy that was dominated by manufacturing. In the 19th and early 20th centuries, industrialisation was the main source of growth for most other European countries and the USA. Since the end of the Second World War, many other countries that have industrialised have experienced fast rates of economic growth. They include China, Indonesia, Japan, South Korea and Turkey. Some economists believe that industrialisation is an essential element in the development of poorer countries.

In the 1950s, the economist W Arthur Lewis argued that LEDCs were often dual economies. He observed that labour productivity in the large, traditional, mainly agricultural sector was low. It was dominated by subsistence production and many agricultural workers were underemployed. The modern, or industrial, sector was small but much more efficient. The Lewis model says that if workers transfer from the traditional sector into the modern sector, which usually involves people moving from rural areas into towns and cities, economic growth and development will result. Higher wages in the industrial sector should attract workers from the agricultural sector. Since many agriculture workers are underemployed, the marginal product of agricultural workers is zero. Therefore, the output of the agricultural sector is not affected by people transferring from farms to factories. Provided firms are able to employ the migrant workers, higher labour productivity in the manufacturing sector means that the total output of the economy will increase. However, for this to happen, there has to be sufficient investment in the industrial sector to create jobs for the migrant workers and the workers must have the right skills.

There are several reasons why productivity in the industrial sector is likely to be higher than in agriculture. The industrial sector generally provides more opportunities for capital investment and for economies of scale. Also, technological progress has meant that, over time, productivity in manufacturing has increased. Manufacturing may also create positive externalities that benefit other firms and sectors of the economy. For example, the benefits of technological progress and investment in human capital can spread from one firm to others.

Industrialisation enables a country to increase its exports and replace some imports by home-produced goods. This allows the country to

> **Key term**
>
> **Urbanisation:** when the proportion of a country's population living in towns and cities is increasing.

> **Key terms**
>
> **Dual economies:** economies with two sectors, a traditional agricultural sector and a modern, more productive, industrial sector.
>
> **Migrant workers:** people who move from one region, or country, to another to try to find a job.

obtain the foreign exchange to buy the essential imports it needs to support its development. Industrialisation also creates jobs for people. Wages in LEDCs are lower than in MEDCs. This gives LEDCs a comparative advantage in **labour-intensive** manufacturing, such as producing textiles, creating employment for people who might otherwise be unemployed.

However, industrialisation is not necessarily the best approach for all LEDCs. As more countries produce labour-intensive manufactures, their price falls and the benefits to countries producing these goods is reduced. Investing to increase productivity in agriculture can be a better option and bring significant benefits by reducing poverty in rural areas. India has benefited from the rapid growth of its service sector and is a major exporter of information technology and business services.

Urbanisation

At present, around half the world's population live in towns and cities and it is forecast that by 2050, about two-thirds will live in urban areas. Urbanisation can bring substantial benefits but many people in the cities in poorer countries live in shanty towns and slums. In slums and shanty towns, the quality of housing is poor and there is a lack of basic services such as clean drinking water and electricity. People move from rural to urban areas to try to improve their standard of living. Many are successful but others are unable to find work and are trapped in poverty.

Urbanisation can lead to **economies of agglomeration**, helping to increase the growth of the economy and support economic development. There are various advantages when firms and people are located in the same area. The growth of towns and cities increases the size of the market providing the opportunity for greater specialisation and economies of scale. It is easier for firms to find workers and for workers to find jobs. Workers develop the skills that are required by the firms located in the area. Specialist firms set up to supply the parts needed by the major enterprises located in the area. Contacts between different firms and between workers can lead to the sharing of knowledge and innovation. As a result, productivity, efficiency and competitiveness should improve.

The concentration of firms in a local area also makes it economic for the government to provide the infrastructure required. However, urbanisation can lead to traffic problems, poor air quality and other forms of pollution. These increase firms' costs and reduce people's quality of life.

▲ **Figure 8.2.10:** The rush hour in Jakarta

The rule of law, property rights, good governance, corruption, political instability, war and conflict

The growth and development of an economy is not only affected by economic factors. The country's institutions, the rule of law and political factors have a major impact on business and people's lives.

The rule of law and property rights

Clearly defined property rights and the ability to enforce contracts are necessary for markets to work. The rule of law provides a means of resolving disagreements. In most cases, economic agents sort out problems themselves but an effective legal system is needed to deal with disagreements that cannot be resolved. If businesses and individuals believe that there is a significant risk that people will not pay for goods and services, trade and the growth of the economy will be restricted.

Transnational corporations are unlikely to invest in a country where property rights are not protected and, for example, there is a risk that their assets might be taken over by the state. Similarly, if economic agents are not confident that contracts can be enforced, foreign firms are unlikely to do business in the country.

Laws help to prevent crimes of violence and protect people's rights. Environmental laws can make sure that natural resources are extracted in a sustainable manner and the damage to local communities is minimised. They can also help to ensure that the benefits are shared fairly. The rule of law can contribute to economic development by protecting people's quality of life.

Good governance

If a country is governed well, it will help to support economic development. Governance is concerned with the quality of management by political leaders and public officials. Good governance involves creating an environment in which businesses can flourish but also implementing policies that deal effectively with market failures. It is concerned with the ability of the state to invest in projects that make good use of the money raised through taxation and to bring about changes that improve people's well-being.

Corruption

Corruption is not only morally wrong but it is also likely to harm economic development. It often means that contracts are awarded to friends or family or to those who pay the biggest bribes, and not to the most competitive firms. If bribes are paid, it also increases the costs of the firm that is awarded the contract. Corruption in government means that spending on public sector projects is higher than it needs to be and, as a result, taxes are higher too. Corruption benefits a few people in positions of power and is likely to increase inequality.

Political instability, war and conflict

A country suffers from political instability when governments often collapse and the country's political system does not provide for a well-ordered transfer of power. A change in government brought about by regular elections does not indicate an unstable political system. Political instability is sometimes caused by conflict and by disagreements between groups of people with very different interests and opinions.

The collapse of a government usually leads to a change in economic policy and creates uncertainty. This is likely to reduce investment and economic growth. If political instability leads to war and conflict, it can prevent a country from developing. Several countries in Africa have suffered in this way. For example, the Democratic Republic of Congo has experienced a number of conflicts since it gained independence from Belgium in 1960 and remains one of the poorest countries in the world, despite being rich in natural resources.

Link

Property rights were explained in 5.3 "Positive and negative externalities in consumption and production" in the AS book.

Key term

Governance: the quality of management by political leaders and public officials.

Key term

Political instability: when governments often collapse and the political system does not provide for a well-ordered transfer of power.

Progress questions

18 Explain how external borrowing can benefit a country that has a savings gap.

19 What is meant by 'the marginal product of labour is zero'?

20 State **two** possible benefits of industrialisation for an LEDC.

21 Urbanisation in many LEDCs is increasing. State **two** possible disadvantages of increased urbanisation.

This section will develop your knowledge and understanding of:

→ demand-side and supply-side policies

→ the difference between market-based and interventionist strategies

→ how market-based strategies include: trade liberalisation, privatisation, deregulation, encouraging foreign direct investment (FDI), low taxes and minimising state involvement in the economy, floating exchange rates

→ how interventionist strategies include: protectionism, public ownership, industrial strategies, government spending on infrastructure, education and health care, managed exchange rates

→ the advantages and disadvantages of FDI

→ the use of buffer stocks to stabilise commodity prices

→ microfinance and fairtrade schemes

→ the types of foreign aid, including debt relief, and the role of foreign aid in helping development

→ the role of remittances

→ the promotion of tourism

→ the role of the World Bank, IMF and non-governmental organisations (NGOs) in promoting development.

Demand-side and supply-side policies

Demand-side policies

Demand-side policies are monetary and fiscal measures that are used to influence aggregate demand (AD). Expansionary demand-side policies are measures to increase AD. Contractionary demand-side policies are measures to reduce AD. Demand-side policies are mainly used to affect national output, employment and inflation but they may also be used to affect the balance of payments. Expansionary monetary policy measures include reducing interest rates, quantitative easing (QE), reducing reserve ratios and allowing the exchange rate to fall. Expansionary fiscal policy measures include increasing government spending, cutting taxes and increasing the government's budget deficit. To reduce AD, these measures would be reversed, for example the central bank could increase interest rates or the government could cut its spending and raise taxes.

Expansionary monetary and fiscal policy measures could be used if the government wants to increase national output and reduce cyclical unemployment. Contractionary monetary and fiscal policy measures could be used to reduce inflationary pressures. Demand-side policies are short-term measures that are used to try to keep the economy close to its normal capacity level of output. Expansionary demand-side policies are used to a close a negative output gap and contractionary demand-side policies are used to a close a positive output gap.

Figure 8.3.1 illustrates the effect of expansionary demand-side policies in eliminating a negative output gap and reducing demand-deficient, or cyclical, unemployment. Figure 8.3.2 illustrates the effect of contractionary demand-side policies in eliminating a positive output gap and reducing demand-pull inflationary pressures.

> **Key term**
>
> **Demand-side policies:** monetary and fiscal measures that are used to influence aggregate demand (AD).

> **Link**
>
> Demand-side policies were explained in 9.1 "Monetary policy" and 9.2 "Fiscal policy" in the AS book.

Although demand-side policies are essentially short-term policies that are used to affect how much of an economy's productive capacity is employed, they may also have some effect on the rate of growth of productive capacity. For example, measures to increase AD to close a negative output gap may increase confidence and have an accelerator effect on investment, which should increase the economy's normal capacity level of output. However, if AD is too high, the result is likely to be inflation which can reduce confidence and the growth of the economy.

Supply-side policies

Supply-side policies are measures designed to increase an economy's long-run rate of economic growth. If successful, supply-side policies will lead to supply-side improvements in the economy and should contribute to sustainable economic development.

Figure 8.3.3 shows an increase in an economy's productive capacity, as long-run aggregate supply shifts from $LRAS_1$ to $LRAS_2$. This means that more goods and service can be produced. Provided the population increases more slowly, people will be able to satisfy more of their needs and wants. However, as explained earlier, economic development also depends on the types of goods and service produced and not just the total volume of output. Reducing poverty and protecting the environment are also important if a country is to achieve a sustained improvement in people's well-being.

Both demand-side and supply-side policies have a role to play in helping an economy to develop. Without supply-side improvements, an LEDC will not be able to achieve a sustained improvement in living standards. Unless aggregate demand is managed to ensure that the economy is producing close to its productive capacity, factors of production will be unemployed, living standards will be lower and the degree of inequality will be higher than necessary. If aggregate demand is too high and inflation is allowed to get out of control, this is likely to reduce economic activity and prevent sustainable development. Managing aggregate demand is an important element in ensuring macroeconomic stability. A stable macroeconomic environment is important for encouraging investment and enterprise.

The difference between market-based and interventionist strategies

Market-based strategies to promote economic development are policies that rely on the operation of market forces to encourage the growth and development of the economy. Economists in favour of market-based strategies believe that government involvement in the economy is likely to prevent the economy working efficiently. They believe that government intervention should be kept to a minimum.

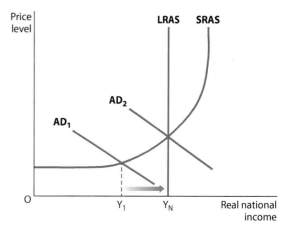

▲ **Figure 8.3.1**: Expansionary demand-side policy

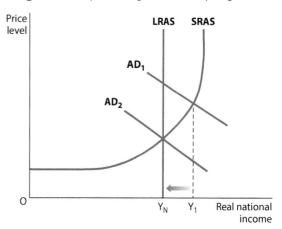

▲ **Figure 8.3.2**: Contractionary demand-side policy

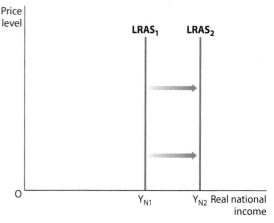

▲ **Figure 8.3.3**: Supply-side policies increase an economy's productive capacity

An interventionist strategy is one where the government provides some important goods and services and actively intervenes in other markets to affect the allocation of resources. Interventionists believe that markets often fail to allocate resources fairly or efficiently and that the government should play a major role in promoting the development of the economy. Some interventionists believe that economic development is most likely to be achieved in a command economy where the government decides on the allocation of resources and the distribution of income. Other interventionists accept that markets have an important role to play but that market failures mean significant government intervention is needed.

Most governments in LEDCs pursue a mixed strategy. In some parts of the economy they adopt a market-based approach but also intervene when they consider that government involvement in the economy is likely to support development. It is the extent to which the government intervenes that varies between countries. The balance between government involvement and market forces will be affected by, for example, the nature of the country's economy and the political views of the government.

Market-based strategies to promote economic development

Free-market (laissez-faire) economists believe that LEDCs are more likely to achieve an improvement in living standards if they allow market forces to determine the allocation of resources. They believe that economic growth can be increased if the government creates an environment in which economic agents are able to pursue their own self-interest, encouraged by financial incentives and competition. Market-based strategies include a number of elements.

Trade liberalisation

Reducing, or removing, restrictions on international trade allows countries to specialise in producing those products in which they have a comparative advantage, improving the allocation of resources. Specialisation and exporting allows domestic producers to benefit from economies of scale and earns the foreign currency that the country needs to pay for imports. Reducing tariffs and other restrictions on imports allows domestic residents to buy products more cheaply and foreign competition provides the incentive for domestic firms to improve their efficiency.

Privatisation

Free-market economists believe that state-owned enterprises (SOEs) are less efficient than privately owned firms. If SOEs make losses, they are usually subsidised by the government. If private sector enterprises make losses, they are likely to go bankrupt. Therefore, they have more incentive to be efficient, to produce products that satisfy people's needs and wants and to innovate. SOEs are often monopoly suppliers. The lack of competition and government interference can lead to inefficiency. The privatisation of SOEs is a market-based strategy to encourage a more efficient use of the nation's resources, increasing economic growth and living standards.

Link

Supply-side policies were explained in 9.3 "Supply-side policies" in the AS book.

Link

The principle of comparative advantage and the benefits of trade were explained in 6.2 "Trade".

Deregulation

Deregulation is the removal of rules that restrict competition. It means that firms are able to launch new products and enter new markets without being restricted by government-imposed rules and regulations. Deregulation can make it easier to set up a new business. Also, if government involvement in the day-to-day running of firms is reduced, it is likely to reduce the costs for existing firms and may lead to lower prices. Removing price controls is another example of deregulation. Price controls interfere with the functions of the price mechanism. Maximum price controls can lead to shortages and minimum price controls can lead to excess supply and goods being wasted.

However, deregulation does not always contribute to economic development. Removing maximum price controls on essential products may harm the poor and removing regulations intended to ensure safe working conditions and to protect the environment may reduce people's well-being.

Encouraging foreign direct investment (FDI)

Encouraging foreign direct investment (FDI) is another market-based strategy to promote economic development. Reducing government regulations and cutting taxes on firms' profits can lead to an increase in investment by foreign transnational corporations (TNCs). FDI increases an economy's productive capacity and should increase economic growth. Allowing foreign firms to invest in the economy can help to fill the savings gap since FDI is usually financed from company profits or other external sources.

Some LEDCs have set up special economic zones (SEZs) to encourage inward investment. Foreign firms locating in these zones are subject to fewer regulations and pay lower taxes than other firms. In some respects, the creation of SEZs is an interventionist approach since it may involve the government providing subsidies and infrastructure to support firms that invest in the zones. China and India are two of the largest economies in the world that have encouraged FDI by setting up SEZs. However, although FDI has a number of benefits for a country, there are also some disadvantages.

Low taxes and minimising state involvement in the economy

Free-market economists believe that the private sector is better at producing goods and services than the public sector. They accept that governments need to provide public goods, such as defence and street lighting, but consider that the private sector should provide most other goods and services. Reducing government regulation and government provision of goods and services means that public expenditure will be lower. Therefore, the government should be able to balance its budget with lower taxes.

Low rates of taxation on firms should provide the incentive to set up and expand businesses. It should also encourage FDI. Low rates of income tax should mean that people have the incentive to work, to work overtime, to develop their skills and to work hard to gain a more responsible, better-paid job.

Link

The case for and against privatisation and deregulation of markets was explained in 3.12 "Public ownership, privatisation, regulation and deregulation of markets".

Link

The advantages and disadvantages of FDI were explained later in this section.

Activity

Find out all you can about a special economic zone in your country. What do you consider to be the costs and benefits of creating a special economic zone? If your country's government has not created a special economic zone, find out all you can about special economic zones in the Philippines or Kenya.

Laissez-faire economists believe that minimising the state's involvement in the economy will lead to goods and services being provided more efficiently, allowing more to be produced. They also believe that the incentive effects of reducing rates of taxation will increase economic activity and economic growth.

Floating exchange rates

Floating exchange rates should mean that LEDCs can focus economic policy on improving the domestic economy without worrying about the value of the currency and the country's balance of payments position. Flexible exchange rates should help the economy adjust to both internal and external economic shocks, helping to maintain a more stable economy. If the country experiences a higher rate of inflation than other countries, its exchange rate will fall to restore competitiveness allowing economic growth to be maintained. A fixed exchange rate can become overvalued and in a globalised world economy, this can result in capital flight and a financial crisis which damages the domestic economy.

However, there are also problems with floating exchange rates. Floating exchange rates can be volatile and create uncertainty for businesses involved in exporting and importing goods and services. A floating exchange rate regime also requires the government to adopt a responsible macroeconomic policy. A floating exchange rate may allow the government to run a large budget deficit combined with an expansionary monetary policy, leading to a high, accelerating rate of inflation. A commitment to maintain a fixed exchange rate would make it less likely that such a policy could be adopted. Laissez-faire economists are generally in favour of floating exchange rates but they also recommend responsible fiscal and monetary policies.

Interventionist strategies to promote economic development

Interventionists believe that economic growth and development are more likely to be achieved if the government plays a major role in the economy. This might involve the state providing goods and services such as electricity, public transport, education and health care. The government may also intervene to regulate the activities of private sector enterprises and to invest in providing essential infrastructure. Intervention has also been used to promote the growth of industries that it is believed, with government assistance, will develop and be able to compete globally.

Protectionism

Protectionism is an interventionist policy that can be used to support a strategy of import substitution. Imposing restrictions on trade, such as tariffs, increases the price of imports and enables domestic firms to compete better in their home market with foreign firms. Consumers buy fewer imports and more home-produced goods which should create employment and reduce the amount of foreign currency the country needs.

> **Link**
>
> The advantages and disadvantage of different exchange rate systems were explained in 7.2 "Exchange rates".

Restrictions on imports can also be used to protect infant industries and support a strategy of industrialisation and diversification. Without restrictions on imports, the infant industry would not be able to compete with well-established foreign TNCs. Protecting an industry against overseas competitors is often complemented by other forms of government support designed to enable the industry to compete with foreign firms.

Export subsidies and other export promotion strategies, including maintaining a competitive exchange rate, can be used to help domestic manufacturers to grow and compete in world markets. The economic development of countries such as China, Japan and South Korea has been supported by policies to improve industrial competitiveness and encourage the growth of exports.

Public ownership and industrial strategies

Public ownership is when firms or other assets are owned by the government. Publicly owned enterprises are also known as state-owned enterprises (SOEs). In some countries, investment in SOEs is an important part of the government's policy for promoting economic growth and development.

An **industrial strategy** is an interventionist government policy to encourage the development and growth of a particular sector of the economy. It usually focuses on part or all of the manufacturing sector. The industrial policy of many LEDCs concentrates on developing a few industries that have been identified as having the potential to grow and become competitive in world markets.

The case for an industrial strategy in LEDCs is that market forces alone will not create the conditions needed for the industrial sector of the economy to develop, particular when there is well-established foreign competition. Without an industrial strategy, the economies of many LEDCs would have to depend on the production and export of primary products. An industrial strategy allows countries to diversify and transfer resources, including labour, into high productivity sectors that have the potential for rapid growth.

An industrial strategy includes a mixture of different elements and the exact nature of the strategy often varies between countries and/or between industries. An industrial strategy may involve: protectionist measures; subsidies, tax relief, government-funded training programmes; providing cheap loans to finance investment; attracting FDI; government spending on the infrastructure the industry needs; and government funding of research and development. Protectionist policies may be required to help the industry become established but may be relaxed when firms have had time to learn how to produce efficiently and have started to benefit from economies of scale. The setting up of SEZs in many countries around the world is an example of an industrial strategy. Both LEDCs and MEDCs use industrial policies to support particular sectors of their economies.

State-owned enterprises (SOEs) are an important part of the industrial strategy in some countries. SOEs can be used to supply key services, such as coal, steel, transport and electricity, that support

> **Key term**
>
> **Industrial strategy:** an interventionist government policy to encourage the development and growth of a particular sector of the economy, often manufacturing.

the development of private sector enterprises. They may also be used to produce the manufactures that the industrial strategy is attempting to encourage. State-controlled factories were important in China when the rapid growth in its manufacturing sector began in the early 1980s but many of these enterprises are now privately owned. However, SOEs remain important in many key sectors of the Chinese economy.

As LEDCs develop and grow, the nature of the industrial strategy may need to change. Often industrialisation begins with the growth of labour-intensive, low technology industries but to develop further, the country's industrial strategy may need to focus on developing more advanced manufacturing.

Industrial strategy has been successful in promoting the growth and development of a number of countries. For example, Malaysia has pursued a mix of import-substitution and export-orientated industrial strategies. The government has used protectionism but also a range of financial incentives. This has attracted considerable foreign investment. The government has encouraged links between foreign and domestic firms and this has led to positive externalities for the domestic economy, for example in terms of technology, the transfer of skills and management expertise.

However, the industrial policies of some other countries have been less successful. A criticism of industrial policy is that government failure may lead to taxpayers' money being wasted. Governments do not have the information to judge which sectors of the economy should be supported and they may be motivated by political considerations. Free-market economists believe that market forces will create the incentives needed to encourage the development of industries that have a chance of success and are more likely to ensure that resources are used efficiently.

Government spending on infrastructure

Spending on infrastructure contributes to the growth of a country's economy and to the well-being of its people. Infrastructure investment is needed in LEDCs to provide transport systems (roads, railways, ports and airports), power supplies, water and sanitation, telecommunication systems, hospitals, schools and housing. Infrastructure is important for business but it also affects the quality of people's lives. An efficient transport system reduces firms' costs. It reduces the cost of obtaining supplies and of sending products to market. Access to electricity, clean water and sanitation improves people's standard of living.

Some infrastructure projects are provided by the private sector, for example mobile phone networks, but others are provided mainly by governments, for example road and rail networks. Some types of infrastructure are quasi-public goods and are unlikely to be provided, or would be underprovided, by the private sector. This means that government spending is required to provide the infrastructure that the country needs. However, infrastructure projects are expensive and tax revenue is limited. LEDCs often have to find other forms of finance

> **Link**
>
> The causes of government failure were explained in 5.8 "Government failure" in the AS book.

to enable them to build the infrastructure they need to support their development.

Education and health care

Both education and health care are investment in human capital. They should increase labour productivity and the growth of the economy. They also directly increase the quality of people's lives. Investment in education and health care contributes to ensuring that development is sustainable.

Education and training increase the variety of tasks that people are able to perform, they make people more adaptable, increase labour mobility and help to reduce unemployment. Many firms need a skilled labour force, and the growth of the economy is likely to be restricted if firms are unable to hire people with the skills they need. Education and training can be provided by schools, colleges and firms. People also learn and develop their skills by doing a job. They learn from other people too.

Spending on health care should help to make the labour force more productive and reduce the time that people are unable to work. Poor health is a source of poverty and inequality. Children who suffer from poor health may not attend school, affecting their skills and how much they are able to earn when they join the labour force.

Education and health care are merit goods with positive externalities in consumption. They are likely to be underprovided without government support. Government spending on education and health care can make a significant contribution to the development of an economy. However, the cost of providing education and health care is high and many of the benefits occur in the future.

Managed exchange rates

A managed exchange rate is when a country's central bank intervenes in the foreign exchange market to influence the value of the currency. A managed exchange rate can support a country's industrial policy because the exchange rate affects the price of exports and imports. Maintaining the exchange rate at a low level can help to ensure that firms are competitive in their home and export markets. A competitive exchange rate supports a policy of export-led growth but also encourages import substitution. A low (undervalued) exchange rate benefits manufacturing because manufacturers produce **tradable goods**. Factors of production will be attracted into the high-productivity industrial sector of the economy which should increase economic growth. A low exchange rate is likely to attract FDI. It means the cost of investing in the economy is lower in terms of foreign currency and goods produced and exported from the economy will be more competitive. FDI will also support the growth of the economy, creating jobs and increasing people's incomes.

However, an undervalued exchange rate increases the cost of importing essential items and adds to inflationary pressures. If inflation increases, a fall in the exchange rate will be needed to

Link

Reasons why merit goods are likely to be underprovided without government intervention were explained in 5.4 "Merit and demerit goods" in the AS book.

Key term

Tradable goods: products that can be sold in a location that is different from where it was produced, for example in a different country.

restore competitiveness and keep the real exchange rate at the same level.

Keeping the exchange rate stable is also important because it helps to ensure that firms are able to predict the price they have to pay for imports and how much they receive for exports. This should increase investment since firms' profits will not be affected by unexpected changes in the exchange rate.

Maintaining a stable, competitive exchange rate requires intervention by the country's central bank and may mean that interest rates have to be kept low to reduce short-term capital inflows. Low interest rates can lead to high inflation. However, low interest rates may be avoided if the government is willing to allow its foreign exchange reserves to rise and to invest abroad, perhaps through a sovereign wealth fund.

A stable, competitive exchange rate can support the growth of an economy, but it will only help if the other conditions necessary for economic development are present. It is just one element of an interventionist development policy.

Case study: Special economic zones

A special economic zone (SEZ) is the term given to an area in a country that has been set up by the government to encourage more business, investment and exports. The objective is to increase the country's rate of economic growth. There are different types of zone but they usually offer incentives to business such as government subsidies and low or no taxes. Some domestic laws or regulations do not apply to firms located in the SEZs. They aim to attract foreign investment from transnational corporations (TNCs) and may be managed at state or local level. By 2019, there were over 5,000 SEZs in nearly 150 countries.

The first four SEZs in China were set up in 1980 as part of their market-based reforms. Since then, a variety of SEZs has been established. According to a World Bank article published in 2015, SEZs in China have created over 30 million jobs, contributed 22% of China's GDP, 45% of foreign direct investment and 60% of exports.

India set up its first Export Processing Zone (EPZ) to promote exports in 1965 and introduced its SEZ policy in 2000, based on the Chinese model. By early 2021, there were 265 SEZs in India. Sri Lanka's position off the southern tip of India makes it an ideal location for international trade and it has 12 EPZs with three more planned. These EPZs have helped to increase Sri Lanka's exports, particularly of clothing.

However, not all SEZs have been successful. In some zones, there have been claims that public money has been wasted and that there has been corruption. Expensive infrastructure may have been built but with limited success in attracting new firms to the area. Some countries have been affected by war and political problems, putting off TNCs from locating there.

1   What is meant by a "special economic zone (SEZ)"?
2   Why might an LEDC create special economic zones?
3   What are the disadvantages of creating special economic zones?

Advantages and disadvantages of foreign direct investment (FDI)

Foreign direct investment (FDI) is when a firm sets up, expands or buys a business in a different country. Transnational corporations (TNCs) invest abroad to expand their business and to increase profits. Reasons why TNCs invest in LEDCs include lower production costs, access to raw materials and the chance to enter a new and growing market. FDI can have many benefits for the country receiving the investment, but there can be disadvantages too.

Advantages of FDI for a developing economy include:

- **Savings gap** – foreign investment helps to fill the savings gap and expands the productive capacity of the economy.

- **Employment** – it creates jobs, and TNCs are likely to invest in human capital, improving the skills and abilities of the labour force. Many of the skills are likely to be transferable and will, in the long run, benefit other firms.

- **Multiplier effect** – the increase in investment, and the output produced by the firm, will have a positive multiplier effect, leading to a further increase in the country's national income.

- **Benefit local firms** – TNCs are likely to develop links with local firms. They may, for example, buy components from local suppliers or sell their products through local businesses. This will create jobs and is also likely to support local firms in improving their efficiency.

- **Technology** – there is likely to be a transfer of technology that will benefit the local economy and may lead to the development of new, local firms in related industries.

- **Skills and finance needed to extract natural resources** – TNCs can provide the finance and the skills that enable a country to extract primary products such as oil, natural gas, copper and other minerals. Without investment from a TNC, these natural resources, which can contribute to the growth and development of an LEDC, may be left in the ground.

- **Infrastructure** – it is likely to lead to increased investment in infrastructure. This might include, for example, transport and communication links. Some of the infrastructure might be paid for by the TNC and other economic agents will also benefit.

- **Exports** – TNCs are likely to export some of the goods produced and may also supply import substitutes. This will help the country's balance of payments and generate the foreign exchange needed to pay for the imports required to achieve the country's development plan.

- **Tax revenue** – FDI is also likely to lead to an increase in the government's tax revenue which can be used to pay for public and merit goods that help to support economic development and improve people's well-being.

Disadvantages of FDI for a developing economy include:

- **Loss of local firms** – investment by TNCs may mean that domestic firms are unable to compete, and some local firms may go out of business. FDI may also make it hard for new firms to

Progress questions

1 What is meant by "demand-side policies"?

2 Explain the difference between market-based and interventionist policies to promote economic development.

3 What is meant by "trade liberalisation"?

4 What is the main objective of an industrial strategy?

5 Why might a managed exchange rate support the growth of an economy?

Link

The importance of foreign direct investment in the global economy was explained in 6.1 "Globalisation".

become established affecting the ability of local people to develop entrepreneurial skills.

- **Footloose** – investment by TNCs is footloose (location can be changed easily) and if market conditions change, the firm may move to a different country, perhaps one with lower costs, leading to unemployment and a reduction in national income.
- **Cost to the government** – the government may have to provide subsidies and/or tax relief to attract FDI and this will mean that the government has less money to spend on other projects that contribute to the country's economic development. It may also have to relax regulations that protect people and the environment. The government may have to change other policies to attract and retain the investment, giving the TNC too much influence over the government.
- **Outflow of profits** – some or all of the profits made from the investment may be paid to people abroad and not invested in the local economy. This can lead to a continuing outflow of foreign exchange.
- **Exploitation** – FDI does not always create many jobs for local people and/or local workers may be exploited. They may be paid very low wages and the working conditions may be poor.
- **Environmental costs** – some FDI, for example when used to extract natural resources, may result in damage to the natural environment.

The use of buffer stocks to stabilise commodity prices

Many LEDCs depend on the production and export of primary products for a significant part of their national income, exports and tax revenue. As explained earlier, fluctuations in the price of primary commodities can harm the development of LEDCs. Although, it is impossible to prevent these fluctuations, buffer stock schemes may be able to reduce the extent to which prices change.

Buffer stock schemes usually set a ceiling price and a floor price. If the market price approaches the ceiling, the buffer stock will release the commodity onto the market, increasing the supply, with the aim of keeping the price below the ceiling. If the market price approaches the floor, the buffer stock will buy the commodity, increasing demand, with the aim of preventing the price falling below the floor.

Reducing the fluctuations in commodity prices should benefit producers and consumers but will also benefit an LEDC that is a major supplier of commodities. If prices are stable, the export revenue and tax revenue that results from the sale of commodities will be more stable. This makes it easier for the government to plan its development strategy. It will have a better idea of how much foreign currency is available to buy essential imports and how much tax revenue is available to finance public expenditure. Stable commodity prices will make it easier for a major commodity exporter to maintain a stable exchange rate, which should also help to support the country's development programme. Stable prices are also likely to lead to more investment by the industry that is producing the commodity, since profits are likely to be more stable and business failures caused by a sudden, expected fall in the price of the commodity are avoided.

Link

The use of buffer stocks to stabilise commodity prices was explained in 5.7 "Government intervention in markets" in the AS book.

Since the Second World War, there have been several international buffer stock schemes, but they have not survived. For example, the International Tin Agreement failed in 1985 and the International Natural Rubber Agreement failed in 1999. Although, a successful buffer stock scheme may benefit commodity producers, so far, the cost and difficulty of maintaining a buffer stock scheme has meant that they have been of limited benefit to LEDCs. Attempts by producers to use buffer stocks to keep prices high usually lead to new suppliers entering the market and/or to the development of substitutes.

The only significant international agreement aimed at reducing commodity price fluctuations that still exists is the Organization of the Petroleum Exporting Countries (OPEC). OPEC is not a buffer stock scheme, but it does attempt to manage the supply of oil on the market. However, even OPEC has had limited success in reducing fluctuations in the price of oil.

Microfinance and fairtrade schemes

Microfinance and fairtrade schemes are approaches to promoting economic development that are independent of governments.

Microfinance

Financial markets in LEDCs are underdeveloped and many people do not have access to the financial services that are available to people in MEDCs. They may be able to borrow from local money lenders, but the rate of interest will be very high. It has been estimated that in 2018 over 1.7 billion adults did not have access to formal financial services and in Sub-Saharan Africa, less than 30% of women had an account with a financial institution. It is a particular problem for those who live in rural areas. If people do not have access to financial services, it will harm the economic development of the country.

The original purpose of microfinance schemes was to provide low-value loans to potential entrepreneurs who wished to set up or develop a small business but were unable to obtain credit. Today, microfinance schemes also provide other financial services such as insurance, savings accounts and payment systems. Many also provide financial and business advice to their clients. Microfinance is a bottom-up approach to development rather than a top-down approach. It supports people's efforts in their communities rather than being provided for them by their government.

Muhammad Yunus is generally regarded as the person who started the modern microfinance movement. In 1976, he created the Grameen Bank (Bengali for "Village Bank") in Bangladesh to provide loans to small groups of people in rural areas. The group took joint responsibility for the loan and most loans have been paid back. The borrowers were very poor and were not required to provide any collateral. The bank has supported a variety of small enterprises in a number of different sectors of the economy. For example, in agriculture, loans have been used to buy seeds, fertilisers, equipment and livestock. In 2006, Muhammad Yunus and the Grameen Bank were jointly awarded the Nobel Peace Prize for their contribution to economic and social development. In 2017, the bank had over 9 million borrowers and 97% of them were women.

Key terms

Microfinance: providing financial services, such as small loans and insurance, to people who do not have access to formal financial institutions.

Collateral: an asset that is promised as security for a loan, which may have to be sold to settle the debt if the borrower is not able to pay back the loan.

Link

The role of financial markets was explained in 7.3 "Financial markets".

Activity

Find out all you can about the Grameen Bank.

> **Key term**
>
> **Crowdfunding**: raising money from a large number of people who each contribute a small amount, typically using the internet.

During the past 40 years, microfinance schemes have been established in most developing countries. At first, most microfinance schemes did not aim to make a profit but an increasing number of the schemes are now profit-seeking. There are many different providers of microfinance. They include microfinance companies such as BRAC International, international banks such as Citigroup and charities such as World Vision. In 2018, World Vision's microfinance subsidiary, VisionFund, provided loans to 1.1 million people located in Africa, Asia, Eastern Europe and Latin America. It also provides savings schemes and insurance services that help protect people when crops fail or there are natural disasters. BRAC International provides microfinance in many countries around the world including Myanmar, Sierra Leone, Rwanda, Tanzania and Uganda. **Crowdfunding** microfinance, that operates over the internet, has also grown in recent years. One of the first to use crowdfunding to raise money to provide microloans was KIVA, a not-for-profit organisation that was set up in San Francisco in 2005.

Benefits of microfinance include:

- helping poor people in rural areas, with no collateral, set up and expand businesses that allow them to support themselves and their families
- encouraging the growth of local businesses that create jobs for other people
- a lower rate of interest than would have to be paid to money lenders
- many schemes lend money to women who generally have less access to financial services than men and evidence suggests, are more likely to pay back the loan
- helping people to support themselves and escape from poverty
- encouraging people to save and protect them from the effects of natural disasters and other unexpected events.

While microfinance may have helped many people, the contribution it can make to a country's economic development is limited. For example, investment in human capital, government spending on infrastructure and an industrial strategy to diversify the economy are still needed to achieve a sustained improvement in people's well-being. Providing microloans can encourage some people to borrow money that they find difficult to pay back and some profit-seeking microfinance schemes charge high rates of interest. Some loans are used to buy consumer goods, and although they may benefit people, it does not contribute to the growth of the economy. Also, most institutions that provide microfinance are not regulated and some people have been treated unfairly.

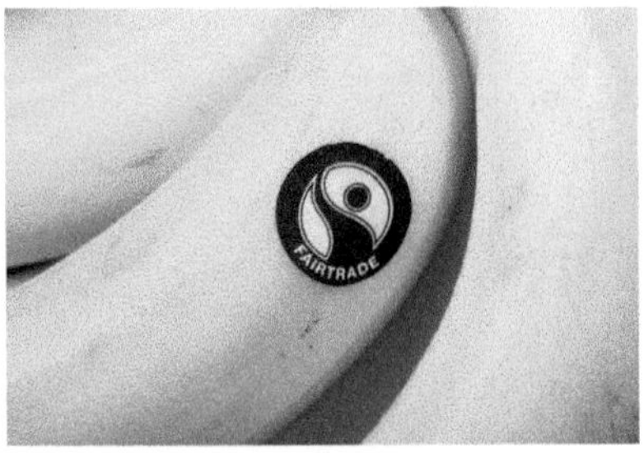

▲ **Figure 8.3.4**: The FAIRTRADE mark

> **Key term**
>
> **Fairtrade scheme**: helps producers obtain higher prices for their products while improving the conditions for workers and protecting the environment. The schemes also encourage consumers to buy fairtrade products.

Fairtrade schemes

The aims of a **fairtrade scheme** include helping producers in developing countries obtain higher prices for their products, improving conditions for workers and protecting the environment. The schemes cover mainly agricultural commodities such as bananas, cocoa, coffee, cotton, flowers, sugar and tea. There are several organisations involved in promoting fair trade and they are usually approved by an international federation such as the FLO (Fairtrade Labelling Organisation) International, usually known as Fairtrade International. Fairtrade International uses a FAIRTRADE mark to identify products that meet social, environmental and economic fair trade standards. The FAIRTRADE mark helps consumers recognise fairtrade products. It encourages people to buy them and so increases the demand for fairtrade products.

A large firm buying from many small suppliers can a have a significant influence over the price they pay. Fairtrade schemes can help to stop small farmers in LEDCs being exploited by large buyers of agricultural products with monopsony power. The abuse of monopsony power is a market failure that may be prevented by fairtrade schemes. Also, small farmers may not be aware of the market price of the commodity they are producing, and this may result in them selling their goods at a price that is below the market equilibrium price. Imperfect information is another example of a market failure that fairtrade schemes can help to prevent.

Fairtrade schemes can also offer farmers some protection against fluctuations in commodity prices. Buyers in fairtrade schemes usually agree to buy a certain amount of the product at a price that is above the market price when the contract is signed. However, if the market price rises above the agreed price, the higher price is normally paid.

Fairtrade schemes also aim to protect workers by ensuring that the working conditions are safe, a fair wage is paid, and that discrimination and the illegal use of child labour are prevented. Another important aspect of fairtrade schemes is that they encourage farmers to use environmentally friendly methods that protect the natural environment, for example they ban the use of harmful chemicals. The objective is to make sure that farming methods are environmentally sustainable.

Fairtrade schemes contribute to economic development by reducing inequality and protecting the environment. Increasing and stabilising farmers' incomes may also lead to more investment in agriculture and help to increase economic growth. Economic growth may also be promoted by education which leads to better and more efficient methods of production.

However, fairtrade schemes may harm farmers who are not in the scheme. They may find it more difficult to sell their produce and if fairtrade schemes lead to an increase in the output of fairtrade products, it could cause the prices of commodities to fall.

Foreign aid and debt relief

Foreign aid

Foreign aid (overseas aid) is when money, goods, technical help or other services are given, or lent, by one country, or international organisation, to another country. Foreign aid is usually provided by rich MEDCs to support the economic growth and development of LEDCs. An important category of foreign aid is Official Development Assistance (ODA) that is defined by the Organisation for Economic Co-operation and Development (OECD) as public (government) money given or loaned on concessional terms and used to support the welfare or development of developing countries. In 1970, the

---

Link

Monopsony was explained in 4.4 "The determination of relative wage rates and levels of employment in imperfectly competitive labour markets".

Key terms

Foreign aid (overseas aid): money, goods, technical help or other services given, or lent, by one country, or international organisation, to another country.

Official development assistance (ODA): public money given or loaned on concessional terms and used to support the welfare or development of developing countries.

Organisation for Economic Co-operation and Development (OECD): a group of 37 mainly developed countries that discuss, propose and monitor, economic and social policies.

Loaned on concessional terms (soft loans): money that is lent at a rate of interest which is below the rate that could be obtained by borrowing on financial markets.

United Nations General Assembly adopted the target that donor countries should contribute 0.7% of their gross national income (GNI) in Overseas Development Assistance, but since that time only a few countries have met that target. Table 8.3.1 shows the largest five **aid donors** in 2019, who are members of the OECD. The table ranks donors in two ways, as a share of GNI donated and in US dollars.

▼ **Table 8.3.1**: Official Development Assistance, 2019 Preliminary figures

ODA as a percent of GNI		ODA US$ billion	
Luxembourg	1.05	United States	34,615.1
Norway	1.02	Germany	23,806.3
Sweden	0.99	United Kingdom	19,365.0
Denmark	0.71	Japan	15,506.7
United Kingdom	0.70	France	12,176.4

Source: OECD, Official Development Assistance (ODA)

Other countries who are not members of the OECD also provide foreign aid. For example, China has provided substantial amounts of aid to countries in Africa and to countries that are part of China's Belt and Road Initiative. The Belt and Road Initiative is designed to develop trade routes between countries and across the continents of Asia, Europe and Africa. Chinese aid has helped to support substantial investment in infrastructure.

Some countries, such as India, provide and receive substantial amounts of foreign aid. The region of the world that receives the most foreign aid is Sub-Saharan Africa.

Types of foreign aid

Foreign aid includes money given as a grant or as a soft loan. Money given as a grant does not have to be paid back. Soft loans (concessionary loans) are provided at a low rate of interest and are often long term. This means that the amount that has to be paid back each year is less than if the money was borrowed on financial markets. The money may be used, for example, to finance spending on roads, schools, hospitals, irrigation schemes or to provide power supplies.

Foreign aid also includes technical support, such as help to improve farming methods or to provide clean water. It may help to provide other services such as education and health care. Aid may support the training of teachers and medical staff. It may provide food and medical supplies when there is a natural disaster, such as an earthquake or when crops fail.

Aid can take various forms and can be **bilateral aid** or **multilateral aid**. Bilateral aid is when one country provides aid to another country, and only two countries are involved. Multilateral aid is when funds are provided by a number of countries and they are usually channelled through an international organisation such as the World Bank or the United Nations. Bilateral aid allows the donor country to choose which countries it wants to support and to have more control over how the funds are used. However, some bilateral aid may be determined by political considerations whereas multilateral aid is less likely to be determined by political factors. The value of bilateral aid provided by donor countries is greater than the value of multilateral aid.

Some of the aid that is provided to LEDCs is **tied aid**. Tied aid is when aid is given on the condition that the money is spent on goods and services produced by the country providing the aid. The value of tied aid is generally less than **untied aid** since the country that receives untied aid can choose the most competitive suppliers of the goods and services it needs.

The benefits of foreign aid to LEDCs

Foreign aid can support the economic development of LEDCs in a number of ways but some economists question how effective it is. Arguments in favour of providing aid include:

- It can help fill the savings gap, providing some of the funding LEDCs need to finance investment.

- Overseas aid provides LEDCs with foreign exchange that they can use to buy the imports they need to support their development programmes.

- Without foreign aid, some LEDCs would be unable to finance expensive infrastructure projects that are needed to support economic growth and development. Investment in infrastructure contributes to short-run and long-run economic growth by increasing AD and the productive capacity of the economy.

- Aid that is used to invest in human capital contributes to long-run economic growth and improves the quality of people's lives. Without foreign aid, investment in schools, hospitals, the training of teachers and medical staff may not be sufficient to support the growing populations of many LEDCs. Training workers can help overcome the lack of skills that restrict the growth of LEDCs.

- Foreign aid can help to get rid of, or control, infectious diseases, for example malaria. According to the World Malaria Report 2020, published by the World Health Organization, the number of deaths from malaria fell from around 736,000 in 2000 to around 409,000 in 2019.

- Aid can be directed at the poorest people in the poorest countries and significantly improve the quality of people's lives.

- **Humanitarian aid** can help countries and people deal with natural disasters that a poor country may not be able to cope with on its own.

To be effective in promoting development, foreign aid must be supported by sound economic policies, and its success will be affected by the extent to which the other conditions needed for economic development are present.

Criticisms and limitations of foreign aid

There is disagreement among economists concerning the contribution that aid can make to encouraging the economic development of poor countries. Some believe that aid creates dependency and prevents market forces providing the incentives that are needed to increase economic growth. For example, providing food aid may lead to lower food prices and harm local farmers, some of whom may go out of business. If a country receives large amounts of foreign aid, it can lead to a rise in the exchange rate, making exports dearer and imports cheaper, damaging competitiveness and domestic business.

> **Key terms**
>
> **Tied aid:** funds that are given on the condition that the money is spent on goods and services produced by the country providing the aid.
>
> **Untied aid:** when the country receiving aid can choose from which country it buys the goods and services it needs.

> **Key term**
>
> **Humanitarian aid:** money, food, equipment and services provided to save lives and reduce suffering. It is often given after a natural disaster or conflict.

Government failure can mean that the money is not well spent. Governments have imperfect information and may not know the best way to support the development of the LEDCs they are trying to help. Funds may be spent on large-scale, prestige projects that provide limited benefit to those who really need help. Corruption and bureaucracy may mean that some of the aid does not get to the people for whom it was intended. Donor governments are sometimes motivated by self-interest. Aid may be given to open up the market of the LEDC to exports from the donor country, for example tied aid. Aid may be given to secure the supply of an essential raw material or to gain political influence rather than to promote economic development.

Providing soft loans can lead to a growing burden of debt. Some LEDCs have found that an increasing proportion of government expenditure has to be spent on servicing government debt. This means that there is less money available for the government to spend on merit goods and public goods needed to support the development of the economy. An increase in the external debt can also mean that a growing proportion of the foreign exchange earned from exports is spent on servicing the debt, leaving less to pay for essential imports.

Some economists consider that encouraging trade is likely to benefit poor countries more than providing aid. Some of these economists believe that LEDCs should be given **preferential access** to the markets of MEDCs. Others are in favour of free trade for all, arguing that the best way to achieve economic growth is to allow countries to produce the goods in which they have a comparative advantage and to open up markets to competition.

Debt relief

Economic development requires investment in physical and human capital. Borrowing to finance investment can help LEDCs grow more quickly and improve people's standard of living. Borrowing is one of a number of ways in which LEDCs can try to close the savings gap. However, if borrowing leads to very high levels of debt, it can become unsustainable. **Unsustainable debt** restricts investment and economic growth.

During the 1970s and 1980s, the governments of a number of LEDCs borrowed large amounts of money which they found difficult to repay. The problem started with the oil crises of the early 1970s and early 1980s which led to big increases in the world market price of oil. Since the demand for oil is price inelastic, countries that imported oil experienced large trade deficits and many LEDCs had to borrow to finance their deficits. High interest rates added to the problem. As a result, the debt servicing costs for these countries increased substantially and became a high percentage of both government spending and export revenues. Some poor countries were paying more to service their debts than they were receiving in foreign aid. In 1982, Mexico announced that it was unable to service its external debt and, according to the Jubilee Debt Campaign, during the 1980s, another 57 countries struggled to service their debts, including Bolivia, Chile, Egypt, Gambia, Morocco and Turkey.

Key terms

Preferential access: when a country reduces, or removes, restrictions on imports from some countries but continues to impose restrictions on imports from other countries.

Unsustainable debt: when debt-servicing costs are so high that they cannot be paid without more borrowing and damage to the development of the country's economy.

High debt servicing costs made it difficult to finance development programmes and some countries had to seek financial support from the IMF (International Monetary Fund). However, the IMF was only willing to lend the money needed to service the debts if the governments of these countries agreed to certain conditions. These conditions were imposed to try to reduce the budget and balance of payments deficits and to improve the competitiveness of the borrowers. The aim was to make governments introduce policies that would improve the performance of their economies and enable them to manage their debts. Policies included cutting government spending, increasing taxes, privatising industries and removing price controls. However, at least in the short run, these policies tended to increase unemployment and make some of the poor worse off.

In 1996, the Highly Indebted Poor Country Initiative (HIPCI) was launched by the World Bank and the IMF to provide debt relief to some of the poorest countries in the world. **Debt relief** is when debts are written off (cancelled) or made easier to pay back by changing the terms of the loan. For example, the rate of interest may be reduced or the time to repay the loan extended. To qualify for debt relief under the HIPCI, countries have to meet strict criteria. Initially, very few countries were able to satisfy the criteria, but the criteria have since been relaxed. In 2005, the HIPCI was supplemented by the Multilateral Debt Relief Initiative (MDRI). Under the MDRI, countries that complete the HIPCI process are allowed to write off debts they have with the IMF, the World Bank and the African Development Fund.

At the start of 2021, debt relief of more than $100 billion had been received by 37 countries, 31 of them African, under the HIPC and the MDR initiatives. Countries that have benefited include Afghanistan, Burundi, Chad, Guyana, Haiti, Malawi, Niger, Togo and Zambia.

In response to the Covid-19 pandemic, the Debt Service Suspension Initiative (DSSI) started on 1 May 2020. This allowed 73 countries to suspend temporarily their debt-service payments to their bilateral creditors. The scheme was adopted to help countries introduce measures to tackle the pandemic and protect people.

Arguments in favour of providing debt relief to LEDCs include the following:

- Debt servicing costs had become unsustainable for some countries and without debt relief, many would have defaulted on their debts.
- A reduction in debt servicing costs means that the government is able to spend more on infrastructure to help increase economic growth.
- Debt relief allows the poorest countries in the world to increase social spending on, for example, health, education and housing, helping to improve the lives of people with very low incomes.
- Some countries had already paid more in interest to lenders than the amount borrowed.
- Many of the debts were incurred many years ago but the debt is being repaid by people who were born more recently.
- Although the debt-servicing costs are significant for the HIPCs, the cost of debt relief is relatively small for the richer countries that lent the money.

> **Key term**
>
> **Debt relief:** when debts are written off or made easier to pay back by changing the terms of the loan.

Link

Moral hazard was explained in 7.3 "Financial markets".

However, there is a risk that countries who have been granted debt relief will behave irresponsibly and take on even more debt, and countries that have not been granted debt relief may be reluctant to repay their debts. This is the problem of moral hazard. Debt relief may also mean that countries are less likely to adopt the sound economic policies that help to support sustainable economic development. It may also mean that economic agents that lend to LEDCs may be less willing to do so in the future. One of the conditions imposed on countries given debt relief under the HICPI and the MDRI is that they manage their debts to ensure that they do not become unsustainable again, but this is difficult to guarantee.

According to the International Debt Statistics Report produced by the World Bank in 2021, the total external debt of the 120 low- and middle-income countries was $8.1 trillion in 2019, equivalent to 26% of their gross national income (GNI). Almost one third of low- and middle-income countries had external debt-to-GNI ratios above 60% at the end of 2019, compared with 23% in 2010. In 9% of countries the ratio exceeded 100%, one-third more than in 2010.

Figure 8.3.5 shows how the external debt-to-GNI ratio for the 120 low- and middle-income countries has changed between 2010 and 2019. Figure 8.3.6 shows the changes in external debt-to-exports ratio, another indicator of sustainability. Both indicators suggest that the sustainability of external debt has fallen over this 10-year period. However, interest rates have also fallen, making it easier for countries to service their debts.

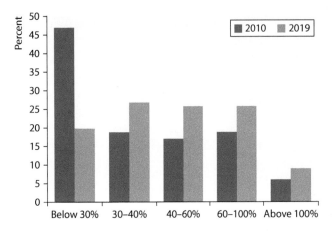

▲ **Figure 8.3.5**: External debt-to-GNI ratio, low- and middle-income countries, 2010 and 2019

Source: The World Bank, *International Debt Statistics 2021*

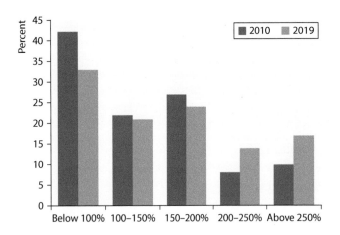

▲ **Figure 8.3.6**: External debt-to-exports ratio, low- and middle-income countries, 2010 and 2019

Source: The World Bank, *International Debt Statistics 2021*

The role of remittances

Remittances are funds transferred to their home country by people living and working abroad. The transfers are usually in cash and are sent by people working abroad to support their families at home. In recent years, remittances have grown rapidly and now represent the largest source of foreign exchange for many LEDCs.

Figure 8.3.7 shows the trends in the main financial flows to low- and middle-income countries between 1990 and 2021. Since the early 1990s, remittances have been larger and growing more rapidly than Official Development Aid (ODA). In 2019, they were more than FDI for the first time since 1993. Until 2019, remittances were a growing, stable and reliable source of funds but as a result of the Covid-19 pandemic, they were likely to fall by around 14% in 2020. Despite this fall, they were expected to be the largest single source of external finance for low- and middle-income countries in 2019, 2020 and 2021. Globalisation and international migration have led to this growth in remittance flows.

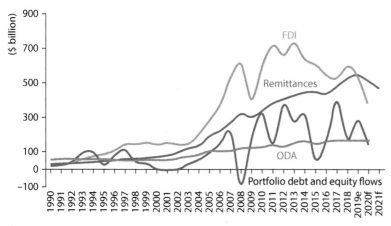

▲ **Figure 8.3.7**: International financial flows to low- and middle-income countries, 1990 to 2021

Note: The data for 2019 are estimates and the data for 2020 and 2021 are forecasts.

Source: The World Bank, *Migration and Development Brief 33*

The benefits of remittances for LEDCs include the following:

- Remittances are an important source of foreign exchange without which many LEDCs would not be able to afford the imports they need to support their development.

- They provide direct support for families, helping to pay for basic necessities and to finance spending on, for example, education and health care.

- Many migrant workers often come from poorer families, and remittances can help to reduce poverty and inequality.

- They may lead to an increase in savings, helping to fill the savings gap.

- Remittances are sometimes used by families to set up a business and as a result, they help to increase investment and the productive capacity of the economy.

- They lead to an increase in spending and an injection of demand into the domestic economy. The multiplier effect of the injection will result in a further increase in national income, and employment.

- Remittances tend to be **countercyclical**. They generally increase when the domestic economy is in recession and decrease when the domestic economy is doing well. When the domestic economy is in recession more people look for work abroad and send more money home to support their families.

- Remittances increase when there is a natural disaster. In these circumstances, people living and working abroad send more money home to help relatives who may be struggling to cope with a very difficult situation. As well as providing immediate relief, after a flood or earthquake, it may also be used to help people rebuild their homes.

- Remittances are a secondary income flow on the current account of the balance of payments and help to reduce the current account deficits experienced by many LEDCs.

- Families receiving remittances are more likely to have a bank account and use other financial services. As a result, they help to

Key term

Countercyclical: an activity that has the opposite pattern to the normal economic cycle and tends to reduce the extent of the usual fluctuations in economic activity.

encourage the development of the financial sector which can have wider benefits for the economy.

However, an increase in remittances may reflect problems in the domestic labour market. People who are unable to find work, or who are paid very little, may choose to look for work abroad. Skilled workers, including doctors, nurses and teachers, are likely to be in demand in many MEDCs. If these workers move abroad, the domestic economy will suffer, particularly if they decide not to return. The substantial investment in human capital will not benefit the LEDC that made the investment. A loss of skilled workers will affect the supply-side performance of the economy and reduce the rate of economic growth and development.

The inflow of remittances will also tend to cause the country's exchange rate to appreciate. The demand for the domestic currency increases when the foreign currency remittances are converted into the domestic currency, leading to an increase in the price of the currency. In countries where remittances are a significant proportion of their foreign exchange earnings, the appreciation in the exchange rate may be large enough to damage the international competitiveness of the economy. There may be a Dutch disease effect which may make it difficult for the economy to diversify and develop its industrial sector.

It is sometimes argued that large inflows of remittances can create moral hazard. If families receive large remittances from relatives living and working abroad, they may be less willing to look for work, increasing the number of people who are economically inactive. Governments may be less likely to provide social welfare or support those who have been affected by natural disasters.

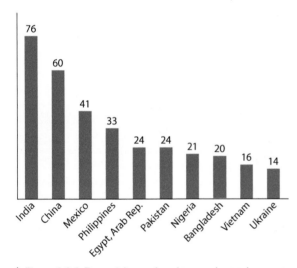

▲ **Figure 8.3.8**: Top recipients of remittances by total amount ($ billion) in 2020

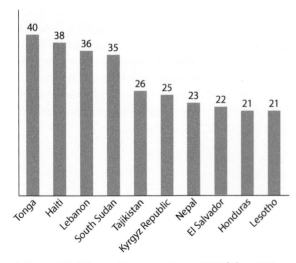

▲ **Figure 8.3.9**: Top recipients by share of GDP (%) in 2020

Source: The World Bank, *Migration and Development Brief 33*

Figure 8.3.8 shows the top 10 recipients of remittances by the total amount of US dollars. India and China receive the most but they only represented 0.4% of China's GDP and 2.9% of India's GDP. Figure 8.3.9, shows the top 10 recipients of remittances as a share of the country's GDP. In 2020, the World Bank estimated that there were 10 countries where remittances were more than 20% of the country's GDP and 25 countries where remittances were more than 10% of the country's GDP.

It is clear from these data that remittances are very important for the economy and the well-being of people in many countries.

The promotion of tourism

According to the World Bank, global expenditure on tourism increased, at current prices, from US$0.527 trillion in 2000 to US$1.575 in 2018 and according to Knoema, in 2018, tourism accounted for over 20%

of the GDP of 32 countries. Many countries around the world, both MEDCs and LEDCs, have identified tourism as an industry that can provide a significant increase in income and employment.

The case in favour of promoting tourism

For many LEDCs, promoting tourism is a way in which they can diversify their economies and reduce their dependence on primary products. For some, it is an alternative to industrialisation but for others, it is just another way of developing their economies. The income elasticity of demand for tourism is high and positive. Therefore, as the world economy grows, tourism is likely to take an increasing share of people's spending.

Tourism is a relatively labour-intensive industry and has the potential to create plenty of jobs for the growing populations of many LEDCs. Tourism employs a high proportion of female workers and for some LEDCs, where the percentage of women in work is significantly lower than for men, this is another advantage. Workers need to be trained and the investment in human capital will, in the long run, benefit other sectors of the economy.

Spending by foreign tourists is an export and an injection into the circular flow of income. It will have a positive multiplier effect on the local and national economy, creating jobs in other industries. A growing tourist industry is likely to be accompanied by an increase in FDI as, for example, TNCs operate hotels and tourist resorts, and car rental services. Investment in infrastructure will be needed and this should also benefit local people. The revenue earned from tourism helps the balance of payments and generates foreign exchange. The increase in the number of tourists provides opportunities for small businesses, for example transporting people, selling souvenirs and supplying food and drinks. Tourism can also create jobs and increase incomes in rural areas, not just in the large towns and cities.

Several countries have seen a significant increase in the percentage of export revenue generated from tourism, for example in Sri Lanka tourism accounted for 9.4% of exports in 2010 and 24.0% in 2019. Over the same period, in Thailand, the percentage of export revenue earned from tourism increased from 10.5% to 20.0%. It is not just LEDCs that have benefited from the growth of tourism, in Greece the share of exports accounted for by tourism increased from 23% to 28% between 2010 and 2019. However, some countries have seen a decline in the share of export earnings from tourism, for example, between 2010 and 2019, it fell from 30% to 23% in Morocco. Also, in 2020, the income from tourism was badly affected by the Covid-19 pandemic but it is expected that the industry will recover and growth return.

Problems resulting from promoting tourism

Like most other industries, the income a country earns from tourism can be affected by unexpected events, a global recession and changes in consumers' tastes and preferences. However, the prospects for the long-run growth in spending on tourism appear to be good.

Foreign TNCs that have invested in building hotels and holiday resorts in LEDCs expect a return on their investment. Therefore, some of the

10 What is the difference between bilateral and multilateral aid?

11 Why is untied aid likely to be of more benefit to an LEDC than tied aid?

12 Explain why debt relief may lead to moral hazard.

13 Explain why an increase in remittances may cause the exchange rate of an LEDC to appreciate.

▲ **Figure 8.3.10**: The Golden Temple in Bangkok

Progress questions

14 What is meant by the "income elasticity of demand for tourism is high"?

15 Explain how an increase in foreign tourism can lead to an increase in a country's real GDP in both the short run and the long run.

16 Explain how the growth in a country's tourist industry is likely to affect its balance of payments in both the short run and the long run.

profits made from tourism are sent abroad, reducing the benefit to domestic residents and affecting the balance of payments.

The growth of tourism can produce negative externalities and damage the natural environment. Tourism inevitably means an increase in transport by air, road and rail, leading to an increase in CO_2 emissions, global warming and other forms of pollution. Too many tourists in rural areas can lead to the destruction of plant and animal life. It may also have a social impact causing a change in the culture of the region and a loss of local customs and traditions.

There is an opportunity cost. The more money the government spends on promoting tourism, the less money it has to spend on health care, education and other social programmes, and on promoting industrial development.

The role of the World Bank, IMF and non-governmental organisations (NGOs) in promoting development

The World Bank

The World Bank was founded in 1944 as part of the Bretton Woods agreement. The World Bank consists of the International Bank for Reconstruction and Development (IBRD) and the International Development Association (IDA). Both institutions provided long-term finance, policy advice and technical help to the governments of developing countries. The IBRD helps middle-income and creditworthy poorer countries, while the IDA supports the poorest countries in the world. The World Bank's twin goals are to end extreme poverty and increase shared prosperity.

In 2020, the World Bank was made up of 189 countries. The member countries are shareholders of the Bank and they also have to be members of the IMF. The World Bank obtains most of its funds by borrowing on international capital markets by selling bonds. It is able to borrow at a low rate of interest because the repayment of the money borrowed is guaranteed by the member countries. It also financed by members' contributions, mainly from the richer countries.

The rate of interest charged by the IBRD is just above the rate at which the World Bank borrows. This rate of interest is lower than the rate an LEDC would have to pay if it borrowed directly from the market. The loans generally have a maturity of between 5 and 15 years.

The IDA provides loans (known as credits) and grants to the governments of the poorest countries. Many countries who borrow from the IDA do not have to pay any interest, but some are charged a very low rate. Typically, loans made by the IDA are repaid over a period of 30 to 40 years.

Originally, the World Bank mainly financed spending on large-scale infrastructure projects but this has changed. It now helps to finance small-scale projects that are designed to improve the well-being of the poorest people in the country. Projects financed by the World Bank include support for rural development, improvements in agriculture, better access to health care, providing safe drinking water and creating jobs through the finance of small businesses. The fundamental objective of the World Bank is to promote the long-term economic development of LEDCs.

The Sustainable Development Goals (SDGs)

The Sustainable Development Goals (SDGs) are 17 sets of global development targets adopted by the member countries of the United Nations in September 2015. They replace the 8 Millennium Development Goals (MDGs) that were set after the Millennium Summit of the United Nations in 2000. The targets are set in areas such as health, education, gender equality, jobs, poverty reduction and protecting the environment. The SDGs reflect the view that development must be economically, socially and environmentally sustainable. The goals are part of Agenda 2030 and are affecting the world's approach to promoting economic development until the year 2030. The World Bank is supporting countries in achieving the SDGs by providing targeted funds and advice.

The International Monetary Fund (IMF)

The main purpose of the IMF is to try to maintain the stability of the international monetary system. A stable international monetary system is important for the prosperity of all countries. A country that is experiencing balance of payments problems can obtain a short-term or medium-term loan from the IMF. Loans provided by the IMF have policy conditions attached. The conditions imposed by the IMF are designed to help the country solve its balance of payments problems and ensure that the loan is repaid. The IMF does not lend money to support development projects in LEDCs, but sound economic policies should assist the long-term development of a country. However, some economists have criticised the IMF for imposing conditions that, at least in the short run, have made some of the poorer people in LEDCs worse off.

Washington Consensus

In 1989, the economist John Williamson identified a set of economic policies that he believed was the generally accepted view of the measures a country should adopt if it wanted to achieve a sustained improvement in its economic performance. These policies reflected the views of many of the economists working at the World Bank and the IMF and were the reforms that a country was expected to adopt as a condition for obtaining a loan from these institutions. Since the head offices of the World Bank and the IMF are based in Washington, this set of economic policies became known as the Washington Consensus. The measures included: avoiding large budget deficits; reducing government subsidies and spending the money saved on health, education and infrastructure; increasing the tax base and reducing marginal tax rates; trade liberalisation; maintaining a competitive exchange rate; opening up the economy to FDI; privatisation of SOEs; and deregulation.

The Washington Consensus is a market-based approach to economic development and has been criticised by those who strongly believe that an interventionist approach is more likely to be successful. They argued that some of these measures are not suitable for many LEDCs and pointed out that China and several other countries in Southeast Asia had grown rapidly by adopting a different approach that included a much greater role for the state.

Activity

Visit the World Bank's website and find out all you can about a project that the Bank is helping to finance in an LEDC of your choice.

Key term

Sustainable Development Goals (SDGs): 17 sets of global development targets in areas such as health, education, gender equality, jobs, poverty reduction and protecting the environment.

Activity

Produce a list of the 17 SDGs. Find out the progress that a country of your choice is making towards achieving the SDGs by 2030.

Link

The role of the IMF was explained in detail in 7.2 "Exchange rates".

Get it right

The World Bank provides long-term loans and other support to help promote the economic development of LEDCs. The IMF provides short-term and medium-term loans to countries with balance of payments problems. The IMF lends to both MEDCs and LEDCs.

Key term

Non-governmental organisations (NGOs): non-profit making organisations that try to achieve social and/or political objectives and are independent of the government.

Progress questions

17 How does the role of the IBRD differ from the role of the IDA?

18 What is the main source of funds for the World Bank?

19 How does the role of the World Bank differ from the role of the IMF?

Non-governmental organisations (NGOs)

Non-governmental organisations (NGOs) are non-profit making organisations that try to achieve social and/or political objectives. They are independent of government but some NGOs do receive significant amounts of money from the state. Many NGOs have been set up to help people in LEDCs and they play an important role in promoting economic development. Oxfam, *Médicins Sans Frontiéres*, Plan International and SNV Netherlands are examples of NGOs involved in improving the well-being of people in developing countries.

NGOs help in three main ways: they are directly involved in projects that improve the lives of people in LEDCs; they make people in MEDCs aware of the problems faced by people in LEDCs; and they try to persuade governments to do more to help. Projects supported by NGOs are varied but they include: providing access to clean water, providing solar panels to allow people who are not connected to an electricity supply system to have a source of power, helping people grow food and look after farm animals, building schools and training teachers, and improving the quality of health care. They also help people recover from the effects of a natural disaster by, for example, providing food, clothing, medical supplies and shelter.

Case study: Peru, an improving economy

▲ **Figure 8.3.11**: Macchu Picchu – a famous site in Peru

The Republic of Peru in South America has a population of over 30 million. Its traditional industries include mining and fishing but manufacturing now provides about 20% of its national income. Instead of exporting raw materials, some are now made into finished goods, such as clothing, before being exported. Over the past 20 years, tourism has also become increasingly important, encouraged by both the government and the private sector. The country includes parts of the Amazon and the Andes plus famous sites such as Macchu Picchu.

Helped by sound macroeconomic policies and supply-side reforms, Peru had an average annual GDP growth rate of around 6.1% between 2002 and 2013. In 2008, it became an upper middle-income country. The average annual growth rate was slower between 2014 and 2019, at around 3.1%, partly due to lower commodity prices, including copper, Peru's main export. The growth in income and employment have helped to reduce poverty, with those in extreme poverty (living on less than $1.90 a day) falling from 16.4% to 2.7% of the population between 2000 and 2018. One of the Millennium Development Goals (MDGs) was to reduce the proportion suffering from extreme poverty and hunger by 50% between 1990 and 2015. In 2019, the GNI per capita of Peru was $6,740 (current USD), up from $1,970 in 2000.

The country's HDI in 2019 was 0.777 (up from 0.679 in 2000) and its IHDI was 0.628. Although Peru has made progress in meeting some of the United Nation's Sustainable Development Goals (SDGs), it still has much to do to achieve many of these targets by 2030. For example, only 54.5% of primary schools had access to basic drinking water in 2018, the rate of electronic waste recycling was 1.5% in 2017 and the land area covered by forest had fallen from 58.8% in 2000 to 56.5% in 2020.

1 Explain two ways in which the extract shows that Peru's economy has become more diversified.

2 Explain why lower commodity prices may have contributed to a fall in Peru's rate of economic growth.

3 What evidence is there to suggest that Peru has become more economically developed since 2000?

4 Why are waste recycling and managing forests important for sustainable development?

Exam-style questions

1 Which one of the following indicates that inequality in a country has increased?

   An increase in the

   A Gini coefficient

   B Human Development Index

   C Inequality-adjusted Human Development Index

   D terms of trade   [1 mark]

2 The table below shows the nominal income per head and the price indices for four countries in 2015 and 2021.

	Income per head ($) 2015	Income per head ($) 2021	Price index 2015	Price index 2021
Country W	2,500	3,000	100	120
Country X	4,000	6,000	100	141
Country Y	6,300	8,400	100	145
Country Z	8,800	9,680	100	102

   Which country had the largest increase in real income per head between 2015 and 2021?

   A Country W

   B Country X

   C Country Y

   D Country Z   [1 mark]

3 The Harrod-Domar model suggests that a country can increase its rate of economic growth by

   A increasing its marginal capital-output ratio.

   B increasing its savings ratio.

   C reducing inequality.

   D reducing the external value of its currency.   [1 mark]

4 Primary product dependency is a problem for some less economically developed countries (LEDCs).

   (i) What is meant by "primary product dependency"?   [2 marks]

   (ii) With the help of a diagram, explain why a fall in the market price of a primary product is likely to lead to a fall in the total revenue received from selling the product.   [4 marks]

   (iii) In April 2021, a country was exporting 9,000 tonnes of a commodity. The price elasticity of demand (PED) for the commodity is −0.8. Between April 2021 and July 2021, the world market price of the commodity increased from $300 per tonne to $360 per tonne. In July 2021, the value of the country's currency against the US dollar was $1 = 17 peso.

   Calculate, in **pesos**, the amount of revenue that the country earned from exporting this product in July 2021.

   You are advised to show your working.   [4 marks]

5 The table below shows the multidimensional poverty index (MPI) and gross national income (GNI) per capita for a selection of five countries in Sub-Saharan Africa in 2018.

Country	MPI	GNI per capita (US$)
Guinea	0.373	850
Lesotho	0.084	1,280
Madagascar	0.384	500
Mali	0.376	830
Zambia	0.232	1,440

(i) Explain why GNI per capita is likely to affect the amount of absolute poverty experienced by a country. (4 marks)

(ii) To what extent do the data in the table support the view that GNI per capita affects the amount of absolute poverty in Sub-Saharan African countries. Use the data in the table to support your answer. (4 marks)

6 Explain the factors that may have contributed to the increase in foreign currency that a country such as Peru has earned from tourism during the past 10 years. (12 marks)

Note: To answer this question as a data response question, use the data provided in the case study "Peru, an improving economy" in 8.3 "Policies to promote development" to support your answer.

7 In 2020, the World Bank classified a country as a low-income country if its GNI per capita was less than US$1,035 in 2019. According to this classification, there were 29 low-income countries including Afghanistan, Ethiopia, Haiti, Niger and Sudan.

Discuss the view that the debts of all low-income countries should be cancelled. (25 marks)

Glossary

A

Absolute advantage: when a country (or other economic agent) can produce a given amount of a good (or service) with fewer resources than another country or when a country can produce more of a good than another country with the same amount of resources.

Absolute poverty: where a person does not have sufficient money to satisfy their basic needs.

Adjustable peg exchange rate system: a system of fixed exchange rates where the exchange rate is allowed to fluctuate within an agreed band and where the par value can be changed if necessary.

Age structure of the population: the distribution of the population among different age groups.

Aid donors: countries, or other economic agents, that provide foreign aid.

Allocative efficiency: producing where price = marginal cost and firms are producing the types of goods and services which best meet people's preferences.

Altruism: when someone acts in the interests of other people, putting their welfare first.

Anchoring: where someone relies heavily on the first piece of information they obtain when making a decision.

Arbitrage: when products can be bought in a cheaper market and resold at a higher price in a more expensive market.

Autarky: where imports are banned and the economy is self-sufficient in a product.

Average cost of labour: the cost of employing each worker, calculated by dividing the total labour cost by the number of workers employed.

Average product or average returns: the output per unit of the variable factor of production, calculated by dividing the total product by the number of units of the variable factor.

Average revenue product: the revenue per worker, calculated by dividing the total revenue product by the number of workers.

Average utility: the satisfaction per item, calculated by dividing total utility by the number of items.

B

Backward vertical integration: where one firm takes over another firm at an earlier stage of production of the same good.

Band: the limits between which an exchange rate is allowed to fluctuate in a fixed exchange rate system.

Banks' balances at the central bank: deposits banks hold with the central bank that can be exchanged for cash or used to pay other banks.

Barometric pricing: a form of price leadership where the price leader is sensitive to market conditions.

Barriers to exit: factors that make it difficult for firms to leave a market.

Beggar-thy-neighbour policies: measures adopted by a country to improve its economy but which harm the economies of other countries, for example imposing tariffs and quotas on imports or devaluing its currency.

Behavioural economics: the study of the effects of psychological, emotional and social factors on economic decision making.

Benefit in kind: something given to an individual or household which does not take the form of money, for example free school meals.

Biases or cognitive biases: systematic errors in thinking based on beliefs and past experience that affect decision making.

Bilateral aid: when one country provides aid to another country; only two countries are involved.

Bilateral loan: when a single lender provides a loan to a single borrower, for example one country lending to another country.

Bilateral monopoly: where there is a single buyer (monopsonist) and a single seller (monopolist) in the market for a product or factor of production.

Birth rate: the number of live births per thousand of the population per year.

Bonds: securities that represent a loan to the government or organisation that issued the bonds. Bonds pay interest to the holder and are usually redeemed at a specified date in the future.

Bounded rationality: the idea that limitations mean that individuals are not completely rational when making choices and economic decisions.

Bounded self-control: the idea that individuals lack full self-control to make decisions that act in their self-interest.

Brain drain: when highly educated and skilled people leave the country.

Bretton Woods System: a global monetary system, agreed in 1944, that set up the International Monetary Fund (IMF) and the system of fixed exchange rates that operated between 1946 and 1973.

C

Capital account (of the balance of payments): a record of transactions that involve the purchase and sale of intangible assets and capital transfers between countries.

Capital flight: when foreign investors rapidly withdraw their money from a country, usually resulting in a large fall in the value of the country's currency.

Capital market: the market that provides medium-term and long-term finance for individuals, firms and governments.

Capital ratios: a bank's capital (equity) as a proportion of its loans.

Carbon tax: an indirect tax levied on the carbon content of fuels. Carbon taxes are used to internalise the external costs of using fossil fuels that release greenhouse gases into the atmosphere.

Cartel: an example of overt collusion, where producers make a formal agreement to control output and/or price.

Choice architecture: a framework or way that choices can be presented to individuals.

Closed shop: where all those doing a certain job must be members of a particular trade union.

Collateral: an asset that is promised as security for a loan, which may have to be sold to settle the debt if the borrower is not able to pay back the loan.

Collective bargaining: where trade unions negotiate and agree pay and working conditions with employers.

Collusion: when rival firms work together for their mutual benefit.

Collusive oligopoly: when some or all of the main firms in an oligopolistic market work together.

Commercial banks: financial institutions that provide financial services to the general public and business. The services provided include accepting deposits, giving loans and providing means of payment.

Commercial bills: short-term securities issued by firms.

Common external tariff (CET): when the same customs duties apply to products imported from non-member countries into any country in a trading bloc. The rates of import duty differ depending on the product and where it comes from.

Common market: a trading bloc where countries have free trade in goods and services and allow free movement of capital and labour between each other. They also have the same restrictions on goods and services imported from non-member countries.

Comparative advantage: when the opportunity cost of producing a good (or service) is lower than in another country.

Competition: when rival firms use strategies to try to increase their sales, market share and/or profits.

Competition policy: state regulation of markets to protect consumers and other firms from dominant firms abusing their monopoly power.

Competitive (or non-collusive) oligopoly: where the firms in an oligopolistic market act individually in their own self-interest.

Computational problems: difficulties in working out the best value for money due to the individual's ability, the time available and the complexity of the issue.

Conduct (of firms): how firms choose to behave or operate in a market.

Conglomerate integration: the combination of two or more firms making unrelated products.

Constant marginal returns: when marginal product stays the same after an extra unit of the variable factor is employed.

Constant returns to scale: when an increase in inputs results in the same proportionate increase in output.

Consumer surplus: the difference between what consumers would be willing to pay for a product and the price paid.

Contestable market: when there are low barriers to entry and exit.

Corporate social responsibility: when businesses behave ethically in relation to their customers, workers, the local community and/or society as a whole.

Countercyclical: an activity that has the opposite pattern to the normal economic cycle and tends to reduce the extent of the usual fluctuations in economic activity.

Creative destruction theory: the replacement of existing products, markets and firms with new ones as an inevitable outcome of technological change.

Credit creation: the process of creating bank deposits/money by giving loans to customers.

Credit crunch: a sudden reduction in lending by financial institutions and an increase in the rate of interest charged on loans.

Crowdfunding: raising money from a large number of people who each contribute a small amount, typically using the internet.

Current account: an active account from which payments are made without any notice of withdrawal and into which there are frequent deposits.

Customs union (CU): a trading bloc where countries do not have any restrictions on trade between each other and each country has the same restrictions on trade with non-member countries.

D

Deadweight welfare loss: the consumer and producer surplus lost when production and consumption are not at the social optimum.

Death rate: the number of deaths per thousand of the population per year.

Debt forgiveness: when a lender cancels or reduces the amount of debt owed by a borrower.

Debt relief: when debts are written off or made easier to pay back by changing the terms of the loan.

Debt: funds raised by borrowing.

Decreasing returns to scale: when an increase in inputs results in a less than proportionate increase in output.

Default choice: where an option is selected in yours or society's interest but you can choose to change this.

Default: when a borrower fails to make a loan repayment or to repay the debt, including interest, when it is due.

Deglobalisation: the reversal of the effects of globalisation, reducing the integration and interdependence between the economies of different countries. It occurs when the volume of international trade and investment decline.

Deindustrialisation: the absolute or relative decline in a country's, or a region's, manufacturing industry.

Demand deposits: money in people's bank accounts that can be spent without giving any notice of withdrawal.

Demand-side policies: monetary and fiscal measures that are used to influence aggregate demand (AD).

Demographic dividend: when the number of people in the workforce is growing relative to the number of people in the dependent age groups.

Dependency ratio: the number of people who are not in the working age group in relation to the number of people of working age.

Deposit account: a savings account that pays interest but may require a notice of withdrawal.

Deposit protection scheme: if a bank fails, the scheme will compensate individuals who have deposited money in the bank, up to an agreed limit.

Destabilising speculation: when the actions of speculators lead to larger fluctuations in the price of an asset than if speculation had not taken place.

Deterioration in the terms of trade: when the average price of a country's exports falls relative to the average price of its imports.

Devaluation: a reduction in the value of a country's currency in terms of other currencies. It is when, in a fixed exchange rate system, the government announces a reduction in the official value of the currency.

Diminishing marginal returns: when marginal product falls after an extra unit of the variable factor is employed.

Discrimination: treating people differently by classifying them into different groups according to particular characteristics.

Diversification: increasing a firm's or country's range of products, to spread risk.

Dividends: money paid by a company to its shareholders out of its profits. Dividends are usually paid twice a year but sometimes more often.

Divorce of ownership from control: when those who own a business are different from those who control it.

Domestic opportunity cost ratio: the amount of a good that has to be given up so that it can produce one unit of another good within an economy.

Dominant firm: a business with a significant market share and a significantly larger market share than its next largest rival.

Dual economies: economies with two sectors, a traditional agricultural sector and a modern, more productive, industrial sector.

Dumping: when a firm exports goods and sells them at a price which is significantly below the price it sells the good in its home market.

Duopoly: a market where two firms control the supply of a good or service.

Dutch disease: when the discovery of a natural resource leads to an appreciation of a country's currency making other sectors of the economy uncompetitive, particularly the manufacturing sector.

Dynamic efficiency: changes in efficiency over a period of time.

E

Economic development: a process that leads to a sustained improvement in the economic wellbeing and quality of life of people.

Economic migrants: people who move from one country to another to try to improve their standard of living.

Economies of agglomeration: the benefits that result from firms and people locating near to each other.

Effective exchange rate index (nominal): a measure of the weighted value of a currency against a basket of other currencies.

Efficiency wage theory: the idea that higher wages can lead to higher labour productivity because workers feel more motivated, increasing the efficiency of the economy.

Environmental Kuznets curve (EKC): a diagram that illustrates an hypothesis of the relationship between economic growth, or real income per head, and damage to the environment.

Equity: funds provided by the owners of the business.

Exchange controls: limits imposed by a government on the buying and selling of foreign currencies.

Expenditure-reducing policies: measures to reduce aggregate demand to reduce spending on imports, and so reduce a deficit on the current account of the balance of payments.

Expenditure-switching policies: measures that change the relative prices of imports and exports, to persuade people to buy fewer imports and to make exports more attractive to people abroad.

External debt: money borrowed from a foreign lender.

External growth: when a firm expands by joining with other firms.

Extractive industries: industries that obtain non-renewable raw materials, such as metals, oil and other minerals, by mining and quarrying. They are part of the primary sector of the economy.

F

Factor endowment: the amount of land, labour, capital and entrepreneurship that a country possesses.

Fairtrade scheme: helps producers obtain higher prices for their products while improving the conditions for workers and protecting the environment. The schemes also encourage consumers to buy fairtrade products.

Financial account (of the balance of payments): a record of transactions that lead to changes in a country's stock of overseas assets and liabilities.

Financial institutions: companies that provide financial services such as banks, insurance companies and investment funds.

Financial markets: where people borrow and lend money, and where they buy and sell financial assets such as shares, bonds, foreign exchange and commodities.

Fire sale: when an organisation is in financial difficulty and has to sell some of its assets at a price that is below their true value.

Firm: an organisation that uses scarce resources to supply goods or services.

Footloose: an industry, or firm, is footloose if its location is not dependent on the availability of particular factors of production. The industry is able to move easily from one location to another.

Foreign aid (overseas aid): money, goods, technical help or other services given, or lent, by one country, or international organisation, to another country.

Foreign exchange market (FOREX): where currencies are bought and sold and their prices are determined.

Forward contract: where traders agree the price and quantity of an item for delivery at a specified date in the future. Payment is made on the agreed delivery date.

Forward market: where forward contracts are bought and sold.

Forward vertical integration: where one firm takes over another firm at a later stage of production of the same good.

Free trade area (FTA): a trading bloc where countries do not have any restrictions on trade between each other but retain their own restrictions on trade with non-member countries.

Freely floating exchange rate system: where the price of a currency is determined by the demand for and supply of the currency on the foreign exchange market, without any government intervention.

G

General Agreement on Tariffs and Trade (GATT): an international treaty to promote international trade by reducing tariffs and other restrictions on imports.

Gini coefficient: a numerical measure of the extent of inequality of a country's income or wealth.

Global supply chain: a worldwide network of suppliers, assembly plants, distribution centres and retailers.

Globalisation: the process through which the economies of the different countries of the world become increasingly integrated and interdependent.

Governance: the quality of management by political leaders and public officials.

Government bailout: when the government provides financial support to a business that would otherwise have gone bankrupt.

Great Depression: the severe global economic depression that began in the USA in 1929 and lasted in many countries until the late 1930s.

H

Harrod-Domar model: an economic model that suggests that the rate of economic growth depends on the savings ratio and the marginal capital-output ratio.

Herding behaviour: when an individual's behaviour is influenced by the behaviour of the group.

Hidden economy: where goods and services are supplied and exchanged but not recorded.

Hit-and-run competition: where firms temporarily enter a market, take advantage of the supernormal profit and then leave when this is no longer available.

Homo economicus: economic man – someone who always acts rationally and in their self-interest.

Horizontal integration: the combination of two or more firms at the same stage of production of the same good or service.

Hot money flows: short-term movements of money between the world's financial centres to achieve the highest possible return for investors.

Human Development Index (HDI): a measure of economic development that is based on life expectancy, education and income.

Humanitarian aid: money, food, equipment and services provided to save lives and reduce suffering. It is often given after a natural disaster or conflict.

Hypothesis of diminishing marginal utility: the idea that the more you have of something, the less satisfaction you gain from consuming an extra unit.

I

IMF quota: an allocation that determines how much a country has to pay to the IMF, its voting rights and its allocation of SDRs.

Imperfect competition: market structures between perfect competition and monopoly, where there is competition between firms but there is not a perfectly competitive market.

Imperfect oligopoly: where a small number of firms dominate the market for a differentiated product.

Import ban (embargo on imports): when no imports of a certain type of product, or products from a particular country, are allowed.

Import substitution: where domestic production replaces foreign imports.

Improvement in the terms of trade: when the average price of a country's exports rises relative to the average price of its imports.

Increasing marginal returns: when marginal product rises after an extra unit of the variable factor is employed.

Increasing returns to scale: when an increase in inputs results in a more than proportionate increase in output.

Industrial strategy: an interventionist government policy to encourage the development and growth of a particular sector of the economy, often manufacturing.

Industrialisation: when the manufacturing sector of an economy grows quickly and the relative size of the agricultural sector declines.

Inequality Kuznets curve: a diagram that illustrates an hypothesis of the relationship between economic growth and the degree of inequality in the distribution of income.

Inequality-adjusted Human Development Index (IHDI): a measure of economic development that is based on life expectancy, education and income but which also takes into account how these three indicators of development are distributed among a country's population.

Inertia or status-quo bias: the tendency to stick with what is familiar, perhaps believing that an alternative will be worse.

Infant industry: an industry that is in its early stages of development.

Infant mortality rate: the number of infant deaths, in the first year of life, out of every thousand live births in that year.

Informative advertising: advertising which aims to increase consumers' knowledge of a product and its features.

Innocent barriers to entry: restrictions on new firms entering the market that occur naturally.

Insolvent: when the value of the liabilities (excluding the equity/ shareholders' funds) of a business are greater than the value of its assets.

Integration of financial markets: when the financial markets of different countries are interconnected and closely linked with each other.

Integration: the combination of two or more firms, through merger or takeover.

Interbank market: short-term lending between banks, usually for a week or less.

Internal debt: money borrowed from a domestic lender.

Internal or organic growth: when a firm expands without joining with other firms.

International mobility of labour: the movement of workers between countries.

Investment banks: financial institutions that help businesses, and sometimes governments, carry out complex financial transactions such as issuing new shares or helping with mergers.

J

J-curve effect: why the balance of trade in goods and services initially deteriorates after a fall in the exchange rate but then improves.

K

Kinked demand curve model: a model of oligopolistic behaviour that assumes if a firm changes its price, other firms will follow decreases but not increases.

L

Labour intensive: where the production of goods and services is carried out mainly by people and where wages are a high percentage of total costs.

Law of diminishing returns: as more units of the variable factor are added to a fixed factor of production, both the marginal and average returns to the variable factor will eventually fall.

Legal tender: money that the law states must be accepted in payment of a debt.

Lender of last resort: when a central bank lends to a commercial bank that is short of liquidity and unable to borrow from other sources.

Liabilities: the amount of money that is owed to individuals, firms, financial institutions, governments and other economic agents.

Life expectancy: the average number of years a person can expect to live.

Limit pricing: where the price is set below the profit-maximising level to act as a barrier to entry.

Liquidity ratios: a bank's liquid assets as a proportion of its customer deposits and other short-term liabilities.

Loaned on concessional terms (soft loans): money that is lent at a rate of interest which is below the rate that could be obtained by borrowing on financial markets.

Localisation of economic activity: when products are made close to where they are sold, using local materials, and designed to suit local tastes and preferences.

Lorenz curve: a graph showing the cumulative distribution of national income or wealth for given percentages of the population.

M

Malthusian catastrophe: when food supplies are not sufficient to feed the population, causing hunger, disease and a fall in the size of the population.

Malthusian trap: a theory that population growth is faster than the growth in the supply of food, leading to a situation where there is not enough food to feed the population.

Managed floating exchange rate system: an exchange rate system where central banks intervene in the foreign exchange market to influence the value of their country's currency.

Mandated choice: being forced by law to make a choice.

Marginal (revenue) productivity theory: the principle that is worth employing additional workers up to the point where their marginal revenue product is equal to their extra cost.

Marginal cost: the change in total cost due to the production of an extra unit.

Marginal cost of labour: the change in a firm's total cost due to the employment of an extra worker.

Marginal physical product: the increase in output due to the employment of an extra worker.

Marginal private cost: the change in private cost due to the production of an extra unit.

Marginal product or marginal returns: the change in total product/output when an extra unit of the variable factor is employed.

Marginal revenue product: the increase in revenue due to the employment of an extra worker.

Marginal revenue: the change in total revenue due to the sale of an extra unit.

Marginal social cost: the change in social cost (private plus external) due to the production of an extra unit.

Marginal utility: the addition to total utility from consuming an extra unit of a product.

Market bubble: when the price of an asset rises rapidly so that it does not reflect its true value. The price then falls rapidly when the bubble bursts.

Market makers: financial institutions or dealers who are always ready to buy and sell certain financial assets, for example particular shares or currencies.

Maturity: the time that a loan lasts for and when it has to be repaid.

Measure of value: a function of money that allows the relative cost of different products to be compared.

Merchandise trade: trade in goods.

Merger: when two or more firms combine on a roughly equal basis to become one new firm.

Microfinance: providing financial services, such as small loans and insurance, to people who do not have access to formal financial institutions.

Migrant workers: people who move from one region, or country, to another to try to find a job.

Minimum efficient scale: the lowest level of output where a firm's long-run average cost is minimised.

Minimum wage rate: the lowest pay that can be offered by law, a wage floor, usually taking the form of the least amount that must be paid per hour of work.

Monetary aggregate: a measure of the money supply.

Monetary economy: an economy that uses money as a medium of exchange when trading goods and services.

Monetary union: an agreement between two or more countries to create a single currency area, to use the same currency controlled by a single central bank with a common monetary policy.

Money market: the market that provides funds to those who want short-term finance.

Money: an asset that fulfils the functions of money.

Monopoly busting: breaking up a dominant firm into smaller separate firms.

Monopsony power: the ability of a single buyer to influence the price or wage rate.

Monopsony: the only or main buyer of a product or factor of production.

Moral hazard: when an economic agent has the incentive to take extra risk because they do not bear the full cost of the risk.

Most-favoured-nation (MFN) clause: when a country agrees to reduce a restriction on trade with one country, the same reduction automatically applies to all other countries.

Multilateral aid: when funds are provided by a number of countries and they are usually channelled through an international organisation such as the World Bank.

N

National minimum wage rate: the lowest pay that can be offered in a particular country per hour or day.

Nationalisation: when private sector firms or industries are transferred from the private sector to state ownership or control.

Natural increase: the difference between the birth rate and the death rate. It shows the annual increase in the number of people per thousand of the population.

Natural monopoly: where due to significant economies of scale, an activity is best carried out by one firm.

Negative marginal returns: when marginal product is negative after an extra unit of the variable factor is employed.

Net advantage: combining the monetary and non-monetary benefits of a job when deciding how much labour to supply.

Net errors and omissions: the net value of the mistakes made when recording the transactions included on the balance of payments account.

New issue market: part of the capital market where securities are offered for sale for the first time.

Non-governmental organisations (NGOs): non-profit making organisations that try to achieve social and/or political objectives and are independent of the government.

Normal profit: when revenue is just sufficient to cover costs, producing where total revenue equals total costs or average revenue equals average costs.

Notice of withdrawal: the depositor must tell the bank in advance when they want to take money out of the account. The period of notice can vary but is typically between 7 days and 3 months.

Nudge: an action that encourages a particular behaviour without removing choice.

O

Official development assistance (ODA): public money given or loaned on concessional terms and used to support the welfare or development of developing countries.

One-way option: in a fixed exchange rate system, when a currency becomes overvalued or undervalued, it is obvious whether the exchange rate will be devalued or revalued, allowing speculators to make very large profits.

Optimum size: producing at minimum long-run average cost, achieving productive efficiency.

Organisation for Economic Co-operation and Development (OECD): a group of 37 mainly developed countries that discuss, propose and monitor, economic and social policies.

Outsource: when a firm buys some of the goods, services or components it needs from another supplier, sometimes in a different country.

Overdrafts: when a bank agrees that a household or firm can withdraw more money from their account than they have paid in. The bank sets a limit on the amount that can be borrowed and charges interest daily on the amount overdrawn.

Overt collusion: when firms have a formal arrangement designed to control the market and reduce competition.

P

Par value: the official value of a currency in a fixed exchange rate system, also known as the parity or central rate.

Pareto efficiency or Pareto optimality: where it is not possible to make someone better off by reallocating resources between products and markets without making someone else worse off.

Pattern of world trade: the types of goods and services that are traded and the share of international trade carried out by different countries or regions of the world.

Per se: a Latin term that means 'by itself' or 'on its own'.

Per se rule or dogmatic approach: a general rule which does not require the individual circumstances to be investigated further.

Perfect or pure oligopoly: where a small number of firms dominate the market for a homogeneous product.

Perfectly contestable market: when there are no barriers to entry or exit.

Performance (of firms): outcomes on which firms may be judged, in terms of how well they are doing.

Persuasive advertising: advertising which aims to influence consumer preferences, encouraging more people to buy one firm's product instead of another's.

Political instability: when governments often collapse and the political system does not provide for a well-ordered transfer of power.

Portfolio investment: the purchase of shares, bonds and other financial assets without any involvement in the management of businesses.

Positional goods: goods and services that people value because of their limited supply and because they are believed to give people status.

Poverty: the state of being very poor.

Poverty line: the minimum level required to not be living in absolute or relative poverty.

Poverty trap: where it is difficult to escape poverty.

Prebisch-Singer hypothesis: over time, the prices of primary commodities fall relative to the prices of manufactured goods.

Predatory pricing: where a firm cuts its price to drive one or more of its rivals out of business.

Preferential access: when a country reduces, or removes, restrictions on imports from some countries but continues to impose restrictions on imports from other countries.

Premium: an amount of money paid for insurance.

Price discrimination: when a firm charges different prices to different consumers for the same product for reasons other than differences in cost.

Price elasticity of demand for labour or wage elasticity of demand: a measure of the percentage change in the quantity demanded of labour as a result of a given percentage change in the wage rate, or simply, the responsiveness of the quantity demanded of labour to a change in the wage rate.

Price elasticity of supply for labour or wage elasticity of supply: a measure of the percentage change in the quantity supplied of labour as a result of a given percentage change in the wage rate, or simply, the responsiveness of the quantity supplied of labour to a change in the wage rate.

Price leadership: where a particular firm changes its price first and other firms in the market then follow, making similar price changes.

Price stickiness or price rigidity: the tendency for prices not to change quickly in response to changes in supply or demand.

Price war: where a price cut by one firm trying to increase its market share leads to a series of price cuts by others.

Principal-agent problem: when there is a conflict of interest between one person or group, the principal, and their representative, the agent.

Producer surplus: the difference between the price sellers are willing to produce each item for and the price they actually receive.

Profit satisficing: where sufficient profit is made but not the most that could have been obtained.

Proprietary trading: when a trader, for example a financial institution, buys and sells securities, currencies and commodities using their own money, rather than on behalf of a client.

Protectionism: imposing tariffs and other restrictions on imports from other countries.

Public ownership: when the government owns a firm, industry or asset.

Purchasing Power Parity (PPP) exchange rate: an exchange rate that reflects what the two currencies are able to buy in their domestic economies.

R

Rationalisation: making a firm more efficient by reorganisation and consolidation.

Real economy: the part of the economy that uses economic resources to produce goods and services to satisfy people's needs and wants. It includes markets for factors of production and markets for goods and services but not financial and money markets.

Real effective exchange rate index: a measure of the weighted value of a currency against a basket of other currencies, adjusted to take into account the different rates of inflation in countries.

Recycling: the process of converting waste into reusable material.

Redeemed: paying back the money borrowed to the holder of a security, usually on maturity.

Relative poverty: where an individual or household has less than a certain percentage of the average income in their country.

Relative wage rate: the pay of one job compared to that of others.

Remittances: funds transferred to their home country by people living and working abroad.

Repatriation of profits: returning profits earned in the host country to the country where the business is owned.

Reserve assets: the assets a country's central bank has available to deal with balance of payments problems. They include official holdings of gold, foreign currency and special drawing rights (SDRs).

Reserve currencies: currencies that are widely used in international trade and that central banks are willing to hold as part of their foreign exchange reserves.

Resource curse: when a country with plenty of natural resources finds it hard to achieve sustainable economic development.

Restrictive practices: actions by a dominant firm or combination of firms to limit competition.

Returns to scale: the relationship between a change in inputs and the resulting change in output when all factors of production are variable.

Revaluation: an increase in the value of a country's currency in terms of other currencies. It is when, in a fixed exchange rate system, the government announces an increase in the official value of the currency.

Ring-fencing: when a bank's commercial and investment banking activities are kept separate from each other.

Rule of reason or pragmatic approach: where individual circumstances are considered and actions, such as having a monopoly, are not illegal unless there is an unreasonable restraint of trade.

Rules of thumb: mental shortcuts, based on experience, which enable individuals to make decisions more quickly and easily.

Run on the bank: when a large number of a bank's customers withdraw their money from the bank at the same time because they are concerned that the bank might fail.

S

Satisficing: achieving a minimum level of a number of variables to satisfy different stakeholders.

Savings gap: when domestic savings are unable to provide the funds required to finance the investment an economy needs.

Secondary capital market: the market where investors buy and sell second-hand securities.

Securities: financial assets that can be bought and sold on financial markets, including shares and bonds.

Service debts: the cash needed to repay the interest and principal due on money that has been borrowed.

Shadow banks: organisations that provide financial services, including giving loans, but are not licensed and do not accept deposits.

Shareholders' funds: the shareholders' stake in the business. It is the value of the total assets minus the value of the other liabilities. The shareholders' stake in the business comes from the money raised by issuing shares plus any profits that have been retained in the business.

Shares: securities that represent ownership of part of a company. Shares pay dividends to the holder depending on the amount of profit made by the company. Shares are not usually redeemed by the company.

Short-termism: when people, firms or the government focus on short-term results rather than their longer-term interests.

Social norms: behaviour consistent with what is considered acceptable in that society at that time.

Sovereign debt: the amount of money borrowed by a country's government.

Sovereign wealth fund (SWFs): a state-owned investment fund that invests in financial and real assets including shares, government bonds, property and foreign enterprises. SWFs generally use foreign exchange reserves, generated by current account surpluses, to buy overseas assets.

Special drawing rights (SDRs): an international reserve asset created by the International Monetary Fund that can be used by central banks to deal with balance of payments problems and can be exchanged for a limited number of foreign currencies (Chinese yuan, euros, Japanese yen, UK pounds and US dollars).

Spectrum of competition: the range of market structures from perfect competition to pure monopoly.

Spot market: where items are traded, delivered and paid for immediately.

Stabilising speculation: when the actions of speculators lead to smaller fluctuations in the price of an asset than if speculation had not taken place.

Stakeholders: those with an interest in the business, including owners, workers and customers.

Standard of deferred payment: a function of money that allows future payments for products bought on credit to be stated clearly.

Stand-By Arrangement (SBA): a facility through which the IMF provides financial help to member countries experiencing balance of payments problems.

Start-up costs: the expenses involved when setting up a new business.

State-owned enterprise (SOE): a business with significant government ownership and control.

Static efficiency: efficiency at a point in time.

Store of value: something that retains its purchasing power over time.

Strategic barriers to entry: restrictions on new firms entering the market that have been created deliberately by existing firms.

Stress tests: an assessment of the ability of a financial institution to cope with difficulties that may arise in financial markets or the wider economy.

Subnormal profit: making less than normal profit, when revenue is not sufficient to cover costs.

Suboptimal: less than optimal, not the best possible outcome.

Subsistence sector: part of the economy where individuals or families provide for their own basic needs, for example they grow their own food.

Sunk costs: costs that have been incurred but cannot be recovered if a firm leaves the market.

Sunrise industry: an industry that is in its early stages of development, often in a new sector of the economy that is expected to grow very rapidly.

Sunset industry: an industry that has been an important part of an economy for many years but has gone into decline.

Supernormal or abnormal profit: any profit greater than normal profit, producing where total revenue is greater than total costs or average revenue is greater than average costs.

Supply of labour: the number of hours that people are willing and able to work at different wage rates.

Sustainable Development Goals (SDGs): 17 sets of global development targets in areas such as health, education, gender equality, jobs, poverty reduction and protecting the environment.

Sustainable economic growth: economic growth that can be maintained over time.

Systemic risk: the possibility that the failure of a large financial institution could have a very damaging effect on other financial institutions and the real economy.

T

Tacit collusion: when firms have an informal arrangement or understanding about their actions, to reduce competition.

Takeover: when one firm buys out or takes control of another.

Tax avoidance: using legal methods to minimise the amount of tax paid by an individual or business.

Tax credit: an amount that can be taken off income to reduce the amount of tax owed.

Tax evasion: illegally not paying the full amount of tax.

Technical efficiency: when a given output is produced with minimum inputs or maximum output is obtained from given inputs.

Technological change: invention, innovation and the diffusion (spread) of new ideas and processes.

Terms of trade (comparative advantage): the rate at which one product is exchanged for another product, for example one orange is traded for two apples.

Terms of trade (for a country): the quantity of imports that a country can obtain for a given quantity of its exports, determined by the average price of exports relative to the average price of imports.

Tied aid: funds that are given on the condition that the money is spent on goods and services produced by the country providing the aid.

Too big to fail: a financial institution that is so important to the economy that the government considers that it cannot be allowed to go bankrupt.

Total product or total returns: the output at different levels of employment of the variable factor.

Total utility: the satisfaction obtained from consuming a particular number of units of a product, the aggregate of the utility for all the units consumed.

Tradable goods: products that can be sold in a location that is different from where it was produced, for example in a different country.

Trade creation gains: when, as a result of joining a trading bloc, production shifts from a higher-cost domestic producer to a lower-cost producer within the trading bloc.

Trade credit: where the seller provides a good or service to a buyer but is not paid until later. It is a type of short-term finance, provided by the seller, to help increase sales.

Trade diversion losses: when, as a result of joining a trading bloc, production shifts from the lowest-cost producer that is not in the trading bloc to a higher-cost producer within the trading bloc.

Trade liberalisation: the removal or reduction of restrictions on international trade, for example reducing tariffs and non-tariff barriers.

Trade union density: the percentage of a particular type of worker in a trade union.

Trade union: an organisation of workers that aims to protect and promote the rights and interests of its members.

Trade war: when countries impose tariffs, quotas or other trade restrictions on each other's exports.

Trading bloc: a group of countries that agree to remove, or reduce, restrictions on trade between themselves whilst keeping restrictions on trade with countries that are not members of the trading bloc.

Transfer price: the price that one part of a business charges another part of the business for goods and services provided.

Transnational corporation (TNC): an enterprise that owns assets, produces and sells goods and/or services in more than one country. Also known as a multinational corporation (MNC).

Treasury bills: short-term securities issued by the government.

Trickle-down effect: where increasing incomes and wealth for the rich leads to the creation of jobs and higher incomes for others.

U

Unemployment trap: where people may be worse off, or little better off, in work than unemployed.

Universal benefit: provided for everyone who fits into a particular category.

Unsustainable debt: when debt-servicing costs are so high that they cannot be paid without more borrowing and damage to the development of the country's economy.

Untied aid: when the country receiving aid can choose from which country it buys the goods and services it needs.

Urbanisation: when the proportion of a country's population living in towns and cities is increasing.

Utility maximisation: obtaining the highest possible satisfaction.

Utility satisficing: where an economic decision provides sufficient satisfaction but not the most that could have been obtained.

Utility: the satisfaction obtained from consuming a good or service.

V

Vertical integration: the joining of two or more firms at different stages of production of the same good or service.

Volatile markets: markets in which there are large, sometimes unpredictable, fluctuations in price.

W

Wage differentials: differences in wages between workers with similar or different skills.

Wage discrimination: when different groups of workers are offered different pay for the same or similar work, for reasons other than differences in their MRP.

Wage rate: the pay for a given time period.

Whistle-blower: a person who informs on another person or organisation that is involved in illegal activities.

World Trade Organization (WTO): an international organisation that regulates international trade and helps countries settle trade disputes.

X

X-efficiency: when a firm uses the ideal combination of factors of production at their lowest cost.

X-inefficiency: when a firm fails to minimise its costs of production.

Z

Zero marginal returns: when marginal product is zero after an extra unit of the variable factor is employed.

Answers

1.1 – Progress questions, Case study

Progress questions

1   Utility is the satisfaction obtained from consuming a good or service.
2   **i.** 60 utils; **ii.** 50 utils.

Case study

The utility of water

1

Cups	Marginal utility (utils)	Total utility (utils)	Average utility (utils)
1	42	42	42
2	28	70	35
3	17	87	29
4	9	96	24
5	4	100	20
6	−1	99	16.5

2   If water is free, Bandile will drink 5 cups to maximise his utility. After this, marginal utility is negative, so total utility falls.
3   Bandile's consumption of water is likely to be less if he had not just completed the parkrun. He is likely to be less thirsty and so will not value cups of water as highly.

1.2 – Progress questions, Case studies

Progress questions

1   The term sometimes used to describe someone who always acts rationally, to maximise their utility, is homo economicus or economic man.
2   Two factors that could influence decision making, according to behavioural economists, are social, emotional and psychological factors (or any explanation or examples of these).
3   "Bounded" means that it is limited.
4   Utility satisficing is when an economic decision provides sufficient satisfaction but not the most that could have been obtained.
5   **i.** social norms; **ii.** altruism; **iii.** inertia (status-quo bias); **iv.** rules of thumb.

Case studies

Boundless exercise?

i   Bounded rationality could be caused by imperfect information about alternatives and their effects; limited ability to process all the relevant information; and limited time to reach the "right" decision. Naomi may not have all the information about alternatives. She had heard that the new gym was better than the sports centre at the end of her street but how reliable was this information? She found "information on the internet" but was this sufficient to make the best decision? She also had not realised that it would take 45 minutes to travel to the new gym. She was choosing between 12 different classes costing different amounts, which was further complicated by the prices varying according to the number of sessions booked. Was she able to process all the relevant information? To obtain the discount, she had no more than 24 hours to make her decision and would need to be able to calculate the discounted prices. Was there enough time available for her to weigh up alternatives?
ii Bounded self-control involves individuals lacking full self-control to make decisions that act in their self-interest. Naomi knew/believed that she would benefit from being fitter and so signed up for the exercise class. However, she only attended three of the twenty sessions, lacking the self-control to turn up every week regardless of the weather, the number of other people attending or other factors that might make it difficult to stick to her plan. Also, "On the way home, she treated herself to a burger and a fizzy drink". She probably knew these would not help her to become fitter but lacked the self-control to do without them.

Workplace pensions in the United Kingdom

1   The United Kingdom workplace pension scheme has a default choice. An opt-in option is selected automatically but an individual can then choose to opt out of the scheme.

2   The increase in take-up rates from 47%, when it was introduced in 2012, to 76% by the time it was fully implemented in 2018, suggests that the scheme has been successful in encouraging people in the United Kingdom to join a workplace pension scheme. However, we do not know what would have happened had the scheme not been opt-out, nor do we know about other factors which may have encouraged individuals to join a workplace pension scheme or not during this time. Perhaps, fewer schemes were available in 2012? It appears to have been more successful in the public sector, perhaps due to more government promotion. It also seems to have been less successful for part-time workers but no figures are provided for this group in 2012 to make a fair comparison.

1.3 – Progress questions, Case studies

Progress questions

1   The models that comprise the traditional theory of the firm are usually based on the assumption that firms aim to maximise profits.
2   Sales revenue maximisation involves gaining the highest possible income from sales (total revenue). It is achieved by producing where marginal revenue is zero.
3   The divorce of ownership from control may lead to a conflict of objectives between owners and managers. The owners will want the firm to maximise profits but the managers may aim, for example, to maximise sales revenue, if this is more in their self-interest. This will affect price, output and other aspects of the behaviour and performance of firms.

Case studies

The rise of Spotify

1   **i.** In the short run, a firm has to cover its variable costs.
    ii. In the long run, a firm has to cover its total costs.
    However, in both cases, firms may continue in production even if not covering the necessary costs, if they believe the situation is temporary and they can make profits in future.
2   It is likely that the objectives of the owners of Spotify may have included growth, maximising sales revenue and/or increasing market share. They may have hoped to maximise their profits but given that they made losses for many years, survival would also have been an important objective.
3   Since it did not make a profit in its first ten years, Spotify has been able to survive by obtaining other sources of money in addition to their advertising and subscription revenue. This included issuing loans and shares in the firm. Others were willing to supply this money because they believed that the company could be profitable in the future.
4   Spotify's continued survival and success require it to cover its total costs in order to survive, to at least make normal profit. This involves either increasing its revenue and/or reducing its costs. Otherwise, it will have to incur more debt, which would only be worthwhile if the firm believed that the situation will improve in future. Spotify may have to offer a greater variety of services to provide more sources of income, perhaps using their insights into people's listening habits, offering podcasts or documentaries, or by providing a better service for the money, to attract customers from its rivals, to increase its subscriptions.

Railways in India

A private sector firm will have owners/shareholders who will be expecting a share of the profits. Therefore, profit is likely to be an important objective of a private sector firm and it must cover all its costs to survive in the long run. However, in large firms, where there is a divorce of ownership from control, there may be profit satisficing as the firm tries to keep its various stakeholders happy.

Indian Railways (IR) is state run and is therefore likely to be operating in the interests of society as a whole. This may involve offering a reliable service to enable people and freight to be transported cheaply and easily around the country. In 2018, it carried over 8 billion passengers and over 1 billion tonnes of freight. This is important for the economy. It is also a significant employer, with over 1.2 million workers.

IR has no shareholders requiring profits and the Indian government could finance its losses, if necessary, or provide money for modernisation or other projects in the long-term interest of the country. For example, all routes are being electrified to reduce imports of fuel and over $1 billion is being borrowed to pay for improvements in the railway infrastructure. However, state ownership of a business may lead to inefficiency and allow the pursuit of other objectives, for example, by workers, managers or politicians.

1.4 – Progress questions, Case study, Exam-style questions

Progress questions

1. Two ways that firms can grow could be by making more of its existing product or extending their range of products. Alternatively, firms may grow because the market for their product is growing or by attracting customers from their rivals. In both cases, this will increase output and require more factors of production. Firms could also grow through internal or external growth or through different types of integration.

2. Two reasons why firms may grow include to increase profit; to lower average cost by taking advantage of economies of scale; to achieve monopoly power; to diversify and become more secure; and for managers to achieve their personal goals.

3. Internal growth is when a firm expands without joining with other firms. External growth is when a firm expands by joining with other firms.

4. Those who may lose out from integration include workers, consumers or other firms. Some workers, including managers, could lose their jobs if they are no longer required. Consumers may have to pay higher prices, especially if the new firm now has considerable market power. Other firms could lose out by having more competition, problems in accessing materials or markets, or by being unable to enter the market.

Case study

The growth of Gepetto's Toys

1. **i.** buying a local coffee shop (a firm making an unrelated product); **ii.** the merger of Gepetto's and Antonio's businesses to form Gean Toys (same stage of production of the same good or service); **iii.** buying Pinocchio Woods, that owns the woodland (different stage of production of the same good or service).

2. Buying Pinocchio Woods is backward vertical integration since it involves taking over an earlier stage of production of the same good.

3. Competition is reduced and the combined firm will have a larger market share. This may give them more influence over the prices they charge. They may be able to take advantage of economies of scale, for example increased division of labour. It is also an opportunity to reorganise their operations. The merger may make the firm more secure and increase their overall profit.

Exam-style questions

1. C. This involves a mental short cut, enabling the individual to make a decision quickly and easily, which, based on past experience, will result in an acceptable outcome.

2. D. In the short run, a firm must be able to cover its day-to-day running costs, its variable costs.

3. C. Conglomerate integration involves the combination of two or more firms making unrelated products. This will spread the risks of trading, since the firm is no longer reliant on one market.

4. **i.** Average utility is the amount of satisfaction per item, total utility divided by the number of items consumed; **ii.** 150 units of utility (2 × 75); **iii.** 50 units of utility (150 – 100).

5. Indicative content is given below:
   - explanation and examples of horizontal integration
   - how it may be an aggressive or defensive move
   - reduction in competition and why
   - increased market share and effect on market power, price, etc
   - take more advantage of internal economies of scale, with explanation, examples and possibly a diagram of lower long-run average costs
   - increase profit
   - rationalisation, with explanation and examples.

6. Indicative content is given below. You should also try to include relevant references to data from the case studies to support your points:
   - meanings of profit and profit maximisation
   - importance of profit
   - need to make at least normal profit in the long run and to cover variable costs in the short run to survive

   - meaning and significance of divorce of ownership from control
   - objective of growth and example of Spotify
   - objective of increasing market share
   - objective of sales revenue maximisation
   - other objectives such as quality and corporate social responsibility
   - profit satisficing and likelihood of a range of objectives
   - what if under state ownership and/or control and example of Indian Railways
   - difficulty of knowing when profits are maximised
   - significance of market structure and degree of competition
   - recognition that maximisation of profit may be the main objective of some firms but not others, including circumstances of when it might or might not be
   - an overall assessment of whether or not the maximisation of profit is likely to be the main objective of firms.

7. Indicative content is given below:
   - distinction between behavioural policies and traditional government policies
   - meaning and examples of merit goods
   - why merit goods are underconsumed
   - analysis of possible behavioural policies – choice architecture, nudges, default choices, etc
   - advantages and disadvantages of behavioural policies
   - analysis of possible traditional policies – subsidies, regulation, etc
   - evaluation of advantages and disadvantages of traditional policies
   - relevance of the nature of the market failure and what would be best to improve the consumption of that particular good or service
   - short-term versus long-term solutions
   - use as complementary policies rather than alternatives
   - an overall assessment of whether or not governments should use behavioural policies rather than traditional policies to increase the consumption of merit goods.

2.1 – Progress questions, Case studies

Progress questions

1. The short run is the time period in which at least one factor of production is fixed in supply.
2. Total product = 60 tonnes (5 × 12).
3. 52 tonnes (60 – 8).
4. Diminishing returns are operating if output is increasing at a decreasing rate.
5. The law of diminishing returns is an input-output relationship.

Case studies

The law of diminishing returns in action

Fixed factor (land in hectares)	Variable factor (workers)	Total product (tonnes)	Average product (tonnes)	Marginal product (tonnes)
1	1	2	2	2
1	2	5	2.5	3
1	3	9	3	4
1	4	14	3.5	5
1	5	19	3.8	5
1	6	21	3.5	2
1	7	21.5	3.1	0.5
1	8	21.5	2.7	0
1	9	21	2.3	−0.5

Returns to scale in action
i. increasing returns to scale, because output increases by a greater percentage (100%) than inputs (50%); **ii.** constant returns to scale, because output increases by the same percentage as inputs (33.3%); **iii.** decreasing returns to scale, because output increases by a smaller percentage (12.5%) than inputs (25%).

2.2 – Progress questions, Case study

Progress questions

1   $394 ($400 – $6).
2   $160 (FC = 8 × $200 = $1600 and $1600 ÷ 10 = $160).
3   $432 (AC = AFC + AVC = $60 + $12 = $72. TC = AC × Q = $72 × 6 = $432).
4   The marginal cost is the same as the addition to the variable cost when an extra unit is produced since these are the only costs that change in the short run.
5   The AFC curve is downward sloping, steeply to start with and then levelling off, as a set amount of costs is spread across an increasing number of units.
6   If marginal cost is less than average cost, this will pull down average cost. If marginal cost is greater than average cost, it will pull up average cost. Marginal cost will cut average cost at the lowest point of the average cost curve.

Case study

Application of short-run costs

1

Units	Fixed cost (FC)	Average fixed cost (AFC)	Variable cost (VC)	Average variable cost (AVC)	Total cost (TC)	Average cost (AC)	Marginal cost (MC)
1	500	500	300	300	800	800	300
2	500	250	560	280	1060	530	260
3	500	167	780	260	1280	427	220
4	500	125	980	245	1480	370	200
5	500	100	1200	240	1700	340	220
6	500	83	1500	250	2000	333	300
7	500	71	1890	270	2390	341	390

2   $500, since there will only be fixed costs at zero output.
3   The marginal cost curve will cross the average cost curve after the 6th unit. Up to and including the production of the 6th unit, marginal cost is less than average cost but with the production of the 7th unit, marginal cost becomes greater than average cost.

2.3 – Progress questions, Case study

Progress questions

1   If a firm is experiencing decreasing returns to scale, its LRAC will rise, other things being equal, since a given percentage increase in inputs will lead to a less than proportionate increase in output, increasing the cost per unit.
2   In the long run, the prices and productivity of factors of production could change as well as the scale of production, perhaps due to technological progress, affecting LRAC.
3   For a U-shaped LRAC curve, LRMC = LRAC at the lowest point of the LRAC curve.
4   If the firm faces a downward-sloping LRAC curve, LRMC must be below LRAC, since the LRMC must be less than the existing LRAC to cause LRAC to continue to fall.

Case study

Alexei's barley farm revisited

1

Land	Labour	Capital	Total product (tonnes)	Total cost ($)	Average cost ($)
1	2	4	50	12000	240
2	4	8	120	24000	200
3	6	12	240	36000	150
4	8	16	300	48000	160
5	10	20	330	60000	182

2   The LRAC curve is U-shaped. LRAC falls, and then starts to rise. This is because there are increasing returns to scale, followed by decreasing returns to scale.

3   Productive efficiency is achieved where Alexei uses 3 units of land, 6 units of labour and 12 units of capital. This produces an output of 240 tonnes of barley at an average cost of $150. This is productively efficient because LRAC is minimised.

2.4 – Progress questions

Progress questions

1   $30 ($450 ÷ 15).
2   €35 (€1022 – €987).
3   ¥19,200 (¥1200 × 16).
4   In perfect competition, the price is set by the market supply and demand, the firm is a price taker and an individual firm can sell as much as it wants at this price. If every item is sold for the same price, both the average revenue and the marginal revenue (the addition to total revenue) will be the same.
5   Total revenue for a monopoly will be maximised where MR = 0. For items sold up to this point, MR will be positive, adding to TR, but for items beyond this, the now negative MR will reduce TR. It is also the quantity where PED is of unit elasticity.

2.5 – Case study

Case study

Not everyone is a winner

1   After a year, Mariana was making normal profit since "the income from sales was only just enough to keep Mariana in business".
2   Profit provides a **reward for risk taking**. Mariana was hoping that her new product would be a success. She risked losing her home if the business was not successful because she had used this as security on her bank loan. Her grandmother was also taking a risk in the hope of receiving some profit. However, her grandmother may have invested in the business to provide her with another **source of income**, through the dividends she hoped to receive. The prospect of profit had acted as an **incentive** to Mariana and also to the rival firm. When the new firm joined the market, there was an increase in **resources allocated** to the production of the good. To start making the product, Mariana was unable to make enough profit for it to act as a **source of funds** but the rival firm may have been able to finance the development of the new product by using past profits they had made on their other products.
3   The other firm was likely to be able to make supernormal profits. With the lessening of competition, it was able to increase its prices. This would have increased the difference between its average revenue and its already low average cost. However, we do not know if this profit margin will be maintained in the long run, since there may be low barriers to entry into the market, for example.

2.6 – Progress questions, Case study, Exam-style questions

Progress questions

1   Invention is the creation of a new idea, product or process, while innovation involves making changes to existing products by introducing new ideas that better satisfy people's wants and/or have been adapted to deal with new requirements.
2   As well as invention and innovation, technological change involves the diffusion (or spread) of the new ideas and processes.
3   Technological change could increase firms' costs in the short run as they spend money on research and development (R&D) and training or have to replace outdated equipment. In the long run, it should reduce the average and marginal costs of the firm.
4   Creative destruction theory is the replacement of existing products, markets and firms with new ones as an inevitable outcome of technological change.
5   Technological change could make markets either more or less concentrated. If the optimum size becomes greater as a result of technological change, a market is likely to become more dominated by large firms, but if the optimum size falls, there could be an increase in the number of small firms.

Case study

Technological change in the automotive industry

1   Assembly-line production is likely to increase labour productivity by making more use of division of labour. Workers can concentrate

on one process in the same part of the factory. Less time is wasted and the worker can become good at what they do more quickly and with limited training. This will speed up the production process and increase the number of items completed per worker in a given time.

2   If more is being produced from a set amount of inputs, the cost of production per item will fall. Alternatively, it may be possible to produce more with fewer inputs. For example, with more division of labour, the equipment required by each worker will fall. Production will become more capital intensive but the increase in the cost of capital will be more than offset by the fall in labour costs.

3   Lower costs enabled the firms to lower the price of their products. This meant that more people could afford to buy them and so the technological change spread to American society as a whole. Other firms are also likely to adopt the technology to reduce their average costs.

Exam-style questions

1   C. Marginal product is increasing and total product is increasing at an increasing rate. It is a short-run situation, when only one factor of production is changing, so there are increasing returns not increasing returns to scale.

2   A. The PED of a downward-sloping straight-line demand curve changes with price becoming less elastic as price falls.

3   A. Normal profit takes account of the owner receiving a reasonable reward. It is the cost of enterprise and is included in the firm's costs.

4   **i.** Fixed costs are costs that do not change with output; **ii.** $600 = (50 + 10) × 10$; **iii.** $25 = (50 × 10) ÷ 20$; **iv.** A diagram such as Figure 2.2.2 can be used to show how AFC falls when output is increased, rapidly to start with and then more slowly. This is because the fixed cost is spread across an increasing number of units as more is produced. This could be supported by referring to two quantities and their respective AFC on the diagram and/or a numerical example.

5   **i.** Some of the points that might be made include:
   - definitions of long run, average cost, LRAC and U-shaped
   - explanation and examples of economies of scale
   - explanation of how increasing the scale of operations could lead to falling LRAC
   - explanation and examples of diseconomies of scale
   - explanation of how increasing the scale of operations could lead to rising LRAC
   - economies followed by diseconomies of scale will cause the LRAC to be U-shaped.

   A diagram such as Figure 2.3.1 could be drawn (LRMC not required) but this is not necessary for full marks.

   ii. Some of the points that might be made include the following:
   - the data generally supports a U-shaped LRAC.
   - initially, as output increases, LRAC falls, for example between Year 1 and Year 4. As output increases each year, LRAC falls from $50 in Year 1 when output is 100 to $20 in Year 4 when output is 400, supporting the possibility of economies of scale.
   - in Year 5, when output rises to 500, LRAC rises to $30, supporting the view that diseconomies of scale have set in.
   - however, LRAC stays the same, at $30, in Year 6 when output rises to 600.
   - in Year 7, rising output is again associated with rising LRAC.
   - there may be other factors at work in Year 6, for example technological progress may have increased productivity, offsetting management diseconomies or a productivity bonus scheme may have been introduced.
   - the likely conclusion is that changes in output cause the firm's LRAC to be U-shaped.

6   Indicative content is given below; you should also try to include relevant references to data from the case study to support your points:
   - meaning and examples of technological change
   - difference between invention and innovation
   - impact on products such as medical advances, mobile phones and the internet
   - assessment of what is meant by "beneficial to an economy"
   - analysis of impact on methods of production and productivity
   - reference to impact of assembly-line production in the car industry and elsewhere
   - analysis of impact on efficiency and firms' costs of production
   - analysis of effect on standards of living
   - analysis of impact on structure of markets
   - creative destruction theory and the reallocation of resources as an inevitable process in free market economies leading to benefits for consumers
   - analysis and evaluation of effects on employment and unemployment
   - evaluation of who may gain and who may lose from technological change

   - role of governments in generating technological change and/or how they can help to support those who lose out
   - significance of the word "always", suggesting that since some individuals and firms could end up worse off, "always" is too strong a claim
   - an overall assessment of whether technological change is always beneficial to an economy.

3.1 – Progress questions

Progress questions

1   A duopoly is a market where two firms control the supply of a good or service.

2   The four main types of market structure are perfect competition, monopolistic competition, oligopoly and monopoly.

3   Examples of barriers to entry into a market include: economies of scale; the amount of advertising needed to compete against well-known brands; the cost of specialist equipment.

3.2 – Progress questions, Case study

Progress questions

1   The demand curve for a firm in perfect competition is perfectly elastic.

2   A firm in perfect competition would not try to sell its products for less than the market price because it can sell as much as it chooses at a higher price. It would sell no more at a lower price and would receive less money per item and in total.

3   Profits will rise if the amount added to revenue from an extra unit (MR) is greater than the amount added to cost (MC), and profits will fall if MR is less than MC. Since normal profit is included in costs, it is therefore just worthwhile producing up to and including the unit where MC = MR.

4   If firms in perfect competition make supernormal profit in the short run, this will attract other firms into the market, since the supernormal profit acts as an incentive and there is perfect knowledge. This will increase the market supply.

5   If some firms make losses in the short run and leave the market, those firms that remain in the market in the long run will have a higher price and quantity sold.

6   Firms making short-run supernormal profits or losses are not productively efficient because AC is not minimised (AC ≠ MC) at the profit-maximising output in both diagrams.

7   Firms in perfect competition may not be allocatively efficient if there are externalities. For allocative efficiency, price must equal MSC, but a firm will only consider the MPC when deciding how much to produce.

Case study

The Tsukiji fish market
- Large numbers of buyers and sellers? Tsukiji was the largest wholesale fish and seafood market in the world with about 900 wholesale fish sellers in the inner market. This is likely to have attracted a large number of buyers, suggesting that each had a very small percentage of the market, but we do not know this for certain. However, for the tuna auctions, buyers needed a licence which is likely to have limited the number of buyers in that section. If they are buying for a food-processing firm, they may also buy a relatively large quantity but a large amount was sold each day overall (about $14 million).
- Homogeneous goods? For a particular type of fish/seafood of a particular size, the goods were probably almost identical but there may have been some variation in quality. The price per kilogram for a particular species of fish was likely to be similar, if not the same, at a given time, but we have no information about this. It only says that "there are plenty of similarly-priced stalls" which suggests the prices are not all the same and there could be some variation in the product.
- Free entry and exit? There may be nothing to stop buyers and sellers entering or leaving the market but there is no information about how much it costs to have a stall there. Also, for the tuna auction, buyers needed a licence. Did the cost of this act as a barrier to entry and/or was the number of buyers limited? Also, for the tuna, a large sum of money would be needed to buy one fish ($632,000 for one tuna in 2017), too expensive for most potential buyers. The tuna auction relates to the wholesale market, which does not fit as well with the market for perfect competition, due to the quantities bought and sold and other limitations.
- Perfect information? It is likely that buyers and sellers will be well informed, for example about the price of a particular species of fish

and that these will be displayed on the stalls. The price in the tuna auction is less certain but previous prices were known to all.

Overall, parts of the market (but not the tuna auction) seem to fit some of the characteristics of a perfectly competitive market quite well, but more information is required.

3.3 – Progress questions, Case study

Progress questions

1   Price elasticity of demand for a product in monopolistic competition is likely to be elastic, meaning that for a given percentage change in price, there will be a larger percentage change in quantity demanded. This is because there are so many close substitutes. For example, if Firm B raises its price, many (but not all) of its buyers will switch to other firms.

2   Cross elasticity of demand for products is likely to be high, meaning that for a given percentage change in price of one firm's good, there will be a larger percentage change in demand for another/other firms. This is because the products are similar and buyers will switch to and from other firms if their relative prices change.

3   A firm in monopolistic competition is a price maker, since it controls the supply of its brand or version of the product. However, since there are many close substitutes, it may have to set its price at a similar level to other firms.

4   Firms can only make normal profit in the long run because if supernormal profits are made in the short run, this will attract other firms into the market, who will know this is happening and can easily enter the market. This will increase competition and the market supply, reducing price and eliminating the supernormal profit.

5   If you were starting a business as a cleaner or gardener, ways that you could differentiate your business to attract customers and to build up brand loyalty include: giving your business a memorable name; making people aware of what services you specialise in; being flexible with when you can work; offering a discount for regular bookings, etc.

Case study

The market for tuk-tuks

i.   There is a large number of potential buyers – a population of over 20 million, plus tourists and work from businesses for transporting goods or advertising. There is also a large number of sellers – 1.2 million tuk-tuks, about 1 per 18 people of the country's population.

ii. The tuk-tuks are similar products in terms of their capacity and what they offer but they look slightly different - painted in a variety of colours and often decorated with ornaments. Some drivers will also make the experience more or less enjoyable than others.

iii. We are not told the cost to buy a tuk-tuk, either new or second hand, but since they are usually bought with a loan and second-hand vehicles and spare parts are plentiful, this suggests that there are relatively low barriers to entry and exit.

iv. Fares in Sri Lanka are not controlled by the government and are usually negotiated between the driver and passengers. Fares are likely to be similar but a buyer will not know all the different prices being charged for a particular journey.

On balance, the market for tuk-tuks in Sri Lanka seems to fit the model of monopolistic competition well considering each of the four main characteristics.

3.4 – Progress questions, Case study

Progress questions

1   A five-firm concentration ratio of 60% means that the largest five firms have 60% of the market (probably sales) between them.

2   The key features of an oligopoly include: a small number of relatively large firms; product differentiation; significant barriers to entry; interdependence and uncertainty; non-price competition.

3   Interdependence is when two or more things, for example firms, depend on each other. In an oligopoly, there are only a few relatively large firms. This means that the actions of one could have a significant impact on the others. Each is affected by the actions and reactions of others. They are not independent of each other, they are interdependent.

4   Conduct is about how firms choose to behave, for example: whether they are using price or non-price competition; the extent of innovation; whether they are colluding; and their pricing strategies. Performance refers to how well they are doing, for example: in terms of profit; different types of efficiency; or any judgement against the firm's objectives.

5   Collusion is when firms work together so they can both benefit from the arrangement. This could include agreeing prices or not competing against each other for contracts.

6   The kinked demand curve model predicts that firms will not follow price rises but will follow price cuts. Therefore, if a firm changes its price, its sales revenue will fall. This suggests that prices are likely to be fairly stable and "stick" at their present level unless there is a considerable change in the market affecting other firms as well.

7   Examples of non-price competition include: advertising; sponsorship; brand image; styling; slogans; packaging; after-sales service; loyalty rewards; free gifts.

8   Predatory pricing involves a firm lowering price to try to drive one or more of its rivals out of business. Limit pricing is where the price is set below the profit-maximising level to act as a barrier to entry. Both involve setting a lower price but for different reasons.

9   Strategic barriers to entry include: spending large amounts of money on advertising and/or creating a strong brand image; selling a large number of differentiated products; and limit pricing. Innocent barriers include: economies of scale/a large minimum efficient scale; high start-up costs; specialist equipment with no alternative use.

10 It is difficult to generalise about the advantages and disadvantages of oligopoly because every real-world oligopoly is different. There is no single model of oligopoly. Much depends on the degree of concentration, product differentiation, ease of entry and whether the firms collude or not.

Case study

An example of a cartel – OPEC

1   If production targets are cut, less will be supplied. The market supply of oil will decrease/shift to the left (as in Figure 3.2.9). At the old equilibrium price of p, there will now be excess demand, which will bid up the price to p_1.

2   Countries may want to join a cartel such as OPEC to be part of an organisation which has more power over the market and to benefit from higher and/or more stable prices and incomes, if these can be controlled by the cartel. Being a member of a cartel also reduces the uncertainty of how rivals may act and react and what could happen in future if the country is part of the decision-making process.

3   The success of a cartel partly depends on how many members join and the size of their market shares. For example, a cartel is likely to be more successful, the larger the market share it controls and the higher the barriers to entry into the market. This makes it less likely that its prices can be undercut by non-members or new entrants. However, it will be easier to coordinate and reach agreements if there are only a few firms in the industry. It also depends on how much the members trust each other to stick to the agreements.

4   A cartel such as OPEC continues to exist despite collusion being illegal in most countries, because its members are countries rather than individual firms. With state immunity, a state cannot usually be sued in a court of another country, so no individual country is able to stop the arrangement.

3.5 – Progress questions, Case study

Progress questions

1   If a monopoly chooses the amount it wishes to sell, the price is determined by the firm's AR = D curve, since this shows how much consumers are willing to pay for a given quantity.

2   A natural monopoly is where an activity is best carried out by one firm and it would be a waste of resources to have more than one firm, for example where there is expensive infrastructure required and/or significant economies of scale available.

3   LRMC is below LRAC in a natural monopoly because even if one firm produces all the goods or services required, this is not enough output to reach the lowest point of LRAC, where LRMC would then cut, and rise above, LRAC.

4   Advertising can increase monopoly power by increasing barriers to entry. If the existing firms spend large sums of money on advertising, it may put off potential new entrants to the market. They may not be willing or able to spend the money required to promote their products against well-known brands, with no guarantee of success.

5   If a monopoly is in the public sector and controlled by the government, it is likely to have different objectives. The firm is likely to be run more for the benefit of society and not to maximise profits. This may involve producing a greater quantity at a lower price than would happen in the private sector. Other differences include that funds for investment do not necessarily have to come from profits; and some of its operations may be subsidised, for example rail links to rural areas.

Case study

Microsoft

1 Microsoft has "regularly developed and launched new and improved software and other products". The firm was only founded in 1975 but has since developed a range of software, web browsers and other devices, which have been updated and improved. This suggests that despite its monopoly power (dominating the personal computer operating system market by the mid-1980s and having 80% of the global internet usage market in 2012), Microsoft has undertaken considerable research and development.

2 Microsoft has been fined over $1 billion for anti-competitive practices by the EU, and the US government threatened to split up the firm. This suggests that there must have been significant abuse of its monopoly power. $94 billion gross profit for the year to March 2020 also seems very high.

3 The Case study illustrates the concept of creative destruction in terms of the development and success of the Android system. Although only launched in 2008, nine years later it had become the leading operating system for global internet usage. In five years, from 2012 to 2017, Microsoft's share of this market fell from 80% to 37.91%. The concept is also illustrated by the development of smartphones to carry out many of the functions of desktop computers or even the development of computer technology generally.

3.6 – Progress questions, Case study

Progress questions

1 Price discrimination is when a firm charges different prices to different consumers for the same product for reasons other than differences in cost.

2 An airline may charge less for a flight six months before it is due to leave because the airline is unsure how high demand will be on that date and it will also receive payment for the flight earlier. If there are only a few seats left a week before, people's demand may be more inelastic and they may be willing to pay more.

3 Examples of economic agents who may gain include:
   - the price discriminating firm, which will increase its sales and profits and possibly barriers to entry, strengthening its position in the market
   - those paying the cheaper price, who may also be those on lower incomes
   - potentially all consumers if lower average costs are passed on in the form of lower prices or the extra profits are used for R&D, leading to new or improved products.

   Examples of economic agents who may lose include:
   - suppliers, who may now be in a weaker bargaining position
   - firms who may want to enter the market, since they may now find it more difficult
   - consumers who pay a higher price than would be charged without price discrimination.

Case study

Price discrimination in the pharmaceutical industry

1 Firms in the pharmaceutical industry can price discriminate because if the products are patented, they will be the sole supplier. They can also separate their markets, charging different prices in different countries, according to ability to pay.

2 The difference in price between countries could be due to the fact that some markets may cost more to supply than others, for example due to higher transport costs or having to comply with local regulations. There may be tariffs (taxes on imports) and other taxes added in some countries, which could increase the price. Also, some national health services may be able to negotiate lower prices because of the large quantities of medicines that they buy.

3 There are advantages and disadvantages of price discrimination for different economic agents, which either support the case for pharmaceutical firms using price discrimination or suggest it should be stopped – both sides should be considered. Money is needed for R&D into new medicines and firms need to gain the money back that they have already invested in this. This will require them to try to charge as much as they can in different markets, for as long as the patent lasts. It could be argued that those with lower incomes are generally likely to receive the products for a lower price than would be paid in a single market. This means that fewer people may use ineffective or poisonous cheap copies. However, some people will pay more than would be charged without price discrimination. This could be considered unfair and exploitation.

3.7 – Progress questions

Progress questions

1 A perfectly contestable market is one with no barriers to entry or exit.

2 A monopoly may or may not be a contestable market – it depends on the extent of barriers to entry and exit. There may also be the possibility of creative destruction. A monopoly is likely to have considerable barriers to entry and/or exit but this does not necessarily apply.

3 Hit-and-run competition, or the threat of this happening, is likely to make firms behave more competitively. They will probably charge lower prices and make less profit (at least in the short run) than if there was no chance of hit-and-run competition. They are also likely to be more efficient, operating closer to their minimum average cost.

4 The internet has enabled some markets to become more contestable by reducing barriers to entry. Firms may not need a physical outlet/shop, reducing start-up costs and more people will know about them more easily and cheaply, requiring less spending on advertising.

3.8 – Progress questions, Case study

Progress questions

1 Benefits to consumers from competition between firms include: lower prices; more innovation; better quality products; better quality service; more awareness of what is available; higher living standards.

2 A firm may be able to maintain monopoly power in the long run, if there are high barriers to entry and/or exit. These may be natural barriers such as high start-up costs or economies of scale. Alternatively, they may be artificial barriers, for example limit pricing or sunk costs such as high advertising expenditure to create a strong brand image and brand loyalty. This makes hit-and-run competition unlikely. The firm may also put money into research and development to try to constantly improve their products, so they stay on top of technological changes and are not replaced by new firms.

Case study

Uber

1 The benefits of Uber offering taxi services mainly result from the increased competition. There are more taxis available and prices are usually lower. Taxi rides are easy to book using the app. It has also created more jobs, increasing the incomes of some people.

2 Uber made use of mobile phone technology to offer a different and easy way of finding the price and availability of a taxi. Uber rents cars to drivers or drivers can use their own, which has overcome some of the barriers to entry into the market. The firm has also applied its way of operating to other related services, such as car sharing and food delivery, increasing availability and undercutting the prices of similar services. By trialling driverless cars, Uber hopes to be one of the first firms that can offer this new service.

3.9 – Progress questions

Progress questions

1 Static efficiency is concerned with a type of efficiency at a point in time – how well are resources allocated? Dynamic efficiency looks at efficiency over a period of time.

2 Two facts about marginal and/or average costs which apply when a firm is productively efficient is that AC is at its lowest and MC = AC.

3 A firm must be technically efficient to be productively efficient because it cannot minimise its costs if it is not producing the most it can from its resources and/or it is paying more than necessary for them.

4 Two factors which can influence a firm's dynamic efficiency are availability of finance and competitive pressure. A firm is more likely to be dynamically efficient if it can access money to pay for research and development, etc. Similarly, if the firm is under more competitive pressure, it may feel more need to be dynamically efficient. This may be the case in a competitive oligopoly, or if the market is contestable, or if creative destruction is likely – these could be discussed as separate influencing factors on a firm's dynamic efficiency, as could market structure.

3.10 – Progress questions

Progress questions

1 Consumer surplus is the difference between the price consumers are willing to pay and what they actually pay.

2   Price discrimination leads to a loss of consumer surplus because the prices charged are closer to the highest price that consumers are willing to pay. This reduces the difference between the price they are willing to pay and the price they actually pay.

3   If a market is transformed from perfect competition to a monopoly, there is usually a loss of consumer surplus. Some of this is transferred to producers, increasing producer surplus.

4   Having a monopoly in a market, rather than perfect competition could lead to an increase in welfare if there are economies of scale and/or more dynamic efficiency, leading to lower costs and prices. The gains in consumer and producer surplus may more than offset the deadweight welfare loss.

3.11 – Progress questions, Case study

Progress questions

1   A dominant firm is a business with a significant market share and a significantly larger market share than its next largest rival.

2   Problems that could arise from a firm dominating a market include: less choice, higher prices and/or poorer quality products for consumers; restrictive practices which could increase barriers to entry for other firms; a less efficient allocation of resources.

3   Measures a competition authority could use to reduce the potential problems of a monopoly include: make monopolies illegal if they use anti-competitive practices; fine firms that are found to be using restrictive practices and stop them from continuing to behave in this way; use controls on prices or profits; stop mergers that would lead to firms becoming monopolies.

4   A country may have a competition policy to deal with mergers and takeovers because they may lead to a dominant firm being formed, that then has the potential to exploit its monopoly power. Competition may be reduced.

5   Examples of restrictive practices include: firms not competing against each other in certain locations; price fixing; any action which makes it more difficult for new firms to enter the market.

Case study

Competition policy in Brazil

1   The reforms made in Brazil may reduce the potential problems of dominant firms and restrictive practices by:
- having a single body rather than three separate agencies
- the body being independent
- introducing a merger pre-notification system
- modernising its cartel enforcement programme
- having higher fines
- working with other international competition policy agencies.

2   Other measures the Brazilian government could use to encourage more competition in markets include:
- taking more action against dominant firms and restrictive practices, for example by providing more money to hire staff, including experts
- enabling infrastructure, such as pipes or cables, to be shared, so that barriers to entry are reduced and more firms can compete to supply the service
- deregulation
- offering financial support, for example investment grants and subsidies for other firms to set up or expand.

3.12 – Progress questions, Case study, Exam-style questions

Progress questions

1   Nationalisation is the process when a private sector firm or industry is taken over by the government.

2   Advantages of state-owned enterprises (SOEs) include:
- public goods can be provided, which would otherwise be a missing market due to their non-excludability and non-rivalry in consumption
- provision of merit goods such as education and health can be increased, to help those who cannot afford them and to help increase economic growth
- being able to take advantage of the benefits of natural monopolies in key industries without consumers being exploited.

Disadvantages of SOEs include:
- decisions being made for political rather than economic reasons and that this may make long-term planning difficult
- inefficiency, due to the lack of competition
- the difficulty of not knowing how much to produce for the social optimum.

3   Regulation involves laws or rules that control the behaviour and activities of individuals and firms. It may be used for a privatised industry to stop it exploiting its monopoly power, perhaps charging higher prices than necessary or stopping other firms from entering the industry.

4   Advantages of privatising state-owned enterprises include:
- more incentive to be efficient, to increase profits and strengthen their position in the market
- being free from direct government interference, enabling them to make longer-term plans
- revenue is raised for the government, which may be used to increase their spending, cut taxes or pay off debts.

Disadvantages of privatising state-owned enterprises include:
- it may result in a private sector monopoly able to exploit its monopoly power by charging higher prices
- a loss of economies of scale, raising long-run average costs, if the market share of a natural monopoly is reduced
- the need for effective regulation, to set rules and enforce good behaviour, but then regulatory capture may occur.

Case study

Privatisation in the Philippines

1   USD 4 billion (200.76 × 0.02 = 4.0152).

2   Advantages of privatisation covered by the case study include: the government can focus on fewer areas; the country is more able to access loans from the IMF and World Bank; increased competition; increased investment; more government revenue, to pay off debts.

Disadvantages of privatisation include: use for political reasons rather than economic; rising prices and a lack of competition (after electricity privatisation); inadequate regulation and regulatory capture; concerns about whether vital services should be left to the private sector; job cuts.

Exam-style questions

1   D. Total revenue is increasing at a constant rate, so this means that $P = MR = AR = \$30$. This would apply to a firm in perfect competition, where it can sell as much as it likes at the market price. In other market structures, firms face a downward-sloping demand curve, where, to persuade people to buy more, the price needs to be lowered.

2   C. The conditions for a perfectly contestable market are that there are no barriers to entry or exit, so there will be no sunk costs. Although perfect competition is a perfectly contestable market with a large number of firms, each of which has a perfectly elastic demand curve, these are not requirements of a perfectly contestable market.

3   A. Productive efficiency occurs when a firm minimises its long-run average cost. This is also the point where $MC = AC$.

4   i. Consumer surplus is the difference between the price consumers are willing to pay and what they actually pay.

ii. A diagram such as Figure 3.10.1 can be used to show the initial consumer surplus (the area between the demand curve and the equilibrium price). An increase in labour costs shifts the supply curve to the left, since firms will now charge a higher price for a given level of output. This will raise the equilibrium price and reduce the consumer surplus triangle because people will now be paying a price closer to the highest price they were willing to pay for given quantities and less will be sold in total.

5   i. Some of the points that could be made include:
- identification of number of firms with different market structures, for example one being a pure monopoly, two and six being oligopolies with two a duopoly
- different degrees of monopoly power/ability to control price, with the general assumption that the fewer the firms/the larger the market share, the greater the power to increase price
- the nature of the electricity market as a possible natural monopoly and explanation of the features of a natural monopoly, economies of scale and falling average cost
- impact on average costs if the market is divided between more firms
- link between average costs and prices
- possibility of sharing of cables if electricity is regulated.

ii. Some of the points that could be made include:
- the increase in price is highest when there are fewest firms (60% for one firm) but also the most firms (70% for 50 firms)

- this supports the view that with a pure monopoly, the firm will have more power to increase price, even though its average costs are lower
- this also supports the view that with many smaller firms, average costs may be higher, making prices higher but does this explain the higher increase in price over the 10-year period, if the number of firms has stayed the same?
- the lowest price increase (30%) occurs in the country with 6 firms, which may suggest that the firms have access to economies of scale but are competing rather than colluding with each other
- however, the data apply to five countries which may be very different, for example: with different inflation rates (are the data in real or nominal terms?); do countries have similar populations, making potential economies of scale comparable; has the number of firms within each country changed over the 10-year period?; is there an equal amount of regulation, enabling all firms to access the cables?; have costs increased by the same amount in each country?; there is no information on the market shares, for example are the six firms of a similar size?
- the likely conclusion is that the number of firms does affect the percentage change in price over the period but there may be other factors which are also, or possibly more, important and we would need further information to be able to reach a more definite conclusion.

6 Indicative content is given below; you should also try to include relevant references to data from the case study to support your points:
- meaning of competition
- methods of competition and motives, including example of Uber
- explanation of the effects of price competition and a price war in the short run and long run, both on consumers and taxi drivers, using examples from the case study
- explanation of the likely effects of competition on consumer choice, costs, prices, efficiency and the allocation of resources
- impact on innovation, for example the development of a mobile app for booking
- impact on quality of service, including quality of the car and the driver plus safety concerns.

7 Indicative content is given below; you should also try to include relevant references to data from the case study to support your points:
- meaning and examples of oligopoly
- significance of interdependence and uncertainty in oligopoly
- difference between collusive and competitive oligopoly
- innocent and strategic barriers to entry
- kinked demand curve
- examples of collusion – tacit, overt and cartels, with possible reference to OPEC
- analysis of effects of collusion, again with possible reference to OPEC
- examples of price and non-price competition
- analysis of effects of competition
- impact on spending on research and development and whether collusion could involve cooperation
- evaluation of advantages and disadvantages to consumers
- awareness that there is no single model of oligopoly and that whether oligopolistic industries benefit consumers will vary from one industry to another
- an overall assessment as to whether oligopolistic industries benefit consumers.

8 Indicative content is given below:
- characteristics of perfect competition
- meaning of an efficient allocation of resources
- meanings and conditions for different types of efficiency – static, dynamic, productive, allocative
- firms as price takers
- possible perfect competition situations for a firm in the short run, probably with a diagram
- analysis of whether firms in the short run are efficient, when making supernormal profit or a loss
- long-run equilibrium situation for a firm in perfect competition, probably with a diagram
- analysis of whether firms in the long run are efficient, when making normal profit
- possibility of externalities
- analysis and evaluation of impact of externalities on efficiency in perfect competition
- possibility of an activity having significant economies of scale
- analysis and evaluation of impact of significant economies of scale on efficiency

- awareness that the model of perfect competition provides a yardstick for judging extent to which real-world markets perform efficiently but is unlikely to exist in its extreme form
- an overall assessment as to whether, and in which circumstances, perfect competition results in an efficient allocation of resources.

4.1 – Progress questions, Case study

Progress questions

1 The demand curve for labour is a derived demand because the demand for labour results from the demand for the product it makes.
2 34 (€374 ÷ €11).
3 £150 (£2,700 ÷ 18).
4 **i.** an increase in demand/shift to the right of the MRP = D curve, because it is likely that increased training will increase labour productivity/MRP; **ii.** a movement back up the MRP = D curve/contraction in demand, because the demand for labour shows how many workers the firm would be willing and able to employ at different wage rates.
5 If the demand for the product is elastic, then a small change in its price will lead to a larger proportionate change in demand and also in the demand for labour to produce it, making the demand for labour more elastic as well.
6 PED = –0.8 (–12 ÷ 15). When the percentage change in the wage rate is greater than the percentage change in the quantity demanded of labour, giving a value for PED between 0 and –1, demand is inelastic.
7 The demand for workers who deal with payments into a bank is likely to be more elastic than the demand for hairdressers. This is because it may be easier to use a machine to do the work of those in the bank, but hairdressing involves an individual personalised service where each customer/hairstyle is different. If the relative costs of the factors of production change, it is easier to substitute capital for labour in the bank.

Case study

Marginal revenue product

1

Number of workers employed	Total physical product, TPP	Marginal physical product, MPP	Total revenue product, TRP ($)	Marginal revenue product, MRP ($)
1	30	30	300	300
2	57	27	570	270
3	81	24	810	240
4	102	21	1020	210
5	120	18	1200	180
6	135	15	1350	150

2 **i.** Gepetto should employ 5 workers at a wage rate of $155 because up to and including this number of workers, their MRP is greater than the wage rate but the next (6th) worker's MRP is less than their wage rate, so they are not worth employing; **ii.** 2 workers if the wage rate is $260, for the same reason; **iii.** no workers because even the MRP of the 1st worker is greater than their MRP.

4.2 – Progress questions, Case study

Progress questions

1 The supply of labour is the number of hours that people are willing and able to work at different wage rates.
2 The supply of labour is directly related to the wage rate, since a rise in the wage rate will increase the quantity supplied.
3 Factors that could influence the supply of labour to a particular occupation include the following (three from the same bullet point would be acceptable):
- monetary considerations – the higher the wage rate, the more people are likely to want to work in that job
- education, skills and experience – if an occupation involves more education, skill or experience, this is likely to reduce the number of people able to offer their services
- job satisfaction, working conditions, hours and promotion prospects – if a job offers more job satisfaction, better working conditions,

normal working hours and good promotion prospects, it is likely to attract more people than those that do not

- pension schemes and other benefits – if an occupation offers a generous pension scheme or other benefits, this will increase the number of people willing to do this work.

4   PES = 1.5 (15 ÷ 10). When the percentage change in the wage rate is less than the percentage change in the quantity supplied of labour, giving a value for PES greater than 1, supply is elastic.

5   The supply of doctors is likely to be less elastic than the supply of cleaners because a doctor requires more education, skills and qualifications than a cleaner. If, for example, the wage rate rises, there will be a smaller percentage increase in the supply of doctors because there will be fewer extra people able to meet the requirements of the job.

Case study

Bruce's Boards

1   Changes that Bruce could make to attract more applicants include:
- lowering the requirements for educational qualifications and training
- offering a higher wage rate or other financial reward such as a larger commission
- improving other non-monetary factors such as offering better working conditions, more paid holiday, shorter working hours or increased benefits.

2   PES = 7.5 (150 ÷ 20). The percentage change in the quantity supplied is greater than the percentage change in the wage rate, making supply elastic.

4.3 – Progress questions, Case study

Progress questions

1   Characteristics of a perfect labour market include: a large number of buyers and sellers of labour; homogeneous/identical workers; free entry and exit; perfect information.

2   In a perfectly competitive labour market, an individual firm faces a perfectly elastic supply curve for labour.

3   AC_L = \$20 an hour; and MC_L = \$20 and hour (w = MC_L = AC_L).

4   The diagram requires the original demand (D_L) and supply (S_L) curves for lawyers, showing the equilibrium wage rate. If more qualifications are required, S_L decreases (shifts to the left) and if demand increases for their services, D_L increases (shifts to the right). The new equilibrium wage rate will be higher than before (but depending on how much each curve is shifted, the number employed may be higher, the same or lower than before).

Case study

Fruit picking in New Zealand

- Large number of buyers and sellers of labour – there are many different farms wanting to employ fruit pickers and many individuals willing and able to work ("thousands of jobs available"). There is no mention of trade unions being involved in the labour market.
- Homogeneous/identical workers – it seems unlikely that workers will be identical in their skills and abilities but although fruit pickers have to be physically fit, the job requires no experience.
- Free entry and exit – there is nothing to prevent workers from starting to become fruit pickers or leaving this work. Potential workers are likely to be fairly mobile and work contracts may be for short time periods, giving flexibility to both workers and firms. It may be relatively easy to start this business on a small scale or to sell the business but we have no information on the costs involved.
- Perfect information – jobs are widely advertised on the internet, so everyone knows what wage rate is being offered and it appears to be the same or similar in different locations.

On balance, the New Zealand fruit-picking market fits the characteristics of a perfectly competitive labour market fairly well, although we would need more information to be able to judge more accurately the extent to which it meets the requirements of this type of labour market.

4.4 – Progress questions, Case study

Progress questions

1   A monopsonist is the only or main buyer of a product or factor of production.

2   Workers might join a trade union to try to obtain higher pay, better working conditions or for support when needed. A trade union will

have more power to bring about changes than an individual worker, especially if dealing with a large or dominant buyer of labour.

3   The marginal cost of labour is greater than the average cost when there is only one buyer of a particular type of labour because the firm faces an upward-sloping supply curve of labour. The firm will have to offer a higher wage rate to attract more workers and this higher wage rate will also have to be paid to its existing workers, adding to the amount paid as a result of employing an extra worker.

4   The two main ways that a trade union can obtain a higher wage rate are by limiting the supply of labour available to firms and negotiating that all the workers are paid a wage higher than the equilibrium wage rate.

5   A trade union could negotiate a higher wage rate for its members without employment falling if it is dealing with a monopsonist and/or if workers' MRP rises.

6   The new demand curve for labour will need to be to the right of D_L and intersect w_1 at q.

Case study

The impact of a trade union

Closed shops being made illegal will weaken the new trade union's power, but a strike may be more likely because it requires only 51% to vote in favour instead of the previous figure of 67%. There are many small firms in the industry, so they will have less power than if there is one employer of workers in the shoe-making industry. The joining fee may be too expensive for some workers but 55% of local shoe workers have joined the union so far. The higher the trade union density, the more effective the union is likely to be.

Shoe firms "have done well in recent years", so they may be able to pay more or improve working conditions, by using past profits or by increasing the prices of the shoes. However, if the country's unemployment is rising, this may affect the shoe industry and firms may be unable or unwilling to pay their workers more at this uncertain time.

Overall, how effective the new trade union is likely to be in improving pay and working conditions for those employed in the local shoe industry depends on the importance of these different factors in the relative bargaining power of the trade union and the local employers.

4.5 – Progress questions, Case study

Progress questions

1   Wage discrimination is when different groups of workers are offered different pay for the same or similar work, for reasons other than differences in MRP.

2   Wage discrimination can affect the type of employment of different groups of workers if they are more or less likely to be offered this work and whether they receive positive or negative discrimination according to the characteristics of this group.

3   Disadvantages for a firm if it discriminates against a certain group of workers include: having to pay a higher wage rate if there are fewer workers to choose from or if they overvalue some workers; higher costs; lower profits and efficiency; reduced competitiveness.

Case study

Management quotas for women

Advantages include:
- increased opportunities for women/discriminated groups
- may be considered fairer if 'disadvantaged' groups have more chance of promotion
- more role models could encourage more of that group to aim for, or apply for, these jobs.

Disadvantages include:
- some from the discriminated group may be appointed even though other candidates are better qualified
- could also be considered unfair as some individuals lose out to others less well qualified
- successful candidates may be unsure if they were appointed on merit or to meet the quota.

4.6 – Progress questions, Case study, Exam-style questions

Progress questions

1   A minimum wage rate is a price floor (the lowest amount that can be paid).

2   Reasons why MRP may increase after a minimum wage has been introduced include: increased productivity, perhaps due to more motivation or concern about losing their jobs; increased training; increased demand for the product; a higher price being charged.

3   The introduction of a minimum wage rate might worsen the international competitiveness of firms because this will increase their costs. Firms may then have to increase prices to pay for the higher wages, making them less price competitive, both at home and abroad. They may also have less profit left to improve the business.

Case study

Minimum wage rates in Thailand

1   6 (48 ÷ 8 or 42 ÷ 7).

2   38.5 baht (308 ÷ 8).

3   The Thai government might have increased the minimum wage rate between 2013 and 2020 because the cost of living has increased. Prices may have risen, requiring more income to maintain the same standard of living. Alternatively, or as well, the Thai government may have decided to raise the minimum reward for work.

4   Having different minimum wage rates in different regions of a country enables workers to earn more in areas where the cost of living is higher. This enables all workers to have a similar minimum standard of living wherever they work. However, it may be difficult to decide which areas should have a higher minimum wage and how much higher this should be. Also, workers may receive the higher minimum wage rate for working in a particular area even though they live outside it. Similarly, the reverse may be true. Another consequence may be that firms may move from high labour cost areas to those with a lower minimum wage, affecting employment opportunities in the different areas.

5   The Thai government may have set a higher minimum wage rate for certain skilled jobs to encourage more workers to qualify for, and work in, these jobs. They may be jobs where there is a shortage of workers, perhaps because it takes time and money to obtain the necessary qualifications. Alternatively, these jobs may have monopsonist employers who could pay less than the MRP.

Exam-style questions

1   B. The other three options are influences on the supply of labour.

2   D. There need to be many buyers of labour, identical workers and perfect mobility of labour.

3   C. The monopsonist will choose the number of workers where MC = MRP, Q_1 workers, but only needs to offer a wage rate of W_3 to attract this number of workers.

4   **i.** $12.55 per hour (average of middle two values when arranged in order, $13.10 and $12); **ii.** $13.60 per hour (total of $81.60 divided by 6, the number of countries); **iii.** a diagram such as Figure 4.3.2 can be used to show the perfectly elastic supply of labour for a firm in a perfectly competitive labour market, at the wage rate determined by the market supply and demand for this particular type of labour (but no need to draw this diagram as well). The firm will face a downward-sloping MRP = D curve and the number of workers a firm will choose to employ is where this intersects the supply of labour. If it employs fewer workers, the firm is losing out on workers whose MRP is greater than their cost and beyond this level, an extra worker will add more to the firm's cost than its revenue.

5   Indicative content is given below:
   - meaning of a national minimum wage
   - explanation of effects on demand and supply of labour, perhaps supported by a diagram such as Figure 4.6.1
   - explanation of effect on labour costs plus possible need to reduce costs and employment and/or put up prices
   - impact on profits and competitiveness
   - more workers to choose from
   - explanation of why workers may be motivated to work harder
   - effects of changes in productivity
   - impact on incentive to train workers
   - consideration of competitive and imperfectly competitive labour markets.

6   Indicative content is given below; you should also try to include relevant references to data from the case studies to support your points:
   - meaning and examples of wage discrimination
   - possibility of both positive and negative wage discrimination
   - conditions necessary for wage discrimination
   - application to opportunities of obtaining particular types of job and/or promotion, with possible reference to women in management
   - analysis of effects on wage rates and employment in labour markets where discrimination occurs and knock-on effects on those where it does not, perhaps supported by diagrams such as Figure 4.5.1 and/or Figure 4.5.2

   - analysis of effects on costs and competitiveness of firms
   - impact on incentive to work and possible effect on welfare payments
   - effects and desirability of positive wage discrimination, for example setting quotas for different groups, such as women in management
   - equity and efficiency arguments
   - whether wage differentials between different groups is necessarily due to wage discrimination
   - an overall assessment of whether governments should make all types of wage discrimination illegal.

5.1 – Progress questions, Case study

Progress questions

1   One factor that influences both the distribution of income and the distribution of wealth is age or government policy. A third possible example is pensions, in terms of the entitlement to pensions for the distribution of income and the amount of pension wealth for the distribution of wealth.

2   One other factor that influences the distribution of income is income from work. People may or may not work and they receive different amounts of pay according to the type of job and how many hours they work. Access to health and education will affect their ability to work and their productivity, which will affect their pay. The distribution of wealth affects people's income because many assets, for example savings, generate an income. Pension entitlement will also add to a person's income after they retire.

3   The distribution of income affects the distribution of wealth because those with higher incomes will be more able to save and buy assets, adding to their wealth.

4   Absolute poverty is when someone does not have enough money to satisfy their basic needs, currently considered to be less than $1.90 a day, according to the World Bank. Relative poverty is when an individual or household is considered poor compared with others in that society at that time. It usually means that they have less than a certain percentage of the average income, for example less than 50% of the average income.

5   Two groups who may be poor and why include: children and old people who have no or few sources of income or wealth; those with limited education or poor health who will be less productive and/or unable to obtain well-paid jobs; the unemployed, who may be relying on low benefit payments for their income or may have no income at all; those in low-paid jobs, who are receiving low incomes and are not able to save.

6   People may disagree about whether a country's income or wealth should be more or less equal, depending on what they think is fair and how much income and wealth the household has. They may also disagree, for example, about the extent of the trickle-down effect if the distribution becomes less equal.

Case study

The Gini coefficient

1   Canada's Lorenz curve would be drawn closest to the line of equality because it has the lowest Gini index, which indicates the least inequality of the seven countries.

2   Brazil has the most unequal distribution of income because its Gini index is the highest at 53.9.

3   Canada has the lowest Gini index, showing the least inequality, at 33.3 and the second highest GNI per capita at US$46.370. Only the United States has a higher income per head, at US$65.760, together with the third lowest GNI index, at 41.1. Brazil has the highest Gini index, at 53.9 and the third lowest income per head at US$9,130, whereas Honduras has the lowest income per head at US$2,390 and the second highest Gini index at 52.1. There is therefore some evidence, based on the rank order of the countries, to suggest that for these seven countries a higher income per head is associated with a lower Gini index but the rank order does not follow exactly and there is a large difference in the incomes per head of the United States and Canada compared with the other five countries, which might be expected to lead to a more significant difference in their Gini indices.

5.2 – Progress questions, Case study, Exam-style questions

Progress questions

1   Universal benefits are given to everyone who fits into a particular category. For example, they may be given to everyone with children. Means-tested benefits are given to those whose income or wealth is below a certain level and have particular needs.

2 Progressive income tax takes a greater sum of money and a greater percentage from those who have higher incomes. This will narrow the gap between the rich and the poor, both as a sum of money and relatively. The tax revenue can also be used to pay for benefits to those with less income and wealth, further narrowing the gap.

3 Absolute poverty can, at least in theory, be eliminated if enough money is given to everyone to enable them to pay for their basic needs. However, relative poverty compares people's income to the average for that society at that time. As incomes rise, so does the relative poverty line, so relative poverty is unlikely to be eliminated.

4 Disadvantages include:
- welfare benefits – if universal, they will be given to the rich as well as the poor, adding to their financial cost and opportunity cost; if means-tested, they have to be claimed, so some people may miss out; if paid in cash, they may not be used to address the problem, for example buying enough food
- state provision – again, if given to everyone, the scheme will be expensive, adding to the cost and opportunity cost; it is difficult to know exactly what to provide and how much
- taxation – if the rates are too progressive, there may be disincentive effects, for example on work and saving; it is difficult to tax wealth because of valuation problems
- wage and price controls – a minimum wage increases costs to firms, may lead to some unemployment and harm their international competitiveness; they prevent the operation of the free market; they need to be enforced, with penalties, to be effective.

Whichever method is used, there will be different moral and political perspectives.

Case study

Negative income tax

1 $10,000 (50% of $20,000).

2 A negative income tax system may reduce the incentive to work, either for as many hours or maybe not to work at all. For example, using the figures in the Case study, someone with no income would receive $10,000 but someone who earns $12,000 would end up with a total of $16,000. For every dollar earned, a person would only be $0.50 better off. It will be difficult to set both a reasonable minimum income and a low rate of payment for every dollar below the cut-off point, to reduce the disincentive effect of earning more. A decision also needs to be made about whether the unit the system is based on is an individual or a household. It could also be argued that some benefits are better paid in kind than in cash.

Exam-style questions

1 D. $1.90 a day is a measure used for absolute poverty; many people without a job are not in relative poverty; relative poverty is when people have less than a certain percentage of the income, not a set percentage of the population.

2 B. A Lorenz curve is a graph showing the cumulative distribution of national income (or wealth) for given percentages of the population.

3 A. Means-tested benefits are paid depending on a person's income or wealth and their needs, so they can focus on those most in need. Universal benefits are paid to everyone who fits into a particular category, such as having children.

4 **i.** Income is a flow of money received by an economic agent over a period of time, for example income from work.

ii. A diagram such as Figure 5.1.2 can be used to show area A, between the Lorenz curve and the line of perfect equality, and area B, underneath the Lorenz curve. The Gini coefficient is then calculated as $\frac{A}{(A + B)}$. The Gini coefficient therefore measures the area between the Lorenz curve and the line of perfect equality as a proportion or percentage of the total area under this line.

5 **i.** Some of the points that could be made include:
- meaning of minimum wage and annual GDP per capita
- justification for a minimum wage
- why a positive relationship may be expected, with a lower annual GDP per capita associated with a lower minimum wage per hour
- explanation of how a higher GDP per capita is likely to indicate a higher standard of living and why this could lead to a higher minimum wage
- link with relative poverty – minimum wage needs to be higher if average incomes are higher
- why a higher minimum wage is more affordable when the annual GDP per capita is higher
- explanation of how a higher GDP per capita could reflect a higher cost of living and why this could lead to a higher minimum wage.

ii. Some of the points that could be made include:
- the highest two minimum wage rates per hour ($20 and $18.50) are in the countries (A and B) with the highest annual GDP per

capita ($55,000 and $60,000) but they are in the opposite rank order.
- country C has both the lowest annual GDP per capita of $10,000 and the lowest minimum wage rate of $8.
- the lowest three countries – D, E and C – are in rank order in terms of the higher the annual GDP per capita, the higher the minimum wage, for example an income of $40,000 in Country D as opposed to $15,000 in Country E is associated with a wage of $13.10 as opposed to $10, although the relative differences are not the same.
- this supports the view that countries with a higher annual GDP per capita are likely to have a higher minimum wage per hour.
- however, the data apply to five countries which may be very different in other respects, for example: is the annual GDP in terms of PPP, taking account of the cost of living in the different countries?; the amount paid (or even whether to have a minimum wage) depends on moral and political judgements which will vary between countries; do the countries have a different minimum wage in different parts of the country or does this figure apply for all areas?
- the likely conclusion is that the differences in annual GDP per capita will contribute to differences in the minimum wage per hour but that there are also other reasons why the minimum wage varies between countries.

6 Indicative content is given below:
- meaning and examples of wealth
- inheritance
- success in business
- significance of pension wealth
- impact of house ownership
- explanation of link with distribution of income
- age distribution of the population
- government policy, for example whether there is a wealth tax.

7 Indicative content is given below:
- meaning and types of poverty
- justification for government intervention to reduce poverty
- specific examples of policies used in different countries
- analysis and evaluation of use of benefits, including universal, means-tested, in cash and in kind
- analysis and evaluation of state provision of different goods and services
- analysis and evaluation of use of taxation
- analysis and evaluation of wage and price controls
- impact on incentives
- equity issues
- other unintended consequences
- whether either type of poverty can be eliminated
- relevance of extent of and combination of measures used
- an overall assessment of the desirability and effectiveness of alternative policies that may be used to reduce poverty.

6.1 – Progress questions, Case studies

Progress questions

1 Globalisation is the process through which countries around the world have become more integrated and interdependent, for example through the increase in world trade, the movement of capital between countries and the growth of TNCs.

2 Trade liberalisation is the process of removing or reducing restrictions on international trade, such as tariffs and quotas.

3 A TNC is a transnational corporation, sometimes known as a multinational corporation. TNCs are enterprises that own assets and sell goods and/or services in more than one country.

4 Foreign direct investment (FDI) contributes to globalisation because it involves foreign companies, financial institutions and individuals acquiring assets in different countries. As a result, they produce, trade and employ workers throughout the world. Production in one country may rely on inputs from a different country making countries more interdependent.

5 A trading bloc is a group of countries that agree to remove, or reduce, restrictions on trade between each other while keeping restrictions on trade with countries that are not members of the trading bloc.

6 Technological developments in transport have reduced the costs of transporting goods between countries. If transport costs are low, prices are likely to be closer to the cost of producing the products. People can benefit from buying products from low-cost producers. This means

that the benefits of international trade should increase. Trade between countries is a key part of globalisation.

7   A barrier to international trade is anything which makes trade between countries more difficult. Common barriers to trade include: tariffs, quotas, government regulations and high transport costs.

8   If countries specialise in producing those goods and services that they are relatively more efficient at producing, costs and prices for consumers should be lower. Specialisation and trade can also make it more likely that producers benefit from economies of scale, leading to further reductions in costs and prices. Specialisation and trade should increase world output and so improve average living standards.

9   Examples of benefits that may result from increased international mobility of labour include: people who are unemployed in one country could move to another country to find employment; labour shortages in countries can be reduced by recruiting workers from abroad; firms are more likely to be able to find the most suitable workers to fill job vacancies.

10 Increased competition from LEDCs, where labour and other costs are often low, may lead some firms in MEDCs to go out of business. This can result in structural unemployment. Also, companies in MEDCs may outsource some of their production to LEDCs which can lead to job losses in MEDCs.

11 A footloose industry is one that is able to move easily from one location to another.

12 Globalisation reduces the degree of inequality between countries when poorer countries grow more rapidly than richer countries. This may happen for a number of reasons including: FDI in LEDCs has led to a more rapid increase in growth; transfers of technology have allowed LEDCs to grow more quickly; freer trade and greater access to the markets of MEDCs has benefited LEDCs; TNCs have located in LEDCs to take advantage of lower production costs and this has increased employment and the rate of growth of some LEDCs.

13 Ways in which globalisation may have damaged the natural environment include: use of fossil fuels to transport goods increasing CO_2 emissions and global warming; overuse of renewable resources, for example overfishing depleting stocks of fish; extraction of raw materials scarring the landscape; the creation of waste.

14 As non-renewable resource are depleted, they become scarcer and prices are likely to rise. This will increase the price people are willing to pay for recycled resources, increasing the profits earned from recycling.

15 Investment by a TNC in a LEDC is likely to improve the balance of trade. The TNC is likely to export some of the cars produced and some of the cars sold in the domestic market will replace imports.

16 A TNC may set up in an LEDC to reduce its costs of production. This may lead to redundancies and plant closures in a MEDC as production is transferred from the MEDC to the LEDC. People who lose their jobs in the MEDC may be occupationally and geographically immobile, and so structural unemployment increases.

Case studies

Ford, a global car manufacturer

1   Ford is based in the USA but it assembles and sells motor vehicles in many countries around the world. It manufactures parts for its cars in a number of different countries and has also outsourced the manufacture of car parts to firms located in other countries. This global operation and supply chain mean that the Ford Motor Company is a TNC. The case study also mentions the investment of around $200 million in India. FDI is another feature of a TNC.

2   Reasons why FMC assembles cars at different locations include:
   • Some locations may have been chosen because production costs are lower than in the USA, where FMC's headquarters is located.
   • The costs of transporting cars can be quite high and it may be better to locate production near to the market.
   • Each assembly plant is likely to produce a limited range of models and it might be possible to gain most of the benefits from economies of scale at each plant.
   • The governments of the countries where the assembly plants are located may have provided subsidies to FMC.
   • If Ford cars are manufactured locally, consumers may be more willing to buy a Ford car.

3   There is a number of reasons why FMC might outsource the production of some car parts but probably one of the most important reasons is cost. For example, it is probably cheaper for Ford to buy sliding sunroofs from a company in Germany than to make them itself. The German company probably supplies a variety of car manufacturers and is able to reap significant economies of scale. It is also likely to have developed expertise in the design and manufacture of this component which also helps to reduce average costs.

Vietnam has prospered during the past 35 years

1   An open economy trades with other countries, exporting and importing goods and services. A mixed economy has a private sector

and public sector. The public (government) sector often supplies public goods and merit goods and may include state-owned enterprises (SOEs) providing key services such as energy. In a mixed economy, the government may also regulate the activities of private firms, for example to protect the health and safety of workers and to protect the environment. To summarise, an open mixed economy trades with other countries and has both private and public sectors.

2   The evidence in the case study that shows that Vietnam has become part of the globalised world economy includes: Vietnam's membership of the WTO; liberalisation of trade; membership of AFTA; the agreement with the EU to reduce restrictions on trade; 12% average annual growth in exports for 30 years; and the large inflows of FDI.

3   Possible benefits identified in the case study include: Vietnam has been transformed from one of the world's poorest nations into a middle-lower income economy; the large increase in GDP per capita; 45 million people lifted out of poverty; and export-led growth creating millions of jobs. Vietnam may also have benefited in other ways, for example, from cheaper imports and the benefits of inward FDI. However, these benefits may also have resulted from other changes that have taken place during the past 35 years. It is difficult to determine the extent to which the improvements have resulted from Vietnam being part of the globalised world economy or from other changes that have taken place.

Global electricity generation is changing but is it changing fast enough?

1   If the world economy is growing rapidly, more is being produced and consumed and people's real incomes are rising. More output, consumption and higher incomes cause the demand for energy, including electricity, to increase.

2   Improving technology has helped to lower the cost of producing solar panels and wind turbines. Also, as demand and output have increased, firms have been able to reap the benefit of economies of scale, reducing average costs. Standardisation has helped to lower production costs too. As the technology becomes more widely available, competition develops. Lower costs and increased competition lead to lower prices.

3   As the prices of solar panels and wind turbines fall, the cost of supplying energy from sources that do not produce greenhouse gases also falls. As costs and prices fall, people are likely to switch away from fossil fuels. However, there is already a substantial investment in power stations that use fossil fuels and the changeover may not happen as quickly as many would like.

4   There are many ways in which governments could encourage firms to switch away from using fossil fuels to generate electricity, they include: subsidising solar panels and wind turbines; increasing indirect taxes on fossil fuels; introducing/extending a system of pollution permits; banning the use of fossil fuels; supporting research into green technologies.

Electric bicycles – a growing global business

1   **i.** The profit in Country A is $[(100 − 80) × 20,000)] = \$400,000$ and the profit in Country B is $[(450 − 290) × 20,000] = \$3,200,000$.
    ii. The tax in Country A is $\$400,000 × 0.1 = \$40,000$ and the tax in Country B is $\$3,600,000 × 0.3 = \$1,080,000$.
    iii. The total amount of tax is $\$1,120,000$.

2   **i.** The profit in Country A is $[(200 − 80) × 20,000)] = \$2,400,000$ and the profit in Country B is $[(450 − 390) × 20,000] = \$1,200,000$.
    ii. The tax in Country A is $\$2,400,000 × 0.1 = \$240,000$ and the tax in Country B is $\$1,200,000 × 0.3 = \$360,000$.
    iii. The total amount of tax is $\$600,000$.

3   To minimise the tax paid, the company should charge a transfer price for the electric motors that ensures that all the profits are made in Country A, where the tax rate is lower. Therefore, it should charge a price of $260 for each electric motor. At that price, the company does not make any profit in Country B, and its profits in Country A are $[(260 − 80) × 20,000)] = \$3,600,000$. The total tax payable is $\$3,600,000 × 0.1 = \$360,000$.

6.2 – Progress questions, Case studies

Progress questions

1   David Ricardo.

2   Comparative advantage is when a country (individual, firm or region) has a lower opportunity cost of producing a good or service than another country (individual, firm or region).

3   If a country has an absolute advantage in the production of a good, it can produce more of that good than another country with the same amount of resources **OR** it can produce the same amount of the good with fewer resources.

4   The slope of a country's production possibility boundary shows the opportunity cost of producing each product. If the slopes of the

production possibility boundaries of two countries are different, this means that the opportunity costs of production in each country are different and shows that each country has a comparative advantage in producing one of the goods.

5 A country's factor endowment is the amount of land, labour, capital and entrepreneurship that a country possesses.

6 Investment and training should improve the efficiency and productivity of the industry. Other things being equal, improvements in productivity will reduce the opportunity cost of production and this might result in a change in comparative advantage.

7 The terms of trade measure the quantity of one good that can be exchanged for a given quantity of another good, for example 1 orange will buy 2 apples.

8 Country B will benefit from trade because through trade, Country B can get 2 kg of apples for each 1 kg of oranges exported whereas if Country B had produced apples itself, it would only be able to produce 1.5 kg of apples for each 1 kg of oranges it gave up producing. (The opportunity cost of producing 1 kg of oranges in Country B = (225 ÷ 150) = 1.5 kg of apples.)

9 As countries specialise and trade, they supply the goods in which they have a comparative advantage for **both** their home **and** export markets. As a result, there is an increase in the total output of these goods. If there are increasing returns to scale, the percentage increase in output will be greater than the percentage increase in factor inputs. This means that the opportunity cost of producing these goods falls, increasing the benefit of specialisation. As productivity increases, average costs fall which allows firms to cut prices.

10 When the pattern of comparative advantage changes, a country may start to import a product that it used to produce for its home market and for export. The industry will decline and workers will be made redundant. If labour is occupationally and/or geographically immobile, workers will not move to the expanding industries and may remain unemployed for a long while.

11 A tariff is an indirect tax on imports whereas a quota is a limit on the quantity (or the value) of a good that can be imported.

12 A tariff increases the price of the product in the domestic market and the price elasticity of demand (PED) determines by how much the quantity sold falls. If PED is elastic, the tariff will lead to a significant reduction in imports whereas if PED is inelastic, the reduction in the quantity of the product bought and imported will be much smaller.

13 Consumer surplus is the difference between the amount consumers would be willing to pay for a product and the amount they have to pay. A quota reduces the supply of the product in the domestic market, leading to a rise in price and fall in the quantity sold. Since consumers are buying less of the product at a higher price, consumer surplus will fall.

14 Without protection, competition from established foreign firms might mean that a new industry cannot get started in a country. If the industry is protected, it can survive. After a period of time, it may become more efficient, benefit from economies of scale and be able to compete with foreign firms.

15 Dumping is when a firm sells its products abroad at a price which is lower than the price it charges in its home market. Sometimes the overseas price is below the cost of production. Dumping can be a predatory pricing strategy or a way to dispose of surplus stocks.

16 Retaliation is when a country imposes trade restrictions, for example a tariff, on another country's exports in response to that country imposing restrictions on its exports.

17 The commodity structure/pattern of world trade is concerned with the types of goods and services that are exported (traded between countries).

18 The geographical distribution/pattern of world trade is concerned with the countries or regions that are exporting (and/or importing) goods and services.

19 Probably the most significant change in the geographical pattern of world trade is the increase in the proportion of world merchandise exports originating in Asia. Asia's share of world merchandise exports has increased from 24.48% to 40.79%. There is a corresponding fall in the proportion of world merchandise exports originating in Europe, from 48.04% to 38.37%, and America, from 19.76% to 16.67%. Africa has also seen a fall in its share of world merchandise exports, from 5.92% to 2.45%.

20 The formula for the terms of trade is: Index of export prices ÷ Index of import prices × 100.

21 The terms of trade in the base year is always 100

22 The terms of trade has improved. If the numerical value increases, it means that export prices must be rising relative to import prices.

23 If export prices are rising relative to import prices, it may mean that the country is becoming less competitive in world markets. This could lead to a fall in the volume of exports sold and a rise in the volume of imports bought. The balance of trade deteriorates when the value of exports minus the value imports falls. What happens to the value of exports and imports depends on changes in both the price and volume of exports. For example, if the price of exports rose by 10% and the volume fell by more than 10% (demand is price elastic), the value of exports would fall.

24 The main difference between a free trade area and a customs union is that all members of a customs union have the same restrictions on trade with non-member countries whereas members of a free trade area each have their own individual restrictions on trade with non-member countries.

25 A monetary union is where a group of countries adopt the same currency, controlled by a single central bank with a common monetary policy.

26 The formation of a trading bloc leads to trade creation gains when production shifts from a high-cost producer to a lower-cost producer within the bloc whereas trade diversion losses occur when production shifts from the lowest-cost producer outside the trading bloc to a higher-cost producer within the trading bloc.

Case studies

Absolute and comparative advantage in the production of rice and wheat

1 Country Y has an absolute advantage in producing rice because it can produce more rice with a given amount of resources than Country X, 18 tonnes rather than 16 tonnes.

2 The opportunity cost of producing a tonne of wheat in Country Y is 2 tonnes of rice.

3 Country X has a comparative advantage in the production of rice. The opportunity cost of producing a tonne of rice in Country X is 0.25 tonnes of wheat whereas the opportunity cost of producing a tonne of rice in Country Y is 0.5 tonnes of wheat. The opportunity cost of producing rice in Country X is lower than in Country Y.

Northland and Southland

1 Southland has an absolute advantage in the production of both doors and windows because Table 6.2.11 shows that it is able to produce more doors and more windows than Northland with the same amount of resources.

2 The opportunity cost of producing 1 door in Northland is 2 windows.

3 The opportunity cost of producing 1 door in Southland is 4 windows.

4 Northland has a comparative advantage in producing doors because it has a lower opportunity cost of producing doors than Southland. Northland only has to give up producing 2 windows for each door it produces whereas Southland has to give up producing 4 windows to produce a door.

5 Southland has a comparative advantage in producing windows because it has a lower opportunity cost of producing windows than Northland. Southland only has to give up producing 0.25 doors for each window it produces whereas Northland has to give up producing 0.5 doors to produce a window.

6 Northland has a comparative advantage in producing doors. If it gives up producing doors to produce windows, it can only produce 2 windows for each door it gives up producing. If it produces doors and trades them for windows, it can obtain 3 windows for each door traded. This is a net gain of 1 window for each door traded.

7 Southland has a comparative advantage in producing windows. If it gives up producing windows to produce doors, it can only produce 0.25 doors for each window it gives up producing. If it produces windows and trades them for doors, it can obtain 0.5 doors for each window traded. This is a net gain of 0.25 doors for each window traded.

Trade restrictions increase in 2019

1 If stricter customs procedures are imposed, it may be more difficult and/or more expensive to export products to a country. Some firms from abroad will be deterred from exporting to that country and the volume of imports is likely to fall.

2 A tariff is an indirect tax and is likely to raise the domestic price of imports immediately. Other restrictions will reduce the supply of imports and, since demand is likely to exceed supply, lead to higher prices. Some restrictions will increase the cost of producing and/or selling goods into the overseas market and lead to higher prices.

3 An increase in restrictions on trade will, at least in the short run, benefit domestic producers who are, at least to some extent, protected from foreign competition. They will be able to charge higher prices, and sales and profits are likely to increase. Overseas firms will suffer, sales will fall and they may have to accept lower prices to be able to compete in the market that has had trade restrictions imposed. Consumers will be worse off as they will almost certainly have to pay higher prices and will have less choice. Home-produced goods and services might also be of inferior quality. The extent of these effects will depend on the severity of the trade restrictions imposed.

The banana wars

1. ACP countries are able to export bananas to the EU without any tariff being charged. This means that their bananas are likely to be more competitive in the EU than bananas from countries that are subject to the tariff. Reducing the tariff may mean that demand switches from the ACP countries to other suppliers and the ACP countries are likely to have to accept lower prices for their bananas.

2. Producers in Latin America are more likely to be able to sell bananas in the large EU market. They may be able to produce bananas at a lower cost than some ACP countries and with the reduction in the tariff, will be more competitive in this market. Latin American banana producers are likely to experience an increase in sales and profits.

3. EU households that buy bananas will be better off since the reduction in the tariff and the increase in the supply of bananas will lead to lower prices and increase consumer surplus.

Destination of merchandise exports from African countries

1. 2008 = [(186 + 357) ÷ 16135] = 3.37%; 2013 = [(274 + 300) ÷ 18997] = 3.02%; 2018 = [(250 + 227) ÷ 19414] = 2.46%.

2. 2008 = 186:357 = 0.52:1; 2013 = 274:300 = 0.91:1; 2018 = 250:227 = 1.10:1.

3. Between 2008 and 2018, Africa's share of world merchandise trade fell from 3.37% to 2.46% and the overall value of merchandise exports also fell, from $543 billion to $477 billion. Over the whole period, African merchandise exports to developing economies grew from $186 billion to $250 billion whereas the value of merchandise exports to developed economies fell from $357 billion to $227 billion. The proportion of African merchandise exports to developing relative to developed economies increased from a ratio of 0.52:1 to a ratio of 1.10:1.

Australia - a major exporter of primary products

1. The terms of trade measures the amount of imports that a country can obtain for a given quantity of exports. This is determined by comparing the average price of exports with the average price of imports. The balance of trade is the difference between the value of exports and the value of imports.

2. Terms of trade in 2019 = (127.8 ÷ 98.2) × 100 = 130.1.

3. Index of export prices in 2017 = (116.4 × 99.0) ÷ 100 = 115.2.

4. Between 2015 and 2019 Australia's terms of trade improved from an index of 100 to 130.1. Export prices rose by 27.8% while import prices fell by 1.8% meaning that Australia was able to buy more imports for a given quantity of exports in 2019 than in 2015.

5. A fall in the exchange rate makes exports cheaper and imports dearer. Other things being equal, this should lead to a deterioration in the terms of trade. However, despite the fall in the value of the Australian dollar between 2013 and 2019, Australia's terms of trade improved. Clearly, there were other factors affecting export and import prices.

The European Union and Canada negotiate a trade agreement

1. A trade deal is an agreement between two or more countries to reduce or eliminate restrictions on trade between each other, for example by reducing tariffs on imports.

2. A tariff is a tax on imports whereas a quota is a limit on the quantity of a good that can be imported.

3. CETA has resulted in a reduction in tariffs and quotas on imports. Canadian firms that were protected by these restrictions on imports will face increased competition from EU firms. The Canadian firms may have to lower their prices and accept lower profits. If they are unable to compete, some Canadian firms may close down and there may be job losses.

4. Intellectual property means creations of the mind. There are lots of people working in creative industries who might benefit from improved protection for intellectual property. These include authors, musicians and song writers. Other people who might benefit include inventors and designers.

5. Consumers benefit because reducing restrictions on trade leads to more competition and lower prices. More competition helps to reduce prices, but prices also fall because the tariff duty does not have to be paid to the government. More competition should also provide consumers with more choice and a greater variety of products. In the long run, freer trade may lead to increased specialisation, economies of scale, lower costs and more invention and innovation.

Exam-style questions

1. A. Foreign direct investment is a key feature of globalisation.

2. B. It takes fewer resources to produce a radio in Country X than Country Y and it takes fewer resources to produce a television in Country Y than Country X.

3. C. A quota will reduce the quantity of the good imported from abroad and is likely to lead to an increase in the domestic production of the good. This should result in more jobs being created.

4. **i.** The terms of trade deteriorates when the price of imports rises relative to the price of exports and therefore more has to be exported to obtain a given quantity of imports.

   ii. The terms of trade (Jan 2020) = $\frac{\text{Index of export prices}}{\text{Index of import prices}} \times 100$

   $= \frac{100}{120} \times 100$

   $= 83.3$

   $= \underline{\textbf{83}}$ to the nearest whole number

   iii. The percentage change in the price of imports $= \frac{-30}{120} \times 100 = -25\%$

   Price elasticity of demand $= \frac{\text{\% change in quantity demanded}}{\text{\% change in price}}$

   $-1.3 = \frac{\text{\% change in quantity demanded}}{-25\%}$

   % change in quantity demanded $= -1.3 \times -25\%$

   $= \underline{\textbf{32.5\%}}$

5. Start by defining the key terms in the question in an opening paragraph, for example: trading bloc, trade creation gains and trade diversion losses. The removal of trade restrictions between members of the trading bloc should result in trade creation gains. Countries in the bloc will start to specialise in producing those goods and services in which they have a comparative advantage over other countries in the trading bloc. High cost producers will stop producing the goods and services in which they have a comparative disadvantage and these products will be produced and imported from lower cost producers within the trading bloc. Trade diversion occurs because the removal of restrictions on trade with member countries may mean that it is now cheaper to import some goods and services from producers within the trading bloc rather than from the lowest cost producers outside the trading bloc. The continuing, or new, restrictions on trade with non-members will mean that it is now cheaper to buy from a higher cost producer within the bloc than from the lowest cost producer outside the trading bloc. Some trade will be diverted from the lowest cost producers to higher cost producers, leading to a worse allocation of resources.

6. Start by explaining what is meant by a transnational corporation (TNC) using some of the data in the case study to support the explanation. Explain why a TNC invests overseas and consider using examples from the case study. Identify factors to be considered when assessing whether the US economy is likely to benefit, for example the effect on growth, employment, the balance of payments and the distribution of income.

   Possible benefits to the economy of the USA include:
   - inflows of profits made from the investment
   - shareholders in the TNC may get higher dividends
   - benefit to the US balance of payments when profits are sent back to the TNC
   - increased production in factories overseas may lead to components produced in the USA being shipped abroad, increasing employment in the USA
   - products produced abroad may be cheaper, benefiting US consumers
   - the investment may support the sale of products made in the USA
   - the investment may finance the extraction of raw materials that are needed in the USA
   - may create jobs for US citizens who work overseas for the TNC.

   Possible costs to the economy of the USA include:
   - less investment in the USA
   - slower growth than if the TNC had invested in the USA
   - fewer jobs created in the USA
   - deterioration in the US balance of payments when the investment occurs
   - the USA may import goods and service produced overseas by the TNC
   - loss of exports that may have occurred if the TNC had invested in the USA
   - may lead to a transfer of technology to competitors
   - use of transfer pricing could lead to a loss of tax revenue for the government of the USA.

   The various benefits and costs should be analysed and evaluated to provide a supported assessment of whether the economy of the USA benefits from overseas investment by a TNC that is based in the USA. Consider using AD/AS diagrams to support some aspects of the analysis, for example the impact on economic growth.

7. To provide a comprehensive answer to this question, there are lots of issues to consider. The time available must be taken into account

when deciding how many issues to discuss and how much time is devoted to each one. However, when discussing the benefits of trade, an explanation of the principle of comparative advantage is important. The benefits of international trade include:

- countries can specialise in those products in which they have a comparative advantage
- where each country has a comparative advantage, specialisation and trade can be mutually beneficial – include a numerical example to explain why
- specialisation and trade can lead to a better allocation of world resources, increasing total output and living standards
- may result in economies of scale, leading to lower costs
- leads to increased competition resulting in lower costs, lower prices, better products, invention and innovation
- greater variety of products and more choice
- reduces the monopoly power of domestic producers that might otherwise dominate their home market and exploit consumers
- may increase economic growth and employment.

The costs of international trade include:

- may lead to an increase in structural unemployment
- some countries may be too dependent on a few products, for example some LDCs are too dependent on a few primary products
- may be difficult for LDCs to compete with MDCs and develop industries that would benefit their economies
- international trade makes countries more interdependent and vulnerable to economic shocks that start in other parts of the world
- environmental costs such as those associated with transporting products.

A good answer to this question would analyse and evaluate the issues raised, and consider both benefits and costs.

7.1 – Progress questions and Case studies

Progress questions

1. The balance of payments account must balance because it is constructed using a double-entry bookkeeping system. Every transaction is entered twice, once as a debit and once as a credit. Therefore, the sum of the debit and credit entries must be equal.

2. Direct investment is when the investor has a controlling interest in the investment whereas portfolio investment is where the investor buys financial assets to earn income but does not get involved in the management of the enterprise in which the funds are invested. Foreign direct investment includes buying, or building, a factory abroad whereas portfolio investment abroad includes buying overseas government bonds to earn interest.

3. The balance of payments account includes a figure for net errors and omissions because, given the large number of transactions, it is inevitable that some transactions that should be included in the account will be missed out and some transactions will be recorded incorrectly. Since the account as a whole must balance, the difference between the total of the debit and credit entries must equal the net sum of the errors and omissions.

4. The current account balance = Balance of trade in goods and services + Primary income balance + Secondary income balance. Therefore, $35 billion = Balance of trade in goods and services + $18 billion – $6 billion. Balance of trade in goods and services = $(35 – 18 + 6) billion = $23 billion.

5. A current account deficit usually means that the country is importing more goods and services than it is exporting. This suggests that domestic firms are not as competitive as foreign firms in export markets and foreign firms are more competitive than domestic firms in the country's home market. However, if the current account deficit is due to deficits on the primary and secondary income balances, this may not be the case.

6. A current account surplus means that exports are greater than imports. Exports are an injection into the circular flow of income and imports are a withdrawal. If the injection from exports is greater than the withdrawal through imports, this will increase aggregate demand. Also, AD = C + I + G + (X – M) and if (X – M) is positive, this will increase AD.

7. An increase in interest rates means that those who invest in interest-earning assets, such as government bonds, will earn a higher rate of return on their investments. As a result, some investors will move their money from other economies, where the expected rate of return is lower, and invest in the economy where interest rates have increased.

8. If an outflow of hot money leads to a fall in the exchange rate, the rate of inflation is likely to increase. The fall in the exchange rate will increase the domestic currency price of imports, adding to cost-push inflationary pressures. A lower exchange rate may also increase AD. Exports will be more competitive and, as the price of imports rises, domestic residents may buy more home-produced goods. The increase in AD will add to demand-pull inflationary pressures.

9. A tariff is a tax on imports. Imposing a tariff will increase the price domestic residents have to pay for imports but it does not directly affect the price paid to the foreign firms selling the goods. The increase in price will reduce the quantity demanded of the products upon which the tariff is imposed. The fall in the quantity sold will reduce spending on imports and therefore the size of the current account deficit, even if PED is inelastic. However, the more elastic the demand, the greater the fall in the value of imports.

10. Deflationary policies are contractionary monetary and fiscal measures used to reduce AD, for example increasing taxes, cutting government spending, increasing interest rates and restricting the growth of money and credit. Devaluation is when, under a fixed exchange rate system, the government decides to reduce the official value of the country's currency in terms of other currencies.

11. Reasons why deflationary measures may reduce a country's balance of trade include:

- deflationary policies are likely to increase unemployment and reduce household incomes, this will reduce spending on imports
- as AD and output fall, firms will buy fewer raw materials and components from abroad
- reducing AD is likely to reduce inflation which should, over a period of time, help to make the country's products more competitive abroad and in their home market, increasing exports and reducing imports
- a fall in AD will create spare capacity and encourage firms to try to sell more abroad, leading to an increase in exports.

12. A fall in the exchange rate reduces the foreign currency price of exports and increases the domestic currency price of imports. These price changes will benefit the balance of trade in goods and services most when they lead to a large increase in the volume/quantity of exports sold and a large reduction in the volume/quantity of imports purchased. Therefore, the more elastic the demand for exports and imports, the greater the benefit to the balance of trade in goods and service.

13. Export subsidies should increase exports and therefore aggregate demand. The increase in AD should help to reduce unemployment and increase economic growth but, depending on the state of the economy, it might add to demand-pull inflationary pressures. Export subsidies also increase government spending and, unless taxes are increased, they are likely to lead to a larger budget deficit or smaller budget surplus. Also, export subsidies may lead to retaliation and prove to be ineffective.

14. When a country is in recession, national output is falling, unemployment rises and inflation is likely to fall. Expenditure-reducing policies would lead to further falls in national output and would increase unemployment and so they are not suitable. Expenditure-switching policies should increase the demand for home-produced goods and services, which should help to increase economic growth and reduce unemployment. When an economy is in recession and there is a negative output gap, the inflationary effects of expenditure-switching policies are likely to be limited. Therefore, expenditure-switching policies are more appropriate than expenditure-reducing policies.

Case studies

France's balance of payments account

1. The balance of trade in goods and services in 2019 was a deficit of €25.2 billion (−€46.8 + €21.6 = €25.2).

2. The deficit on the trade in goods improved by €1.3 billion but this was offset by a reduction in the surplus on the trade in services (€3.2 billion) and a reduction in the surplus on the primary and secondary income balance (€1.1 billion). Overall, €(1.3 − 3.2 − 1.1) billion = −€3.0 billion.

3. In 2018, France's net portfolio investment overseas was €9.4 billion whereas in 2019 net portfolio investment in France was €93.0 billion.

4. In 2018, France's holdings of reserve assets increased by €10.4 billion.

5. The sum of the current and capital account balances should equal the financial account balance. In 2019 the combined current and capital account balance was a deficit of €14.3 billion (−16.2 + 1.9). However, the financial account shows that there was a net inflow of €28.9 billion to finance this deficit. This means that the net value of the errors and omissions on the account must be €14.6 billion. For example, it might mean that the current account deficit was larger than shown.

Does Indonesia's persistent deficit on the current account of its balance of payments matter?

1 The primary income balance is: [the income a country earns on its overseas assets plus remittances from its nationals working abroad] MINUS [the income the country pays to people abroad on the assets they own in the domestic economy plus remittances sent abroad by foreign nationals working in the domestic economy].

It could also be defined as the net flow of profits, interest and dividends from investments in other countries and net remittances from migrant workers.

2 The primary income balance is part of the current account. A deficit on the primary income balance will increase the overall current account deficit or offset the surplus on other parts of the current account.

3 If Indonesia has a deficit on its current account, it has to finance that deficit. To finance the deficit, it can: attract investment from abroad, sell its overseas assets, borrow from abroad or use its foreign exchange reserves. Each of these policies will add to Indonesia's net overseas liabilities.

4 The two expenditure-reducing policies mentioned in the extract are contractionary monetary policy and contractionary fiscal policy. The two expenditure-switching policies mentioned are allowing the exchange rate to depreciate and imposing import restrictions.

Exam-style questions

1 B. The financial account shows where the money comes from to pay for the current account deficit or how the deficit is financed.

2 A. The current account balance is the sum of the balance of trade in goods and services and the primary and secondary income balances. Therefore, the primary and secondary income balance must equal the current account balance minus the balance of trade in goods and services. The primary and secondary income balance = $(540 − 625) billion = −$85 billion.

3 B. A tariff increases the price of imports. If the price elasticity of demand for imports is elastic, it will lead to a proportionately larger fall in the quantity of imports bought.

4 **i.** Reserve assets are the assets a country's central bank has available to deal with balance of payments problems. They include official holdings of gold, foreign currency and Special Drawing Rights.

ii. The balance of trade in goods and services = $(9.6 − 19.0) billion = a deficit of $9.4 billion.

The balance of trade in goods and services as a percentage of GDP = (9.4 ÷ 745) × 100 = 1.26% of GDP, to two decimal places.

iii. The current account balance + capital account balance + errors and omissions must equal the financial account balance. Therefore, the capital account balance = financial account balance − current account balance − errors and omissions = $(14.1 − 9.6 + 1.7) billion.

Capital account balance = $6.2 billion

5 Indicative content is given below:
- meaning of recession and balance of trade in goods and services
- a recession leads to lower incomes and employment
- explanation of why a fall in income will reduce the demand for imports
- significance of the income elasticity of demand for imports (or the MPM)
- link between the fall in demand for imports and the balance of trade in goods and services
- explanation of why a recession is likely to lead to disinflation and possibly deflation
- impact of disinflation on price competitiveness
- how disinflation and improvements in price competitiveness are likely to affect both exports and imports
- explanation of why a recession usually leads to lower investment in physical capital, human capital and research and development (R&D)
- impact of lower investment on competitiveness in the long run and the effects on the balance of trade in goods and services.

6 Indicative content is given below (although there may not be enough time to consider all the policies listed); you should also try to include relevant references to the data from the case study to support your points:
- meaning of deficit on the current account of the balance of payments and recent experience of Indonesia
- difference between expenditure-reducing and expenditure-switching policies plus examples
- examples and analysis of effects of contractionary monetary policy on the current account balance, and impact on other macroeconomic policy objectives
- evaluation of the suitability of contractionary monetary policy, given the current state of Indonesia's economy

- examples and analysis of effects of contractionary fiscal policy on the current account balance, and impact on other policy objectives
- evaluation of the suitability of contractionary fiscal policy, given the current state of Indonesia's economy
- analysis of the effects of a fall in the exchange rate on the current account balance, and on other policy objectives, with reference to the fall from 2012 to mid-2020
- significance of price elasticities of demand for exports and imports and the possibility of capital outflows
- evaluation of the suitability of a lower exchange rate, given the current state of Indonesia's economy
- examples and analysis of the effects of direct controls on the current account balance, and on other policy objectives
- evaluation of the suitability of direct controls, given the current state of Indonesia's economy and the possibility of retaliation
- examples, analysis and evaluation of the impact of supply-side policies
- significance of the cause, size and duration of Indonesia's current account deficit
- an overall assessment of the relative merits of the different policies that Indonesia might use to try to reduce the deficit on the current account of its balance of payments.

7.2 – Progress questions and Case study

Progress questions

1 An increase in the value of exports means that, to pay for the exports, overseas buyers must convert more of their currency into the currency of the firms supplying exports. This leads to an increase in the demand for the currency on the FOREX.

2 When there is an outflow of FDI, domestic firms investing abroad must obtain foreign currency to pay for the investment. They obtain foreign currency by exchanging their own currency for the foreign currency, increasing the supply of their currency on the FOREX.

3 A substantial inflow of FDI will lead to an increase in the demand for the country's currency, shifting the demand curve to the right. The diagram should be the same as Figure 7.2.4.

4 If the world market price of copper falls, since the demand for copper is price inelastic, the value of the country's exports will also fall. This will reduce the demand for the country's currency and cause the exchange rate to depreciate.

5 If it is believed that a country's exchange rate is going to depreciate, speculators are likely to sell the currency hoping to buy it back when the price has fallen. Hence, the supply of the currency on the FOREX will increase, adding to the pressure for the exchange rate to depreciate.

6 In a freely floating exchange rate system the exchange rate is determined by market forces without any central bank intervention. In a managed floating exchange rate system, the central bank intervenes in the market to influence the exchange rate but the nature and the amount of intervention can vary.

7 The exchange rate will depreciate when there is excess supply of the currency on the FOREX. The central bank can use its foreign exchange reserves to purchase its own currency, adding to the demand for the currency and eliminating the excess supply.

8 Other things being equal, a fall in interest rates will make it less rewarding for overseas residents to buy interest-earning assets (for example, saving in a bank account) and so the demand for the currency will fall. Also, it will be more rewarding for domestic residents to invest abroad, increasing the supply of the currency on the FOREX. The fall in the demand for the currency and the increase in the supply of the currency will cause the price to fall, the exchange rate depreciates.

9 If a country has a balance of payments surplus, the demand for the currency exceeds the supply of the currency on the FOREX and the exchange rate will appreciate. A rise in the exchange rate increases the price of exports and reduces import prices. The demand for exports will fall and the demand for imports will increase. Provided the demand for exports and imports are sufficiently price elastic, the balance of payments surplus will fall.

10 If a country has a permanently higher rate of inflation than other countries, its products will become increasingly uncompetitive at home and abroad. As a result, its balance of payments on current account will deteriorate. The demand for its currency on the FOREX will fall and the supply will increase, leading to pressure for the exchange rate to depreciate. In the short run, the central bank can prevent the exchange rate falling by using its foreign exchange reserves to buy up the surplus currency. Eventually, it will run out

of foreign exchange reserves and the government will have to adopt deflationary policies to reduce the current account deficit and restore competitiveness.

11 If a country has a balance of payments surplus, the demand for the currency on the FOREX will exceed the supply of the currency. The central bank can prevent the exchange rate from appreciating by supplying its currency and buying foreign currencies, adding to its foreign exchange reserves. It can also keep interest rates low, reducing inward portfolio investment. In addition, the government may set up a sovereign wealth fund to invest the surpluses on the current account in overseas assets.

12 A fall in the exchange rate will lead to an increase in import prices and adds to inflationary pressures. If a household's nominal income does not change, its real income will fall.

13 If a firm buys raw materials and components from abroad, a rise in the exchange rate will reduce the amount it has to pay for these items and reduce its costs. Other things being equal, this will increase the firm's profit.

14 The main way in which the IMF raises funds to provide loans to member countries is through the quota system. Each member country has to pay the IMF 25% in SDRs or other widely accepted currencies and 75% in its own currency.

15 SDRs (Special Drawing Rights) are assets, created by the IMF, that can be exchanged for any of the five major world currencies. They are part of a country's foreign exchange reserves.

Case study

Mexico's exchange rate system

1 The phrase means that the Mexican government adopted a fixed exchange rate system by specifying the value of the Mexican peso against the United States dollar, known as the peg. With a pegged exchange rate, the Mexican central bank intervenes in the FOREX to maintain the value of the currency.

2 Under a fixed exchange rate system, if a country has a higher rate of inflation than other countries, its goods and services become uncompetitive and the balance of payments is likely to deteriorate. This will lead to an excess supply of the currency on the FOREX and pressure for the exchange rate to fall. Speculators will realise that the currency is overvalued and sell the currency. If this situation continues, it is unlikely that the central bank will have enough foreign currency reserves to prevent the exchange rate falling. The government will have to devalue the currency or allow it to float.

3 Between January 2013 and July 2014, the US dollar and Mexican peso exchange rate was fairly stable, $1 = 12.70 peso in January 2013 and $1 = 12.99 peso in July 2014, with little variation. However, between July 2014 and January 2017, the value of the peso fell from $1 = 12.99 peso to $1 = 21.35 peso. This is a significant depreciation in the value of the peso.

4 Mexico is a major oil exporter and a fall in the price of oil would have reduced the value of Mexican exports and reduced the demand for the peso on the FOREX. Also, the expectation that interest rates in the USA were going to increase would increase the demand for dollars. Investment by overseas financial institutions and other economic agents in interest-earning assets in the USA would increase. The fall in the demand for the peso and the increase in demand for the dollar would lead to a depreciation in the value of the peso compared to the dollar.

5 Between July 2015 and January 2017, the value of the Mexican peso depreciated against the US dollar. This would have increased inflation in Mexico. The Mexican central bank is likely to have increased its official rate of interest to try to prevent the exchange rate falling further and to reduce inflationary pressures.

7.3 – Progress questions and Case studies

Progress questions

1 Money avoids the need for a double coincidence of wants.

2 In a monetary economy there would be 30 different prices, one for each product. In a barter economy there would be (30 × 29) ÷ 2 = 435 different prices.

3 Shares are not generally accepted in exchange for goods and services and their value can change significantly from one day to another. Therefore, they are not a medium of exchange or a good store of value.

4 The money market provides short-term finance whereas the capital market provides medium-term and long-term finance.

5 Bonds are a loan and pay interest to the holder. Shares represent part-ownership of a company and pay dividends which depend on the profit made.

6 A spot market is where items are traded, delivered and paid for immediately whereas in a forward market, the price of an item is agreed now but it is delivered and paid for at a specified date in the future.

7 Savings provide funds that can be loaned by financial institutions to firms that wish to invest. Investment increases productive capacity and supports the growth and development of an economy.

8 The main way in which governments borrow is by selling bonds but they may also borrow short term by selling treasury bills.

9 Differences between equity and debt include:
- equity is money put into a business by the owner whereas debt is borrowed money
- providers of equity get a share of the profits (in a company, the shareholders receive dividends) whereas providers of debt finance receive interest
- interest is a fixed cost for the business and is paid to those who provide debt finance before any profit is calculated whereas dividends are a share of the profit and do not have to be paid
- if the business goes bankrupt, providers of debt will get their money back before the owners get any money.

10 The three main functions of a commercial bank are: to accept deposits; provide loans and overdrafts; and provide an efficient means of payment.

11 A bank creates credit when it gives a loan to its customers. When a bank agrees to give a customer a loan, it increases the deposit in the customer's account by the amount of the loan. The bank deposit can then be used to pay for goods and services. Bank deposits are money, they are a medium of exchange and store of value.

12 Activities of an investment bank include: arranging new issues of shares and bonds; advising firms about mergers and takeovers; advising governments who want to privatise SOEs; they buy and sell securities for clients; providing wealth-management services; commodity trading; trading foreign exchange.

13 Sources of funds for commercial banks include: share issues; retained profits; bond issues; borrowing on the money markets; and usually most important, customers' deposits.

14 Reasons why a bank may become insolvent include: a rise in the number of customers failing to repay their loans and a fall in the value of the other assets that the banks own. A bank will become insolvent if a fall in the value of its assets eliminates its equity/shareholders' funds.

15 A central bank is a financial institution that is responsible for monetary policy and maintaining the stability of the financial system. Most central banks are state-owned.

16 The two main ways that commercial banks use their accounts with the central bank are: to withdraw cash – the central bank supplies them with banknotes and debits their accounts; to settle debts between each other.

17 Lender of last resort means that a central bank will lend to a commercial bank when it is short of liquidity and is unable to borrow from other sources.

18 If the owners and managers of a financial institution believe that the government will bail them out if they go bankrupt, they may choose to take too many risks. Taking risks can be very profitable when the investment succeeds and may mean that those who work for the financial institution earn large salaries and bonuses. If the government bails out a failing financial institution, the owners and employees do not bear the full cost of their decisions when they go wrong.

19 Herding means that people follow the behaviour of other people and do not necessarily behave rationally. A market bubble is caused when the price of an asset rises rapidly, until it is well above its true value. Herding behaviour means that when some investors start to buy an asset, others follow suit and demand rises very quickly. The increase in demand leads to a rise in price which is followed by further increases in demand and price. When some investors realise that the asset is overvalued, they will sell the asset and the price will start to fall. Herding means that other investors will also sell and the bubble will burst.

20 If a bank has a high capital ratio, the value of its assets can fall significantly before the equity in the bank is wiped out and so it is less likely to become insolvent. A high liquidity ratio means that if there is a run on the bank, the bank is less likely to run out of cash.

21 The percentage increase in the size of the shadow banking market is $(52 − 30) trillion ÷ $30 trillion x 100 = 73%.

22 Reasons why problems in financial markets may reduce aggregate demand include: households and firms may not be able to borrow as easily, as banks restrict lending, and so consumption and investment may fall; interest rates may rise, increasing the cost of borrowing; household and business confidence may fall; asset prices may fall, reducing people's wealth; some people may lose their savings if one or more banks fail; some people may start to save more to pay off their debts.

23 If the availability of credit decreases and the cost increases, investment may fall. This includes investment in physical capital, human capital and in R&D. The reduction in confidence resulting from problems in financial markets may have similar effects. Less investment means that the productive capacity of the economy will grow more slowly.

Case studies

Hyperinflation in Venezuela

1 Hyperinflation is when the rate of inflation is very high, typically more than 50% per month.

2 **i.** Some people stopped accepting bolivars in exchange for goods and services and so money was no longer able to fulfil its role as a medium of exchange; **ii.** Rapidly rising prices, for example, over 65,000% in 2018, meant that the bolivar was unable to maintain its value over time. It was not an effective store of value; **iii.** Restaurants and shops stopped displaying their prices and so money was no longer effective as a measure of the value of different goods and services.

3 Many people had to use dollars to buy goods and services because traders were unwilling to accept bolivars. Traders were unwilling to accept bolivars because high inflation meant that the bolivar was losing value very quickly.

Northern Rock

1 Interbank loans are short-term loans made by one bank to another. A bank with surplus cash will lend money on the interbank market and a bank that is short of cash will borrow on the interbank market. Most loans are for 7 days or less.

2 The money Northern Rock borrowed on the international money markets was short term. This meant, Northern Rock had to keep taking out new loans to finance the mortgages (long-term loans) it had provided for people. In the financial crisis, banks stopped lending to each other because they lacked confidence in the ability of other banks to repay the money borrowed. The interbank market stopped working. As a result, Northern Rock was unable to raise the funds it needed to repay the money it had previously borrowed on the international money markets.

3 A run on a bank is when depositors lose confidence in a bank and they try to withdraw their money at the same time.

4 Banks lend long term and borrow short term from depositors. This means that if lots of people who have deposited money with the bank start to withdraw their money at the same time, the bank will not have enough liquid assets to get the cash it needs to pay its depositors. This can happen even when a bank is making a profit.

Exam-style questions

7 D. Portfolio investment overseas is recorded on the financial account of the balance of payments.

8 C. An increase in exports increases the demand for the currency on the FOREX shifting the demand curve to the right. A decrease in imports reduces the supply of the currency on the FOREX and shifts the supply curve to the left.

9 A. Both equity and debt are sources of funds for a bank.

10 **i.** The balance of payments is a record of a country's financial transactions with the rest of the world.

ii. A growing surplus on the balance of trade in goods and services is a net injection into the circular flow of income and would lead to an increase in aggregate demand. An AD/AS diagram should be used to illustrate the effects on the macroeconomy. The diagram should be the same as Figure 7.1.3 except that the AD curve should be shifted to the right, leading to a higher price level and an increase in real national income.

iii. The original cost of buying $45,000 on the forward market (when the exchange rate was €1=$1.15) was €(45,000 ÷ 1.15) = €39,130. If the dollars had been bought on the spot market (when the exchange rate was €1=$1.20) they would have cost €(45,000 ÷ 1.20) = €37,500/. Therefore, in this case, buying the dollars on the forward market would have reduced the firm's profit by €39,130 − €37,500 = €1,630.

11 **i.** Some of the points that might be made include:
- If the Chilean central bank increases the Monetary Policy Rate, it is likely to lead to an increase in other interest rates in Chile.
- An increase in interest rates will increase the demand for the Chilean peso on the FOREX since it is more rewarding for overseas residents to invest in Chilean interest-bearing financial assets.
- An increase in interest rates will also tend to reduce the supply of Chilean peso on the FOREX because it is also more attractive for Chilean residents to invest in Chilean interest-bearing financial assets rather than overseas.
- The increase in the demand for the Chilean peso and the fall in supply should lead to an appreciation in the exchange rate.

ii. Some of the points that might be made include:
- The data are consistent with the hypothesis that the Monetary Policy Rate (official interest rate) set by the Chilean central bank affected the Chilean peso exchange rate the over the period shown.
- Between June and December 2010, the Monetary Policy Rate increased from 1.00% to 3.25% and the Chilean peso exchange rate appreciated against the US dollar. In June, 537 pesos were needed to buy 1 US dollar but in December, only 475 pesos were needed to buy 1 US dollar.
- The Monetary Policy Rate increased every month and each month, the peso exchange rate appreciated. For example, between August and September, the Monetary Policy Rate rose from 2.00% to 2.50% and the exchange rate appreciated from 509 pesos per US dollar to 494 pesos per US dollar.
- However, a given increase in the Monetary Policy Rate did not always have exactly the same effect on the exchange rate. Between June and July, the Monetary Policy Rate increased by 0.5% and 5 fewer pesos were needed to buy one dollar. However, between July and August, the Monetary Policy Rate also increased by 0.5% but 23 fewer pesos were needed to buy one dollar.
- While the data are consistent the view that the increase in the Monetary Policy Rate led to an increase in the Chilean peso, there may have been other factors that caused the exchange rate to appreciate over this time period.

12 Indicative content is given below:
- meaning of a minimum liquidity ratio
- meaning of a minimum capital ratio
- inadequate liquidity and insolvency as causes of bank failures
- explanation of the significance of banks borrowing short term and lending long term
- explanation of a run on a bank and why this can cause a bank to fail
- explanation of why imposing a minimum liquidity ratio makes it less likely that a run on a bank will cause the bank to fail
- explanation of insolvency
- causes of insolvency
- explanation of why imposing a minimum capital ratio makes it less likely that a bank will become insolvent
- explanation of why imposing a minimum capital ratio may make a run on a bank less likely.

13 Indicative content is given below; you should also try to include relevant references to data from the case study to support your points:
- differences between a commercial bank and an investment bank
- explanation of the importance of banks to the economy
- reasons why a bank might fail, with possible reference to Northern Rock
- explanation of how a central bank acting as the lender of last resort can support a bank that is failing due to a shortage of liquidity
- explanation of why a financial crisis might lead to a well-run bank running out of liquidity
- assessment of the case for a central bank acting as lender of last resort to a solvent bank that is short of liquidity
- explanation of how the government might bail out a bank
- meaning of systemic risk
- relevance of the size and importance of the failing bank and whether its failure would pose a systemic risk
- analysis of how the failure of one bank may lead to the failure of other banks
- assessment of the effects of bank failures on the macroeconomy
- assessment of bank failures on depositors, other lenders, shareholders and employees, with possible reference to Northern Rock
- meaning of moral hazard
- assessment of whether the risk of moral hazard means that central banks and governments should not support a failing bank
- discussion of whether a central bank acting as lender of last resort is less damaging than a government bail out
- discussion of whether or not a commercial bank should be supported but an investment bank should be allowed to fail
- an overall assessment of whether central banks and governments should or should not support a failing bank.

8.1 – Progress questions, Case studies

Progress questions

1 Economic growth is the rate of increase in the total output of an economy whereas economic development is a much broader concept.

Economic development occurs when there is a sustainable increase in people's well-being. It takes into account the ability of people to satisfy their needs and wants but also the degree of inequality, people's health and education, and the environment in which they live and work.

2   The three aspects of human development included in the HDI are: the standard of living, health and education (or GNI per head, life expectancy and years of schooling).

3   The IHDI takes into account the degree of inequality in income, health and education but the HDI does not.

4   Sustainable development means that progress is being made in improving the well-being of the current generation of people without reducing the ability of future generations to satisfy their needs.

5   National income measures the monetary value of the total output of an economy.

6   Living standards depend on people's ability to consume goods and services. As more is produced, more can be consumed. Money national income can increase either because output has risen and/or because the price level has risen. Changes in real national income reflect the change in the total output of the economy, the effects of inflation have been removed, and therefore it is a much better indicator of changes in living standards.

7   A PPP exchange rate is when the exchange rate reflects the relative domestic purchasing power of the two currencies. For example, if 100 Turkish lira spent in Turkey will buy the same basket of goods as 200 South African rand spent in South Africa, then the PPP exchange rate is 1 Turkish lira = 2 South African rand.

8   Measures of national income may not include, or record accurately, the size of the subsistence sector in an economy. Measures of national income include those goods and services that enter into exchange. Even if a country attempts to estimate the value of subsistence production and include it in national income, the estimate is likely to be inaccurate. Therefore, if one country has a small subsistence sector and the other country has a large subsistence sector, the estimate of GDP per capita at PPP exchange rates in the country with a large subsistence sector is likely to be an inaccurate measure of the country's output per head and, so people's standard of living.

9   Environmental limits to economic growth include: the finite quantity of non-renewable resources; too much use of renewable resources; pollution from production; pollution and waste from the consumption of goods and services; greenhouse gas emissions and global warming.

Case studies

Botswana: selected indicators, 2000-2018

1   GDP per head in 2000 = (45,655 ÷ 1.643) pula = 27,788 pula. GDP per head in 2018 = (89,798 ÷ 2.254) pula = 39,839 pula.

2   The percentage increase in GDP per head was [(39,839 − 27,788) ÷ 27,788] × 100 = (12,051 ÷ 27,788) × 100 = 43.4%.

3   Between 2000 and 2018, the degree of inequality fell in each of the years shown in the table. In 2000, the richest 1% of the population had 29.6% of the total income but by 2018 this had fallen to 22.6%. The poorest 50% of the population's share of total income increased from 5.5% in 2000 to 8.7% in 2018. Nevertheless, even in 2018, there was still a high degree of inequality in the distribution of income.

4   Real GDP per head has increased by over 43%, indicating that, on average, people in Botswana were able to consume more goods and services in 2018 than in 2000. Over the same period, the share of total income of the poorest 50% of the population has increased, indicating that they have benefited from rising material living standards. The fall in the share of total income going to the richest 1% of the population also suggests that the majority of the population has seen their standard of living improve. The substantial increase in mobile phone subscriptions may be partly explained by changes in technology and availability, but nonetheless, it still suggests that people in Botswana are better off. Average life expectancy has also increased significantly, from 50.6 years to 69.3 years, showing that people are living healthier lives. The improvement in well-being is also supported by the increase in Botswana's HDI from 0.581 to 0.730. The only indicator that might suggest that living standards have not improved is the increase in CO_2 emissions per capita. This might mean, for example, that air quality has got worse, but more power is needed to increase output, for transport and for people's homes.

Comparison of living standards in four countries in 2019

1   Using PPP exchange rates to convert each country's GNI per capita into US dollars means that the differences in GNI per capita should reflect accurately the different amounts of goods and services that can be purchased by the average person in each country.

2   In poor LEDCs, a high proportion of the population is usually employed in the subsistence production of agricultural goods. Agricultural productivity in LEDCs is usually much lower than in MEDCs. As a country develops, people usually move out of the agricultural sector into manufacturing and the service sectors. In poor LEDCs, some people in the agricultural sector are not fully employed and as employment switches away from the agricultural sector, agricultural productivity increases. Hence, a high level of employment in agriculture, as in Burundi (92%), indicates low productivity, subsistence production. The low level of employment in agriculture in Belgium (1%), indicates a high productivity agricultural sector with most of the population employed in high value-added manufacturing and services.

3   Bolivia appears to have the most unequal distribution of income. It has the highest Gini coefficient and the difference between its HDI and IHDI is the largest of all four countries. However, the MPI for Bolivia is lower than in Bangladesh and Burundi suggesting that the level of poverty is higher in these two countries but that partly reflects the lower levels of GNI per capita. Also, the figures for MPI are not for the same years.

4   Most of the key indicators suggest that average living standards are higher in Bolivia than Bangladesh. For example, GNI per capita is nearly 72% higher in Bolivia than Bangladesh, meaning that the average person is able to consume more material goods and services. The HDI and IHDI figures are also higher. However, despite the lower percentage of GDP spent on health care, life expectancy in Bangladesh is higher (72.6 years) than in Bolivia (71.5 years). The Gini coefficients indicate that income is more evenly distributed in Bangladesh. This suggests that the higher income per capita in Bolivia overstates the extent to which the average person in Bolivia is better off than the average person in Bangladesh.

8.2 – Progress questions, Case studies

Progress questions

1   An increase in the capital stock means there is an increase in the supply of one of the factors of production. This increases the productive capacity of the economy. An increase in productive capacity means that the economy is able to produce more goods and services, represented by a rightward shift in the PPB.

2   An increase in the savings ratio is likely to mean that total savings have increased. Savings provide funds for firms that wish to invest and should mean that investment increases. Other things being equal, an increase in investment should lead to an increase in a country's growth rate. Also, a high savings ratio means people are forgoing current consumption and therefore more of the country's resources can be used to produce capital goods rather than consumer goods.

3   A fall in the marginal capital-output ratio means that the productivity of capital has increased. As a result, other things being equal, the country's growth rate should increase.

4   The equilibrium growth rate = s ÷ k = 0.1 ÷ 2.5 = 0.04 = 4% per annum.

5   The savings ratio required to achieve a growth rate (g) of 5% when the capital-output ratio is 3 is calculated as follows: g = s ÷ k and so 0.05 = s ÷ 3 and therefore s = 0.15.

6   Ways in which financial markets can help an economy to grow include: providing an efficient means of payment; helping people to save; providing funds to finance investment; providing insurance services.

7   Ways in which climate may affect a country's economic development include: how easy/difficult it is to grow crops; the likelihood of infectious diseases; the chances of natural disasters occurring.

8   The birth rate is the number of live births per thousand people per annum.

9   The natural increase in the population is (22 − 7) per 1000 people = 15 per 1000 people = 1.5%.

10 Reasons why a growing population may be good for an economy include: that it increases the supply of labour; might lead to a younger population that may be more flexible and mobile; is good for business and encourages investment; increases the size of the market, allowing for more specialisation and economies of scale.

11 Investment in human capital is spending on education and training to improve the knowledge, abilities and skills of people.

12 Investment in human capital helps to support economic development because it should lead to an increase in productivity and the economy's potential output of goods and services. It may help people set up and manage firms and contribute to technological change. It can also help people lead more interesting and satisfying lives.

13 The hypothesis illustrated by the inequality Kuznets Curve is that at first economic growth leads to an increase in inequality but, after a certain point, further economic growth will lead to a more equal distribution of income.

14 Reasons why economic growth may damage the environment include: more non-renewable resources are used up in producing the output; some renewable resources may be overused; more production and

consumption can lead to an increase in pollution and there is more waste.

15 The discovery of a primary commodity such as oil might mean that much of the country's investment goes into the extraction and sale of the resource. As a result, investment into other sectors of the economy may be reduced. Also, as the product is exported, the demand for the country's currency will increase and the exchange rate will appreciate. The appreciation in the exchange rate will reduce the competitiveness of other sectors of the economy.

16 The Prebisch-Singer hypothesis suggests that, in the long run, the prices of primary commodities will fall relative to the prices of manufactured goods and so commodity-dependent LEDCs will experience a deterioration in their terms of trade.

17 Exports are an injection into the circular flow of income and a component of aggregate demand (AD). If exports increase, AD and the incomes of those involved in supplying exports will also increase. The increase in incomes in the export sector will lead to an increase in the demand for other goods and services. Therefore, factor incomes in these sectors of the economy will also rise, leading to further increases in AD, output and income. Overall, the initial increase in exports will lead to a larger increase in national income. This is the multiplier effect of the increase in exports.

18 The savings gap is when domestic savings do not provide enough funds to finance the amount of investment the country needs for its economic development. If a country is able to borrow from overseas, this will provide some of the additional funds required for investment. For example, the government might borrow from abroad to finance infrastructure projects or domestic firms might borrow from foreign financial institutions to finance the building of a new factory.

19 The marginal product of labour is the change in total output when one more or one fewer workers is employed. As long as the marginal product of labour is zero, a reduction (or increase) in the number of workers employed will not affect total output.

20 The benefits of industrialisation include: productivity in manufacturing is often higher than in agriculture and therefore total output increases if workers move from agriculture to manufacturing; technological progress may be more likely in manufacturing; creates employment; the income elasticity of demand for manufactures may be higher than for primary products and so the switch to manufacturing is more likely to lead to economic growth; less dependent on the production of primary products whose prices are volatile; exports of industrial products earn foreign exchange; industrialisation can lead to import substitution which means less foreign currency is needed to pay for imports.

21 Disadvantages of urbanisation include: the creation of slums and shanty towns; not enough basic amenities to cater for the growing population; unemployment will increase if the firms in the towns and cities are unable to create enough jobs; urban poverty; pollution, congestion and overcrowding.

Case studies

Thailand and Togo

1 The phrase "much of the population depends on subsistence agriculture" means that many people in Togo grow crops to meet their own needs and the needs of their family.

2 A much higher proportion of Togo's merchandise exports are commodities (72% as opposed to 27%) and so a fall in the price of commodities is likely to cause a larger deterioration in Togo's terms of trade than Thailand's terms of trade. However, the table does not state the proportion of each country's imports that are commodities. The impact on the terms of trade will also depend on which commodities fall in price and by how much, and which commodities the two countries export and import.

3 There is a variety of indicators that suggest that Thailand is a more developed country than Togo. Probably the three most significant indicators are GDP per capita (Thailand $6180, Togo $655), the HDI value (Thailand 0.755, Togo 0.503), and life expectancy (Thailand 76.9 years, Togo 60.7 years), in the two countries. The 2015 Gini indices show that income is more evenly distributed in Thailand (36.0) than Togo (43.1) which also suggests that Thailand is probably a more developed economy. In addition, the lower proportion of GDP produced by the agricultural sector (Thailand 8%, Togo 28%) also supports the view that Thailand is a more developed country than Togo.

Argentina's debt crisis

1 External debt is the amount of money that the government, firms and residents of a country have borrowed from abroad.

2 The extract states that Argentina failed to pay around US$500 million of interest to holders of government bonds showing that the country's government has defaulted on its debt. It has also agreed a deal with a group of private bondholders to change the terms of its debt and is trying to change the terms of its US$44 billion loan with the IMF.

A change in the terms upon which money has been borrowed may indicate that the country has defaulted on its debt.

3 In January 2020, around 60 Argentinian peso were needed to buy 1 US dollar but by January 2021, around 86 peso were needed to buy 1 US dollar. Since much of Argentina's debt is likely to be in dollars, the cost of repaying the debt in terms of domestic currency has increased. It is likely that Argentina will need to export more to obtain the foreign currency needed to service its external debt, that is to pay the interest and to repay the loans when they mature.

4 Most of the evidence in the table to suggests that Argentina's ability to pay its external debt got worse between 2015 and 2019. Argentina's total external debt as a percentage of its GNI increased from just over 30% to almost 65%. In 2015, its stock of debt was equal to 2.45 years' worth of exports but by 2019 its stock of debt had increased to 3.26 years' worth of exports. Also, the proportion of its annual exports need to service its debt increased from 25% to 47%. However, short-term debt as a percentage of Argentina's total debt fell (from 34% to 24%) and Argentina's foreign currency reserves also increased slightly as a percentage of its external debt (from 13% to 15%). The reduction in the proportion of short-term debt and the increase in the percentage of foreign currency reserves suggest that Argentina might be more able to service its external debt.

8.3 – Progress questions, Case studies

Progress questions

1 Demand-side policies are monetary and fiscal policies that are used to influence aggregate demand.

2 Market-based policies to promote economic development are those that allow market forces to determine the allocation of resources. Supporters believe that economic growth will be increased by the government creating an environment in which economic agents can pursue their self-interest, encouraged by financial incentives and competition. Interventionist policies involve the government providing some important goods and services and actively intervening in other markets to affect resource allocation.

3 Trade liberalisation is the reduction or removal of restrictions to international trade to allow countries to specialise in products in which they have a comparative advantage.

4 The main objective of an industrial strategy is to encourage the development and growth of a particular sector of the economy, often manufacturing.

5 A managed exchange rate is where the government and/or central bank take action to reduce fluctuations in the exchange rate. A more stable and predictable exchange rate will remove some of the uncertainty associated with international trade and should encourage investment and exports, supporting the growth of the economy.

6 When the investment takes place, there is likely to be an inflow of foreign exchange to acquire the domestic currency needed to pay for the investment. Later, the transnational corporation (TNC) is likely to export some of its output which will also lead to an inflow of foreign currency. It may produce import substitutes which will reduce the amount of foreign currency needed to pay for imports. However, it is also likely that some of the profits made by the TNC will be paid to overseas residents, resulting in an outflow of foreign currency.

7 A buffer stock scheme will buy the commodity when prices are falling. This will reduce the excess supply on the market and help to stop the price falling. When prices are rising, the buffer stock will sell from its stock of the commodity and increase the supply on the market. This will reduce the excess demand and help to stop the price rising. Therefore, the extent to which prices fluctuate should be reduced.

8 Benefits of microfinance schemes include: allow people with no collateral to obtain loans to support their business; allow people to borrow to deal with unexpected events, such as crop failure; people do not have to borrow from moneylenders at high rates of interest; provide financial services to people in rural areas who do not have access to formal financial services; may help people save; may provide people with a means of payment; may provide insurance services; support the growth of local business and may result in new jobs being created.

9 Businesses that belong to a fairtrade scheme have to provide safe working conditions and pay a fair wage to their employees. They must agree that they will not discriminate against any group of workers and that they will not use child labour. Some fairtrade schemes insist that businesses that are part of the scheme must recognise trade unions who can help to protect workers' rights.

10 Bilateral aid is when one country provides aid to another country and only the two countries are involved. Multilateral aid is when aid is provided by a number of countries and it is usually channelled through an international organisation such as the World Bank or the United Nations.

11 Untied aid is likely to benefit an LEDC more than tied aid because the LEDC receiving the aid can spend it where it wants and is likely to be able to buy the goods and services it needs at a lower price.

12 If a country's debts are reduced or written off, it may encourage the country to take on more debt because it has not had to pay all the interest or to repay the amount borrowed.

13 If the amount of remittances a country receives from abroad increases, the foreign currency will have to be converted into the country's own currency. This will increase the demand for the domestic currency and will, therefore, increase the price of the currency (the exchange rate).

14 If the income elasticity of demand for tourism is high, it means that a given percentage increase in income will lead to a larger percentage increase in the demand for tourism.

15 An increase in foreign tourism is an injection into the circular flow of income and it will lead to an increase in AD. It will also have a multiplier effect because those people whose income increases as a result of the increase in tourism will spend at least some of their extra income. This will lead to a further increase in AD and a further increase in real national income (GDP). An increase in tourism will also require an increase in investment in the industry, for example more hotels will have to be built. This increase in investment will also have a multiplier effect and lead to a short-run increase in real GDP. In the long run, the increase in investment in both physical and human capital will increase the productive capacity of the economy and its ability to sustain the growth in demand from foreign tourists. It is also likely to increase the capacity to supply complementary goods and services such as transport, entertainment and souvenirs.

16 In the short run, an increase in tourism will show as a credit item on the current account of the balance of payments. It is shown as a service. If the growth in tourism leads to an increase in FDI, this will show as a credit item on the Financial Account. In the long run, as the tourist industry produces profits for foreign investors, there will be a debit item on the primary income section of the current account. The growth of tourism will also lead to other transactions that affect the balance of payments, for example more coaches and other means of transport may be imported from abroad.

17 Both the IBRD and the IDA provide long-term finance to support the economic development of LEDCs. However, the IBRD lends money to middle-income and creditworthy poorer countries whereas the IDA provides grants, interest-free loans or loans at very low rates of interest to the poorest countries in the world. Loans provided by the IBRD are usually for a period of between 5 and 15 years whereas loans provided by the IDA are usually repaid over a period of 30 to 40 years.

18 The main source of funds for the World Bank is borrowing on international capital markets by selling bonds.

19 The main role of the World Bank is to provide long-term finance to support the economic development of LEDCs whereas the IMF provides short-term and medium-term loans to countries experiencing balance of payments problems with the main aim of maintaining the stability of the international monetary system. The IMF lends to LEDCs and MEDCs.

Case studies

Special economic zones

1 A special economic zone (SEZ) is an area set up by the government to encourage more business, investment and exports.

2 An LEDC might create special economic zones to support the industrialisation and diversification of the economy. The objective is to promote economic growth and development. Reliable infrastructure, subsidies, less regulation and no or low taxes may attract more businesses to locate there, particularly foreign transnational corporations (TNCs). More investment can increase the country's productive capacity and could lead to more jobs, income and exports.

3 Disadvantages of creating special economic zones include: the financial cost, and the opportunity cost, particularly for countries with limited tax revenue; the potential for waste, for example expensive infrastructure may have been built but few new firms attracted; the risk that other factors, such as conflict or political problems, may put off foreign investors; the possibility of corruption in some areas; the choice of location and sectors to support may be taken for political rather than economic reasons, with governments not necessarily having all the information needed to choose the best approach.

Peru, an improving economy

1 The extract states that Peru's traditional industries include mining and fishing. It produces and exports primary commodities, particularly copper. However, the extract also states that manufacturing now provides 20% of Peru's national income and that tourism has become increasingly important during the past 20 years. The growth of manufacturing and tourism is a clear indication that Peru's economy has become more diversified.

2 Peru is a major exporter of primary products and since the demand for such products is likely to be price inelastic, a fall in commodity prices will reduce Peru's export revenue. Exports are an injection into the circular flow of income. A fall in injections will have a downward multiplier effect and tend to reduce national income. Therefore, the fall in commodity prices is likely to have contributed to a fall in Peru's rate of economic growth.

3 There is plenty of evidence in the extract to suggest that Peru has become more economically developed since the year 2000. The average rate of economic growth has been strong between 2000 and 2019 (6.1% between 2002 and 2013, 3.1% between 2014 and 2019) and the extract states that it became a middle-income country in 2008. Extreme poverty has fallen from 16.4% of the population in 2000 to 2.7% in 2018. Between 2000 and 2019, GNI per capita increased from US$1970 to US$6,740 and even taking into account inflation, this is a large increase. Over the same period the HDI has increased from 0.628 to 0.777, providing further support for the view that Peru has become more economically developed since 2000.

4 An important aspect of sustainable development is protecting the environment. If economic growth causes serious damage to the natural environment it will not be sustainable. The extract states that Peru is only recycling 1.5% of its electronic waste which suggests that too many electronic products are not being disposed of in a sustainable way. The lack of recycling will also mean that non-renewable resources are used up more quickly. The reduction in the area of land covered by forest is likely to affect animal habitats and global warming.

Exam-style questions

1 A. The Gini coefficient is a measure of inequality and an increase in the Gini coefficient indicates that the degree of inequality has increased.

2 D. The real income per head for Country Z rose from $8,800 to $(9,680 \times 100/102) = \$9,490$. That is an increase of 7.8%. The real income per head for Country Y fell, for Country W it was unchanged and for Country X it rose by 6.4%.

3 B. According to the Harrod-Domar model, an increase in the savings ratio will lead to an increase in investment, resulting in a more rapid increase in the country's productive capacity. The equilibrium (or warranted) rate of economic growth is $(s \div k)$ where s is the savings ratio.

4 **i.** Primary product dependency means that the country produces mainly commodities such as tea, sugar, rice, copper and zinc. It is likely to earn most of its foreign currency from exporting a few primary products.

ii. The demand for most primary products is price inelastic. If the price of the product falls, it leads to a smaller percentage increase in the quantity sold and therefore total revenue falls. This can be seen in the diagram. When price falls from P_1 to P_2, the quantity sold only increases from Q_1 to Q_2. The total revenue $(P_1 \times Q_1)$ is more than $(P_2 \times Q_2)$.

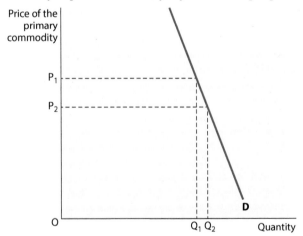

iii. The percentage increase in the price of the commodity between April 2021 and July 2021 is 20%. Since the PED is –0.8, the percentage fall in the quantity sold is 16%. Therefore, the quantity sold in July 2021 is 9,000 tonnes × 0.84 = 7,560 tonnes. The revenue in US dollars is 7,560 × $360 = $2,721,600. Since $1 = 17 pesos, the total revenue, in pesos, earned from exporting the commodity was 2,721,600 × 17 = 46,267,200 pesos.

5 **i.** An increase in GNI per capita is likely to lead to a fall in absolute poverty. Absolute poverty means that people are not able to afford essential goods and services such as food, clothing, housing, health care and education. As GNI per capita rises, on average, people's incomes increase and they are more likely to be able to afford enough food so that they do not go hungry. They are also more likely to

be able to afford other necessities. Therefore, the percentage of the population suffering from absolute poverty is likely to fall. As GNI per capita increases, the government is also likely to raise more tax revenue and so it could spend more money on merit goods such as education and health care, allowing more people to benefit from these essential services, reducing absolute poverty.

ii. The higher the value of the multidimensional poverty index (MPI), the greater the amount of poverty in a country. For the countries in the table, generally, the higher the GNI per capita, the lower the MPI and therefore the lower the amount of absolute poverty. Madagascar has the lowest GNI per capita ($500) and the highest MPI (0.384) which supports to view that GNI per capita affects the amount of absolute poverty in Sub-Saharan Africa. Zambia has the highest GNI per capita ($1,440) and the second lowest MPI (0.232). The country with the lowest MPI is Lesotho (0.084) and it has the second highest GNI per capita ($1,280). Guinea's GNI per capita ($850) is slightly higher than Mali's ($830) and Guinea's MPI (0.373) is slightly lower than Mali's MPI (0.376) which is consistent with the proposition that an increase in GNI per capita leads to a reduction in the degree of poverty. The data are not totally consistent with the proposition and although Madagascar has a significantly lower GNI per capita than both Mali and Guinea, its MPI is not very different. Also, the table only includes five countries from Sub-Saharan Africa and without data from the other countries in Sub-Saharan Africa it is not possible to come to a definite conclusion.

6   Indicative content is given below; you should also try to include relevant references to data from the case study to support your points:
  - growth in the world economy has led to rising real incomes
  - tourism has a high, positive income elasticity of demand (YED)
  - rising incomes mean that there will be a more than proportionate increase in the demand for products with a YED of more than +1. As a result, countries are likely to earn more foreign exchange from foreign tourists
  - the case study indicates that tourism has been encouraged by the government of Peru. Perhaps the government has subsidised the building of hotels, infrastructure and the provision of other services that might attract tourists. It may also have spent money on marketing Peru as an attractive tourist destination
  - the case study also indicates that tourism has been encouraged by the private sector. It is likely that there has been investment by TNCs which could make Peru more attractive as a tourist destination
  - a depreciation in a country's exchange rate would also make the country more attractive as a tourist destination and, provided demand is sufficiently price elastic, increase the amount of foreign currency earned
  - a fall in the price of flights to the country could increase tourism and the amount of foreign currency earned
  - the development of various attractions that encourage foreign tourists to visit the country and to spend their money in the country.

7   Indicative content is given below:
  - the meaning of debt cancellation
  - the different types of debt, for example multilateral loans, bilateral loans, loans from private sector financial institutions
  - the significance of these differences for debt cancellation, for example private sector financial institutions may not be willing to write off countries' debts
  - the moral case for helping the very poorest people in the world
  - for some countries, debt servicing is a high percentage of government spending and export revenues
  - would save the foreign currency used to service the debt
  - debt servicing may be a high percentage of the money given in foreign aid, meaning that the country is not getting much benefit from foreign aid
  - some of the money saved could be used to finance social programmes such as relieving poverty and providing education and health care
  - some of the money saved could be used to finance spending on essential infrastructure
  - the debt may have been incurred many years ago and yet the current generation of people is having to pay off the debt
  - the interest some countries have already paid is more than the amount that was borrowed
  - without some form of debt relief, some countries may default on their debts and this may be more damaging than if some debts were cancelled
  - policies that may have to be introduced to allow countries to continue to service their debts may reduce economic growth and hurt the very poor
  - the cost of cancelling all the debts of the poorest countries in the world is not very significant for the richer countries of the world
  - the problem of moral hazard and the risk that if debts are cancelled, countries may just take on more debt
  - the difficulties involved in monitoring and ensuring that countries do not take on more debt
  - if debts are cancelled there is less pressure on countries to adopt sound economic policies
  - if private sector financial institutions believe that there is a risk that they will not get their money back, they may not be willing to lend money to low-income countries in the future
  - debt relief may help to a limited extent but it does not solve the problems faced by the world's poorest countries
  - alternatives to the complete debt cancellation of all low-income countries, e.g. phased debt relief that depends on certain conditions being met, cancelling the debts of countries that meet certain conditions
  - the opportunity cost of debt cancellation
  - discussion of other policies that might help low-income countries and whether they might be more effective
  - an overall assessment of the case for and against cancelling the debts of all the world's low-income countries.

Index

Page numbers in **bold** indicate key terms boxes.